MARY LOU BURTON

Bravo! ®
PUBLICATIONS, INC.

BRIDAL RESOURCE GUIDE

THE AREA'S MOST COMPREHENSIVE GUIDE TO WEDDING-RELATED SERVICES

1999 Bravo!®
Bridal Resource Guide

The brides who have used the Bravo!® Resource Guide say it best.

"I used the Bravo!® Resource Guide for every aspect of my wedding planning. I honestly don't know what I would have done without it. It was invaluable!"
~Kappy Hodges

"This Guide had everything. It saved me hours of phone calls!"
~Carmen Hunter

"I looked through many publications, but none were as complete or user friendly as the Bravo!® Resource Guide! Even my fiancé likes it! Don't plan a wedding without it!"
~Melissa Mercer

"My daughter lives in Chicago. She used the Bravo!® Resource Guide and made appointments with places she thought would work for the reception site, photographers, cake, and flowers. We did all the planning, right down to the flowers being selected, signed all the contracts, AND IT WAS ALL ACCOMPLISHED IN JUST FOUR DAYS!!!!"
~Judy Daniels

"As a recent Father-of-the-Bride, your Resource Guide was the answer to a father's prayer. We were able to plan every detail, set and follow a budget, and pull off the whole thing without the anxiety I have seen with other Friends' Children's weddings.
~Ed Casey

"The Bravo!® Resource Guide makes a wedding day wonderful not woeful."
~The Oregonian

Bravo!® Publications, Inc.
7165 S.W. Fir Loop, Suite 106
Portland, Oregon 97223
(503) 684-1379, (800) 988-9887; Fax (503) 684-1037
E-mail: bravo7165@aol.com

Visit our Web sites:
http://www.bravowedding.com/ & http://www.bravoevent.com/

ISBN 1-884471-21-8

TABLE OF CONTENTS

Banquet & Reception Sites continued...

TABLE OF CONTENTS

Honeymoon, Travel & Accommodations continued...

TABLE OF CONTENTS

ACKNOWLEDGEMENTS

This Guide would not have been possible without the hard work, dedication, and endless hours from the following people:

Account Managers
Carinne McCulloch
Anne Ryan

Public Relations & Marketing
Helen Kern
Amy Waetjen

Seattle Sales
Marion Clifton
Janet Meinheit

Copy Writing & Production Support
Amy Waetjen

Layout & Print Production
Kieley Malueg, *Publications Plus*

Prepress & Printing
Paramount Graphics, Inc.
Beaverton, Oregon U.S.A.

Title Page
Photographs provided by:
top center: "bride and groom"
   © *C Studio, See page 484*

top left: "bride"
   © *Adams & Faith Photography, See page 476*

top right: "at the beach"
   © *Photography by Peter Paul Rubens, See page 508*

bottom left: "just married"
   © *C Studio, See page 484*

bottom right: "ring bearer"
   © *red door studio, See page 511*

Cover Design
Roz Pasion, *Roz & Co.*

Cover photographs provided by:
top left: "wedding cake"
   © *Joseph Photographer, See page 496*

top right: "dancing bride and groom"
   © *Joseph Photographer, See page 496*

middle: "bride holding bouquet"
   © *red door studio, See page 511*

lower right: "sunflowers"
   © *Edmund Keene Photographers, See page 489*

bottom: "blowing bubbles"
   © *Photography by Peter Paul Rubens, See page 508*

Spine photograph provided by:
"bride and groom in the rain"
   © *C Studio, See page 484*

Back cover photographs provided by:
top: "bridesmaids"
   © *red door studio, See page 511*

middle: "bride and groom in car"
   © *Adams & Faith Photography, See page 476*

bottom: "reception table"
   © *Custom Chair Covers, See page 517*

Visit our Web sites:
http://www.bravowedding.com/
http://www.bravoevent.com/

Mary Lou Burton

Mary Lou began Bravo! Publications, Inc. in 1989 after planning her own wedding for 550 Italian relatives. On the honeymoon, she and husband, John, realized the hundreds of hours they'd spent researching businesses could be helpful for other brides and grooms doing the same research. Mary Lou and Marion Clifton researched and created the first *Bravo! Bridal Resource Guide* in 1990. In 1994 an additional guide using the same concept and format was created specifically for meeting and event planners — *Bravo! Event Resource Guide.*

Front row: Amy Waetjen, Carinne McCulloch, Jake Ryan, Kieley and Katie Malueg **Back row:** *Helen Kern, Mary Lou and Will Burton, Anne Ryan*

© *Joseph Photographer*

Mary Lou graduated from the University of Portland in 1985, with a bachelor's degree in communications management. She has appeared as a guest speaker for Nordstrom and Meier & Frank, as well as appearing on AM Northwest and other local broadcasts. She has written and contributed to several national and local publications. Over the last nine years as Bravo! has grown, so has her family. Her three sons are a wonderful source of inspiration: Alex, 8; Nick, 6; and Will, 19 months.

Anne Ryan

Anne joined the Bravo! Team in 1994 after planning her wedding. Her excitement and professionalism have brought energy and growth to Bravo! Anne has believed in the Bravo! concept and philosophy and has helped develop several products including the Bravo! Meeting & Event Planners' Trade Show. Anne is a native Oregonian. She is a graduate of University of Portland, with a bachelor's degree in liberal arts, with a minor in psychology, business and history. She married Scott Ryan in 1994, her hobbies include her two year old son, Jake, gardening, skiing and oil painting.

Carinne McCulloch

Carinne worked in the recreation industry for several years and was a client of Bravo! She decided to make a move and Bravo! was fortunate to be the place that she chose. No project is ever impossible with Carinne's "can-do" attitude. Her enthusiasm and easy-going personality has contributed to Bravo's growth while maintaining quality. Carinne graduated from Oregon State University in 1991 with a bachelor's degree in both business and human performance. Carinne and her husband, Derek, enjoy wakeboarding, sailing and skiing.

Kieley Malueg, Publications Plus

Kieley has worked with Bravo! Publications for three years designing, typesetting, planning and managing print production. She's a native Portlander and a 1989 graduate of the University of Oregon. Her experience includes marketing, design and print production in the recreation and tourism industries. Her attention to detail and professional expertise has enhanced Bravo!'s efforts to continue to produce affordable, high-quality, user-friendly publications. She's married to Ken Malueg, and they have one daughter. They enjoy traveling, fishing, crabbing, gardening, cooking, and spending time with their families.

Amy Waetjen

Amy joined Bravo! this year as our production and office manager. She has brought copywriting skills to our appreciative clients. With such a small office we wear many hats, and Amy has been able to combine production with on-line maintenance, marketing, customer service plus a variety of other tasks. Amy graduated from Valparaiso University in Indiana with a bachelor's degree in communication. She grew up in Eugene and enjoys running, hiking, skiing and writing.

Helen Kern

Helen, Mary Lou's mother, joined Bravo! this year as well. She is in charge of human relations, always bringing some tasty treat or beautiful flowers to the office. She is our public relations ambassador and helps out with many projects around the office. Her words of wisdom inspire us each day! Helen is the mother of eight children — and her most important accomplishment of all is the faith and hope she gave to all of her children.

Spread The Word!

We need your help. To continue to supply this Guide we rely on you, the reader, to let the businesses and services in this book know that you heard about them through the *Bravo! Bridal Resource Guide*. Our featured businesses will recognize the Bravo! name.

Pass it on to a friend. Before they walk away with *your* copy, let them know they can fill out the order form on page 23 to receive their own copy.

The Bravo! Difference

- ## Location... Location... Location!
  This Guide will help you find the perfect spot for your ceremony or reception, whether at an intimate garden setting or a downtown glamorous ballroom—it's all right at your fingertips.

- ## All the important details about the sites
  From cost and terms to what's included and what's extra, the *Bravo! Bridal Resource Guide* includes descriptions of each facility for easier selection based on what you need. By the time you call a facility, you're thoroughly informed.

- ## The ultimate tool for brides and grooms
  From listings of over 450 ceremony and banquet sites to exceptional caterers, decorators, rental equipment, and entertainment. You'll find everything for your upcoming wedding in this one resource guide.

- ## This is a book you will rely on
  Everything has been thoroughly researched to ensure that you have the most current information, updated annually. Everyone we've included is outstanding!

Take A Look At Our Web Site
www.bravowedding.com
If you like our guide... you'll love our Web pages

- ## Search by area, capacity, and type of service
  You'll be able to search our site for the type of product or service you need. Find all downtown facilities that will accommodate more than 500 guests or a gift basket company that will deliver to Beaverton.

- ## We're putting the Guide on-line
  Every client in the book is listed on our Web site with location, phone number, contact and type of business or service. We are in the process of activating many client pages on-line as well, with the same easy-to-read format.

- ## Links to event services and facilities
  Many of our client pages have direct links to their home pages with more details and photos of their facility or service. You can get more detailed information or communicate with many of these services easily on-line or through e-mail.

- ## Guest book and order form
  We'd love to hear from you. Sign-in to our guest book and let us know what you like about the Bravo! products or services. We love suggestions of what we could do better. You can order any of our products on-line.

IF YOU LOVE THE BRAVO! BRIDAL RESOURCE GUIDE, WAIT UNTIL YOU BROWSE OUR BRAVO! BRIDAL WEB SITE!

Check out the Bravo! Publications Web sites at:
http://www.bravowedding.com/ *and* http://www.bravoevent.com/

The Bravo! Web site is:
- **Easy to use!**
- Features all the **detailed information** you're used to seeing in your Bravo! Bridal Resource Guide!
- Has its own **"search engine"** so you can find things easily by category or location!
- Features **color photographs**!
- Has a comprehensive **Calendar of Events** that will let you know when and where the next bridal shows will be taking place.

The Bravo! Wedding and Event Web sites will be...
growing and changing weekly, so be sure to browse them often so you can see what's new!

ADD BRAVO! TO YOUR ROLODEX!
(Just cut out the card below and staple or slip it into your Rolodex.)

Bravo! Publications, Inc.
7165 S.W. Fir Loop, Suite 106
Portland, OR 97223

Bravo!®

Phone: (503) 684-1379; **Toll Free:** (800) 988-9887
Fax: (503) 684-1037
E-mail: bravo7165@aol.com
Web sites: http://www.bravowedding.com/
http://www.bravoevent.com/

BRAVO!® RESOURCE GUIDES

When You Want Information, Not Glossy Ads—You Want Bravo!

Bravo!® Publications is proud to offer four regional resource guides for planning meetings, events and weddings. Each of the guides featured on this and the following page is filled with important information and details about the area's finest businesses and services providers, and is presented in easy-to-read, résumé style formats, alphabetically, by category. Designed to be user-friendly, each of these guides truly are your planning *Resource*!

Portland • Vancouver • Salem
and outlying areas
Bravo!® Bridal Resource Guide

Churches, Chapels, Banquet & Reception Sites, Caterers, Florists, Photographers, Videographers, Invitations, Bridal Attire, Tuxedo Rentals, Bridal Registry, and more…

The 1999 Edition features 608 pages
of easy-to-read, resumé-style write-ups on area businesses and service providers, listings of Banquet and Reception Sites, how-to's, check lists, and all the helpful hints!

Suggested Retail: $9.95

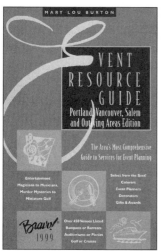

Portland • Vancouver • Salem
and outlying areas
Bravo!® Event Resource Guide

Venues, Attractions & Activities, Accommodations, Audience Participation, Gifts & Promotional Items, Food & Beverage, Rental Services, and more…

The 1999 Edition features 592 pages
of easy-to-read, résumé-style write-ups on area businesses and service providers, listings of Banquet and Event Sites, how-to's, checklists, and all the helpful hints.

Suggested Retail: $8.95
Complimentary to pre-qualified Meeting and Event Planners.

Say You Saw It In Bravo!
Every business or service needs to track where their business is coming from. By letting them know you are using one of the *Bravo!® Resource Guides*, you not only ensure that Bravo!® will be available for meeting and event planners or brides in the future, but you also let the businesses or services know where their business is coming from.

TO ORDER CALL (800) 988-9887

Bravo!® Organizers

The step-by-step system to track every detail of your event.

Organizers feature:

- Detailed worksheets designed to double as contracts
- Time schedules, checklists and calendars
- Detailed budget worksheets and "who pays for what forms
- "To Do" forms and "Delegating Duties" lists

Bravo!® Wedding Organizer
Suggested Retail: $22.95

Bar/Bat Mitzvah Organizer
Suggested Retail: $22.95

Greater Puget Sound
Bravo!® Bridal Resource Guide

Churches, Chapels, Banquet & Reception Sites, Caterers, Florists, Photographers, Videographers, Invitations, Bridal Attire, Tuxedo Rentals, Bridal Registry, Favors, Accessories, Consultants and more…

The 1999 Edition features 544 pages
of easy-to-read, resumé-style write-ups on area businesses and service providers, listings of Banquet and Reception Sites, how-to's, check lists, and all the helpful hints!

Suggested Retail: $9.95

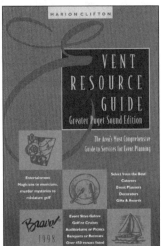

Greater Puget Sound
Bravo!® Event Resource Guide

Venues, Attractions & Activities, Accommodations, Audience Participation, Corporate Gifts & Awards, Food & Beverage Services, and more…

The 1999 Edition features 608 pages
of easy-to-read, résumé-style write-ups on area businesses and service providers, listings of Banquet and Event Sites, how-to's, checklists, and all the helpful hints.

Suggested Retail: $8.95
Complimentary to pre-qualified Meeting and Event Planners.

TO ORDER CALL (800) 988-9887

If you are planning a wedding,
getting married or know someone who is, order
what every bride needs to plan a perfect wedding!

Bravo!
Bridal Resource Guide &
Wedding Organizer Package
$22.95

This special offer is 33% off the cover price. You will receive the *Bravo! Bridal Resource Guide*—including everything you want and need to know about the area's finest wedding-related businesses, over 450 reception and ceremony listings, traditions and helpful hints. In addition, you'll get the *Bravo! Wedding Organizer*—awarded *"one of the five best wedding organizers available"* by *Bridal Guide* magazine. This professional step-by-step system keeps track of every detail of your wedding. The sturdy loose-leaf, three-ring binder includes worksheets that double as contracts, time schedules, checklists and calendars, and budget and expense worksheets.

❒ *Package: Bravo! Bridal Resource Guide & Wedding Organizer* $22.95

❒ *Bravo! Bridal Resource Guide only* $9.95

Please select Bridal Guide edition:

❒ *Portland • Vancouver • Salem '99 Edition*

❒ *Puget Sound '99 Edition*

Shipping and handling additional—$3 per package $_____

TOTAL: $_____

METHOD OF PAYMENT:

❒ Check or money order enclosed ❒ Charge to: Visa or Mastercard

Name of card holder:_____

Account No:_____

Exp. Date: _____ Signature:_____

Please allow 7 to 10 days for delivery

Name: _____

Address: _____ **Mail Stop:** _____

City: _____ **State:** _____ **Zip:** _____

Phone: _____ **Fax:** _____ **E-mail:** _____

Wedding date: _____

Send order to: **Bravo! Publications, Inc.**
7165 S.W. Fir Loop, Suite 106 • Portland, OR 97223
(503) 684-1379, (800) 988-9887; Fax (503) 684-1037; E-mail: bravo7165@aol.com
Web Sites: http://www.bravowedding.com/ & http://www.bravoevent.com/

Please fill in this survey and send to Bravo! Publications.

Your input is very important for the continued success of this publication. Please take the time to fill out this survey and send it back to us.

1. How has the *Bravo!® Resource Guide* been helpful to you? (Examples)

_____

_____

_____

2. Please list the businesses and services (by name) that you have found and are working with out of the *Bravo!® Resource Guide* (caterer, facility, musician, etc.).

_____

_____

_____

_____

3. Your experiences can help others. To ensure the quality of this publication for future users, we'd like to know if you had good or bad experiences with the businesses listed in the Guide.

_____

_____

_____

_____

4. Please add any additional ideas, thoughts or recommendations for how *Bravo!®* can improve this Guide for you.

_____

_____

_____

_____

Name: _____ **Phone:** _____

Address: _____

Wedding Date: _____ **Approx. budget:** _____

From the rehearsal to the wedding, reception, and honeymoon, these special events should be fun, memorable, and perfect. In other words, the events that people remember for years to come are the events that have been planned down to the last detail. That's exactly what this book is about.

It comes from a real-life need—and a real-life situation. In 1988 Mary Lou Burton had a wedding and a reception for 500 Italian relatives. In the months leading up to the wedding, she learned enough through experience to write a book. So the week after the honeymoon, she sat down with her friend, Marion Clifton, and planned the first *Portland–Vancouver Bridal Guide*. Now in its ninth year, this book has become a best seller—the largest, most complete bridal, event, and party resource guide in the Pacific Northwest.

The goal of the *Bravo!® Bridal Resource Guide* is to help brides and event planners like yourself find the facilities, caterers, florists, bakers, photographers, musicians, and other specialty services best able to fit their precise needs. Before any business is listed in this guide, it's screened to make sure the information is reliable, descriptive, and factual. It's then organized in clear and detailed descriptions and easy-to-read formats that allow you to quickly and easily make apple-to-apple comparisons of similar services.

This edition has grown to include over 450 ceremony, reception, and event sites in the Portland, Vancouver, and Salem areas, by location and capacity. Hundreds of additional business and service listings are at your fingertips, saving you countless hours of research time. Unlike other guides that simply compile advertisements and photographs, we have tried to create a bridal and event resource guide that's filled with truly useful information. We've even included pages of helpful hints that help you check references, protect deposits, secure dates, decorate inexpensively, and much more.

The *Bravo!® Bridal Resource Guide* is designed to fit in most handbags. It's easy to carry with you and includes spaces for notes. That's why so many brides call it their "Bridal Bible." And the free gifts and discounts offered by many of the companies will more than pay for the cost of the book as you use it in planning your big event!

HOW TO USE THIS BOOK

Congratulations! You've just purchased the most complete wedding, party, and event planning resource in the Pacific Northwest. Before you start, here are some tips on how to use it to your best advantage.

DISCOVER YOUR OPTIONS

Over 500 businesses, services, and resources are listed in this book. It provides detailed information about companies that can help you plan everything from engagement to the honeymoon. Within these pages you'll find a variety of resources with descriptions, services, and policies listed in detail. You'll appreciate the wealth of knowledge and be amazed by the talents and services our area supports, including outstanding caterers and exquisite florists as well as special services like talented seamstresses and unique gift shops.

IT'S EASY TO FIND THE SERVICES YOU NEED

Each page is designed to read like the résumé of a company. It's up to you to select the services that meet your needs and requirements.

As you explore your options, be sure to view samples, ask questions, get written estimates, and take notes. Make sure you feel absolutely comfortable that the companies you select will be able to provide the services or deliver the merchandise you're requesting. If you have any doubts, go to the next business on your list.

Remember, you're the customer. Use this book to help you create exactly the kind of wedding, party, or special event you've always dreamed of having!

IT'S EASY TO COMPARE THE SERVICES YOU FIND

As you start working your way through this book, you'll find it's filled with key information organized in a consistent format that allows you to compare and reference the various services easily.

For example, if you've invited 500 guests to your reception, you'll find only a few facilities that can accommodate that large of a group. That quickly narrows down the number of phone calls you'll need to make. In the *Bravo!*® *Bridal Resource Guide*'s "Rehearsal, Banquet & Reception Sites" section on pages 69 to 209, you'll find capacity listed first.

All the basic facts are listed at the top of each page, including company name, address, phone number, business hours, and contact person. The rest of the page describes the company's services, costs, deposits, reservation requirements, etc., and a special note. The Portland, Vancouver and Salem edition contains information on over 450 churches, chapels, parks, and reception sites. This puts the key facts you need right at your fingertips.

USE THE HELPFUL HINTS

Most sections start with a Helpful Hints page. They're there to save you time, money and headaches!

Professional planners with years of knowledge and experience in wedding planning and event coordination share their secrets on how to avoid the pitfalls and offer ways to make everything run smoothly. At one time or another, they've seen or tried it all! Some of the tips have come from brides who told us, "If only I had it to do over again, I would..." All the tips are worth reading. Some will apply, some won't. But by reading through the pages, you'll find creative and inspiring ideas that you can incorporate into your event—whatever the size or style!

USE IT AND ABUSE IT. THIS IS *YOUR* WORKBOOK!

This book is designed to fit in your purse or briefcase. Keep it handy so you can make phone calls on your coffee breaks, or book appointments during lunch. It lies flat for easy note-taking. Use Post-it notes as bookmarks. Tear pages out, doodle on it or scream into it! (Its special muffle-guard paper spares you any embarrassment.)

We know this book will make planning easier, leaving you more time to enter into the festivities surrounding your special event. So relax, and let the Bravo!® Bridal Resource Guide work for you!

The *Bravo!*® *Wedding Organizer* offers a more detailed workbook for organizing all the details of your wedding. More detailed information can be found on page 22.

The order form is located on page 23 of this guide.

Spread The Word!

We need your help. To continue to supply this Guide we rely on you, the reader, to let the businesses and services in this book know that you heard about them through the *Bravo! Bridal Resource Guide*. Our featured businesses will recognize the Bravo! name.

Pass it on to a friend. Before they walk away with *your* copy, let them know they can fill out the order form on page 23 to receive their own copy.

Organizational Tools

•

Budgeting Tips

•

Schedules and Checklists

•

Etiquette

•

Blank Calendars

•

Start a Wedding Tradition

•

Wedding Day Survival Kit

SO NOW I'M ENGAGED—WHAT DO I DO NEXT?

He proposed—the day you've been waiting for has finally arrived! You have to tell your parents, his parents, call all your friends, call the church, get time off for the honeymoon, buy a wedding dress, find a caterer.... STOP!

First things first! Before all the hustle begins, do yourself a favor and **sit down with your fiancé and ask yourselves the following questions:**

- Are your families large or small?
- What is your budget?
- What style of wedding would you prefer to have—do you like intimate gatherings, large parties, or impromptu, unique events?
- Do you want a romantic theme or a formal affair?

Work together so that you both agree on the same things, and then commit your thoughts to paper so that you will have a plan.

ONCE YOU MAKE YOUR PLAN, STICK TO IT!

Everyone seems to become an expert on wedding planning when they find out you're engaged. You'll receive loads of unsolicited advice, and everyone will try to sway your thinking. Don't let anyone steer you away from what's important to you and your fiancé. If you do, your wedding will be a combination of everyone else's dreams but your own!

GET ORGANIZED...
WITH THE *BRAVO!® WEDDING ORGANIZER*

Every event planner has his or her own way of getting organized. Over the years of publishing this book, we've encountered a lot of systems, both personally and professionally. From that experience and exposure, we have developed a special *Bravo!® Wedding Organizer* that incorporates the best of all the plans—along with some specially designed forms of our own. Everything you need is included:

- 40 detailed worksheets designed to double as contracts for reception site, caterer, photographer, florist, musicians, and more
- Time schedules and checklists
- "To Do" lists and forms
- Financial responsibilities guidelines
- "Delegating Duties" lists
- Guest and gift lists
- Business card holders
- Helpful Hints
- Pockets for swatches, samples, coupons, and receipts

In short, everything you need to keep you organized, on budget, and on schedule has been thought of and incorporated into the 14 tabbed sections of the *Bravo!® Wedding Organizer.* The tab headings serve as a reminder and makes it convenient to organize and store information. When it's time to deal with each element of the event, the information is there at your fingertips. Just three-hole punch and slip everything into your three-ring binder, and you're as organized as you can get.

To order your *Bravo® Wedding Organizer*
Send **$22.95 for Organizer with notebook** (plus $3 for postage and handling) to:

Bravo! Publications, Inc.
Bravo!® Wedding Organizer
7165 S.W. Fir Loop, Suite 106
Portland, Oregon 97223
(Please look for order form on page 23.)

A CONSULTANT CAN EASE THE STRESS

Hiring a consultant is a wise idea, especially if there is arguing between mother and daughter, between families, divorced parents and even attendants. This is an emotional time and if you can have an objective opinion of a consultant buffering between the two, it can sometimes ease the pressure. Money can be one of the biggest problems and obstacles. If a third party is involved, such as a consultant, they can collect the money without it being embarrassing. Many times these arguments result from lack of communication, emotional overload and misconceptions. The two parties just need to communicate; sometimes writing it down and having someone calm present to the other half is a good way to deal with it. They say you hurt the ones you love the most, the stresses of a wedding can truly test your relationships with family, friends and even your fiancé, remember to keep focused on what's important that day!

DELEGATE DUTIES

Every bride thinks, "If I don't do it, it won't get done the way I want it!" This may be true, but you'll soon realize you can't do it all and keep your sanity. You and your fiancé have figured out the plan, now delegate duties to family and friends. Everything can and will be done the way you want it if you give a clear description of what you need accomplished and when. Family and friends will enjoy knowing they helped contribute to making your special day a success!

RELAX AND ENJOY YOUR WEDDING DAY!

We suggest you get someone to coordinate all the details on the day of your wedding. Hire a professional or ask a trustworthy friend or family member who is not directly involved in the wedding party to oversee and coordinate delivery and setup of flowers, rental equipment, decorations, etc. Provide this person with a comprehensive list of everything he or she will need to keep an eye on, including the arrival of musicians and where they need to set up, where and when the formal photographs will be taken, phone numbers with a contact name for all the businesses providing services, etc. Your months of planning and coordination will pay off! You and your groom should be concerned and consumed only with the joy of the day and your love for each other!

If you don't read any other page from top to bottom, make sure to read this one. The following suggestions will ensure that your wedding turns out the way you want it while keeping your budget in line.

The most important advice we can offer both you AND your parents is **DO NOT GO INTO DEBT!** Weddings come in a variety of types and sizes; one is not necessarily better than the other based on the size or how much money you spend. Whatever you do, don't start your married life in debt.

BE REALISTIC WITH YOUR BUDGET

Your wedding budget should be handled like a business budget. If your boss said, "The budget for the Christmas party is $5,000," you would use only those services that would keep you within budget. The same is true for your wedding. Find the services that can accomplish what you want within the budget you've designated. Be realistic about your budget. If you have only $2,000 for your reception, it's unlikely you're going to be able to afford a full sit-down dinner for 300 guests, but a buffet with hot and cold hors d'oeuvres may work very well. Follow your budget allocations as closely as possible. This will eliminate financial stress.

SAMPLE BUDGET SHEET

Service	Budget	Actual	Deposit	Due	Balance	Due
Caterer	$2,500	$2,750	$500	5/5	$2,250	8/6
Florist						
Photos						

SETTING UP A BUDGET

It is recommended you set up a separate bank account for your wedding. This way funds can be tracked and kept separate from regular finances. Always pay businesses or services with a check or credit card for better records and tracking of expenses. Allocation of your budget depends on what is most important to the bride, groom and family contributing. Some spend more on music and entertainment or photography than others. The following is a percentage break-out of what the average dollar spent is:

• Reception—40%
• Honeymoon—15%
• Engagement rings—14%
• Photography—9%
• Miscellaneous (clergy fees, rehearsal dinner, attendants gifts, limos)—8%
• Bride's and groom's attire—5%
• Music—4%
• Flowers—3%
• Invitations—2%

WAYS TO SAVE MONEY

It's amazing how fast wedding costs can exceed the planned budget. If you find yourself in the position of needing to trim back to make everything fit within your budget, consider the following:

- **Avoid peak wedding days and seasons.** You can save money by having your wedding during the months considered to be "off-season" (January–May and late October–November) and on a Thursday or Friday evening or Sunday during the day. Because these times are in less demand, many businesses and services provide what you are looking for at reduced prices. You're also more likely to get your first choices!

- **Consider a daytime versus evening wedding.** Friday and Saturday weddings are becoming popular as well. Considering a Friday or Saturday wedding gives additional options for your wedding date. Food and alcohol costs are considerably less for daytime events than evening events. People don't drink as much if at all, and the food itself is far simpler and therefore less expensive.

- **Cut back on the guest list.** Guest lists can be the first thing to get out of control. Everyone wants to invite anybody and everybody they ever knew. Be firm with your figures of how many guests for each family. If that doesn't work, go back to the old formula of immediate family first, close personal friends second, etc., or have everyone review the list and cut back by 10%, 20%, or whatever is necessary to bring things back in line.

- **Determine what is most important to you** and put your money into that, but trim back on other areas. If fabulous flowers have always meant the most to you, spend a little less on your wedding gown or wear your mother's, sister's, or a friend's gown. If you've always wanted the most incredible dress in the world, cut back on the flower budget and have a DJ instead of a band.

- **Don't be afraid to shop around.** A little time on the phone could save you a lot of money. There can be a considerable difference in prices between different businesses for the same items or services. Just make sure that you are going to receive exactly the same item or level of service from the less-expensive company and that no short cuts are being taken at your expense.

If you're very clear about what budget you have to work with from the beginning, you'll find that the people in the wedding industry can be very helpful with all kinds of clever ideas on how to save money. Don't be afraid to ask for suggestions or ideas.

CONTRACTS

Contracts can be the most confusing and difficult part of planning a wedding. Keep in mind that this is a business arrangement. You're the customer and you are contracting with certain businesses to provide the services you request on a certain date, at a certain time, and within a certain budget. Contracts are a **MUST** when doing business with the many types of wedding-related services. Your wedding is an emotional experience, but remember—money is changing hands. A contract will spell out everything in black and white. It will also clarify any grey areas. If the business doesn't have a formal contract, write up your own and have them sign it. Estimates are a good first step, but they aren't final. Many brides have been shocked a week before their wedding when a supplier has said, "We had a price increase in the last six months; now it will cost this much for what you want." Remember, you carry a book filled with other options. **BEWARE** of contracts you feel pressured to sign! Make sure you don't sign something that you haven't thoroughly read or don't understand. Never sign a contract that makes you feel uncomfortable or that you can't afford. A contract is a legally binding document that commits you to the service or provider. Be well informed about what you are signing; ask questions, or take a copy of it home to look over if you have any hesitation at all.

CHECK OUT REFERENCES

The best way to research a business is to ask for references and then take the time to call them. This way you will rapidly discover if the services or merchandise were provided or delivered as promised. **There are state and private agencies that can provide information on a business's reputation. Don't be afraid to call them.**

DEPOSITS

In most cases a deposit is required to place an order formally or to reserve a certain date. Brides and grooms make the common mistake of assuming that the reception site is reserved based on a verbal commitment for date and time. **The agreement is not always valid, let alone recorded, until after the deposit has been received.**

YOU'RE THE CUSTOMER!

Always remember that you're the customer! Even though this can be an emotional time, **don't settle for less than what was contracted for.** Insist on the best service and accept nothing less. You may be spending more money on this one day than most people spend in a year! Make the most of your investment and do it your way.

WEDDING EXPENSES

The division of expenses depends on the financial ability of the bride, groom, and their respective families. Sit down and discuss the type of wedding you want to have and use the following list of items so each participant can choose what he or she would like to pay for. Remember that the reception can sometimes amount to 50% or more of your total expenses. If your costs need to be reduced, you may want to change to a less formal reception.

The bride and her family's expenses traditionally include:
- the wedding gown and accessories
- invitations and personal stationery
- flowers for the church, reception, and wedding attendants
- photographs
- reception, including room charge, food, servers, refreshments, and wedding cake
- music
- transportation for wedding attendants to church and reception
- gifts for bridesmaids
- accommodations for bridesmaids, if necessary

The groom and his family's expenses are normally:
- groom's wedding attire
- the clergy or judge's fees
- the marriage license
- all honeymoon expenses
- rehearsal dinner
- bride's bouquet and going-away corsage and both mothers' corsages
- boutonnieres for groomsmen
- groomsmen gifts
- accommodations for attendants

The wedding attendants' expenses are:
- wedding attire
- traveling expenses
- wedding gift

YOU'VE WAITED A LONG TIME TO GET MARRIED.

Your wedding date is a year away—it seems like an eternity! As formal weddings have become more and more popular, you should allow about one year for planning. Many reception facilities are reserved as far as a year in advance during the summer months and December. The size and formality of your wedding will play an important part in determining your date and schedule. Even if your wedding is small and less formal, allow yourself a minimum of three months. The more time you have to plan, the better your chances of reserving your first choices. On the biggest day of your life, who wants to settle for less? With all you have to do, time will fly quicker than you think!

The following schedule and checklist provide you with the basis for organizing your planning time and ensure that all the details will be handled. These are strictly recommendations; we encourage you to look on the following pages to see when the businesses themselves say they need to be reserved.

AFTER ENGAGEMENT—SIX MONTHS AND BEFORE

❏ Select a wedding date and time (be flexible).

❏ Buy a wedding notebook (see the Bravo® Wedding Organizer info on page II).

❏ Figure out your budget and write it down.

❏ Determine type of wedding and reception: formality, size, colors, and theme.

❏ Decide on the ceremony site and make an appointment with the clergy.

❏ Reserve a reception facility; if there's no in-house catering, you will need to find a caterer.

❏ Start compiling names and addresses of guests.

❏ Decide on wedding attendants (bridesmaids and groomsmen).

❏ Shop for your wedding gown and headpiece.

❏ Select a professional photographer.

❏ Start collecting favorite photographs from both of your childhoods through present that you'll want to use in your wedding video or multi-image slide program.

❏ Select dresses for your bridesmaids.

❏ Find a florist.

❏ Mail out engagement announcements.

❏ Send an announcement to your local paper.

❏ Register at the bridal registry stores of your choice (more than one is fine).

❏ Reserve a band or orchestra for your reception (if you choose).

❏ Decide on honeymoon destination; if it's a popular area, make reservations now.

FOUR TO FIVE MONTHS BEFORE

❏ Compile the final guest list; delete or correct as needed.

❏ Make sure all deposits are paid for services reserved.

❏ Finish planning the honeymoon.

❏ Order bridal attire; some manufacturers require up to six months for delivery.

❏ Order the wedding cake.

❏ Have groom, groomsmen, and ushers fitted for formal wear.

❏ Purchase your wedding rings.

❏ Order invitations, thank-you notes, imprinted napkins, and wedding programs.

❏ Ask people to handle certain duties like candle lighting, guest book, cake serving.

❏ Select musicians for ceremony

TWO TO THREE MONTHS BEFORE

❏ Plan ceremony rehearsal and rehearsal dinner.

❏ Address invitations (mail four to six weeks prior to wedding).

❏ Organize details with service providers: reception facility, photographer, etc.

❏ Check accommodations for out-of-town guests; send them information.

❏ Make beauty appointments: hair, nails, massage, facial, and makeup.

❏ Arrange for final fittings for your gown and bridesmaids dresses.

❏ Make your transportation arrangements for the wedding day.

❏ Purchase gifts for your attendants.

❏ Shop for your trousseau, lingerie, and going-away outfit.

❏ Give a bridesmaids' luncheon or bachelor party (optional).

❏ Send thank-yous for gifts received early.

❏ Get accessories: garter, unity candle, toasting goblets, ring-bearer pillow, etc.

ONE WEEK TO A MONTH BEFORE

❒ Change your name (if you choose) on your driver's license and Social Security card; organize which credit cards and bank accounts will be used.

❒ Decide where you'll be living and send change-of-address cards to post office.

❒ Confirm accommodations arranged for out-of-town guests.

❒ Get your final count of guests to caterer.

❒ Delegate last-minute errands and details.

❒ Make any necessary lists for photographer and musicians.

❒ Ask a responsible person to coordinate services and people on the wedding day; give them a list of who and what is supposed to be where and when.

❒ Get your marriage license. *Note: if your were married before, you'll need to know the date and place of the divorce or annulment. You may also need to have paperwork proof of divorce or annulment.

❒ Pick up your wedding rings; make sure they are the correct sizes.

❒ Pick up wedding attire; try it all on one last time to make sure it fits.

❒ Make sure bridesmaids have their dresses and they all fit.

❒ Keep up on writing thank-yous; don't let them pile up.

❒ Pamper yourself and make sure you eat right and get enough sleep.

THE WEDDING DAY

❒ Eat a good breakfast.

❒ Relax and enjoy getting ready for your big day.

❒ Go to hairdresser or start fixing your hair a few hours prior to the wedding.

❒ Put all the accessories you will need for dressing in one place.

❒ If pictures are being taken before ceremony, be ready at least two hours before.

❒ Just enjoy the day! All your months of planning will make your day perfect!

MONTH:

MONDAY	TUESDAY	WEDNESDAY	THURSDAY	FRIDAY	SATURDAY	SUNDAY

Today, wedding etiquette is good manners and a blending of traditional customs with contemporary ones. When you incorporate good manners into your wedding planning, you add a special touch of caring and thoughtfulness into everything you do, because you're making others involved in your special day feel special too.

Knowing the proper things to say and do also gives you greater confidence that you can handle any unexpected or awkward situation.

Let the following helpful tips show you how to incorporate good manners and proper etiquette into every aspect of your wedding duties—from addressing envelopes properly for invitations to knowing when to send thank-you notes. Good luck!

ANNOUNCING YOUR ENGAGEMENT

Share your good news with your families as soon as possible—it's only right that they hear it from you first. If you'd also like to announce your engagement formally in both your and your fiancé's hometown papers, contact the lifestyles editor to learn the appropriate way to prepare your information. Ask if photos are also accepted. The simplest, customary form of preparing your announcement is to type it on an 8 1/2 x 11 sheet. The following sample will give you an idea of how to write your copy:

Mr. and Mrs. Dennis Brown of Dayton Avenue announce the engagement of their daughter, Ann Marie, to John Smith, the son of Mr. and Mrs. Thomas Smith of St. Louis. No date has been set for the wedding (or, The wedding will take place in December).

ORDERING INVITATIONS

Order your invitations at least three months in advance to give you plenty of time for printing, addressing, and mailing. If it's a very formal wedding, choose a rich, creamy paper. If it's semiformal, you have many options in paper stocks and colors from which to choose. It's also acceptable to include more personal touches such as a poem, a Bible verse, or other sayings.

ADDRESSING INVITATIONS

Create a master list of names in order to avoid duplications. Make sure all names and titles are spelled correctly and addresses are accurate. Below are some typical examples of different addressing styles.

When addressing invitations to married couples, use the following format:

Mr. and Mrs. John Smith
1022 Robins Court
City, California 12345

Keep in mind that many women have retained their maiden names or prefer to be called by their titles or professional names. In these cases, you may send one invitation to both husband and wife, putting her name above his on the envelope. Follow the same rule for couples with different last names or unmarried couples living together.

Ms. Jane Smith
Mr. Joseph Thomas
122 Maple Street, Apartment R-10
Dayton, Ohio 12345

Be sure to write out in full the names of streets, cities, and states as well. Don't send an invitation to a couple and "family." Instead, on the inner envelope, include the name of each child invited as:

Mr. and Mrs. Smith
Kevin, Brian, and Amy

Adult members of a family who are over 18 should always receive separate invitations. You may, however, send one invitation to two sisters or brothers living together at one address. Generally, the rule is each invited guest should receive a personal invitation to your wedding, so avoid wordings like "and guest." Make an effort to find out the address of the guest and send a separate invitation.

MAILING INVITATIONS

Invitations are usually mailed four to six weeks before the wedding. Do send invitations to your wedding official, your fiancé's immediate family, all members of the wedding party, and a guest list made up of both your friends and his, as well as other relatives and coworkers with whom you want to share your day. Keep in mind your budget limitations and refrain from letting your list get out of control. Selection may sometimes be difficult, but it is best to stick as closely as possible to your list.

If you haven't received an RSVP by two weeks before the wedding, have a family member call and check. When each invitation is accounted for, tell your caterer how many guests to expect.

POSTAGE FOR INVITATIONS

Remember before purchasing stamps for your invitations to go to the post office and have the invitation weighed. Normally the postage will be 33 cents, but if the invitation has many inserts or is a larger size it might require more postage. Also, it is fun to have your invitations post-marked at a special location (i.e. Bridal Veil in Oregon is a popular place). You can either mail the entire finished package of invitations there or hand deliver the package with special instructions.

SAVE-THE-DATE LETTERS:

Inform out-of-town guests about the upcoming wedding date far enough in advance, so if they need to take time off work or save for the trip they will have time. This letter can also give details about hotel accommodations in different budgets, special wedding rates and who to contact at the destination and the 1-800 number.

BANQUET AND RECEPTION SITES

Rehearsal Dinner: The rehearsal dinner is usually hosted by the groom's parents. This is either formal or casual and follows the ceremony rehearsal the night before the wedding, although many brides and grooms are choosing to have the rehearsal two days before the wedding. It is the beginning of the festivities and an opportunity for all wedding party attendants and family to get to know each other. Invitations should be sent or telephoned at least three weeks prior and should be extended to all those participating in the wedding: attendants and groomsmen and their spouses, the clergy, parents of any children, immediate family and out-of-town guests who have arrived. The best man begins the toasts following dessert and then the gifts are presented to the wedding party and any other special helpers. Slide shows or videos can be shown of special memories of the bride and groom as individuals and then as a couple for their family and friends. This evening usually ends early so everyone can get a good night's sleep. See "Rehearsal Dinner Sites" section on pages 67–86.

Outdoor weddings: Always play it safe with an outdoor site—make sure you either have a back-up location or rent and set up tents. In the wonderful Pacific Northwest you can never be too sure of the weather. These tents or canopies can be expensive; don't forget to figure this into your budget.

Non-traditional sites and times: Saturdays are the most popular day to get married, and most businesses and services will charge top dollar for this prime time. Consider Friday nights or Sunday weddings as an option; some services will give a considerable discount for booking this off-day. Also, sites such as restaurants, parks, historical sites and beaches can be non-traditional, but also very fun and exciting with atmosphere and unique cuisine.

ROLES MEMBERS OF THE WEDDING PARTY PLAY

Maid of Honor: Although she has no prewedding responsibilities, she is expected to assist the bride whenever she can. She lends moral support and plays a big role in making sure the other bridesmaids are dressed to perfection and they all make it to the church on time. She is responsible for her own wedding outfit and pays for everything except the flowers. She also attends all prewedding parties and may even give one herself. The maid of honor is usually one of the witnesses required by law to sign the marriage certificate. Walking down the aisle, she precedes you and your father, arranges your train and veil, carries the groom's ring if there is no ringbearer, and holds your bouquet during the ceremony. She also stands next to the groom in the receiving line and sits on his left at the bride's table.

Best Man: His duties are many and varied and carry a lot of responsibility to ensure the wedding runs smoothly. The best man serves as the personal aide and advisor to the groom, supervises the ushers, carries the bride's ring and the marriage certificate, which he also signs, tips the altar boys in a Catholic ceremony, and acts as a right-hand man to the groom on his special day. The best man sits at the right of the bride and, as official toastmaster of the reception, proposes the first toast to the new couple, usually wishing them health, happiness, and prosperity. His final duties are to ensure the new couple takes off for the honeymoon without a hitch and that all the ushers return their rented formal wear on time.

Bridesmaids: Although they don't have any prewedding responsibilities either, they often will volunteer to help with any errands or duties that need to be accomplished. They are invited to all prewedding parties and may also give one if they wish.

Ushers: Their responsibility is to seat guests at the wedding ceremony and act as escorts for the bridesmaids. To avoid seating delays, there should be at least one usher for every 50 guests. They also attend all prewedding parties the groom goes to and are required to provide their own wedding clothes, renting the proper formal attire if they do not own it. If formal wedding portraits are not being taken before the ceremony, ushers should arrive fully dressed in their formal wear 45 minutes before the ceremony and assemble near the entrance. As guests arrive, each usher should offer his right arm to each woman and escort her to her seat on the left or right of the aisle, depending on whether she is a friend of the bride or groom.

The Bride's Mother: Your mother usually helps compile the guest list and arranges the details of the ceremony and reception. It is her responsibility to keep the bride's father and future in-laws informed about wedding plans. She should also inform the groom's mother of her wedding attire so that their dresses are similar in length and style. The mother of the bride is privileged to sit in the very first pew on the bride's side. She is the last to be seated and the first to be escorted out of the church after the ceremony. She also greets all guests in the receiving line and sits in a place of honor at the bride's parents' table at the reception.

The Bride's Father: Your father rides in the limousine or car with you on the way to the church and escorts you down the aisle. He is also seated in the first pew behind the bride during the ceremony and later stands in the receiving line greeting and thanking guests. At the reception, he should dance the second dance with the bride and will usually make a short toast or welcoming speech to all the guests.

The Groom's Parents: Your fiancé's mother should be invited to all showers and both his parents should be included in the rehearsal dinner, if they don't host it themselves. They should also contribute to the guest list for the wedding and reception and may or may not offer to share expenses. The groom's parents are honored guests at the ceremony and are seated, just before your mother, in the first pew on the groom's side of the aisle.

WHEN PARENTS ARE DIVORCED

Dealing with divorced parents may add a complication to your wedding plans, but if handled well, everything can still work out just the way you planned. The key is to provide separate places of distinction at the ceremony, in the receiving line, and at the reception to ensure their happiness and enjoyment of the day.

GUIDELINES FOR DIVORCED PARENTS

- **Invitations:** Invitations are usually issued by the parent you have currently lived with. If both parents have contributed, then both names and stepparents can be mentioned.
- **Ceremony seating:** For seating at the ceremony there are two options: if parents are friends and they are not remarried, they can sit side by side in the front pew. Otherwise the parent you have lived with would sit in the front pew with his or her spouse, and the other parent sits in the second or third pew with his or her spouse.
- **Photographs:** Each set of parents will most likely want to have a photo taken with the bride and groom; it is important to spell this out to the photographers earlier. This can take longer for photographs so appropriate time needs to be allocated.
- **Down the Aisle:** Walking down the aisle can be more than just a scary walk when trying to decide whether your father or stepfather should escort you. Consider whether you have remained close to your father and if you want him to fulfill this traditional role; or if your stepfather has filled the role of your father you may decide this is more appropriate. If your father and stepfather get along, you may ask both. If the decision is impossible, choose neither and ask your mother to walk you down.
- **Receiving Line:** For the receiving line and reception, customarily the parent who is paying for the wedding greets the guests with you. The other parent can be mingling. At the reception a good solution to feuding families is to have two different parent tables.

RECEIVING LINE

Usually held at the beginning of the reception, this event allows parents and the wedding party members to greet guests and receive their good wishes. The line traditionally begins with your mother, followed by the groom's mother, the bride and groom, your maid of honor and the rest of the bridesmaids. The fathers can join in and, if so, should stand to the left of their wives. **If your parents are divorced**, your mother stands alone or with your stepfather, while your father circulates among the guests. Or, to avoid confusion, decide not to include fathers in the line. The important thing is to avoid hurt feelings or misunderstandings. Another alternative is to have your father and his new wife stand on the other side of the groom. If you feel it becomes too difficult to orchestrate, it is **perfectly acceptable to mingle and greet your guests during the reception rather than have a receiving line**. Whatever works well for your situation is fine.

SEATING ARRANGEMENTS AT THE RECEPTION

The bride's table, which should be the focus of the reception, can be of any shape and is sometimes elevated so everyone can see the wedding party. The groom usually sits to the bride's left with the maid of honor on his left. To the right of the bride is the best man, and the rest of the bridesmaids and ushers sit at the table male, female, male, female. If it's a small wedding party, the officiant and husbands and wives of the wedding party may also sit at the bride's table. Otherwise, a separate table for parents is set where your mother heads the table and the groom's father sits at her right and the wedding officiant sits at her left. The groom's mother sits on your father's right. However, if your parents are divorced, consider arranging a separate table for each set of parents.

DON'T FORGET THANK-YOU NOTES!

You and your groom must send personal, handwritten notes of appreciation thanking everyone who gave you and your new husband a gift. It is suggested you begin sending thank-you notes immediately upon receiving your gifts. Try to acknowledge each gift within two weeks of its arrival. The customary note is written in blue or black ink on a quality notepaper in white or ivory. Colored or decorated notes are also acceptable. Whatever you choose, the most important thing is that the note be timely and sincere.

If you need more information or advice, several excellent books by the editors of popular bridal magazines and by etiquette experts are available at libraries and book stores. Bridal consultants and bridal-shop personnel are also sources of lots of useful tips and information.

Weddings make us all sentimental. By including a special item or tradition in your ceremony and reception that has been used by other family members, or that you yourself may wish to pass on to future generations, you allow family and friends to share in your joy as well as the traditions of your family.

Here are some ideas that you may wish to incorporate into your wedding:

- Select a Bible that you can comfortably carry down the aisle with you. At the completion of the ceremony, you and your groom can sign your names and your wedding date in the front of the Bible as well as the location and time of your marriage. As each future bride and groom uses it, their names will be added.

- The kneeling cushions and ring-bearer's pillow used during the ceremony can be made from the wedding gown of one of the bridal couple's mothers or grandmothers or from fabric selected for the occasion, and then passed on to future generations of family brides and grooms.

- If you decide not to use your mother's wedding dress, what about using her veiling and attaching it to the headpiece you have selected? This gives you the "something old" to use with your wedding attire.

- Many brides choose to carry a family memento during their wedding. A handkerchief made from the lace of a family member's gown or veil can be easily carried with your bridal bouquet.

- Your wedding garter can be made from satin and lace used by other family members in their wedding attire. Just make sure you have a backup garter for the groom to throw at the end of the reception.

- Instruct your florist to design your bridal bouquet with two detachable flowers that you can give to your mother and mother-in-law as you return down the aisle.

- Since the first toast at the reception signifies the celebration and coming together of two families as well as the beginning of a new one, silver or pewter toasting goblets make wonderful gifts to be passed on to future family brides.

- Your cake knife and server are something you will want to save and pass on.

- The day of your wedding, plant a tree or a rose bush that you can watch grow throughout the years of your marriage.

- A perfect gift from the groom can be a charm bracelet. With each year, in celebration of your wedding anniversary, a new charm can be added.

When you've returned from your honeymoon and have packed away your dress, you'll want to get a special box in which you can carefully pack all of your wedding treasures. Someday you can share them with your daughter(s) and future daughters-in-law.

You will want to put some things together a few days before your wedding to take to the church. We call it the "Wedding Day Survival Kit." It includes all those little odds and ends that you'll need for quick repairs and to cover the things others may have forgotten.

- ❑ Scissors
- ❑ Needles and thread (in the colors of your bridal and attendant gowns)
- ❑ Safety pins
- ❑ Iron and ironing board (if none is available at church or ceremony site)
- ❑ Makeup kit (for light touchups)
- ❑ Hand mirror and makeup mirrors
- ❑ Kleenex
- ❑ Smock or towels to protect dresses from last-minute makeup touchups
- ❑ Electric curlers and curling iron
- ❑ Bobbie pins and combs to anchor veils and headpieces
- ❑ Hair spray
- ❑ Deodorant or antiperspirant
- ❑ Dress shields
- ❑ Extra nylons in the appropriate colors
- ❑ Extra socks for groomsmen and ushers (someone is bound to forget)
- ❑ Toys to keep flower girls and ring bearers busy in a quiet way
- ❑ Smocks for flower girls and ring bearers to wear over their wedding attire until it's time for the photos or ceremony (kids will get dirty!)
- ❑ Masking tape (for last-minute fix-up jobs on decorations)
- ❑ Scotch tape for taping cards to gifts so they don't fall off
- ❑ Lightweight wire (for last-minute repairs on decorations)
- ❑ Super glue
- ❑ Breath freshener
- ❑ Aspirin
- ❑ Smelling salts (just in case one of your attendants faints)
- ❑ Refreshments (pop, ice tea, juice....everyone is bound to get thirsty)
- ❑ Straws (never drink directly from a glass or can; you will undoubtedly spill)
- ❑ A hand-held fan for those hot summer months

Put all your supplies for your "Wedding Day Survival Kit" into a carryall bag and put it next to the things that are going to the church. You'll be glad you have it!

One final tip. Find out whether your church has a stool that you can use in the dressing room. If not, bring one with you. You'll get tired of standing after you've dressed in your gown. If you sit in a chair, you'll wrinkle your gown. This is where the stool comes in handy! Drape your gown skirt and train over the stool, then sit; no wrinkles!

GIVING AWAY
THE BRIDE

The custom of the bride

being given away by her

father has its origins in

ancient times when women

were considered to be

owned by and slaves to

men. The marriage was

treated as a property

transaction, with the right

of ownership being passed

from one man to another.

HELPFUL HINTS

- **You will have the opportunity to attend several excellent bridal shows throughout the year.** The advantage to these shows is that it is a perfect time to meet and talk with area businesses and services and see what they have to offer all in one place.

- **Be prepared!** It's very helpful if you have a **target list** of items and services you will need to have to make your wedding day complete. Don't wander. Have a **plan of action** and go and find the booths that have the services you are looking for.

- **Take notes.** You will receive a lot of information as you are touring the booths, and it can get confusing. Be sure to write down the names of the companies that impress you the most, so that you can come back to the booth to talk with them later. If you are collecting information as you go, **fold down the corners of the brochures or hand-outs** of the companies you like so that you can go directly to their material when you need it.

- **Keep information organized!** *The Bravo!® Wedding Organizer* is the perfect place to store all the valuable information you gather. After the show, pull out the important information and discounts and put into appropriate categories in *The Bravo!® Wedding Organizer*…it's the perfect system. For more information see page 23.

- **Dress comfortably.** Make sure you wear comfortable shoes and clothing. You'll be on your feet for a long time.

- **Take your mother or a friend to help you.** If you have an assistant, they can carry all the information you are gathering so that you can **keep your hands free** to take notes and review information.

    (**Note:** Don't take too many people with you. You'll end up spending all your time trying to find them as they wander off or start talking with other people and you won't accomplish what you set out to do.)

- **Have sticky labels or mail labels with your name and address.** You'll be signing up for a lot of door prizes. It's very quick and easy if you have a label to put on the entry forms.

- **Fashion shows.** This is always one of the biggest features of Bridal Shows. You'll see all the latest fashions for the entire wedding party, in addition to resort wear, attire for mothers of the bride and groom, and more. Most shows will provide you with a program. Keep it in-hand so that if you see something you fall in love with, you'll know where to go to find it after the fashion show is over.

For more assistance with staying organized during the wedding planning process, check out the Bravo! Wedding Organizer. Detailed question worksheets double as contracts. This step-by-step system will keep every detail of your wedding organized. To order, refer to the order form on page 23 in this Guide.

Extraordinary Events

"Willamette Valley's Finest Event Professionals"

Second Annual Fall Bridal Event

Sunday, November 7th, 1999
1–3p.m.

Willamette Valley Vineyards
Great Room
8800 Enchanted Way, S.E.
Salem, Oregon

Featuring shops and services from nine wedding professionals

Act One Linen Rentals
Beaver Tents
Class Act Wedding Coordinators
Daniel's Photography
Elegant Creations Cakes and Confections
Green Thumb Florists
Music Express Disc Jockey Service
Tomorrow's Treasures Invitations and Accessories
Willaby's Catering

For more information call:
Susan Adkins or Jean Williamson
(503) 371-5470

The date is tentative and subject to change.

MEIER & FRANK

Upcoming Bridal Events

Wednesday, January 27 • 6:30 p.m.
Washington Square Bridal Event
9300 S.W. Washington Square Road, Tigard

Saturday, January 30 • 8:30 a.m.
Vancouver Mall Mother & Daughter Bridal Breakfast
4917 N.E. Thurston Way, Vancouver

Thursday, February 11 • 6:30 p.m.
Vancouver Mall Bridal Event
4917 N.E. Thurston Way, Vancouver

Wednesday, March 10 • 6:30 p.m.
Clackamas Town Center Bridal Event
12100 S.E. 82nd Ave., Portland

Wednesday, April 7 • 6:30 p.m.
Lloyd Center Bridal Event
1100 Lloyd Center, Portland

Thursday, April 8 • 6:30 p.m.
Salem Center Bridal Event
400 High St. N.E., Salem

These dates are tentative and subject to change.
Please call for more information and a 1999 fall calendar of events.
(503) 241-5194

Two Great Wedding Shows

1 ◇ 9 ◇ 9 ◇ 9

Mid~Willamette Valley Bridal Show

January 9th and 10th, 1999
Jackman Long Building
Oregon State Fairgrounds
Salem, Oregon

HOURS:
Saturday, January 9th • 10 a.m. to 5 p.m.
Fashion Shows at 11 a.m. and 2:30 p.m.

Sunday, January 10th • 11 a.m. to 5 p.m.
Fashion Shows at 12:30 p.m. and 3 p.m.

  Admission $6

SCHOOL OF
PROFESSIONAL DEVELOPMENT
and Models Agency

—◇—

Linn Benton Bridal Show

October 9th and 10th, 1999
Linn County Fairgrounds
Albany, Oregon

HOURS:
Saturday, October 9th • 10 a.m. to 5 p.m.
Fashion Shows at 11 a.m. and 2:30 p.m.

Sunday, October 10th • 11 a.m. to 5 p.m.
Fashion Shows at 12:30 p.m. and 3 p.m.

Free Parking • Free Admission

 *produced by:*
(800) 537-9396

the *1999* Pacific Northwest

Wedding Showcase
for Him & for Her

winter show February 27th & 28th

summer show July 25th

10 a.m. to 5 p.m.
at the Oregon
Convention Center

Tickets $7 available at Fred Meyer Fastixx or at the show. Good for $1.00 off Admission with this ad

More than just a bridal fair

The all new 1999 Pacific Northwest Wedding Showcase has something for brides and grooms alike. You'll find traditional wares as well as exciting alternative ideas for planning the most special day of your life... Your wedding.

Over 100 specialty exhibitors

Romance specialists from the Northwest will offer tips on how to plan your wedding. Two daily fashion shows will highlight the latest in bridal gowns, tuxedos and other wedding party attire. Mark your calendar and plan to attend our exclusive Wedding Showcase.

*Your presence is the only gift we request.
to RSVP for exhibit space or for more information, call
(503) 295-8587*

produced by

media sponsors

CorEvents

K103 fm
Soft rock for a busy world.

Please let this show know that you heard about them from the Bravo! Bridal Resource Guide.

$1 OFF DISCOUNT COUPON

107.5 THE BEAT *sponsors*

The Original

Portland Bridal Show

The "Bride's Bridal Show"
with the Bridal Fashion Premiere
of the Season

Don't Miss It!!
This is Portland's *Big* Bridal Show

Plan your entire wedding with over 130 "Wedding Related" Exhibitors

Saturday & Sunday - January 9th & 10th, 1999
Oregon Convention Center

Win!
A Romantic Honeymoon Get-Away at the

Columbia Gorge Hotel

will be given away at **each show**!
Some Restrictions May Apply

Showtimes:

Mornings	Afternoons	Evening
Doors Open 10:30 am	Doors Open 2:00 pm	Doors Open 5:00 pm
Fashion Show 12:30 pm	Fashion Show 3:30 pm	Fashion Show 6:30 pm
(Each Day)	**(Each Day)**	**(Saturday only)**

Tickets:

Admission $7 at the Door - $6 with this Ad
for Adults _and_ Children

No Strollers Allowed

One Coupon per person - _Not Valid_ for Saturday 10:30am (Morning) show

Shows sell out early! - Advance Tickets Guarantee Admission

Advance *Tickets* at
FASTIXX

For Additional Show Information Call (503) 274-6027
Tentative Year 2000 Show Dates: January 8th and 9th, 2000

Portland's Premiere Bridal Tea

— Top Wedding Professionals —
— Fashion Show —
— Guest Speaker —
— Luncheon —

Held at the beautiful

Downtown Embassy Suites Hotel

319 S.W. Pine Street

Saturday, February 20, 1999

11 a.m. to 2 p.m.

$19.95 per person

For tickets contact Crystal Lilies

(503) 221-7701

Seating Limited

Elegance · Presentation · Selection · Answers to your Questions

Bridal Show
January 16, '99
presented by

WeddingLink
Your Link to Wedding Professionals

Plan the wedding of your dreams with a little help from some of Portland-Vancouver's top wedding professionals. Look at the great ideas, see exciting new products and services and best of all talk directly to the experts. This is the show where you get the answers and personal help you're looking for.

We invite you to take all the time you need. The show runs form 9am to 6pm. Enjoy our gourmet fare, hors d'oeuvres, cakes, pastries and other delicacies. Plus one of the most elegant bridal fashion shows in the Northwest at 10am, 1pm and 4pm. Arrive early for best seating.

COUPLES.
Free honeymoon package from Couples the complete Jamaican Resort, from "Unforgettable Honeymoons".

Plus many more wedding products and services ...

Win the entire package worth $10,000

DoubleTree Hotel at the Quay
Just off I-5 on the Columbia River
Vancouver, WA

Free Parking
admission $6, $5 with can food donation

Weddings of Distinction

*Weddings of Distinction is a
nonprofit group of select professionals
dedicated to excellence in bridal services.*

Calendar of Events

•

**5th Annual
Weddings of Distinction Bridal Tea & Fashion Show**
Saturday, January 23rd • Noon
The Benson Hotel

•

**8th Annual
Zell Bros Bridal Show**
Saturday, April 10 • 11 a.m.–3 p.m.
Zell Bros

•

*Call to receive more information on
planning the wedding of your dreams and
our updated calendar of events.*

•

**(503) 227-8471
Zell Bros**

These dates are subject to change. Please call for confirmation.

TRADITIONS

In Roman times a man gave

his bride-to-be a coin or

gold ring as "down

payment" for the bride and

to show his good intentions

to wed her.

•

The bride stands to the

groom's left because in

Medieval times he needed

to keep his sword hand free

(a) to fend off attacks from

those not wanting the

wedding to take place

and/or (b) to keep an

unwilling bride at his side.

Child Care
To Go, Inc.
"We bring the quality to you."
7933 S.E. Morrison
Portland Oregon 97215
(503) 254-1319
E-mail: LMROBERTS@juno.com
Web site: http://www.marketing1.com/ChildCareToGo

Child Care To Go, Inc. provides a full range of **on-site** child care services, taking care of your child care needs. We provide high quality care for weddings, receptions, meetings, conferences, special occasions, or just anytime you want an adult-only event. Child Care To Go, Inc. also provides individual family care. Perfect for business people wanting to bring their families with them on their business trips.

We've been in the child care industry since 1988, providing quality care to children in the Portland area. This service allows parents to bring their children to your function and know that they are well cared for and close by.

Child Care To Go, Inc. brings all equipment needed to care for and entertain the children. We also have cots and playpens available for sleeping. All you need to do is provide the space and we will do the rest.

Base Charge for Group Care
◆ $35 set-up fee
◆ $35 per hour, this price includes: one care provider, changing table, playpens and/or cots, and play equipment for up to 3 children under 1 year, 4 children up to 2 1/2 years, 6 children up to 6 years, and 8 children over 6 years

Base Charge for Individual Care
◆ No set-up fee
◆ $25 per hour, for single family care only. Multiple family care is charged at group rate

Additional Charges
◆ $25 per hour for each additional care provider needed for group care

Service Agreement
◆ Child Care To Go, Inc. will come and set up and be ready to receive children 1/2 hour before your event.
◆ All care providers provided are well trained and have been cleared with a criminal background check.
◆ 3 hour minimum time required for services.
◆ CCTG reserves the right to have final approval of site. Space provided must be appropriate for the needs of the children.

BRIDESMAIDS TEA

Traditionally, a cake that had a special ring baked into it was served to all the bridesmaids at a tea. The bridesmaid who was served the lucky slice was believed to be the next one to marry.

HELPFUL HINTS

- **A consultant can ease the stress:** Hiring a consultant is a wise idea, especially if there is arguing between mother and daughter, between families, divorced parents and even attendants. This is an emotional time, an objective opinion of a consultant can sometimes ease the pressure. Money can be one of the biggest problems and obstacles. If a third party is involved, such as a consultant, they can collect the money without it being embarrassing. Many times arguments result from lack of communication, emotional overload and misconceptions. The two parties just need to communicate; sometimes writing it down and having someone calm present to the other half, is a good way to deal with it.

- **A consultant can save money and mistakes:** Brides and grooms sometimes feel a consultant can be an additional expense that they cannot afford. In fact a consultant can be your best investment especially if you are on a strict budget. An experienced consultant can help a couple avoid common mistakes. Working with vendors can be costly if the right questions are not asked, and a bride and groom with the help of a consultant will never feel pressured into booking a service, because the consultant knows the timeline and whether a sales pitch is just that or not.

- **Services available:** Wedding consultants and event planners can arrange as little or as much of your event or wedding as you want. How they bill for their services varies. Even though you are paying them for their time, in most cases they can save you money in other areas because of their familiarity with different services and discounts that are available to them as frequent customers.

- **Why hire an event planner or consultant?** People are often under the misconception that planning your own event and preparing the food, setup, decorating and cleanup will save money. In fact it can sometimes cost more—not just in money, but in time and headaches as well. A good consultant can work with you and your budget, saving valuable time and money allowing you to enjoy the event.

- **Selecting a consultant:** Talk to different consultants before making your final decision and find out who is familiar with providing the types and level of service you're looking for. Don't be afraid to ask questions or to see portfolios and ask for references. The person or company you select should be the one you feel most comfortable with personally and professionally.

- **Finding a banquet, reception, or ceremony site:** Qualified consultants have been to and seen locations that you may never have heard of, but that are perfect for your event. Some consultants have videotapes and photographs of various sites, so you can preview a variety of locations without having to drive all over town. Once you have made your selection, your consultant can make sure your date and time are available, and arrange for you to visit the location.

- **NOTE:** Be specific about the services you want and what your budget is. From this information a consultant will be able to offer you a variety of suggestions that will work for you and your wedding plans. Be sure to read any and all contracts before signing them so that there is no confusion at a later date about who is responsible for what and how much it will cost.

For more assistance with staying organized during the wedding planning process, check out the Bravo! Wedding Organizer. Detailed question worksheets double as contracts. This step-by-step system will keep every detail of your wedding organized. To order, refer to the order form on page 23 in this Guide.

Class Act

EVENT • COORDINATORS

Full-Service Event Planners
Contact: Susan Adkins, Owner
Portland *(503) 295-7890*
Salem *(503) 371-8904*
Fax (503) 589-9166
Business Hours: Mon–Fri 8am–5pm
Web site: http://www.open.org/classact/
E-mail: classact@open.org

WEDDINGS • REUNIONS • HOLIDAY PARTIES
SEMINARS • FUND RAISERS

Class Act is a full-service event management agency offering planning-to-cleanup services for successful parties and programs. Class Act's skilled event coordinators help you with budget preparation, site selection, rental arrangements, decorations, entertainment, food and beverages, setup, takedown, and post-event arrangements.

Specialties

- **High school reunions:** we manage everything from start to finish, including memory yearbook preparations.
- **Weddings:** we design weddings and receptions to match the unique preferences of each couple.

Service Fee and Consultation

- **Reunions:** Class Act charges based on the number of people attending, and the fee includes all services, from early organization to post-event mailings. Organizers should meet with us at least a year before the event to guarantee the greatest range of options.
- **Other events:** Class Act bids a flat fee based on project size. Fees include all services. We recommend that brides begin meeting with us between a year and nine months before the wedding.

Experience and Business Network

Class Act has been operating since 1987, coordinating events large and small for individuals, families, reunion classes, and businesses. We encourage you to call our references to ask about their successful experiences with our event planning services. Our network of quality florists, entertainers, bands, disc jockeys, caterers, and related service providers offer a range of products and pricing.

WE TAKE CARE OF DETAILS!

Class Act is committed to personalized service. Your event should match your style, your vision, and your budget. That's why we spend time just listening to you about your preferences, your goals, and your expectations. Based on your ideas, we recommend creative themes and decorating suggestions, and identify the best people and vendors to implement every aspect of your unique project.

We love to help you create the most successful event while relieving you of the responsibility of details. We want you to enjoy the event as much as your guests will.

Tualatin, Oregon
Contact: Heather K. Willig
(503) 692-8555; E-mail: idowedd@teleport.com
Business Hours: by appointment

WHY "I DO" WEDDINGS?™

Creative Design/Innovation
Where do your wedding dreams take you? Jumping from an airplane? A private reception at a local vineyard? Or perhaps yachting on the Columbia? *"I Do" Weddings*™ works within your budget to make your special day memorable!

No Rookies
With over 10 years of event coordination experience, we can arrange for anything from an intimate wedding for 25 to a reception for 500.

Have Fun!
At *"I Do" Weddings*™, we're as excited as you are for your big day. So to give you the attention you deserve, we only work with a certain number of brides per year. Call *"I Do" Weddings*™ today to pamper yourself.

"Day of" Packages
Have you taken care of the big items but need assistance with the details? Do you need someone to take over where you've left off? Let *"I Do" Weddings*™ organize your details for you! We'll be the first to arrive… and the last to leave!

Vendor Relationships
Are you looking for the perfect, but unusual party favor? How about the best place to find a 3-tiered cheesecake? Is your budget limited, but your ideas are not? Let *"I Do" Weddings*™ find the perfect caterer, DJ, photographer, etc. for you. No pressure, no hassles. You decide who you can afford and feel most comfortable with.

Peace of Mind
Relax… *"I Do" Weddings*™ will assist with every detail from the day you say "yes", to the day you say "I Do." You can count on us to work within your budget and to provide a stress-free wedding.

Competitive Pricing
Call *"I Do" Weddings*™ for pricing on our "Day of" and "Full-service" packages.

Certification
"I Do" Weddings™ is a member of the Association of Bridal Consultants, a national organization committed to creating high standards of professionalism in the bridal consulting industry.

Party Pleasers
Wedding/Event Planning Services
Keri Baird
Professional Consultant
663-0772

FULL-SERVICE PLANNING
WITH PERSONALIZED SERVICE

Planning a special occasion takes time and detail, with a knowledge of available resources.

Party Pleasers specializes in planning all of the details of your special event by comparing prices, visiting facilities, making phone calls, and meeting with vendors to bring you quality services and savings, to save you time, money and stress.

Types of Events Include

- Complete wedding and event planning (You make the decisions; we will take care of all the details.)
- On-site coordinator for events, rehearsals, weddings, and receptions
- Planning and organizing the perfect location for rehearsal dinners
- Personalized bridal showers, baby showers, or luncheons
- Memorable anniversary and birthday parties (includes shopping for that special gift)
- Festive holiday parties
- Fun-filled company picnics and seminars

Experienced Business Networks

Party Pleasers recommends professional, detail-oriented vendors to provide the following services for your special event:

- Budget
- Site Selection
- Post-event Arrangements
- Catering (food and beverages)
- Bartending Services
- Florists
- Decorations and Party Supplies
- Entertainment
- Invitations, Announcements, and Programs
- Transportation
- Hotel and Travel Accommodations
- Photographers and Videographers
- Formal wear
- Makeup Artistry
- Registry and Gifts
- Rental Arrangements
- Complete Setup and Takedown

EXPECT ONLY THE BEST WITH PARTY PLEASERS!

R.S.V.P.

event planning made simple

Contact: Lisa Komer
(503) 624-8395; Fax (503) 620-4106
E-mail: lkomer@classic.msn.com

R.S.V.P. is a complete event planning service. Whether you are planning a wedding, Christmas party, business luncheon or anniversary party, R.S.V.P. caters to all of your needs.

Services Offered include
- Ceremony and Reception location and coordination
- Caterer
- Photographer
- Florist
- Cakes and candies
- Rental equipment
- Decorations
- Invitations, including custom-made
- Music
- Transportation
- Honeymoon
- Bridal attire and formalwear
- Bridesmaid dresses
- "Day of" event coordination

Fees
Since every event is unique, fees are based on services required. Please contact Lisa Komer to schedule a free consultation.

Planning a wedding is an exciting, as well as, stressful event. R.S.V.P. is here to alleviate your stress so you can sit back and enjoy one of the most important events of your life.

You have the image of your dream wedding... Together we will make all your dreams come true. I look forward to working with you to create a truly memorable wedding day.

Contact Lisa Komer for a consultation.
(503) 624-8395; Fax (503) 620-4106
E-mail: lkomer@classic.msn.com

Marilyn Storch

Special Occasion Consulting
P.O. Box 219293
Portland, Oregon 97225-9293
(503) 520-9667; Fax (503) 644-5991
E-mail: mstorch@teleport.com

© Jamie Bosworth

You're engaged! Now what do you do? You know Who. Now all you need to decide is When? Where? What? How? and How Much?

You and your fiancé should look forward to the big day with the least amount of stress possible. After all, this "business" of a wedding is quite an undertaking! It involves your closest friends, your loving families, legal documents, months of planning, coordinating and deadlines, the hiring of many professionals, emotional overload...and You, the Star.

Do you really want to be the director at your own wedding? Do you really want to have your mother, aunt, and friends handle the details? Wouldn't it be nicer to have your mother, aunt and friends by your side, relaxing and enjoying your day along with you?

Let Marilyn relieve you from hundreds of details, allowing you the luxury of experiencing your extraordinary day the way you should. Trained by the best in the industry, Marilyn feels your excitement and anticipates your wedding day along with you. With her calm nature and professional demeanor, Marilyn will lift the load off of your shoulders and into her hands, resulting in a wedding day that flows smoothly. Her behind-the-scenes guidance will put polish on your special day and allow you to shine.

Marilyn loves what she does and would like to help you have the wedding of your dreams. And she's only a phone call away...

careful • professional • calm

VARIOUS PACKAGE OPTIONS

Elizabeth Toscano
Wedding Planner

Portland (503) 226-6700
Mosier (541) 478-4455
E-mail: cherryhill@gorge.net

Experience

After more than a decade of coordinating weddings and events, Elizabeth Toscano is now offering her services to brides and grooms who want expert help in planning their Portland area wedding or commitment ceremony. As owner of Cherry Hill, the premier outdoor wedding venue in the Columbia River Gorge, Toscano has handled the myriad of details for hundreds of celebrations—from intimate gatherings of five, to black tie occasions for over 300 guests.

Professional Wedding Planning

Because of her complete familiarity with local wedding services, Toscano knows where and how to get the best of everything—photographers, pastry chefs, caterers, florists, musicians and officiants. Her expertise will ensure your wedding runs smoothly and is everything you hoped it would be.

Fees

At the initial complimentary telephone consultation, Toscano will discuss with you all elements that go into the planning of your event and their approximate cost. You will then have the option of hiring her on an hourly consultation basis or you may choose to have her handle all the details of your wedding for a fixed fee.

"Everyone I have talked to has said it was the best wedding they have ever been to!"
—Ellen Stevenson, bride, Vancouver, Washington

*"A **huge** thank you for all you did to make July 25th a special day, not only for Sara and Stephen, but all our families and friends."*
—Susan Renwick, mother of the bride, Pasadena, California

"Toscano's matter-of-factness, combined with an impeccable sense of taste and organization, has helped her to become the Martha Stewart of Gorge weddings."
—*Hood River News*, August 20, 1997

See page 119 under Banquet & Reception Sites.

Weddings by Linda

ॐ

19093 S. Beavercreek Road, Suite 348
Oregon City, Oregon 97045
(503) 557-0282, (888) TO SAY I DO (867-2943)
Fax (503) 557-3253
E-mail: tosayido@northwest.com
Web site: http://www.weddingsbylinda.com

Congratulations on your engagement! Weddings by Linda knows that planning your wedding can be confusing, overwhelming and stressful. Having a professional wedding consultant assist can save you time and money. Preparing for that special day can be fun and rewarding when Weddings by Linda is helping you fulfill your wedding dreams.

The relationship between Linda and her vendors is one of trust, reliability, customer service and superb excellence in their field. She has high standards and knows her clients can rest assured they will have top priority.

Whether you need referrals or a full-service planner and coordinator, Linda is always available to assist in any way she can. There are many questions you may have regarding wedding etiquette or traditions, please feel free to call Linda anytime and she will gladly help you find the information you are looking for.

ॐ How Linda Got Started

Linda began her wedding career singing in choir and professionally for weddings in 1977 at age 12. In the 1980s it blossomed into more than just singing…she was assisting with her friends' and family's weddings and receptions, and she was having a blast. Then in 1993, Linda was married and realized how naturally it all came to her. Maintaining a career in the corporate world, she knew there was more to life than this, and one day while sitting at her desk, she asked herself once again, what can I do as a self-employed person that would entail working with people and having fun? Voila! Wedding consultant! She called her accountant, found out the logistics of what she would need to get started and by the time she got home that evening she had a business started. She hasn't looked back since and is having the time of her life!

ॐ Linda's Pricing

Linda bases her fee on the needs of each job, whether you need referrals beginning at $25 or full-service planning, Linda's fees are competitive and reasonable. You won't be disappointed when Linda is working for you.

ॐ Linda's Area of Expertise

Linda specializes in rehearsal dinners, wedding ceremonies and receptions but also loves to assist in the honeymoon arrangements, living arrangements for out-of-town guests, etc. She has a great relationship with the local hotels and inn keepers who work with Linda and give special discounts to her clients. She makes sure your out-of-town guests are provided with tourist literature for those who might have an interest in checking out the local hot spots.

Your Day Your Way

Personalized Wedding Planning
Specializing In Unique Ceremonies & Celebrations
Contact: Sarah Schurr
(503) 771-8221
E-mail: sure@europa.com

Have Fun At Your Own Wedding!
Your Day Your Way can help to plan the wedding that is just right for you, reflecting your own individual style and personality.

Don't Know Where To Start?
Your Day Your Way can help you in planning a wedding you can be proud of and enjoy. I provide recommendations to prescreened vendors in a variety of styles. I will work with you to put together a truly unique event.

Help On The Big Day!
I can attend your rehearsal and wedding to assure that everything goes according to your plan, providing a calm, friendly resource for any questions. You will be free to enjoy your wedding with family and friends.

Affordable, Flexible Rates!
Your Day Your Way can provide as much or as little service as you want. I charge on a flat hourly rate, making it easy to purchase only the hours you need. Choose only rehearsal and wedding day service, only planning services, or help from beginning to end. I offer a free initial visit for brides to check out my service risk-free with no obligation.

Unique and Personal Weddings Are My Specialty
Second marriages, blending families, multicultural weddings, commitment ceremonies, holy unions...I love to help make your wedding day special. From small artistic weddings to large theme weddings, all get my personal attention.

For your free initial consultation
call Sarah Schurr at
(503) 771-8221
or e-mail at
sure@europa.com

Check out the *Your Day Your Way* web site at
http://www.europa.com/~sure/

JEANNE LAPP

2925 Ascot Circle
West Linn, OR ❦ 97068
(503) 657-1070 ❦ Fax: 557-8825

Your Perfect Wedding

E-mail: yourperfectweddingjelap@aol.com

You want your wedding to be perfect—each part carefully planned so that the special activities of the day flow smoothly, happen at the right time and never appear awkward. Whether you've decided on a small, intimate gathering or a grand celebration, Jeanne Lapp will help make your wedding day a dream come true.

Specialties

Weddings, and only weddings, are Jeanne's expertise. She devotes herself to helping each bride fulfill her special wedding dream. Caring, friendly and attentive to each bride's needs, she is dedicated to finding the right wedding professionals to work within a bride's vision, time frame and budget. Since producing weddings are her joy, you can rest assured that the end results will far exceed your own expectations.

Experience

Jeanne offers over ten years experience as a wedding consultant in the Portland area. Five of those years were spent as wedding coordinator at The Old Church. She has planned and carried out Bridal Faires and has given her own bridal workshops. Her customers know her as a consummate professional.

> *"Jeanne, thank you for making our wedding possible. Because of your time, patience, understanding, and organization, we had a perfect wedding day."*
> Troy and Lori MacKenzie

> *"You made our wedding perfect. You were helpful and encouraging from the very beginning. We feel fortunate to have had your services."*
> Teresa and Jeff Cumpston

From the moment you have your first conversation with Jeanne, until the final day when you prepare to walk down the aisle, you can take comfort in knowing that every detail of your special day will be handled professionally, carefully, and thoughtfully.

Fees

Call Jeanne to schedule a consultation to determine your needs. A fee will be quoted for the services you desire.

Dreams are fragile...place them in competent hands

Notes

TRADITIONS

*The handkerchief carried
by farmers' wives was a
good luck charm. The tears
cried at the wedding would
bring rain for the crops. It
was also said that "she
who cried at her wedding
wouldn't shed another tear
afterwards."*

•

*Amongst the Romans a kiss
was the bond to a legal
agreement. At a wedding
ceremony, however, it was
the transfer of the power of
the souls.*

*Romantic mansion located on
two wooded acres overlooking the Willamette River*

Amadeus
at the FERNWOOD

*2122 S.E. Sparrow (Off River Road Exit)
Milwaukie, Oregon 97222
Contact: Kristina (503) 659-1735, (503) 353-8948
Business Hours: Seven days a week,
5pm–midnight; Sunday Brunch 10am–2:30pm*

Capacity: 300 people

Price Range: lunches $20; full course sit-down or buffet style dinners $27; plus gratuity

Catering: full-service in-house catering

Types of Events: bridal luncheons, rehearsal dinners, **on-location wedding ceremonies**, ceremonies and receptions, large group luncheons

Availability and Terms

We are here for your personal needs to make your rehearsal dinner celebration the most romantic and elegant. Reservations should be made as soon as possible to ensure availability. A deposit is required at the time of booking. Half the deposit is refundable if cancellations are made at least six months prior to your event. **No** cost for using the facility, bartending services, linens, flowers, and candles.

Description of Facility and Services

Seating: table and chairs provided for up to 300

Servers: provided with catering services

Bar facilities: full-service bar with bartender provided; host/no host; liquor provided according to OLCC regulations

Linens: cloth tablecloths and napkins provided in cream color

China and glassware: fine china; variety of glassware

Cleanup: provided by Amadeus at the Fernwood

Decorations: early decorating available; fresh flowers for guest tables provided by Amadeus; please discuss ideas with banquet representative

Parking: ample free parking; valet service

ADA: disabled access available

FACILITY OVERLOOKING WILLAMETTE RIVER

Amadeus at the Fernwood is the perfect setting for a romantic rehearsal dinner or wedding reception. You and your guests will enjoy fine continental dining in a wonderful old mansion on two wooded acres, filled with antiques, fireplaces, crystal chandeliers, candlelight and fresh flowers, overlooking the Willamette River. We offer a full bar with a wide variety of Oregon and international wines, and outdoor dining and wedding ceremonies on our patio is available. A classical pianist is featured nightly and during Sunday brunch.

SUNSET DINNER SPECIAL: Daily • 5–6:30pm • $9.95

Please let this business know that you heard about them from the Bravo! Bridal Resource Guide.

BUFFALO GAP SALOON & EATERY

6835 S.W. Macadam (just north of the Sellwood Bridge) • Portland, Oregon 97219
(503) 244-7111; Fax (503) 246-8848
Business Hours: Mon–Fri 7–2:30am, Sat 8–2:30am, Sun 9–2:30am
Office Hours: Mon–Fri 7am–5pm
Web site: http://www.citysearch.com/pdx/buffalogap

Capacity: groups from 20 to 50 people

Price Range: typically $10–$15; customized menus available; room fees range from $35–100

Catering: full in-house catering exclusively

Types of Events: receptions, rehearsal dinners, parties, social events, business meetings

Availability and Terms

Early reservations strongly encouraged. The Buffalo Gap's "Attic" can be utilized as a completely private space, with full bar, private restrooms, and sundeck (weather permitting).

Description of Facility and Services

Seating: tables and chairs provided

Servers and bartenders: included in price

Bar facilities: two full-service bars; beer and wine

Linens and napkins: white or colored linens can be ordered

China and glassware: provided by Buffalo Gap

Decorations: table decorations are permissible

Cleanup: included at no extra charge

Parking: free on-site and adjacent parking available

Special Services

The Gap has one of the most beautiful and intimate (up to 30 guests) garden patios in the city, an upstairs sundeck, two full-service bars, a game and billiards room, a very accommodating staff, and live music five nights a week.

A GREAT GATHERING PLACE
WITH SOMETHING FOR EVERYONE

The Buffalo Gap's building is over 100 years old, and has been used, among other things, as a private residence, rooming house, brothel and saloon. In business for over 25 years, with over 150 menu items to choose from, the gap is conveniently located and a wonderful experience for a diverse group of people.

1331 S.W. Washington
Portland, Oregon 97205
Contact: Christine, Bob or Mercedes
(503) 223-0054

A Portland Favorite since 1979!

Cassidy's Restaurant is located in a historic building in the heart of downtown Portland. Our exceptional menu features regional cuisine of delicious seafood, premium-cut meats, fresh pastas, seasonal salads and more.

Capacity: up to 70

Private Banquet Room

Cassidy's private banquet room is warm and inviting, and your guests will enjoy all the privileges of our restaurant service. The room is accented with beveled glass windows, natural woodwork and original art by Northwest artists. It is the perfect place for your rehearsal dinner.

Services

- **Food**   From a sit-down dinner or extensive buffet to appetizers and desserts, we offer our fresh Northwest specialties. We'll help you plan a menu just right for your occasion.
- **Beverage**   Cassidy's Restaurant offers a wide assortment of spirits, beers, wine and nonalcoholic beverages.
- **Staff**   Cassidy's staff of experienced restaurant professionals also services our special events.
- **Cost**   Cost is based on your choice of menu. There is no room charge for use of the banquet room or restaurant.
- **Linens**   White tablecloths and napkins available at no additional cost.

Catering

Cassidy's offers full-service catering at the location of your choice.

RESERVE THE ENTIRE RESTAURANT
FOR AFTERNOON WEEKEND RECEPTIONS!

Call Bob, Mercedes or Christine for a consultation.

See page 297 under Caterers & Ice Carvings.

CHART HOUSE®

5700 S.W. Terwilliger Boulevard
Portland, Oregon 97201
(503) 246-6963
Business Hours:
Mon–Fri 11:30am–10pm;
Sat 5–10pm; Sun 5–9pm

Capacity: 20–200
Price Range: please call for current prices
Catering: in-house
Types of Events: ceremonies, receptions, rehearsal dinners, bar mitzvahs, birthday parties and wakes

Availability and Terms

The entire facility is available for private functions on Saturdays and Sundays until 3:30pm, semi-private dining areas are available during lunch and dinner operating hours. Special event reservations are secured with a deposit.

Description of Facility and Services

Seating: we can create seating arrangements appropriate for any event
Servers: staff included in price; 18% gratuity on food and beverages
Bar facilities: full or limited bar available
Dance floor: 30-person capacity; electricity available for band or disc jockey
Linens: tablecloths and napkins available in many colors for a minimal charge
China and glassware: white china; clear glassware
Decorations: schedule early decorating; no limitations if decorations do not harm wood, plants, or paintings; flowers and candles available for arrangements; no confetti, please
Parking: complimentary valet parking
ADA: on entrance level; restroom for disabled

Special Services

Chart House offers a unique wedding and reception setting. Our banquet facility is located in a cozy room with a stone fireplace, bar and magnificent views of the city and mountains. We would be happy to offer help in arranging your event and recommending bakeries, florists and photographers. Cake cutting is complimentary.

SPECTACULAR VIEWS!

The Portland Chart House is perched high in the west hills with panoramic views of Mount Hood, Mount St. Helens, the Willamette River and the city lights below. The restaurant boasts a spectacular view coupled with the finest quality food and beverage, and a professionally trained staff that will ensure a memorable dining experience.

2229 S.E. Hawthorne Boulevard
Portland, Oregon 97214
Contact: Jane Meredith or Charlie Slate (503) 239-4002
Business Hours: Mon–Thu 11:30am–10pm; Fri–Sat 11:30am–11pm; Sun 5–10pm

Capacity: 40 banquet, 120 restaurant
Price Range: $6–$15
Catering: in-house catering for groups of 20-40; several menus available
Types of Events: rehearsal dinners, wedding receptions, business meetings, office parties, banquets

Availability and Terms
The banquet room is available during all operating hours with the exception of Friday and Saturday evenings. Seventy-two-hour notice required.

Description of Facility and Services
Seating: tables and chairs provided
Servers: full staff available
Bar facilities: full-service bar on the premises
Linens and napkins: variety available with prior notice
Decorations: welcome
Cleanup: provided
Parking: plenty of street parking available
ADA: fully accessible

FRESH SOUTHWESTERN CUISINE
Minutes away from downtown Portland and the Oregon Convention Center, Chez Grill offers fresh, innovative, and inexpensive Southwestern cuisine. We feature fresh homemade tortillas, and our full bar provides Portland's best margaritas.

ITALIAN RESTAURANT

8544 S.W. Apple Way
Portland, Oregon 97225
Contact: Gwen Tiemeyer (503) 292-0119; Fax (503) 292-6451
Business Hours: Mon–Thu 11am–10pm; Fri 11am–11pm; Sat 4:30–11pm; Sun 4–10pm

Capacity: seating from 20 to 150, depending on requirements

Price Range: room rental and setup fees may be waived when meal minimums are met; ranges $9.95–$18.95

Catering: full service in-house and on-location catering

Types of Events: wedding receptions, rehearsal dinners, meetings, luncheons, banquets

Availability and Terms

Advance reservations of two to six months are recommended, however, we will try to accommodate last minute events when possible. A deposit is required to secure the room.

Description of Facility and Services

Seating: variety of seating options available for up to 150

Servers: provided

Bar facilities: host/no-host bars available; restaurant supplies all liquor and bartender

Dance floor: available upon request

Linens: cloth linens available in limited colors at no additional cost; special colors can be ordered for a fee

China and glassware: included in the cost of food and beverage

Decorations: standard decorations including helium balloons acceptable

Parking: ample free parking

ADA: meets all standards; all meeting rooms on ground level

CONVENIENT BEAVERTON LOCATION

Our new restaurant (between Jesuit High School and Zupans on Beaverton-Hillsdale Highway) features spacious dining rooms, a full-service lounge and gorgeous meeting/banquet rooms. Three generations of Italian recipes including fresh pasta, veal, chicken, pizza, calzone and charbroiled steaks. We feature banquet menus that include both Italian and American food, and we know you'll find the service and atmosphere first class. Accessible from both I-5 and Highway 217 and only 10 minutes from downtown Portland.

102 Oak Avenue
Hood River, Oregon
97031

Reservations
(800) 386-1859

Sales
(541) 386-1900

E-mail: HRHotel@gorge.net; Web site: www.hoodriverhotel.com

A unique location for your rehearsal dinner—
the Hood River Hotel

Capacity: 5 to 200 guests
Price Range: price varies according to room, time of year, and menu selection
Catering: full-service in-house catering or off-premise
Types of Events: weddings, receptions, rehearsal dinners; informal hors d'oeuvres to formal sit-down dinners; off-site catering available

Availability and Terms
Hood River Hotel's ballroom can accommodate up to 250 people. Additional areas are available for groups of 20 or fewer. We suggest that you book early to ensure availability. A deposit is required at time of booking to secure your date with the balance due the day of your event.

Description of Facility and Services
Seating: tables and chairs for up to 200 people
Servers and cleanup: included in catering cost
Bar facilities: full liquor service from Pasquale's Ristorante and Wine Cellar Bar; bartender included in price quote; extensive selection of wines and champagnes
Dance floor: accommodates up to 55 people
Linens and napkins: cloth linens available in a variety of colors
China and glassware: traditional pattern; assorted glassware
Decorations: floral supplies available upon request; early decorating by prior arrangement; some restrictions apply; in-house florist available
Parking: on-street and designated off-site parking
ADA: fully accessible

Special Services
- Baby Grand piano
- Dance floor and stage
- Wine Cellar
- Built-in sound and PA system
- Full bar
- Wood burning fireplace

ROMANTIC AMBIENCE
The Hood River Hotel offers the romantic ambience you're looking for. With our Baby Grand piano and built-in sound and PA system, you can enjoy a variety of music at your event. Use our Wine Cellar for a wine tasting party or entertain your guests by our wood burning fireplace.

Il Fornaio

115 NW 22nd Avenue
Portland, Oregon 97210
Contact: Faith Chhim, Event Coordinator
(503) 248-4324 or (503) 248-9400; Fax (503) 248-5678
Business Hours: Mon-Thu 11:30am–10pm; Fri 11:30am–11pm;
Sat 10:30am–11pm; Sun 10:30am–10pm
Web site: http://www.ilfornaio.com

Capacity: Private Dining Room up to 28 guests; Piazza (room) up to 55 guests; Piazza and the Private Dining Room combined accommodate up to 80 guests; Sala delle Luci (front window room) up to 75 guests, receptions from 2–6 p.m. up to 150 people

Price Range: varies according to menu selection; no room rental fee; a customized menu can be created to meet your specific needs and budget

Types of Events: full sit-down dining is available for rehearsal dinners, weddings, receptions, bridal showers, parties, and other special occasions

Availability and Terms

Il Fornaio has an intimate Private Dining Room that can accommodate up to 28 people. In addition our indoor Piazza garden room with a fireplace and a retractable roof provides a warm setting for groups up to 55 guests. This room is available year round and can be combined with our Private Dining room to accommodate 80 guests. The Sala delle Luci area is a semi-private room filled with light that pours in from huge windows that look out onto Mount Hood. This room holds a maximum of 50 people for a sit-down dinner and 75 for cocktail parties.

The authentic Italain menu features wood fired pizzas, rotisserie meats, mesquite grilled local fish, and fresh regional pastas. Each meal includes house baked breads made fresh throughout the day

Description of Facility and Services

Seating: provided to accommodate group size
Servers: provided
Bar facilities: full bar, extensive Northwest and Italian wines and full service cafe-bar
Linens: white linen
Decorations: flowers, displays and decorative items are welcome
Parking: valet parking
ADA: elevator available

IL FORNAIO OFFERS AUTHENTIC ITALIAN CUISINE

With friendly and professional service in a setting that is comfortable and intimate. Bring your next special occasion to Il Fornaio with award-winning authentic Italian food and wine. Our friendly and knowledgeable staff will work with you to create a menu that is befitting to your group. We look forward to helping you plan a memorable occasion.

Portland	Clackamas	Hillsboro
0715 S.W. Bancroft	*12725 S.E. 93rd Avenue*	*18925 N.W. Tanasbourne Dr.*
Portland, Oregon 97201	*Clackamas, Oregon 97015*	*Hillsboro, Oregon 97124*
(503) 222-5375	*(503) 653-7949*	*(503) 617-7614*

Capacity: 75 to 150 guests
Price range: $5–$9 per person
Catering: in-house
Types of events: rehearsal dinners, team awards banquets, going away parties

Availability and Terms
Reservations are taken for groups of 25 or more

Description of Facility and Services
Seating: tables and chairs for 75–150
Servers: provided
Dance floor: possibly can be arranged; please inquire
Linens: please inquire
China and glassware: white china and house glassware provided
Audio visual: available by arrangement
Equipment: available by arrangement
Cleanup: provided by The Old Spaghetti Factory

EXCEPTIONAL FOOD AT AFFORDABLE PRICES
What keeps customers coming back to The Old Spaghetti Factory? It's exceptional food at affordable prices in an extraordinary atmosphere of antiques and fun. Our distinctive decor includes a vintage trolley car and other antiques from around the world. Our menu features a spaghetti dinner (entree, salad, bread, beverage and dessert—all for one low price) and other pasta-based specialties. Join us for your next gathering and enjoy our fare and fun!

RESTAURANT · BAR
FUN DINING · PLUSH BOOTHS · GENEROUS COCKTAILS

1309 N.W. Hoyt
Portland, Oregon 97209
Contact: Joseph Moreau (503) 833-5060

Office Hours: Tues–Sat 11am-6pm
Restaurant Hours: Open every day

Capacity: 20–150 guests
Price Range: determined by type of event
Catering: full-service in-house; off-site events
Types of Events: receptions, rehearsals, lunch and dinner parties; you may select full
sit-down service, buffet or cocktail party

Availability and Terms
The entire facility is available for private functions. Upper dining room and private room
available separately or together. Deposit required to secure the date. Final payment due on the
date of the event.

Description of Facility and Services
Seating: indoor seating for up to 100 guests; outdoor seating for up to 25 guests
Servers: provided by Paragon
Bar facilities: full bar or limited bar
Dance floor: 20 person capacity; stage and electrical available for musicians
Linens: white linen; other colors available for minimal charge
China and glassware: white china; clear glassware
Decorations: candles provided; schedule early decorating; no nails, tacks, tape or confetti
Cleanup: provided by Paragon
Parking: ample street and pay lot parking; valet parking negotiable
ADA: fully accessible

Special Services
We are happy to assist you in all aspects of your special day including menu selection,
decorations, music and any other details to make your event especially memorable. We are
pleased to recommend photographers, florists and bakeries.

RUSTIC NORTHWEST CUISINE
Based upon the concept of a quintessential "neighborhood" restaurant and bar, Paragon
Restaurant features rustic Northwest cuisine, a fun, full-service bar and friendly staff. Paragon
is located in the heart of the Pearl District, the home of Portland's art community,
sophisticated urbanites, and vintage brick warehouse buildings—all just five minutes from
downtown. Paragon's design mixes the timeless elements of a traditional grill-style restaurant
with modern artistry in a converted warehouse. The unique private banquet room seats up to
22 people and features a slide-up wall to adapt to your privacy needs. The upper dining room
is available for special events and can seat up to 50 people. Paragon also has ample patio
seating for outdoor dining. Our chef is happy to work with you to create a menu that matches
your needs. Whether it is a cocktail party, a sit-down meal, buffet or business meeting,
Paragon is the perfect venue for a memorable event.

319 S.W. Broadway
Portland, Oregon 97205
Contact: Ray Colvin
(503) 525-0945; Fax (503) 525-0946
Business Hours: Mon–Fri 11:30am–midnight; Sat–Sun 4pm–11pm

Capacity: Antinori private dining room up to 40 people; Piedmont private dining room up to 30 people; main floor available for up to 110.

Price Range: varies according to menu selection; no room rental fee

Catering: in-house

Types of Events: banquets, rehearsal dinners, receptions

Availability and Terms
Reservations advised 30 days in advance. Piatti requires a 72-hour cancellation notice; deposits required only in December. Credit card number reserves the space.

Description of Facility and Terms
Seating: provided to size of group
Servers: provided
Bar facilities: full bar available; extensive wine list
Linens: white linens provided at no charge
China and glassware: provided
Decorations: floral and decoration services available
Audio visual: available
Cleanup: provided at no charge
Parking: validated parking; valet parking available
ADA: approved facility

Special Services
We can coordinate overnight accommodations in the historic Benson Hotel, adjacent to the restaurant.

AWARD-WINNING CUISINE
PAIRED WITH PROFESSIONAL SERVICE
Piatti on Broadway is owned by restaurant Hall of Fame member Claude Rouas, formerly of Maxims in Paris and L'Etoille in San Francisco. Known for award-winning cuisine and professional service, Piatti on Broadway is a perfect choice for your special guests.

Here's what the critics say
"...really one of the best restaurants in downtown Portland."
~ Sarah Perry, KINK Radio

"Superb Italian food."
~ Travel & Leisure

"A menu that makes the most of fresh food and terrific preparation."
~ Our Town

7424 S.W. Beaverton-Hillsdale Highway
Portland, Oregon 97225
Contact: Tim Larrance (503) 296-0110
Business Hours: Mon–Thu 11:30am–11pm; Fri 11:30am–midnight;
Sat 8am–midnight; Sun 8am–9pm

Capacity: 100 sit-down, 150 reception
Price Range: $10–$20 per person
Catering: in-house catering only
Types of Events: casual parties, brewer's dinners, rehearsal dinners, wedding receptions

Availability and Terms

Inside party room next to brewery, outside patio reception area with built-in bar and kitchen holds up to 200 people. Both are reserved on a first-come, first-served basis (evening dinners and receptions only). A 50% deposit is required upon booking.

Description of Facility and Services

Seating: tables and chairs provided
Servers: provided by Raccoon Lodge
Bar facilities: complete full bar, bartenders, and liquor liability provided by Raccoon Lodge
Linens and napkins: provided in limited colors
China and glassware: banquet china and glassware provided
Cleanup: provided
Parking: parking available, day parking limited Monday through Friday
ADA: fully accessible

Special Services

Our party room is also available for sporting events, beer/food tastings, holiday parties and birthdays.

VISIT OUR NEW NEIGHBORHOOD PUB

Our chef will make your event one to remember. Our brewmaster features beers only available at this public brewery house. The Raccoon Lodge menu features meats, chicken, and seafood cooked on our large rotisserie and smoker. We offer a lodge breakfast on Saturday and Sunday from 8–11 a.m.; express lunch on the weekdays; fun and creative dinners served nightly.

Visit our Web site at: www.raclodge.com

RHEINLANDER

5035 N.E. Sandy Blvd.
Portland, Oregon 97213
Contact: Banquet Staff
(503) 288-8410
Business Hours: Mon–Fri 9am–5pm

Capacity: 20 to 100 people; 150 people for stand-up
Price range: please call for current prices, customized menus available
Catering: full in-house catering; call for information regarding outside catering
Types of Events: sit-down dinners, hors d'oeuvres, rehearsal dinners, anniversaries, birthdays, retirements, meetings and corporate functions

Availability and Terms

Our beautifully remodeled banquet rooms can accommodate up to 100 people. We recommend reserving a room as soon as possible, but welcome you on short notice—space permitting! We require a deposit which is applied to the balance.

Description of Facility and Services

Seating: round or rectangular tables available depending on your size and needs
Servers: staff included
Bar facilities: host or no-host bars with a minimum setup fee; bartender included; cocktail service provided at no charge
Linens and napkins: linen tablecloths, napkins, and skirting in a variety of colors
China and glassware: white china with lovely burgundy pattern; all glassware and stemware provided; silver serving items and cake cutting service included in price
Cleanup: provided by Rheinlander
Decorations: pre-approved by the banquet staff; tape only; early access for decorating. Ask about our additional decorating services!
Parking: free parking; private banquet entrance
ADA: Rheinlander is entirely handicap accessible

Special Services

We specialize in wedding rehearsal dinners, small receptions, and corporate functions. We want your event to be perfect and exactly how you imagined it to be. Our experienced banquet staff will work with you on every detail. Please call for an appointment to view rooms, look at samples or even taste the food!

BEAUTIFUL BANQUET ROOMS ENHANCED BY DELIGHTFUL ENTERTAINMENT!

The Rheinlander is proudly celebrating 35 years in Portland. We have remodeled our banquet rooms to offer rich mahogany surroundings, offset by delicate lighting. We offer authentic German cuisine and fresh continental specialties including poultry, beef, seafood and pork. Strolling accordionists and singers complement your evening with their beautiful music.

ON THE COLUMBIA

3839 N.E. Marine Drive
Portland, Oregon 97211
Contact: Dorothy Lane
(503) 288-4444; Fax (503) 284-7397
Web site: http://www.saltys.com

Restaurant Hours:
Lunch Mon–Sat 11:15am–3pm; Dinner Mon–Thur 5–10pm, Fri–Sat 5–10:30pm;
Sunday Brunch 9:30am–2pm; Sunday Dinner 4:30–9:30pm; winter hours vary

Capacity: up to 200 guests
Price Range: call for current prices
Catering: full-service catering
Types of Events: rehearsal dinners, wedding receptions, bridal showers, anniversary celebrations and other events; private breakfasts, sit-down dinners and luncheons, seafood and brunch buffets, cocktails and hors d'oeuvres

Availability and Terms

We recommend reserving your space three to six months in advance. But if you need assistance with last minute planning—we can help! A deposit is required to reserve your date. Room fees are waived with a minimum purchase of food and beverage.

Description of Facility and Services

Seating: a variety of table sizes and seating options
Servers: after a specified minimum gratuity or 18%, servers provided at no additional charge
Bar facilities: full-service bar provided courtesy of Salty's; host/no-host; liquor, beer and wine
Linens: house colors available at no additional charge
China and glassware: restaurant silver, china and glassware available
Audio visual: overhead and slide projector with screen; TV, VCR, flip charts available for rent
Cleanup: handled by Salty's staff
Parking: plenty of free parking; complimentary valet service available Mon–Sat nights
ADA: first floor accessible for handicapped; Wine Room and North Shore View Room are on second floor

Special Services

Our catering director works closely with you to ensure your event's success. We print a personalized menu for you and your guests. We are happy to refer you to bakeries, florists, DJs and musicians. At Salty's, we pride ourselves on catering to your every whim.

GIVE YOUR WEDDING A BETTER POINT OF VIEW!

Salty's is located on the riverfront only 15 minutes from downtown Portland. We provide the perfect recipe for memorable occasions; rehearsal dinners, wedding receptions, or bridal showers for up to 200 guests. Salty's exceptional Northwest cuisine, warm hospitality, and spectacular views of the mighty Columbia and majestic Mount Hood will make your event a very special occasion! We're easy to get to, and ready to serve you the very best seafood, steaks, Sunday Brunch, and riverfront view in Portland.

Sayler's OLD COUNTRY KITCHEN

4655 S.W. Griffith Drive   *10519 S.E. Stark*
Beaverton, Oregon 97005   *Portland, Oregon 97216*
Contact: Sally Kanan (503) 252-4171 or (503) 644-1492

Capacity: 10-300
Price range: $7-$20
Catering: in-house
Types of events: receptions, rehearsal dinners, meetings, banquets

Availability and Terms

West: Two private rooms available day and night. Outside patio available day and night. The entire restaurant is available Mon–Fri 7am–2pm and can be split into five separate areas.

East: Six rooms are available or the entire restaurant is available Mon–Fri 7am–4pm and Sat 7am-2:30pm.

Not available on Sunday. Reservations are on a first come, first obtained basis and should be made no later than two weeks before the event. A 50% deposit is requested with signed contract.

Description of Facility and Services

Seating: tables and chairs provided
Servers: provided by Sayler's
Bar facilities: main or portable bar available; bartenders, liquor and liability provided
Dance floor: 12' x 12' floor can be rented; electrical available
Linens: white available for no charge; colored linens available at extra charge
China and glassware: white china and glassware provided
Decorations: flexible; please inquire
Cleanup: provided by Sayler's staff; charge will be applied for any damage
Parking: plenty of free parking
ADA: ADA approved

Special Services

The entire restaurant is available during the day with plenty of free parking. Every function has its own host to look after any group needs.

WE SERVE A GREAT AMERICAN MEAL

The Old Country Kitchen is perfect for small daytime meetings, Monday through Friday, large daytime receptions and small banquets or rehearsal dinners in the evening. We specialize in great, affordable, American food. Try our prime beef, exceptional seafood and home-style chicken. Buffets, sit-down or food stations, are our specialty. You get all the amenities of a restaurant but lots of privacy for your meetings.

SYLVIA'S ITALIAN RESTAURANT & CLASS ACT DINNER THEATRE

5115 N.E. Sandy Blvd. • Portland, Oregon 97213
Contact: Norm Stone (503) 288-6828
Dinner: Sun–Thurs 4–10pm; Fri, Sat 4–11pm
Dinner Theatre: Thurs–Sat 6:30pm dinner, 8pm show
Sun Matinee 11:30am brunch, 1pm show;
5:30pm dinner, 7pm show

Web site:
http://www.sylvias.net

Enjoy the abundance of hospitality and generosity served up at one of Portland's foremost and popular Italian restaurants. Sylvia's has been a family tradition since 1957 offering quality Italian food and providing friendly service in an authentic and pleasant atmosphere.

Capacity: Piazza Room, 80 people; Dinner Theatre, 100 people (limited evenings)
Price Range: $9 and up (including room)
Catering: up to 500 people; off-premise up to 5,000 people
Types of Events: rehearsal dinners, family feasts, wedding receptions, sit-down, buffet, cocktails, hors d'oeuvres, meetings

Availability and Terms

Sylvia's can be reserved on an as-available basis, with a minimum $100 nonrefundable deposit. We request a minimum of two-weeks notice for cancellations.

Description of Facility and Services

Seating: tables and chairs provided
Servers: staff included if you use in-house banquet facilities; 16% gratuity added
Bar facilities: full bar
Dance floor: available on request; extra charge
Linens and napkins: burgundy cloth linens and napkins at no charge; other colors available for extra charge
China and glassware: white dinnerware and restaurant glassware available for in-house banquets
Decorations: brass lanterns provided; table decorations provided for a charge; early decorating welcomed; please no confetti
Cleanup: provided by Sylvia's
Parking: parking available at no additional cost
ADA: fully accessible

Sylvia's
"a place to celebrate food, a place to cherish friends."

The
Wild Berry
Room

3220 S.E. Milwaukie Avenue
Portland, Oregon 97202
Contact: Charles E. Barker
(503) 234-1978
Fax (503) 239-7168

Capacity: 50 reception, 30 seated; patio seats an additional 20 guests during summer months

Price Range: $14–$22

Catering: in-house only

Types of Events: rehearsal dinners, personal and professional celebrations

Availability and Terms

Reservations can be made by calling London Catering at (503) 234-1978. Rental fee is $40 an hour with a maximum fee of $120.

Description of Facility and Services

Seating: tables and chairs provided
Servers: available
Bar facilities: full-service bar; bartenders provided
Linens and napkins: available
China and glassware: included
Audio visual: available
Cleanup: included in rental fee
Parking: plenty of free street parking
ADA: fully accessible

A CLASSIC NORTHWEST
HAND-CRAFTED PRIVATE DINING ROOM

Our exquisite central courtyard is the perfect setting to hold your rehearsal dinner during the summer months. French doors open to a brick terrace, complete with a sculptured stone fountain and polished granite buffet.

WILF'S
Restaurant and Piano Bar
at Historic Union Station

N.W. Sixth and Irving
Portland, Oregon 97209
(503) 223-0070; Fax (503) 223-1386
Web site: http://www.citysearch.com/pdx/wilfs

Capacity: up to 160 reception-style; 150 seated; private rooms up to 35 guests
Price range: starting at $15 per person; customized menus to meet your specific needs and budget
Catering: full-service in-house catering plus off-premise catering
Types of events: sit-down luncheons or dinners, hors d'oeuvres reception-style, brunch, cocktail parties, off-site catering

Availability

Wilf's offers our main dining room for up to 130 guests, or our private rooms for up to 35, decorated in warm rich colors to complement the feel of the historic Union Station. Reserve early; last minute reservations welcome, as space allows. Advance deposit required on parties of 10 or more; cancellation terms vary.

Description of Facility and Services

Seating: tables and chairs for up to 175 on-premise; off-premise rentals available
Servers: waitstaff provided; off-premise at additional charge
Bar facilities: full-service bar on-site with liquor, wine, beer, nonalcoholic, bartender, and liquor liability; off-site Wilf's or host can provide liquor, liability to be discussed
Dance floor: 30- to 100-person capacity; available at additional charge
Linens: cloth napkins and tablecloths in a variety of colors
China and glassware: ivory china; appropriate glassware
Cleanup: included in rental charge
Decorations: special needs may be accommodated; please no tape or nails
Parking: free parking spaces 1–36 only or valet parking offered
ADA: fully accessible

Special Services

Your rehearsal dinner is just as important as your wedding day and at Wilf's, we'll make it perfect! Choose a sit-down dinner or luncheon, or hors d'oeuvre-style cocktail party, all served in the warm, comfortable atmosphere of Wilf's, or let our catering department come to your special location for an afternoon or evening affair. Casual or formal, our staff can take care of every detail… flowers, special decor items, music… just let us know… we can make it perfect!

WILF'S… FOR YOUR DAY AND STYLE!

Since 1975, the Portland area has enjoyed fine food, impeccable service, and a warm, relaxed atmosphere at Wilf's. Classic steak and seafood blended with seasonal creations customize your style and needs. Enjoy our renowned jazz and Sinatra-style piano bar while you dine for your family celebration. If your plans require our expert catering services, you can count on Wilf's to make it perfect while making you a star! Free parking is available at Union Station, in the Pearl District.

WORLD TRADE CENTER
Two World Trade Center Portland
25 S.W. Salmon Street • Portland, Oregon 97204
Reservations: (503) 464-8688 • Office Hours: Mon–Fri 8am–5pm

Capacity: inside: 400 reception, 300 seated; **outside:** 800 reception, 500 seated; **Flags riverfront space:** 125 reception, 80 seated

Price Range: please call for specific price information

Catering: We can host a rehearsal dinner or reception, or we can package your entire wedding, handling all the details for you! Full-service in-house catering available. Menus flexible to client's choices.

Types of Events: sit-down, buffet, hors d'oeuvres

Availability and Terms
A variety of rooms are available to meet your specific needs. Choose between the glassed-in Mezzanine or our covered Plaza for your outdoor ceremony or reception. Our new riverfront banquet space offers a fantastic view of the river and Tom McCall Waterfront Park. There is also a 220-seat auditorium for indoor ceremonies. Reservations are suggested at least six months in advance—particularly during spring and summer months. Deposit of half of the total room rental is required at the time of booking.

Description of Facility and Services
Seating: seating capacity based on room(s) selected and seating arrangement; table and chair setup included in rental price

Bar facilities: fully OLCC licensed

Dance floor: dance floor upon request at standard rental rate; electrical hookup for bands or disc jockey available

Decorations: inquire about limitations; nothing that will damage the walls or ceiling

Parking: underground daytime and evening parking available in the building

ADA: all rooms are disabled accessible

INVITE YOUR GUESTS TO SEE THE WORLD
There's nothing like holding your reception, or even the whole wedding, in Portland's showcase—at the World Trade Center. Located in the heart of the city between S.W. Salmon and Taylor streets, First and Front avenues, this award-winning facility has a commanding view of the beautiful Tom McCall waterfront and provides the finest in facilities. You'll enjoy our cooperative and helpful staff, prepared to do whatever it takes to make your special time a wonderful experience. Call for a complete tour and information packet.

THE NOISIER THE BETTER

In order to chase away

any evil spirits that

may be lurking about,

rehearsal dinners were

a melee of broken glass and

china, reaffirming the belief

that the more noise made

the better when it came to

disposing of evil spirits.

HELPFUL HINTS

- **Begin looking for your reception, banquet, or meeting site immediately:** As soon as the engagement is announced, the first decision to be made is where to hold the event. Meet first with your clergyman to find out the days and times available at your church or synagogue.

- **Visit the location:** When you narrow down the options of sites available, view the room in person before you reserve it or send a deposit. Oftentimes the look and feel of a room or location will sway a decision one way or another. It is also easier to plan an event by keeping the room's layout and size in mind.

- **Be flexible:** If you are insistent about a certain date and time, you may spend weeks searching all over town for a place to accommodate your needs. By the time you finally discover that no options are available your first choice may also be booked on your alternate dates.

- **Be honest about your budget:** Do not be afraid to tell the facility coordinator or event planner what your budget is. This very important information can be used as a guideline and can save time and effort. Trust the person in charge to help create a successful event. They can offer time- and budget-saving recommendations based on experience.

- **Deposits are important:** Remember that when you reserve a facility, a deposit is usually required. Even though you thought your date was secure, the site is not formally reserved until a deposit is received. Many brides have lost their reception site by overlooking this fact.

- **Host or hostess for your wedding:** Ask someone to be the host or hostess for the reception. The family usually doesn't arrive at the reception until after the guests. If you have a host or hostess to greet the guests and direct them to the punch or coat rack, they will feel more comfortable.

- **Gift table:** Assign a reliable person to be in charge of gifts at the reception. He or she should have scotch tape handy to tape cards securely to packages. It is very frustrating and embarrassing to open gifts and not know who they were from. When a card is given as a gift, many times it will have cash or a check inside. These cards should be placed in a box marked "card only." Rental shops rent a wishing well with a slit in the top to slip cards through, or wrap a box and put a slit in the top. Make sure you have a vehicle to take the gifts to a safe place an hour or so after the reception begins.

For more assistance with staying organized during the wedding planning process, check out the Bravo! Wedding Organizer. Detailed question worksheets double as contracts. This step-by-step system will keep every detail of your wedding organized. To order, refer to the order form on page 23 in this Guide.

Afternoon Tea
by
Stephanie

Serving Tea with
A Touch of Romance Ltd.

530 First Street • Lake Oswego, Oregon 97034
Contact: Stephanie or Gail (503) 636-0179
Business Hours: Tues–Sat 10am–6pm; closed Sunday–Monday
Tea served: Tues–Fri 11am–3pm; Saturdays by advance reservation only

Capacity: up to 25
Price Range: prices vary according to menu selection
Tea Catering: available in-house and off-site
Types of Events: bridal showers, bridesmaids luncheons, bridesmaids teas, getting-aquainted teas, baby showers, and of course, any occasion special to you; walk-in service welcome

Availability and Terms
A deposit and advance reservation are required for special event teas.

Description of Facility and Services
Charm and elegance is your first impression as you enter the cozy tea room located in downtown Lake Oswego. Classical melodies soften the mood for a return to an era of loveliness.
Seating: antique chairs
Servers: provided by Afternoon Tea
Linens: cloth linens available at no charge
China and glassware: fine china and silver flatware provided
Parking: street parking and parking lot
ADA: not accessible

Bridal Accessories and Flowers
After having tea, take care of your bridal accessory and wedding flower needs at
A Touch of Romance, ltd., "Truly a Unique Shop."

- Wedding florist on-site
- Bridal jewelry
- Bridal books and planners
- Bridesmaid gifts
- Wedding consulting services included with floral package
- Flower girl baskets
- Invitations
- Photo albums
- Plume and guest book pens
- Ring bearer pillows
- Favors, garters and hankies

And much more!

A Video Guide To Portland Region Wedding Sites

Sunshine Enterprises
2703 N.W. 91st Street
Vancouver, Washington 98665
(360) 574-5096

Best Places
To Say
"I Do"
Portland, Oregon Region

Best Places To Say "I Do"

From the famous Columbia Gorge Hotel to Timberline Lodge on Mount Hood, to the wineries of the Willamette Valley, this video guide features 23 of the area's most unique sites for weddings and receptions. A full video portrait of each location gives you a preview of its amenities. Also included is a fact sheet for each site.

Save yourself time and gas money by previewing over 23 locations. Included are Ballrooms, Gardens, Museums, Wineries, Farms, and Private Homes—many with historical designations. From the elegant to the funky, to the breathtaking, this video guide will show them all to you.

Professionally videotaped and narrated with full music background, this video will take the headaches out of looking for the right location for your "dream" wedding.

Cost

$24.95 plus $3 shipping

To Order

- Phone (360) 574-5096
- Write to Sunshine Enterprises
    2703 N.W. 91st Street
    Vancouver, Washington 98665

"Columbia Gorge"
P.O. Box 307
Cascade Locks, Oregon 97014
(503) 223-3928

THE CASCADE STERNWHEELERS

Owned & operated by the Port of Cascade Locks

Capacity: 200 sit-down, 375 reception
Price Range: varies depending on number of guests and length of cruise; minimum of two hours; please call
Catering: full range of catering services provided including menu selections for champagne toasts, complete dinners and hors d'oeuvres
Types of Events: plated, buffet, hors d'oeuvres, cake, champagne toasts

Availability and Terms
We offer a variety of accommodations for wedding parties up to 375. Two fully enclosed heated decks provide a comfortable setting for any time of year. A 25% nonrefundable deposit is required upon booking; final payment is due 30–120 days prior to scheduled event depending upon the season.

Description of Facility and Services
Seating: tables and chairs provided
Servers: provided
Bar facilities: two to three full-service bars with bartenders available
Dance floor: dance area available; full electrical hookup
Linens and napkins: cloth linens and napkins; color coordination available
China and glassware: house china available with our catering service
Decorations: elegant turn-of-the-century motif requires little decoration
Cleanup: provided courtesy of the Sternwheeler crews
Parking: *Cascade Locks:* free parking; *Portland:* City Center and off-street parking available for a fee
ADA: disabled accessible

Special Services
With two rivers and an abundance of breathtaking views to choose from, the Cascade Sternwheeler "Columbia Gorge" continues to provide a unique venue for your wedding/ceremony and reception.

As a unique wedding site, we can provide catering and menu selection, music and entertainment. The Cascade Sternwheeler can also coordinate a performance of your ceremony by one of our credited Captains. Please call to arrange a tour of either of the Cascade Sternwheeler "Columbia Gorge" or our 20-acre Marine Park and Private Island.

CRYSTAL DOLPHIN

1200 N.W. Front Avenue, Suite 120
Portland, Oregon 97209
(503) 226-2517
Fax (503) 226-2539

Capacity: 90 guests (April–September); 75 guests (October–March); 180-seat outdoor deck facility

Price Range: $525–$800 per hour (two-hour minimum); off-season discounts and wedding packages available

Catering: four exclusive caterers

Types of receptions: rehearsal dinners, weddings, receptions and many corporate events

Availability and Terms

"84-foot luxury charter yacht" available for private events year-round. To book your date, a 25% nonrefundable deposit is required.

Description of Facility and Services

Seating: for up to 90
Servers: provided
Bar facilities: full-service bar, bartenders , liquor and liability provided by Crystal Dolphin
Dance floor: space available with electrical
Linens: linen and cloth provided
China and glassware: nautical selections of china
Cleanup: provided by Crystal Dolphin
Decorations: Crystal Dolphin is magnificently decorated; other decorations are permitted
Parking: free for each guest
ADA: handicapped friendly

Special Services

We always include fresh floral arrangements in your colors. We have a beautiful private bridal changing area with two private restrooms. Our amenities are superior to and unlike any other tour vessel in our area.

UNMATCHED FACILITIES FOR WEDDINGS AFLOAT

Champagne wishes and caviar dreams await you aboard Portland's most prestigious and luxurious yacht, the Crystal Dolphin.

You will be pampered by our professional crew on your special day. We have unmatched facilities for weddings afloat.

We feature the finest in gourmet selections, a unique variety of entertainers, an exclusive selection of Oregon wines and microbrews.

Our crew will cater to your guests' every need. Your special day will be the event of a lifetime. Sit back, relax and experience the ultimate in private luxury charters.

PORTLAND SPIRIT & WILLAMETTE STAR

Sales Office:
110 S.E. Caruthers
Portland, Oregon 97214
Contact: Sales
(503) 224-3900,
(800) 224-3901
Web site:
http://www.cruiseawi.com

Offering spectacular views, outstanding service and first-class Northwest cuisine, prepared on board in each ship's galley. Our event planning services ensure that not one detail is overlooked, from a rehearsal dinner for 25 to an elegant sit down dinner reception for 340. A cruise on the **Portland Spirit** or **Willamette Star** will guarantee the perfect place for your special day.

Availability, Price and Terms

The Portland Spirit vessels are available year round from downtown Portland. You may charter the entire **Portland Spirit** vessel or one deck rentals are available. The **Portland Spirit** also offers public cruise schedules. The **Willamette Star** is available for private charter. Deposit and signed contract confirms cruise date. Prices depend on time of day, season of year and number of guests. NOTE: Capacity recommendations on each vessel depend on time of year, menu selected and type of wedding planned. Please call for specific recommendations.

Portland Spirit

130 foot, three level yacht, two outside decks
Available for full boat charter, one deck rental
Capacity: up to 540 guests
Seating: tables and chairs for 350,
    plus outside seating
Dance floor: large marble dance floor

Willamette Star

75 foot, two level yacht, two outside decks
Available for private charter
Capacity: up to 120 guests
Seating: tables and chairs for 80,
    plus outside seating
Dance floor: available

Description of Vessel Services and Facilities

Enclosed decks are temperature controlled
Linens: linen tablecloths and napkins provided
China: our house china and glassware provided
Servers: included with food and bar service
Bar facilities: full service bar, liquor, bartenders and liability insurance
Cleanup: provided
Parking: commercial and street parking available
ADA: limited with assistance

A DREAM COME TRUE...
A ROMANTIC WEDDING CRUISE ON A LUXURY YACHT

Imagine exchanging your vows on board Portland's most luxurious yachts. As the sun sets behind the city, your guests celebrate in style on the gorgeous waters of the Willamette River. Choose from the **Portland Spirit** or the more intimate **Willamette Star**. Our captain can perform your ceremony for that nautical touch, or choose to join us for the most wonderful reception available in town. Our wedding coordinator can help you with all the details so you can relax and enjoy your wedding cruise.

See page 182 under Banquet & Reception Sites.

THE STERNWHEELER ROSE
PORTLAND STEAM NAVIGATION CO.

6211 N. Ensign
Portland, Oregon 97217
Contact: Judy (503) 286-ROSE (7673)
Business Hours: Mon–Fri 8am–5pm

ROMANTIC RIVER SETTING

Cruising aboard *The Sternwheeler Rose* is a unique way to make your wedding special. It's also a festive place for a rehearsal dinner, bachelor party or a bridal shower. We offer a standard wedding package that includes boat charter, ceremony by Captain, elegant hors d'oeuvre buffet, champagne, flowers, invitations, napkins and wedding cake. Of course, you are welcome to create your own package. Our experienced caterer can provide you with suggestions or create the specific menu of your choice—you're limited only by your imagination and budget! Additionally, our staff, crew and captains are available to help you plan every step and execute every detail to make your wedding a wonderful and memorable event.

Capacity: up to 130 people; you may reserve the entire boat for your private cruise
Price Range: customized wedding packages available; prices vary; please inquire
Catering: licensed, in-house catering available; flexible menus
Types of Events: wedding ceremonies, receptions, dinners, dances, rehearsal dinners, parties

Availability and Terms
The Sternwheeler Rose is Portland's finest year-round charter boat. It cruises on the Willamette and Columbia rivers. A deposit of 50% is required. Terms are available.

Description of Facility and Services
Boarding location: OMSI; other boarding sites can be scheduled
Seating: tables and chairs provided
Servers: provided
Bar facilities: beer, wine, champagne, soft drinks and bartender standard; full-service bar available
Dance floor: floor for up to 80 people; electrical hookups available
Linens and napkins: all colors of linen tablecloths and cloth napkins available
China and glassware: glass plates, glasses and barware available
Decorations: No candles, confetti or propane allowed
Cleanup: complete cleanup courtesy of The Sternwheeler Rose with catering
Parking: free at OMSI

Special Services
Be sure to ask about decorations both for ideas and logistics

We Invite You To Celebrate On
The Sternwheeler Rose

Please call if you have any questions or would like more information.
We at The Sternwheeler Rose look forward to serving you,
and proudly offer you and your guests "...the Best Food on the River."

A Night in Shining Amour Wedding Chapel and Ballroom

115 West Ninth Street
Vancouver, Washington 98660
Contact: Joe and Pam Thielman
(360) 750-7891
Web site: http://www.shining-amour.com
E-mail: jthielm@pacifier.com

Capacity: wedding ceremony: 125, reception: 150; meetings and other events depend on type of setup required (maximum remains 150)

Price Range: varies depending on event and length of time needed; wedding packages from $65 to $1,100; please call

Catering: full range catering services are provided or you can self cater your event with a refundable deposit

Types of Events: specializing in weddings and receptions, management retreats, banquets, employee parties, meetings, seminars, and privately catered family gatherings

Availability and Terms

Call for availability. A 50% deposit is required at time of booking based on the time required at a rate of $100 per hour for the first three hours and $50 per hour thereafter. Balance is due one week prior to event. Four hours minimum on the weekends.

Description of Facility and Services

Seating: all-white wooden chairs with padded seats, rectangular or round tables available and seating arranged as requested

Servers: provided, or as you desire

Bar facilities: arranged on request

Dance floor: beautiful hardwood flooring makes the entire ballroom area a wonderful place to dance

Linen: provided

China: available for rent or you provide

Decorations: beautiful white and gold decor accommodates a wide variety of color schemes

Cleanup: provided or extra charge, depending on package

Parking: street side and several parking lots and garages nearby

ADA: complied

About Us

At your request, we will serve as the host/hostess of your function, attending to every detail. We endeavor to remain as flexible as possible regarding our service to you. We have many resources available to make your event the best it can be and will work with you to control your costs.

Built in 1910, the building has been remodeled, giving it an ambiance and charm of style and grace. You will find the ballroom a wonderful place for your wedding day.

Please let this business know that you heard about them from the Bravo! Bridal Resource Guide.

A PERFECT DAY

Phelps Family Farm
22011 S. Penman Road
Oregon City, Oregon 97045
Contact: Sherri
(503) 722-3267
Business Hours: Mon–Fri 8am–4pm
Evening and weekend appointments available

© Raymond's Catering

Capacity: 300+
Price Range: price depends on type of party and number of guests
Catering: in-house catering by Raymond's Catering & Baking
Types of Events: indoor or outdoor buffets and plated dinners, barbecues, showers, rehearsal dinners, breakfast

Availability and Terms

Seven-hour segments available. One-third nonrefundable deposit required at time of booking.

Description of Facility and Services

Seating: chairs for ceremony and tables and chairs for reception included in site fee
Servers: included with catering
Bar facilities: full service; host or no-host; bartenders required; caterer provides liquor and liquor liability
Dance floor: indoor floor with indoor and outdoor electrical hookups
Linens: tablecloths included; cloth napkins available for an extra charge
China and glassware: included with catering
Decorations: decorating available
Cleanup: included with catering
Parking: free parking
ADA: accessible in most areas

Special Services

Our professional staff will assist in any facet of your event planning. Decorating and bridal party sewing and alterations available. Massage therapist on staff to calm those wedding jitters!

GARDEN ELEGANCE

Garden elegance among the trees! Our 11-acre site offers many choices: an indoor ballroom with a dance floor, charming gazebo, and winding pathways through ivy-covered trees—a photographer's delight. Proprietors Ray and Sherri are the third generation of Phelps to own the farm. Antique farm machinery, in the family for 60 years, is attractively displayed in the landscaping. Our country paradise will make your wedding day the most memorable day of your lives.

THE ACADEMY CHAPEL & BALLROOM

400 East Evergreen Blvd.
Vancouver, Washington 98660
Windsor Wedding Consultants, Suite 216
(360) 696-4884
Business Hours: Mon–Fri 10am–5pm;
evenings by appointment

Capacity: up to 225 guests, ceremony; up to 300 guests, reception
Price Range: beginning at $200 and up for chapel, and $600 and up for ballroom
Catering: no in-house catering; full kitchen facility available
Types of Events: sit-down, buffet, hors d'oeuvres, cake and punch

Availability and Terms

The Academy has a ballroom and a chapel. The ballroom's maximum capacity is 300 people; prices start at $600 for weekday rental. The chapel will hold a maximum of 225 people; $200 fee for weekdays. A deposit is required, and advance reservation of two to six months is recommended.

Description of Facility and Services

Seating: tables and chairs provided
Servers: provided by your caterer or yourself
Bar facilities: portable bar available in ballroom; you provide bartenders, liquor, and liability
Dance floor: 17'x26' dance floor in ballroom
Linens and napkins: can be rented on location
China and glassware: not available from the Academy
Cleanup: included in price
Decorations: inquire about our table decorations
Parking: free parking for 400 cars
ADA: yes

Special Services

We have a variety of items and services to choose from: elegant silk-flower and candle arrangements for rent; invitations, ring pillows, cake tops and unity candles for purchase. Windsor Wedding Consultants will plan all or part of your wedding to perfection while keeping within your budget specifications.

BREATHTAKINGLY BEAUTIFUL

Located in the historic Academy building in Vancouver, Washington, the Academy Chapel features a breathtaking, three-story-high carved altar, beautiful stained-glass windows, and a lovely balcony at the rear of the chapel—perfect for a soloist. The grand ballroom is decorated with elegant wallpaper, chandeliers, and blue-gray carpet. The Academy is only 15 minutes from downtown Portland and is easy to find, with ample free parking. Give Windsor Weddings a call today to tour our facility.

© Adams & Faith

The Adrianna Hill Grand Ballroom

An Enchanting Place of Celebration

918 S.W. Yamhill • Second Floor • Portland, Oregon 97205
Philip Sword or Barbara Abalan (503) 227-6285 • Shown by appointment only

Capacity: up to 300 guests

Price Range: charge varies

Catering: and event planning provided exclusively by Accent on Events; $15.95 per person and up

Types of Events: wedding ceremonies and receptions, corporate and private celebrations, concerts, dances, fundraisers, reunions, holiday parties, proms and more

Availability and Terms

A 50% facility deposit is required to confirm your date at one of the most unique, prestigious and sought-after facilities in the Pacific Northwest. Early reservations suggested.

Description of Facility and Services

Facility rental: includes Victorian ballroom decor, all tables and chairs, dressing room for bridal party, full service bar area, Roman columns, ambiant lighting, gift and guest book tables and coat racks

Event staff: experienced managers, chefs, waitstaff, licensed bartenders and kitchen personnel provided by Accent on Events (included in catering costs)

Bar facilities: all bar services provided by Accent on Events, Inc. (full bar available)

Dance floor: hardwood floors perfect for dancing; custom stereo sound system available for cassette tapes or CDs; bands and DJs welcome

Silverware, china, glassware and linens: included in catering costs

Parking: across the street at 10th Avenue and Yamhill Street—City Center Parking

TURN-OF-THE-CENTURY GRAND BALLROOM

The Adrianna Hill Grand Ballroom resides in an elegant 8,000-square-foot Victorian gallery space with a beautiful restored hardwood floor, suspended "U" shaped balcony and 55 foot-long stage backed by a high cathedral-style wall. Originally built in 1901, this storybook setting with unique architecture is newly remodeled—complete with a 35-foot beamed and vaulted ceiling, large ornate brass chandeliers and elaborate Old World designs along the sculpted balcony. We are proud to offer you a treasured and unforgettable experience in this nonsmoking environment.

"Yes, Cinderella, You Shall Go To The Ball…"

The
ALBERTA STATION
Ballroom
"Renovated Historic Lodge"

Receptions • Events • Meetings

1829 N.E. Alberta
Portland, Oregon 97211
Contact: Patrick Goebel, Manager
(503) 284-8666, (503) 813-2072; Fax (503) 284-8645
Business Hours: Please call for an appointment

Capacity: 4,000 sq. ft., up to 570 (open floor)
Price Range: $800 per day for Ballroom rental
Catering: outside catering welcome
Types of Events: weddings, receptions, corporate and private functions, fund-raisers, holiday parties, concerts and dances

Availability and Terms
Reservations are recommended six months in advance; 60-day prior notice for cancellation. Security and cleaning deposit required.

Description of Facility and Services
Seating: available for rent, setup provided
Servers: available through caterer
Bar facilities: provided through caterer
Dance floor: 4,000 sq. ft. of hardwood floors; capacity: 570 (open floor); electrical available
Linens and napkins: provided by caterer
China and glassware: provided by caterer
Decorations: please inquire
Cleanup: please inquire
Parking: free street parking available
ADA: accessible

Special Services
Our prep kitchen has ample room and provides caterers a refrigerator/freezer, stainless steel work table, and a full-size bar counter. The mezzanine level offers a private dressing room leading to a generous-sized balcony

ELEGANT BALLROOM OFFERING UNIQUE STYLE
Located on Northeast Alberta and 19th Avenue, Alberta Station was built in 1925 as the Odd Fellow Fraternal Lodge. Alberta Station features its' original wood staircase and spacious lobby. The Ballroom offers unique style—soft yellow walls, bold accented columns, and an impressive 18-foot high scalloped ceiling. Its' floor boasts 4,000 sq. ft. of maple hardwoods, and period fixtures lit with dimmers offer total control for lighting.

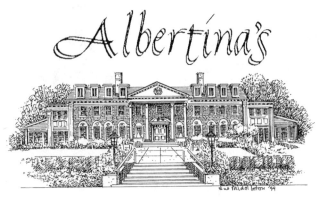

Albertina's

AT THE OLD KERR NURSERY

424 N.E. 22nd Avenue • Portland, Oregon 97232
Contact: Catering Coordinator (503) 231-3909
Business Hours: Mon–Fri 9am–4pm

Capacity: up to 250
Price Range: price determined by event
Catering: full-service, in-house catering
Types of Events: weddings and receptions, anniversaries, retirement parties, birthdays, family reunions, dinners, special events

Availability and Terms

Albertina's offers four rooms to accommodate up to 250 people. Our garden patio is also available on the weekends. Reservations should be made as early as possible, six months to one year in advance is recommended. A $300 deposit will secure your date.

Description of Facility and Services

Servers: hostess and servers provided by Albertina's
Bar facilities: champagne, wine, beer; bartenders provided by Albertina's
Dance floor: dance floor available at additional cost; ample electrical hookups
Linens: cloth tablecloths for service tables and paper napkins provided by Albertina's
China, glassware and silver service: provided by Albertina's
Decorations: beautiful fresh floral arrangements in colors of your choice; please discuss your decorating ideas with the Albertina's catering coordinator
Parking: on-site parking
ADA: fully accessible

CHARMING SETTING FOR SPECIAL OCCASIONS

Barely a mile from downtown Portland stands the stately, three-story Georgian-style Old Kerr Nursery. The building was erected in 1921 with the money of canning jar magnate Alexander Kerr and over a period of 55 years provided shelter, medical care, and schooling to thousands of children. Closed as a nursery in 1967, the building reopened in 1981 after having been lovingly restored by loyal volunteers. The Old Kerr Nursery has been placed on the National Register of Historic Places and is an official Portland Historical Landmark. Equally beautiful inside and out, the intriguing Nursery is a charming setting for your most special occasion. Experience the history and unique qualities preserved within its four walls. Albertina's at The Old Kerr Nursery is operated as a nonprofit business with all proceeds donated to Albertina Kerr Centers, whose programs provide services for children and youth at risk, families in need, and individuals with disabilities.

ALFIE'S WAYSIDE COUNTRY INN
ALFIE'S LE CHARDONNAY WINE CELLARS

1111 Highway 99 West
Dundee, Oregon 97115
Contact: Alfie or Bonnie (503) 538-9407

Capacity: 400
Price Range: prices vary according to menu selection
Catering: available in-house and off-site
Types of Events: weddings, anniversaries, birthdays, reunions, holiday parties, business meetings, brunches, luncheons

Availability and Terms

Advance reservations of six months to a year recommended; however, we will accept reservations on short notice if date is open. Deposit required to hold date; 30-day cancellation policy.

Description of Facility and Services

Seating: provided for 400
Servers: full staff
Bar facilities: staffed, full-service bar
Dance floor: parquet wood; accommodates up to 50; PA and microphone available
Linens: burgundy and white; other colors available for extra cost
China: ivory china; glasses and stemware vary
Cleanup: included
Decorations: call for limitations; decorating by prior arrangement
Parking: plenty of free parking on site
ADA: yes

Special Services

Event planner on site to assist you

IN THE HEART OF
OREGON'S WINE COUNTRY

Classic, elegant setting in the heart of Oregon's wine country. Beautifully decorated banquet rooms. Adjoining is the finest tasting room and wine store in the entire valley.

Romantic Mansion located on
two wooded acres overlooking the Willamette River

Amadeus
at the FERNWOOD

2122 S.E. Sparrow (Off River Road Exit)
Milwaukie, Oregon 97222
Contact: Kristina (503) 659-1735, (503) 353-8948
Business Hours: Seven days a week,
5pm–midnight; Sunday Brunch 10am–2:30pm

Capacity: 300 people
Price Range: lunches $20; full course sit-down or buffet style dinners $27; plus gratuity
Catering: full-service in-house catering
Types of Events: bridal luncheons, rehearsal dinners, **on-location wedding ceremonies**, ceremonies and receptions, large group luncheons

Availability and Terms

We are here for your personal needs to make your wedding the most romantic and elegant. Reservations should be made as soon as possible to ensure availability. A deposit is required at the time of booking. Half the deposit is refundable if cancellations are made at least six months prior to your event. **No** cost for using the facility, bartending services, linens, flowers, and candles.

Description of Facility and Services

Seating: table and chairs provided for up to 300
Servers: provided with catering services
Bar facilities: full-service bar with bartender provided; host/no host; liquor provided according to OLCC regulations
Dance floor: accommodates up to 50 people
Linens: cloth tablecloths and napkins provided in cream color
China and glassware: fine china; variety of glassware
Cleanup: provided by Amadeus at the Fernwood
Decorations: early decorating available; fresh flowers for guest tables provided by Amadeus; please discuss ideas with banquet representative
Parking: ample free parking; valet service
ADA: disabled access available

FACILITY OVERLOOKING WILLAMETTE RIVER

Amadeus at the Fernwood is the perfect setting for a romantic wedding reception or rehearsal dinner. You and your guests will enjoy fine continental dining in a wonderful old mansion on two wooded acres, filled with antiques, fireplaces, crystal chandeliers, candlelight and fresh flowers, overlooking the Willamette River. We offer a full bar with a wide variety of Oregon and international wines, and outdoor dining and wedding ceremonies on our patio is available. A classical pianist is featured nightly and during Sunday brunch.

SUNSET DINNER SPECIAL: Daily • 5–6:30pm • $9.95

Events at Arnegards

Ninth and Hawthorne
1510 S.E. Ninth • Portland, Oregon 97214
Contact: Robin Andersen
(503) 236-2759; Fax (503) 231-8837
Business Hours: Mon–Fri 10am–2pm
After-hour appointments always available

Capacity: our entire facility can accommodate up to 450 people; we have two ballrooms and a meeting room available

Price Range: Ballroom rental rates $600–$1,200; discounts available Monday–Thursday

Catering: catering is supplied by renter, or you may choose from our list of caterers

Types of Events: wedding ceremonies and receptions, private parties, cocktail parties, luncheons, dinners, banquets, holiday parties, retirement parties, meetings, all-day seminars, corporate parties, and any other event imaginable

Availability and Terms

Newly open, some premium dates still available. Please reserve rooms as early as possible. Short notice reservations depend on availability. A 50% deposit is due at time of booking with the balance due two weeks prior to event.

Description of Facility and Services

Seating: tables and chairs; provided up to 220; banquet tables, guest book table, and cake table included

Servers: provided by caterer

Bar facilities: provided by caterer or renter; stunning bar area located off The Winnington Ballroom

Dance floor: large dance floor available; capacity: 300+, electrical: supplied

Linens: provided by caterer or client

China: provided by caterer or client

Decoration limitations: establishment is well decorated; we are flexible to your needs; no tape, tacks, or nails on walls; please consult Event Coordinator prior to decorating

Cleanup: renter or caterer is responsible for cleanup; security deposit required

Parking: some off-street parking available; plenty of street parking

Special Services

We have a large stage available with dressing rooms.

NEWLY RESTORED
1920s BALLROOM AND CONFERENCE ROOM

Our newly renovated 1920s ballroom will be open and available to rent November 1st, 1998. We are located conveniently in Southeast Portland. Have your next event in any of our three rooms: *The Winnington Ballroom:* This maple hardwood-floored ballroom has a stage, 14-foot high ceilings, lighted ceiling fans and great acoustics. It can accommodate up to 320 people. *The Grace Ballroom:* This maple hardwood-floored ballroom is perfect for company functions, holiday parties, banquets or receptions and can accommodate up to 100 people. *The Meeting Room:* Can accommodate up to 28.

THE ATRIUM

100 S.W. Market Street
Portland, Oregon 97201
Contact: Catering Director
(503) 220-3929
Business Hours: Mon–Fri 7am–4pm;
evenings and weekends by appointment

Capacity: reception, 100 to 250+; sit-down dinner, 100 to 150
Price Range: food starting at $14 per person plus room rental
Catering: The Atrium provides all catering services tailored to your special day
Types of Events: hors d'oeuvres, dinner, sit-down, and buffet

Availability and Terms

Our magnificent two-story glass building and convenient location one block from Front Avenue in the heart of downtown Portland make The Atrium a popular facility for wedding receptions and other special events. To ensure reserving the date you want, plan to make your reservations six months to a year in advance. The $800 room-rental fee is required at the time of booking and is also considered the deposit for your event. A 120-day advance cancellation in writing is required for a full refund.

Description of Facility and Services

Seating: tables and chairs for 250+
Servers: full wait staff
Bar facilities: full bar service, bartenders, servers and all alcoholic beverages
Dance floor: 200-person, 1,200-square-foot dance floor with full electrical hookups
Linens and napkins: linen, cloth napkins and tablecloths in assorted colors; included in room rental
China and glassware: provided
Cleanup: included
Decorations: though our policies are fairly liberal, please call for restrictions
Parking: ample free parking
ADA: yes

GET THE FEELING OF BEING OUTDOORS YEAR-AROUND IN OUR MAGNIFICENT TWO-STORY GLASS STRUCTURE

The Atrium's unique structure offers a beautiful setting. Its two-story windows and lush greenery as well as the glass-covered roof along with the back patio and two fountains in a beautiful parklike setting will have a profound impact on all its guests. The Atrium is easily accessible on the corner of First and Market, one block from the Marriott Hotel and Front Street, and only three blocks from the RiverPlace Alexis Hotel. Please call our Catering Director at (503) 220-3929 for information or reservations.

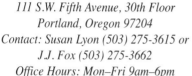

111 S.W. Fifth Avenue, 30th Floor
Portland, Oregon 97204
Contact: Susan Lyon (503) 275-3615 or
J.J. Fox (503) 275-3662
Office Hours: Mon–Fri 9am–6pm
Restaurant: Mon–Thurs 5–11:30pm; Fri 5pm–12:30 am; Sat–Sun 5pm–12:30am

Capacity: 10 to 300 people
Price Range: $21.50 per person and up
Catering: full-service in-house catering
Types of Events: full sit-down meals, buffet, cocktails and hors d'oeuvres, rehearsal dinners, wedding ceremonies

Availability and Terms

Atwater's has six separate dining rooms that can be used individually or in combination to host as many as 300 guests. Atwater's requires a deposit ($100–$500) in advance to reserve space for your reception. For cancellations within 180 days of the event, Atwater's will refund the deposit only if another event can be booked in your place.

Description of Facility and Services

Seating: tables and chairs for 300 available
Servers: included
Bar facilities: fine selection of wines and liquor; liquor liability, bar and bartenders provided courtesy of Atwater's
Dance floor: dance floor can be rented; large space available
Linens and napkins: cloth napkins and linens; ask about colors
China and glassware: china is white with trim; many types of glassware
Cleanup: we do it all
Decorations: please inquire about available table decorations; early decorating possible; decorations must conform to Portland's building and fire codes
Parking: garage and street parking available
ADA: fully accessible

YOU SHOULD SEE OUR VIEW ON WEDDINGS

Atwater's six dining rooms with panoramic views of downtown Portland can be used individually or in combination to host as many as 300 guests. Our 30th floor private dining suites provide an intimate and elegant setting for groups up to 100. Our 11,000-square-foot banquet room on the 41st floor has a fresh, new, elegant look and a breathtaking panoramic view of downtown. It can accommodate groups of up to 300 guests. Atwater's serves American cuisine featuring the bounty of the Pacific Northwest. Our catering staff can help you plan all aspects of your reception including: menu, decorations, and entertainment. We'd also like to share with you our view on rehearsal dinners or your wedding ceremony.

AVALON
at St. James Place

4607 N.E. St. James Road
Vancouver, Washington 98663
(360) 906-0960, (888) 806-0960
Fax (360) 906-0998
Business Hours:
By appointment; please call for a tour;
we can accommodate all schedules

Capacity: chapel seats 220; reception area accommodates up to 300
Price Range: wedding and reception packages in various price ranges
Catering: full-service in-house catering featuring Northwest cuisine
Types of Events: weddings and wedding receptions, from cake and punch to formal
  dinners; we also offer bridal teas, luncheons, rehearsal dinners and parties for all occasions

Availability and Terms

A $500 deposit is required to book your space. Reservations are accepted up to one year in advance. We suggest that you book as soon as possible to secure your date.

Description of Facility and Services

Seating: round tables and upholstered chairs provided
Servers: professional service staff in formal attire
Bar facilities: full beverage service available—host or no-host; Avalon to provide
  professional bartenders and all beverages
Baby grand piano: our house pianist is available for your event
Dance floor: 15' x 18' available at no charge
Linens and napkins: ivory damask provided; other colors available for an additional charge
China and glassware: ivory china with gold band; flatware and stemmed glassware provided
Decorations: brass and crystal lamps on 18" round mirrors provided
Covered patio: off our Fireside Room
Cleanup: provided by Avalon at no charge
Parking: ample off-street parking in our lot
ADA: fully accessible

Special Services

Complete wedding planning is available from the day you book your date through the wedding day!

VANCOUVER'S PREMIER EVENT FACILITY
WHERE GRACIOUS SERVICE AND CLASSIC ELEGANCE
CREATE THE PERFECT WEDDING

No detail was overlooked in creating this facility. Spacious dressing rooms are available for the entire bridal party. The bride's room is beautifully appointed with an 8' dressing table and three stools, a loveseat, tables and chevel mirror. We have a child care room available for those younger guests. We offer a coat and package check.

Our elegant chapel with its soaring vaulted ceiling, decorative pillars, unique lighting, baby grand piano, sound system and altar area was created to be the perfect setting for your wedding. Our Fireside reception room features a beautiful fireplace area—perfect for photos—and French doors to our covered patio area. Our hand-picked staff offers the best service in the industry! We are conveniently located just off I-5, 5 minutes north of the bridge. Turn east on SR 500, left on St. Johns Road and go half a mile—we're on the left.

RESTAURANT

4630 S.W. Macadam Avenue
Portland, Oregon 97201
Contact: Kimberly Lang
(503) 227-4630; Fax (503) 796-2704
Business Hours: Open daily, 11:30am–11pm
Web site: www.avalonrest.com

Capacity: from an intimate gathering of eight, to 250 (including the entire facility and outdoor patio)

Price Range: individually customized menus starting at $30 per person

Types of Events: elegant sit-down or buffet brunch, lunch or dinner; cocktail and hors d'oeuvre receptions; rehearsal dinners; outdoor ceremony site available in summer months

Availability and Terms

Avalon has five rooms of varying sizes, which can be used individually or in combination to host from eight to 250 guests. A facility fee is required to hold the reservation. Cancellation policy is based on the size of the group.

Description of Facility and Services

Seating: up to 250

Servers: provided by Avalon and included in price

Bar facilities: full-service host or no host bar; bartenders and liquor liability provided by Avalon

Dance floor: available

Linens and napkins: provided in a variety of colors

China and glassware: in-house china, crystal and silver available

Cleanup: provided by Avalon

Decorations: accommodating staff will be happy to discuss needs and ideas, or you may bring your own

Parking: ample parking available; valet optional

ADA: fully accessible

Special Services

The attentive staff at Avalon Restaurant will ensure your event is executed with precise detail, and look forward to providing you with a memorable affair.

PROVOCATIVE FOOD, COSMOPOLITAN ELEGANCE AND NATURAL BEAUTY...

The stunning Avalon Restaurant overlooks the scenic Willamette River through expansive floor-to-ceiling windows, and provides an exceptional venue to host an event to remember! Nationally acclaimed Chef Roy Breimen will create an unforgettable menu for your guests to enjoy, while our attentive staff will pamper you with service. If you are looking for exquisite food, gracious service, and a memorable event, Avalon Restaurant will exceed your expectations.

BeckenRidge Vineyard

300 Reuben-Boise Road
Dallas, Oregon 97338
Contact: Becky Jacroux, Owner/Manager
(503) 831-3652
Business Hours: Tue–Sat 10am–5pm;
evenings and weekends by appointment

Capacity: 1,825 sq. ft. event room seats 120, plus 1,200 sq. ft. covered patio

Price Range: $1,400 for the entire day; ask about midweek discounts

Catering: we have a list of preferred caterers; fully equipped kitchen

Types of Events: weddings, receptions, reunions, business meetings and team-building events

Availability and Terms

Opening in April 1999. Located just west of Dallas, 18 miles from Salem. Open year-round; closed in January. A 50% deposit holds your reservation.

Description of Facility and Services

Seating: round tables and chairs for guests; rectangle accessory/serving tables

Servers: provided by caterer

Bar facilities: BeckenRidge and Airlie wines are exclusively served; bottled beer and champagne available upon request; server provided

Dance floor: hardwood floor throughout; stereo sound system available

Linens: ivory cloth tablecloths provided; quality paper napkins available in choice of color

China and glassware: fine china, silver and glassware provided to complement any function

Decorations: silk flower arrangements available at no charge; bubbles provided; please no rice, confetti, or birdseed

Cleanup: we assist with setup and cleanup

Parking: complimentary parking on site

ADA: fully equipped to accommodate ADA requirements

Special Services

BeckenRidge Vineyard produces five varieties of grapes and our custom-labeled wines are produced by Airlie Winery. Both Airlie and BeckenRidge wines are featured at our events and are also available for individual purchase by attending guests.

CELEBRATE YOUR SPECIAL OCCASION
NESTLED IN THE BEAUTY OF THE VINEYARD

You will enjoy our serene, country setting and be delighted with our facility specifically designed for events. BeckenRidge has a warm, friendly lodge-like atmosphere with a commanding view of the vineyard and the Willamette Valley. Special features include a vineyard patio, rock fireplace and grand piano. Personal attention from the owner will help you create a memorable event for you and your special guests.

H O T E L · P O R T L A N D

309 S.W. Broadway at Oak Street
Portland, Oregon 97205
(503) 295-4140; Fax (503) 241-3757
Office Hours: Mon–Fri 8am–6pm
Available all other times by appointment
Web site: www.citysearch.com/pdx/bensonhotel

We look forward to making an appointment with you.

Begin your reception with cocktails in front of the fireplace and experience the Old World charm of our grand lobby. Then move into the Crystal Ballroom to celebrate your first dance under crystal chandeliers where your romantic wedding will be captured forever in your heart. The Mayfair Ballroom is found at the top of our grand staircase, on the mezzanine, and is the perfect setting for larger wedding groups with a built-in stage showcasing a baby grand piano. The mirror on the staircase landing came from Paris in 1883 and was designed for the Royal Palace in Honolulu; it has been with the Benson since 1958 and remains a photography favorite. For more intimate weddings and a view of Broadway, enjoy the classic Cambridge Room. Complete event with a romantic honeymoon night with our "Champagne Kisses" package.

Capacity: seated dining for up to 400 guests; stand-up reception for up to 500 guests

Price Range: brunch and luncheon receptions starting at $25 per person; evening receptions starting at $30 per person

Catering: full-service in-house catering; preferred caterer for the Portland Art Museum and Central Library

Types of Events: sit-down, buffet, hors d'oeuvre receptions, rehearsal dinners; brunch and luncheon receptions also offered

Availability and Terms

We are able to book your wedding date one year in advance. A nonrefundable deposit of 20% is required to make your booking definite. Full payment is due one week before your reception. We encourage you to call as soon as possible to secure your desired date.

Description of Facility and Services

Seating: chairs provided, gold Chivari chairs available at additional charge; round tables seating 4 to 10 guests are provided

Servers: all servers and support staff included at no charge

Bar facilities: full-service bar; we provide all bartenders, servers and beverages

Dance floor: provided in a variety of sizes at no additional charge

Linens and napkins: fine linens and napkins provided at no additional charge

China and glassware: fine china, glassware and silver provided

Parking: ample free parking available, rates vary; valet available upon request

ADA: yes

BRENTWOOD-DARLINGTON COMMUNITY CENTER

7211 S.E. 62nd Avenue
Portland, Oregon 97206
Contact: Mary Davis
(503) 306-5961 ext. 223
Fax (503) 306-5946
Center Hours: Mon–Fri 8am–5pm

Capacity: event space can be divided into three smaller spaces, plus living room. Total capacity is up to 130

Price Range: hourly base of $25-$100

Catering: outside catering or your own arrangements

Types of Events: suitable for family reunions, receptions, anniversary parties, retirement or going-away parties, birthday parties, baby showers, workshops, classes, conferences, dinners, holiday parties, concerts and more

Availability and Terms

Call to check on available dates and times. A cleaning fee of $50 and a $100 refundable damage deposit are needed to hold the date and time.

Description of Facility and Services

Seating: 95 stackable chairs, 15 rectangular tables seating six, five round tables seating eight, 10 wooden armchairs, two bistro tables; specific equipment requirements are requested on our application form

Servers: renter or caterer provides

Bar facilities: renter or caterer to provide beer and wine only, bar, bartender, and liquor liability insurance

Dance floor: tiled floor suitable for dancing; electrical outlets available; renter must provide P.A. system

Linens and napkins: renter or caterer provides

China and glassware: renter or caterer provides

Cleanup: renter responsible for removing all decorations and sweeping floor; tables and chairs must be returned to original locations

Decorations: refer to Building Use Rules in application packet for guidelines

Parking: free parking; additional overflow parking available on weekend by prior arrangement

ADA: yes

Special Services

The Center will provide a hostess on duty during your event to assist with building operations and troubleshooting.

A PLACE FOR CELEBRATIONS!

The large windows, expansive view of Brentwood Park, high ceilings, and tree-lined outdoor space provide a warm, welcoming, light-filled environment for any event. The center is an air-conditioned, nonsmoking facility. Guests have access to the community living room with a gas fireplace, a modern kitchen, changing area, cloak room and accommodating restrooms.

Overlooking The Historic
Columbia River Gorge
P.O. Box 5
Bridal Veil, Oregon 97010
Contact: Jennifer Miller
(503) 981-3695 or (503) 982-0944

Capacity: 150 indoor (800 sq. ft. pavilion); 1,000 outdoor
Price Range: price varies according to event
Catering: renter may select caterer of choice
Types of Events: corporate events and meetings, company picnics, reunions, anniversaries, rehearsal dinners, weddings and receptions

Availability and Terms
We suggest that you book your event one year in advance; we only schedule one event per day Fridays, Saturdays, Sundays and holidays. A $500 refundable deposit is required at booking, with full payment due 30 days before your event. Full refund 60 days prior to event. Months of operation are March–October; please inquire for off-season pricing.

Description of Facility and Services
Seating: chairs available at additional charge or renter may make own arrangements; picnic tables for 100+
Servers: provided by caterer
Bar facilities: caterer or renter provides licensed bartender, liquor, and liability insurance
Linens: provided by caterer
China and glassware: provided by caterer
Dance floor: 800 sq. ft. available in pavilion for dancing
Decorations: no rice, paper or metallic confetti; nails, tacks, or staples may not be placed on building surfaces
Cleanup: renter/caterer is responsible for leaving grounds as found
Parking: ample parking available; parking attendants strongly suggested
ADA: accessible

Special Services
Bridal Veil Lakes has a number of RV spaces available.

NATURAL BEAUTY IN ITS MOST SPECTACULAR FORM
Nestled in the heart of the historic Columbia River Gorge, just 30 minutes east of Portland, natural beauty is in its' most spectacular form at Bridal Veil Lakes. Beautiful wildflowers and lush forest are the perfect backdrop for your lakeside wedding. The view of the Columbia River Gorge and the serene lakeside setting add just the hint of romance that will make your wedding memories last a lifetime. The photo opportunities are endless! Bridal Veil Lakes recreational area is protected from the Columbia Gorge east wind and our Lakeside Pavilion is wonderful for indoor events. Please call and make an appointment to visit our exclusive and private setting for the wedding of your dreams.

The Historic
Broetje House

3101 S.E. Courtney
Milwaukie, Oregon 97222
Contact: Lorraine or Lois
(503) 659-8860
Business Hours: Mon–Fri 10am–4pm;
weekends by appointment

Capacity: 150 inside or outside
Price Range: $150 to $6,000; please call for specific price information
Catering: in-house catering only
Types of Events: sit-down, buffet, garden, cocktails and hors d'oeuvres, cake and punch

Availability and Terms
Rental hours are 8am to 9pm Sunday through Friday; Saturday from 9am to 2:30pm (11am ceremony), and 3:30pm to 9pm (5pm ceremony). A one-third deposit is required on booking.

Description of Facility and Services
Seating: tables and chairs for 150
Servers: provided as needed during the event
Bar facilities: bar facilities available; provide your own bartender and liquor; bottled or canned beer, wine, champagne only—no hard liquor
Dance floor: yes
Linens and napkins: linen or cloth in many colors for an added charge
China and glassware: variety of china and wine/champagne glassware
Cleanup: included in package price
Decorations: special arrangements must be made for early decorating
Parking: plenty of free parking space; valet parking also available
ADA: yes

Special Services
Our in-house catering, use of our serviceware, china, glass stemware, coffee pots, punch bowls and ladles, serving dishes, chafing dishes, and silverware are provided with the package price. You'll also find lovely honeymoon suites and rooms available for changing or an overnight stay.

ENJOY TURN-OF-THE-CENTURY ROMANTIC AMBIANCE
Enjoy the romantic ambiance offered by this magnificent, turn-of-the-century, Queen Anne–style bed and breakfast. Built in 1890 by John F. Broetje, the house features a unique four-story, 50-foot-high water tower. Over an acre of picturesque grounds with a gazebo grace this elegant estate, making it an ideal setting for your wedding and reception! Each event is specially designed to meet the needs of the bride and groom.

The Burdoin Mansion

For Weddings &
Special Occasion Celebrations

18609 N.E. Cramer Road
Battle Ground, Washington 98604
Contact: Rob or Becky Neuschwander
(360) 666-4828
Business Hours: Tues–Sat 10am–5pm;
closed Sunday and Monday

AN ATMOSPHERE THAT REFLECTS
ALL THE ELEGANCE AND GRACE OF THE VICTORIAN ERA

Capacity: indoors 65, outdoors 200
Price Range: $990 and up
Catering: outside catering or by your own arrangement
Types of Events: banquets, receptions, wedding ceremonies, bridal teas

Availability and Terms
A 50% deposit is required to reserve your date.

Description of Facility and Services
Seating: 150 white wooden fold-up chairs, twelve 5' round tables, 4' x 6' banquet tables
Servers: provided by caterer
Bar facilities: provided by caterer; Washington state liquor permit required
Dance floor: 12' x 16'
Equipment: full PA system available, 20' x 30' tent
Linen and napkins: white
China and glassware: 150-piece crystal set
Cleanup: provided
Parking: 20 on-site spaces and parking available one block away
ADA: limited due to the historic nature of the home

Special Services
DJ services and decorative consulting available.

A UNIQUE TURN OF THE CENTURY VICTORIAN MANSION
Situated in a storybrook setting of forest and country homes, The Burdoin Mansion provides a unique atmosphere for your event, reflecting the elegance and grace of the Victorian Era. Our 30 years combined experience in pastoral ministry, weddings, and decorative design will give you the security and confidence to relax and enjoy your celebration.

Canterbury Falls

P.O. Box 156 • Molalla, Oregon 97038
Contact: Judy Hall (503) 829-8821
Closed Monday and Tuesday;
Shown by appointment only

Capacity: up to 400
Price Range: $2,395 up to 200 guests; multiple provisions; only one event per day
Catering: very large reception area includes expansive lawns, floral settings, romantic evening lighting, dance floor, plus a 28'x58' summerhouse; 12'x20' Catering Alcove includes a large, commercial cooler and more; may choose no food, cake only, family prepared, or catered
Types of Events: weddings, receptions, theatre, concerts, poetry readings, storytelling, seminars and hot air balloon launch area; wedding rehearsal is included in the fee

Availability and Terms

Canterbury Falls offers the perfect spacious setting for a romantic English garden wedding. The gardens are available June through September. A natural setting of ferns, white flowering shrubs, and perennials nestle against the 400-square-foot Gothic Pavilion. Many colored theme gardens border the lawns. Event is reserved upon receipt of a $500 deposit. Availability is limited; reserve early.

Description of Facility and Services

Seating: amphitheatre seating for 350; round guest tables for 200; chairs for 250
Linens: beautiful table linens and centerpiece containers; other items provided
Servers, china and glassware: caterer to provide
Cleanup: setup and cleanup included
Decorations: exquisite items provided; no decoration needed
Wedding coordinators: experienced assistance is included in fee
Florists: Victorian elegance to country; we will provide your floral and decorating needs, creatively designed to accommodate your style
Watercolorist: Judy Hall offers professionally accurate, original bridal-floral portrait paintings; this is a unique and lovely wedding gift; price range: $900 to $2,600; inquire for details
Sound system: available in pavilion
Parking: ample parking; parking attendants included
ADA: yes

AN ENCHANTINGLY ROMANTIC ENGLISH GARDEN

Located just 40 minutes south of Portland, or 30 minutes east of Salem, this charming setting (although easily accessible) is hidden well from the public. Canterbury Falls is approached following a 3/4 mile lane through the woods. You arrive in a secluded glade of pervading, Country-Gothic, English influence. The 80 acres include the resident's stone house, streams and waterfalls with two arched footbridges, flower gardens, forests, and meadows. The elegant pavilion boasts eight white lanterns, which enhance a Cinderella effect. In daytime hours it rests in the shade below an amphitheatre seating where your guests can experience nature's art, an unforgettable bridal entry, and your most memorable day. (Information is subject to change.)

CAPTAIN AINSWORTH HOUSE
BED & BREAKFAST

19130 Lot Whitcomb Drive • Oregon City, Oregon 97045
Contact: Claire Met (503) 655-5172
Tues–Sat 10am–4pm; evenings and weekends by appointment

Capacity: 100 stand-up reception; 70 sit-down reception May–Oct; 70 rest of year
Price Range: price varies depending on function and size of group
Catering: no in-house catering; small, fully equipped kitchen available with a large commercial refrigerator; you also may do your own catering.
Types of Events: sit-down, buffet, cake and punch receptions; reunions, teas, and other social or business functions

Availability and Terms

Open year-round. Reserve as early as possible. A one-third deposit reserves your special day.

Description of Facility and Services

Tables and chairs: round tables and chairs for 100; rectangle accessory/serving tables
Servers: provided by caterer or renter
Bar facilities: caterer or renter provides bartender, liquor, and liability insurance; canned or bottled beer, white or blush wine and champagne only
Dance floor: electrical outlets provided; stereo system available
Linens: ivory linen tablecloths; quality paper napkins available in choice of color
China, glassware and serviceware: glass plates and glassware to complement any function; china and antique silver service available at an additional charge
Cleanup: we help with setup and cleanup; catering cleanup excluded
Decorations: silk floral table centerpieces provided; inquire about limitations; no rice, birdseed, or confetti please
Parking: free on- and off-street parking
ADA: completely accessible

Special Services

Our reception facility has been elegantly decorated to complement any event. A black-and-white tiled floor, ivory silk rose garlands, and brass fixtures can easily blend into any color scheme. French doors lead to 20'x30' covered patio area. Our two acres of picturesque grounds provide a lovely setting for photographs and outdoor weddings.

SOUTHERN HOSPITALITY WITH A NORTHWEST FLAIR

The Captain Ainsworth House Bed and Breakfast is a carefully restored 1851 Greek Revival mansion with massive two-story columns. Carefully chosen period antiques create an elegant ambiance. Two of the four bedrooms, each with a private bath, are available to be used as dressing rooms. We offer elegant overnight accommodations for your out-of-town guests. Please ask about our special B&B wedding package.

CAVANAUGHS®
HILLSBORO HOTEL

3500 N.E. Cornell Road
Hillsboro, Oregon 97124
(503) 648-3500
(800) 325-4000

Capacity: up to 150 people for receptions or dinners
Price Range: varies depending on size and length of event; please call
Catering: full range of catering services including sit-down, buffet, cocktails, hors
d'oeuvres, picnics, theme or custom parties, meetings, seminars; ideal for conventions and
retreats with hotel; on-premise outdoor events available

Availability and Terms:
Groups up to 150 people. A six-month advance reservation is recommended; deposit is
required upon booking. Deposit can be refunded with 60-day written cancellation notice.

Description of Facility and Services
Seating: tables and chairs provided for any set up
Servers: provided with our catering service
Bar facilities: full-service bars available with bartenders ($50 setup fee required)
Dance space: dance floor available; full electrical hookup
Linens and napkins: cloth linens and napkins available with food service
China and glassware: house china and stemmed glassware available
Decorations: we can assist you, and we allow decorations prior to event
Cleanup: provided and included in catering cost
Parking: plenty of free parking
ADA: complied

HIGH QUALITY SERVICE
WITH A PERSONAL TOUCH
Nestled in the heart of the Oregon Silicon Forest, Cavanaughs Hillsboro Hotel offers the
perfect location for small to mid-size weddings and receptions. Their specialty is providing
high quality service with a personal touch. From cocktail and hors d'oeuvre receptions to
formal sit-down buffets—every detail is checked and rechecked to assure our clients that each
function becomes a success.

For the honeymoon, be sure and visit our
Washington, Idaho and Montana locations.

(800) 325-4000

www.cavanaughs.com

DISTINCTIVE
CATERING

CATERING AND RECEPTION FACILITY

Part of the Home Builders Association of Metro Portland
15555 S.W. Bangy Road
Lake Oswego, Oregon 97035
Contact: Barb Chirgwin
(503) 684-1880; E-mail: barbc@bbamp.com
Business Hours: Mon–Fri 8am–5pm

Capacity: 50-200 seated; 50 to 300 reception
Price Range: room rental charge varies per event and season
Catering: catering starts at $9.95 per person (plus gratuity) in-house or at your location
Types of receptions: sit-down, buffet, theme, cocktails and hors d'oeuvres, barbecue, picnic or special requests

Availability and Terms

Spacious reception hall/auditorium featuring patio, stage, dance floor, and optional bar. Please make your reservations with as much advance notice as possible.

Description of Facility and Services

Seating: as many tables and chairs as you need
Servers: we provide complete staff
Bar facilities: full-service bar and bartender available; host or no-host; liquor, beer, wine, and champagne
Dance floor: we have a dance floor and stage with optional media equipment
Linens and napkins: full array of tablecloths and napkins ranging from fine linen, cloth or paper (available in any color)
China and glassware: white china with trim; matching glassware available
Cleanup: cleanup staff provided
Decorations: rooms are accessible for early decorating
Parking: plenty of free parking, including handicapped parking
ADA: yes, handicapped accessible

CELEBRATE YOUR NEXT EVENT WITH US!
PHONE NOW FOR YOUR PRIVATE CONSULTATION
FOR MEMORIES THAT WILL LAST A LIFETIME!

We look forward to making your wedding reception a total success. Excellent facilities, friendly staff, easy freeway access and ample parking.

CENTRAL LIBRARY

801 S.W. Tenth Avenue
Portland, Oregon 97205
Contact: Sandra Lahti
(503) 306-5578
Business Hours: Mon–Fri 9am–5pm
Web site:
http://www.multnomah.lib.or.us/lib/rentals/

Capacity: seated dining for up to 300; stand-up reception for up to 1,200
Price Range: $600-$3,600 plus security; please call for specifics
Catering: select the licensed caterer of your choice
Types of Events: ceremonies, receptions and rehearsal dinners

Availability and Terms

Central Library's lobbies, reading rooms and meeting rooms are available for after-hours weddings and receptions. A 50% deposit is required to hold space.

Description of Facility and Services

Seating: limited number of banquet tables, round tables, and stacking chairs
Servers: provided by caterer
Bar facilities: provided by caterer; no hard alcohol or red wine
Dance floor: provided by caterer
Linens: provided by caterer
China and glassware: provided by caterer
Cleanup: provided by caterer
Decorations: no helium balloons, glitter, confetti, candles or fog/bubble machines; all
decorations must be approved in advance by Central Library
Parking: available on street or in nearby lots
ADA: handicap accessibility and facilities in all areas

IMAGINE YOUR WEDDING IN OUR "GARDEN OF KNOWLEDGE"

Experience the grandeur of Central Library as never before. After a $24 million, three-year renovation, this historic 1912 building is a masterpiece and an exquisite setting for weddings, receptions, parties, rehearsal dinners, bridal teas and brunches. The building's grand lobbies and unique spaces are an elegant backdrop for any event. Enter the building and enter "The Garden of Knowledge," a theme echoed in the building's public art and unique interior detailing. Imagine your reception or rehearsal dinner in the Library's reading rooms surrounded by the works of your favorite authors. Your guests will welcome a visit to Central Library's garden paradise.

Cherry Hill

located in the
Columbia River Gorge National Scenic Area
1550 Carroll Road • Mosier, Oregon 97040
Contact: Elizabeth Toscano
(541) 478-4455; Fax (541) 478-4457
Business Hours: Mon–Fri 8am–5pm

Capacity: up to 80 inside; 200 in the garden
Price Range: varies according to type of event
Catering: full-service in-house catering
Types of Events: sit-down, buffets, cocktails and hors d'oeuvres, picnics

Availability and Terms
Cherry Hill is available for your private use from April 15 through October 31. A $500 deposit holds your day and is refundable if we can rebook.

Description of Facility and Services
Seating: tables and chairs for up to 200
Servers: service staff included in catering costs
Bar facilities: full-service bar provided: liquor, beer, and wine
Dance floor: available with electrical outlets
Linens and napkins: heirloom, banquet, or casual linens available
China and glassware: china and glassware provided
Cleanup: provided by Cherry Hill
Decorations: staff will decorate to your theme
Parking: on and off-street parking
ADA: limited

Special Services
The experienced coordinators at Cherry Hill look forward to helping you organize any aspect of your wedding or reception. Our on-site florist, caterer, and pastry chef work closely together to ensure that no detail is overlooked and that all is in the best of taste.

COUNTRY GARDEN SETTING
Whether you imagine an intimate wedding or a grand reception, Cherry Hill is the premiere outdoor event site in the Columbia Gorge. Our turn-of-the-century farmhouse is perched on an orchard-covered hillside with panoramic views. Ceremonies take place on the shaded lawn under the spreading limbs of towering Oregon oaks. Receptions are held beneath starry skies or in our classic American red barn. Brides and grooms often choose our Wedding Weekend, including rehearsal and dinner, ceremony and reception, with every detail thoughtfully arranged by the staff at Cherry Hill.

> "Toscano's matter-of-factness, combined with an impeccable sense of taste and organization, has helped her to become the Martha Stewart of Gorge weddings."
> —*Hood River News,* August 20, 1997

CHIEF OBIE LODGE

Boy Scouts of America
Scout Office
2145 S.W. Naito Parkway
Portland, Oregon 97201
Contact: Volunteer Services (503) 225-5759
Lodge Location
11300 S.E. 147th • Portland, OR 97236
(must contact Scout Office for viewing)
Business Hours: Mon–Fri 8:30am–5:30pm; Sat 10am–4pm

Capacity: up to 250 guests
Price Range: $750 for facility rental (10am to 11pm)
Catering: client provides outside catering service
Types of Events: any type of nonalcoholic event

Availability and Terms
We recommend that the Chief Obie Lodge be reserved at least six months in advance. A $500 refundable cleaning deposit is required to hold your reservation.

Description of Facility and Services
Seating: tables and chairs for up to 250
Servers: provided by caterer or client
Bar facilities: alcohol is prohibited
Dance floor: 250-person dance floor; electrical outlets available
Linens, china and glassware: provided by caterer or client
Cleanup: client and/or caterer is responsible for leaving Lodge as it was found
Decorations: please discuss decorating ideas with our staff; no candles
Parking: on-site parking; short walk to Lodge
ADA: limited access

Special Services
The Chief Obie Lodge offers two dormitories to accommodate up to 75 overnight guests.

PANORAMIC VIEW
A Mount Hood panorama awaits you at Chief Obie Lodge, where weddings, family reunions or corporate events will find the perfect setting. The Lodge, set on a knoll overlooking 190 acres of field and forest, is easy to find—only a five-minute hop from I-205 and Clackamas Town Center. The Great Room in the majestic building holds 250 guests under a huge cathedral ceiling. Those wishing overnight accommodations for up to 75 guests can also reserve the upstairs consisting of two large dormitories with shower facilities. Two lawn areas, fringed with fir and alder, serve well for outdoor activities.

Portland
503•231•9915

Vancouver
360•253•8326

Mailing address:
13 S.E. Grand Avenue • Portland, OR 97214
Portland (503) 231-9915; Vancouver (360) 253-8326
Fax (503) 231-7985
E-mail: gsabin@teleport.com; Web site: http://www.citygrill.com

Capacity: if you haven't selected a location for your wedding reception, we can help; our *new* **Tualatin** restaurant has an outdoor area that can accommodate 2,200 people on the lake adjacent to the Century Hotel; inside, there is room for 150 people; our *new* **Gresham** restaurant has banquet space for 240 people; City Grill Restaurant in **Vancouver** has two banquet rooms—one for 90 people and the other for 40 people; our event planners also have access to hundreds of venues, many of which you may not have realized are available for receptions

Price Range: call for information; many of our restaurant spaces are free with menu order minimums

Catering: full-service in-house catering with customized menus

Types of Events: wedding receptions to private parties; whether casual or formal, we know the perfect spot for your reception; outdoor weddings are our specialty

Availability and Terms

Please call to book your event.

Description of Facility and Services

Seating: classroom, buffet, full-service or custom seating arrangements
Servers: banquet captain to attend to your individual needs
Bar facilities: full-service bar at each restaurant location; full-service portable bars also available
Dance floor: available upon request
Linens and napkins: linens and napkins included; large selection of custom linens and colors available for a reasonable fee
China: provided; optional patterns available on request
Decorations: wide range of decorations available; have a great idea?—we can make it work!
Parking: on-site parking available
ADA: accessible

WHEN EVERYTHING HAS TO BE RIGHT

Our professional staff is available to help you plan the banquet or reception of your dreams. With the help of our creative planners, anything is possible. Whether you just need a few ideas or would like us to handle all the details, we're here for you.

We look forward to hearing from you.
Give us a call for our brochure to get some ideas.
We can meet with you personally to discuss your plans.

4000 Westcliff Drive • Hood River, Oregon 97031
Contact: Erika, wedding consultant
(541) 387-5405, (800) 345-0931
Business Hours: Mon–Fri 9am–5pm

Columbia Gorge Hotel

Capacity: 10 to 200; 40 guest rooms; 3 function rooms
Price Range: prices vary according to wedding package
Catering: full-service catering, on- or off-premise
Types of Events: outdoor and indoor weddings, banquets, informal hors d'oeuvre receptions to formal sit-down dinners

Availability and Terms
Early reservations required, especially for summer garden weddings. Advance deposit required to secure space.

Description of Facility and Services
Seating: accommodating up to 200 guests
Servers: included in price quote
Bar facilities: full-service bar for alcoholic and nonalcoholic beverages available; extensive selection of liquor, beer and wine
Dance floor: for 50 people; electrical hookups available
Linens and napkins: white linen tablecloths and napkins available
China and glassware: china, glassware and silverware provided
Cleanup: included in price quote
Flowers and decorations: professional in-house florist to take care of all your special needs
Parking: ample free parking

Special Services
Complete wedding services; on-site wedding consultant. Detailed wedding packages for your convenience.

ROMANCE AND ELEGANCE WITH A PERSONAL TOUCH
Experience the natural grandeur and the picturesque views from our historic country inn. Let the Columbia Gorge Hotel and your very own Professional Wedding Coordinator help plan one of the most important days of your life. Enjoy the option of four outdoor wedding lawns that are situated on five acres overlooking the mighty Columbia River. Savor our exquisite dining, voted one of Oregon's best restaurants, and stay in one of our distinctive guest rooms. Our personal style and uniqueness will ensure ever lasting memories.

© Julian Gable 1997

© Holland Studios

THE CROWN BALLROOM & GARDEN COURT
"The Fine Art of Weddings & Receptions"
918 S.W. Yamhill and Ninth Avenue • Portland, Oregon 97205
(diagonal from the downtown Nordstrom, on the top floor of the historic Pythian Building)
(503) 227-8440, (800) 852-1443; Fax (503) 227-2654
Business Hours: by appointment only; offering after-hours showings

The Crown, proudly atop the downtown Pythian Building consists of The Crown Ballroom—an elegant Victorian hall built in 1901 in the tradition of a European Grand Salon, boasting rich mahogany paneling, a beamed cathedral ceiling and full stage for beautiful wedding ceremonies. And for smaller receptions—the artful and ever romantic Garden Court.

Capacity: The Crown Ballroom: 225 guests/sit-down; Garden Court: 60 guests/sit-down; rooms may be booked together for a facility capacity of 275 sit-down or 400 cocktail-style

Price Range: $700 to $3,050, depends on room, date, type of event and number of guests

Catering: four professional in-house catering services to assist in menu/event planning for cocktail parties, buffets or formal sit-downs; can work with all budgets and themes from intimate tea parties to formal dances and concerts to black tie galas

Types of Events: elegant wedding ceremonies and receptions; corporate celebrations and banquets; famous for Casa Blanca and Titanic theme parties

Availability and Terms
While only three years old, The Crown is regularly booking 6–12 months in advance. Half the rental fee will reserve either or both rooms. Rooms are reserved for 3- to 10-hour time blocks.

Description of Facility and Services
Banquet seating: tables and double-padded black dining chairs for up to 275 guests
Bar facilities: full bar services; host/no-host with bartenders and liquor liability provided by our in-house caterers or yours; two full-service cocktail bars; one espresso/champagne bar
Dance floors: three hardwood floors with spotlights, mirror balls, gels and accommodates two to 200 guests
Decorations: this fully decorated 10,000-ft facility is tastefully designed with Victorian architectural themes, large tropical plants, impressive chandeliers and large candelabras, while French-lace curtains on king-size windows open up to spectacular midtown city views
Convenient parking: 7-level parking structure adjacent to building with economy rates

Special Features
The Champagne Room for the Bride's party features a vanity bar, a guest phone, three sofas and city views. The in-house Black Wing Gallery for the groom's party includes a water fountain, walk-in closet and private lounge/restroom. Large gold grand piano for cake cutting ceremony; 26-foot serpentine buffet table and full-service kitchen. Full stage with raised and lighted dance floor, full-length formal velvet curtain for ceremonies, receiving lines and grand entrances! Ask for Anne, our Director, for a private tour of this showcase venue.

CROWNE PLAZA®

HOTELS · RESORTS

14811 Kruse Oaks Boulevard
Lake Oswego, Oregon 97035
For banquet reservations:
Linda Goss (503) 624-8400 ext. 253
Sleeping room rates:
Mandy Marsh (503) 624-8400 ext. 251

Capacity: groups of 20 up to 300
Price Range: inquire about prices
Catering: incredible full-service custom catering
Types of Events: sit-down dinner, buffet, cocktails and hors d'oeuvres, luncheons, any custom party

Availability, Terms, and Location

One ballroom and one boardroom are available for banquets and receptions. We recommend making reservations as early as possible. The Crowne Plaza is conveniently located at the intersection of Interstate 5 and Highway 217. Its accessibility to Portland, Beaverton, Tigard, and Lake Oswego makes it ideally situated for your wedding and reception.

Description of Facility and Services

Seating: tables and chairs for up to 250 people
Servers: included
Cleanup: handled by The Crowne Plaza
Bar facilities: full-service bar facilities; bartenders available for private reception
Dance floor: space available for band; large dance floor
Linens and napkins: all colors available (some extra charge)
China and glassware: classic styles
Decorations: inquire about decorations we can provide for an extra cost
Parking: plenty of free parking; valet parking available
ADA: fully accessible

Special Services

• **Weddings:** Our six-story atrium with cascading waterfalls makes a beautiful setting for your wedding ceremony. **When booking your reception, a complimentary suite will be provided for the bride and groom.** Special rates are available for your out-of-town guests.

LUXURIOUS AND ELEGANT

The luxurious and elegant Crowne Plaza features a six-story waterfall in the atrium and 161 tastefully decorated rooms. Other amenities include an indoor-outdoor pool, spa, sauna, exercise facility, and gift shop. This hotel is ideal for rehearsal dinners, bridesmaid luncheons, and wedding receptions.

See page 383 under Honeymoon, Travel & Accommodations.

THE CRYSTAL BALLROOM

132 W. Burnside
Portland, Oregon 97209
Contact: Mary Hendrickx
(503) 492-2777
Business Hours: Mon–Fri 9am–5pm;
tours weekends and by appointment

Capacity: 1,000 persons concert-style; 350 seated

Price Range: $5,000 Monday–Thursday to $8,500 Friday–Sunday; food and beverage minimum required to waive rental; based on day of week and time of day

Types of Events: weddings, receptions, reunions, meetings, seminars, exhibits, banquets, concerts, dances, holiday parties

Availability and Terms

We suggest that you book your event six months to one year in advance for a weekend date and three to nine months in advance for weekday functions. Function deposits are 25% of room rental cost. Deposit is due 30 days after booking.

Description of Facility and Services

Seating: eight 8-top round tables available for assorted seating, 130 folding chairs; additional tables and chairs may be rented; fixed seating in the ballroom, including theatre seats in the mezzanine and benches surrounding the ballroom totals 190

Servers: staff included in price; 17% gratuity added to the bill

Bar facilities: full-service cocktail bar featuring McMenamin's beer and wine

Dance floor: The Crystal's most remarkable featuring is its maple "floating" dance floor; one of the last of its kind, it is said to have the ability to make a good dancer out of a bad one

Live music: live music is welcome to compliment your event; the cost is the responsibility of the renter, but recommendations will gladly be made

Linens and napkins: assorted linen and napkin colors are available to rent

China and glassware: silverware and plates included; due to the nature of the "floating" dance floor, some glassware is discouraged

Decorations: responsibility of renter

Cleanup: included in price

Parking: street parking is available and several paid parking structures are in close walking distance

BEAUTIFULLY RENOVATED HISTORIC BALLROOM

The historic Crystal Ballroom boasts 7,500-square-feet of floating dance floor. Its eclectic and festive decor make it an ideal setting for events ranging from an award banquet to a wedding reception. The unique Crystal had been a forum for music, dancing, and personalities that have helped define several eras. Extracting inspiration from over 80 years of history, a team of artists have added dimension to the Crystal's walls by painting murals throughout the building and the on-site brewery.

CRYSTAL SPRINGS RHODODENDRON GARDEN

S.E. 28th North of Woodstock
Mailing Address: 7215 S.E. Hawthorne
Portland, Oregon 97215
Contact: Rita Knapp, Event Coordinator
(503) 256-2483
Business Hours: please call for appointment

Capacity: 150 maximum

Price Range: varies according to size and time use (must include setup, takedown, rehearsal time, and photography session)

Catering: no kitchen; catering by family or caterer; separate entrance for deliveries

Types of Events: weddings, receptions, reunions, seminars, memorials; mainly on lawn; rustic building available in rainy weather

Availability and Terms

Outdoor events may be scheduled between May and mid-October. In the event of inclement weather, building may be used. Reservations are accepted up to one year in advance. Fee is 50% of agreed terms, balance due 30 days prior to event date. For cancellation, a sliding scale for 90, 60, and 30 days ahead.

Description of Facility and Services

Seating: tables and chairs for up to 50 available on-site; larger groups must get seating from rental company

Servers: provided by caterer

Bar facilities: alcohol-free facility

Dance floor: rustic floor for indoor facility; floor may be rented for outdoors; 70 decibel sound restriction outdoors

Linens, china, and glassware: provided by caterer

Cleanup: site to be clear of refuse–dumpster on site; refundable deposit

Decorations: no tiny metallic pieces, please; only birdseed for confetti

Parking: two parking lots

ADA: through service entrance; $25 fee for use of road with three locked gates

Special Services

Building may be used for dressing if not used for reception or serve as your "base of operations."

WORLD-CLASS BOTANICAL GARDEN

This world-class botanical garden bounded by a sparkling lake filled by 13 natural springs invites a wide variety of both water and land birds. Lush greenery of mature trees and shrubs combine with winding pathways to provide unsurpassed beauty throughout spring and summer, followed by outstanding fall colors. Three "created" waterfalls enhance the garden's natural beauty. An atmosphere of peace, seclusion, solitude, and at-one-ness with nature characterizes the garden.

DOUBLETREE
HOTELS · GUEST SUITES · RESORTS™
COLUMBIA RIVER

1401 N. Hayden Island Drive
Portland, Oregon 97217
Contact: Sales Office (503) 283-2111
Office Hours: Mon–Fri 8am–6pm, Sat 9am–4pm

Capacity: up to 1,200 guests
Price Range: price will vary depending on type of event and menu selection
Catering: full-service in-house catering provided by the hotel exclusively
Types of Events: from light hors d'oeuvres receptions to elegant luncheon and dinner affairs, including rehearsal dinners and bridal showers

Availability and Terms

The hotel offers many separate ballrooms to accommodate any size wedding party. Several ballrooms have floor to ceiling windows which allow for a dramatic view of the mighty Columbia River and its awesome beauty. It is suggested that reservations be made as soon as possible. A deposit is required at time of booking. Please call the Catering Office for details.

Description of Facility and Services

Seating: your choice of banquet rounds or informal cabaret style
Servers: staff included in catering costs
Bar facilities: full beverage service; hotel offers all beer, wine, and liquor
Dance floor: available for our guests
Linens and napkins: an extensive array of linen colors at no additional charge
China and glassware: white china; stemmed glassware
Cleanup: provided by hotel staff
Decorations: lattice, silk plants, mirror tiles, votive candles, and bud vases available; access for early decoration by prior arrangement
Parking: 750 complimentary parking stalls
ADA: yes

Special Services

The hotel provides complimentary deluxe accommodations for the bride and groom the night of your wedding reception, along with a complimentary bottle of champagne. In addition, we offer special group rates for your guests' sleeping needs.

BEAUTIFUL RIVERFRONT LOCATION
PROFESSIONAL AND QUALITY SERVICE

By selecting this hotel on Hayden Island, you will benefit from the unique and dramatic setting on the majestic Columbia River, as well as true professional wedding coordinators who will assist with all your planning needs. From menu planning to room decor and design, our experienced and friendly staff are specially trained to ensure a memorable and worry-free event. Just north of downtown, our convenient location and ample parking make attending your special event easy for your guests. Experience the difference of the DoubleTree Hotel Columbia River, and your memories will be endless.

Please let this business know that you heard about them from the Bravo! Bridal Resource Guide. **127**

DOUBLETREE HOTEL™

PORTLAND • DOWNTOWN

310 S.W. Lincoln • Portland, Oregon 97201
Contact: Sales Office (503) 221-0450; Fax (503) 225-4303
Business Hours: Mon–Fri 8am–6pm; Sat 9am–1pm

Capacity: 250 people maximum
Price Range: $18 per person and up; customized packages available
Catering: full-service in-house catering exclusively
Types of Events: receptions; bridal showers; rehearsal dinners; luncheons; and dinner affairs

Availability and Terms

The DoubleTree Hotel Portland • Downtown's elegant Columbia Falls Ballroom will accommodate up to 250 people for a reception and dance. We recommend that you make your reservation as soon as possible. A $500 nonrefundable deposit is required.

Description of Facility and Services

Seating: tables and chairs provided; banquet round tables
Servers: staff included in catering costs
Bar facilities: portable bars; host/no-host; beer, wine, mixed drinks, champagne, and soft drinks
Dance floor: complimentary; electrical outlets available
Linens and napkins: linen tablecloths and napkins in a variety of colors at no additional charge
China and glassware: white china; stemmed glassware
Cleanup: provided by hotel staff
Decorations: lattice, silk plants, mirror tiles, votive candles available; access for early decorating by prior arrangement
Parking: complimentary on-site parking available
ADA: yes

A MEMORABLE OCCASION...

...Awaits you at the DoubleTree Hotel Portland • Downtown! With all the planning, choosing and coordinating, you need a hotel that can accommodate and foresee your wedding reception needs. Our Columbia Falls Ballroom combines simple elegance and versatility to reflect a variety of wedding themes. We offer creative menus to tantalize all taste buds and our professional and friendly staff will do all the work so that you will feel comfortable and confident as you visit with friends and family who have come to share your special day.

The DoubleTree Hotel Portland • Downtown is conveniently located on the southwest side of downtown directly off major interstate access. We offer complimentary parking and airport shuttle, a complimentary suite for the bride and groom on the night of the wedding, and we will arrange a discounted room rate for out-of-town guests.

Sweet dreams abound at the DoubleTree Hotel Portland • Downtown. Come see how memorable your wedding reception can be!

DOUBLETREE
HOTELS · GUEST SUITES · RESORTS™
AT THE QUAY

100 Columbia Street • Vancouver, Washington 98660
Contact: Sales and Catering Office (360) 694-8341
Business Hours: Mon–Fri 8am–6pm; Sat 9am–1pm

Capacity: 14 meeting rooms to accommodate weddings and receptions from 10 to 600 guests; indoor and outdoor settings with riverview and patio seating available

Price Range: each event is individually priced with custom menu and services to meet your specific needs

Catering: full-service in-house catering exclusively

Types of Events: our events are as unique as our customers; offering a variety from light hors d'oeuvre receptions to elegant luncheon and dinner events

Availability and Terms

Please contact the sales and catering office to discuss space availability and terms.

Description of Facility and Services

Seating: tables and chairs provided by hotel

Servers: staff included in catering costs

Bar facilities: full beverage service; hotel provides all alcoholic beverages

Dance floor: complimentary; electrical outlets available; staging available for band or disc jockey

Linens and napkins: linen tablecloths and napkins in a variety of colors at no additional charge

China and glassware: white china; stemmed glassware

Decorations: lattice, silk plants, votive candles, and bud vases available; access for early decorating by prior arrangement

Cleanup: provided by hotel staff

Equipment: podiums, risers, and staging available at no charge

Parking: complimentary

ADA: all meeting rooms are accessible

Special Services

The DoubleTree Hotel at the Quay offers 160 guest rooms and 3 suites. Your guests will enjoy the many "extras," including coffee, coffee maker, iron and ironing board available in each room, no access charge for calling card calls and upgraded terrycloth towels. Special group rates are available for ten or more rooms per night.

EXPERIENCE THE DIFFERENCE

By selecting the DoubleTree Hotel at the Quay, you will benefit from our unique and dramatic setting on the Columbia River, as well as our professional wedding consultants, who will assist you with all your planning needs. From menu planning to room decor and design, our experienced and friendly staff are trained to ensure a memorable and worry-free event. Our convenient location at the Washington/Oregon border situates us perfectly to accommodate friends and family from both states. Experience the difference of the DoubleTree Hotel at the Quay and plan the most memorable day of your life!

DOUBLETREE HOTEL™

PORTLAND • JANTZEN BEACH

909 N. Hayden Island Drive
Portland, Oregon 97217
Contact: Sales Office (503) 283-4466
Office Hours: Mon–Fri 8am–6pm; Sat 8am–5pm

Capacity: up to 1,400 guests
Price Range: price will vary depending on type of event and menu selection
Catering: full-service in-house catering provided by the hotel exclusively
Types of Events: from light hors d'oeuvres receptions to elegant luncheon and dinner affairs, including rehearsal dinners and bridal showers

Availability and Terms

The hotel offers many separate ballrooms to accommodate any size wedding party. Several ballrooms have floor to ceiling windows which allow for a dramatic view of the mighty Columbia River and its awesome beauty. It is suggested that reservations be made as soon as possible. A deposit is required at time of booking. Please call the Catering Office for details.

Description of Facility and Services

Seating: your choice of banquet rounds or informal cabaret style
Servers: staff included in catering costs
Bar facilities: full beverage service; hotel provides all beer, wine, and liquor
Dance floor: available at no additional charge
Linens and napkins: an extensive array of linen colors at no additional charge
China and glassware: white china; stemmed glassware
Cleanup: provided by hotel staff
Decorations: lattice, silk plants, mirror tiles, votive candles, and bud vases available; access for early decoration by prior arrangement
Parking: complimentary parking
ADA: accessible

Special Services

The hotel provides complimentary deluxe accommodations for the bride and groom the night of your wedding reception, along with a complimentary bottle of champagne.

BEAUTIFUL RIVERFRONT LOCATION
PROFESSIONAL AND QUALITY SERVICE

By selecting this hotel on Hayden Island, you will benefit from the unique and dramatic setting on the majestic Columbia River, as well as true professional wedding coordinators who will assist with all your planning needs. From menu planning to room decor and design, our experienced and friendly staff are specially trained to ensure a memorable and worry-free event. Just north of downtown, our convenient location and ample parking make attending your special event easy for your guests. Experience the difference of the DoubleTree Hotel Jantzen Beach, and your memories will be endless.

DOUBLETREE HOTEL™

PORTLAND • LLOYD CENTER

1000 N.E. Multnomah • Portland, Oregon 97232
Contact: Catering Office (503) 249-3130
Business Hours: Mon–Fri 8am–6pm; Sat 9am–noon

Capacity: up to 1,100 guests
Price Range: price will vary depending on type of event and menu selection
Catering: full-service in-house catering provided by the hotel exclusively
Types of Events: light hors d'oeuvre receptions to elegant luncheon and dinner affairs, including rehearsal dinners and bridal showers

Availability and Terms

The DoubleTree Hotel Portland • Lloyd Center offers <u>four</u> separate ballrooms to accommodate any size wedding party. The Northwest Ballroom, our newest addition, offers floor to ceiling windows that overlook the pool and outside patio. Reservations are suggested six to nine months in advance with a deposit. Please call the catering office for details.

Description of Facility and Services

Seating: your choice of banquet rounds or informal cabaret style
Servers: staff included in catering costs
Bar facilities: full beverage service available; DoubleTree Hotel Portland • Lloyd Center to provide all beer, wine, and liquor
Dance floor: available at no additional charge
Linens and napkins: an extensive array of linen colors at no additional charge
China and glassware: white china; stemmed glassware
Cleanup: included in price
Parking: parking for over 750 cars; rate is discounted for all guests attending; maximum charge of $3 per car
ADA: yes

Special Services

The DoubleTree Hotel Portland • Lloyd Center provides a complimentary Bridal Suite the night of your wedding reception along with a complimentary bottle of champagne. In addition, we offer special group rates for your guests' sleeping needs.

RELAX AND ENJOY THE MOMENT

Choose the DoubleTree Hotel Portland • Lloyd Center. Our professional wedding coordinators can accommodate all your planning needs. From menu planning to room decor and design, our experienced and friendly staff are specially trained to take the stress and pressure out of planning your wedding. Our convenient location and ample parking make attending your special event easy for your guests. Our new Northwest Ballroom, with beautiful window-views of the outdoor pool and patio area, provides the perfect setting to make your wedding day memorable. Let us plan this special event while you relax and enjoy the moment.

9957 S.E. 222nd • Gresham, Oregon 97080
Contact: Karen Reed, owner (503) 667-7069; Fax (503) 666-6636
or Kay Oft, manager (503) 667-6121; Fax (503) 666-9769
(3.9 miles south of Gresham on Regner Road)

East Fork
Country Estate

Capacity: up to 250 seated ceremony and reception
Price Range: please call for specific prices on wedding packages
Catering: in-house catering
Types of Events: full-service wedding receptions with sit-down buffet dinners; traditional cake, coffee, and punch receptions

Availability and Terms
Friday evening weddings are from 5 p.m. to 11 p.m. Saturday bookings are from 9 a.m. to 3 p.m. (11:30 a.m. ceremony, followed by a reception from noon to 3 p.m.) and from 4:30 p.m. to 10:30 p.m. (6 p.m. ceremony, followed by a reception from 6:30 p.m. to 10:30 p.m.). Sunday weddings are any six-hour period until 9 p.m. Open April 1–October 15.

Description of Facility and Services
Assistance: your personal, professional wedding consultant is included in our package price
Bar facilities: beer, wine, and champagne available
Dance floor: yes, with electrical hookups
Linens and napkins: many colors to choose from
China and glassware: clear glass china with a pattern; glass coffee cups and stemware
Cleanup: included in our wedding packages
Decorations: included in our wedding package price; the gardens include hundreds of bedding plants, roses, and willow and fir trees
Parking: ample free parking is available
ADA: yes

Special Services
You may wish to reserve our horse and white vis-à-vis carriage as part of your wedding processional. Each event is given special, thoughtful, caring attention. We specialize in "stress free" weddings.

THE ESTATE FACES MOUNT HOOD
AND OVERLOOKS A SERENE FARM VALLEY
Your guests will be seated under white canopies on lawn areas in front of the gazebo. The Estate includes a large, beautifully decorated indoor reception area with hardwood floors and oriental carpeting, several covered patios, four canopies on the lawn areas, and spacious bride and groom changing rooms.

Your guests will arrive to find terraced lawns and flowering gardens facing Mount Hood, horses grazing on the Estate's pastures, and a view overlooking a farm valley, the Cascade foothills, and Mount Hood. The result is a warm, relaxed country setting.

EASTMORELAND GRILL AT THE EASTMORELAND GOLF COURSE

2425 S.E. Bybee Boulevard
Portland, Oregon 97202
Contact: Jerilyn Walker
(503) 775-5910: Fax (503) 775-6349
Office Hours: 9am–5pm

Capacity: 125 for a sit-down dinner; 175 for a reception
Price Range: $250 to $500 room-rental charge, depending upon the size of the event; $10 to $30 per person; the menu will be created especially for you by our staff
Catering: full-service catering available in-house
Types of Events: cocktails, hors d'oeuvres, cake and champagne, buffet, sit-down

Availability and Terms

The Eastmoreland Grill encourages your reservations up to one year in advance. A deposit is required and is nonrefundable. Half-payment is required 30 days in advance, with the remaining half payable on the day of the event.

Description of Facility and Services

Seating: tables and chairs provided for up to 125 sit-down guests
Servers: full staff available; a gratuity will be added to food and beverage purchases
Bar facilities: full-service bar and staff bartender provided upon request; host/no-host; liquor, beer, and wine
Dance floor: we can provide a dance floor for 30 to 40 people on request, with 110-volt electrical hookups
Linens and napkins: cloth tablecloths and napkins available in some colors
China and glassware: white china; glassware available in plastic or glass, as required
Cleanup: cleanup provided
Decorations: our catering manager will discuss with you and help develop your decoration plans
Parking: large parking lot with overflow area
ADA: full facilities

Special Services

The Eastmoreland Grill will cater to your every need in order that your day be just as you would have it to the last detail.

GRACIOUS STYLE OVERLOOKING LUSH GREENS

The lush, beautiful greens of the Eastmoreland Golf Course are the setting for our gorgeous new Tudor-style clubhouse. The banquet room overlooks the tenth tee and has a large, gracious veranda for outdoor entertaining. Winter events are equally blessed with a handsome fireplace where guests love to gather. Our staff has extensive experience in wedding receptions, rehearsal dinners, corporate events, anniversaries, birthdays, and reunions, and we will create a personal menu exactly to your specifications. A telephone call to our staff will start you on your way to a carefree and beautiful event.

EMBASSY SUITES

EMBASSY SUITES HOTEL—PORTLAND AIRPORT

7900 N.E. 82nd Avenue • Portland, Oregon 97220
Contact: Sales and Catering Offices (503) 460-3000; Fax (503) 460-3030
Business Hours: Mon–Fri 7am–6pm; Sat 9am–5pm

Capacity: Portland Grand Ballroom: 8,450 sq. ft. accommodates 563 in rounds of 10, 994 theatre-style; Cedars Conference Room: 2,144 sq. ft. accommodates 143 in rounds of 10, 252 theatre-style; two dedicated boardrooms and convention office—14,000+-sq. ft. total

Price Range: negotiable—dependent upon guestroom block and meal/catering function

Catering: full-service in-house catering, with off-site capabilities; flexible menus

Types of Events: weddings and receptions, parties for all occasions, ballroom and atrium availability, seasonal outdoor, all corporate, exhibit and social events

Availability and Terms

Reservations can be made up to six months in advance; 30–60 day sliding scale cancellation fee. Minimum deposits required with full payment in full 72 hours prior to all events.

Description of Facility and Services

Seating: 563 round tables with 16' ceiling height in Grand Ballroom; 143 round tables with 12' ceiling height in Cedars Ballroom

Servers: one server per 20 guests; one bartender per 75 guests

Bar facilities: in-house; one lobby bar and portables available

Dance floor: two 30' x 30' dance floors (900 sq.ft. each)

Linens: in-house linen (white, burgundy, cream) optional colors available at additional cost

China: in-house white hotel china and dress plates; other options available at additional cost

Cleanup: provided by hotel

Parking: complimentary; 24-hour airport shuttle

ADA: nine fully accessible suites; facility meets ADA requirements

100% Satisfaction Guarantee!

BREATHTAKING VIEWS
COMBINED WITH LUXURY AND CONVENIENCE

Bring the outdoors in with the eight-story, open-air, skylit atrium lobby. Sparkling waterfalls and streams flow throughout the lobby from the central glass elevators. Towering trees and lush foliage with a colorful array of flowering plants contribute to the garden atmosphere, topped off with the gentle strains of a baby grand piano in the lobby bar.

Located one mile from the terminal, two miles from the golf course, minutes from downtown and 45 miles from skiing on Mount Hood. All 251 suites include breathtaking views of Mount Hood, Mount St. Helens and the Columbia River. We offer creative and magical packages for your special evening. Celebrate your day in style, while you treat your family like royalty at the *new* Embassy Suites Hotel at Portland Airport!

EMBASSY SUITES PORTLAND DOWNTOWN

319 S.W. Pine Street • Portland, Oregon 97204
Contact: Lisa Bonner (503) 279-9000 ext. 6169; Fax (503) 497-9051

EMBASSY SUITES

Capacity: 220 sit down; 300 reception
Price Range: from $12.95 for luncheons, from $17.95 for dinners and average of $20 for receptions
Catering: complete in-house catering only
Types of Events: wedding receptions, rehearsal dinners, bridal brunches and luncheons

Availability and Terms

Two large ballrooms plus a ceremonial room and six smaller rooms, great for rehearsal dinners. Most rooms have large windows and are decorated with the elegance and style of the historic Multnomah Hotel, including all of the amenities in an Embassy Suites. Once an event is confirmed, a deposit is required.

Description of Facility and Services

Seating: all tables and chairs provided
Servers: professional service staff available
Bar facilities: hotel provides bar facilities and professional alcoholic beverage servers
Dance floor: 15' x 15' floor available with electrical hookups
Linens, napkins, china and glassware: provided by hotel
Decorations: please check with catering representative
Cleanup: provided by hotel
Parking: valet and parking garage
ADA: all facilities handicapped accessible

Special Services

Let our catering representative help in making your occasion one to remember. With the elegance and style of our restored historic hotel, you will find table decorations included with rooms and a professional staff that is flexible in helping you set up your function with confidence. Enjoy the use of our bridal suite for the bride and her attendants as well as a complimentary honeymoon suite for the bride and groom.

WHERE HISTORY MEETS HOSPITALITY

Come discover Portland's premier historic hotel where you will find contemporary amenities in a classic setting. Along with nine meeting rooms, the hotel has 276 guest suites all designed and furnished to complement the hotel's early 20th century architecture. First opened in 1912 as the Multnomah, the hotel was the hub of Portland society. The same holds true today. Plan your event at the new Embassy Suites Portland Downtown and be a part of history.

EMBASSY SUITES®

PORTLAND—WASHINGTON SQUARE

9000 S.W. Washington Square Road
Tigard, OR 97223
Contact: Lisette Crepeaux
(503) 644-4000

Capacity: up to 1,200 people
Price Range: price to be determined by event and menu selections
Catering: full service catering
Types of receptions: elegant served dinners or buffets, hors d'oeuvres receptions and special private parties

Availability and Terms

The Embassy Suites Hotel has a wide variety of banquet facilities for your special event. Our function rooms can accommodate from 10–1,200 guests.

Description of Facility and Services

Seating: provided for up to 800 guests
Servers: included in catering cost
Bar facilities: full service hosted or no host bar; beer, wine and champagne service; we provide all beverages, bartenders and servers
Dance floor: dance floor provided at no additional cost
Linens and napkins: fine linens available in colors to coordinate with banquet room decor
China and glassware: fine china, silver and glassware provided
Cleanup: included in catering charges
Decorations: limited decorations available at no additional charge
Parking: complimentary parking
ADA: fully equipped to accommodate ADA requirements

Special Services

The Embassy Suites Hotel provides a complimentary Presidential Suite ($500 value) for that special bride and groom on the night of the wedding. Special rates are available for your out-of-town guests in our luxurious suites. Contact our Catering Professionals to see why Embassy Suites is the perfect setting for your memorable occasion.

EOLA HILLS
WINE CELLARS

501 S. Pacific Highway 99W • Rickreall, Oregon 97371
Contact: LJ Gunderson (503) 623-2405; Fax (503) 623-0350
Business Hours: Daily 10am–5pm

Conveniently located just 10 minutes from
downtown Salem in the heart of Oregon's Wine Country

Capacity: 10–250 (more if event is both indoors and outdoors)
Price Range: $350–$1,200 (facility)
Catering: in-house catering available
Types of Events: weddings, receptions, brunch served every Sunday

Availability and Terms

A $350 deposit is required. We are able to arrange functions on short notice if necessary, 30-day minimum preferred. Currently booking events up to one year in advance.

Description of Facility and Services

Seating: provided
Servers: Eola Hills staff ($15/hr.)
Bar facilities: wine and beer service provided by Eola Hills only
Dance floor: dance floor available
Linens: variety of colors available for an additional cost
China and glassware: both on-site and rental available for an additional cost
Decorations: flexible; wine barrels give a great ambiance to facility
Cleanup: may require additional charge
Parking: plenty of parking available (up to 300 vehicles)
ADA: accessible; small flight of stairs leading to restrooms

Special Services

Full event planning services available. Each event is customized to meet your individual needs. The Tasting Room and Gift Shop are open daily from 10am–5pm.

BRING TOGETHER FINE WINE, FOOD AND FUN!

No event is too big, too small, too out in left field-in fact, the bigger the challenge put before us, the more we shine! When it comes to putting on the Ritz and creating an atmosphere designed just for you, let LJ, our Special Events Manager, go to work and it'll happen. Eola Hills has become a popular event facility because of the great winery atmosphere backed up by LJ's personality, creativity, and commitment to make you shine at your own event. It's a special place where you can be a guest at your own party!

Eola Hills Wine Cellars
"We've been discovered—
and for good reasons"

FIFTH AVENUE SUITES HOTEL
Red Star Tavern and Roast House
506 S.W. Washington • Portland, Oregon 97204
Contact: Margie Yager, Director of Catering
(503) 417-3377
Business Hours: Mon–Fri 8am–5pm

Capacity: 6,000 square feet of meeting/private dining space; intimate parties of 16; receptions up to 200

Price Range: three-course lunch entrees from $14 and three-course dinner entrees from $19 per guest

Catering: enjoy "re-kindled American classics" in-house catering from Red Star Tavern and Roast House's Executive Chef Rob Pando

Types of Events: wedding ceremonies and receptions, rehearsal dinners, bridal luncheons

Availability and Terms
Space should be reserved as soon as possible—minimum of 72 hours notice. A deposit equal to one half the estimated expense is required. Cancellation terms apply.

Description of Facility and Services
Seating: tables and chairs provided
Servers: provided
Bar facilities: bartender provided; Red Star provides all beverages
Dance floor: will be rented
Linens: ivory, white and other linen colors available
China: in-house china available; other patterns will be rented
Decorations: no decorations to be attached to walls or ceilings
Cleanup: fees vary
Parking: valet parking available at Fifth Avenue Suites Hotel, 24 hours
ADA: yes

Special Services
Complimentary evening wine tasting in our fireside lobby, complimentary coffee service, fitness center, 24-hour room service, concierge, Aveda spa. Our catering consultants are available and happy to assist you in making your event successful and memorable.

THE PICTURE OF
COMFORT AND SOPHISTICATION
Historic 10-story 1912 building, formerly a distinguished department store, is the picture of comfort and sophistication. Of the hotel's 221 rooms, 135 are spacious 550-square-foot suites. As part of a $25 million renovation, the hotel has the residential feel of a turn-of-the-century American country home.

Our banquet rooms are located on the main, second and third floors of the hotel. Within these rooms, you will find a decor filled with classic lines and warm ambiance.

FINE HOST

777 N.E. Martin Luther King Jr. Blvd.
Portland, Oregon 97232
Contact: Fine Host Catering Dept.
(503) 731-7851

FINE HOST
CORPORATION

OREGON
CONVENTION
CENTER

Capacity: meeting rooms for 10-650; elegant ballrooms for 10-1,200
Price Range: price determined by event and specific menu
Catering: full-service catering provided by Fine Host exclusively
Types of Events: from intimate champagne receptions to elegantly appointed full-service multi-course dinners, bridal showers, and rehearsal dinners

The **SKYVIEW TERRACE**, located in the Twin Points, offers a breathtaking panoramic view of Portland's city scape, providing two full-service bars and a reception area. A perfect location for that memorable wedding reception. The **PLAZA** offers a unique setting for an outdoor wedding ceremony or reception surrounded by beautiful roses (outdoor canopies available).

Availability and Terms

We offer a wide selection of rooms to fit your needs. A deposit of 50% of the total bill is due at the time of the booking. Final payment is due one week prior to event.

Description of Facility and Services

Seating: tables, chairs, and head tables provided
Servers: staff included in catering costs
Bar facilities: full beverage service available; host/no host; Fine Host to provide all beer, wine, champagne, liquor, soft drinks, and bartenders
Dance floor: available with electrical outlets; extensive audiovisual systems; call for pricing
Linens and napkins: wide variety of colors; various types of linens and napkins
China and glassware: white china; stemmed glassware
Cleanup: included in price
Decorations: water fountains, multi-tiered buffet tables, mirrored bases, floral displays, and theme decorations available at no additional charge. Ice sculptures, floral arrangements, silver service, votive candles available for a fee.
Parking: off-street parking and a 830 space parking lot available
ADA: entire facility is ADA approved

Special Services

If you book your bridal shower or rehearsal dinner with us at the same time as your wedding reception, we will provide complimentary Oregon wines served at your bridal shower or rehearsal dinner (two-hour limit). Since most weddings occur on Saturdays, Fine Host offers additional incentives for bookings other days of the week.

WE BRING SOMETHING EXTRA TO EVERY RECEPTION

Nothing is more important to the success of your wedding than careful, detailed planning. Our staff is experienced in helping you plan your wedding and is sensitive to your needs. We know the questions to ask, the details to cover, and the arrangements to make. Our attention to detail and quality service will make your wedding a celebration to always remember.

The Fountains Ballroom

223 S.E. 122nd Avenue
Portland, Oregon 97233
Contact: Denise or Becky
(503) 261-9424; Fax (503) 261-2989
Web site: http://www.lum.com/fountainsballroom

We do it all for weddings!!!

**Ceremonies + Receptions + Catering + Photography + Wedding Cakes + Invitations + Flowers
And much more!**

Capacity: up to 300 with beautiful outside garden patio

Price Range: $600 to $1,200 (most packages reflect an 8-hour booking); please add $200 if having a wedding ceremony and wedding reception

Catering: in-house; affordable buffet menus up to elegant plated dinners

Terms

A 50% nonrefundable deposit is requested; remaining balance due 10 days prior to event.

Description of Facility and Services

Seating: 15 round tables and 200 white wedding chairs

Servers: professional staff in formal attire

Bar facilities: full bar, espresso and formal champagne toast available (liability insurance provided)

Dance floor: three optional dance floors

Linens and napkins: linen available as well as personalized napkins; most colors

Decorations: table decorations available as well as extended decorating services

Photography: on-site professional studio (**Negatives are included** in all wedding packages)

Flowers: professional on-site florists

Parking: free parking and surrounding street parking (valet services available)

1999 SPECIAL PACKAGE

Why not call The Fountains Ballroom where most everything for your wedding can be provided in one low-cost package? We have a special offer for the 1998-1999 season that includes the following: room rental, garden patio, full catered dinner buffet, servers, custom wedding cake, professional photography package including all negatives, complete floral package, partial bar, professional DJ with sound system and lights, invitations, bride and groom food basket for the honeymoon night and *five free gifts* including food platter for before ceremony, three 8 x 10 portraits, table decorations, throw bouquet, and additional 10% off invitations!!! You should not need to purchase anything extra for this package! All this plus much more is only $4,999 (based on 100 guests). Upgrades are available. Or you may choose the individual services you would like to use! It is all up to you and your needs.

We look forward to serving you and your family on your very special day! Please call today for a free consultation. (subject to availability)

**See page 296 under Caterers & Ice Carvings.
See page 484 under Photographers.**

THE
G EORGIA N
RESTAURANT

MEIER & FRANK
DOWNTOWN

621 S.W. Fifth Avenue
Portland, Oregon 97204
(503) 241-5162 or (503) 241-5163; Fax (503) 241-5251

Capacity: up to 200 sit-down, 250 reception; The Grill: 24' x 32', seats 48;
The Party Room: 17' x 22', seats 20; The Georgian Tea Room: 54' x 62', seats 150

Price Range: price varies according to type of event

Catering: full-service in-house catering-from sandwiches to steaks, we have it all

Types of Events: banquets, receptions, rehearsal dinners, bridal teas, anniversaries, business lunches, corporate meetings, fund-raisers, class reunions, bus tour groups

Availability and Terms

Reservations recommended as early as possible. Please inquire for specific price and terms.

Description of Facility and Services

Seating: tables and chairs provided
Servers: provided by The Georgian Restaurant
Bar facilities: complete selection of Northwest wines and local microbrews
Linens and napkins: white standard; colors optional
China and glassware: provided by The Georgian Restaurant
Cleanup: provided by The Georgian Restaurant
Parking: street and parking garages nearby
ADA: fully accessible

Special Services

We are conveniently located on the 10th floor of Meier & Frank, in the center of downtown Portland along Tri-Met MAX light rail and Fareless Square. The Georgian Restaurant's prime location makes it an easy place for all your guests to find. Our staff will be happy to assist you in any way possible.

A PORTLAND TRADITION FOR GENERATIONS

Located in the historic Meier & Frank building, built in 1909, The Georgian Restaurant has always been the restaurant where celebrations are made just a little more special. The restaurant has a quiet atmosphere with décor reminiscent of the classic colonial days.

JAKE'S CATERING
A T   T H E
GOVERNOR
H O T E L

611 S.W. 10th Avenue
Portland, Oregon 97205
(503) 241-2125; Fax (503) 220-1849
Web site: http://www.mccormickandschmicks.com

Capacity: 600 reception; 450 sit-down dinner
Price Range: $28 to $50
Catering: Jake's Catering is the exclusive caterer for The Governor Hotel; off-premise catering available
Types of Events: from stand-up cocktail/appetizer receptions to fabulous buffet presentations to complete sit-down dinners for groups and gatherings of all sizes

Availability and Terms
Our Italian Renaissance style rooms offer variety and flexibility for groups of 20 to 600. The majestic Ballroom, Renaissance Room, Fireside Room, Library, and five additional rooms gracefully complement the charm of The Governor Hotel. We require a 50% deposit to confirm your event and payment in full 72 hours prior to event for estimated charges.

Description of Facility and Services
Seating: tables and chairs for up to 450
Servers: all servers included as hotel service
Bar facilities: full-service bar and bartender
Linens and napkins: cloth napkins and linens provided in a variety of colors
China and glassware: fine china and glassware provided
Decorations: please inquire about specific decoration ideas and needs
Parking: ample parking available near hotel
ADA: committed to full service for guests with disabilities

Jake's Catering… A Tradition
Jake's Catering at The Governor Hotel is a division of McCormick & Schmick Management Group and "Jake's Famous Crawfish." Jake's is one of the most respected dining institutions in the Portland area, and Jake's Catering at The Governor Hotel upholds this prestigious reputation.

Known for offering extensive Pacific Northwest menu selection, including fresh seafood and fish, pasta and poultry dishes, and prime cut steaks, Jake's Catering at The Governor Hotel has the flexibility and talent to cater to your needs.

CLASSIC ELEGANCE AND SERVICE
Listed on the National Register of Historic Places, The Governor Hotel is an architectural beauty. Built in 1909 and renovated in 1992, the hotel has been completely restored to its original grandeur. The original design and ornate craftsmanship of the grand banquet space area were preserved in the original Italian Renaissance styling. The room's chandeliers, high vaulted ceilings, marble floors, and black-walnut woodwork and walls are truly unique.

1922

Grand Oregon Lodge

Vintage Ballroom & Meetinghouse

604 Seventh Street, Second Floor
Oregon City, Oregon 97045
(503) 722-4190; Fax (503) 722-8090
E-mail: grandoregonlodge@worldstar.com

Capacity: up to 299 total capacity
Price Range: $800–$1,800
Catering: select your own or we can provide a caterer
Types of Events: receptions, parties, meetings, presentations, classes, fund-raisers, ceremonies, banquets, concerts, dances, shows, casino events

Availability and Terms
The Lodge is available Monday through Sunday, days and evenings. Fifty percent of the rental fee is required to hold your date. Remaining balances and deposits are due 60 days prior to the event.

Descriptions of Facility and Services
Seating: new 60" and 8' tables, new banquet chairs
Servers: provided by caterer or client
Bar facilities: available
Dance floor: full vintage ballroom available for dancing
Linens: white available
China and glassware: available through caterer
Cleanup: kitchen wiped and mopped, trash taken away, floor swept; cleanup deposit required
Decorations: classic and elegant decor throughout facility; special decor requirements are accommodated, subject to restrictions; please inquire
Parking: city lot next to building, good on-street availability
ADA: new bathroom facilities, chair lift entrance

VINTAGE ELEGANCE IN CHARMING HISTORIC DISTRICT
After 75 years of private ownership, this architectural treasure is finally opening for the public to use and enjoy. Built in 1922 as a Fraternal Lodge, this restored 6,000 square-foot facility offers generous rooms designed specifically for public celebrations. Nostalgia graces the vintage ballroom with its grand proportions and classic details. The adjacent Red Room elegantly stages buffet and refreshments adjoined by the service kitchen. This room also functions as a smaller meeting room for classes, presentations or additional dining. Our Billiard Room includes two magnificent 9' antique Brunswick pool tables refurbished in oceans of royal red felt and honey leather pockets. These bright and elegant rooms all contain 15' ceilings, plaster crown moldings, chandeliers, transoms, wood floors and vintage detail.

Gray Gables Estate

Year-round Wedding Gardens
3009 S.E. Chestnut
Milwaukie, Oregon 97267
(503) 654-0470; Fax (503) 654-3929
Business Hours: Mon–Fri 9am–5pm
Under New Management

Capacity: up to 275
Price Range: various wedding and reception packages
Catering: in-house catering
Types of Events: weddings, receptions, rehearsals, banquets, costume balls, anniversaries, proms, office parties, fund raisers, picnics

Availability and Terms
The Gray Gables takes bookings for its facility up to one year in advance, but shorter notice can be accommodated if space is available. A $500 deposit is required to hold your reservation date.

Description of Facility and Services
Consultation: every package includes bridal consultation and event coordination
Seating: tables and chairs provided for up to 275 people
Servers: all parking and service attendants included
Bar facilities: extensive selection of beer, wine, and champagne available
Dance floor: accommodates up to 125 people; electrical outlets available
Linens and napkins: elegant linen tablecloths and skirting; quality paper napkins; specialty linens available at additional cost
China and glassware: clear crystal china, appropriate glassware; silver service available at an additional cost
Cleanup: provided by Gray Gables staff
Decorations: we are proud to offer a variety of decorating options, or you may provide your own; canopies with seating for 200 are provided in case of inclement weather
Parking: ample free parking

Special Services
We can provide and assist with invitations, cakes, ministers, photographers, videographers, florists, musicians, disc jockeys and live musicians. We are the Northwest's premier full-service event center. Our consultants understand the significance of your special day. We assist you in planning and executing all details, to make your event a unique and wonderful occasion.

HISTORIC, COLONIAL ESTATE AND MANOR HOUSE
The staff of Gray Gables looks forward to the opportunity to serve you. Our historic, colonial estate and manor house are the perfect settings for any day or evening event. Our picturesque English and botanical grounds, complete with waterfalls, ponds, and fountains, make a beautiful setting for an indoor or outdoor wedding. We are conveniently located just eight miles from downtown Portland. Please call for a guided tour of our lovely facility.

404 S.W. Washington
Portland, Oregon 97204
Contact: Ted Papas (503) 224-2288
Business Hours: Mon–Thurs 7am–midnight;
Fri and Sat 7am–2:30am

Capacity: up to 500
Price Range: varies by number of persons and menu selection
Catering: in-house catering only; off-premise catering always available
Types of Events: wedding ceremonies and receptions, rehearsal dinners, banquets, holiday parties; you may choose from sit-down dinners, buffets, cocktails and hors d'oeuvres

Availability and Terms

Please make reservations as soon as possible. Short-notice reservations gladly accepted upon space availability.

Description of Facility and Services

Seating: tables and chairs for up to 500
Servers: provided
Bar facilities: provided by Greek Cusina
Dance floor: available; with electrical hookups
Linens: available upon request
China: fine china available at no extra charge
Decorations: we can decorate or client can
Cleanup: provided by Greek Cusina
Parking: available on street or in adjacent parking structure
ADA: accessible

Special Services

Music—come see what's making the Greek Cusina *the* place for entertainment. Live Greek performances at no charge!
Off-premise catering—let us cater your next event, whatever the occasion, whatever the location. Have your event Sunday through Thursday and get the band for yourself at no charge!

A TOUCH OF GREECE IN THE HEART OF PORTLAND

Our new Minoan Room is now open and awaiting you. Decorated in warm hues of gold and stunning architecture, The Minoan Room is inviting as well as elegant and romantic—the ideal place for your special day.

Let us dazzle you with our exceptional food as you enter a world of Mediterranean charm and flavor.

Our new Minoan Room
"A Must See Event Facility"

The Greenwood Inn

S.W. Allen Blvd. at Hwy. 217
Beaverton, Oregon
Contact: Catering
(503) 643-7444 ext 726 or 727
Office Hours: Mon–Fri 8am–5pm

Capacity: 10 to 500 people

Price Range: Room rentals may be waived depending on food order. We make every effort to work within your budget and offer great flexibility in meeting your special needs. We're happy to custom design a menu for you.

Catering: full-service in-house catering

Types of Events: elegant sit-down or handsome buffet meals, hors d'oeuvres or simple cake-and-punch receptions, bridal luncheons, and rehearsal dinners

Availability and Terms

The Greenwood Inn has nine private rooms accommodating a variety of group sizes. Advance reservations of two to six months are recommended. A deposit is required at the time of confirmation, with the full amount applied to your bill.

Description of Facility and Services

Seating: tables and chairs provided at no additional charge

Servers: included in the cost of food or room rental

Bar facilities: host or no-host bars available; hotel supplies all liquor and bartender

Dance floor: spacious dance floor available at no additional charge

Linens and napkins: cloth linens provided in limited colors at no additional cost; special colors can be ordered for a fee

China and glassware: included in the cost of food, beverage, or room rental

Cleanup: handled by The Greenwood Inn at no additional cost, assuming normal usage

Decorations: limited supply of decorative items available for your use at no additional charge. Elaborate themed events can also be arranged by our staff of professionals.

Parking: 1,000 free spaces available for your use

ADA: all private rooms are on main level and have easy access

Special Services

Access to your room is at least one hour prior to the start of your function. In most cases we will set up your table decorations for you. Please ask about special room rates for your out-of-town guests.

OVER 20 YEARS
OF EXCELLENT SERVICE

The Greenwood Inn offers a resort-like atmosphere with a convenient location for you, your family and guests. From rooms for your out-of-town guests to complete reception planning and services, we're here for you. It's our pleasure to be a part of your special day—a day to remember.

HALLMARK
INNS & RESORTS, INC.

Regional Sales Office
15455 Hallmark Drive
Lake Oswego, Oregon 97035
Contact: Sharon Grosse
(503) 635-4555; Fax (503) 635-6007

Cannon Beach	*Newport*
1400 S. Hemlock	*744 S.W. Elizabeth*
Cannon Beach, Oregon 97110	*Newport, Oregon 97365*
(503) 436-1566, (888) 448-4449	*(541) 265-2600, (888) 448-4449*

Web site: www.hallmarkinns.com

Capacity: *Cannon Beach:* up to 150 reception; *Newport:* up to 200 reception
Price Range: varies depending on size and length of event; please call
Catering: full range of catering services on premise; outdoor events available with tent
Types of Events: business meetings, company retreats, seminars, banquets

Availability and Terms

A six-month advance reservation is recommended; deposit is required upon booking. Deposit can be refunded with 30-day written cancellation notice.

Description of Facility and Services

Seating: tables and chairs provided
Servers: provided with our catering service
Bar facilities: full-service bars available with bartenders ($30 setup fee required)
Dance floor: dance floor available, full electrical hookup
Linens and napkins: cloth linens and napkins available with food service
Decorations: we can assist you, and we allow decorations prior to event with special arrangement
Cleanup: provided and included in catering cost
Parking: ample free parking available

OCEAN BREEZES AND BEAUTIFUL VIEWS

Cannon Beach, Oregon

This oceanfront Hallmark Resort offers 128 of the most beautifully located guest rooms on the Northern Oregon Coast. Just outside your room is the famous Haystack Rock, and the resort is within walking distance of Cannon Beach attractions and shops. Accommodations range from cozy rooms for two to family-designed two-bedroom suites for six. In addition to guest rooms, there are five houses available for beachside retreats and group getaways.

Newport, Oregon

Hallmark Resort at Newport offers 158 of the most beautifully appointed oceanfront guest rooms and luxury suites on the Central Oregon Coast. Close to Newport's attractions, golf courses and shops. All guest rooms and suites overlook the Pacific Ocean.
Accommodations range from cozy rooms for two to spacious guest rooms with in-room two-person spa, fireplace and oceanfront balcony.

HEATHMAN PRIVATE DINING

THE HEATHMAN HOTEL

1001 S.W. Broadway at Salmon Street • Portland, Oregon 97205
Contact: Catering Manager (503) 790-7758

Capacity: 140 people reception; 80 people seated
Price Range: $150 to $1,000 room rental fee
Catering: full-service in-house catering
Types of Events: sit-down meals, buffets, receptions

Availability and Terms
Early reservations are strongly encouraged. Deposits are required upon booking space.

Description of Facility and Services
Seating: tables and chairs for up to 80 people
Servers: provided, with 18% service charge
Bar facilities: full-service bar with bartenders available for your event; The Heathman
supplies the liquor, beer, and wine
Dance floor: 40-person-capacity dance floor with electrical outlets
Linens and napkins: white tablecloths and napkins
China and glassware: fine china, silver, and crystal supplied
Decorations: candles available; no nails, tacks or tape permitted
Cleanup: included in your Private Dining charges
Parking: parking available; price varies
ADA: fully accessible

Accommodations
The Heathman features seven private, distinctive rooms, accommodating intimate weddings,
rehearsal dinners, private parties, holiday celebrations, and receptions.

THE HEATHMAN LODGE

7801 N.E. Greenwood Drive • Vancouver, Washington 98662
Contact: Catering Office (360) 254-3100 or (888) 475-3100
Business Hours: Mon–Sat 8am–5pm

Capacity: 5 to 400 people
Price Range: room rentals vary depending on food order; event room rates available
Catering: full-service, upscale catering
Types of receptions: elegant, sit-down or handsome buffet meals, hors d'oeuvres or simple cake and punch receptions, bridal luncheons and rehearsal dinners

Availability and Terms

The Lodge offers 5,000 square feet of banquet and reception space. The ballroom is divisible into three rooms, each with pre-function space. Two additional smaller banquet rooms are available as well. The Lodge also offers a 1,230-square-foot Grand Suite and three large suites for more intimate receptions.

Description of Facility and Services

Seating: tables and chairs provided at no additional charge
Servers: included in cost of food or room rental
Bar facilities: host/no-host bars available; hotel supplies all liquor and bartender
Dance floor: available
Linens and napkins: available
China and glassware: included in cost of food, beverage or room rental
Cleanup: handled by the Lodge at no additional cost
Decorations: limited decorative items available at no additional charge; elaborate theme events can be arranged
Parking: ample free parking
ADA: meets all ADA standards; all banquet rooms are on ground level

Special Services

A night in one of the 121 guest rooms or 22 suites is a truly memorable experience. Old-world craftsmanship is evident in stretched leather lampshades and hand-crafted mirrors and frames. Hickory and pine furnishings lend comfort to the surroundings.

The Heathman Lodge is Vancouver, Washington's newest full-service upscale hotel. An unexpected urban retreat, the Lodge offers travelers and locals from the Portland/Vancouver area a blend of heart-felt service, business amenities and rustic, mountain lodge comfort. Inspired by authentic Pacific Northwest decor and cuisine, the Lodge provides each guest a calm refuge and a memorable experience.

HAND-HEWN HOSPITALITY

Hilton
Portland

921 S.W. Sixth Avenue
Portland, Oregon 97204
Contact: Catering
(503) 220-2684
Business Hours: Mon–Fri 8:30am–5:30pm

Capacity: 12 to 1,200 people
Price Range: customized menus at varying prices
Catering: full-service catering
Types of Events: luncheons, hors d'oeuvres, served dinners and buffets

Availability and Terms

The Hilton Portland has many different reception rooms of varying sizes to accommodate any event from small rehearsal dinners to large wedding receptions. We feature our elegantly appointed new Pavilion Ballroom, ideal for 250 to 350 guests. Our new Broadway Room is suited for groups of fewer than 150 guests.

Description of Facility and Services

Seating: your choice of banquet rounds or informal cabarets
Servers: included in catering cost
Bar facilities: hosted or no-host bar; beer, wine, and champagne service; we provide all
    beverages, bartender, and servers
Dance floor: appropriately sized inlaid parquet dance floor
Linens and napkins: fine linens in colors to coordinate with room decor; specialty linens also
    available
China and glassware: white china and stemmed glassware; ornate silver chafing dishes and
    urns
Cleanup: included in catering charges
Decorations: votive candles at no charge to complement your floral centerpieces
Lodging: complimentary deluxe room with champagne for the bride and groom; special
    group rate for your out-of-town guests; based on availability
Parking: parking available; costs vary
ADA: fully equipped to accommodate ADA requirements

We Accommodate All Your Needs

The Hilton Portland is a full-service hotel, conveniently located in the heart of downtown Portland. Our reputation for superior service is built on 75 years of combined banquet experience. We can accommodate your guest room needs, rehearsal dinner, and reception.

ON-SITE WEDDING SPECIALISTS

Our on-site Wedding Specialists will assist you in planning a perfect reception. Fresh, local cuisine and specialty menu items, custom-designed wedding packages, newly renovated guest rooms, and courteous, prompt service make The Hilton Portland your best choice!

Portland Airport
Hotel and Trade Center
8439 N.E. Columbia Boulevard
Portland, Oregon 97220
(503) 256-5000; Fax (503) 256-5631
E-mail: HIPDXSALES@aol.com

Capacity: maximum of 1,200 guests
Price Range: customized to meet your needs
Catering: full-service catering on or off premise; wedding packages available
Types of Events: we offer a large number of rooms to accommodate your rehearsal dinner, ceremony or reception and will cater everything from a simple cocktail party to an elaborate, multicourse sit-down dinner

Availability and Terms

We offer a wide selection of rooms to fit your needs. Advance reservations are strongly encouraged. Deposits are required and are refundable with 60 days written notice.

Description of Facility and Services

Seating: all types of tables and chairs
Servers: staff included in catering cost
Bar facilities: full beverage service available; Holiday Inn Portland Airport to provide all beer, wine and liquor
Dance floor: cost varies per size of dance floor
Linens and napkins: variety of colors
China and glassware: white china and stemmed glassware
Decorations: silk plants, mirror tiles, votive candles, ficus trees and bud vases
Cleanup: included in price
Equipment: podium, risers and specialty props
Sleeping accommodations: 286 modern guest rooms with 17 suites; we offer special rates for your out-of-town guests
ADA: accessible
Parking: free parking for 900 cars

Special Services

Our professional sales and catering staff are ready to assist you with all your needs. Allow the Holiday Inn Portland Airport to take the stress out of your next event. The success of your event is our ultimate goal.

YOUR EVERY EXPECTATION WILL BE EXCEEDED!

The Holiday Inn Portland Airport is part of the John Q. Hammons Hotel Corp., one of the nation's largest. It has 286 modern guest rooms with the largest meeting facility 5 minutes from the airport. In addition to the 12 meeting and banquet rooms totaling 33,607 square feet of flexible meeting space, we have the ability to fulfill any client's needs or challenges. The staff at the Holiday Inn Portland Airport is well versed at accommodating your personal needs on the most special day of your life; you can rest assured that your every expectation for your wedding will be exceeded. We welcome the opportunity to give you 100% guest satisfaction.

Holiday Inn SELECT℠

25425 S.W. 95th Avenue
Wilsonville, Oregon 97070
Contact: Catering Department
(503) 682-2211
Business Hours: Mon–Fri 7:30am–5:30pm; Sat by appointment

Capacity: up to 850 standing; 600 sit-down
Price Range: please ask our catering specialists for current menu prices
Catering: full-service in-house catering
Types of Events: sit-down, buffet, cocktails and hors d'oeuvres, luncheons, brunch, dinner, cake and punch

Availability and Terms

Five separate rooms are available to accommodate from 10 to 850 guests. In addition, our Atrium with its various sized terraces can accommodate gatherings of up to 500. Our catering specialists will be happy to assist you with our current event policies.

Description of Facility and Services

Seating: tables and chairs for 600
Servers: staff included in catering costs; gratuity will be added to final bill
Bar facilities: full-service bar; minimum liquor sales; liability insurance provided
Dance floor: available at minimum charge
Linens and napkins: white linen tablecloths and napkins; special colors extra charge
China and glassware: white china and stemmed glassware
Decorations: no glitter, confetti, birdseed, or rice inside the facility please
Cleanup: provided by the Holiday Inn; please remove your own decorations immediately
Parking: complimentary
ADA: banquet rooms and Atrium fully accessible; elevator to guest rooms

Special Services

The Holiday Inn Select Portland South offers a complimentary suite for the bride and groom on their wedding night. Special rates are available for out-of-town guests.

A "SELECT" BRAND OF EXCELLENCE

The **Holiday Inn Select Portland South** was recently acquired by the IMPAC Hotel Group and has undergone a five million dollar capital improvement project. Upgrading includes every area of the hotel from the inside-out. The result is the first **"Select"** brand Holiday Inn in the city designed to fulfill your every wish. Please let our professional staff assist you in planning a wedding event that you and your guests will relive with the fondest of memories.

102 Oak Avenue
Hood River, Oregon
97031

Reservations
(800) 386-1859

Sales
(541) 386-1900

E-mail: HRHotel@gorge.net; Web site: www.hoodriverhotel.com

Capacity: ballroom and mezzanine available; 5 to 250 guests

Price Range: price varies according to room, time of year, and menu selection

Catering: full-service in-house catering or off-premise

Types of Events: weddings, receptions, rehearsal dinners; informal hors d'oeuvres to formal sit-down dinners; off-site catering available

Availability and Terms

Hood River Hotel's ballroom can accommodate up to 250 people. Additional areas are available for groups of 20 or fewer. We suggest you book early to ensure availability. A deposit is required at time of booking to secure your date with the balance due the day of your event.

Description of Facility and Services

Seating: tables and chairs for up to 200 people

Servers and cleanup: included in catering cost

Bar facilities: full liquor service from Pasquale's Ristorante and Wine Cellar Bar; bartender included in price quote; extensive selection of wines and champagnes

Dance floor: accommodates up to 55 people

Linens and napkins: cloth linens available in a variety of colors

China and glassware: traditional pattern; assorted glassware

Decorations: floral supplies available upon request; early decorating by prior arrangement; some restrictions apply; in-house florist available

Parking: on-street and designated off-site parking

ADA: fully accessible

Special Services

- **Special Honeymoon Packages:** to suit budget and needs
- **Wedding Services:** on-site consultant and packages available to fit most budgets
- **Fireside Weddings:** have a romantic ceremony by a warm, crackling fire
- **Baby Grand piano and built-in stereo system**

EUROPEAN-STYLE CHARM

This charming European-style 1913 hotel offers 41 rooms and is listed on the National Register of Historic Places. Conveniently located in the heart of historic downtown Hood River and the Columbia River Gorge National Scenic Area, our banquet facility offers a unique location for your special event. Decorated in a wine cellar theme, the Hood River Hotel offers a full bar and the finest Italian and Northwest cuisine in the Columbia Gorge. Our warm European charm and friendly staff will ensure a wedding your guests will remember forever.

Hostess House, Inc.

10017 N.E. Sixth Avenue
Vancouver, Washington 98685
(360) 574-3284

Featured in *Modern Bride Magazine*
as the place to have your wedding
in the Pacific Northwest!

Open seven days a week;
please call for an appointment

Capacity: chapel holds 200 guests; reception area holds up to 300 in good weather

Price Range: wedding and reception packages starting at $1,195

Catering: full in-house catering and bakery

Types of Events: all types from cake and punch to sit-down dinners

Availability and Terms

A $500 deposit reserves your date and applies toward purchases. Reservations are taken as far as a year in advance; however, we can occasionally accommodate reservations on short notice.

Description of Facility and Services

Seating: as many chairs and tables as needed; plus patio

Servers: we provide all serving attendants and any additional personnel needed

Bar facilities: full-service bar and bartenders; we provide all alcoholic and nonalcoholic beverages and liquor liability

Dance floor: oak dance floor for 75 to 100 people; house DJ available for $150

Linens and napkins: lace tablecloths and engraved napkins

Serviceware: fine china; long-stem crystal; silver serving pieces

Cleanup: Hostess House provides at no extra charge

Decorations: chapel and reception facility will be decorated throughout with floral arrangements in your colors. A 15 unit candelabra with flower arrangement, two sprays of flowers, and six pew arrangements decorate the chapel. A fresh flower arrangement will be at the guest book and fresh bud vases on every dining room table.

Parking: ample free parking provided

ADA: completely disabled accessible

INTRODUCING THE HOSTESS HOUSE...THE FIRST FULL-SERVICE WEDDING CENTER IN THE NORTHWEST

The candle-lit chapel seats 200 guests and looks out onto a beautiful garden with a waterfall. Now you can have the excitement and joy of a perfectly planned wedding with none of the work or worry. Our bridal consultants will assist you with every detail. The reception center is absolutely gorgeous! It has an indoor fountain, oak dance floor, and a fireplace. The covered decks open onto a lovely landscaped yard with a beautiful gazebo. The Hostess House — where the bride's wedding dreams come true! DIRECTIONS: We are located 10 minutes North of Portland. From I-5 North or South, take the 99th Street exit (#5) and go West two blocks. Turn right onto Sixth Avenue.

See page 228–229 under Bridal Accessories & Attire.
See page 329 under Ministers.

112 S.W. Second Avenue
Portland, Oregon 97204
Contact: Brad Yoast
(503) 227-4057; Fax (503) 227-5931

PORTLAND'S IRISH RESTAURANT & PUB

E-mail: portland@kellsirish.com • Web site: http://www.kellsirish.com
Business Hours: Mon–Sat 11:30 am–2 am; Sundays noon–midnight

Capacity: **Dining room:** 80 seated; **Pub:** 150 people; **Banquet:** four separate private banquet rooms, from 10–150 people or combine entire second floor, over 2,500 square feet

Price Range: Price varies according to the time, size of party and menu selection. We can custom tailor a menu to suit your budget!

Catering: Full-service in-house catering and off-premises catering

Types of Events: Sit-down dinner and luncheon, buffet, cocktails and hors d' oeuvres

Availability and Terms

Kells entire restaurant is available for booking with advance notice. The dining room, pub and private banquet rooms may be reserved separately or all together. We accept major credit cards. A deposit is required to secure the date with the remaining balance due upon completion of services.

Description of Facility and Services

Seating: tables and chairs provided

Servers: Kells will provide servers

Bar facilities: full service bar dispensed according to OLCC regulations; largest single malt selection in the northwest, full range of microbrews, fine cigars also available

Dance floor: 20' x 20' dance floor, electrical hook ups, stage, state-of-the-art sound system

Linens and napkins: linens available in green and ivory, other colors available with notice

China and glassware: white china with glassware to complement

Cleanup: provided by Kells

Decorations: early decorating by prior arrangement

Parking and ADA: parking available, ample street parking, disabled access and facilities

PORTLAND'S FAVORITE
IRISH RESTAURANT & PUB

Kells has become a Portland landmark since its opening in 1990. One of Portland's favorite nightspots, Kells offers a great menu of New World Irish cuisine mixing traditional favorites with fresh, northwest seafoods, produce, and all-natural ingredients. Kells also features live Irish music seven nights a week, a grand stone fireplace and comfortable cigar room. All this and the warm, friendly service and atmosphere of a genuine Irish Pub.

LAKESIDE GARDENS

16211 S.E. Foster Road
Portland, Oregon 97236
(3.4 miles east of I-205 on Foster Road)
(503) 760-6044; Fax (503) 760-9311
Business Hours: Mon–Fri 10am–2pm;
evenings and weekends by appointment
Web site: http://www.citysearch.com/pdx/lakesidegardens

Capacity: 225 people—sit-down wedding at gazebo; 180 people—sit-down wedding inside; 300 people—buffet reception; 120 people—sit-down buffet

Price Range: price is determined by the event and menu selection

Catering: full-service in-house catering only

Types of Events: elegant wedding receptions all year-round, birthdays, anniversaries, barbecues, corporate parties, business meetings, or seminars

Availability and Terms

Please make your reservations as early as possible; we recommend six months in advance. A $500 booking fee will hold the date and time frame scheduled for your event.

Description of Facility and Services

Seating: tables and chairs are provided; terrace and garden seating available

Servers: we provide all serving attendants

Bar facilities: beer, wine, and champagne; we provide beverages and bartenders

Dance floor: hardwood dance floor with electrical hookups for DJs and bands

Linens and napkins: linen tablecloths; linen and paper napkins available

Serviceware: fine china, glassware, and silver serving pieces available for your use

Cleanup: provided by Lakeside Gardens

Decorations: elegant building requires little decoration

Parking: plenty of convenient free parking

ADA: completely disabled accessible

THE IDEAL PLACE RIGHT IN YOUR OWN BACKYARD

Lakeside Gardens is a Private Event Facility situated on approximately seven acres. We schedule events year-round. Outside, Lakeside Gardens blends tall cedars, weeping willows, mute swans, and lakes surrounded by a garden paradise. During cooler weather Lakeside Gardens also offers a complete inside facility. Inside amenities consist of beautiful chandeliers, brass railing, an elegant oak and marble fireplace, a black ebony baby-grand piano, and mirrored wall that reflects an inspiring panoramic view of the lake and surrounding gardens. We are conveniently located only minutes from downtown Portland and the Portland International Airport. Lakeside Gardens offers superb catering. We are able to provide ice sculptures and other decorations to create the setting of your choice. A knowledgeable wedding consultant or program coordinator will work with you to plan and execute everything. Please call us for more details and personal assistance as you plan your next event.

LAKEWOOD CENTER FOR THE ARTS

368 S. State Street
Lake Oswego, Oregon 97034
(503) 635-6338
Business Hours: Mon–Fri 9am–5pm
Web site: http://www.lakewood-center.org

Capacity: 150 for sit-down dinner, 225 for cocktail party
Price Range: $450 for the room
Catering: provided by renter; kitchen available
Types of Events: banquets, receptions, reunions, office parties, business meetings.

Description of Facility

Lakewood Center is conveniently located on State Street (Highway 43) at the south end of Lake Oswego. The Community Meeting Room, on the lower level at the Center, has windows on two sides and is decorated with a forest green and cream color scheme. A full-catering kitchen is attached to the space. The room comes with tables, chairs and place settings for up to 150.

Availability and Terms

Reservations should be made as soon as possible, six months to a year in advance. A security deposit is required to reserve your date. This fee is nonrefundable if you cancel your date. Your room fee balance of $450 is due one week before your event. The security deposit will be refunded, 2–3 weeks after your event, if there is no damage and the room is clean.

Description of Reception Services

The Lakewood Center is the perfect facility for those who wish to coordinate the details for themselves or bring in their own consultant or catering company. The room is ideal for banquets, receptions, reunions, office parties and business meetings.
Seating: up to 150
China: place settings of plate, salad plate, coffee cup, water glass and silverware for up to 150 are included
Dance floor: room is carpeted; many groups dance on the carpet or rent a dance floor from outside sources
Decorations: please inquire; no tape, tacks, or nails please
Cleanup: done by the renter
Parking: paved lot behind facility
ADA: full handicap accessibility
Special note: the Center rents only the room, tables and chairs, and place settings for up to 150. Items such as linens, silver, crystal, serving utensils, coffee urns, and dance floor need to be arranged with other vendors.

LINN COUNTY FAIR AND EXPO CENTER

3700 Knox Butte Road • Albany, Oregon 97321
Contact: Jill Henderson (541) 926-4314, (800) 858-2005; Fax (541) 926-8630
Business Hours: 8am–5pm; E-mail: fairexpo@co.linn.or.us

Capacity: Conference Center can accommodate up to 6,000 guests; Willamette Events Center: 48,600 sq.ft.; Santiam Building: 21,000 sq.ft.; Calapooia Arena: 48,600 sq.ft.; Warm-up Arena: 21,000 sq.ft.; Cascade Lifestock Pavilion: 42,000 sq.ft.;
Price Range: $40–$1,600
Catering: in-house catering available; contracted and flexible
Types of Events: receptions, weddings, parties, showers, conventions, conferences, expositions, and more

Availability and Terms
Currently booking into 2005. Please call for availability.

Description of Facility and Services
Seating: provided according to event; up to 3,000
Servers: provided; contracted out
Bar facilities: contracted out through caterer
Dance floor: available at market rate
Linens: available in a variety of colors
China and glassware: contracted out
Decorations: some limitations apply; please inquire
Equipment: A/V carts, cords, podiums, sound; anything can be arranged
Parking: approximately 2,000 public parking spaces available
ADA: fully accessible

Special Services
Service is extreme here! On-site assistance with local contacts and arrangements. The Linn County Fair and Expo Center is a full-service conference center, exhibit hall, and fairgrounds facility with a professional "can do" staff.

MALLORY HOTEL

729 S.W. 15th Avenue • Portland, Oregon 97205
Contact: Catering Department (503) 223-6311
Business Hours: seven days a week

A RETURN TO ELEGANCE

When you wish to revive the era of gracious service and elegant surroundings, *The Mallory Hotel* is ready to accommodate you. Our banquet and reception facilities are spacious and beautifully appointed with *crystal chandeliers, mirrors and decorative gilding*. We have been creating memorable celebrations in Portland for more than 84 years.

Our *Executive Chef, Ann E. Grassi*, leads a team of creative culinary professionals in designing menus specifically suited to your function. Whether you're planning a *sumptuous brunch buffet*, a *simple business luncheon*, a *cocktail reception* or an *elaborate five-course dinner*, we offer the best of *local ingredients* and *"au courant"* preparations to dazzle and delight. Our servers are professional, discreet and eager to assist your guests with any needs or desires. For groups from *eight to 125* our flexibility and dependable service results in satisfied clients who return time and again for special celebrations and events to remember. Please contact our Catering Department to schedule a tour of our facilities or receive details on available menus.

Capacity: 8–90 for sit-down meals; 125 for cocktail receptions and meetings
Price Range: varies according to menu selections
Catering: full-service, in-house catering only
Types of Events: weddings, receptions, rehearsal dinners, bridal showers, banquets, reunions, office parties, business meetings and seminars

Availability and Terms

Reservations are recommended six months to one year in advance. We accommodate groups on very short notice when space is available. A deposit is required at the time of booking with the balance due the day of your event. Deposit is refundable if cancellation is received at least 60 days prior to your event date.

Description of Facility and Services

Seating: sit-down service for up to 90 guests; standing service for up to 125 guests
Servers: professional serving staff included in catering cost
Bar facilities: full-service bar dispensed according to OLCC regulations; bartender provided at no additional charge for hosted or non-hosted bar
Linens: damask tablecloths and napkins provided; special orders accommodated
China and glassware: fine china and appropriate stemware included in cost
Cleanup: provided by The Mallory Hotel
Decorations: limitless possibilities
Parking: complimentary covered parking available at Mallory Park, across from the hotel on Yamhill.
ADA: full disabled accessibility

Special Services

With your reception, The Mallory Hotel will provide a complimentary Bridal Suite. With our 140 suites and large guest rooms, The Mallory Hotel can accommodate your out-of-town guests.

Please let this business know that you heard about them from the Bravo! Bridal Resource Guide. **159**

1401 S.W. Naito Parkway
Portland, Oregon 97201
Contact: Nancy VanLaningham or Mark Sanders
(503) 499-6361; Fax (503) 221-1789
Business Hours: Mon–Fri 7am–6pm; Sat 9am–4pm

Capacity: up to 1,000 people
Price Range: price will be determined by event and specific menu
Catering: provided by the hotel exclusively
Types of Events: from intimate champagne receptions to elegant multicourse dinners, including rehearsal dinners and bridal showers; the addition of the beautiful Mt. Hood Room offers a new view on Portland; overlooking the Willamette River and Mount Hood, the perfect room with the perfect view will enhance your special day

Availability and Terms
The Portland Marriott Hotel offers a wide selection of rooms to fit your specific wedding needs. Since most weddings occur on Saturdays, we suggest reserving your reception site as soon as possible.

Description of Facility and Services
Seating: tables, chairs, and head tables provided
Servers: included in price
Bar facilities: full beverage service available; Portland Marriott Hotel to provide all beer, wine, liquor, and bartenders
Dance floor: available at no charge
Linens and napkins: extensive linen selections at no charge
China and glassware: Marriott Hotel uses only fine china, crystal, and silverplated flatware
Cleanup: included in price
Parking: limited valet parking available in hotel; plenty of public parking adjacent to hotel
ADA: yes

Special Services
The Portland Marriott Hotel provides **a complimentary deluxe upgraded king room the night of the wedding** for that special bride and groom.

WEDDING CELEBRATIONS
At Marriott, we bring something extra to the wedding party—a tradition of care, concern, and service that assures peace of mind for the bridal couple and a memorable reception for everyone. After playing host to hundreds of bridal couples and their families, Marriott has the art of reception planning down to a science. Let us assist you in planning the wedding celebration of your dreams.

THE MARSHALL HOUSE

1301 Officers' Row
Vancouver, Washington 98661
Contact: Julie Garver or Frances Anderson (360) 693-3103
Business Hours: Mon–Fri 9am–5pm; Sun by appointment

Capacity: 25 to 225 inside; more if verandas or gardens are used
Price Range: $100 to $850
Catering: caterers from Marshall House's approved list only; caterers required for any food, beverage, or cake service
Types of Events: sit-down, buffet, hors d'oeuvres, cake and punch, or garden

Availability and Terms

You may rent as many rooms as you need (up to 4) to accommodate from 25 to 350 guests for as many hours as you need. Standard weekend rental periods are from 11am to 6pm, and from 6pm to 1am. Reservations should be made as soon as possible—six months to one year in advance for the busy summer months. A $50 deposit is required to hold your date.

Description of Facility and Services

Seating: antique tables and chairs
Servers: must be provided by caterer; one per every 50 guests/minimum of two
Bar facilities: champagne, white wine, and bottled or canned beer only (no hard liquor or kegs); must be served by an approved bartender; no self-serve alcohol
Dance floor: 20'x30' hardwood dance floor; electrical hookup available
Linens and napkins: linen rental available
China and glassware: your caterer provides
Cleanup: we provide; extra charge for extra cleanup
Decorations: no tape, tacks, staples, or wire; you carry liability for damage; rooms not available for early decorating except within rental time
Parking: 60 spaces adjacent to building, additional parking one block away
ADA: yes

Special Services

The Marshall House encourages the unique and will be happy to help you create the perfect arrangements for your event. With four spacious rooms, the verandas, and the lawn, the possibilities are endless. Antique furnishings and candelabra are available at no extra charge. Linens, coffee urns, and punch bowls are available for rent. Call for a tour and an information packet. Our staff will assist you from planning through party.

IN THE ELEGANT VICTORIAN STYLE

Picturesque Officers Row features 21 grand houses on 21 acres of lawn, trees, and gardens. The George C. Marshall House stands as a centerpiece on the Row in the historic Queen Anne style. With wide verandas, rich colors and textures, 11-foot ceilings, and a magnificent central staircase, the Marshall House is sure to provide a most elegant backdrop for your memorable day.

2126 S.W. Halsey • Troutdale, Oregon 97060; Contact: Sales Office (503) 492-2777
Business Hours: Mon–Fri 9am–5pm; Sat–Sun 10am–5pm, tours by appointment

Capacity: 200 people seated; 250 people reception style
Price Range: $100 to $3,500 food and beverage minimum required; based on size of room and day of week
Catering: in-house catering only; plated, buffet, and hors d'oeuvre; prices vary
Types of Events: wedding ceremonies and receptions, rehearsal dinners, bridal showers and parties

Availability and Terms

Edgefield has several beautiful and unique locations for wedding ceremonies and receptions, accommodating both small and large parties. Several large banquet rooms are available for receptions, seating between 100 to 200 people each. The movie theater makes an ideal room for ceremonies, or try a natural setting outdoors. Additional set-up fees for outdoor receptions and ceremonies. For the best availability, we suggest booking summer or holiday weekend events at least one year prior. Our dedicated wedding coordinators can assist you in booking and planning your event. Deposit equals 25% of estimated food and beverage total and is due 30 days after booking.

Description of Facility and Services

Seating: round and rectangular tables for assorted seating; cushioned banquet chairs
Servers: staff included in price; 17% gratuity added to bill
Bar facilities: full-service cocktail bar featuring Edgefield ales and wines
Dance floor: hardwood or concrete floors in two separate banquet rooms
Linens and napkins: assorted tablecloth and napkin colors; no charge
China and glassware: china, glassware, and flatware; no charge
Cleanup: included in price
Decorations: client responsibility
Parking: free
ADA: 11 out of 12 banquet rooms are accessible

Special Services

Built-in stereo systems in most rooms; 103 bed & breakfast rooms; two on-site restaurants — three in summer.

EUROPEAN-STYLE VILLAGE

McMenamins Edgefield is the classic gathering place for weddings. The historical Main Lodge building is surrounded by auxiliary buildings and spectacular gardens and landscaping, making the 25-acre property a virtual paradise and providing beautiful backdrops for photographs. Included on-site is a winery, brewery, movie theater, gift shop, sports bar, artisans, special events and tours daily. Edgefield is 25 minutes from downtown Portland and only 15 minutes from the airport. Call the Group Sales Office for a complete banquet packet.

THE MELODY BALLROOM

615 S.E. Alder • Portland, Oregon 97214
Contact: Kathleen Kaad (503) 232-2759; Fax (503) 232-0702
E-mail: melody.ballroom@mci2000.com
Business Hours: Tue–Fri 10am–2pm or by appointment

Capacity: two rooms, up to 1,100 people; used separately, 300 and 800 people
Price Range: varies, please call
Catering: in-house catering and beverage services only
Types of Events: sit-down, buffet, theme, cocktails and hors d'oeuvres

Availability and Terms
The Melody Ballroom requires a $600 or $1,200 deposit to reserve your date. Reservations are accepted one year or more in advance. Catering cost must be paid one week prior to the event.

Description of Facility and Services
Seating: tables and chairs provided as needed
Servers: staff included in catering costs; gratuity on food and beverage
Bar facilities: full-service bar provided; host/no-host; liquor, beer, and wine
Dance floor: 30'x30'; 300 capacity; two large stages; can accommodate full touring bands
Linens and napkins: cloth and linen tablecloths and napkins; limited colors
China and glassware: china and glassware
Cleanup: included in catering cost
Decorations: no limitations; we can provide fresh flowers and limited decorating accessories
Parking: free street parking

Special Services
The Melody Ballroom rents on a per day basis, giving our clients the flexibility for decorating and music set up at your convenience. Our event coordinators will be happy to help you plan and execute your event to perfection…just ask.

EXTRAORDINARY FOOD AND FRIENDLY SERVICE
WILL MAKE YOUR EVENT A SUCCESS!

The Melody Ballroom is a unique, historic facility, owned and operated by a professional chef. Our philosophy is to say "Yes!" and to make your event truly individual. We work with diverse menus and styles—even your favorite recipes! Our caring staff provides friendly service that will make your guests feel as if they were in your own home.

MILWAUKIE CENTER/
SARA HITE MEMORIAL ROSE GARDEN

5440 S.E. Kellogg Creek Drive
Milwaukie, Oregon 97222
Contact: Lin Dahl (503) 653-8100
Please call for an appointment

Milwaukie Center and the Sara Hite Memorial Rose Garden are located in beautiful North Clackamas Park. The new outdoor Rose Garden is available for weddings, receptions and photo opportunities. The Center is an air conditioned, nonsmoking facility; perfect for any size group up to 400 for a sit-down dinner. In addition to the space, there are many "extras" available. Our Facility Use Coordinator will help to make your event a pleasant experience.

The Milwaukie Center's full-service commercial kitchen and two Pullman kitchens are available for you or your caterer to prepare food for your event. The Center Nutrition Program has affordable prices and will provide you service that will please your guests if you do not have a caterer.

ROSE GARDEN:
Capacity: to 150 people
Price Range: call for prices
Seating: chairs for 100; eight 6' tables; 20' x 20' canopies available at an additional fee
Availability and Terms: call for schedule availability; a 50% deposit is required to hold your date

MILWAUKIE CENTER:
Capacity: North Wing: 200 standing, 125 seated; South Wing: 600 standing, 350 seated
Price Range: call for specific price information
Catering: your own catering arrangements or the Center Nutrition Program has affordable prices for catering with no additional cost for the use of the commercial kitchen
Alcohol: use of alcohol is allowed if renter agrees to follow all rules; must provide proof of liability insurance and take legal responsibility for guests; $100 fee
Availability and Terms: make your reservation as soon as your date is established; a 25% deposit is required to hold your date

Description of Facility and Services
Seating: chairs for 500; tables for 400; equipment request (number of tables and chairs) required at time of application
Servers: renter or caterer provides; or provided through contract with Nutrition Program
Bar facilities: renter or caterer to provide bar, liquor, bartender, and liability insurance
Dance floor: available; PA system also available
Linens and napkins: renter or caterer provides
China and glassware: Melamine china and silverware for 250; no glassware
Cleanup: renter responsible for removing all decorations and cleanup
Decorations: please discuss your decoration ideas with the Facility Use Coordinator
Candles: tapered and birthday candles are not allowed due to fire safety; votive candles may be permissible; request must be made on application and reviewed with Facility Use Coordinator
ADA: yes

Special Services
The Milwaukie Center will have a Building Coordinator on duty during your event to assist with necessary details

MONTGOMERY PARK

2701 N.W. Vaughn Street
Portland, Oregon 97210
Contact: Paula Person, event director (503) 228-7275
Office Hours: Mon–Fri 8:30am–5pm

Capacity: 15 to 1,200 people (up to 400 seated, 1,200 standing); 15,400 square feet

Price Range: $65 to $2,700

Catering: inside catering contracted to Food in Bloom; outside catering through one of four approved caterers: Jake's, The Best of Everything, Briggs & Crampton, or Eat Your Heart Out

Types of Events: weddings, receptions, buffets, meetings, trade shows, corporate events, business parties

Availability and Terms

Montgomery Park has two reception halls, a large banquet facility, a beautiful atrium and two meeting rooms. Deposits or reservation fees may be required. Book up to one year in advance. Available hours are flexible.

Description of Facility and Services

Seating: tables and chairs provided (one setup included in room cost)

Servers: provided by caterer

Bar facilities: bar services and liquor provided by caterer

Dance floor: dance floor in the Atrium accommodates 500+ people with electrical hookup for bands or disc jockeys available

Linens, china and glassware: caterer provides

Decorations: no helium balloons or tape; table decorations must be obtained from caterer, florist, or other source

Cleanup: you must remove all materials you bring in; some or all of your deposit may be kept for damage or extra labor for cleanup

Equipment: podium, easel, risers, table cloths, flip chart, whiteboard, overhead projector, ladder and phone service, and full audiovisual service available

Parking: 2,200 free spaces available on weekends and evenings

Special Services

An event coordinator, security or maintenance personnel will be available depending on the time of the event.

SOARING ATRIUM AND MODERN DECOR

Montgomery Park, a beautifully renovated historic building, features a 135-foot soaring atrium, a light airy atmosphere, and a contemporary black-and-white decor. It is an impressive site for your function. Montgomery Park is located in Northwest Portland at the bottom of the northwest hills, providing a beautiful setting for your special event.

MOUNTAIN VIEW GOLF CLUB

27195 S.E. Kelso Road
Boring, Oregon 97009
Contact: Sally Drew (503) 663-5350

Capacity: our versatile room design enables us to provide meeting and banquet space for 20 to 350 people; 200 sit-down; 300 cocktail receptions

Price Range: price varies with menu choices and services

Catering: professional chef on staff

Types of Events: wedding receptions, bar/bat mitzvahs, business meetings, golf tournaments, wedding receptions, seminars, and more

Availability and Terms

We encourage reservations as early as possible and book up to one year in advance. Deposit required at time of booking with full payment due 10 days prior to event.

Description of Facility and Services

Seating: provided for up to 350 guests
Servers: provided by Mountain View
Bar facilities: full bar service
Dance floor: 18' x 18'
Linens: full linens and skirting available; variety of colored napkins
China and glassware: white china with full selection of glassware
Decorations: centerpieces available; no confetti, rice, birdseed or open flames
Cleanup: included in room charge
Parking: plenty of free parking available
ADA: fully accessible

Special Services

A Bridal Basket with assorted buffet food, cake, sparkling wine or cider, and fluted glasses are packed and sent with the bride and groom. Espresso bar and soda bar available.

PEACEFUL VIEWS AND ACCOMMODATING STAFF

Mountain View Golf Club is located less than five miles from the quaint and restful town of Sandy, Oregon, just a short drive from the scenic forests and lakes of majestic Mount Hood. Our newly completed multi-million dollar club house welcomes the public to enjoy the best of casual to fine dining, peaceful views form our second-story decks, while sipping Northwest wines and microbrews. We can accommodate intimate to large gatherings and will coordinate your event from beginning to end.

MT. HOOD BED & BREAKFAST

8885 Cooper Spur Road • Parkdale, Oregon 97041
Contact: Jackie Rice (541) 352-6885
Office Hours: Mon–Fri 8am–7pm

Capacity: up to 200+ (indoors or outdoors)
Price Range: available upon request
Catering: local catering
Types of Events: receptions with country elegance, buffets, barbecues

Availability and Terms

Four guest rooms and outdoor gardens are available for weddings and receptions. Deposit is 50% of total with balance due 30 days prior to event.

Description of Facility and Services

Seating: for up to 200+
Servers: service staff included with catering
Dance floor: available with electrical outlets; accommodates 200+
Linens: provided by caterer
China and glassware: provided by caterer
Decorations: early decorating possible; cleanup to be immediately after event
Cleanup: client and caterer responsible
Parking: off-street
ADA: limited accessibility

ENCHANTING COUNTRY SETTING
WITH SPECTACULAR MOUNTAIN VIEWS

Mount Hood Bed & Breakfast has everything you need for your wedding or event. Situated on the north shoulder of Mount Hood just out of the Columbia Gorge, the facility offers spectacular views of Mount Hood, Adams and Rainier. Our 7,200-square-foot sports barn can be used to move to the indoors in case of inclement weather. Come see us on the sunny side of Mount Hood. A little more than one hour from Portland.

See page 378 under Honeymoon, Travel & Accommodations

NORTH STAR BALLROOM

635 N. Killingsworth Court
Portland, Oregon 97217
Contact: Harriet Fasenfest (503) 240-6088
Business Hours: Mon–Fri 10am–2pm;
or call for an appointment

Capacity: from 20 to 375
Price Range: $75–$1,500
Catering: on-site available, in-house with outside caterers welcome
Types of Events: sit-down dinners, buffet, cocktails and hors d'oeuvres, themes

Availability and Terms

Ballroom, salon/bar, dining room, reception area, private parlor and meeting room available. Rooms to be reserved up to two years in advance. A 50% deposit is required at the time of reservation, refundable under terms. A refundable cleaning/damage deposit is required.

Description of Facility and Services

Seating: tables and chairs provided for up to 300
Servers: caterer to provide
Bar facilities: bar available; caterer or bar service to provide liquor and liability
Dance floor: large maple floors up to 250; up to 220 volt
Linens and napkins: caterer to provide
China and glassware: caterer to provide
Cleanup: responsibility of caterer
Decorations: upon approval
Parking: free off-street parking available; valet parking can be arranged for an additional cost
ADA: handicap ramp to lower level; one handicap accessible bathroom

Special Services

The rooms are accessible for early decorating. Sound and lighting equipment available. Video services can be arranged at an additional cost.

URBAN SOPHISTICATION AND ECLECTIC MEDITERRANEAN STYLE

Not your typical romance and wedding? Then why choose a typical wedding hall? The North Star Ballroom is proud to offer a stunning new facility that is as unique as you are. Discover the hidden treasures of Portland's only "neighborhood villa," conveniently located just off I-5 less than ten minutes from downtown Portland. The North Star Ballroom has a variety of rooms that capture the spirit of its Italian Renaissance architecture. The Ballroom and adjacent bar have 3000 sq. ft. of beautifully refinished maple floors, large multi-paned windows, warm colors, rich fabrics and many designer details throughout. The lower level offers a dramatic dining room and reception area, private parlor with antique vanity and armoire and a private kitchen for outside caterers. Very competitively priced with wedding packages available, the North Star Ballroom is a perfect choice for those contemporary celebrations of the heart.

O'CALLAHAN'S
RESTAURANT & CATERING

AT QUALITY INN HOTEL & CONVENTION CENTER

3301 Market Street N.E.
Salem, Oregon 97301
Contact: Sales and Catering
(503) 370-7835 or (503) 370-7997

Capacity: up to 450

Price Range: will vary with menu selection; customized to fit your budget

Catering: full-service in-house catering, customized menus, ice sculptures, beverage services and off property catering

Types of Events: weddings, receptions, bridal luncheons, rehearsal dinners, buffets, cocktails and hors d'oeuvres, formal sit-down, complete hotel services, private parties, corporate meetings and seminars, retirement, anniversary, birthday, and office parties, reunions, bar/bat mitzvahs, proms, bachelor/bachelorette parties

Availability and Terms

Quality Inn Hotel offers 10 banquet rooms that will meet a variety of group sizes. Early reservations are recommended, but we welcome short notice, space permitting. Full payment of guaranteed number of guests is required one week prior to event. Off property catering also available.

Description of Facility and Services

Seating: provided for up to 450

Servers: appropriate service staff provided

Bar facilities: full-service bar and bartender; award winning wines, micro-brews, beer and liquor

Dance floor: up to 24'x24'

Linens and napkins: cloth tablecloths and napkins available in selected colors

China and glassware: white china; variety of glassware

Cleanup: provided by O'Callahans

Decorations: please discuss decorating plans with our catering coordinator; early access when possible

Parking: ample free parking

ADA: yes

SALEM'S ONLY FULL-SERVICE HOTEL AND CONVENTION CENTER

Elegantly Suited to Meet All Your Wedding Needs.
Specializing in groups from 15 to 450.
Offering in-house and off property catering and conference space.
Easy access from I-5.

O'CALLAHAN'S
RESTAURANT & CATERING

at
RAMADA INN
PORTLAND AIRPORT
6221 N.E. 82nd Avenue
Portland, Oregon 97220
Contact: Ann Conger
(503) 253-2400; Fax (503) 253-1635
Business Hours: Mon–Sat 8am–6pm

Capacity: Executive Ballroom: 300 sit-down, reception 350pp; Upstairs Ballroom: 200 sit-down, reception 250pp; rooms can be combined to accommodate up to 500 guests

Price Range: reception $11.95 to $21.95; banquets $9.95 to $21.95

Catering: full-service in-house and off-premise catering; references available

Types of Events: weddings, anniversaries, receptions

Availability and Terms

O'Callahan's offers two ballrooms, the Executive Ballroom (4,200 square feet) and the Upstairs Ballroom (2,800 square feet). Reservations should be made 6 to 12 months in advance. Reservations are made for five-hour segments. A 25% deposit is required to secure your date with the balance due 72 hours prior to your event. A 60-day cancellation notice is required for deposit refund.

Description of Facility and Services

Seating: chairs for up to 600 guests

Servers: appropriate service staff available

Bar facilities: full-service bar with bartender; portable bar available; liquor and liability provided by O'Callahan's

Dance floor: portable dance floor with 550 capacity; 110 and 220 outlets available

Linens and napkins: linen tablecloths and napkins available in a variety of colors

China and glassware: white china; variety of glassware

Decorations: early decorating (two hours prior) available; decorations to match our room colors available; please no scotch tape, thumb tacks or rice

Parking: ample free parking

ADA: bathrooms, elevators, and guest rooms

Special Services

A complimentary bridal suite is available for the bride and groom following their reception at O'Callahan's with a minimum purchase. We also offer group rates for your out-of-town guests.

THE POSSIBILITIES ARE ENDLESS!

O'Callahan's has been part of the Northwest scene for over 20 years. During that time we have catered numerous wedding receptions and rehearsal dinners—casual to very formal. We are also happy to cater your event off-premise. With our reputation for personalized and professional service...the possibilities are endless!

OAKS PARK
HISTORIC DANCE PAVILION
at Oaks Park

Portland, Oregon 97202
Contact: Volanne (503) 233-5777
Business Hours: Mon–Fri 8am–5pm

Capacity: dance pavilion with formal seating for 275; festival setup with dancing for 500; outdoor gazebo area for 1,000

Price Range: pavilion rental for a minimum of three hours at $75 per hour, five hours for $350, 10 hours for $600; outdoor gazebo area is $405 plus a $45 waste-removal fee

Catering: our in-house catering menus are individually designed to suit your own taste, personality, and style. Our goal is to give you exactly what you want. If you are using an outside caterer, we will charge you a fee of 20% of their final bill

Types of Events: full-line catering, buffet, hors d'oeuvres, and cake and punch

Availability and Terms

Our indoor facility is available for bookings on any day or evening. Our outdoor gazebo and grounds are extremely popular; please don't hesitate to call and inquire. A deposit of 10% is required on the day of booking.

Description of Facility and Services

Seating: we can formally seat 275 people

Servers: we can provide any equipment necessary and the personnel to guarantee your event will run smoothly and at a level of service you expect

Bar facilities: Oaks Park Association provides liquor at the liability of the renter; it is Oaks Park's policy to provide a staff bartender

Dance floor: 99'x54' dance floor with a capacity for 500 people

Linens and napkins: all colors of linen and cloth napkins and tablecloths available for an additional cost

Decorations: we enjoy your personal style—and offer the bonus of fanciful historic carousel horses

Parking: ample free parking

ADA: yes

A LOVELY, ROMANTIC, AND HISTORIC SETTING

Join us in our historic riverside park on the Willamette River and let us create the perfect memory for you and your guests. Our beautiful lighted gazebo is framed by a forested setting and mystic city skyline backdrop. The gazebo offers a lovely, romantic setting for your wedding or reception. In case of chilly weather, our historic, multiwindowed dance pavilion is just steps away. Our facility is ideal for weddings, reunions, receptions, birthdays, and anniversaries. It is our policy to work with you and offer exemplary step-by-step service all during the celebration, allowing you to enjoy the day.

See page 322 under Ceremony Sites.

OREGON MUSEUM OF SCIENCE AND INDUSTRY

1945 S.E. Water Avenue
Portland, Oregon 97214
Contact: Event Sales Office
(503) 797-4671; Fax (503) 797-4566
Event Sales: by appointment

Capacity: 50 to 4,000
Price Range: call for cost estimates on rental fees and catering
Catering: exclusive, full-service in-house catering available; creative menus are based on budget requirements and/or type of food and beverages served
Types of Events: social events; receptions set among the exhibits as well as sit-down breakfasts, luncheons and dinners; most areas offer a spectacular view of the downtown city skyline and the river

Availability and Terms
The riverfront science center has five exhibit halls: Turbine Hall, Changing Exhibit Hall, Information Science Hall, Life Science Hall and Earth Science Hall. For additional space and entertainment the Auditorium, Copeland Lumber Dining Room, Outside Courtyard, Murdock Sky Theater and OMNIMAX® Theater are also available. A 50% nonrefundable deposit of estimated charges is due upon signing an agreement. The balance is due the day of your event.

Description of Facility and Services
Seating: tables and chairs in current inventory are available for use at no additional charge. Any equipment that OMSI does not have may be rented for you at an additional cost.
Bar facilities and servers: provided by Fine Host Corporation
Dance floor: may be rented from outside source
Linens and china: our Event Sales department strives to create events that are visually stunning. We provide a wide variety of specialty linens, china, tableware, and floral arrangements that will make your event at OMSI stand alone.
Parking: no charge
ADA: meets all ADA requirements

Special Services
Our experienced event planners will assist you with virtually all planning aspects of your event. Creative menu planning, outstanding service, specialty decor expertise and close attention to detail will provide you with a magnificent event—one your guests will not soon forget.

OMSI'S WORLD CLASS SCIENCE CENTER
OMSI's world class science center is available for private special events. The museum features interactive hands-on exhibits to educate, entertain, and amaze your guests. Also featured: an OMNIMAX® Theater that shows educationally rich and sensory thrilling motion pictures on its five-story domed screen; the Murdock Sky Theater that features astronomy and laser light shows; and a 219' submarine that is available for tours.

Visit our Web site:
http://www.omsi.edu

OREGON CITY GOLF CLUB

20124 S. Beavercreek Road • Oregon City, Oregon 97045
Contact: Rose Holden, Event Coordinator
(503) 656-2846, (503) 656-0038
Business Hours: Mon–Sun 8am–6pm
E-mail: OCGC@IPNS.com

Capacity: 125 seated; 160 standing; can accommodate additional guests depending on season

Price Range: $200 to $1,000

Catering: we work with an approved list of caterers

Types of Events: wedding receptions, bridal showers, private parties, baby showers, graduations, retirements, birthdays, tournaments, meetings, seminars

Availability and Terms

We suggest that you reserve as early as possible but we are sometimes able to accommodate parties on short notice. A deposit is required to secure your date.

Description of Facility and Services

Seating: round or adjustable tables with double padded white chairs for 125+ guests

Servers: appropriate staff will be provided

Bar facilities: host or no-host; beer, wine, champagne available; bartenders provided; compliance with all local and state liquor laws; liquor liability provided

Dance floor: available; CD player provided; electrical available

Linens: linens available; a variety of colors available from caterer for an additional cost

China and glassware: clear glass china available; variety of crystal glassware available

Cleanup: provided by Oregon City Golf Club

Decorations: no staples, nails, tacks or tape; artist's putty may be used

Parking: free parking

ADA: yes

Special Services

Our event coordinator will work with you in planning and executing all details, to make your event a total success.

SOCIAL EVENTS TO TOURNAMENTS

Oregon City Golf Club was built in 1922 and is the third oldest public golf course in the State of Oregon still in operation. With our newly remodeled clubhouse and banquet facility, we can handle all of your social events and tournament needs.

25700 S.W. Pete's Mountain Road
West Linn, Oregon 97068
Contact: Catering Department (503) 650-6900
Business Hours: 8:30am–5pm

Capacity: up to 500 people sit-down dinner
Price Range: customized reception package
Catering: full-service, in-house catering
Types of Events: sit-down, buffet cocktail and hors d'oeuvres, outdoor garden setting
reception and ceremonies

Availability and Terms

Please make reservations as early as possible. One large banquet room is available. An advance deposit is required; payment is due seven days in advance.

Description of Facility and Services

Seating: tables and chairs provided for up to 500 guests
Servers: provided
Bar facilities: full-bar service provided
Dance floor: 18' X 18' floor; electrical available
Linens and napkins: provided; in all colors
China: fine white china provided
Decorations: we will be happy to discuss your specific need
Cleanup: provided by The Oregon Golf Club
Parking: free parking
ADA: yes

Our private country club setting, the natural beauty and charm, the exceptional service and attention to detail will allow you to have a first-class event that you and your guests will thoroughly enjoy.

Nestled in the Willamette Valley against a backdrop of the majestic Cascade Mountain Range, The Oregon Golf Club boasts an exceptional reputation. Inspired by the Scottish traditions of golf's birthplace and enlivened by the beauty of the Pacific Northwest, our spectacular facility is an ideal location for your wedding and reception.

4001 S.W. Canyon Road
Portland, Oregon 97221
Contact: Kristen Backsen or Lisa Schur
(503) 220-2789; Fax (503) 220-3689
E-mail: BACKSENK@metro.dst.or.us
Business Hours: Mon–Fri 8:30am–5pm

OREGON ZOO

The Oregon Zoo has always been a dramatic, fun and surprisingly elegant place to host your special events. Our new Cascadian-style ballroom, coming in September 1998, gives you one more wonderful choice for a romantic gathering in the heart of Portland's favorite playground. Like a private alpine lodge, the new ballroom is grand yet intimate, accommodating up to 500 people for banquets or up to 800 reception guests. Warm colors, rich textures, and thick, plush carpets ensure the comfort of your family and guests. The Grand Staircase in the heart of the facility provides the perfect backdrop for keepsake photographs of the beautiful bride.

Join the couples who have discovered the zoo as Portland's ideal wedding and reception site. The Oregon Zoo is located on the MAX light rail only five minutes from downtown. A portion of all event fees is used in endangered species research and protection.

Capacity: indoor up to 800; outdoor up to 6,000
Price Range: price varies according to menu selections
Catering: in-house catering; award-winning chef
Types of Events: buffet or sit-down; weddings, rehearsal dinners, corporate events, outdoor barbecues, indoor banquets, theme parties…anything is possible!

Availability and Terms
Our banquet room can accommodate up to 800 people. Our outdoor facility can accommodate groups up to 6,000. A deposit is required to confirm reservation. Book early, as our facilities are very popular.

Description of Facility and Services
Seating: tables and chairs included in cost
Servers: provided by the zoo
Bar facilities: host or no-host bar available
Dance floor: we can rent one for your event for an additional fee
Linens and napkins: assorted colors of tablecloths and napkins available at no additional charge
China and glassware: 9" and 6" plates with border design; clear glass stemware
Cleanup: included in catering costs
Decorations: no balloons allowed because of the animals
Parking: large lot adjacent to entrance
ADA: yes

THE OVERLOOK HOUSE

3839 N. Melrose Drive
Portland, Oregon 97227
(503) 823-3188
Business Hours: Mon–Fri 9am–4pm

Capacity: winter (November-April) up to 75; spring, summer, and early fall months (May–October) up to 150

Price Range: call for current information

Catering: select your favorite caterer; we provide complete kitchen facilities

Types of Events: buffet, patio cocktails and hors d'oeuvres, cake and punch weddings and receptions

Availability and Terms

The entire home and grounds are included in a six-hour rental period, 11am to 5pm or 6pm to 12 midnight. Reservations may be made as soon as the date of your event is determined up to a year in advance. A deposit is required, with a portion refundable if we have a minimum of 30 days' notice. Rental fees are due 30 days in advance of the event. Tours by appointment or Tuesdays between 5–7pm.

Description of Facility and Services

Seating: tables and chairs provided

Servers: provided by your caterer or yourself

Bar facilities: you provide your own beverages and liquor liability; please, bottled or canned beer, wine, and champagne only—no hard liquor allowed

Linens and napkins: provided by your caterer or yourself

China and glassware: white china and glass punch cups and trays available

Cleanup: cleanup is your responsibility

Decorations: please inquire about restrictions or for details on early decorating

Parking: on-street parking available

ADA: facilities available

Special Services

Overlook House personnel are on site at all times to make sure everything is taken care of and running smoothly. The use of our serviceware, china, glassware, silverware, coffee pots, punch bowls, and ladles is included in the rental fee.

THE ROMANCE AND ELEGANCE
OF A MANSION AND GARDENS

The Overlook House is a 1927 brick, English Tudor–style home located on more than an acre of beautifully landscaped grounds overlooking the Willamette River and the Portland West Hills. The grounds are graced by a rose garden and trellis, making it an ideal setting for an outside wedding and reception during the spring, summer, and early fall months. Inside, the original woodwork and fireplace make the living-room area a lovely site for an intimate wedding or gathering. The Overlook House is also an ideal setting for weekday business retreats.

NCP PANTHEON BANQUET HALL

5942 S.E. 92nd Avenue • Portland, Oregon 97266
Contact: Effy Stephanopoulos (503) 775-7431, Fax (503) 775-3068
Business Hours: Mon–Fri 10am–6pm; or by appointment

Capacity: up to 500
Price Range: various packages available; call for details
Catering: in-house catering
Types of Events: weddings, rehearsal dinners, bridal showers, birthdays, anniversaries, retirement, proms and holiday parties; corporate functions and business meetings

Availability and Terms

Our two banquet rooms are available any day of the week. Please make reservations as soon as possible, but we always try to accommodate receptions on shorter notice. Pantheon Banquet Hall accommodates up to 500 people and our smaller banquet room accommodates up to 150 people.

Description of Facility and Services

Seating: tables and chairs provided for up to 500
Servers: professional serving staff
Bar facilities: full-service bar; bartender
Dance floor: 18'x18' up to 24'x60'; electrical outlets available
Linens and napkins: tablecloths and napkins in an assortment of colors
China and glassware: china and crystal glassware provided
Cleanup: provided by Pantheon Banquet Hall
Parking: ample parking available

WE MAKE WEDDINGS SPECIAL

Every wedding is special and exciting, says Effy, banquet coordinator, as we can focus on each bride attending to every detail to make this day the most perfect day of her life. Enjoy our finest cuisine prepared by our professional chefs. Also a private bridal room awaits you, along with a complimentary bottle of champagne or nonalcoholic champagne and limousine service to and from the Pantheon Banquet Hall, compliments of Saki, the owner.

Fairytale Experience

"Anyone that employs your service can expect, after arriving in your MAGICAL COACH, to walk through your doors into a WONDERLAND of special treatment. The PRINCE AND PRINCESS are introduced with a spotlight entrance into the PANTHEON HALL, which is nothing less than CINDERELLA'S BALLROOM. I have many friends who still are discussing how this FAIRYTALE atmosphere was hidden in a structure centrally located in the middle of the Rose City."
~Mrs. Judy Stowell

PAZZO

R I S T O R A N T E

HOTEL VINTAGE PLAZA

422 S.W. Broadway • Portland, Oregon 97205
Contact: Private Dining
(503) 412-6316
Business Hours: Mon–Fri 9am–5pm

Capacity: 100 people reception; 80 people seated
Price Range: varies with menu selection, call for details
Catering: full-service in-house and off-premise catering from Pazzo Ristorante
Types of Events: sit-down, buffet, hors d'oeuvres

Availability and Terms

The Hotel Vintage Plaza has banquet rooms available to accommodate functions of many sizes. These rooms are located on the second floor of the hotel and display the same European decor seen throughout the hotel lobby, restaurant, and guest rooms. Also available is the Pazzo Cellar which has the capacity for seating up to 80 guests, 100 for a reception The Pazzoria bakery can accommodate up to 30 people for an evening event.. We encourage you to reserve as soon as possible to secure your desired date. A deposit is required to confirm your space.

Description of Facility and Services

Seating: up to 80
Servers: serving attendants available; 18% gratuity
Bar facilities: full-service bar with liquor, beer, and wine provided
Linens and napkins: linen and cloth tablecloths and napkins available in ivory, burgundy, sage, and hunter green; paper napkins also available
China and glassware: ivory china with green bistro banding; sheer-rim wine glasses and flute champagne glasses available
Cleanup: included in catering charges
Decorations: we have votive candles available for your use; we'll also assist you with any floral arrangements and decorations you may need
Parking: valet parking available; $7 per car for short-term parking; $15 per call for all day; parking garage located across the street for self-park
ADA: yes
Guest rooms: Hotel Vintage Plaza has 107 guest rooms and suites; each evening the hotel serves an Oregon Wine Reception in the lobby; call (503) 412-6313 for details

TUSCAN CUISINE IN SUMPTUOUS STYLE

From the warm and friendly greetings of the doorman to the pampering from our wait staff, our guests experience cozy European elegance and personalized service. Pazzo Ristorante offers exquisite food that embraces the warmth of Northern Italian Tuscan cuisine with artistic presentation and quality services. We will be happy to assist you in custom designing a menu to meet the needs of your function.

See page 385 under Honeymoon, Travel & Accommodations.

500 S.E. Butler Road
Gresham, Oregon 97080
Contact: Mark Wallace (503) 667-7500
Business Hours: Mon–Fri 8am–5pm
Web site: http://www.persimmongolf.com

Capacity: up to 300 sit-down, more for stand up receptions
Price Range: varies
Catering: in-house by Persimmon Grille
Types of Events: weddings, receptions, rehearsal dinners

Availability and Terms

Persimmon features an elegant reception area for entertaining 300-person banquet facility. Reserve space up to one year in advance. A deposit is required to reserve space.

Description of Facility and Services

Seating: tables and chairs provided for up to 300
Servers: included in catering cost
Bar facilities: Persimmon has alcoholic beverages and bartenders available
Dance floor: accommodations available; electrical outlets available
China and glassware: white china; glass or plastic beverage ware available
Linens and napkins: white tablecloths and napkins; colors available at additional charge
Decorations: please inquire with events coordinator
Cleanup: courtesy of Persimmon
Parking: free on-site parking
ADA: disabled accessible

Special Services

Persimmon's precise attention to detail will assure your wedding day is flawless. Please inquire regarding accessibility for early decorating. Valet parking available at an extra charge.

THE PERFECT SETTING
FOR WEDDINGS AND RECEPTIONS

Persimmon offers a wide variety of services in an elegant relaxed environment set among spectacular scenery overlooking magnificent views of Mount Hood.

PORTLAND ART MUSEUM

NORTH WING

1119 S.W. Park Avenue • Portland, Oregon 97205-2486
Contact: Scott Parker (503) 226-2811 ext 290
Business Hours: Mon–Thurs 10am–4pm;
Call for an appointment

The Portland Art Museum's North Wing Building offers unique and magnificent rooms for any kind of gathering. Situated in the heart of Portland's Park Blocks, this architectural beauty is listed on the National Historical Register. Selection includes two large ballrooms, one banquet room, and several meeting rooms–each with a gracious and distinctive style! Arrangements can be made to view the current exhibition or tour galleries in conjunction with your event.

Capacity: 15 to 1,000 with very flexible configurations; or the entire building for up to 1,500

Price Range: varies according to room; please call for specific information

Catering: choose from our list of preferred caterers

Types of Events: every imaginable possibility, from wedding ceremonies, elegant receptions, full-dress balls, parties, and reunions to business meetings, seminars, fund raisers, training sessions and more. Corporate sponsors enjoy additional benefits of using the Belluschi Building and the North Wing.

Availability and Terms

Reserve your room up to one year in advance. A refundable deposit confirms your reservation. Liability insurance and a nominal security fee are required.

Description of Facility and Services

Seating: tables and chairs available; set up according to your floor plan
Dance floor: hardwood dance floors and stages in all ballrooms
Linens, china, glassware, service and setup: all provided by caterer
Bar service: available through caterer
Decorations: elegant facilities need little decoration
Parking: available on street or in several nearby lots
ADA: handicap accessibility and facilities in all areas

RESERVE THE PORTLAND ART MUSEUM
FOR A TRULY ARTFUL AFFAIR!

PORTLAND CONFERENCE CENTER

300 N.E. Multnomah Street • Portland, Oregon 97232
Contact: Sales Coordinator (503) 239-9921
Business Hours: Mon–Fri 8am–5pm or by appointment
E-mail: info@portlandcc.com; Web site: http://www.portlandcc.com

Capacity: accommodate groups from 50 to 400 for sit-down and 600 for standing reception
Price Range: various packages available; please call for specific information
Catering: full in-house service and off-site catering available
Types of Events: ceremonies, receptions, rehearsal dinners, special events

Availability and Terms
A newly remodeled Grand Ballroom together with a variety of rooms to meet your specific needs. Reserve your room anytime from two years to two weeks in advance; we will make every effort to accommodate you. We require a deposit to confirm your reservation.

Description of Facility and Services
Seating: tables and chairs provided
Servers: provided in formal attire
Bar facilities: full service bar and bartender
Dance floor: Grand Ballroom complete with hardwood dance floor plus portable parquet flooring available
Linens and napkins: variety of colors available included with catering package
China and glassware: white china and glassware provided with catering
Decorations: need little decoration; our policies are fairly liberal; early decoration sometimes available; we will handle basic cleanup; we can provide fresh flowers; ask about our inventory
Parking: ample parking and MAX lightrail stops at our door
ADA: main and mall levels comply

Special Services
Full-service amenities from on-site and off-site catering to consultants who gladly assist in planning perfect events to ensure your satisfaction.

"PORTLAND'S BEST KEPT SECRET"
We welcome the opportunity to individualize your special occasion,
for a truly memorable affair!

PORTLAND SPIRIT & WILLAMETTE STAR

Sales Office:
110 S.E. Caruthers
Portland, Oregon 97214
Contact: Sales
(503) 224-3900,
(800) 224-3901
Web site:
http://www.cruiseawi.com

Offering spectacular views, outstanding service and first-class Northwest cuisine, prepared on board in each ship's galley. Our event planning services ensure that not one detail is overlooked, from a rehearsal dinner for 25 to an elegant sit down dinner reception for 340. A cruise on the **Portland Spirit** or **Willamette Star** will guarantee the perfect place for your special day.

Availability, Price and Terms

The Portland Spirit vessels are available year round from downtown Portland. You may charter the entire **Portland Spirit** vessel or one deck rentals are available. The **Portland Spirit** also offers public cruise schedules. The **Willamette Star** is available for private charter. Deposit and signed contract confirms cruise date. Prices depend on time of day, season of year and number of guests. NOTE: Capacity recommendations on each vessel depend on time of year, menu selected and type of wedding planned. Please call for specific recommendations.

Portland Spirit	**Willamette Star**
130 foot, three level yacht, two outside decks	75 foot, two level yacht, two outside decks
Available for full boat charter, one deck rental	Available for private charter
Capacity: up to 540 guests	**Capacity:** up to 120 guests
Seating: tables and chairs for 350, plus outside seating	**Seating:** tables and chairs for 80, plus outside seating
Dance floor: large marble dance floor	**Dance floor:** available

Description of Vessel Services and Facilities

Enclosed decks are temperature controlled
Linens: linen tablecloths and napkins provided
China: our house china and glassware provided
Servers: included with food and bar service
Bar facilities: full service bar, liquor, bartenders and liability insurance
Cleanup: provided
Parking: commercial and street parking available
ADA: limited with assistance

A DREAM COME TRUE...
A ROMANTIC WEDDING CRUISE ON A LUXURY YACHT

Imagine exchanging your vows on board Portland's most luxurious yachts. As the sun sets behind the city, your guests celebrate in style on the gorgeous waters of the Willamette River. Choose from the **Portland Spirit** or the more intimate **Willamette Star**. Our captain can perform your ceremony for that nautical touch, or choose to join us for the most wonderful reception available in town. Our wedding coordinator can help you with all the details so you can relax and enjoy your wedding cruise.

See page 93 under Banquet & Reception Sites—Boats.

THE DAVID COLE
QUEEN ANNE
VICTORIAN MANSION

1441 NORTH MCCLELLAN
PORTLAND, OREGON 97217
PHONE 1-503-283-3224
FAX 1-503-283-5605

Capacity: 200 seated at outdoor gazebo (glassed in for winter months); 300 reception

Price Range: weekend, weekday and holiday rates available. Please call for specific price information; range from $300–$1,750

Catering: select from closed list of six professional caterers for any food service (except cake); alcohol must be served by attendant; kitchen available for warming, but no on-site cooking

Types of Events: weddings, receptions, rehearsal dinners, buffets, cocktail parties, corporate meetings, fund-raisers, class reunions, picnics, birthdays, anniversaries, memorials, photo shots, movies, and many other events

Availability and Terms
The mansion is a 6,300-square-foot Victorian with a 42' round enclosed gazebo. Reserve as early as possible. Reservations have a 90-minute and six-hour time limit per function. Available year-round, the mansion is conveniently located just minutes north of downtown Portland, just off I-5.

Description of Facility and Services
Seating: tables and chairs for up to 300 guests included in rental fee
Servers: provided by caterer
Dance floor: space for 200+ guests in the enclosed gazebo
Bar facilities: provided by Queen Anne
Cleanup: provided by the Queen Anne staff
Decorations: completely decorated in Victorian era antiques, silk floral garlands and arrangements throughout the home; meticulously landscaped gardens outdoors
Parking: plenty of free parking

Special Services
Lovely appointed dressing rooms for the bride and groom. Chauffeur-driven, 1951 Bentley, in Anniversary Silver, available by the hour.

A MAGICAL STORYBOOK PLACE
Every bride deserves perfection on her wedding day whether it is informal, formal, or a simple family ceremony. Easily accessible and very private, the Queen Anne Victorian Mansion is a beautiful location for creating your perfect day. Built in 1885 by David Cole as a wedding gift for his wife, the house is truly a work of art. The home is listed on the Historic Register. It features two-tone wood and spooled gingerbread throughout. It has three English coal-burning fireplaces and one of the largest private collections of Povy stained glass windows in the world. Come celebrate your special day with us!

RAM RESTAURANT & BIG HORN BREWING CO.

320 Oswego Pointe Blvd. • Lake Oswego, Oregon 97034
(503) 697-8818; Fax (503) 697-7743
Business Hours: Sunday–Thursday 11:30am–midnight;
Friday and Saturday 11:30am–2am

BREWING COMPANY

Capacity: Trolly Room, up to 30 people; Dolphin Deck, up to 70 people
Price range: please inquire
Catering: in-house
Types of events: wedding rehearsals and dinners or any type of party

Availability and terms

For groups of up to 70, reservations are accepted anytime; deposit is required upon booking. Deposit will be refunded seven days prior to event.

Description of facility and services

Seating: tables and chairs provided
Servers: service staff provided
Bar facilities: bartender provided with each party
Dance floor: available in upstairs Game Room
Linens: cloth table linens and napkins provided
China and glassware: house china and glassware available
Decorations: are welcome; we can assist you
Cleanup: included in rental cost
Parking: plenty of free parking
ADA: complied

Special services

Our event coordinator will help you plan a great event with a perfect menu. We know the importance of each event and plan them as if they are our own.

OVERLOOKING THE WILLAMETTE

The Ram Big Horn Brewing Company offers a full-service facility overlooking the beautiful Willamette River. You can't help but love the view.

RAMADA PLAZA HOTEL

1441 N.E. Second Avenue
Portland, Oregon 97232
Contact: Lucy Mitchell,
Sales and Conference Services Manager
(503) 233-2401
Business Hours: Mon–Fri 8am–6pm, Sat 7am–3pm

Capacity: 10–200 guests; three spacious, private reception rooms with private access option; the foyer area is perfect for your receiving line, buffet dinner and guest bars

Price Range: varies; please inquire

Catering: full-service in-house catering exclusively to fit your specific wedding reception needs

Types of Events: elegantly served dinners or buffets, hors d'oeuvre receptions and private parties

Availability and Terms

Early reservations are strongly recommended. Please call the Catering Office for additional details.

Description of Facility and Services

Servers: appropriate service staff provided in catering costs

Bar facilities: portable bar; complete bar set-up stations; host/no-host; beer, wine, mixed drinks, champagne, and soft drinks

Dance floor: complimentary; electrical outlets available

Linens and napkins: cloth tablecloths and napkins available in a variety of colors at no additional charge

China and glassware: white china, stemmed glassware

Decorations: early access for setup prior to your event; banquet staff will set up tables and chairs according to your specifications

Cleanup: included at no extra charge

Parking: ample free parking available

ADA: fully accessible

Bridal suite: Ramada Plaza Hotel provides a complimentary "Bridal Suite" the night of the wedding for the bride and groom based on space availability; otherwise an executive king room on our executive floor will be offered; we would be happy to assist you with a guest room block for your visiting family and friends at a special wedding reception rate

Special Services

The Ramada Plaza Hotel will work within your budget. Call now and let us help make your reception plans memorable.

BACKED WITH EXPERIENCED
RECEPTION AND MEETING COORDINATORS

The Ramada Plaza Hotel has a warm traditional atmosphere with a convenient location for you, your family and guests. We are near the Rose Quarter, Rose Garden arena, Oregon Convention Center and shopping at Lloyd Center. The 10-story hotel has 238 guest rooms, each featuring a view of the city, the Willamette River, the West Hills or Mount Hood. We also offer a full-service restaurant and lounge. We look forward to making this a memorable day for you and your guests!

1510 S.W. Harbor Way
Portland, Oregon 97201
Contact: Sales & Catering
(503) 423-3111
Web site: http://www.RiverPlaceHotel.com

RIVERPLACE HOTEL

Capacity: 10 to 400 guests; 400 reception; 200 sit-down meal
Price Range: varies according to room and services
Catering: meal prices starting at $15 per person for lunch and $24–$50 for dinner; full-service in-house and off-premise catering
Types of Events: ceremonies and receptions; sit-down dinners and buffets; catered affairs outdoors in Tom McCall Waterfront Park or onsite courtyard

Availability and Terms

The hotel's ballroom as well as its waterfront Esplanade Restaurant and Grand Suite, Private Dining Room, and Courtyard are available for weddings and special events. Each provides a unique space whether for 10 or 400 guests. A nonrefundable deposit is required to confirm space.

Description of Facility and Services

Seating: variety of seating customized to meet your needs from 10 to 200
Servers: included as hotel service
Bar facilities: host/no-host bar; alcohol /nonalcoholic beverages available; liability provided
Dance floor: complimentary dance floor; electrical hookups available
Linens and napkins: white napkins and cloths; inquire about color selection
China and glassware: ivory china with wine-colored border and gold band; crystal glassware; only silver chafing dishes and flatware are used
Cleanup: included with full-service catering
Decorations: discussion of your ideas and needs welcomed
Parking: Master Account Parking may be arranged; garages within close proximity
ADA: fully accessible

Special Services

Silver candlesticks with white candles are provided by the hotel. Rooms are frequently available one-and-a-half hours prior to the function for early decorating—earlier if no prior functions are scheduled. Specialized menus are easily created to accommodate your tastes for whatever occasion you may be planning. We also have special guest room rates for your out-of-town guests and honeymoon packages.

A WATERFRONT LOCATION IN DOWNTOWN PORTLAND

The elegant RiverPlace Hotel overlooks the marina on the Willamette River, a perfect setting for a Northwest wedding.

ROCK CREEK COUNTRY CLUB CLUBHOUSE

5100 N.W. Neakahnie Avenue
Portland, Oregon 97229-1964
Contact: Helen or Diane
(503) 690-4826; Fax (503) 614-8801

Capacity: two private areas, seating 50 to 250 people
Price Range: standard menus begin at $11.95; room charges start at $300
Catering: full-service in-house catering
Types of Events: from simple hors d'oeuvre receptions to buffet and sit-down dinners

Availability and Terms

The Clubhouse can accommodate groups ranging from 10 to 300 people in two separate facilities. Our main banquet room is a spacious open area for 300 guests. Our upper floor features a deck overlooking the golf course and large skylights, providing an open-air feeling and accommodating 130 people. All facilities have access to the surrounding grounds of the golf course. Rooms should be reserved six months in advance. A non-refundable fee of $300 is required to reserve a facility.

Description of Facility and Services

Seating: variety of table sizes and seating options
Servers: included in your catering cost; 15% additional gratuity charge
Bar facilities: full-service bar in all facilities; bartender, liquor, and liquor liability provided by Rock Creek Country Club Clubhouse
Dance floor: 12' x 12' parquet dance floor; $75 rental fee
Linens and napkins: cloth tablecloths and napkins available in all colors
China and glassware: white china, stemmed glassware
Cleanup: cleanup is provided by Rock Creek Country Club Clubhouse
Parking: ample parking available
ADA: disabled facilities available

Special Services

We offer complete event planning, including catering, beverages, decorations, entertainment, flowers, cake, photographers, video services, plus much more.

WE SPECIALIZE IN WEDDING RECEPTIONS

The Rock Creek Country Club Clubhouse, on the grounds of Rock Creek Country Club, is located 15 miles northwest of downtown Portland, between Beaverton and Hillsboro. The Clubhouse is situated adjacent to the 10th tee and 18th fairway, providing a lovely backdrop for your wedding photos. We pride ourselves in making each catering event as unique as the individual planning it. We welcome the opportunity to make special arrangements or work with your individual needs. Our experience and facilities are unmatched in the Washington County area.

JUST 10 MINUTES FROM PDX
1554 N.E. Third Avenue
Camas, Washington
(360) 834-9467

ROCKET CITY NEON ADVERTISING MUSEUM AND RECEPTION HALL

Capacity: 50-300
Price Range: starting at $400; smaller groups inquire
Catering: we will provide catering or you may use your own caterer; call for menu and prices
Types of Events: reunions, wedding receptions, anniversaries, business parties, meetings

Availability and Terms

Rocket City is the most unique reception facility in the Greater Portland metropolis. Step back in time with 6,000 square feet of advertising from America's hey day. A full-size replica of a gas station, a corner market dairy, a 1950s-style diner and a famous neon clock producer provide the backdrop for walls and displays full of antique neon, vending machines, old gas pumps and juke boxes. Bring your dancing shoes and enjoy our hardwood dance floor with music provided by Wurlitzer. The fun never stops, and the place books up fast, so plan to make your reservation four months to a year in advance to ensure the date you want.

Description of Facility and Services

Seating: tables and chairs for up to 150 included in rental fee
Servers: included in catering
Bar facilities: beer, wine and champagne available
Dance floor and stage: large dance floor; electrical hookups on stage
Linens: available on request
China and glassware: available on request
Decorations: few or no decorations are needed with our festive atmosphere
Cleanup: provided by caterer
Parking: ample parking
ADA: fully ADA complied

NOT JUST THE SAME OLD THING

Our unique atmosphere is the perfect setting for any festive event. Rocket City's friendly and experienced staff will work with you from decor and design to menu planning, ensuring an event you and your guests will always remember. When your planning time is running short, we can recommend a variety of qualified photographers, musicians, DJs and florists. Take a step back and let Rocket City help you create a day of exceptional memories.

(360) 834-9467

SALEM INN

1775 Freeway Court, N.E. • Salem, Oregon 97303
Contact: Sales Office (503) 588-0515 or (888) 305-0515; Fax (503) 588-1426
Business Hours: Open 7 days a week

Capacity: *Capitol Room:* 621 sq. ft.; *meeting room:* 800 sq. ft. (accommodates up to 50 people)

Price Range: $125 per day; 10 or more rooms rented, meeting room is free

Catering: outside catering welcome

Types of Events: wedding receptions, reunions, seminars, meetings, corporate functions

Availability and Terms

No deposit required. Cancellation notice required 48 hours before function. Reservations should be made as early as possible.

Description of Facility and Terms

Seating: tables and chairs provided by Salem Inn
Servers: provided by caterer
Bar facilities: no bar facilities on site
Linens: fee for linens
China and glassware: dishes, flatware and glassware available
Cleanup: provided in rental fee
Parking: ample parking available
ADA: accessible

Special Services

Our friendly staff will strive to make your stay as comfortable and enjoyable as possible. We offer a complimentary continental breakfast each morning. Executive suites available.

CONVENIENT LOCATION

Located at the Market Street exit off I-5, the Salem Inn is close to the State Capitol, State Fairgrounds, Wallace Marine Park, Lancaster Mall and Volcanoes Stadium.

Directions: *I-5 south*, exit 256, turn right and hotel will be on your right. *I-5 north*, turn left, proceed one block and hotel will be on your right.

SETTLEMIER HOUSE

355 N. Settlemier Avenue
Woodburn, Oregon 97071
Contact: Sharon Walsh
(503) 982-1897
Business Hours: open by appointment

Capacity: inside the house: 60 to 85; outdoors: 300+
Price Range: starting at $400, facility rental varies; midweek discounts available
Catering: we recommend professional caterers or you may select your own
Types of Events: weddings, receptions, rehearsal dinners, buffets, cocktail parties, meetings, picnics, office parties, family reunions, fund-raisers, class reunions, birthdays, anniversaries, memorials, photo shoots, movies, and many other events

Availability and Terms
A 25% deposit is due at time of booking.

Description of Services and Facility
Seating: some tables and chairs provided
Servers: provided by caterer or client
Bar facilities: client provides bartender, beverages, and liquor liability; beer, wine, and champagne only—no hard liquor allowed
Dance floor: gazebo; capacity: 25+; electrical outlets available
Linens and napkins: provided by caterer or client
China and glassware: available in limited quantity
Cleanup: responsibility of client, unless other arrangements are made
Decorations: please inquire about restrictions and details on early decorating
Parking: free street parking

Special Services
The Settlemier personnel are on site at all times to answer questions and make sure that everything is taken care of and running smoothly.

A LOVELY ROMANTIC SETTING PLEASANTLY SITUATED IN THE HEART OF THE WILLAMETTE VALLEY

The Settlemier House is an 1892 Victorian home located on nearly an acre of beautifully landscaped grounds. The backyard is surrounded by a photinia hedge with a gazebo, offering a romantic and private setting for an outdoor wedding and reception during the spring, summer, and early fall months. It is our policy to provide friendly service—we want you and your guests to feel welcome and to have a truly memorable experience. The Settlemier House is located 30 minutes south of Portland and 20 minutes north of Salem, making it ideally accessible for all your guests.

SHELDON'S CAFE
at the Grant House — on Officers' Row

1101 Officers' Row
Vancouver, Washington 98661
Contact: Gary
(360) 699-1213
Business Hours:
Tues–Sat 11am–2pm, 5pm–8pm;
Sundays, weddings only

Capacity: 20 to 100+
Price Range: food starting at $10 per person; room charge $400
Catering: full-service catering available in-house or off premise
Types of Events: ceremonies and receptions, rehearsal dinners, family reunions, birthdays, anniversaries, meetings, etc.

Availability and Terms
House rental includes main dining room, sunroom, covered veranda, as well as the herb and flower garden patio. A $250 nonrefundable deposit is required to guarantee your reservation.

Description of Facility and Services
Seating: all indoor, veranda and patio seating provided
Servers: included in price; 15% gratuity on all food and beverages
Bar facilities: Cafe provides liquor, regional beers and wines
Dance floor: outdoor patio only; accommodates 40+ people
Linens: cloth and paper products available
China: fine china and glassware available
Decorations: the Grant House's historic elegance reduces the need for expensive decorations; we are glad to discuss your specific decorating needs
Cleanup: included at no extra cost
Parking: ample free parking; easy access to I-5
ADA: Yes

Special Services
We excel at helping you have a fun and memorable event. Save time and reduce stress by letting us host both the ceremony and reception.

Sheldon's Cafe is located in the historic and elegant Grant House on Officers' Row in Vancouver. Built in 1850 and listed on the National Register of Historic Places, the Grant House features wrap-around verandas, a main dining room with two fireplaces, a private dining room, and a sunroom that looks upon our herb and flower garden patio.

4575 N. Channel • Portland, Oregon 97217
Contact: Orrin Johnston (503) 289-1597
Business Hours: Mon–Fri 8am–6pm;
Sat 9am–5pm; or by appointment

Capacity: ballroom seats 400, 560 in entire facility; 800+ reception
Price Range: our complete menu packages start at $9.95 (lunch) and $14.95 (dinner)
Catering: full service, in-house Northwest specialty, custom tailored to your needs
Types of Events: buffet and sit-down breakfast, lunch or dinner, cocktail and hors
d'oeuvres, offered for wedding ceremony and receptions, rehearsal dinners, birthday and
retirement parties. Use our facility to impress family, friends and business associates for
these and other events.

Availability and Terms

The entire facility includes four tastefully appointed rooms available for your use.
Reservations should be made as soon as possible to ensure availability. A nonrefundable,
nontransferable deposit is required within 30 days of confirming reservations.

Description of Facility and Services

Seating: all tables and chairs provided and set to your specifications
Servers: our professional staff is provided with a customary service charge
Bar facilities: full service, host/no-host bars include large oak bar for ballroom, variety of
portable bars for smaller rooms
Dance floor: 1,200-square-foot oak dance floor located in ballroom with electrical hook ups
Linens and napkins: available in a variety of colors at no additional charge
China and glassware: white china and stemmed glassware at no additional charge
Cleanup: included in service
Decorations: Shenanigans' picturesque view requires little decoration. Table candles, mirror
tiles, bud vases and punch fountain are provided at no charge. You are welcome to bring
your own decorations.
Equipment: podiums, microphones, risers and easels provided by us at no charge
Parking and ADA: ample free parking; disabled access available

Special Services

Shenanigans' offers a wedding package consisting of hors d'oeuvres, as well as a variety of
options and ideas. Our flexibility coupled with 50 years of combined experience is sure to
make this special day a truly memorable and unique one.

SPECTACULAR RIVERSIDE SETTING

Shenanigans' is conveniently located on the scenic banks of the Willamette River, in the
bungalow style Ports O' Call complex, only minutes from downtown Portland. Please come in
and see for yourself the exquisite panoramic view and impressive hospitality that makes
Shenanigans' the perfect place for the beginning of a life time of happiness. Exit 303 off I-5,
follow the signs to Swan Island, left on N. Port Center, take immediate right and we're just to
your left.

Sheraton
Portland Airport
H O T E L

8235 N.E. Airport Way
Portland, Oregon 97220-1398
Contact: Julie Bradford
(503) 249-7642
Business Hours: Mon–Fri 8am–9pm

Capacity: 25 to 450 seated; 750 standing
Price Range: $14 to $24 per person
Catering: full-service in-house and off-site catering
Types of Events: sit-down, buffet, cocktails and hors d'oeuvres, rehearsal dinners

Availability and Terms
The Sheraton features 16 reception rooms on the lobby level for entertaining. Facilities may be reserved 18 months in advance with a $500 deposit. Cancellations must be made at least six months in advance for a refund of your deposit.

Description of Facility and Services
Seating: tables and chairs for 700
Servers: included
Bar facilities: full-service bar with bartenders provided; Sheraton provides liquor, beer, wine, and champagne
Dance floor: included in price
Linens and napkins: large selection of colors at no additional cost
China and glassware: white china provided; all types of glassware provided
Cleanup: included in price
Decorations: Sheraton supplies centerpieces, silver punch fountain, white lace skirting on cake and beverage tables, large floral arrangement; special arrangements needed for early decorating
Parking: complimentary parking available
ADA: yes

Special Services
A special wedding night package is included with your wedding reception. Enjoy spending this evening in a deluxe guestroom, upgraded to a suite upon availability, enhanced with champagne and chocolates.

"AFFORDABLE EXCELLENCE"

SHILO INN—
PORTLAND/BEAVERTON

9900 S.W. Canyon Road
Portland, Oregon 97225
Catering Office (503) 297-1214
Business Hours:
Mon–Fri 8am–6pm; Sat 9am–5pm
Web site: http://www.shiloinns.com

Capacity: up to 160 people in meeting space; 142 suites and mini-suites
Price Range: please call for specific price information
Catering: full-service catering with an array of selections, including traditional and gourmet Northwest specialties
Types of Events: from intimate parties to multicourse dinners—we can do it all!

Availability and Terms

Our refurbished Oregonian Ballroom holds up to 160 people. For gatherings up to 90 people, choose our Patio/Terrace room which overlooks our patio, outdoor pool, gazebo and fountains. The Canyon room is ideal for more intimate get-togethers, accommodating 30 to 40 guests. We encourage you to make your reservation as soon as possible. Our Executive Board Room can accommodate up to 15.

Description of Services and Facility

Seating: tables, chairs, and head tables provided
Servers: staff included in the price of catering
Bar facilities: host/no-host bars, bartenders included, with a minimum bar setup fee
Dance floor: available upon request; $95 setup fee
Linens: linen tablecloths and napkins available in a wide array of colors
China and glassware: white china and stemmed glassware available
Decorations: suggestions and referrals available for all your decorating needs
Parking and ADA: ample free parking; special access available
Sleeping accommodations: 142 suites and mini-suites; special packages and group rates

Suites and Mini-suites

Featuring 142 suites and mini-suites with microwave, refrigerator, coffee maker, ironing unit, and hair dryer. Complimentary full breakfast. Voice mail, data ports, seasonal pool and spa, amenities galore.

PERFECT OUTDOOR EVENT FACILITIES

Shilo Inn—Portland/Beaverton offers Northwest hospitality in a unique, "country" setting. Extensive, manicured courtyards with fountains and flowering shrubs offer the perfect event setting. Our gazebo will host intimate ceremonies with up to 150 guests. Whether you are planning a meeting, wedding, event or private getaway, Shilo Inn ensures comfort, quality and affordable excellence.

SUITES HOTEL

Restaurant and Convention Center—
Portland Airport/I-205
11707 N.E. Airport Way
Portland, Oregon 97220-1075
Contact: Sales/Catering Office
(503) 252-7500, ext 270
Business Hours:
Mon–Fri 8am–5:30pm;
Sat by appointment

Capacity: banquet rooms to accommodate up to 350 reception guests
Price Range: packages to fit most budgets
Catering: full-service at our deluxe hotel or your special location
Types of Events: ceremonies and receptions; rehearsal dinners and family brunches,too!

Availability and Terms
You are invited to visit our facility to discuss your needs.

Description of Facility and Services
Seating: banquets of up to 350 guests
Servers: professional, full-service staff for all events
Bar facilities: hosted or no-host bars and table service
Entertainment: musician and DJ referrals available
Dance floor: beautiful wood floor at $50 setup fee
Linens: included to complement your colors
China and glassware: included; styled to complement formal and informal themes
Cleanup: setup and cleanup by our staff
Decorations: chandeliers, mirrored walls, table and buffet decorations included
Guestroom accommodations: 4-Diamond/AAA rated, all-suites hotel with 200 guest rooms;
 special wedding packages and group rates available; kitchenette and two full dressing
 vanities in every room.
Parking: free parking available on-site
ADA: banquet rooms and guest suites

Special Services
Our professional catering coordinators will assist you in planning the ceremony and/or
reception of your dreams. We offer the convenience of a full-service banquet facility,
restaurant and deluxe hotel on one property.

OUR TRADITION OF
AFFORDABLE EXCELLENCE CONTINUES
Newly Remodeled

SILVER FALLS
VINEYARDS
4972 Cascade Highway, S.E.
Sublimity, Oregon 97385
Contact: Duane Defrees
(503) 769-5056

Capacity: 150 inside, 250 inside and outside
Price Range: $250–$1,050; limited to one event per day
Catering: your choice of caterer; excellent selection of caterers recommended upon request
Types of Events: weddings, receptions for any occasion, reunions, business meetings, company parties, proms, holiday parties

Availability and Terms
Reservations are recommended as early as possible for summer, fall, and holiday events. Setup may take place the day before if facility is not booked. Deposit required.

Description of Facility and Services
Seating: tables and chairs provided for 50 guests; list of rental services available
Servers: provided by caterer or client
Bar facilities: bar facilities on premises; licensed caterer or client must provide bartender, liquor, and liability
Dance floor: inside dance floor; capacity: 75
Linens and napkins: ivory tablecloths provided
China and glassware: provided by caterer or client
Cleanup: responsibility of client or caterer; refundable cleaning deposit required, amount varies with type of event
Parking: ample free parking available
ADA: yes

Special Services
The facility includes a bridal party lounge with a great mirror, leather furnishings and oriental rug. The vaulted and beamed reception area has a piano, CD sound system, wood stove, French doors, and a stained glass entry. The kitchen is equipped with a range, refrigerator and microwave. Several charming bed & breakfasts are located within 10 miles of the site.

A GREAT PLACE FOR A GREAT TIME
Silver Falls Vineyards is an elegant, old-world rustic facility surrounded by a horse ranch, vineyard, and miles of rolling countryside. Conveniently located 12 miles east of Salem in a private setting, Silver Falls Vineyards is a unique, versatile place to hold your wedding and reception.

STOCKPOT RESTAURANT & CATERING COMPANY

8200 S.W. Scholls Ferry Road
Beaverton, Oregon 97005
Contact: Gary or Murray (503) 643-5451
Business Hours: 9am–2am DAILY

Capacity: indoors, three rooms; up to 350 guests
outdoors, two patios and the green; up to 600 guests
Price Range: will vary depending on food services required
Catering: in-house only
Types of menus and specialties: The Stockpot Restaurant specializes in custom menus designed to complement your style of reception. A variety of buffets—traditional fare and many ethnic styles are available, as well as full-course sit-down dinners, hors d'oeuvre selections, or even a Southwest barbecue on the patio.

Availability and Terms

The entire restaurant is available for private use on Saturday during the day. The patios overlooking the ninth green are available during the spring and summer months. Reservations are taken at your convenience with a $200 nonrefundable deposit at time of booking.

Description of Facility and Services

Seating: all tables and chairs provided
Servers: professional staff included in catering costs
Beverages: full beverage service offered; liquor liability included
Dance floor: available for you and your guests; ample electrical outlets for bands
Linens: provided with catering costs
China and glassware: a full selection of china and disposable available
Decorations: table decorations available; however, you may bring your own; rooms open for early decorating
Parking: free parking space for 600 cars; handicapped parking available

Special Services

Our desire is to give your reception those personal touches that reflect your style and personality. Menu planning, service, and other minute details are all part of the process. We don't forget whose wedding it really is.

PATIO OVERLOOKS THE GOLF COURSE

The Stockpot Restaurant is a unique catering facility with an elegant indoor reception room and spacious patios that overlook the ninth green. Enjoy your rehearsal dinner or wedding reception indoors, outdoors, or a combination of both. The Stockpot Restaurant at the Progress Downs Golf Course looks forward to making your event a great success.

The Sweetbrier Inn

7125 S.W. Nyberg Road (Exit 289 off I-5)
Tualatin, Oregon 97062
Contact: Sales & Catering Office
(503) 692-5800, (800) 551-9167; Fax (503) 691-2894
Office Hours: Mon–Fri 8am–5:30pm; Sat 9am–12pm

Capacity: 250 for dinner; 300 for reception
Price Range: creative, customized menus to fit your budget
Catering: full-service in-house catering
Types of Events: cocktails and hors d'oeuvres, buffets, sit-down luncheons or dinners, rehearsal dinners, wedding receptions, anniversary, special event celebrations, holiday parties

Availability and Terms

Four separate rooms are available; we can seat 250 for dinner or host 300 for a reception. You can reserve for day or night with a $500 deposit. Deposits are refunded if a cancellation is made six months prior to the event.

Description of Facility and Services

Seating: tables and chairs
Servers: staff included in catering costs
Bar facilities: full-service bar available
Dance floor: 270 square feet of dance floor; PA systems and outlets available; risers available
Linens: white linen tablecloths and colored napkins; white skirting
China and glassware: white china; assorted glassware
Decorations: creative catering staff to assist you
Parking: ample free parking
ADA: elevator, restrooms and guest rooms

Hotel Features

The Sweetbrier Inn offers 131 guest rooms and luxury two-room suites. Honeymoon packages are also available.

PARKLIKE SETTING

The Sweetbrier Inn in Tualatin has a full-service restaurant, meeting, and banquet facility with hotel rooms, convenient for your out-of-town guests. The garden setting provides the perfect atmosphere for your rehearsal dinner and reception and furnishes ideal surroundings for those special photographs. A spiral staircase in the main lobby is also available for photographs.

TALLINA'S
GARDENS & CONSERVATORY

15791 S.E. Hwy. 224
Clackamas, Oregon 97015
(503) 658-6148
Business Hours: Mon–Sat 8am–4pm
Closed to Weddings November 1 through May 30
Contact Our Facility For More Information

Capacity: Rose Garden, seating for 200; "The Park," seating for 300; Glass Conservatory, seating for 160

Price Range: $450 to $1,800

Catering: you provide caterer; kitchen is available for warming food, but no on-site cooking or barbecues please

Types of Events: weddings, receptions, anniversaries, birthdays

Availability and Terms

Conservatory includes a main room and dressing/rest rooms are available. The Gardens are open for viewing dawn to dusk 365 days per year. The Conservatory is open for viewing Monday through Saturday 8am to 4pm provided no event is going on. It is best to call first for availability. A deposit of 50% of the total bill is required at the time of booking. Final payment is due three weeks prior to your event.

Times available to rent: Noon–5pm, 6pm–11pm, Noon–10pm or 11am–9pm. Additional time is $100 per hour or any part thereof.

Provided that cancellations are made six weeks in advance, we will gladly refund 75% of your deposit.

Description of Facility and Services

Seating: up to 300 chairs available (depending on area rented) and up to 20 round tables available (depending on area rented)

Servers: provided by caterer

Bar facilities: ONLY wine or champagne allowed; renter must provide liability insurance

Linens, china and glassware: provided by caterer

Cleanup: caterer or client to clean up; must be left as found to receive deposit refund

Decorations: please, no loose sequins, confetti, rice, birdseed, rose petals or potted plants, etc.

Parking: 150 paved parking and 200 grass parking

ADA: limited

Special Services

Complete gardens can be rented for pictures only for $50—provided not already rented.

BEAUTIFUL GARDEN SETTING

Tallina's extensive gardens are beautifully landscaped with over 1,200 rose bushes. The French rose garden, Oriental garden, cottage garden, English vegetable garden and five ponds are the perfect settings for a romantic wedding or any festive event. Our indoor Victorian Glass Conservatory gives you that outdoor feeling in colder months. We are now introducing "The Park," a wonderful natural grassy setting. Tallina's assures you of a setting that will forever enhance your most treasured memories.

TIFFANY CENTER

1410 S.W. Morrison
Portland, Oregon 97205
(503) 222-0703 or (503) 248-9305
Office Hours: Monday–Friday 9am-5pm.
Appointments recommended;
after hours and Saturday appointments available

Capacity: from 10 to 1,300 people; seven rooms and two elegant grand ballrooms ranging from 200 to 6,918 square feet

Price Range: call for price schedule

Catering: exclusively by Rafati's Elegance in Catering, prepared on-site in their commercially licensed kitchen. Rafati's full-service catering can assist you with your selection of the perfect menu for your wedding. From brunch to casual or formal reception services, all events are customized to reflect each bride's individual taste and style. Rafati's offers personalized menu planning in all price ranges.

Types of Events: wedding ceremonies, receptions, rehearsal dinners, private parties, dances, concerts, theater productions, exhibits, fund-raising events, corporate meetings and seminars

Availability and Terms

The Tiffany Center has three ballrooms with dance floors, stages and dressing rooms. Early reservations are suggested, but short notice reservations will be accommodated with space availability. A refundable deposit is required at the time of booking. Client must provide liability insurance.

Description of Facility and Services

Seating: table and chair setup included in room rental
Servers: provided by Rafati's Elegance in Catering
Bar facilities: provided by Rafati's Elegance in Catering; fully licensed
Dance floor: accommodates up to 700 people
Parking: convenient street and commercial lot parking; located on MAX line
ADA: all event rooms are fully ADA accessible

Special Services

The Tiffany Center's expert staff can provide you with complete event planning services. From candle and floral centerpieces, wedding cakes, decorated ice carvings, place cards and balloons to musicians and limo services and much more.

PORTLAND'S PREMIER WEDDING FACILITY

The Tiffany Center features traditional charm and elegance in a centrally located historic downtown building. Large ballrooms and cozy foyers together with gilded mirrors, gleaming hardwood floors and emerald green accents will provide you with an elegant setting for your wedding ceremony and/or reception. Our experienced, professional staff will provide you with everything you need to ensure that your once-in-a-lifetime event is a treasured memory.

See page 311 under Caterers & Ice Carvings.

TIMBERLINE LODGE

Timberline, Oregon 97028
Catering Sales Office
(503) 622-0722; Fax (503) 272-3708
Business Hours:
Tues–Sat 10am–6pm
http://www.timberlinelodge.com

Capacity: up to 200 seated, 400 standing, four banquet rooms, outdoor patio
Price Range: packages begin at $32.95 per person
Catering: in-house only
Types of Events: ceremony, reception (buffet or sit-down), cocktails, lodging

Availability and Terms

The Raven's Nest, capacity of 175 theater-style, is a loft-style room with cathedral ceilings and large picture windows that provides a perfect setting for a ceremony. Also available is the Ullman Patio, with majestic Mount Hood as a backdrop, for an outdoor ceremony. On the floor below the Raven's Nest, the Ullman Hall banquet room has a dance floor, picture windows and seating for 200 people. Silcox Hut is also available for up to 45 people. Packages are for a four-hour duration (from start of ceremony to end of reception) and include food and beverage services and a wedding cake. A deposit is required upon reservation. Contact the Catering Office for a complete wedding packet.

Description of Facility and Services

Seating: round tables and chairs are available for up to 200
Servers: Timberline has a full staff of professional servers and bartenders
Bar facilities: full-service bar available
Dance floor: 400-square-foot dance floor in Raven's Nest; 300-square-foot dance floor in Ullman Hall; electrical outlets available
Linens and napkins: cream or white tablecloths and napkins
China and glassware: fine china; glassware of all types available
Decorations: two-hour setup time for decorating included; no confetti, glitter, rice or birdseed, please; inquire about special restrictions
Parking: Sno-Park permit required during winter months
ADA: disabled facilities available, with the limitations of a historic building

Special Services

Timberline, a National Historic Landmark, has 70 guest rooms available for your event. Your guests can enjoy the convenience of the ceremony and reception at one site plus the unique overnight experience this historic lodge provides.

TIMBERLINE—A CLASSIC FOR OVER 60 YEARS

For over 60 years, Timberline has been a favorite destination for millions of visitors from around the world. Located just 60 miles from Portland on the 6,000-foot level of Mount Hood, Timberline is the epitome of the classic alpine ski lodge. Unique lodging, gourmet dining and panoramic views of the Cascade Mountain Range welcome guests year-round.

Tuality Health Education Center

Facilities for your special events.

A member of the Tuality Healthcare family.

334 S.E. Eighth Avenue
Hillsboro, Oregon 97123
(503) 681-1700
Business Hours: Mon-Fri 9am-5pm

Capacity: rooms range in size from 270–3,100 square feet and can accommodate up to 400 people or 250 in banquet/seating format

Price Range: price varies according to event

Catering: choose from one of our preferred caterers.

Types of Events: receptions, banquets, parties, meetings, seminars

Availability and Terms

A 50% rental deposit and signed license agreement reserves your space up to one year in advance. Day, evening and weekend space is available. Minimal kitchen fee per person.

Description of Facility and Services

Seating: tables and chairs provided and set up to your specification
Servers: provided by caterer
Bar facilities: provided by caterer
Dance floor: dance floor available up to 18' x 18'
Linens: provided by caterer
China and glassware: white Wedgwood china; variety of glassware available
Decorations: no rice, birdseed or confetti; enclosed dripless candles only
Cleanup: handled by caterer
Parking: ample free parking
ADA: fully accessible

Special Services

Choose from our preferred caterers who have access to our cold kitchen, china, silverware, glassware, and some table decorations. Early decorating my be arranged with the caterer. Equipment such as a CD player, rear or front screen projection of video, slides, computer screen or satellite broadcast may be rented. An audiovisual technician can be provided.

PERFECT FOR SMALL OR LARGE EVENTS

The Tuality Health Education Center features a beautiful sunlit foyer area that is perfect for cake and buffet service tables. The combination of skylights and foliage in our lobby is a perfect setting for your guests to mingle. Moveable walls allow for creating a space that is just the right size for your event.

THE VIEWPOINT INN

40301 E. Larch Mountain Road
Corbett, Oregon 97019
Contact: Geoff Thompson (503) 695-3256

Capacity: The Great Room: 140 people seated, 160 standing; indoor/outdoor: up to 350
Price Range: varies according to event
Catering: in-house catering
Types of Events: weddings, receptions, corporate events, fund-raisers, seminars, meetings

Availability and Terms
A $250 deposit is required for private dinner events.

Description of Facility and Terms
Seating: seating available for 150 people
Servers: one server to every 10-12 guests
Bar facilities: provided by The Viewpoint Inn
Linens: white linen available
China: provided by The Viewpoint Inn
Dance floor: dance floor available, capacity: 150
Audiovisual: no audiovisual equipment available on site
Cleanup: room must be left in good condition
Parking: parking available for 100 vehicles
ADA: accessible

Special Services
The Viewpoint Restaurant offers spectacular food, including blackened salmon, New York steak and roasted pork tenderloin. Four unique guest rooms and suites are available, ranging from $75 to $175 per night including breakfast. The Inn closes to the public during special events.

VIEW SPECTACULAR SUNSETS AND TRANQUIL STARLIT NIGHTS
Situated above the Vista House at Crown Point and overlooking the mighty Columbia River Gorge, The Viewpoint Inn has been visited by royalty, celebrities and political leaders during its 73-year history. This historic manor is only 25 minutes from downtown Portland, offering a unique setting for weddings and receptions. Built in 1924, The Viewpoint Inn is on the National Register of Historic Places and is the only inn of its kind featuring Arts and Crafts style architecture left intact on the Columbia River Gorge.

THE WEDDING HOUSE

2715 S.E. 39th Avenue
Portland, Oregon 97202
Contact: Joan Ormsby (503) 236-7353
Business Hours: Mon–Fri 10am–4pm
evening appointment available

Capacity: 100 seated for ceremony; up to 150 for reception
Catering: in-house catering available; outside catering services also welcome
Types of Events: weddings, receptions, anniversaries, parties, business meetings

Availability and Terms

Reservations are available at The Wedding House in six-hour segments; 10am to 4pm for morning bookings, and 5pm to 11pm for evening bookings. A nonrefundable deposit is required to secure your date and does apply to purchases. Balance is due two weeks prior to your event date.

Description of Facility and Services

Seating: tables and chairs provided as needed
Servers: included in catering cost
Bar facilities: host or no-host bar available upon request
Dance floors: available upon request; electrical outlets
Linens and napkins: white tablecloths and napkins; colors available upon request
China and glassware: available upon request
Cleanup: provided by The Wedding House
Decorations: please discuss decorating ideas with our staff; early access for decorating available by prior arrangement
Parking: free parking
ADA: yes

Special Services

If you prefer to have your wedding at your home and not at ours, we will be happy to assist in the planning and executing aspects.

- Catering
- Flowers
- Cakes
- Music
- Limousine
- Photography
- Wedding Dance Instruction
- Bridal and Formal Wear Boutique
- DJ Service
- Invitations
- Something special…just ask

COMPLETE WEDDING SERVICES

A beautiful historic home with a fireplace, ballroom, and large staircase with banister, The Wedding House will add romance to any elegant occasion. Kitchens and reception facilities are available for small and large groups. We offer complete wedding packages that can be catered to your individual needs.

In The Willamette Athletic Club
4949 S.W. Landing Drive • Portland, Oregon 97201
Contact: Catering (503) 225-1068

Capacity: up to 250 for buffets; 100 for sit-down dinners
Price Range: $11 and up for food per person
Catering: in-house only
Types of Events: wedding receptions, rehearsal dinners, anniversaries, reunions, showers

Facilities

The Willamette Cafe in the Willamette Athletic Club offers three rooms accommodating up to 250 people. A terrace with a view to the Willamette River is available for outdoor parties.

Rates

Minimum food charge is $11 per person. A $500 deposit is required to secure the facility. The deposit is refundable if notice of cancellation is given 90 days prior to event.

A room charge of $250 takes care of everything except the dance floor. All tables are set with linen, fresh flowers and votives. All stemware, silverware and china are provided as well as all skirted tables. We'll provide a 12-foot skirted table for the wedding cake decorated with silver champagne bucket, silver candelabra, silver goblets and silver serving set. We'll also cut, plate and serve your wedding cake. All setup and cleanup are complimentary and there's plenty of free parking.

Description of Facility and Services

Servers: no additional charge including wedding cake cutting service
Gratuity: 17% service charge on food and beverage for buffets and 20% for plated dinners
Bar facilities: beer and wine—full-service bar available (minimum sales of $300)
Linens: linen skirting, tablecloths and napkins available at no additional charge
China and glassware: bone china and crystal glassware provided at no additional charge
Dance floor: available at an additional charge
Cleanup: provided by Willamette Cafe at no additional charge
Entertainment: beautiful baby grand piano available; outside contractors welcome
Parking: ample free parking available
ADA: yes

CUSTOMIZED SERVICE

The Willamette Cafe offers white tablecloth service and excellent food combined with years of experience catering wedding receptions and rehearsal dinners. All table arrangements, seating and menus can be customized to suit your specifications. Your every need will be attended to by our first class staff so that you, your family and friends can relax and enjoy the festivities of the day.

Willamette Gables

Riverside Estate
10323 Schuler Road
Aurora, Oregon 97002
Contact: Laurel and Scott Cookman
(503) 678-2195

Wedding receptions and special events in an intimate country setting on the banks of the Willamette River

Willamette Gables is a five-acre country estate on the banks of the Willamette River, 30 minutes south of Portland and 30 minutes north of Salem. This beautiful southern plantation-style home provides the perfect backdrop for your wedding and reception.

The adjacent gardens and manicured grounds overlook the meandering Willamette River, offering gorgeous views and solitude.

Willamette Gables is shown by appointment only on Saturdays and Sundays from 9am to 5pm. The property will not be shown if an event is taking place.

Capacity: we can accommodate up to 200 in our outdoor setting
Price Range: $2,000
Catering: choose your own caterer or choose from our list
Types of Events: weddings, receptions, picnics, garden parties, teas, anniversaries and private parties

Availability and Terms

Our outdoor setting is available Saturday and Sunday June-September by reservation only. All reservations must be accompanied by a 50% deposit; the balance is due 45 days prior to your scheduled event. Time limit: any six-hour period between 10am and 9pm; we schedule only one event per day in order to give you the personal attention you deserve.

Description of Facility and Services

Seating: round tables for 200; chairs for 200; rectangular tables for accessories
Servers: provided by caterer
Bar facilities: caterer or renter provides licensed bartender and liability insurance; beer , wine and champagne only
Linens and table service: provided by caterer
Setup and tear down: provided; caterers are expected to provide their own cleanup and trash removal
Decorations: many items are provided; little decoration needed; no rice, birdseed or confetti
Sound system: provided by your musicians
Photographers: we suggest you choose a photographer who specializes in outdoor weddings and events
Parking: ample parking; parking attendants included in the fee

Special Services

- **Covered Area:** 40' x 60' canopy included in the fee
- **Wedding and Event coordination:** experienced assistance included in the fee

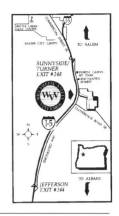

WILLAMETTE VALLEY VINEYARDS

8800 Enchanted Way S.E. • Turner, Oregon 97392
Contact: Hospitality Coordinator (503) 588-9463;
Fax (503) 588-8894; Toll free (800) 344-9463
Business Hours: 11am–6pm daily

Capacity: up to 600 inside and outside

Price Range: $150 to $1,800

Catering: exclusively by Willaby's Catering, prepared on-site; Willaby's full-service catering can assist you with your selections of the perfect menu for your wedding; all events are customized to reflect each bride's individual taste and style; Willaby's offers personalized menu planning in all price ranges

Types of Events: indoor and outdoor weddings and receptions. The indoor facility and outdoor facility can be utilized together. Other events include showers, rehearsal dinners, business meetings, class reunions, all-day seminars, family gatherings, and more

Availability and Terms

Reservations should be made as soon as possible. We require a 50% deposit at the time of rental.

Description of Facility and Services

Seating: tables and chairs are available

Licensed servers: Willamette Valley Vineyards arranges for wine servers for both indoor and outdoor events

Liquor liability: we are not licensed to serve any alcoholic beverages other than wine and beer on premise. Our award-winning wines are available for purchase in our tasting room.

Music and dance floor: amplified music is allowed, and dance floor areas are available both inside and outside the facility

Linens and glassware: available for rent

Cleanup: client or caterer to provide

Decorations: no nails, rice, or birdseed please

Parking: free parking available to Willamette Valley Vineyards patrons

ADA: access to restrooms, tasting room, and event rooms

Special Services

Personalized neck labels attached to your choice of Willamette Valley Wines are available for purchase prior to your event. This personalized touch is a special remembrance for your guests and attendants. Complimentary tours by arrangement.

PANORAMIC VIEW

Our newly built Visitor Center with panoramic view of the Willamette Valley and Coastal Range is the perfect location for any event.

SKY ROOM AND TERRACE

Top Floor of the Holiday Inn
1021 N.E. Grand Avenue • Portland, Oregon 97232
Contact: Mary Baskerville at Catering Office (503) 820-4160; Fax (503) 235-0396
Office Hours: Mon–Fri 8am–5pm; other times by appointment

Capacity: Ballroom: up to 250 people; Windows Sky Room: up to 200 people; Terrace: up to 100 people

Price Range: prices vary with size and menu selection; we will work with you and your budget

Catering: provided by the hotel exclusively

Types of Events: full sit-down, buffet, cocktails and hors d'oeuvres, rehearsal dinners and wedding ceremonies

Availability and Terms

Grand Ballroom has four separate reception rooms that can be used individually or in combination to host as many as 250 guests. Windows Sky Room with floor-to-ceiling windows offers a spectacular view of downtown Portland. Our open-air terrace is also available for private functions. All banquet facilities are located on the top floor of the Holiday Inn Portland—Downtown. A deposit is required to reserve space with the deposit applied to the final bill.

Description of Facility and Services

Seating: tables and chairs provided
Bar facilities: full beverage service; hotel provides all alcoholic beverages
Dance floor: dance floor and electrical hookups available at an additional charge
Linens: linens and cloth napkins available in a variety of colors, complimentary basis with catering
Cleanup: provided by Windows at no charge
Parking: complimentary parking; street and lot parking nearby

Special Services

Windows catering staff offers personalized attention to every detail of your reception including customized menu planning, private space for rehearsal dinners, and lovely honeymoon suites with a spectacular Portland city view for the bride and groom as well as special guestroom rates for your out-of-town guests. You may also hold your wedding ceremony here.

ELEGANCE AND SPECTACULAR CITY VIEW

Windows is a full-service banquet facility. In addition to our 4,000-square-foot ballroom, Windows Sky Room with its panoramic view, is also available for private affairs. Our open-air terrace provides a beautiful setting for a wedding and/or a reception. Windows catering serves fine Northwest cuisine highlighting fresh foods of the Pacific Northwest. Whether an intimate gathering or a full reception, your event is special to us.

WORLD TRADE CENTER
Two World Trade Center Portland
25 S.W. Salmon Street • Portland, Oregon 97204
Reservations: (503) 464-8688 • Office Hours: Mon–Fri 8am–5pm

Capacity: inside: 400 reception, 300 seated; **outside:** 800 reception, 500 seated; **Flags riverfront space:** 125 reception, 80 seated

Price Range: please call for specific price information

Catering: We can host a rehearsal dinner or reception, or we can package your entire wedding, handling all the details for you! Full-service in-house catering available. Menus flexible to client's choices.

Types of Events: sit-down, buffet, hors d'oeuvres

Availability and Terms
A variety of rooms are available to meet your specific needs. Choose between the glassed-in Mezzanine or our covered Plaza for your outdoor ceremony or reception. Our new riverfront banquet space offers a fantastic view of the river and Tom McCall Waterfront Park. There is also a 220-seat auditorium for indoor ceremonies. Reservations are suggested at least six months in advance—particularly during spring and summer months. Deposit of half of the total room rental is required at the time of booking.

Description of Facility and Services
Seating: seating capacity based on room(s) selected and seating arrangement; table and chair setup included in rental price

Bar facilities: fully OLCC licensed

Dance floor: dance floor upon request at standard rental rate; electrical hookup for bands or disc jockey available

Decorations: inquire about limitations; nothing that will damage the walls or ceiling

Parking: underground daytime and evening parking available in the building

ADA: all rooms are disabled accessible

INVITE YOUR GUESTS TO SEE THE WORLD
There's nothing like holding your reception, or even the whole wedding, in Portland's showcase—at the World Trade Center. Located in the heart of the city between S.W. Salmon and Taylor streets, First and Front avenues, this award-winning facility has a commanding view of the beautiful Tom McCall waterfront and provides the finest in facilities. You'll enjoy our cooperative and helpful staff, prepared to do whatever it takes to make your special time a wonderful experience. Call for a complete tour and information packet.

Notes

ILLUSION OF BEAUTY LAW

A law was passed in 1775 stating that a young woman couldn't wear makeup at her wedding. If she did, her marriage would not be considered legitimate, because the groom would have been "ensnared" by the illusion of beauty made by the makeup.

HELPFUL HINTS

- **Eat right and get enough sleep:** It gets very hectic prior to the wedding with all the planning and parties. Be sure to take care of yourself! You'll need every ounce of energy. Eat right and get enough sleep to look your very best on this special day.

- **Pamper yourself:** A couple of weeks before the wedding, take time to pamper yourself. Schedule a massage to relieve tension and stress. A facial is wonderful for your skin, but be sure to allow some time for your face to benefit from it. Avoid using unfamiliar products too close to the wedding in case your skin has an allergic reaction. Prepare your hands and nails with a manicure. A pedicure will do wonders for your feet and toes for the honeymoon.

- **Hair consultation:** When you have selected your headpiece, make an appointment for a consultation with your hairdresser. This allows time to experiment with different hairstyles that complement your face and work well with the headpiece. This way there are no "surprise" hairstyles the morning of your wedding. You and your hairdresser should agree on the style and look well in advance. Also make sure your hairstyle will look nice even when you take off the headpiece.

- **Makeup consultation:** A makeup consultation can help you apply makeup in a natural and flattering way to highlight your features. The photographer may ask for a heavier application for the photos. Ask the consultant how to obtain the best look without overdoing it.

- **Bridesmaid lunch and manicure:** A fun idea is to take your bridesmaids to lunch and then treat them to a manicure. This usually takes place a day or two before, or the morning of the wedding. For parties of three or more it is best to schedule an appointment at least three months in advance.

- **On-site beauty service:** Many salons and beauty consultants offer hairstyling and makeup for you and your bridesmaids at the ceremony site. Fees are based on services, number of people, and travel time.

For more assistance with staying organized during the wedding planning process, check out the Bravo! Wedding Organizer. Detailed question worksheets double as contracts. This step-by-step system will keep every detail of your wedding organized. To order, refer to the order form on page 23 in this Guide.

By appointment only
(503) 244-2885, (503) 287-1272, (503) 515-5323

We are an ensemble of professional stylists/makeup artists, that come to you on location with experience. We are fully equipped to handle all of your needs down to the smallest detail.

Our Services include

- **A complimentary consultation** to discuss what your needs are, so that a proper package can be designed for you, and book any necessary appointments at that time.
- **A personal consultation** to discuss any haircare preparation (hair shaping, retexturizing, coloring, and conditioning treatment) necessary to be done prior to the wedding.
- **A trial run with the bride** to go over makeup selection and application as well as a practice style and headpiece placement.
- **A package designed** to suit your needs

On-site

- Bridal/formal up-do's
- Full makeup application
- Manicure/polish changes
- Assistance through the ceremony

Services in the Salon We Offer

- Haircutting
- Shampoo and styling
- Color and weaves
- Manicures and pedicures
- Artificial nail services
- Permanent waves and retexturizing
- Special occasion styling and up-do's
- Hairstyling lessons
- Color cosmetic application
- Eyelash tinting

Off-site Referrals for

- Facials/full body massage

30 day notice preferred.
Short notice inquiries and services are welcomed.
Deposit required.

VISA MasterCard and personal checks accepted.

MAKE-UP BY J.J.

P.O. Box 19534 • Portland, Oregon 97280
Contact: Janice Johnson (503) 604-4221 or (503) 452-8399

International Experience

With over 12 years experience in the industry, including international experience in London and Greece, I've worked in film, television, and print, for fashion runway shows and weddings.

Specializing in the Natural Look

I specialize in the natural look, though I can create any look you desire for your special day. I work as a team on location with some of the leading hair stylists in the industry to help create the perfect look for your wedding day.

Clients Include

- Nordstrom
- Fred Meyer—television and print
- Nike, Inc.
- Hearst Productions—television movies
- Disney Films
- Columbia Sportswear
- Rosey 105
- Pacific Trail
- Eddie Bauer
- Precor
- Tunturi
- AVIA Sportswear
- KPTV—Channel 12
- Studio 3, Inc.
- Tyee Productions
- Generator Industries
- Bruce Gillette Studios

A portfolio of my work is available upon request. A deposit is required upon booking my services. Please call for availability.

E-mail: toli@spiretech.com

PARADISE
DAY SPA & SALON

2905 N.E. Broadway
Portland, Oregon 97232
(503) 287-7977

PARADISE BEFORE THE HONEYMOON

Seduce your senses, soothe your body, surrender your stress for the most important day of your life.

Our staff of professional licensed therapists and practitioners invite you and your chosen loved ones to our beautiful facility to be nurtured and beautified for your special day.

We Welcome You to Paradise

We are a unique spa and salon that caters to brides, grooms and your entire wedding party. Specializing in beauty consultation, wedding day hair and veil, makeup application, nails, etc. Our spa treatments complement your experience to soothe you with facials, massage and body treatments. When you visit our salon, you'll be in a vintage house with portraits of our satisfied bridal customers on the wall.

Bridal Packages

The Lotus Blossom is a package specifically designed for the bride. You'll receive a complimentary consultation, hairstyle, makeup application, and manicure—all done on the wedding day.

When Should You Schedule?

Brides should schedule their consultation one to two months prior to the wedding day. This will allow time for specific hairstyles (colors, cuts or perms) and to discuss your makeup and hair needs. On-site services on your wedding day are available with advance booking.

CALL FOR MORE INFORMATION ON OUR
FULL RANGE OF SERVICES AND WEDDING BROCHURE.
WE WILL BE HAPPY TO ASSIST YOU
IN ANY WAY POSSIBLE.

Professional Make-up Services

Kim Lane • Carrie Wilson
(503) 287-5205; Fax (503) 287-5299

We specialize in makeup only. At your location, we offer our seven years experience, including weddings, runway, print and film. We have had extensive training, in addition to working for MAC cosmetics for five years. We are knowledgeable in techniques for enhancing features on all skin tones and our expertise in color theory will enable us to choose the best colors for you and your wedding party. We work quickly and efficiently to eliminate any stress on your special day.

• On-site Services
- We use products specially formulated for film, video and photography
- Engagements, rehearsal dinners and other special events
- Entire wedding parties—including men and mothers, too
- Waterproof mascara and false eyelashes (if desired) at no extra charge
- Lessons available

In Advance
Prior to your wedding, we will meet for a consultation to discuss the details and choose your look. At this time we can schedule any additional appointments that will best suit the needs of you and your wedding party.

SASSÉ SALON & SPA

630 S.W. Alder
Portland, Oregon 97205
(503) 228-8266,
(800) 882-8261
Business Hours:
Mon 10am–7pm;
Tues–Fri 8am–8pm;
Sat 9am–6pm
Sun—Parties by appointment only

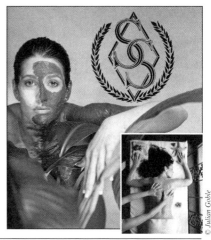

© Julian Goble

SPA BRIDAL PARTIES

Sassé Salon and Spa offers everything from hair care to six-hour day spa packages, Sassé can fit into any budget. Newly expanded—now a 5,000 sq. ft. facility in the heart of the city.

Salon Options

- Hair care and design
- Nail care
- Hydrobaths
- Vichy showers
- Facial therapy/skin care
- Massage
- Swedish showers
- Spa treatments
- Waxing
- Wolff suntanning
- Ayurvedic steam
- Juice/espresso bar

Spa Treatments

- **The Ultimate Day Spa:** unique six-hour experience (includes lunch)
- **Quintessential Spa Treatment:** relaxing, purifying four-hour spa experience (includes lunch)
- **Revitalizer:** two-hour getaway of therapeutic bliss (includes lunch)
- **Thallaso Hydromassage Bath:** hydrobath combined with oils and sea algae
- **Ayurvedic Herbal Steam Treatment:** with Himalayan scalp massage
- **Vichy Shower Massage Treatment:** invigorating shower aligned with spine
- **Aromatherapy Massage:** rare essences and oils are used to relax and invigorate
- **Sea Algae Body Treatment:** rehydrates, refines and tones
- **Herbal Body Wrap:** relaxing detoxifying treatment.
- **Fango Mud Pack:** for the breakdown of cellulite and body detoxification
- **Salt Glow Body Scrub:** invigorating massage leaving skin baby soft
- **European Back Treatment:** invigorating skin care treatment for the back
- **Full European Facial:** deep pore cleansing, facial massage, and personal masque
- **Specialty Treatment Facials:** individually tailored
- **Pedicure Pals Room:** where friends can enjoy their pedicures together

DISCOVER THE NATURAL WAY TO BEAUTY

At Sasse Salon and Spa we are dedicated to the art of beauty and well being in a professional and satisfying atmosphere. We believe that Earth's natural ingredients, rather than chemicals, offer a holistic solution to individual beauty problems. Extensive research has proven that natural elements such as extracts, organic clays, and flower essences have a positive effect on the skin and well-being. Visit us at Sasse Salon and Spa and let your body discover the natural way to a healthier, more radiant face and body.

VITALITY

7365 S.W. Barnes Road, Suite-A
Portland, Oregon 97225
(503) 297-2277

AVEDA™

8511 S.W. Terwilliger Boulevard, A
Portland, Oregon 97212
(503) 244-4404

Services We Offer

- Haircutting
- Colour and weaves
- Special occasion styling and up-do's
- Manicures and pedicures
- Colour cosmetic application
- Facials *(available only at Vitality)*
- Full body massage *(available only at Vitality)*
- Day of beauty spa package *(available only at Vitality)*

- Shampoo and styling
- Permanent waves and retexturizing
- Hairstyling lessons
- Artificial nail services
- Hair styles on video

In Advance… to Start with

- Initial 30-minute complimentary consultation
- All other appointments for bridal party will be made
- Discuss an appropriate bridal package that would best accommodate your needs

Two Months Before

- A consultation with your stylists to discuss appropriate haircare preparation

One Month Before

- Colour and/or retexturize hair, along with deep conditioning treatments and haircut
- Practice style with hairpiece
- Makeup selection and application

Two Weeks Before

- Facial
- Full body massage
- Haircuts for men in bridal party

One Week Before

- Natural or artificial nail services
- Pedicure
- Waxing (lip, brow, underarm, leg, and bikini)

Wedding Day

- Makeup application
- Bridal up-do
- All remaining bridesmaids shampoo and style

OUR PROMISE

You can feel confident that our well-trained staff
will provide you with the quality service you deserve.
We look forward to working with you on
that very special day…your wedding day!

TALISMANS

Talismans a bride may

choose to wear or carry on

her wedding day came

about from a mix of

tradition and superstition.

Something Old
to bring a sense of
continuity

Something New
adds an optimistic note

Something Borrowed
the superstition that
happiness rubs off

Something Blue
for purity, fidelity and love

A Penny In Your Shoe
to help ensure a life of
fortune

BRIDAL ACCESSORIES

- **How to make candles burn slower and drip less:** If you plan to use candles at your event or wedding, put them into a freezer in a foil-wrapped box the night before. This prevents the candles from burning down too far while the photographer is taking formal portraits before the ceremony. An alternative is to bring an extra set of candles. You don't want it to look like the candles were already used before the wedding actually begins.

- **Guest-book pen:** Bring an extra pen for the guest book. Sometimes fancy plume pens run out of ink or don't write well. You want to make sure you have a complete list of who attended your wedding.

- **Money tree or money bag:** If you choose to have a "money tree" at your reception, it's a good idea to have envelopes on hand to put the money in. Guests can attach their gifts to the tree along with their names (no one likes to give an anonymous gift). If you choose the tradition of a "dollar dance," a money bag to carry on your arm will eliminate pin marks on your beautiful wedding gown.

- **The unity candle:** Unity candles used during the ceremony are not only symbolic, but can be enjoyed for many years to come to celebrate your anniversaries.

- **Wedding gown slips:** These slips can be very expensive to wear for just one day. Some shops have slips available for rent.

- **Shoes:** Comfort is number one—style is second. Find a pair of shoes that will be comfortable, and then customize them with lace, beading, and pearling. Clip-on accessories are also available to dress them up. If you buy a satin shoe, many stores offer free dyeing after the wedding so that you can wear them again.

- **Garters:** It is nice to buy two garters, one to throw and the other to keep as a fun memento.

- **Toasting goblets:** You'll find a variety of glass, crystal, pewter, or silver goblets and toasting glasses to choose from. You can have them engraved with your names or initials and your wedding date. Your florist will be able to provide decorations such as ribbons and fresh flowers to place around the stems of your glass or goblet. These are mementos you'll want to keep for years to come, or to pass on to the next generation.

- **Something old:** Ask your mother or grandmother for something she carried at her wedding: a lace hankie, Bible, or piece of sentimental jewelry you can wear or carry.

- **Bubble shower:** A new trend is providing containers of bubbles that can be blown as the bride and groom leave the ceremony. The bottles can be customized with the names and wedding date for guests to keep as a keepsake.

For more assistance with staying organized during the wedding planning process, check out the Bravo! Wedding Organizer. Detailed question worksheets double as contracts. This step-by-step system will keep every detail of your wedding organized. To order, refer to the order form on page 23 in this Guide.

NORDSTROM

Downtown Portland	*Lloyd Center*
(503) 224-6666	*(503) 287-2444*
Clackamas Town Center	*Washington Square*
(503) 652-1810	*(503) 620-0555*
Salem Center	*Vancouver Mall*
(503) 371-7710	*(360) 256-8666*

AT NORDSTROM,
WE HAVE A BEAUTIFUL SELECTION
OF FINISHING TOUCHES FOR YOUR SPECIAL DAY

Hosiery

You'll find a variety of styles and colors to complement you and your attendants' bridal attire from Givenchy, Classiques Entier, and Donna Karan.

Fashion Jewelry

You'll enjoy an extensive selection of Austrian Crystal jewelry from Swarovski and Christian Dior, as well as freshwater pearl designs from Lily Rachel.

Fashion Accessories

Finishing touches for your bridal party are easy with our extensive accessory collection, including decorative hairpieces and satin gloves. We are also happy to place special orders for your individual needs.

Lingerie

Complete your trousseau with selections from our beautiful collection of bridal lingerie, including bustiers, garter belts with matching panties, peignoir sets and garters.

Handbags

Our handbag section features a unique selection of styles including satin, velvet, and beaded handbags from $28 and up.

Fine Jewelry

Whether you're shopping for an engagement ring or wedding set, you'll find a breathtaking array of contemporary and traditional rings. Custom jewelry designing is also available in selected stores.

Westside
*4775 S.W. Watson Avenue
Beaverton, Oregon 97005
(503) 643-9730*

Downtown
*423 S.W. Fourth Avenue
Portland, Oregon 97204
(503) 827-4578*

The most enormous selection of elegant accessories from economical to extravagant.

A trip to The Wedding Cottage is a must for anyone planning a wedding. The variety and beauty of the wedding accessories are like no other in the Pacific Northwest. There is so much to see, that brides return again and again.

The Wedding Cottage carries many lines including Beverly Clark, Marcela, Lillian Rose, Cathy's Concepts and the new Toccata line. Many items are custom-made or customized to fit a bride's individual or wedding theme.

An extensive amount of inventory is on hand. However, we take pride in our ability to special order items not in stock in the exact color or style needed.

Every bride receives a Bride's Card that allows her a $10 instant credit every time her cumulative purchases reach $100. Brides who do all their shopping at The Wedding Cottage find they have substantial savings.

- ♥ Bridal books and planners
- ♥ Guest and memory books
- ♥ Unity candles and holders
- ♥ Bridal jewelry
- ♥ Knives and servers
- ♥ Custom cake tops and charms
- ♥ Bubbles and cameras
- ♥ Favors and candies
- ♥ Personalized napkins and ribbons
- ♥ Toasting goblets
- ♥ Invitations and announcements in over 50 books, including Crane

- ♥ Bridesmaid and groomsmen gifts
- ♥ Plume and guest book pens
- ♥ Ring Bearer pillows
- ♥ Flower Girl baskets
- ♥ Garters, hankies, gloves
- ♥ Photo albums
- ♥ Custom veils, headpieces, and hats
- ♥ Purses and money bags
- ♥ Shower invitations and games
- ♥ Rehearsal invitations
- ♥ Specialty and Anniversary Gifts

Our main store is located in Beaverton, with a second smaller location in downtown Portland, inside the Ania Collection.

See page 397 under Invitations & Announcements.

HELPFUL HINTS

- **Selecting your bridal gown:** Take the time to try on the various styles available at different shops. Most importantly, pick the dress you feel the best and most comfortable in. Many people will try to influence your preference one way or another. Just remember you're the one wearing it and your fiancé is the one you're wearing it for! **NOTE:** Allow at least six months to order your wedding gown.

- **Bridesmaid dresses:** There are several factors to keep in mind when selecting bridesmaid dresses. Colors and fabrics vary with the seasons. The style usually complements the bridal gown. The formality is based on whether it is a daytime or evening wedding. Choose a dress color and style that will be flattering on all the bridesmaids, and keep in mind that the main focus will be on the backs of the dresses during the ceremony.

- **Formal and evening attire:** Many bridal shops carry a nice selection of formal and evening gowns for special occasions and pageants. Bridal salons may carry one-of-a-kind gowns or a limited selection.

- **Guideline for lengths:** The bridesmaid dresses should never be longer than the bride's gown. The mother's dresses should never be longer than the bridesmaid dresses.

- **Headpieces and veils:** Pick a headpiece that enhances your face and hairstyle; it should complement, not overwhelm. If you attempt to press your own veil, be extremely careful. Press the veil between white tissue. Do not put an iron directly on the veiling. Ask about care when you buy the veil.

- **Accessories:** Most bridal shops carry a nice selection of bridal accessories, including garters, slips, gloves, jewelry, shoes, albums and guest books.

- **Looking good all day long:** You may want to consider the fabric for your dress more closely, depending on how long you will be in the dress. There is no way to avoid wrinkling a dress once it is put on; however certain fabrics wrinkle more easily. Here are a few ways to preserve your dress: Get dressed at the ceremony site, eliminate traveling in dress before ceremony, bring a stool to the ceremony site for sitting on, and make sure there is an aisle runner if you have a long train. Detachable trains and veils make it easier to travel about and dance at the reception. Just remember, this is a day to enjoy, don't worry if your dress is tattered and stained at the reception; with a cleaning and preservation service most stains and problems can be fixed.

- **Picking up your dress:** It might be smart to leave the dress at the bridal shop even if the dress is ready in far in advance of the wedding day. The bridal shop may be better equipped to store and keep the dress fresh and pressed.

- **IMPORTANT NOTE:** The following recommendations are for your protection: 1) be careful about where you buy your wedding dress. Ask your friends and family about where they went and what their experiences were; 2) make sure the delivery date of your dress is well in advance of your wedding; 3) get a copy of the order or receipt with a guarantee of delivery date to keep with your wedding records; 4) if a contract is used, **read it carefully** (even the fine print) before signing! If you have any questions or concerns about the company, check it out with organizations that keep track of the reputations of companies.

Alameda BRIDAL FAIRE

5707 N.E. Fremont
Portland, Oregon 97213
(503) 282-4430
Business Hours:
Mon–Fri 10am-6pm; Sat 9am–5pm

© Photography by Fudge

Wedding Flowers

Whether your wedding dreams include an enchanted garden, a cathedral or fireside at home, Alameda Floral can help make them come true. Free personal consultation to create the ambiance you want for your wedding day.

Photography

The photographer who captures the memories of a perfect day should be #1 on your list. Alameda Bridal Faire has only the best and we can help you here!

Travel Agency

We offer hundreds of packages of romantic travel for couples, from intimate hideaways to luxury cruises. Personal planning and service are top priority.

Wedding Gowns, Veils and Accessories

Our selection of the finest gowns and veils are available for viewing at all times. When it comes to accessories, we travel to New York to find the latest, fashionable and most reasonably priced toasting flutes, cake knives, guests books, pillows, and gifts for the wedding party.

Invitations

Receive the personal help and attention to detail that is so very necessary in ordering your printed stationery. The first that your guests will see of your style and taste.

Disc Jockey Service

Need a great DJ? Our goal is to provide a smooth flowing event where everyone has a good time! You will be amazed and excited to see how special your event can be.

Tuxedos

Excellent service combined with genuine joy for your event is the reason men of distinction rent their formal attire at the Alameda Bridal Faire.

Custom Cakes and Catering

Food your guests will be talking about for many years to come and dream wedding cakes delivered with pride and perfection.

Wedding Officiate

Get married at the Alameda Bridal Faire, by our non-denominational officiate, from Vegas style to an intimate affair.

To add to your shopping enjoyment,
we feature a full-service espresso bar and deli.

AniA
Collection
愛 婉 雅 禮 服
A n d r e a & A i l e e n
419 S.W. Fourth Avenue
Portland, Oregon 97204
Contact: Aileen (503) 796-9170
Business Hours: Mon–Sat 11am–6pm

Styles and Selections

AniA has all styles in stock: traditional, sheath, halter, informal, off-shoulder, sleeveless, etc. The boutique features an international selection including French and English designer gowns. Sizes carried are 8-26.

Description of Wedding Gowns

White, candlelight, ivory; newer styles are featuring colors such as rum pink and yellow greens. Fabrics include silk — satin and shantung, Italian matte satin, tulle, organza and crepe. We carry the Diamond Collection, St. Pucchi, Jim Hjelm Couture, Carmela Sutera, Alfred Sung, Manalé, Designer Collection (England Designers), Pronovias, Marisa, Jasmine, Moonlight, Mika Inatome, Vera Wang, Watters & Watters and Belsioé.

Service

We will steam your dress and give you a garment bag for your dress. For alterations, we have a pool of seamstresses we can recommend.

Headpieces

We can custom design headpieces if you do not see one you like in stock or in a catalog. In-stock styles include halos, bun keepers, mantilla, headband and crown tiara. Designs range from simple elegance to very ornate. Price range: $50 to $300.

Bridal Attendant Attire and Mothers' Dresses

We carry traditional to contemporary styles for bridesmaids featuring the Jim Hjelm Couture and Occasions lines. One company has selection styles available for a two-week turnaround. Mothers' dresses are available from Watters & Watters and Belsioé. Delivery time is 2-14 weeks depending on the company. Price range: $50 to $500.

Special Occasion Dresses

Our special occasion dresses can cross over to bridal or bridesmaid dresses. Sizes range from 8–26. We attempt to carry gowns appropriate for the symphony or a black tie affair. Price range: $190 to $500.

Accessories

Kenneth Cole shoes, Colorifics (dyeable shoes), garters, Christian Dior jewelry, Carolina Amato gloves, ring bearer pillows. Holo pieces from England.

TOTALLY COMMITTED TO CUSTOMER SERVICE

AniA Collection is located downtown to cater to business people and downtown shoppers. Step in off the busy streets and enter our boutique where we our totally committed to customer service. We aren't pushy and our prices are up front. Customer layaway is available.

**We recommend appointments to ensure personalized service,
but walk-ins are welcomed warmly.**

Please let this business know that you heard about them from the Bravo! Bridal Resource Guide.

BELLE AND BOW TIE TUX

Bridal and Formal Wear

Northeast	Eastside
4300 N.E. Hancock	*Ross Center*
(at 43rd & Sandy)	*11211 S.E. 82nd Ave.*
(503) 284-5969	*(503) 652-7076*
Mon–Sat 9am–7pm	*Mon–Sat 10am–7pm*

Styles and Selections of Wedding Gowns

Over 60 gowns to select from in each store. We feature Alfred Angelo Dreammaker gowns.

Description of Wedding Gowns and Ordering

- **Colors:** white and eggshell
- **Fabrics:** satin, lace, taffeta and peau de soie
- **Styles:** chapel length, sweep train, street length, sheath, off the shoulder and more
- **Sizes:** 4 to 44 are carried in the store
- **Price range:** $350 to $1,500

It usually takes from three to six months to order your gown. A 50% down payment is needed upon ordering; deposits are nonrefundable.

Service

Alterations are done at our Northeast store. Our locations are available for bridal portraits. And for a $60 charge, you can bring your gown back for preserving and boxing.

Headpieces

Wreaths, face framers, hats and crowns are just some styles available at two of our three locations. **Price range:** $70 to $220.

Bridal Attendant Attire

Alfred Angelo bridesmaid dresses, sizes 4 to 44. **Price range:** $180 to $300. Alfred Angelo junior bridesmaid and flower girl dresses in sizes 3 to 12. **Price range:** $120 to $200.

Accessories

Bridal and bridesmaid gloves, jewelry and rental slips.

WEDDING GOWNS TO FORMAL WEAR

Two convenient locations in the Portland area, where we help with your bridal-attire needs from wedding gowns to formal wear. Come visit us today and see the number of ways Belle & Bow Tie can make your wedding day easier.

See page 257 under Tuxedos & Formal Wear.

Bodas El Grande

1725 S.E. 122nd Avenue • Portland, Oregon 97233
Contact: Nelly Rodriguez (503) 256-2432
Business Hours: 9am–9pm; open 7 days a week every day of the year

Specializing in Hispanic Weddings and Wedding Attire

Bodas El Grande carries a selection of over 90 styles of gowns including formal, halter, informal, sheaths and additional wedding dresses. Prices for our gowns start as low as $150, and range to $650. We can custom-order your wedding dress in sizes 4 to 34. White, cream, ivory and non-traditional colors are all available on short notice. We can have a dress ready for you in as little as seven days.

Additional Services

We offer extra services to the bride including a reception site available for rent; wedding invitations in English, Spanish, or in both languages; steam pressing; garment bags; and in-house alterations.

Headpieces

Bodas El Grande has a variety of headpieces in stock. From traditional to contemporary, we can custom-design all styles, including halos, bun styles, tiaras, Spanish mantillas, hats and combs. Prices range from $14 to $140.

Attendant Attire

Bridal attendant and mother-of-the-bride and groom dresses are available in sizes small to XXXL, in a wide variety of colors including the latest fashion trends. Prices range from $50 to $200.

Special Occasion Dresses

Our vast selection of special occasion dresses are often selected for bridesmaid dresses. We carry dresses in all styles and lengths as well as a wide selection of beaded gowns under $100.

Accessories

Special accessories such as bras, garters, bustiers, gloves, dyeable shoes, and 14k gold and costume jewelry are available at very affordable prices.

We at Bodas El Grande are totally committed to helping the bride and the members of the wedding party.

THE BRIDAL ARTS BUILDING

10017 N.E. 6th Avenue
Vancouver, WA 98685
(360) 574-7758
Business Hours: Mon–Sat 10am–6pm;
open late Thursday night until 8pm;
Sun noon–5pm; closed most holidays

Styles and Selections of Wedding Gowns

Come visit and experience our truly elegant and complete Bridal Salon. We offer nationally advertised designer gowns at affordable prices. Select from over 300 gowns in stock. Bridal Arts also offers a beautiful line of rental wedding gowns and slips.

Ordering Your Gown

Allow three months after your gown has been ordered for delivery. A 50% deposit is required when you place your order, with monthly payments on balance available. Ask about our layaway plan. Rush orders are welcome.

Description of Wedding Gowns

- **Colors:** white, ivory, blush, pink and rum
- **Fabrics:** satin, taffeta, silk, lace, peau de soie and tulle
- **Styles:** cathedral, chapel length, sweep train, floor length, and street length
- **Sizes:** 3 to 44
- **Price range:** from under $300 to $2,000

Service

Because you are so special to us, we pay the sales tax for Washington buyers. We also include a garment bag to protect your gown, can store your gown until your wedding, and professionally steam your gown, so it's perfect for your wedding. We will match any other store's prices and services.

Headpieces

We offer a large selection of premade headpieces and veils, or can custom design one to your specifications. **Price range:** starting from $60.

Bridal Attendant and Mothers of the Bride Attire

We feature nationally advertised designer bridesmaid gowns in all the popular styles, fabrics, and colors. A 50% deposit is required for special orders. **Sizes:** 4 to 44. We cater to mothers for informal to formal attire for weddings. **Sizes:** 4 to 24. Also be sure to see our complete line of holiday and cruise attire.

Tuxedos

We carry the complete line of Black Tie Tuxedos. The finest quality at the best price...that's "Black Tie."

Exquisite Wedding Cakes

Our cakes are scrumptious. Always baked fresh—never frozen, and custom decorated to your specifications. $1.75 per serving for most flavors. Fresh-flower decor and fountain setups are available. We deliver and set up (fee depending on distance).

Bridal Arts Florist

Our florists truly specialize in gorgeous wedding arrangements at affordable prices. We will even meet with you at your church to design your flowers to your needs. Always a free toss bouquet with your order. We are "the" experts in this field. We have done hundreds of weddings—each one very unique and special.

Special Bonus

When you order both your cake and flowers from us, we will waive the delivery and setup fee and include a fountain setup under the cake at no extra charge.

FULL-SERVICE WEDDING FACILITY

The Hostess House and Bridal Arts Building is the first full-service wedding facility in the Northwest. We have everything for your wedding, including a candle-lit chapel that seats 200 guests and an absolutely gorgeous reception center; wedding attire for the entire wedding party; dyed-to-match shoes; jewelry, gloves, and slips; invitations and imprinted napkins; party supplies and decorations; custom-designed cake tops and unity candles; gift shop and bridal registry; DJ services, musicians, and vocalists. Other services include catering, photography and video services, plus much more.

Directions: located 10 minutes north of Portland. From I-5 north or south, take the 99th Street exit (#5) and go west two blocks, turn right onto Sixth Avenue.

See page 154 under Banquet & Reception Sites.
See page 329 under Ministers.

Bridal Showcase

I-5 to Exit #9, next to Clark Co. Fairgrounds
Vancouver, Washington
Contact: Donna or Dorothy
(360) 573-2817 or (503) 289-6324
Business Hours: Tues–Fri 10am–6pm; Sat 9am–5pm

Styles and Selections of Wedding Gowns

Bridal Showcase carries gowns from 27 manufacturers. This special collection has been carefully selected for today's bride.

Ordering your Gown

It takes an average of four months to order your gown. A 50% deposit is required. Charges for cancellations of special orders are assessed.

Description of Wedding Gowns

All colors, fabrics, and styles. **Sizes:** 4 to 30, larger sizes upon request. **Price range:** $200 to $1,300.

Service

We have in-house alterations for your convenience. Charges for alterations will vary depending on what needs to be done. Complimentary steaming of gowns is included.

Bridal Attendant Attire

Dresses from sizes 4 to 24. **Price range:** $95 to $200.

Dresses for Mothers of the Bride and Groom

Moms can choose from a large selection of dresses in a variety of colors, styles, and fabrics in sizes 4 to 26. We also carry a large selection of petites. **Price range:** $70 to $350.

Accessories

• Headpieces • Shoes • Undergarments

Silk Beaded Gowns

We have a wide range of silk beaded gowns that are perfect for cruises, fund raisers, pageants, or any formal event.

FINEST MERCHANDISE AND CONSULTANTS

Our business truly serves the community from Salem to Seattle with the finest merchandise and consultants trained to meet each individual's personal needs. We're just 10 minutes from Portland, conveniently located next to the Clark County Fairgrounds. Take I-5 or 205, exit #9.

♥ *Member of Weddings of Distinction*

See page 246 under Dress Design, Alterations & Custom Veils.

Bride's World, USA & Ambrosia Catering

17943 S.W. Tualatin-Valley Highway
Aloha, Oregon
(503) 649-9583
Mon, Wed, Fri, Sat 11am–6pm;
Tues, Thurs 11am–8pm; Sun 11am–4pm

Styles and Selections of Wedding Gowns

Bride's World USA offers hundreds of wedding gowns in stock for purchase. We feature gowns from many manufacturers, including beautiful gowns from tea-length informals to the traditional cathedral-length gown shimmering with thousands of beads and sequins. Special orders taken gladly.

Alterations Service

In-house alterations for your convenience. Charges for alteration will vary depending on work to be done.

Accessories

We have a complete line of bridal and bridesmaid shoes, bras, slips, gloves and jewelry. We also carry a wide range of ring bearer pillows, invitations, goblets, knives, and bridesmaid gifts.

Description of Wedding Gowns and Ordering

- **Colors:** white, ivory, eggshell, pink, rum
- **Fabrics:** satin, taffeta, silk, shantung and more
- **Styles:** cathedral, chapel length, sweep trains and tea length; necklines include Queen Anne, V-neck, bateau, Sabrina and off the shoulder
- **Sizes:** 4 to 44
- **Price range:** $110 to $2,000

Special orders generally require two to four months to arrive. If your wedding is only a few weeks away, we're happy to call the manufacturer to see if they have the gown in stock, so we can get it in seven to ten days. A 50% nonrefundable deposit is required.

Ambrosia Creative Catering Cost and Services

Ambrosia Creative Catering offers a full line of catering services that are tailored to your needs. Choose from complete event packages (including crystal plates, linens and more) or let us design a package especially for you. Prices start as low as $9.95 per person for a full-service buffet, complete with wedding cake. Our staff provides complete setup and cleanup for your event. A deposit is required to secure your event date. A 15% gratuity will be added to the final bill. We provide a fully-licensed kitchen where your food is professionally handled and prepared.

Our Promise to You…

We promise to create an exquisitely designed occasion for you and your guests, with your budget in mind.. Ask to see our full-color portfolio and reference list.

We Do the Work…You Don't Worry

We take pride in helping you plan and design your special occasion.

ONE STOP CAN FULFILL ALL YOUR WEDDING NEEDS!

8925 S.W. Beaverton-Hillsdale Hwy
Portland, Oregon 97225
(503) 297-9622; Fax (503) 297-9061
call for your personal appointment
Business Hours:
Mon–Fri 11am–8pm; Sat 10am–5pm

We are the "Dream Makers"

In our fairytale setting, a tradition carried on by Charlotte's Weddings, we help make your dream come true. We currently have over 400 gowns in stock that can be purchased off the rack or special ordered. Sizes: 4-44. Prices range from $150 to $2,500. Choose from famous designer gowns or from our "simply elegant" gowns at prices you can afford. You will find splendid attire for every member of your bridal party, from the maid of honor to the littlest flower girl, and styles that are appropriate for mothers and guests too. Not to forget the groom and his attendants, we will fit them in fabulous tuxedos in the most famous styles offered today.

Wedding specialties and services

- Professional bridal consultant who will give the personal attention you deserve; no waiting; private rooms with ceiling to floor mirrors in every room
- Elegant designer wedding gowns
- Large selection of informal dresses for garden weddings and other informal settings
- For the budget-oriented bride we have a budget room with prices under $500
- Discounts on bridesmaid dresses, invitations, tuxedos, and more with the purchase of a wedding gown
- Rentals of beautiful bridal gowns, veils, slips, and a wide selection of fabulous silk floral arrangements
- Wide selection of veils, hats, and headpieces (designer or custom)
- Wonderful selection of accessories—shoes, jewelry, hosiery, gloves, bras, garters, and bustiers
- Guest books, pens, cake tops, cake knifes and servers, and much more
- Professional seamstress who will work with you by appointment

INDIVIDUAL ATTENTION

At Charlotte's Weddings, everything is made so easy. You will have so much fun that you will not believe it until you experience it for yourself. Call and schedule an appointment, so that we can give you the professional assistance and attention you deserve.

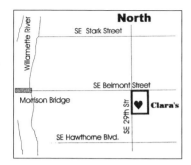

916 S.E. 29th • Portland, Oregon 97214
(at the corner of 29th and S.E. Belmont Street)
(503) 234-3484; Fax (503) 234-0404
Business hours: Mon–Fri 11am–8pm; Sat 10am–6pm
E-mail: claraswe@sprynet.com

EVERY BRIDE DESERVES A GUARDIAN ANGEL!

Clara's Wedding Establishment Ltd. is Portland's unique bridal shop. At Clara's, we take all of the stress out of planning your wedding. We have several designer gown lines to choose from. However, if your dream gown is not on any rack, don't worry—we custom-make gowns to your exacting wishes. And, brides get a **free hour** of limousine service with the purchase of a bridal gown.

Free Wedding Coordination Service

Clara's is truly the one place to come to plan your wedding. Along with all of the retail items you need, we offer wedding planning and coordination at no cost to you. From start to finish, you can plan your entire wedding without leaving Clara's comfortable surroundings. Let us handle all of the details from making appointments for meetings at Clara's to taking notes in those meetings so you can totally concentrate on making your dreams come true.

Visit our shop soon to learn about our unique services. Brides are always encouraged to drop by Clara's at any time to relax with a cup of tea. We look forward to seeing you soon.

Wedding Specialties and Services

- ♥ **Wedding gowns and wedding party attire:** Clara's carries several well known gown lines. We also custom-design and make gowns and veils, bridesmaid and flower-girl dresses. If you can't find that perfect gown...come talk to us!
- ♥ **Free wedding coordination:** Let Clara's help you find just the right site, florist, caterer, photographer, bakery, etc. to make your day perfect. And, all at no cost to you!
- ♥ **Limousine service:** White stretch limousines attended by well groomed, courteous, professional drivers. No minimum hours for weddings.
- ♥ **DJ Service:** Clara's own Ultimate Entertainment offers complete music for your ceremony and reception. Packages include music, lighting, bubble machine.
- ♥ **Accessories:** We have it all! Wedding-party gifts, goblets, serving sets, guest books and pens, ring pillows, and much more. All available in traditional or modern styles.

"LET CLARA'S BE YOUR GUARDIAN ANGEL!"

See page 452 under Disc Jockeys.
See page 530 under Transportation.

Gown pictured by LAZARO

437 N.W. 23rd
Portland, Oregon 97210
(503) 827-0667; Fax (503) 827-0668
Business Hours: Mon–Tues 10am–6pm;
Wed–Thurs 11am–8pm; Fri–Sat 10am–6pm;
October – May: Sundays 12:30–4pm;
Appointments required
E-mail: divinedesigns@ipns.com

Divine Designs—the Showroom Collection with Style, Simplicity, and One-of-a-Kind Lines:

- Allin rae
- Bianchi
- Carmi
- Christo's
- Christian Dior
- Diamond
- Demetrios
- Givenchy
- Janell Berte
- Jessica McClintock
- Jim Hjelm
- Jasmine
- Lazaro

- Lezu Atelier
- Maggie Sottero
- Monique L'Huillier
- Nancy Issler
- Pricilla
- Reem
- Robert Legere
- Stephanie's
- Siri
- Van Lear
- Vera Wang
- Watters & Watters
- And many more!

For more information call
Divine Designs (503) 827-0667
Custom Designs Offered.

Divine Designs will not be undersold.

Elegant Moments Bridal

Oregon City Shopping Center
1900 S.E. McLoughlin Boulevard
Oregon City, Oregon 97045
(Off I-205, Oregon City exit #9)
(503) 650-GOWN
Business Hours:
Mon 11am–8pm; closed Tuesdays;
Wed–Thurs 11am–8pm; Fri 11am–6pm;
Sat 10am–5pm; Sun noon–4pm
Web site: http://www.elegantmoments.com

One of the Largest Bridal Salons in the Northwest

Premier Bridal Salon

Elegant Moments Bridal is true to its name. An atmosphere of elegance is only one part of the difference you can enjoy while selecting your wedding gown. With comfort in mind, the large fitting areas are perfect for a single bride or large groups. From our spacious dressing rooms and exquisite fitting areas, friends and family can relax in comfort and elegance. Selection, comfort, personal attention, and our commitment to service are only some of the reasons to visit us.

Newest Bridal Fashions

Our store is filled with the newest styles from many of today's top designers. We carry a wide selection of styles ranging from informal to formal, halter tops to long sleeves, and traditional to modern. We also provide a very complete assortment of bridesmaids, mother-of-the-bride, flowergirls and special occasion dresses.

Veils, Shoes, Jewelry, Gloves, Garters, and More

We have an extensive selection of veils, custom veils, bridal shoes, dyeable shoes, gloves and bridal accessories to put the finishing touches on your special day. Our knowledgeable bridal consultants will help you make your wedding day perfect. Our assortment of ring bearer pillows, garters, gloves, guest books and pens, unity candles, cake knife sets, toasting goblets, and attendant gifts make a visit well worth it.

Full-service Bridal

Come and experience the best full-service salon in the Northwest. Bridal consultants help you to find your fashion style and locate your ultimate wedding dress. We are here to serve our customers and we will always take the extra time you need to give you the service you deserve. Each gown is always hand-pressed and ready to walk down the aisle. Alterations are available by our on-site seamstress. Appointments are never needed.

WE LOVE WHAT WE DO FOR YOU... AND IT SHOWS

Come to Elegant Moments Bridal for the most important dress decision of your life and experience our commitment to giving you the personal attention that you deserve. Our bridal consultants are here to help you in all aspects of finding your perfect gown, wedding party attire, or just putting the finishing touches together for your special day. We truly love what we do for you and it shows.

Elsie's

VICTORIAN BRIDAL

739 S.W. Evans Street
Portland, Oregon 97219
Contact: Elsie E. Bartling
(503) 244-4098
Business Hours: Mon–Sat;
call for appointment

One-of-a-Kind Period Gowns

Elsie's Victorian Bridal designs one-of-a-kind period gowns from the early 1800s through the 1970s. "I specialize in natural-fiber fabrics and antique laces, hand crochet, and embroidery." Everything is custom made; nothing is manufactured. Select from over 60 dresses in stock or have a custom design made especially for you.

Ordering your Gown

Choose a dress available in the shop, or allow one month for the gown design you select to be made. A 50% deposit is required. Since each gown is custom designed, there are no refunds or exchanges.

Description of Wedding Gowns

- **Colors:** white, ivory, eggshell, pink, blue, lavender or rose
- **Fabrics:** silk, satin, lace, linen, cotton or net
- **Styles:** chapel length, sweep train, floor length or tea length
- **Sizes:** 6 to 20 (also custom orders)
- **Price range:** $295 to $1,995

Restoration of Antique and Vintage Gowns

In addition to custom designing wedding gowns, Elsie can restore antique or vintage gowns your mother or grandmother may have worn. All alterations to reconstruct and fit the gown to your specifications are done with expert handwork. Elsie's provides consultation on Old World customs and offers an ideal Victorian setting for wedding portraits.

Bridal Attendant Attire, Headpieces, Mothers' Gowns, and Parasols

Custom-order bridesmaid dresses in all sizes. **Price:** $250. Junior bridesmaid and flower-girl dresses by custom order. **Price:** $195. One-of-a-kind, custom-order dresses in all sizes. **Price:** $295 to $695. Victorian-style hats, antique headpieces, garlands, and headpieces of handmade silk roses to complement your dress are on hand or can be custom made. **Price range:** $225.

CREATING FAMILY HEIRLOOMS

For over 24 years, Elsie's Victorian Bridal has been designing for the bride who wants that nostalgic touch of "something old"—something unique and reminiscent of days gone by. Each one-of-a-kind gown is designed and made by Elsie with exquisite embellishments of handmade antique imported lace, hand embroidery, and French hand sewing, making it a timeless creation that will become a family heirloom to be treasured for years to come.

HERE WE GO AGAIN

9519 S.W. Barbur Blvd.
Portland, Oregon 97219
Contact: Chris Gauger (503) 244-0855
Business Hours: Mon–Sat 10am–6pm;
Thurs 10am–8pm; Sun noon–4pm
E-mail: hwga@europa.com
Web site: http://www.hwga.com

Congratulations on your upcoming wedding! This should be an exciting, fun time for you, planning your celebration. At Here We Go Again, we wish you much joy, happiness and the perfect wedding. We'd love to help!

Gorgeous Gowns!

Although our selection changes constantly, we get designer gowns such as Demetrios, House of Bianchi, Venus, Moonlight, Scaasi, Diamond Collection, Alfred Angelo, Jessica McClintock, Mori Lee and many others. Occasionally we have European designers as well.

Our gowns come from a variety of sources. Most are consigned by women like you who, for whatever reason, don't wish to keep their gowns. Others come from bridal boutiques as overstock or floor samples. Still others come direct from manufacturers as overcuts or closeouts to supplement our stock and complete our size selection.

Great Value

Don't think for a moment we accept just any gown for consignment! We carefully screen all gowns, accepting only current styles that are cleaned and in perfect condition. We know you don't have time to sort through a bunch of out-of-date dresses to find the few gems. We inspect each gown to ensure quality and often send them to be cleaned a second time if they don't meet our standards. We're as picky as you are!

Impeccable Service

Shopping for a gown should be a fun experience. You don't have to spend a fortune to be treated like someone special — we love helping you! Regardless of your budget or size, we want to help you find the perfect gown. At Here We Go Again, you'll find unexpected extras: expert in-house alterations, convenient 7-day-a-week hours, layaway and flexible payment options, and noncommission sales people who really care — not about making the sale but about helping you find what you want.

Wish List Service

Since our stock changes rapidly, we might not have your gown today. We understand you're busy and can't come in every week to check. Give us an idea of the styles you like and your budget, and we'll review incoming gowns for a match. If the right gown comes in, we'll call you! This simple service can save you time — and might get you the perfect gown.

Check us out on-line at
http://www.hwga.com!

When you

Dream of the perfect dress...

Rosewood Bridal

we can make it happen.

11545 S.W. Durham Road
Tigard, Oregon 97224
Contact: Gail Herschbach (503) 603-0363
Business Hours: Mon–Tues 11am–7pm; Wed–Fri 11am–5:30pm; Sat 10am–5pm
Open Sundays January–March

ROSEWOOD BRIDAL ESTABLISHED ELEGANCE

Magnificent Selection of Wedding Gowns

Whether you're looking for sophisticated silk, an elaborate organza or a simple design, Rosewood Bridal has many styles, fabrics and colors to choose from. Rosewood Bridal not only features gowns from such designers as Jessica McClintock, Demetrios, Mon Cheri and many more, but also has an in-house design team who will help create your very own original gown.

Special Services

We provide services including alterations and shoe dyeing. All fittings are done at Rosewood Bridal. Wedding gowns are steamed and pressed at no charge and wedding gowns are stored at the shop to ensure their safety, also free of charge.

Bridal Attendant Attire and Mothers' Dresses

Rosewood offers a sophisticated line of bridesmaids' dresses in chiffons and velvets with a wide variety of styles and sizes available through special order. You will also find a large selection of flower girl dresses in Cinderella styles of silk and satin, and mothers have a selection of dresses to choose from in classy styles and colors. Not to leave out the groom, Rosewood Bridal carries an entire line of tuxedos.

Accessories

Rosewood Bridal carries a variety of accessories that you'll need for the finishing touch, including shoes, gloves, headpieces and jewelry. And for last-minute items, look no further. You'll find everything from wedding books, pens, ring pillows, goblets and cake cutters.

Genuine Pampering and Nurturing

Rosewood Bridal never pressures a client or pushes for a sale. The Rosewood associates work as a team to meet each bride's needs. There's no sales commission, no competition to force a sale—just true care and concern shown through personal attention. "It's a tradition a bride shares with her mom and closest friends...we do everything we can to enhance that experience," says Gail Herschbach, owner.

When to Visit Us

Rosewood Bridal will help you find the perfect dress in time for your wedding. Although we recommend visiting the shop at least six months before your wedding. Rosewood Bridal can often rush an order or fit a bride at the last minute with a gown off the rack. Rosewood Bridal strongly suggests making your first appointment at least one year before your wedding date if you plan to have a gown custom-designed at the store.

5331 S.W. Macadam Avenue
Portland, Oregon 97201
(503) 274-8940; Fax (503) 274-9843
Business Hours: Mon, Tue & Thu 10am–7pm; Wed 10am–8pm;
Fri 10am–9pm; Sat 10am–6pm; Sun noon–5pm

Congratulations on Your Coming Wedding

Your wedding day is one of the most unique and romantic days of your life. Planning your special day combines the talents of many people who wish to help make it the most memorable day for you to remember. Tower Bridal's friendly, well-trained consultants are dedicated to providing you and the members of your wedding party the best service available.

Wedding Gowns and Attendant Dresses

Our collection of gowns include romantic silk to traditional satin, crisp taffeta to floaty tulle. All are from designers you'll recognize from the pages of current Bridal Magazines: Priscilla of Boston, Galina, House of Bianchi, Jim Hjelm, Lila Broude, Alfred Sung and Alfred Angelo, to name a few. There are over 300 gowns to select from and they may be purchased from off the rack or you may special order to your specific size and color. Prices range from $150 to over $3,000.

Tower Bridal has a wide variety and selection of dresses that your attendants will enjoy wearing, available in all styles, fabrics and colors; from semi-formal to formal. Perfect complements to your gown and style. Flower girls and Mothers-of-the-Bride and Groom are not forgotten with a very special selection awaiting their choice.

Accessories

Veils, cathedral length or short and sassy; custom designed headpieces and tiaras from top designers; an excellent selection of shoes-all available in various fabrics and styles. We also offer lacy garters, lingerie, petticoats, ring bearer pillows, guest books and other select accessory items.

Special Service... with a smile

In-house alterations are available to give you that perfect fit with complimentary pressing to perfection, ready to go down the aisle. Charges for alterations will vary according to the work being done. Tuxedos, accessories and groomsmen gifts are available, the finest quality at the best price. Open 7 days a week with plenty of free parking.

We look forward to seeing you at Tower Bridal and we are committed to helping make your wedding day the happiest day in your life.

Unique Bridal Fashions

11906 N.E. Halsey
Portland, Oregon 97220
(503) 252-3973; Fax (503) 252-4212

In our 21st year as a family owned and operated business

In serving brides in the Northwest over the years, our gowns have been shipped to brides in other countries as well as all over the United States. In all our years in the bridal business, we have never missed a wedding yet!

Styles and Selection

Our customers tell us we have the best selection and prices. Our gowns are personally selected at the bridal markets by three generations, thus supplying a greater variety of styles to choose from. Our gowns start at around $300 and we stock sizes 4 through 44. If your wedding is soon we can always call to see if the manufacturer has the gown in stock, and if not, we will gladly sell you the one we have in the shop. Manufacturers we carry include Alfred Angelo, Mon Cheri, P.C. Mary's, Bridal Originals, Justine, Jacqueline, Jessica McClintock, Majestic, Golden Gate, On Fashions, Andrea by Lizzette Creations, Casablanca and Do You Love Me.

Visa, MasterCard and Discover are accepted. Our prices are always very reasonable.

A nonrefundable deposit is required to order. Convenient layaway is available for in-stock gowns. We stock five to six dozen headpieces at all times.

Special Services

We have dozens of bridesmaid dresses in the shop available in many sizes and colors. Prices start at $98 with a discount on orders of three or more. Many styles also have matching flower girl dresses.

We carry "Dyeable," "Colorific," and "Special Occasion" shoes, including children's sizes. We stock "Flattering Me" and "Goddess" foundation garments.

Our seamstress is in the shop on Tuesdays and Thursdays. Alterations are done efficiently, quickly, and at an affordable price.

We carry bride and groom t-shirts and caps. T-shirts are available for most members for the wedding party. You'll find other unique gifts in our store as well as boxed jewelry sets starting at $9.50.

It would be our pleasure to help you with your bridal needs while staying within your budget. We are conveniently located off I-84 and I-205.

TRADITION

By the 14th century, the bride's garter became so highly valued that guests would rush the bride at the altar to gain the garter's possession.

Today, things have settled down considerably. Now the groom throws the bride's garter to the unmarried men at the reception.

DRESS DESIGN AND ALTERATIONS

- **Dress design:** If you haven't found the dress of your dreams or if the dress you have in mind doesn't exist, take your ideas, pictures, and dreams to a dress designer. Designers offer a variety of options, taking a sleeve from one dress and a bodice from another to design a gown especially for you. Many expensive original designer dresses with designer prices can be copied, allowing you to stay within your budget.

- **Hemming:** Consult with a seamstress on hemming your dress. Many dresses can be lifted at the waistline to avoid taking lace off the entire hemline, and without distorting the lines and design of the dress. Also ask about ways to bustle up the train so it is comfortable and convenient for you to get around in at the reception.

- **Reserving alterations services:** As soon as you have selected your gown, be sure to make an appointment to reserve services for alterations. Many bridal-alterations specialists are booked months in advance. Your bridal shop can recommend a reliable seamstress or may have someone they work with. Brides should be prepared to pay for alterations and include this in their budget. They are never included in the price of the gown.

- **Making bridesmaid dresses:** You should buy the fabric all at once, even if each bridesmaid is paying for her own dress. Fabric comes in different dye lots and is difficult to match. Make sure that all the different fabrics you buy come from the same bolts to be sure everything matches. Remember to buy extra fabric, especially if you are working with delicate fabrics such as velvet or chiffon. This is not the time to come up short. Also, have the dresses made by the same seamstress to keep the dresses similar.

  NOTE: It's a good idea to make a demo dress in the style and fabric that you have selected, just to make sure you are getting what you want.

- **Length of bridesmaid dresses:** After you determine the length, hem all the dresses by measuring up from the floor. When marking the hemlines, be sure each bridesmaid is wearing the shoes she will be wearing for the wedding. This way, even though your bridesmaids are different heights, all the hemlines will align in the photographs.

For more assistance with staying organized during the wedding planning process, check out the Bravo! Wedding Organizer. Detailed question worksheets double as contracts. This step-by-step system will keep every detail of your wedding organized. *To order, refer to the order form on page 23 in this Guide.*

August Veils

4609 S.E. 35th Avenue
Portland, Oregon 97202
(503) 788-5280; Fax (503) 788-5281
Web site: www.augustveils.com

Congratulations! In the near future you will be realizing one of life's most rewarding moments—your wedding. Rewarding? Yes! Stressful, most definitely! Here at August Veils we can appreciate the planning and endless attention to detail that contribute to a wedding. The kind of details that make your experience uniquely yours.

Experience and Attention to Detail

Our staff specializes in the kind of skills and experience to help you create the headpiece or veil that is just right for your occasion. Relax and let August Veils guide you through creative choices, playful suggestions, all guided by technical expertise that will help make your decisions a reality. Imagine creating an elegant headpiece embellished with Austrian crystals, pearls, and sequins. Working with your designer to incorporate lace from your gown, bringing together the past and present by adding memories from your mother's or grandmother's wedding dresses—the choices are only limited by your imagination.

Affordable Elegance

You'll be surprised at the affordability and luxury of your own custom design. All of our special attention and quality custom work does not take as much time as one might think. August Veils prides itself not only on its craftsmanship, but also in ensuring customers with prompt service. Quick turnarounds are no surprise to us!

Call today for more information on how you can begin your design experience, or visit our Web site for viewing and on-line ordering information.

AniA
Collection
愛 婉 雅 禮 服
Andrea & Aileen

419 S.W. Fourth Avenue
Portland, Oregon 97204
Contact: Aileen (503) 796-9170
Business Hours: Mon–Sat 11am–6pm

Services

Designer Aileen can turn your vision of the perfect wedding gown into a reality. She can create a contemporary dress design using a New York Couture bridal studio to make the custom, one-of-a-kind design gowns. She uses only fine silk fabrics when making her designs. Bring in a photo, drawing or a description of what you would like, and Aileen will work with you to create an original wedding gown or bridesmaid dress.

Experience

Aileen did her design schooling in Taiwan and has been designing for over 10 years. She and her friend Andrea Hoyt recently opened their bridal boutique in downtown Portland.

Ordering and Cost

Brides or bridesmaids should plan to make an appointment and spend at least an hour with Aileen if working on an original design. It is recommended that you place an order four to six months before the wedding. Charges will vary depending on quality of fabric and intricacies of work.

Alterations

AniA Collection can recommend a number of experienced seamstresses for any needed alterations.

**We recommend appointments to ensure personalized service,
but walk-ins are welcomed warmly.**

fletcher artworks
ATELIER
and custom clothiers

Studio	Correspondence
1012 N.E. Brichwood Drive	P.O. Box 6614
Hillsboro, Oregon 97124	Aloha, Oregon 97007

Contact: Paula Smith-Danell
(503) 693-7725
Business Hours: by appointment

Services

We can help you create the dress of your dreams if you've been unable to find it or if you've found it but it is a costly haute couture original. If you have no idea what you want we can still help create a look for you that is unique.

We can create the perfect dress for you from just a drawing or one or more magazine cuttings; or you may want to peruse the vast fashion library for ideas, both contemporary or historical. If you are planning to wear your mother's or grandmother's dress but find you can't zip it up, we can alter or reconstruct the gown to fit you.

European Couture Experience

Paula has her bachelor's degree in Fashion Design from the American College for Applied Arts in London, England. She graduated summa cum laude and was awarded most outstanding graduate for her graduating class.

She has been in the fashion industry since 1984 and has been designing custom clothing and bridalwear since 1986. A portfolio is available for viewing by appointment, and references are available upon request.

Ordering your Dress

Please call for an appointment, and bring all your design ideas or plan to spend time looking through the many volumes of dress designs that Paula has spent years acquiring and cataloging. An estimate will be given at the time of the design selection, and a 50% deposit will be required when the dress is ordered. The balance will be due on receipt of the completed dress. Please plan on placing your order at least four months before your wedding date.

A series of measurements will be taken at our first meeting and will be turned into a flat pattern that will fit only you. It is helpful to bring the foundation garments that you are planning to wear as well as a shoe in the heel height that you are considering.

We will make a mock-up of your dress, so you can decide if this is the style you want. Any changes that you desire will happen at this point. Then it's on to the final fabric and final fitting, and you will have the dress of your dreams to wear on your special day.

Specializing in custom bridalwear
and women's tailored suits

Bridal Alterations by
Nahideh Nadjaran
(503) 590-7121
Business Hours: Appointment only

Nahideh has over 25 years experience in creative sewing, tailoring and alterations. She has been working on couture lines of bridal gowns such as Vera Wang, Lazaro Christo's and Amsale for more than 10 years. On your first visit with her, you will find out that her main focus is on creating the best fit possible for your gown.

Services
Nahideh also offers redesigning and alterations on new and antique gowns, bridesmaid, mother of the bride and flower girl dresses.

Appointments
Please make your reservation at least one month before the wedding.

Testimonials
"I just wanted to thank you on your beautiful and patient work on my gown. It is perfect! Even better than the dress, was working with you. Thank you for making this so very special."
— Lennette Lagler

"Thank you for all your help with my wedding gown. I feel I could not have worked with anyone better. Your knowledge, workmanship and personality make you someone very special. Thank you again."
— Robin Francisca

Bridal Showcase

I-5 to Exit #9, next to Clark Co. Fairgrounds
Vancouver, Washington
(360) 573-2817 or (503) 289-6324
Business Hours: Tues–Sat; call for an appointment

Description of Service and Experience
Most manufactured gowns are made for women who are size 10 and 5'8" tall. Since most of us aren't that size, it can be hard to find the perfect gown. Let Bridal Showcase fix it for you. From the simplest to the most difficult changes, our staff seamstress, Barbara Miller, can alter that dream gown to fit you perfectly. Custom-made gowns and complete makeovers of vintage gowns are also available. We begin with properly fitting bras to ensure a good fit, then design from a pattern, a sketch, or a picture of just an idea. We always make sure everything meets your specifications and tastes.

Our staff has years of experience in all areas of the bridal business. Our inventory of laces, appliqués, and trims makes selection easy. Come ask questions and look at our albums of previous projects and samples of our work. We gladly supply references.

Ordering and Cost
Most alterations take one week, but call for an appointment at least four to five weeks before your wedding. Custom-made and vintage-gown makeovers take 12 weeks, longer during the busy times of year. Each customer receives a firm bid in writing before any work is started.
♥ *Member of Weddings of Distinction*

"I DO" WEDDINGS™

Tualatin, Oregon
Contact: Heather K. Willig
(503) 692-8555; E-mail: idowedd@teleport.com
Business Hours: by appointment

The PROFESSIONAL ASSOCIATION of Custom Clothiers

Weddings™

CUSTOM SEWING • ALTERATIONS

Custom Dresses For Your Entire Wedding Party

Can't find the perfect bridesmaid's dress in the color of your choice without spending $200, not including alterations? We specialize in helping each bride accomplish their dream day wedding by creating custom made dream dresses for your attendants and flower girls *within your budget* and *on time*! Call *"I Do" Weddings™* today for an initial complimentary appointment!

No Rookies

With over 20 years of sewing experience, *"I Do" Weddings™* can also alter your off-the-rack wedding gown and attendants' dresses to create a custom fit dress just for you!

Availability

Out-of-town bridesmaids flying in at the last minute? Not a problem…just order your gowns no less than three months in advance because our calendar fills quickly.

Certification

"I Do" Weddings™ is a member of the Professional Association of Custom Clothiers, Oregon Chapter, a nonprofit organization formed to create unity among professional in the sewing industry.

Jennifer's Creations

"Designing one-of-a-kind Bridal Gowns"

Located in Vancouver, Washington
Contact: Jennifer (360) 573-2933

Description of Service

Jennifer's Creations specializes in designing and creating the gown of your dreams! You can choose everything including special sleeves, necklines, skirts, special effects and more. Size is no problem as your gown will be custom fit.

Ordering and Cost

A down payment of 50% will be required to begin your gown and reserve your date. The balance will be due when you pick up your finished gown. Call soon for a free consultation!

Other Services Include

• Alterations, bustling and exquisite beadwork
• Invitations, jewelry, gloves and accessories
• Authorized representative for Discount Bridal Service, Inc.® "A Personal Buying Service for Brides"—saving you 20%–40% on nationally advertised bridal gowns, bridesmaids and flowergirls.

Notes

THE BRIDE'S VALUE

The bride's value was judged by her beauty, ability to work, to produce children and by the size of her dowry. The more household goods, land and money the bride had in her dowry, the higher esteem she was held in.

HELPFUL HINTS

- **Creating your own dress:** There are two reasons for creating your own dress: when you can't find exactly what you are looking for at a bridal shop (but know exactly what you want from pictures you may have seen), or if you want to save money by creating your wedding gown yourself or with the help of a seamstress. An additional way to save money is to purchase the lace, sequins, and beading at a fabric store or craft shop and sew it on yourself. If you don't feel comfortable with this, your mother or grandmother may enjoy taking the time to hand sew beading and sequins. An original gown becomes one of sentimental value to be treasured and passed on to future generations.

- **Finding a seamstress:** Your fabric store, friends, or family may be able to recommend a good seamstress or dress designer who specializes in bridal gowns or evening attire. Or look under the section in this book for alterations and dress design. It is a good idea to work with someone who has experience. Working with an inexperienced seamstress can be a costly experiment, with the prices of special-occasion fabrics and laces.

- **Mock dress:** Make the bodice pattern you've chosen in a less expensive fabric to be sure it is the style you want. Alterations in the pattern can be made at this time to check the fit to your figure. Ask your seamstress what the cost will be for this extra step.

- **Buy extra fabric:** Always purchase a couple of extra yards of fabric in addition to the recommended amount on the pattern. You may choose to change a feature or add accessories. To find the exact fabric dye lot can be difficult a couple of months later. When making bridesmaid dresses, purchase the fabric all at once, even if the bridesmaids are paying for their fabric individually.

- **Creative, time-saving ideas:** If you're making your wedding gown or special-occasion attire yourself, ask your fabric store for suggestions. The clerk can answer your questions, offer new ideas, and save you time. Some fabric stores may even offer classes and seminars on fabrics, helpful hints and special accessories you can create.

- **Bridal accessories:** Fabric stores may also carry headpieces, caps, frames, and veiling for you or your seamstress to create your own unique headpiece or veil. Inquire about all the additional accessories they may be able to provide.

For more assistance with staying organized during the wedding planning process, check out the Bravo! Wedding Organizer. Detailed question worksheets double as contracts. This step-by-step system will keep every detail of your wedding organized. To order, refer to the order form on page 23 in this Guide.

AMERICAN SHOWCASE
Fabric • Trim • Bridal

3604 S.W. Macadam Avenue
Portland, Oregon 97201
(503) 242-9373
Business Hours: Mon–Sat 10am–6pm

Whether you're a last-minute bride or planning months in advance, American Showcase offers unique bridal fabrics and supplies. Come visit our showroom and see why other fabric stores refer their customers to us.

Comments
"Ohhh…it's just like eating chocolate."
"There are other fabric stores, but I come here because of the personal service."
"You always know exactly what I need."
"You don't come in here just to buy fabric—you know you'll leave with a total look."
"You know more of what I need than I do."
"If they don't have what you need, they'll bend over backwards to find it."

"I've Heard So Much About American Showcase"
This we hear all the time. American Showcase Fabrics is known not only for its wedding and bridal supplies but also as the place for fabrics for Miss Oregon, Miss Teen Oregon, Miss Rodeo Oregon and other pageants.

From time to time you'll run into famous celebrities and designers from Disney, sports, TV, movies, stage, opera, skating and dance looking for that perfect thing.

We Provide
- The finest imported fabrics, trims, rhinestones, pearls, beads, tiaras, headpieces, veils, gloves, feathers and jewelry
- Custom sewing, specializing in brides' and bridesmaids' dresses and veils
- Alterations
- Women's resale
- Rental: bridal, pageant and evening dresses
- Famous, expert designers
- Specializing in bridal, performing arts, worldwide pageants and competitions of any kind
- Unique, hard-to-find and specialty fabrics
- 39 years in business

Wholesale/Retail
American Showcase offers a very generous discount of 30–40% off "Bridal Fabric Package" to all brides who purchase fabric from us for their entire bridal party. Special orders included!

PROMPT SHIPMENT ANYWHERE IN THE WORLD

134 N.W. 8th Avenue
Portland, Oregon 97209
(503) 222-9033
Business Hours: Mon–Sat 10am–6pm; Sun 1-5pm

Fabrics and Patterns Available

- **Bridal-gown fabrics:** silks, satin, jacquard, brocade, taffeta, chiffon, organza, organdy, georgette, silk and cotton batiste, damask, velvet, dupioni, beaded and embroidered crêpes, and failles
- **Bridal gowns:** a selection of ready-made bridal dresses is available for try on and special orders; most dresses 30% off regular price
- **Patterns:** a full line of patterns available
- **Wedding party:** a large variety of fabrics for your bridesmaids, flower girls, and mothers of the bride and groom; from ornate to simply elegant, regardless of the season, you're sure to find the perfect fabrics **Price range:** $6 to $80 per yard. Special orders are encouraged.

Lace and Trims

- **Laces:** largest selection of beaded and plain Alençon and Venice laces in the Northwest **Price range:** $8 to $180 per yard.
- **Trims:** beaded or Venice frontal pieces, appliqués, pearls, sequins, ribbons, beaded fringe, and a large selection of trims

Headpieces and Veils

Unique finished headpieces and veils are available, or select from a full range of widths of illusion veiling. Many styles of wire and buckram frames are available to use with our extensive supply of flowers and pearl sprays.

Special Services and Bridal Accessories

Daisy Kingdom offers free demonstrations on bridal accessory design. For Daisy Kingdom customers, we have names of seamstresses specializing in weddings who are available to design or duplicate a gown or headpiece. Bridal gloves, garters, pillows, wedding books, slips, ribbon roses, and more are available.

AN EXCLUSIVE LOOK FOR YOUR WEDDING

At Daisy Kingdom, we've built our excellent reputation by carrying unique fabrics and accessories, providing superb service, and living by the philosophy of quality first! We enjoy working with brides to make sure they find the designs and fabrics to create the bridal gown and wedding party attire of their dreams.

700 S.E. 122nd • Portland, Oregon 97233
Contact: Bridal Department
(503) 252-9530
Visit our Web site: http://www.fabricdepot.com/

Fabrics and Patterns Available

- **Bridal-gown fabrics:** satin, brocade, shantung, taffeta, chiffon, organza, jacquard, georgette, Swiss batiste, damask, velvet, and linen.
- **Wedding party:** satin, taffeta, velvet, lamé, jacquard, silks, faille, crêpe, silk, and shantung.
- **Specialty silk:** dupioni, suiting, crêpe de chiné, beaded
- **Patterns:** full line of patterns available at 50% off every day

Lace, Trims and Accessories

Fabric Depot has almost every kind of lace in fabrics and trims. Many of our laces are available with beads and sequins, and in a large array of colors.

Laces: Galloon, Florence, Alençon, Venice, Chantilly, and embroidered organza

Trims: specialty trims include sequins, beaded dangle, satin piping, pearl edging, rhinestone strands, and button loops

Appliques and Motifs: huge variety of bodice motifs, collars, collar appliqués with and without beads and sequins

Buttons: large selection of fabulous special occasion buttons

Headpieces and Veils

We carry a large assortment of tiaras, hats, and headpieces. We also have a fabulous selection of tulle and netting in many colors and in 54", 72", and 108" widths. A variety of veiling including illusion, point de esprit, and Russian.

Special Services

The Palmer Pletsch International School of Serving Arts, located in our huge classroom, offers many specialized sewing classes to help with your bridal sewing projects, including classes in fit, cutwork, and couture sewing.

Discounts and Ordering

Fabric Depot offers a 40% discount off our already low retail prices when a "full bolt" (10–25 yards) is purchased. Special orders are available on most fabrics and notions.

OFFERING THE LARGEST SELECTION IN THE WEST

Fabric Depot has the largest in-stock quantities of fabrics, trims, and notions in the West. Our 40,000-square-foot retail store is an awesome display of every kind and type of fabric and notion available in the industry. Our fully stocked 30,000-square-foot attached warehouse allows us to provide large quantities of fabrics and notions.

Notes

THE BACHELOR PARTY

The traditional purpose of the bachelor party was to raise a special fund so that the groom could continue to go drinking with his buddies after the responsibility of the household budget had been taken over by the bride.

HELPFUL HINTS

- **Selecting formal wear:** There are a variety of formal wear styles available. The formal wear shop you decide to work with can offer suggestions for styles and colors that will appropriately fit the time of day. Even though etiquette books are very specific about what the groom and groomsmen should wear, in this day and age just about anything goes. Accessories to match the bridesmaid dresses are available for rent or purchase, or can be special ordered. Although the bride may help in deciding what the groom will wear, make sure that he is comfortable with the style selected.

- **Questions to ask:** Is the formal wear stocked locally? Are the locations convenient for the groomsmen? What is the price, and what does that include? Do you feel comfortable and confident that the formal wear store will deliver what you ordered?

- **Customized look for groom and groomsmen:** There are ways to bring out the personality of the groom and groomsmen and not sway too far from tradition. Paisley, plaid or polka dot cummerbunds and bow ties are a special flair that give a custom look. At the reception the groom can escape from the formal and put on sporty or Disney character accessories.

- **She keeps the gown, why shouldn't he keep his tux?:** A wonderful surprise for your groom is to purchase the tuxedo for his wedding present. This will make your groom feel as special as you do on the wedding day, with a tuxedo tailored to fit only him. There will be occasions to wear this tuxedo following the wedding day, many more occasions than a bride would have to wear her dress.

- **Buying a tuxedo:** Check into the purchase prices at your formal wear shop. If a tuxedo is worn four or more times per year for special occasions, it may be more cost-effective to own your own.

- **Final fitting and pickup date:** You must instruct each member of the wedding party to pick up his own tuxedo. Make sure they try on the entire outfit at the store. This will avoid the most common problem with formal wear—proper fit. If adjustments or replacements need to be made, they can usually be done right on the spot, or arrangements for substitutions can be made.

- **Out-of-town groomsmen and ushers:** If some of the groomsmen and ushers live out of town, the formal wear shop can supply you with measurement cards to mail back to them. Any clothing or alterations shop in the groomsman's home town should be able to do a complimentary fitting. It is imperative that these gentlemen take the time to try on their entire tuxedos when they pick them up!

- **Bring extra socks:** Have the groom buy a couple of extra pairs of socks to match the formal wear. Be sure these extra socks are on hand where the groomsmen plan to dress. It never fails that someone will show up with only white athletic socks. This may seem minor, but they stick out like a sore thumb in photographs.

- **Group rates and discounts:** Many formal wear shops offer special group rates, discounts or rebates for black-tie or black-tie-optional events. Ask about setting up a special rate for all the guests who will attend.

For more assistance with staying organized during the wedding planning process, check out the Bravo! Wedding Organizer. Detailed question worksheets double as contracts. This step-by-step system will keep every detail of your wedding organized. To order, refer to the order form on page 23 in this Guide.

BELLE AND BOW TIE TUX
Bridal and Formal Wear

Westside	*Northeast*	*Eastside*
8112 S.W. Beaverton-	*4300 N.E. Hancock*	*Ross Center*
Hillsdale Highway	*(at 43rd & Sandy)*	*11211 S.E. 82nd Ave.*
(503) 292-3557	*(503) 284-5969*	*(503) 652-7076*
Mon–Sat 8am–7pm	*Mon–Sat 9am–7pm*	*Mon–Sat 10am–7pm*

Formal Wear Styles

Twenty-seven different tuxedos to choose from, featuring Pierre Cardin, and Lord West. Some styles include tails; shawl collars; spencer waistcoats; double-breasted, notch, and peak lapels. Small boys' sizes available in most styles. Any style can be ordered for the larger sizes.

Price

- **Price range:** $75 to $95
- **Included** in price are coat, pant, shirt, shoes, jewelry (studs and cuff links), and all basic colors of bow ties and cummerbunds plus a few exotic ones
- **Optional items:** scarves, canes, gloves, and pocket squares reasonably priced
- **Alterations:** included in price and done in store

Ordering and Pickup

Reserving your tuxedos two months in advance is enough time. The groom and his party are registered upon ordering, and a file is kept to keep track of each person's measurement as he comes in. It is a must that each individual pick up his tuxedo and try it on. Usually, if there is a problem, a replacement can be made the same day.

Out-of-town Attendants

Belle & Bow can supply you with out-of-town sizing cards. These cards can be mailed to out-of-town attendants, who can get measured where they live and mail them back to the formal wear store where you registered.

Retail Accessories and Additional Services

The various retail items for sale are shirts, suspenders, vests, socks, pocket squares, top hats, scarves, gloves, jewelry, specialty bow ties, and cummerbunds.

Accessories in special colors can be ordered upon request. Belle & Bow Tie consultants can help you pick the suit appropriate for your wedding. We stock all tuxedos in our local Hollywood store, so last-minute orders are no problem.

ALL YOUR BRIDAL-ATTIRE NEEDS

We can help you with your bridal-attire needs from wedding gowns to formal wear for your entire wedding party. Come visit us today and see the number of ways we can make planning your wedding easier!

See page 226 under Bridal Accessories & Attire.

gingiss®
FORMALWEAR

You chose wisely.

Beaverton Town Square
(503) 643-7022

Clackamas Corner
(503) 653-7668

Web site:
http://www.gingiss.com

Vancouver Mall
(360) 256-6424

World's Largest Renter of Men's Formalwear

Formalwear Styles

Gingiss carries an assortment of name brands such as Lord West, Christian Dior, Perry Ellis and Oscar de la Renta. Our sizes range from 4 to 70. Because we have 275 stores nationwide, we have the ability to special order larger sizes and up-to-date styles to fit your wedding needs.

Price

Gingiss makes pricing easy. We run wedding specials each season. Gingiss offers a base price including coat, two styles of pants, standard tuxedo shirt in white or ivory, four choices of jewelry, solid color cummerbund and tie and suspenders. Then Gingiss gives you the option of upgrading using vests, hosiery, two styles of shoes, pocket squares, and button covers.

Gingiss Provides The Right Fit

Two people measuring the same person could come up with two different sizes. Why? Because measuring is an art not a science. At Gingiss, there is one nationwide measuring technique followed up with the final fitting one to two days before the wedding. If adjustments are needed to lengthen pants or shorten sleeves, it's not a problem. All Gingiss Formalwear consultants are trained to do alterations while you wait. *No appointments necessary.

Out-of-town Attendants and Guests

Out-of-town attendants are easy to handle with Gingiss Formalwear. Since we're the only nationwide formalwear specialist, we can ensure proper fitting for all your attendants, no matter where they live, through our Travel Tux Service.

Additional Services

Gingiss carries all merchandise in the stores. This allows us to provide try-ons, ability to do last-minute orders in as little as 20 minutes and fix an improper fit on the spot.

THE DIFFERENCE IN BLACK AND WHITE

With more than 275 stores and over 62 years of formalwear experience, the Gingiss name has been a hallmark of quality for more than half a century. When you register your wedding with Gingiss, you're assured of having the widest selection, the highest level of service and the most expert attention to detail and fit. We are "The Difference in Black and White."

Your Formal Wear Specialists

28 locations—also serving Corvallis and Eugene area

GRAND AVE	HOLLYWOOD	GRESHAM
(503) 232-1542	(503) 287-1725	(503) 667-6299
CLACKAMAS	**LAKE OSWEGO**	**PROGRESS**
(503) 659-2337	(503) 636-8911	(503) 626-6483
HILLSBORO	**EAST SALEM**	**SOUTH SALEM**
(503) 640-1838	(503) 371-7970	(503) 399-7989
MALL 205	**BEAVERTON**	**VANCOUVER**
(503) 254-1841	(503) 643-2661	(360) 253-9637

JANTZEN BEACH **HAZEL DELL**
(503) 247-9301 (360) 574-7768

MORE BRIDES TRUST MR. FORMAL
THAN ANY OTHER COMPANY

Why Trust Mr. Formal?
- ✦ Trust our **22 years of experience** in the formalwear business
- ✦ Mr. Formal is the largest formalwear company in the Northwest
- ✦ Largest inventory with over 15,000 tuxedos and accessories
- ✦ Professional formalwear staff to assist with your selection

Create the Look You Want
- ✦ Mr. Formal offers over 50 elegant tuxedo styles
- ✦ The elegant Oscar De La Renta and After Six lines
- ✦ Largest inventory of designer vests, jewelry, and accessory colors
- ✦ Our sizes range from 4 to 70

We Fit Your Budget
- ✦ **Price range:** start as low as **$69.95**
- ✦ **Included in price:** coat, pant, shirt, jewelry, cummerbund and tie
- ✦ **Enhancement items:** shoes, suspenders, pocket squares, hosiery and designer vests
- ✦ **Alterations:** included in price; alterations person is on staff
- ✦ **Price Promise:** We promise quality tuxedos at the best price available

The Convenience of Mr. Formal
- ✦ 28 convenient locations throughout the Puget Sound area and Oregon
- ✦ Out-of-town ordering is easy with our custom measurement cards
- ✦ Toll free number and fax machines available
- ✦ Tuxedos are locally stocked, so last minute changes are never a problem

OUR PRICE PROMISE
Our policy is "buyer's assurance." We promise quality tuxedos at the best price. If you find a better price elsewhere, we will match that price on the same manufacturer and style.

**Let Mr. Formal enhance the atmosphere of your
next event or fund raiser with our special group discounts.**

THE WEDDING TORCH

In ancient times the wedding torch—a symbol of life and love—was carried ahead of the bridal procession.

HELPFUL HINTS

- **Preparing your gown for the wedding day:** After alterations are performed on a new gown, have it cleaned, pressed, and padded with tissue so it is perfect and ready to go on your wedding day. Make an appointment for cleaning or pressing a new gown at least two weeks before the wedding.

- **Preserving your precious gown:** Your wedding dress is a sentimental and costly investment. Saving this investment means special handling, packaging, and dry cleaning by experts. You should not only clean the gown, but preserve and save its beauty as an heirloom for future generations. Many brides today have the pleasure of wearing their mother's or grandmother's dress on their wedding day because it was properly cleaned and preserved.

- **Dealing with stains:** When you bring your gown to your dry cleaner, it is important to point out any stains. Different stains require different treatments. Champagne stains in particular can be very difficult to discover, because they do not show up right away, but darken with age.

- **Choosing a wedding-gown specialist:** Today's wedding gowns feature beading, sequins, and pearls that require delicate care and special handling. Be sure to select a cleaner that specializes in gown cleaning and preservation.

- **Restoring heirloom dresses:** For brides choosing to wear an heirloom dress, don't be discouraged if it has become yellowed with age. In many cases a professional cleaner can restore the dress to 90% of its original color. Bring the dress in for an evaluation, and allow a month for this process to be done.

- **Avoiding common mistakes:** Avoid hanging your wedding gown over a prolonged time. This may cause the gown to stretch and sag. Fragile gowns should not be put in plastic bags, because moisture can form inside and promote mildew and fabric rot. Strong light, heat, or open air are other factors that will cause deterioration.

For more assistance with staying organized during the wedding planning process, check out the Bravo! Wedding Organizer. Detailed question worksheets double as contracts. This step-by-step system will keep every detail of your wedding organized. To order, refer to the order form on page 23 in this Guide.

TAILORS & CLEANERS SINCE 1951

939 S.W. 10th
Downtown at the corner of 10th & Salmon
Portland, Oregon 97205
(503) 227-1144
Business Hours: Mon–Fri 6:30am–6pm; Sat 7:30am–12:30pm

Unique, High Quality Cleaning Solvent

We are the only dry cleaner in the entire metro area to use the solvent Valclean. This solvent is guaranteed to be gentle to delicate wedding dresses. **It is proven not to harm beading, lace and handwork, or melt sequins on wedding gowns, formals, or special occasion dresses.** This solvent, as clear as water, is the safest method for properly cleaning your dress.

We clean all wedding dresses separate from any other clothes to ensure the best results. We produce the whitest, cleanest dress available because it is our policy not to compromise, and to go the extra step for our customers.

Professional Pressing

We pride ourselves on having one of the finest silk pressers in the city. With over 18 years of experience, you can be assured that your gown will be perfectly pressed for your special day.

Simply call to schedule, or bring in the dress a few days before the wedding, and we will have it pressed, delicately filled with tissue, and enclosed in plastic ready for your wedding day. Delivery to the church is available in certain areas. Fees begin at $55.

Expert in Preservation

We feel strongly that your special day should be remembered far into the future. After expertly cleaning your gown, we pack it in the highest quality box available with an acid-free liner and a mailing box, so that it may be easily shipped if necessary.

Between each fold we use museum approved, acid-free tissue and a bodice form, so that many years from now, when the time comes to pass it to the next generation, your gown will be as fresh as the day it was worn. Preservation fees begin at $125.

A Long History of Service

We have been in business for 47 years with the same ownership. Because of this, we are well into our second generation of brides and wedding parties. We have perfected gown cleaning and preservation like no other cleaner in the area. Come see for yourself!

> **Bee Tailors & Cleaners was voted by a Downtown newspaper as "Best Dry Cleaner" in Portland for four years in a row.**

Notes

WEDDING SHOWERS

The custom of giving wedding showers began in Holland, when friends or even entire communities gathered together to "stake" a young bride of modest means for all her household goods. The lack of dowry was considered to be an impediment to marriage.

HELPFUL HINTS

- **Unique shops for registry:** There are many wonderful stores where you can register. The china, glassware, flatware, and special accessories you select will be with you the rest of your lives. Look at the many registry stores in this book and remember, you can register at more than one.

- **Why you should register:** By registering, you let your family and friends know the gifts you would most like to have, and will ensure that what you receive will suit both your tastes and styles. Even if you and your fiancé can't imagine using fine china, stemware, and flatware in the near future, you'll appreciate them in years to come. It is very expensive to invest in formal china down the road. Family and guests enjoy giving gifts knowing they will be treasured and eventually passed on to future generations.

- **Mixing and matching:** Many shops allow you to mix and match your patterns to design your own dishware theme. Ask about ideas they may have. Most important, have fun selecting items that you and your fiancé will enjoy using.

- **When to register:** Soon after you become engaged is the best time to register. If your friends want to send engagement gifts, you can tell them where you are registered. Or for showers, your guests can select from a variety of items that you have on your "wish list."

- **Check with your registry:** It is a good idea to check your registry list periodically and keep it up to date with items you have received. Some gift givers will be making purchases in your behalf from other stores or will forget to let the store you are registered at know whom they are buying the gift for. It's nice for your guests to know what items you have or haven't received so they may plan their purchases accordingly.

- **Damaged items:** No business can be responsible for gifts that get broken after they leave their store. If gifts are damaged or broken, it usually happens in shipping. Packages that are carefully packed will reach you intact. However, if you find breakage upon unpacking, please call your delivery carrier (Postal Service or U.P.S.) for an inspection and claim. **NOTE:** Most shippers require that all packing, boxes, and wrappings be retained for inspection, so be sure to keep everything!

- **Thank-you notes:** It is important and proper etiquette to send thank-you notes immediately after receiving a gift. This way you let the gift giver know that the gift was received. Keep up with the many thank-you notes you will need to write, rather than waiting until after the honeymoon.

For more assistance with staying organized during the wedding planning process, check out the Bravo! Wedding Organizer. Detailed question worksheets double as contracts. This step-by-step system will keep every detail of your wedding organized. To order, refer to the order form on page 23 in this Guide.

the Wonder of it All.

Second Floor Home & Gift Collections

731 S.W. Morrison at Park
Portland, Oregon 97205
(503) 223-7121; Fax (503) 223-9754
Toll Free (800) 284-2044
Business Hours: Mon–Fri 10am–6pm; Sat 10am–5pm
Web site: http://www.carlgreve.com

WHY IS CARL GREVE
THE BRIDE'S FAVORITE STORE?

CHINA
- Bernardaud
- Calvin Klein
- Christian LaCroix
- Christofle
- Gien
- Hermes
- Lavre Japy
- Lynn Chase
- Mottahedeh
- Pickard
- Puiforcat
- Raynaud
- Richard Ginori
- Rosenthal
- Royal Worcester
- Spode
- Tiffany & Co.

- Vietri
- Villeroy & Boch
- Wedgwood

SILVER
- Christofle
- Gorham
- Jean Couzon
- Lunt
- Puiforcat
- Reed & Barton
- Retroneu
- Tiffany
- Wallace

CRYSTAL
- Baccarat
- Daum
- Hoya
- Kosta Boda
- Lalique
- Orrefors
- St. Louis
- Tiffany
- Waterford
- William Yeoward

GIFTWARE
- Anichini Linens
- Annie Glass
- Mariposa
- Nambé

EXCLUSIVE TO PORTLAND: Tiffany china, silver and crystal; Lynn Chase tableware; Hoya crystal; and William Yeoward crystal.

Services
- Table-Setting Seminars
- Exquisite Complimentary Giftwrap
- Interior and Home Design Services
- Designer Events and Trunk Shows
- Lavish Service
- A Knowledgeable Staff
- Exchanges Gladly
- Parking Validation

CARL GREVE
SECOND FLOOR HOME & GIFT COLLECTIONS
Bridal Registry • Distinctive Tablewares
Fine Bed, Bath and Table Linens • Distinctive Home Furnishings

COOK'S
CHINA, CRYSTAL & SILVER SHOP LLC

8538 S.W. Apple Way
(off Beaverton-Hillsdale Hwy.
next to Jesuit High School)
Portland, Oregon 97225
(503) 292-4312 • Fax (503) 292-3908
Business Hours: Mon–Fri
10am–5:30pm; Sat 10am–5pm

Cook's features one of the largest selections of china dinnerware, crystal stemware, and flatware in the Portland area since 1984. Our knowledgeable staff will assist couples in selecting patterns that they will use during their lives together. Registering at Cook's will benefit you and your guests. Congratulations on your upcoming wedding and best wishes to you both.

Cook's Features

- Arthur Court
- Baldwin Brass
- Belleek
- Block
- Christian Dior
- Colonial Candles
- Dansk
- Denby
- Eureka
- Gorham
- Hagerty
- Henckels
- International
- Kirk Stieff

- Kusak
- Lenox
- Lunt
- Marquis
- Minton
- Nambé
- Noritake
- Oneida
- Pickard
- Pimpernel
- Portmeirion
- Reed & Barton
- Riedel
- Rosenthal

- Royal Albert
- Royal Crown Derby
- Royal Doulton
- Royal Worcester
- Sasaki
- Schott
- Spode
- Towle
- Villeroy & Boch
- Wallace
- Waterford
- Wedgwood
- WMF Fraser
- Yamazaki
- and much more…

Cook's Services

- Specializes in everyday savings, quality, and service
- Features a modern, spacious showroom
- Employs knowledgeable bridal consultants to assist you with important selections
- Offers a convenient location with free parking
- (800) 574-1329 for your out-of-town guests
- Provides UPS delivery and gift wrap at a minimal charge
- Welcomes special orders at no extra charge

Bridal Registry/Completion Program

We offer a completion program which entitles all registered brides to an additional discount off already low prices on dinnerware, crystal and stainless/silverplate flatware patterns. This one-time purchase can include as many pieces as you need from our tabletop department and is good up to three months after your wedding. *An appointment is helpful to save you time.*

DISCOVER OUR VALUES!
Visit our Web site: http://www.cookschina.com

JCPENNEY

Clackamas
12300 S.E. 82nd Avenue
Portland, Oregon 97226
(503) 653-8830 ext. 231

Washington Square
9500 S.W. Washington Square Road
Portland, Oregon 97223
(503) 620-0750 ext. 234

Vancouver
8900 N.E. Van. Mall Drive
Vancouver, Washington 98662
(360) 254-3800 ext. 215

Salem
305 Liberty Street
Salem, Oregon 97301
(503) 585-4535 ext. 274

Eugene
300 Valley River Center
Eugene, Oregon 97401
(541) 342-6211 ext. 234

Also available at any of our 1,200 stores nationwide!
Call our national Gift Registry seven days a week: (800)-JCP-GIFT (527-4438)

How our Registry Works

JCPenney's complimentary gift registry offers you an opportunity to register at your convenience in your home or with one of our experienced consultants in our stores. In addition to what is available in our stores, we have gift registry catalogs and regular store catalogs to use when selecting your gifts. Our registries are immediately updated during the sale so as to eliminate gift duplication. JCPenney's toll-free number makes it effortless for family and friends to use our nationwide "SENDS Program" in the purchase and shipping of your gifts. Free gift boxes and wrap are also available for in-store purchases. Our consultants will assist you in the store with your selection of the items you and your intended have chosen for your future home. The process is quick and easy with the use of our scanners as you walk the store with the consultant. We also provide you with our "Registered At" cards to insert in your shower or bridal invitations. A complimentary wedding portfolio/planner is also given upon registration. Guest may also access your registry via the Internet at http://www.JCPenney.com.

The Best Way to Register

By registering with JCPenney, you can make your gift selections readily available to family and friends across the country. Just give us a call to make an appointment with one of our gift consultants. This ensures that you will never be rushed and the consultants can help you choose from a wide assortment of gift favorites found in our stores and catalogs. Although we recommend an appointment with a consultant, you may pick up a gift selection book from the gift registry and choose the "Do-It-Yourself" option if you are pressed for time. Whichever you choose, once you sign up, your gift list becomes easily accessible through JCPenney's nationwide gift registry network.

Returns and Exchanges

It's easy to return or exchange any gifts purchased through the gift registry at any of over 1,200 JCPenney stores. We have your gift registry on file for three months after your wedding, with a record of what items were purchased for you. Not only can we help you with your returns, but we can help you finish out items on your registry you wanted but did not receive. Handling returns or exchanges with your ease and satisfaction in mind is as important to us as selling you a gift that meets your needs. *JCPenney Gift Certificates Also Available!*

Items Available for Registry

- **Formal and casual china:** Mikasa, Noritake, Royal Doulton, Fitz & Floyd, Lenox, Pfaltzgraff, Villeroy & Boch, Nikko
- **Flatware and stemware:** Oneida, Reed & Barton, Towle, Wallace, Pfaltzgraff, Divinci, Royal Crystal Rock
- **Home accessories:** Martex, Croscill, Braun, Royal Velvet, Fieldcrest, Revere, Farberware, T-Fal, Crown Corning, Pyrex, Cuisinart, Kitchenaid, Oster, Braun, Black & Decker, Krups and many more

www.kitchenkaboodle.com

DOWNTOWN
SW 6th & Alder, second floor (503) 464-9545

BROADWAY
NE 16th & Broadway (503) 288-1500

CLACKAMAS TOWN CENTER
Across from Eddie Bauer (503) 652-2567

NORTHWEST
NW 23rd & Flanders (503) 241-4040

PROGRESS SQUARE
SW Hall Blvd. & Scholls Ferry Rd. (503) 643-5491

Order Toll Free: (800) 366-0161
e-mail: weddings@kitchenkaboodle.com

EVERY WEDDING IS SPECIAL. SHOULDN'T YOUR GIFTS BE, TOO?

Kitchen Kaboodle's Bridal Registry — like each of our five convenient Portland area stores — is brimming with a dazzling array of the kinds of things that give your house its special character. The kinds of things that make your house a home.

We carry just about everything you'll need as you begin your lives together. From high-quality cookware to decorative accessories, gorgeous dinnerware to finely-crafted furniture, Kitchen Kaboodle carries a wide variety of:

- Dinnerware
- Barware
- Stemware
- Cookware
- Bakeware

- Kitchen Appliances
- Gadgets & Utensils
- Cutlery
- Cook Books
- Table & Kitchen Linens

- Candles & Candlesticks
- Decorative Accessories
- Lamps & Rugs
- Furniture
- Much, much more

WE'VE DONE THE WORK SO YOU DON'T HAVE TO.

We know this is a busy time for you, so we burned the midnight oil to make sure our Bridal Registry is convenient and easy to use. Registry forms are available for you to complete at home or in the store. Each store updates your registry daily with items purchased at other locations, so your registry is always current. We'll even keep your registry list on file for one year following your wedding date.

BRIDAL SPECIALISTS IN EACH STORE.

In addition to the Bridal Specialists available in each of our five stores, our Bridal Consultant is available—(503) 243-5043 ext. 214, or (800) 366-0161 ext. 214—for free consultation. Our specialists will be happy to sit down, discuss your wants and needs, and recommend the products that will best meet those needs. They'll tap their years of experience to help you decide what items to include on your list.

All this and a free gift, too.
Mention the Bravo! Bridal Guide when you register with us and receive a free gift.

MEIER&FRANK

RIDAL REGISTRY
NATIONAL NETWORK
1-800-452-6323

Downtown
(503) 241-5158

Washington Square
(503) 620-3311, ext. 5158

Lloyd Center
(503) 281-4797, ext. 5158

Clackamas Town Center
(503) 653-8811, ext. 5158

Vancouver
(360) 256-4411, ext. 5158

Salem
(503) 363-2211, ext. 5158

The Best Way to Register

After you've set a wedding date, make one with our Bridal Registry. Come in together, four to six months before your wedding. You can scan the gifts you most want and need with the help of our professional bridal consultants or on your own. Choose from our large selection of china, crystal, flatware, kitchen items, bed and bath linens and more. With so many options, you won't need to register anywhere else!

How Our Registry Works

Our complimentary computerized registry makes your gift preference list available at nearly 300 May Company Department stores nationwide. It's all part of our coast-to-coast network that's convenient for all your family and friends wherever they live. Your Meier & Frank registry will be available at any of these fine May Company Department stores:

- **Famous-Barr** in Missouri, Illinois and Indiana
- **Filene's** in Massachusetts, New York, Connecticut, Maine and New Hampshire
- **Foley's** in Texas, Oklahoma, Arizona, Colorado and New Mexico
- **Hecht's** in Washington D.C., Virginia, Maryland, North Carolina and Pennsylvania
- **Kaufmann's** in New York, Pennsylvania, Ohio and West Virginia
- **L.S. Ayers** in Indiana
- **Robinsons-May** in California, Arizona and Nevada

Our bridal consultants will answer all your questions and provide as much, or as little assistance as you would like. Purchases made for you are recorded instantly and removed from your list in order to avoid gift duplication. We will also provide announcement cards to inform you family and friends that you are registered at Meier & Frank.

Policies

- Damages/Duplicates: we will gladly exchange duplicates or damaged gifts.
- After-Wedding Completion Offer: as a special offer to our registered couples, we offer a completion-discount program to assist you in completing your registry.
- Tabletop Club Plan: use our plan to complete your china, crystal, and flatware patterns. When you purchase $100 or more, you'll have up to one year to pay without finance charge when a minimum monthly payment is made when due.

Services

Your bridal registry will remain in our computer for 13 months after the wedding. Update us if you receive gifts purchased elsewhere; friends and family enjoy the convenience of calling and getting an updated gift list as your anniversary approaches.

We can also help your out-of-town guests with their gift purchases with our convenient toll-free number. By calling (800) 452-6323.

See page 46 under Bridal Shows & Events.

DOWNTOWN
901 S.W. Yamhill • Portland, Oregon 97205
(503) 223-9510

WASHINGTON SQUARE
9610 Washington Square • Portland, Oregon 97223
(503) 620-2243

Also located in the Oregon Market at the Portland Airport

We offer you the opportunity to let your wedding guests know about those unique items you've been dreaming of. At your convenience, come in and fill out a registry card with your chosen colors, themes or artists' work. We'll keep your information on file to guide your guests in their selection of a truly memorable wedding gift. Our knowledgeable and creative sales staff will help you choose items that you will love to receive and your guests will enjoy giving.

Everything you Need to Furnish your New Home with your Own Personal Style
- Fanciful and functional ceramics
- Art glass stemware
- Unique kitchen accessories
- Exotic wood humidors and jewelry boxes
- Creative lighting in wood, ceramic and glass
- One-of-a-kind garden accessories including fountains, lighting and chimes
- Handcrafted furniture

Services/Policies
- Layaway Available
- Gift Certificates
- Packing and Shipping
- Gift wrap available for a small fee

NO CASH REFUNDS, but exchanges gladly given within 10 days with a receipt or original gift box

See page 404 under Jewelry & Gifts.

If you're planning a wedding, plan a trip to Club Wedd.®

Think practical. Think fun. Think Club Wedd.

It's the best way to register for the things you need and, better yet, the things you want.

Registering is a breeze, so you and your fiancé can just have fun creating your wish list together.

Your guests will love the convenience of Club Wedd, too, since they can print your registry and pick out a gift at any Target store.

Registering is easy–here's how:

1) Just go to the Club Wedd kiosk at your nearest Target store and follow the simple instructions.
2) Next, stop by the Guest Services desk to pick up a bar code scanner.
3) Then, just stroll down our aisles and scan the items you want to appear on your list.

No appointment necessary.

Remember, everything's fair game. We've got your household covered. From a set of **dishes** to a pair of **mountain bikes**, a set of **tools**, the **camera** with the zoom lens, a classic **romantic movie** (don't forget the popcorn popper.) Just have fun.

It's quick.

After you've scanned all your requests, you're automatically registered. You can review your list and make any changes, then take a printout home with you that day!

The announcement.

Once you've registered with Club Wedd, let your friends and family know your wish list is ready for them at all Target stores across the country.

And it's only at Target.

ZELL BROS
Jewelers -.- Platinumsmiths

800 S.W. Morrison Street • Portland, Oregon 97205
(503) 227-8471 or (800) 444-8979; Fax (503) 223-8546
Business Hours: Mon–Fri 10am–5:30pm; Sat 10am–5pm

The Largest Selection of Fine China, Crystal, and Flatware in the Western U.S.

Mix Portland's early history with one of the city's most delightful traditions, and you have Zell Bros Jewelers. Since 1912, brides have been coming to Zell Bros to make their selections. Now we have more to offer than ever before! Choose from more than 450 patterns by over 100 manufacturers, for example:

- Royal Worcester & Spode
- Lalique
- Georg Jensen
- WMF
- Raynaud
- Saint Louis
- Nambé
- Wallace/Tuttle
- Allan Adler
- Denby
- Baccarat
- Thomas
- Buccellati
- Old Newbury Crafters
- Reed & Barton

- Waterford Marquis
- Orrefors
- Kosta Boda
- Jean Couzon
- Hutschenreuther
- Ginori
- Laure Japy
- Philippe Deshoulieres
- Gien
- Lunt
- Crane Stationery
- Lladro
- Christofle
- Royal Crown Derby
- Waterford

- Rosenthal
- Sasaki/Christian Dior
- Wedgwood
- Royal Doulton
- Herend
- Lenox
- Royal Copenhagen
- Villeroy & Boch
- Haviland
- Coquet
- Dansk
- Hermés
- PresenTense
- Puiforcat

Superior Personal Service

You can count on all the personal service you need and careful attention to detail. Here are just a few of the services we offer you:

- Bridal registry
- Complimentary gift wrap
- Full-service Stationery Department

- Exchanges gladly within 180 days
- Free jewelry inspection/cleaning
- Parking validation with purchase

WE HAVE EXACTLY WHAT YOU WANT.

See page 405 under Jewelry & Gifts.

Unforgettable Honeymoons Bridal Registry

Romantic Travel for Couples

5705 N.E. Fremont Street
Portland, Oregon
(503) 249-8444, (888) 343-6413

© Namale Resort 1998

"Well Wishers can contribute to your romantic,
once-in-a-lifetime Honeymoon."

How Our Registry Works

- Call Unforgettable Honeymoons for complimentary copies of our honeymoon planner and various cruise and destination brochures. Schedule your one-hour complimentary honeymoon consultation at our office in Portland (open evenings and Saturdays).
- After finalizing your travel plans, we will secure your reservations and require a minimal deposit of $150–$200 per couple. You'll receive a complete confirmation in writing as well as a destination packet with maps, tips and details about your trip.
- We will provide you with a set of registry cards and honeymoon gift certificate order forms (the first 50 are complimentary). These cards and order forms can be enclosed with your invitations, presented at bridal showers or distributed by your bridal party, family and friends.
- Guests may call us toll free to order honeymoon gift certificates over the phone, or they can mail a check or money order directly to us with the gift certificate order form. Each order form allows a space for them to write a personal message to both of you.
- You will be updated as often as you wish on the status of your registry. We will provide you with a list of the gift certificates purchased. The amount collected for each gift certificate will be placed in a special client trust account until the balance of your honeymoon is due (usually three to four weeks prior to departure).

"Our personalized honeymoon planning service,
combined with our unique honeymoon bridal registry,
will make your honeymoon completely care-free."

MAKE YOUR HONEYMOON DREAMS A REALITY...
CALL UNFORGETTABLE HONEYMOONS TODAY
(503) 249-8444

Please let this business know that you heard about them from the Bravo! Bridal Resource Guide. **275**

Notes

WEDDING CAKES

Wedding cakes can be traced back to ancient Rome. A simple wheat cake or biscuit was broken during the ceremony, with the bride and groom taking the first bites. The remainder was then crumbled over the bride's head to ensure a bountiful life with lots of children.

HELPFUL HINTS

- **The wedding cake:** You'll find many flavors and styles of cakes to choose from. Visit several shops and compare quality, style, and prices. Also, sample different flavors of cakes to help in selecting the flavor you want. The baker is a specialist, so ask for advice and recommendations. Remember, each tier can be a different flavor. Make sure the portfolio and samples you are viewing are work done by the current baker on staff.

- **Order your wedding cake early:** Busy wedding months are June through September; you will need to order your cake four to five months in advance if you're getting married in the summer. At ordering time, you need only an approximate number of guests. Confirm the number two to three weeks before your wedding.

- **Figuring the amount:** The baker will be helpful in advising you on the amount of cake needed based on the number of guests. The price is usually based on a per-slice amount. Be sure to ask about tier sizes and serving portions—are they pieces or slivers of cake?

- **Cake knife, server and instructions:** Don't forget to bring a knife and server to cut the wedding cake or have the caterer supply them. Make sure your baker provides you with instructions for cutting and serving your wedding cake. Because of their size and elegance, wedding cakes can be tricky to serve. Appoint someone to be in charge of cutting and serving and supply that person with the instructions, or ask your caterer if their servers can be available for this task.

- **Fountain cakes:** If you've decided on a fountain cake, an 18-inch bottom is required; you may have to buy a larger cake than you need. Also keep in mind that a fountain cake must be close to a wall outlet.

- **Wedding cake tops & decorations:** Most bakeries and bridal accessory stores have a large selection of cake tops: hand-blown glass, figurines, or ornaments that are permanent keepsakes. Fresh-flower arrangements are very popular and can be coordinated with your baker and florist. If you have chosen colored decorations, bring some color swatches or samples when ordering.

- **Personalized mints** in your color theme are available for your wedding. This is a special touch you may want to consider for your cake table.

- **Edible place cards:** Place cards made from the finest chocolates or cookies are a personalized touch for a formal wedding dinner.

- **Serve the wedding cake:** If you have waiters at your event, it is recommended to serve the cake to each guest rather than just placing cake on a table. This way guests won't take an extra piece or expect seconds.

- **A smaller wedding cake:** To save dollars, order a smaller wedding cake and decorate it with beautiful fresh flowers, ribbons or sugared fruits. Then have sheet cakes to cut for guests. The wedding cake can stay in place until all the sheet cakes are gone.

For more assistance with staying organized during the wedding planning process, check out the Bravo! Wedding Organizer. Detailed question worksheets double as contracts. This step-by-step system will keep every detail of your wedding organized. To order, refer to the order form on page 23 in this Guide.

CHOCOLATERIE
Bernard C.™
Award Winning, Belgian-Style Chocolate

4768 N.W. Bethany Blvd., Suite C-1
Portland, Oregon 97229
(503) 690-8982
Fax (503) 533-8178
Web site:
http://www.citysearch.com/pdx/bernardc

A Sweet Thank-You

A wedding is a magical occasion and you want all of your guests to feel as special as you do. The elegant Bernard C. white, copper or gold mini-box of two-to-four chocolates is a distinct way to say, "thank-you." We will help you choose the perfect chocolates, such as heart-shaped with custom centers and can customize the boxes with the bride and groom's names (printing charges apply).

About the Chocolate

When Bernard Callebaut arrived in Canada from Belgium in 1982, his goal was to produce a line of chocolates with a quality never before experienced by North Americans. In 1998, he became the first North American to be awarded the "Grand Prix International Artisan Chocolatier" at the International Chocolate Festival in Roanne, France. In addition to the grand prize, he captured the award for the best chocolate to accompany fine wines. The Belgian-born chocolate maker is renowned as an innovative creator of unique fillings for his chocolates. The centers the delicious chocolates are the freshest and highest quality available. The assortment consists of approximately 47 different centers with additional seasonal centers offered during the summer months. The chocolates do not contain any artificial additives in order to extend the in-store shelf life.

Where to Find Us

Ron and Barbara Cameron and Laura Adler invite you to try these irresistible chocolates at their Bernard C. Chocolaterie in the Bethany Village Centre. Take Sunset Highway (Hwy 26) to the Cornell-Bethany Boulevard (exit #65); turn right on Bethany Boulevard (north) for one-and-a-half miles to the Bethany Village Centre. We are *"under the clock tower."*

THE CAKE AFFAIR BY JOYCE MOORE

(at the Chic-N-Deli)
11239 S.E. Division Street, Portland, Oregon 97266
Contact: Joyce Moore (503) 256-5131
Business Hours: Mon–Fri 11am–6pm; Sat 10am–5pm

Types and Styles of Wedding Cakes

At The Cake Affair, we offer many special designs and styles of cakes. Or, if you prefer, we can work with your ideas to create your own special look. One of our specialties is fountain cakes with satellite stairways or streamers. We pride ourselves on our tasty and attractive traditional cakes as well.

Flavors include sour cream white or chocolate, German chocolate, Lady Baltimore, poppy seed, carrot, and raspberry swirl. Filling flavors include lemon, cherry, pineapple, fudge, butter cream, mocha, raspberry, strawberry parfait, chocolate, champagne, and many more! A favorite is chocolate marble. The best way to choose the flavor for your cake is to come in and sample our delicious flavors—it may take a while, but it's worth it!

Cost

The Cake Affair has a wide variety of styles and sizes of cakes from which to choose. You can order the very affordable to the ultramodern cake or an elegant creation that will serve 500. Our charges are based on the size and complexity of the order. A flat fee per cake is payable in full one week prior to the wedding.

Experience

We have more than 28 years' experience in the Portland-Vancouver area and have been at this location for the past ten years.

Ordering, Delivery, and Instructions

Orders should be placed six to eight weeks before the wedding, but we can accommodate shorter-notice orders when necessary. We offer free delivery and setup within five miles of our location. An additional fee is charged for delivery beyond five miles. Complimentary cake-cutting instructions are provided with each order.

Additional Items and Decorations

We have an elegant selection of cake tops made of litec, as well as other affordable and beautiful styles and designs. Or if you prefer, we can build a cake top to match your wedding colors and specifications. Grooms cakes are another option available at The Cake Affair, offering you a tasty addition to the food served at your reception—a nice way to recognize the groom on this special occasion.

THE CROWNING TOUCH TO A PERFECT DAY

We want your cake to be the crowning touch to your perfect day. We encourage couples to come in and let us assist them in designing the wedding cake of their dreams! Our decorator takes personal interest in each order. Come in to view our photos and read thank yous from our many happy brides.

Distinctive Weddings
by
Eden's Cakes and Catering

41707 S.E. Porter Road
Estacada, Oregon 97023
Contact: Virginia (503) 630-6131
Any hour by appointment; closed Sundays

Types and Styles of Wedding Cakes

We make wedding cakes in every flavor. Our special banana recipe or chocolate with raspberry filling are favorites with our brides. However, we have a large selection of other flavors available if desired. Every tier can be a different flavor. We'll design a traditional or modern-style cake—tiered or on pedestals, with satellite cakes, stairways, streamers, etc. Eden's will also custom design a cake to the bride's specifications. Frostings can be in white or ivory, with or without floral designs that match the bride's colors.

Cost

Cost is based on a per-head basis. A small deposit is required, with full payment due one week before your wedding. Your deposit is nonrefundable, but we will hold it for a later date if needed.

Service and Ordering

Eden's gives each bride personalized, custom service to make sure every order is exactly to the bride's specifications. Order your cake one to three months before your wedding.

Experience, Samples, Delivery, and Instructions

Eden's is a family-owned and -operated bakery that has specialized in wedding cakes for over 26 years. For us, it's a family tradition. We've recently opened a full-service catering and floral business to better serve our brides. Ask to see our portfolio. Samples are available before selecting.

Each cake is carefully boxed before delivery, so it arrives in the freshest possible condition—no dirt or dust. We'll deliver, set up your cake, and provide you with instructions for cutting at no extra charge.

LOTS OF PERSONAL SERVICE

Eden's is a family-owned, full-service catering and cake service. All our cakes are fresh, not frozen, using only the finest ingredients. We give you lots of personal service to eliminate the chance of error. Call for an appointment. We'll be glad to meet with you at a convenient time and location.

See page 305 under Caterers & Ice Carvings.

HANK'S PERFECTION BAKERY

661 S.E. Baseline
Hillsboro, Oregon 97123
Contact: Patty or Curtis (503) 648-4613
Business Hours: 6am–6pm

For your most special occasion, Perfection Bakery offers a wide selection of truly elegant, elaborate, and unique cake designs, and a knowledgeable staff to assist you in designing your perfect creation.

Our tradition of care and attention to detail has been passed along and refined for more than 65 years, using the finest ingredients available.

Our bakers and designers take pride in offering decadent cake flowers for your enjoyment. We offer the latest in shape designs from traditional rounds, to hearts, squares, rectangle and petal shapes.

We design the custom cake to your guest list needs, and the configuration to fill you heart's desire, including fountain stairs and unique stands.

Our personal one-on-one appointments allow you to sit and sample your cake flowers of choice and talk with a designer to determine your wedding needs.

We request orders 30 days in advance, but may accommodate shorter notice orders at our discretion. Full payment is required two weeks prior to delivery, with a full refund if canceled within five days of delivery the date.

Deliver and setup are free within the Hillsboro, Cornelius, and Forest Grove areas, with minimum mileage charges to Portland Metro Areas.

We encourage couples to come in and meet our knowledgeable and courteous staff and take advantage of our care and experience in planning your special day.

Perfection Bakery is a full-service bakery offering a full line of quality baked goods from pastries, cookies, breads, rolls and sheet cakes to fill your needs.

Call today for your appointment.

"Baking your dreams come true since 1924"
1717 N.E. Broadway
Portland, Oregon 97232
(503) 287-1251
Business Hours: Mon–Sat 6am–6pm

Types and Styles of Wedding Cakes

Helen Bernhard Bakery is known throughout the metro area for beautiful and delicious cakes, pastries, and desserts. We use only the finest and freshest ingredients, including real butter. All our cakes are made from scratch and come in round or square shapes, stacked or separated by pillars. Flavors include Lady Baltimore, yellow butter, chocolate, banana, carrot, poppy seed, pink champagne, white chocolate, and apple spice. Filling flavors include lemon, raspberry, French cream, chocolate, pineapple, mocha, mint, apricot and strawberry. We have a variety of decorating options and offer an excellent selection of cake ornaments that will complement your color theme.

Cost, Ordering, and Delivery

A $10 nonrefundable deposit is requested when ordering your cake, with the balance due two weeks prior to the wedding. We recommend that you come in and select your wedding cake at least 30 days before the wedding. We always try to accommodate the bride's busy schedule, so we do accept orders on shorter notice. No appointment is necessary unless you need to talk directly to a decorator. Delivery throughout the Portland Metro area is offered at no extra charge.

Experience, Service, and Samples

Helen Bernhard Bakery has been providing the finest cakes and confections available in the Portland and Vancouver area for over 70 years through four generations of bakers. We recommend that you come in to sample the different flavors of cakes we offer and to review portfolios of our work. One of our friendly and professional staff members or decorators will be glad to sit down with you to help determine the type, size, and style of cake that will best fit your needs.

Additional Items and Decorations

As a full-service bakery, Helen Bernhard's can create a variety of baked goods for you, including petit fours, sheet cakes, chocolate Genache groom's cake, breads, Danish pastries, donuts, pies, cookies, and cheesecakes. We also have beautiful porcelain, glass, and traditional cake tops from which to choose that can add a crowning glory to your wedding cake.

SERVING OUR THIRD GENERATION OF HAPPY BRIDES

Helen Bernhard Bakery understands how important the wedding cake is to every bride and groom. A wedding cake is not only a long-standing tradition, but will also be the focal point of your reception. We have received great pleasure and satisfaction in creating cakes for many happy brides over the years and look forward to serving you. Let Helen Bernhard's make your wedding day a beautiful and delicious memory!

BAKERY &
CHOCOLATIER

4733 S.E. Hawthorne
Portland, Oregon 97215
(503) 234-8115
Mon–Sat 6:30am–6pm

1997 United States Pastry Alliance gold medal winner
Winner of the Austin Family Business Award

Types and Styles of Wedding Cakes

If you're looking for a beautiful wedding cake, exquisite looking and luscious inside...A place where you can taste a variety of flavors and then select a different flavor for each tier...A place where you can get handmade mints to match your wedding colors...A place where you can get a special first-anniversary cake, just for the two of you, free...Then JaCiva's is your answer.

You can select a rich chocolate groom's cake or an assortment of Victorian tea pastries or chocolate truffles to make your rehearsal dinner or special-occasion event truly unique.

Cost, Ordering, and Delivery

Cost varies depending on the flavor, size, and style of cake. A $50 deposit is required, with the balance due two weeks before the wedding. Early ordering is suggested, especially for summer dates. JaCiva's delivers and sets up your cake free of charge in the local area. There is an additional fee for Sunday, private home and outside the metro area deliveries.

Chocolate and Other Gifts

JaCiva's offers a wonderful selection of wedding favors, groomsmen and bridesmaid gifts.

Wedding Accessories

Featuring the Beverley Clarke and Lilian Rose collection and others including; photo albums, ring pillows, pens, toasting glasses, cake and knife server, garters, etc.

"The cake must be a JaCiva's"

Bridal Connection July–August '96

CALL FOR A CONSULTATION WITH
JACIVA'S
"THE PERFECT PLACE TO FIND
YOUR PERFECT WEDDING CAKE"

♥ *Member of Weddings of Distinction*

Renaissance Wedding Cakes

1160 S.W. McGinnis Court
Troutdale, Oregon 97060
Contact: Karen
(503) 492-4208; Fax (503) 492-2904
E-mail: rwedcakes@aol.com
By appointment only

Types and Styles of Wedding Cakes

If you're interested in personal attention to detail and pride in workmanship then come and see me. All my cakes are made from scratch, from the finest freshest ingredients. Flavors of cake include my moist and luscious carrot and banana, white, butter, lemon, chocolate, German chocolate, poppyseed, spice, pink champagne and mocha. Some of our many fillings are lemon, raspberry, strawberry, fudge, cream cheese and cherry. There are a large variety of styles and shapes to choose from, and every tier can be a different flavor. You can have my light and creamy butter cream or my rolled fondant made from scratch.

Additional Items

Also available are groom's cakes, 1/2 sheets, 1/4 sheets, fountains, stairways, various cake stands and a large variety of ornaments that can be ordered for your convenience.

Cost

Cost is based on a per serving basis. A $50 nonrefundable deposit is required at time of order, with full payment due two weeks prior to the wedding. We like to have orders a month in advance, but we will always try to accommodate short notice.

Experience, Samples, Delivery and Instructions

I have 13 years experience in the Portland/Gresham area. Samples are available at consultations. Consultations are by appointment only. Delivery is available at no charge in the Gresham/Troutdale area. There will be a small charge for delivery elsewhere. Your cake will be boxed for delivery and cake cutting instructions are provided.

Personal Service Is Our Business

Renaissance is a family-owned business that believes very strongly in personal service. Give us a call—we will be glad to arrange a consultation.

YUM! YUM! YUM! YUM!

PIECE OF CAKE

Established in 1979
Winner of Chocolate Safari 1991
7858 S.E. 13th • Portland, Oregon
Contact: Marilyn DeVault, food designer (503) 234-9445
Business Hours: New hours, please call

YUM! YUM! YUM! YUM!

AWARD WINNING! AWARD WINNING!

We provide elegant, classical wedding cakes and fun, unique designs that are custom tailored to your wedding dreams.

Gourmet Cakes from Piece of Cake

◆ **CHEESECAKE WEDDING CAKE:** decadent and beautiful. YUM! Choose from vanilla, chocolate marble, deep chocolate, amaretto, chocolate amaretto, praline and cream, grand marnier, lemon, German chocolate, Kahlua, and white chocolate.

◆ **AWARD-WINNING FANTASY CAKE:** voted favorite of the year. Each tier consists of cheesecake, choice of filling, and cake. What a surprise. YUM!

◆ **CARROT:** a wonderfully moist, spicy carrot cake made with pineapple. YUM!

◆ **IRISH OATMEAL:** a moist oatmeal spice cake with a real homemade texture. YUM!

◆ **DOUBLE CHOCOLATE FUDGE:** the chocolate lover's choice… made with coffee and buttermilk, this cake is almost black with chocolate. YUM!

◆ **POPPYSEED:** made with sour cream and filled with marionberries. YUM!

◆ **CREAM CHEESE POUND CAKE:** a dense pound cake, rich with cream cheese and butter. YUM!

◆ **APPLE RUM:** packed with apples, raisins, and walnuts, then frosted with cream cheese frosting. YUM!

◆ **BANANA PINEAPPLE:** moist banana cake complemented with a hint of rum. YUM!

◆ **ITALIAN CREAM:** coconut, pecans and a taste of Italy. YUM!

TASTE!   YUM! Call (503) 234-9445 YUM!   TASTE!

LOOKING FOR SOMETHING TO ADD TO YOUR PRE-WEDDING FESTIVITIES?
ORDER ONE OF OUR BACHELORETTE OR BACHELOR PARTY CAKES.

CATERING   ◆   CATERING   ◆   CATERING   ◆   CATERING   ◆   CATERING

We Also Provide Classic Rolls Royce Limousine Service!
Chauffeur driven. Vroom! Vroom!

Piece of Cake follows in a three generation family tradition of catering and event services. Marilyn and her staff are food designers, and the cakes are always a work of art.

SUPERSTITIONS ABOUT WEDDING CAKES

It's bad luck for the bride to bake her own wedding cake.

•

The bride who samples her cake before it's cut will forfeit her husband's love.

•

When the bride saves a piece of her wedding cake, she ensures her husband's fidelity for life.

HELPFUL HINTS

- **Alcoholic beverages, alternative beverages, and rental equipment:**
  Distributors, wine shops, and some stores offer variety and savings when purchasing in bulk. In some instances, unused beverages may be returned for a refund. Touring wineries is an excellent opportunity to sample different varieties of wine for your event.

  Try alternative beverages with a flair. Juice and espresso bars feature drinks that can be enjoyable and a budget saver as well.

  Rental companies carry a variety of beverage-service equipment.

- **Hiring professional beverage servers:** Beverage service companies provide professionally trained staff who can handle complete bar services. These bartenders have the training and experience that help control potential liability issues involving the host or coordinator. Each bartender is required to have a permit to serve alcohol. This permit is received only after a course and testing on alcohol awareness is completed.
  Alcohol Service Law In Oregon: Any contracted bartender for pay is required to have the OLCC permit to serve alcohol. Volunteer servers do not need a service permit. **Alcohol Service Law In Washington:** Bartenders are not required to have a permit to serve alcohol for a private function.

- **Oregon and Washington Liquor Control Commission Laws:**
  In Oregon: private hosted bars featuring hard alcohol, beer, and wine do not require any special licensing. Private no-host bars may only feature beer and wine and do require a special day license. OLCC does not allow private no-host service of hard alcohol. Only OLCC licensed food and beverage establishments and caterers may sell hard alcohol. **In Washington:** private hosted bars featuring hard alcohol, beer, and wine do require a WLCC Banquet Permit. The permit must be obtained one week in advance at any Washington state liquor store. Private no-host bars are not allowed. Only WLCC licensed food and beverage establishments may provide no-host bars. For more information, contact: Oregon Liquor Control Commission at (503) 872-5070 or Washington Liquor Control Commission at (360) 260-6115.

- **Liability issues concerning the service of alcohol:** Find out who assumes the liability for alcohol service. Although the event facility and/or caterer carries liability insurance, the host or coordinator may still be considered liable. Make sure all parties involved with the event are properly insured and consult an insurance agent for appropriate coverage for yourself.

- **Banquet versus seated dinner:** It might be surprising, but a seated dinner can be less expensive than a buffet style. Each guest is served a specific portion, rather than guests helping themselves to seconds and thirds. If you schedule the reception in an off-hour, you'll spend less on food and alcohol.

- **Types of food:** Serving less labor intensive food is more cost effective. A baron of beef carved by a server with dinner rolls, salads, cheeses, fruit and veggies will cost less than hors d'oeuvres that take hours of preparation.

- **Catering saving ideas:** Ask your caterer if he/she has other parties they are preparing food for that day, and ask to use the same hors d' oeuvres to take advantage of bulk buying and preparation. Also, ask the waiters to pass the hors d' oeuvres rather than having a station; guests will only take one, rather than fill their plate.

HELPFUL HINTS

- **Menu at your reception:** The time of day will determine what you serve: for a morning wedding or event you will want to serve a brunch menu; hors d'oeuvres are perfect for afternoon receptions; and a sit-down dinner or buffet is appropriate for evening. If your event is at breakfast, lunch, or dinner time it is appropriate to serve food and beverage.

- **Catering guidelines:** It is important not to run out of food at the banquet or reception. Some people will have one plate and others will come back for thirds. Ask the caterers what their guidelines are and how they accommodate for extra people. Some will automatically provide for an additional 10%, for which you will be billed extra. Make sure to get estimates from several different caterers for the same menu to see how the prices vary, what portions, what is and isn't included. **NOTE:** Make sure the prices quoted will be valid for your event!

- **Estimating how many people:** Your caterer can help estimate the number of guests that you will need to serve based on how many people are invited. Some figure that 65% to 75% of the total number of guests invited will actually attend. With the expense of a sit-down dinner it is wise to send an R.S.V.P. card with your invitation, but consider that it is an additional expense and many people forget to send them back.

- **What the caterer supplies:** Caterers generally supply the dishware, flatware, glasses, cups, saucers, and table linens (special requests may be an additional charge). They normally can provide all servers, waiters, and bartenders, although these services may not be included in the quoted price. Make sure you know what all the extras are (including gratuities) and what they cost before signing a contract.

- **Delivery of food:** If the caterer delivers the food, make sure it is transported in warmers and coolers to ensure that it stays at the appropriate, safe temperature.

- **Serving the food:** You may want to instruct your caterer not to uncover food until the guests are through the receiving line. If you are not having a receiving line, prepared food for two servings—one set out and one kept in the kitchen until it is needed. **NOTE:** Do not leave food out for long periods of time unless hot food is in chafing dishes and cold food is on ice. For buffet style, set plates at the beginning of the buffet table and napkins and silverware at the end. This way guests will not have to juggle forks and napkins while getting their food. (See helpful hints for liquor laws, liability and beverage service on page 288.)

- **Food stations:** Food stations can please a wide variety of guests...pasta, Mexican, seafood and vegetarian (15% of your guests will be vegetarians). Stations can also assist in keeping down long lines that occur with only one buffet table.

For more assistance with staying organized during the wedding planning process, check out the Bravo! Wedding Organizer. Detailed question worksheets double as contracts. This step-by-step system will keep every detail of your wedding organized. To order, refer to the order form on page 23 in this Guide.

PROFESSIONAL ICE CARVING

*Sculptor: **Christopher Huessy***
Contact: Dennise Huessy

Warehouse	***Office***
(503) 557-0650	*(503) 654-0075*

Traditional Sizes

• Full Size: 20" by 40" • Half Size: 20" by 20" • Multiple block sizes available
All sizes are available in clear or with color. Some specialty carvings include roses frozen in the ice. Carving detail generally lasts four to six hours.

Professional Background

Professional Ice Carving is a well-established full-time business. Our sculptor, Christopher Huessy, is a talented ice carver with over 25 years of experience. In addition to private affairs, we are currently servicing over 90 of the finest caterers, clubs, hotels, restaurants and professional organizations within the Portland Metropolitan area. Christopher is a leader in his industry, having custom designed and built his own ice block machine that produces 300-pound clear block ice, thus to ensure the quality of our product.

International Competition Medals and Honors

1998 – Competitor – The Nagano Winter Olympics Ice Carving Competition – Karuizawa, Japan
1997 – Sapporo Snow Festival – Sapporo, Japan
1996 – Gold medal – Anchorage, Alaska
1996 – Gold medal – Asahikaiwa, Japan
1994 – Gold medal – Fairbanks, Alaska
1993 – Gold medal – Lake Louise, Alberta Canada
Christopher competes internationally to continue to offer "cutting edge" technology and to remain up-to-date on styles and trends.

Corporate Focus

Ice sculptures are a classic expression of prestige. Our ability to create an image in ice is as vast as your imagination. All sculptures are handcarved with artistic flair, and various images can be created for all kinds of events, from the "traditional" to "contemporary." We pride ourselves on our ability to reproduce business logos, complete with color. From practical shapes to extravagant masterpieces, you can rest assured you are in qualified hands.

Services

We take care of the details. What sets us apart is not just our ice carving but our consulting, delivery, safety, setup and expertise. Call for a personal appointment, and we'll be happy to assist you in creating an extraordinary event. We welcome your ideas and work with you to create the perfect affair!

Endorsements

Golf & Country Clubs	**Hotels & Inns**	**Retail Chains**
Columbia Edgewater Country Club	Benson Hotel	AT&T Wireless
Multnomah Athletic Club	DoubleTree Hotels	Ben Bridge
Oregon Golf Club	Hilton Hotel	Fred Meyer
Portland Golf Club	Holiday Inns	Meier & Frank
Pumpkin Ridge Golf Club	RiverPlace Hotel	Nordstrom
The Reserve Vineyards & Golf Club	Timberline Lodge	Safeway

INTEL • NIKE • OHSU • OMSI • OREGON CONVENTION CENTER • PSU • ROSE FESTIVAL ASSOC. • US BANK

We invite comparison

Please let this business know that you heard about them from the Bravo! Bridal Resource Guide.

(Located inside West Linn Thriftway)
5639 Hood Street • West Linn, Oregon 97068
(503) 656-2981; Fax (503) 650-1230

A "Taste of Holland" Bakeries, Catering and Floral

- works with you in creating a one-of-a-kind masterpiece

- allows you to sample several different cakes and fillings

- provides highly skilled color matching from your samples

- creates the finest quality wedding cakes in the nation as judged by National Retail Bakers Association

- provide a free first anniversary cake

- provide expanded delivery outside of metro area for a nominal fee

- provide elegant catering and flowers for any occasion

Our award-winning bakery team will assist you in selecting from our large assortment of elegant Dutch pastries, gourmet cookies and breads to make your wedding day memorable.

Cost, Ordering and Delivery

We encourage you to come in to order your wedding cake. This allows you to view our portfolio and sample our quality. We request a 20% nonrefundable deposit with your order.

Ask about our

FREE

Anniversary Cake.

Photography by Adams & Faith

918 S.W. Yamhill, Second Floor
Portland, Oregon 97205
Contact: Philip Sword or Barbara Abalan
(503) 227-4061

Accent ON EVENTS, INC.

Full Service Catering and Special Event Production
WEDDINGS, CORPORATE & PRIVATE CELEBRATIONS

Experience

Philip Sword has served 15 years in the catering and special event industry. Nine years were spent in Los Angeles producing high profile events for celebrity clientele. Uniquely qualified in fabulous food, incredible presentations, ambience design, logistics, operations and the ability to "make it happen," Accent on Events, create magical and unforgettable weddings without spending a fortune. We believe our assistance to be invaluable and our experience and knowledge unparalleled. Accent on Events operate The Adrianna Hill Grand Ballroom and serve as its caterer and event coordinator. Our extensive off-premise experience make us available for any facility you may have chosen.

Menu Planning

Although we have numerous pre-planned menus for all occasions, we typically custom design most menus based on personal requests and budgets allowance. From sit-down service and buffet style to hors d'oeuvres receptions, the same meticulous attention to detail is always given.

Cost

Custom designed to meet your specific budget and requests.

Terms

A 50% deposit is required to confirm date and services. Balance due at close of event. Early reservations are suggested.

Alcohol

All dispensing of alcohol is in accordance with current OLCC Rules and Regulations. We hold a Caterers Dispensing license to legally provide and serve beer, wine and spirits at special events and carry full liability insurance.

Additional Services

We can recommend and assist you with any other services you may wish to subcontract (photography, entertainment, bakery, florist, etc.) We know the best.

**You are invited to schedule an appointment
at one of Portland's most unique locations or
at your chosen facility to discuss your wedding.**

Distinctive Catering

AN ELEGANT AFFAIR

P.O. Box 80013
Portland, Oregon 97280
Contact: Melody
(503) 245-2802; Fax (503) 246-4309

Brides…You are cordially invited to An Elegant Affair…Your wedding!

Types of Menus and Specialties

Catering is our only business. An Elegant Affair catering will carefully plan, prepare, and present a tantalizing bill of fare created specifically to fit your wedding budget and needs. Whether it's a formal sit-down dinner, an intimate hors d'oeuvres reception, or a fabulous rehearsal dinner, we are committed to making your wedding an elegant one!

Services and Cost

- **Menu planning:** Our seasoned staff can prepare any type of cuisine in our fully licensed catering kitchen, and we are happy to design a menu that will suit your special occasion.
- **Estimating number of guests:** We can help you determine how many guests to expect to ensure accurate food quantities are ordered.
- **Cost:** Our prices are determined on a per-person basis and vary upon menu selection. A 25% deposit is required to reserve your event date. The balance is due before the event.
- **Beverage service:** Alcoholic and nonalcoholic beverages are available.
- **Linens and napkins:** Buffet table linen and skirting no charge; paper products no charge; white and colored linen tablecloths and napkins available.
- **Serviceware:** Silver serving trays available no charge; china, glassware, paper, plastic available.
- **Riverboat receptions and parties:** Available year-round on the Willamette.
- **Servers:** We supply experienced, professional servers and bartenders in formal black and white attire. Setup, serving, and complete cleanup of all food and beverages are always provided at no extra charge.

For your entertaining ease, let AN ELEGANT AFFAIR help make your special day a worry-free and memorable event.

You'll find hosting a special occasion will never be easier or more enjoyable.

**Call today for a complimentary consultation!
(503) 245-2802**

Applewood Catering

Chef Peter Leigh Gallin

HOOD RIVER, OREGON   VANCOUVER, WASHINGTON

541.386.2144 360.260.0379

E-mail: applwood@pacifier.com

Specializing in Fresh Northwest and International Cuisine

Applewood Catering combines an international flavor with the colorful bounty of fresh Northwest ingredients to bring you healthy and unique menus tailored to fit any palate and budget. Chef Peter Leigh Gallin hand selects the freshest Northwest fruits, produce, meats and seafood to create a meal that will be an enchanting event. Combined with artistic presentation and refined professional service, your wedding will be an occasion you and your guests will never forget.

Full-Service Catering for Any Occasion—From Elegant to Casual

Applewood Catering is a full-service caterer able to work closely with you to ensure your wedding is the celebration you deserve. Whether you need catering for six or 600, we can arrange for every necessity; from all rentals and staffing, to cake, photographer and flowers, as well as the site.

Applewood Catering is experienced in large formal weddings, rehearsal dinners and elegant hors d'oeuvres as well as small intimate repasts and cooking classes. Let Chef Peter and Applewood's trained professional staff handle all the details to make your reception an event you and your guests will truly enjoy.

Chef Peter Leigh Gallin, Creative Catering since 1990

Chef Peter is a graduate of the renowned California Culinary Academy where he studied classical French cooking techniques. In addition, he has traveled and lived throughout the world where he has gained culinary influences from cuisines across the globe.

He is a devotee to better living through healthy eating and is a cooking instructor as well as a caterer. He has worked as Chef du Cuisine at numerous restaurants throughout the Rocky Mountains and now calls the Pacific Northwest home.

Serving Greater Portland, Vancouver and the Columbia River Gorge

Professionalism • Experience • Creativity

Applewood Catering
Call today for a consultation or brochure
(360) 260-0379 or (541) 386-2144
Applwood@pacifier.com

12003 N.E. Ainsworth Circle, Suite A
Portland, Oregon 97220
Contact: Christian or Annette Joly
(503) 252-1718; Fax (503) 252-0178
Business Hours: Mon–Fri 7am–7pm
Web site: http://www.caperscafe.com

If You're Entertaining Very Important People... We Deliver

When you want to electrify a crowd, nothing causes quite the stir like food prepared by Capers Cafe and Catering Company. Bold, imaginative food... presented with both precision and panache. You've probably got some great ideas. So do we. And together we will plan an event that's destined to be remembered and implemented precisely as planned. All foods are prepared from fresh Northwest products with emphasis on taste and appearance.

Banquet and Reception Site

Capers is able to accommodate private rehearsal dinners and receptions up to 150.

Cost

Cost is based on the food selection and type of event. All costs are itemized and on a per-person basis. A 50% deposit is required upon confirmation of event. Cancellations may be made 10 days prior to the event.

Experience

With 25 years experience in the industry, Christian Joly has prepared international events for 2,000, as well as intimate dinners for two.

Services

Capers Cafe and Catering Company is a fully licensed and insured caterer, capable of providing any style of food and beverage that a customer may require. Seven days a week.

Food Preparation and Equipment

Capers Cafe and Catering Company prepares all foods with flair, putting heavy emphasis on taste and visual appearance.

Serving Attendants

To ensure a successful event, we provide all the necessary professionals to prepare, serve, and clean up. Gratuities are optional.

OUR FOODS AND SERVICES
ARE 100% GUARANTEED

Capers Cafe and Catering Company is an extremely successful business because of its employees. Our staff believes in satisfying all the needs of our customers. We never take shortcuts and guarantee our foods and services 100%, or we return your money. *We are at your service.*

CAROUSEL CATERING

223 S.E. 122nd Avenue • Portland, Oregon 97233
Contact: Catering Department (503) 261-9424; Fax (503) 261-2989
E-mail: khandley11@aol.com; Web site: http://www.lum.com/fountainsballroom
Business Hours: Tues, Wed, Thurs 9am–9pm or by appointment

"Stress-Free One Stop Wedding Planning"

Types of Menus and Specialty

Carousel Catering works with you to design a menu that suits your personality, style, and theme. We offer hors d'oeuvres, self-serve buffets, and sit-down meals. We cater anything from large sit-down dinners to a private party for two. All food is beautifully arranged and garnished with freshly carved centerpieces. We offer one stop planning—taking away your stress on the most important day of your life. We offer our own on-site facility located at The Fountains Ballroom. Ask about our photography, flowers, printing and decorating services.

Cost

Packages range from $6.95 to $40 per person. A nonrefundable deposit of $250 is required to reserve your date with the balance due 10 days prior to your event. A 20% gratuity will be added to the final food bill.

Services: On-site and off-site—We're located at The Fountains Ballroom

- **Wedding cakes:** each cake custom-made; choose from over 14 flavors and 12 fillings; each layer can be a different flavor at no additional charge.
- **Espresso:** full-service espresso catering featuring Mochas, Lattés, Italian Sodas and more, offering your guests a unique alternative to alcoholic beverages
- **Beverages:** assorted nonalcoholic beverages available; alcoholic beverages may be added to contract—we are fully licensed and insured; full bar, beer and wine service available
- **Dishes and glassware:** crystal dishes and cups; champagne, beer, and wine glasses available in glass or plastic
- **Linens:** coordinated linens, napkins, and table skirting; personalized paper napkins
- **Serviceware:** silver tea service; silver punch bowl, nut and mint trays, candelabra; silver champagne cooler and toasting glasses
- **Floral arrangements and ice carvings:** elegant floral arrangements for food and cake tables; specialize in freehand ice carvings, any size and design
- **Events:** we are wedding specialists; however, we also do corporate events from formal sit-down to box lunches.

See page 140 under Banquet & Reception Sites.
See page 484 under Photographers.

Restaurant and Catering
1331 S.W. Washington
Portland, Oregon 97205
Contact: Christine, Bob or Mercedes
(503) 223-0054

A Portland Favorite since 1979!

Cassidy's Restaurant is located in a historic building in the heart of downtown Portland. Our exceptional menu features regional cuisine of delicious seafood, premium-cut meats, fresh pastas, seasonal salads and more.

Full-service Catering

Cassidy's is experienced in catering all wedding-related events including rehearsal dinners, wedding brunches and full receptions.

Services

- **Food**   From a sit-down dinner or extensive buffet to appetizers and desserts, we offer our fresh Northwest specialties. We'll help you plan a menu just right for your occasion.

- **Beverage**   Cassidy's Restaurant is completely licensed and insured to serve alcohol and also offers a wide assortment of nonalcoholic beverages.

- **Cost**   We are happy to work within your budget.

- **Staff**   Cassidy's staff of experienced restaurant professionals also services our catered events.

Private Banquet Room and Full-service Restaurant

Cassidy's has a private dining room available for receptions and rehearsal dinners up to 50 people. On weekend days Cassidy's offers the entire restaurant facility to private parties for receptions up to 300 people.

RESERVE THE ENTIRE RESTAURANT FOR AFTERNOON WEEKEND RECEPTIONS!

See page 70 under Rehearsal Dinner Sites.

Contact: Sandra or Karla
(503) 238-8889

Seriously Now...

Catering At Its Best takes quality seriously and continuously pushes it to higher levels. Offering unique blends of Northwest native flavors, uncompromised freshness and meticulous organization—our events and galas sparkle. Exacting standards, gracious professionalism, and a detailed understanding of artful, delicious presentation create wonderful celebrations!

They Say It's All in the Past—We Believe the Best is Yet to Come

Experience has groomed Catering At Its Best. Planning for the unforeseen, preparing for the "what ifs," and asking simple questions set the mark for professionalism. Members of our catering team are proficient, organized and thoughtful. The wait staff offers crisp, groomed service, artistic, bountiful presentation and thorough completion of all tasks. Behind the scenes, the Chefs create works of art with only top grade, fine quality ingredients. Quantities are carefully calculated—unpretentious abundance is the benchmark.

Atmosphere is for the Stars

Regardless of a location's character, the atmosphere can be formalized, refined or made to appear fun and festive. Catering At Its Best inventories a full line of serviceware, providing color-coordinated linens and is home to a wealth of props and decorations. About a month before your event, plan to meet at your site and we will set the plans to make your dreams, ideas and details a reality! Creativity, ingenuity and experience help transform your ideas into realization, props into ambiance, banquet halls into gala ballrooms, and Mother Nature into paradise.

We Get Around!

Catering At Its Best has partied all over town! We are approved to serve in major locations in and about Portland including the Crystal Dolphin, the Jenkins Estate, the Sternwheeler Rose, Canterbury Falls and The Old Church. Catering At Its Best is the exclusive caterer for Kingstad Meeting Centers. We welcome our clients to visit our kitchen, discuss plans and sample flavors and presentation.

Energized for the Future

Because brides and grooms rarely have a chance to eat at their own receptions, we prepare beautiful individual meals and a chilled bottle of champagne just in time to escape for the honeymoon!

Call Now!

Please call Karla or Sandy to arrange a meeting or to receive sample menus.

1972 N.W. Flanders
Portland, Oregon 97209

NO THEME TOO EXOTIC; NO CUISINE TOO ESOTERIC

Types of Menus and Specialty

Our fare ranges from New Age/organic to classical decadence. We can design menus for casual or formal dining—from receptions and rehearsal dinners to bridal showers and anniversary dinners for two. We offer on- and off-premise catering. Ask about our honeymoon packages.

Think of Us for

LIFE CYCLE EVENTS	*CORPORATE FUNCTIONS*	*SOCIAL EVENTS*
Wedding Receptions	Company Picnics/BBQs	Teas/Brunches
Rehearsal Dinners	Holiday Parties	Cocktail Parties
Bar/Bat Mitzvahs	Grand Openings	Reunions
Birthdays/Anniversaries	Business Meetings	Retirements

Cakes

Wedding cakes from the simple to the elaborate; all types of flavors and fillings. Prices start at $1.50 per person. We also can create groom's cakes, first anniversary cakes and cakes for other special occasions. Call for an appointment to view photographs; samples available.

Cost

Reasonably priced. Free consultation and planning.

Experience

Chef du Jour Catering has been in business for seven years. We are the caterer for Congregation Beth Israel in Northwest Portland. We use the freshest available product and classical preparation techniques. Each menu is designed to meet the individual customer's desires and needs.

Service

Chef du Jour is a full-service caterer and can provide linens, glassware, centerpieces or anything else you need for your event. We have a professionally trained staff, attractive and healthy food and innovative food styling. We also offer decorating and florist services and pickup and delivery.

CATERING WITH A DIFFERENCE!

Dale's Catering Service

Always in good taste!

2420 S.E. Belmont Street • Portland, Oregon 97214
(503) 234-9948; Fax (503) 236-9346

Specialized menus for
each client since 1945

Experience

Dale's Catering has been serving Portland and the surrounding metropolitan communities since 1945. We pride ourselves on our commitment to our clients.

Types of Menus and Specialty

Dale's Catering will prepare food for any type of event from the most formal of weddings to large company dinners and sporting events. At Dale's Catering we believe that each wedding has its own unique personality and that the menu and service should reflect that personality. We can provide everything from formal wedding dinners served in courses to very simple hors d'oeuvres prepared, trayed, and delivered to your reception site.

Cost and Services

Because we are a full-service catering company, we can provide you with:

- **A menu designed especially for you.**
- **Equipment:** silver coffee and tea service, silver punch bowl, coffee urn, candelabras, cake knife and server, china, glassware, silverware, linens, linen napkins, paper and plastic supplies, tables, chairs, and much more are available.
- **Beverages:** Assorted alcoholic and non-alcoholic beverages are available. Dale's Catering Service is licensed by the OLCC to serve alcoholic beverages, and all of our bartenders have OLCC service permits.
- **Flowers:** We work with a local florist who can handle all of your floral needs.
- **Cakes:** We do not prepare cakes but will be happy to recommend three custom bakeries, and we can facilitate the ordering and delivery of your cake if you wish.

The cost of catering for your wedding will be determined by the menu, the number of guests, and the service requested. When we supply alcoholic beverages, you will be billed for the amount used.

An advance deposit of $500 is required one month prior to your wedding. You will be billed for the balance the first business day after the event, and the full balance is due upon receipt of the invoice. If you must cancel, your full deposit will be refunded if we are given 72 hours notice.

Comments From Our Clients

"Thank you for a job beautifully done."   *S.B.—Portland*

"The food was wonderful. It was a perfect day and a perfect wedding."   *K.V.—Vancouver*

"Thank you for the wonderful service. The food display was fresh, crisp and colorful."
                                                                    C.P.—Portland

Visit us at our Web site:
www.citysearch.com/pdx/dales

14297 S.W. Pacific Highway • Tigard, Oregon 97224
Contact: Steve DeAngelo (503) 620-9020
Available for catering seven days a week
Call for store hours

Types of Menus and Specialties

DeAngelo's offers all types of menus from self-serve buffets to full-service formal sit-down affairs. We are well-known for our Pasta Bars. On-site cooking is always a hit with attendees. All foods are prepared from scratch. Low-fat and vegetarian menus are happily accommodated. A wide range of ethnic menus are available, such as Asian, Italian, Mexican, African, and Caribbean. Give DeAngelo's Catering a call when planning your wedding reception.

Cost and Experience

Price is based on a per-person basis for full-service events; however, many other options are available. DeAngelo's Catering prides itself on quality food at an affordable price. Delivery available. Food tasting and references provided upon request. Free consultation.

Services

DeAngelo's is licensed and insured to serve alcoholic beverages. Complete event coordination and site-analysis service available. To complete your event, all full-service buffets are decorated at no charge.

Presentation and Service Staff

All foods are exquisitely presented using copper chafing dishes along with granite and marble tiles and slabs. Service staff is available for all types of events. Attire is always appropriate.

Approved Caterer for the Following Locations

- Canterbury Falls
- Capt. Ainsworth House
- The Crown Ballroom
- Elk Cove Winery
- Jenkins Estate (main house and stable)
- Marshall House
- Queen Anne Victorian Mansion
- World Forestry Center

Other Sites which we are Familiar with

- Lakewood Center of the Arts
- The Laurelhurst Club
- Leach Botanical Gardens
- Metger Park Hall
- Oaks Park
- Scouters Mountain Lodge
- Senior Centers: Oregon City, Sherwood, Tigard, Wilsonville
- Sokol Blosser Winery
- North Star Ballroom

A founding member of the Association of Caterers and Event Professionals

FLEXIBILITY TO MEET YOUR NEEDS

DeAngelo's is always willing to work with clients to find a menu that fits within their budget and menu guidelines. We offer flexibility to adapt to special needs and requests. With our wide range of menus and services, we can accommodate your requests.

Decorations provided FREE with all full-service buffets!

Visit our Web site: www.cateringbydeangelos.com

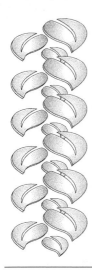

Deja Bree'z Catering
Full Service Catering for all Events

200 Hawthorne Ave., S.E., Suite E-500
Salem, Oregon 97301
Contact: Lisa Shores
(503) 363-7203
Fax (503) 364-6246

Our menus are casual American with flair—buffet, sit-down, hors d'oeuvres to prime rib. Choose from our own menus, or we can design a personal menu especially for your event.

Cost and Terms
Cost is based per person. A 25% deposit is required at time of booking. The final billing is due at the conclusion of your event.

Experience
Established in 1992, Deja Bree'z has the combined experience of over 40 years in the catering business. References are available.

Services
Beer and wine service available, fully licensed and insured. We offer the best wine service in Salem. Our servers are licensed by the State of Oregon. China, linens, ice sculptures, invitations and tear-down service are available.

ENJOY YOUR DAY
Deja Bree'z is a full-service catering company. Our philosophy is, "The day is yours to enjoy." We can plan the event from the ground up, or simply deliver the food to your location. We will work within your budget. We believe that the presentation of the event is as important as the taste. Our staff is fully trained to make your special day worry-free.

833 N.W. 16th Avenue
Portland, Oregon 97209
Contact: Linette True (503) 243-3324
E-mail: delilah@teleport.com
Web site: http://www.teleport.com/~delilah

Classic or Trendy

Your reception reflects your style, just as your bridal gown, flowers and music do. The food we prepare and the table we set show your guests the care you've taken to celebrate your wedding day.

Cuisine

- **Northwest:** Freshly prepared local seafood, meats, fruits and vegetables, changing with the season
- **International:** Authentic ethnic dishes including European, Mediterranean, South American and Asian.
- **Regional American:** Southwestern, Cajun, Heartland, Eastern Seaboard and Southern

Menus

Buffet or formal table service? Brunch, lunch, mid-afternoon or dinner? Winter, spring, summer or autumn? Indoor or outdoor? Cuisine? With this many factors involved in an event, our menus are custom designed to suit the event. Delilah's encourages you to mix and match cuisines to include your favorite dishes. Tasty vegetarian options are available.

Services

- **Staff:** professional waiters, licensed bartenders, chefs for on-site cooking or carving, on-site coordinators
- **Table settings:** china, linen, silver and crystal are available
- **Decoration:** ice carving, floral design, formal or rustic displays
- **Outdoor:** canopies, tents, dance floors, arches, tables, umbrellas and chairs in many styles

Exquisite Presentation

Our luscious food merits a beautiful presentation. We artfully arrange and garnish our dishes to be a focal point for your reception.

DELILAH'S GIFT TO YOU

We know how exciting your wedding day will be, so we prepare a basket as a gift from Delilah's filled with goodies from your reception, for the two of you to enjoy when you're alone.

EAT YOUR HEART OUT CATERING

Monica Grinnell, Proprietor since 1975
1230 S.E. Seventh
Portland, Oregon 97214
Kitchen/Voice Mail: (503) 232-4408

Types of Menus and Specialties

Who better to cater your wedding reception than the co-author of *Newlywed Style: The Cookbook*, first in a series of life-style books for newly married couples. **Eat Your Heart Out Catering** was created in 1975 by two brides, who produced three brides-to-be along the way. Maybe you want to be involved in the menu, or just sit back and be dazzled by choices ranging from **baron of beef with Oregon Pinot Noir sauce and baby baked potato bar to caviar eclairs with lemon cream**. Recommended by **major facilities** including Montgomery Park, World Forestry Center, Jenkins Estate, The Marshall House, Portland Art Museum and Central Library among others—we specialize in all cuisines: ethnic, traditional, or more adventuresome with Northwest fresh products. At the heart of it, Monica Grinnell, the owner, was trained as an interior designer, so **food design and presentation** are as important as the **delicious flavors** we create. Most of all, we specialize in you because we know that **you** want to remember your wedding reception as a wonderful experience, from planning the look and the menu, to the moment you leave your reception with a beautiful food basket tucked under your arm.

Experience

Eat Your Heart Out Catering has had the pleasure to be hired by some of the finest corporations and private clients in the Northwest. Our experience includes 20 years of planning catering events; designing and packaging a line of herbed vinegars; cooking with such noted chefs as Julia Child, Marcella Hazan, Craig Claiborne, and Pierre Franey; teaching cooking classes; and appearing on local television demonstrating and teaching cooking techniques. We would be glad to furnish you a client list or recommendations, and we are happy to show you our beautiful **portfolio**.

Food Presentation, Equipment and Staff

Eat Your Heart Out Catering is a full-service caterer. We provide **dishes**, **linens**, disposable products if you need them, all **serving pieces** both traditional and unusual, **flowers**, **ice sculptures**, even props for **special themes**. Our staff includes **bartenders**, **servers**, even a substitute **"Auntie"** to cut the cake, so yours can enjoy the reception. Most importantly we give you the **confidence** to make your dreams become a reality.

WHAT MAKES US SPECIAL

You make us special. You're going to be whirlwinded, waited on, waited for, honeymooned, brided, groomed–kaazaam, you're married! And **Eat Your Heart Out** will be a part of it.

Distinctive Weddings
by
Eden's Cakes and Catering

41707 S.E. Porter Road
Estacada, Oregon 97023
Contact: Virginia (503) 630-6131
Any hour by appointment; closed Sundays

Types of Menus and Specialty

Eden's can provide all your wedding or reception catering needs, from hors d'oeuvres and canapés to full- or self-service buffets and sit-down luncheons or dinners. Choose from our popular menus—trays, salads, hot dishes, and more—or create your own menu with favorite family recipes you provide. Eden's will prepare and serve them to perfection. Serving sizes are apportioned for hearty appetites. Eden's can also provide your wedding cake as well as all your floral needs. Ask to see our portfolio.

Cost

Cost is determined by the number of guests to be served and menu items selected. A $75 nonrefundable deposit is required when you place your order (however, we will hold for a later date if needed). Our services should be booked one to three months in advance of your wedding.

Services

- **Beverages:** punch, coffee, tea, or soft drinks (no alcoholic beverages)
- **Dishes and glassware:** china and glass used
- **Napkins and linens:** linen, cloth, lace, and quality paper available in your choice of colors; cake napkins also available

Food Preparation, Equipment, and Serving Attendants

We'll provide anything you need for a complete reception and save you the extra footwork and expense of renting things like serving trays, chafing dishes, punch bowls, coffee and tea services, stainless flatware, glass plates, and cake knives. Eden's provides serving attendants and setup and cleanup crews for food services at no additional charge. Servers will stay as long as needed. Taxes and gratuities are included in your event costs.

WEDDINGS ARE OUR ONLY BUSINESS

Eden's Cakes and Catering will work with you and your family to make sure your dreams come true. We can do all or part of the food; if you want Aunt Sally's potato salad, we'll provide the bowls and serve it for you. And we use only the freshest, name-brand products. Nothing is frozen. Let us color coordinate everything, including mints, table settings, and cake, and save you the time and money of running all over town to make arrangements. We can design and make your wedding cake to your specifications and include them in your catering package. Weddings are our only business, and we do a great job!

See page 281 under Cakes & Candies.

FABULOUS FOOD
BY NANCY TAYLOR

3075 N.W. Front Avenue
Portland, Oregon 97210
Contact: Nancy Taylor
Kitchen/Voice Mail (503) 228-5781
Fax (503) 226-6364

Types of Menus and Specialty

Fabulous Food has been in the catering business since 1982, with a fine reputation for producing stress-free entertaining. Nancy's formal training includes classes in France at LaVeran and Le Cordon Bleu and in California from great chefs such as Julia Child, Julee Rosso, and Sheila Lukins of The Silver Palate. Fabulous Food believes in using the best quality ingredients and serving them with style. Whether the occasion calls for a backyard barbecue or formal French dinner service, we'll work with you to create the menu and details that will make your wedding or special event a fabulous affair!

Services

Nancy is happy to sit down with you and help plan details, from recommending an appropriate location to choosing and arranging for the rental of table linens in your color scheme. She prides herself on being flexible when working with her clients so the end result is a great event! After helping two daughters through their weddings, Nancy knows what wedding plans involve and enjoys every aspect.

Cost

The cost is based on a per-guest count and will vary according to your menu selections. A deposit of 50% is required two weeks in advance, with the balance due the day of the event.

Food Preparation and Equipment

We will provide all the service equipment you need from a wide collection of styles, including black lacquer, antique silver, brass, copper, baskets, and more!

Serving Attendants

We will provide all service staff needed, and also will take care of setup and cleanup of food and beverage services. We are fully licensed by the Oregon Liquor Control Commission and provide professionally trained staff.

THE FOOD IS TRULY FABULOUS

Fabulous Food has planned successful parties and receptions ranging from small affairs in private homes to large corporate festivities for U.S. Bank, *Life Magazine*, Air Touch Cellular, Nordstom, and Zell Bros Jewelers. All of Nancy's clients speak highly of her professional attitude, friendly smile and dependability, but most of all they say, "The food is truly fabulous."

♥ *Member of Weddings of Distinction*

Four Seasons Catering

Contact: Kevin Danley
(503) 674-2812

Receptions Without Limitations

Four Seasons Catering specializes in unique wedding receptions that include formal sit-down dinners, casual summer brunches, bountiful hors d'oeuvre buffets, and beautiful dessert buffets. Whether a garden party wedding for 30, or a formal reception for 300 in an historic wedding hall, Four Seasons Catering will create an atmosphere that every guest will remember. Imagine a summer reception at a local vineyard with a menu including flavorful hors d'oeuvres such as Jamaican chicken skewers, goat cheese tarts with grilled vegetables, and smoked salmon crostini.

Creating an Event with Individual Style

Each wedding menu is customized to meet the bride and groom's individual needs. Our staff will meet with each couple to ensure that every detail will be attended to. Following an initial consultation, an itemized estimate will be prepared. Four Seasons Catering can also provide a full line of dinnerware and glassware, linens, floral arrangements, tables, chairs, outdoor lighting, and canopies. All servers are professionally attired, and primed to provide each guest with a memorable event. Four Seasons Catering servers are responsible for setup as well as cleanup.

Attention to Detail Makes Each Event Special

At Four Seasons Catering, each wedding reception is carefully executed to achieve an unforgettable event. Small details create a reception with individual flair, from custom-made napkins to match the bride's color theme, to gift boxes of handmade chocolate amaretto truffles for each guest to take home.

"I'd always enjoyed the idea of entertaining, but working out the technical difficulties was a problem. When I discovered Kevin Danley with Four Seasons Catering, all my problems were solved. I have used Four Seasons Catering for small, intimate dinner parties to large, full-scale corporate affairs, never once being disappointed."

—Curtis Barber, Evolution Hair Design

"Four Seasons Catering catered our daughter's wedding reception in September of 1996. Kevin Danley met with us to hear exactly what the bride really wanted for her reception. He listened to her ideas and incorporated a plan that made our event very elegant. The day of the wedding we had nothing to worry about as Kevin took care of everything."

—Phil and Marsha Cavin

IZZY'S CATERING

Eastport Plaza	*Gateway Mall*	*Gresham*
3846 S.E. 82nd Avenue	*1307 N.E. 102nd Avenue*	*225 N.E. Burnside*
Portland, Oregon 97260	*Portland, Oregon 97220*	*Gresham, Oregon 97030*
Contact:	*Contact:*	*Contact:*
Debbi Schall or Robert Lampson	*Carol Pratt*	*Chris Wiser*
(503) 771-9919	*(503) 255-6364*	*(503) 667-7972*

Types of Menus

Buffet: We specialize in offering a high-quality buffet with an outstanding presentation at a very affordable price. We can feature Izzy's traditional buffet which includes a variety of pan and thin crust pizza, chicken, baked beans, mashed potatoes, wild rice stuffing, cinnamon rolls, salads, desserts and more. We can also customize a menu featuring a wide variety of entrees that are not typically on our restaurant menu. Please call for more details. We are very flexible, conscientious and affordable.

Appetizers: We also can serve you a wide variety of appetizer platters for your special event.

Restaurant Facilities

We have a variety of banquet rooms in our three eastside locations that can comfortably accommodate groups from 20 to 75 for rehearsal dinners, bridal luncheons, or small receptions. Larger portions of the restaurant can be reserved during selected off-hour times.

Catering Services

We have an experienced event coordinator on our staff to help assist you with any of your wedding planning needs.

Cost

On-site
- $6.19 lunch, $7.99 dinner for our traditional Izzy's buffet *
- Prices will vary for customized menus depending on menu items selected.

Off-site
- Pricing on catered buffet packages will vary depending on party size, menu selection and amenities, but packages typically range from $6.50–$10 per person.

* *Price valid as of 1/1/99*

JAKE'S CATERING
AT THE
GOVERNOR
HOTEL

611 S.W. 10th Avenue
Portland, Oregon 97205
(503) 241-2104; Fax (503) 220-1849
Web site: http://www.mccormickandschmicks.com

Type of Menus and Specialty

Jake's Catering at The Governor Hotel is a division of McCormick & Schmick Management Group and "Jake's Famous Crawfish." Jake's is one of the most respected dining institutions in the Portland area, and Jake's Catering at The Governor Hotel upholds this prestigious reputation.

Known for offering extensive Pacific Northwest menu selections, including fresh seafood and fish, pasta and poultry dishes and prime cut steaks, Jake's Catering at The Governor Hotel has the flexibility and talent to cater to your needs.

From stand-up cocktail/appetizer receptions to fabulous buffet presentations, to complete sit-down dinners for groups and gatherings of all sizes, Jake's Catering at The Governor Hotel is always poised and ready to serve.

Enjoy delicious hors d'oeuvres and entrees, delectable desserts and specialty theme menus (upon request), all prepared by our talented chefs and served by our friendly and professional staff.

Customers are encouraged to review our catering menus and to tour the elegant banquet facilities at The Governor Hotel to fully appreciate the total scope of menu options, facilities, and full-service capabilities.

Cost

We base our cost on a per-person count and the type of menu developed. We require a 50% deposit to confirm your event and payment in full 72 hours prior to event for estimated charges. We ask for a guaranteed number of guests three business days prior to the event.

Services

Jake's Catering at The Governor Hotel is the exclusive caterer at The Governor Hotel, which features nine exquisite banquet rooms with an Italian Renaissance decor and the capability to host groups from as small as 10 people up to 450 (seated) and 600 (stand-up reception).

Jake's Catering at The Governor Hotel provides off-premise catering services.

A REPUTATION FOR QUALITY
AND A RESPECT FOR TRADITION

This is the motto for Jake's Catering at The Governor Hotel and McCormick & Schmick Management Group. You are guaranteed the finest quality of food and presentation, a friendly and professional staff, and a personalized customer service. Trust your important event to one of Portland's long-time favorites to ensure a truly memorable and successful experience.

See page 142 under Banquet & Reception Sites.

PHOTO © JULIAN GOBLE

"We are a preferred caterer at The Crown Ballroom"

625 S.W. 10th, Suite 492-C, Portland, Oregon 97205 • (503) 525-0396; Fax (503) 232-8557

Menu Design

Market Street Catering will custom design your menu to suit the needs of your event. We offer all wedding-related events, including rehearsal dinners, receptions, and wedding brunches. Our professional catering staff is experienced in all aspects of menu design. Our fresh, artfully prepared food is served on buffets that are decorated with specialty linens and flowers. We also have the capability to offer sit-down dinners with French service.

Cost

Because we are a full service catering company, the cost of events is based on a per person charge that will depend on the menu selection and type of event.

However, we are capable of working within an individual's budget. A 50% nonrefundable deposit is required upon confirmation of the event and full payment is due 48 hours prior to the event.

Experience

Market Street Catering offers a varied and extensive blend of catering expertise. We have a combined history of over 25 years in customer service, menu planning, preparation and presentation.

Services

Our event planners are happy to help you with all aspects of your wedding and reception planning, from linens, china, glassware and specialty pieces, to flowers and decor. The professional service staff will work with you to make your wedding event successful. Assorted alcoholic and non-alcoholic beverages are available. Market Street Catering is fully licensed by the OLCC and assumes complete liability.

Location

Join us for lunch at our cafe located at 1728 S.E. Seventh Avenue for one of Portland's best kept secrets.

Market Street Cafe is available for your next private party, breakfast meeting, or rehearsal dinner.

Elegance in Catering

TIFFANY CENTER
1410 S.W. Morrison, Suite 600
Portland, Oregon 97205-1930
(503) 248-9305; Fax (503) 243-7147 ; E-mail: rafatis@vr-net.com

Types of Menus and Specialty
Rafati's full-service catering staff can assist you with the selection of the perfect menu for your function. From brunches, picnics in the park, formal dinner service, elegant afternoon tea in sterling silver to the most formal or casual of wedding receptions—we've done it all. Our portfolios are filled with pictures of our work—Northwest and other American Regional cuisines to Continental and Ethnic, mirror displays of whole decorated salmon, seasonal fruits and grilled vegetables, theme buffet presentations, formal dinner services and elegant hors d'oeuvres passed on silver trays.

Cost
The cost is determined by the menu selection, level of desired service and number of guests.

Experience
Operating under the Rafati's name since 1983, our actual catering and food service experience spans more than 25 years. Experience has made flexibility our hallmark.

Food Preparation and Equipment
Rafati's specializes in delicious, freshly prepared foods set in an elegant, lavish and stylish display. From silver, copper, crystal and mirrors to baskets, china, fresh flowers and theme props—we provide all service equipment needs.

Special Services
Service attendants: trained, professionally uniformed service staff to set up, serve and clean up; OLCC licensed, professionally uniformed and equipped bartenders

Beverages: we offer full liquor, extensive wine and champagne selections, bottled and keg beer (domestic, micro and imported) and a full selection of chilled non-alcoholic beverages; OLCC licensed with liquor liability insurance

Dishes and glassware: china, glassware standard, disposables on request

Napkins and linens: linen cloths, napkins and table skirting in range of colors; paper products in selection of colors

Other: fresh flowers; table, hall and theme decorations; ice carvings—full event services.

WHEN GOOD TASTE AND EXPERIENCE COUNT
...COUNT ON RAFATI'S
Rafati's is the exclusive caterer for the Tiffany Center—a centrally located, historic building featuring event floors of traditional charm and elegance with gilded mirrors, polished woods and emerald accents. From our fully licensed commercial kitchen we also provide elegant catering services to many other facilities and venues in the Portland Metro area. Our attention to detail, safe food-handling practices, award-winning chefs, trained professional servers, bartenders and experienced event planners are all dedicated to ensuring your freedom! Freedom to enjoy one of the most momentous days of your life.

West Hills Catering Company

503.228.6822

Visit our Web site:
www.citysearch.com/pdx/whcc

Colleen Ann Schultz
Event Coordinator

Kevin D. Davin
Executive Chef

Portland's Premier Catering Service

Make your wedding reception the talk of the town! With over 40 years combined experience, Executive Chef Kevin Davin and Event Coordinator Colleen Schultz have teamed up to bring catering excellence to Portland. West Hills Catering Company features praise-winning cuisine and first-rate service.

Chef Davin—a consummate professional with a classic European culinary education will create an exclusive menu, tailored to your tastes.

Colleen will tend to all your wedding reception details. From helping you find the perfect location to decorations, custom linens, and silver, her experience will set your mind at ease.

Concerned About What To Serve?

There is no need to settle for a standard package offered by many clubs, caterers, or hotels. West Hills Catering Company offers an extensive variety of menu choices. Or we'll create a customized menu just for you.

We Are Experts At Taking The Show on the Road

Let us transform any site from ordinary to extraordinary! We use only state-of-the-art food preparation, handling, and transportation equipment. This ensures the safest and highest product quality.

Call for Menus and Compare Our Value

Our per person menu pricing is inclusive of service personnel, china, flatware, glassware, beautiful silver serving pieces and candelabras, linens, setup and cleanup.

You do not need to worry about any hidden charges—there are none! Elegant, full-service wedding buffets start as low as $10 per person.

Complete Wedding Reception Planning

Beyond fine cuisine and outstanding service, West Hills Catering Company also offers complete wedding staging, full liquor license, ice carvings, floral arrangements, entertainment, tents, canopies, and more!

Thank you for considering West Hills Catering Company. We truly believe you will feel very comfortable with us and we look forward to being of service to you. Please phone Colleen Schultz. She'll be happy to discuss your plans or answer any questions you may have.

Put West Hills Catering Company to work for you.
We do the work, and you take the bow.

YOURS TRULY CATERERS

1628 S.W. Jefferson Street
Portland, Oregon 97201
Contact: Barbara
(503) 226-6266; Fax (503) 226-7616

A PORTLAND TRADITION
WITH A STANDARD OF EXCELLENCE

Types of Menus and Specialty

At Yours Truly, we specialize in preparing menus to suit each client's needs, always keeping in mind an elegant appearance as well as superb taste—from simple to dishes that please the most discriminating palate. One of our specialties, a poached, glazed, and decorated salmon that would grace any table, is often used as the centerpiece.

Cost

Our costs are based on the menu needs and the size of each function. The amount of the deposit depends on the total amount and is due upon confirmation. Cancellation policies vary according to the circumstances.

Experience and Services

Yours Truly has been successfully catering Portland's most exciting events for almost 50 years. For everything from breakfast meetings to wedding receptions—from bridge luncheons to corporate Christmas parties, Oregonians have relied on Yours Truly. Owner Barbara LaValla was the hostess on Channel 6's *KOIN Kitchen* for three years. Combine this with her outstanding culinary skills, and you're reaching one of the most qualified caterers in the Northwest when you call Yours Truly. A portfolio and references are available upon request.

- **Beverages:** licensed to serve alcohol; you may provide your own beverages, or we will be happy to arrange everything for you, charging only for the amount consumed
- **Dishes and glassware:** an exquisite selection of china, crystal, and silver service for you to use at your wedding—FREE OF CHARGE
- **Napkins and linens:** we can provide the colors of your choice

Food Preparation and Equipment

We provide a wide variety of menus, with dishes always prepared to look as elegant as they are delicious. No matter what the occasion, Yours Truly will handle every detail with an unequaled sense of style.

Serving Attendants

Yours Truly prides itself in providing the most fully trained, efficient, and professional cooks, servers, and bartenders available to handle everything—setup, service, and cleanup. All our serving attendants are fully licensed and are dressed in tasteful tuxedo uniforms. We're prepared to handle any size or style of event.

Please let this business know that you heard about them from the Bravo! Bridal Resource Guide. **313**

Notes

WEDDING RING FINGER

In the 19th century it was

believed that a main artery

ran from the fourth finger

of the left hand directly to

the heart, making that

finger the perfect

appendage on which to

wear the wedding ring.

HELPFUL HINTS

- **Remember the marriage license:** Don't forget to bring the marriage-license packet to the wedding! Assign this task to a trusted friend or family member. A ceremony is not legal and complete without this—some ministers will even make you go home to get it while everyone waits.

- **A handkerchief is a must:** Include a handkerchief in your wedding attire, or have your maid-of-honor carry one for unexpected tears.

- **Make your ceremony special:** The minister or priest can help to make your wedding ceremony meaningful for both of you. Ask how you can personalize the ceremony—writing your own vows, selecting special songs, etc.

- **Ring-bearer pillow:** Practice tying the rings to the pillow so that they will stay on during the walk down the aisle, but will slip off easily during the ceremony.

- **Plan how to start the music:** Prelude music is a nice touch as the guests are being escorted into the church. To start the processional music, have someone signal the musicians at the appropriate time. Setting a specific time doesn't always work because guests are still coming in, or delays get in the way of starting the ceremony on time. One way to handle this is to have your clergyman signal the musicians to start the processional music after a nod from the father of the bride. Also provide your priest, judge, or pastor and the musicians with a cue sheet. The person officiating can unknowingly cut your well-planned music.

- **Approve your music selections with clergy:** Make sure your clergyman is aware of your music selections. Ask whether there are any restrictions on music. Some ministers or priests insist on approving all the music prior to the ceremony. Your favorite love song may seem offensive to the clergyman; neither you nor your musicians will enjoy any last-minute confrontations.

- **Check all the rules:** Make sure you know all the rules and restrictions about the church, chapel, or synagogue. Some have strict rules about photographs or videotaping, candles, and music. Sit down with the clergyman and discuss your ceremony from start to finish, so that any details can be worked out early.

- **Obtaining a marriage license in Oregon:** You must be at least 17 years of age or have written consent from a parent. No exams or blood tests are required. If divorced or widowed, please consult the Marriage License office by calling (503) 248-3523. Cost is $60 with a three-day waiting period. License is valid for 60 days.

For more assistance with staying organized during the wedding planning process, check out the Bravo! Wedding Organizer. Detailed question worksheets double as contracts. This step-by-step system will keep every detail of your wedding organized. To order, refer to the order form on page 23 in this Guide.

OLD LAURELHURST CHURCH

3212 S.E. Ankeny
Portland, Oregon 97214
Contact: Deborra Buckler
(503) 231-0462 ; Fax (503) 231-9429

Old Laurelhurst Church is located at the corner of 32nd and Ankeny, in southeast Portland, just one block south of Burnside, half a block from the Music Millennium store, centrally and conveniently located. The church rose garden and beautiful Laurelhurst Park, just one block from the church, are favorite sites for wedding photography.

Built in 1923, Old Laurelhurst Church is an outstanding example of the Spanish Colonial Revival-style of architecture. Designed by Portland architect F. Manson White, who also designed the Auditorium Building, the church is listed in *Architecture: Oregon Style*, page 163. With an arcaded entrance, curvilinear gables and domed corner bell towers with round-arched openings, the church features wrought-iron balconet and lamps and magnificent cathedral-quality stained glass windows. The live acoustics and warm ambiance provide an intimate feeling complementing the long and stately aisle in the sanctuary, which features the ornate original wooden beams and trim.

A nondenominational Christian church, Old Laurelhurst Church seeks to be of service to the community. The church is available for weddings, receptions, concerts, seminars, and community events. The sanctuary acoustics have been acclaimed by musicians and speakers. The church allows couples to bring in the Christian minister of their choice to officiate, or will provide referrals. The on-site reception facilities accommodate up to 250 guests and include a stage and dance area, separate serving room, and a commercial grade kitchen for caterer's use. Please contact Deborra Buckler, wedding coordinator, to arrange tours and consultation.

A Night in Shining Amour
Wedding Chapel and Ballroom

115 W. Ninth Street
Vancouver, Washington 98660
Contact: Joe and Pam Thielman
(360) 750-7891
Web site: www.shining-amour.com
E-mail: jthielm@pacifier.com

Built in 1910, our facility has been completely remodeled, giving it an ambiance and charm of style and grace. You will find the ballroom a wonderful, warm place to hold your wedding. You will feel elegant on the beautiful hardwood floors within the brick walls, under the crystal chandeliers. An intriguing bubbler makes a wonderful backdrop for that most important day of your life. We have beautifully decorated dressing rooms for both the bride and groom. A loft over the chapel is perfect for video, music, and reception overflow.

We also have a gift shop as a resource for you to find invitations, wedding accessories, or gifts for your attendants. We can even turn your wedding dress into an heirloom bassinet after the wedding.

Our packages range from $65 to $1,100. Flexibility is the backbone of our service. You can simply rent our facility or you can leave the entire wedding in our capable hands. Keeping costs within your budget is our specialty.

ALBERTINA KERR CENTERS' HOOD MEMORIAL CHAPEL

722 N.E. 162nd
Portland, Oregon 97230
Contact: Chaplain Lee Lower
(503) 255-4205
Business Hours: Mon–Fri 8am–5pm;
or by appointment

Our chapel facility includes a lovely sanctuary seating 180 guests, a changing room, and a smoking patio. Although not available for reception use, the fireside room, with kitchenette, provides plenty of preparation space for families and wedding-party members. The chapel is located on the beautiful grounds of Kerr Youth and Family Center in Portland.

The agency chaplain may be available to officiate at the request of bridal couples who have not already selected a minister. The chaplain will assist by conducting the wedding rehearsal and helping to plan the ceremony as needed. Traditional, contemporary, and personalized service planning are available.

A fee of $400 covers up to eight hours of rehearsal and wedding-day time. Chaplain's fees are $100, which covers an initial meeting, the rehearsal, and the wedding. A deposit of $100 reserves your day.

The Burdoin Mansion

For Weddings &
Special Occasion Celebrations

18609 N.E. Cramer Road
Battle Ground, Washington 98604
Contact: Rob or Becky Neuschwander
(360) 666-4828
Business Hours: Tues–Sat 10am–5pm;
. closed Sunday and Monday

All the Elegance and Grace of the Victorian Era

The Burdoin Mansion is a unique turn of the century Victorian colonial mansion, situated in a storybook setting of forest and country homes. The mansion can accommodate up to 65 guests indoors, 200 outdoors.

Pastor Rob Neuschwander has been a licensed minister and sought after vocalist in the Portland/Clark County metropolitan area for over 10 years. He has officiated or participated in over 100 ceremonies and is currently pastoring Point of Grace Fellowship in Vancouver. Please call for additional information or to receive a brochure.

See page 113 under Banquet & Reception Sites.

CANBY PIONEER CHAPEL

N.W. Third and Elm
Canby, Oregon 97013
Contact: Darlene Key (503) 263-6126
Viewing hours by appointment

This is the chapel for the couple who wish to have their marriage memories cherished in the romance of a Victorian country church. Built in 1884, this turn-of-the-century, traditional, steeled church features ornate interior walls of pressed tin in white, with a vaulted ceiling and leaded stained-glass windows. Both the side lawn and front stairway are perfect locations for additional wedding portraits.

The chapel will seat up to 120 guests. The basic fee includes rehearsal time plus three hours on your wedding day. You may select your own minister and musicians, or we will be happy to provide you with a list of referrals.

When it comes to something as special as your wedding, the church or chapel you select will set the tone for the day. We'll work closely with you to make sure everything is just as you've always dreamed it would be.

The Carus House
Historic Wedding Chapel

23200 S. Highway 213
Oregon City, Oregon 97045
(503) 631-7078; E-mail: carushs@aol.com
Business Hours: Please call for an appointment

Historic Elegance • The Carus House Wedding Chapel is a beautifully restored Queen Anne Vernacular-style chapel originally constructed circa 1880. A registered historic landmark, it is located just outside of historic Oregon City. **Intimate and Romantic** • Our main chapel seats 125 guests (additional seating available) and includes hardwood floors and a romantically adorned arbor. A small indoor reception area contains four tables with linens, seating six guests each, and two bar tables. Our main chapel area is also available for setup as a reception area to accommodate your needs. A full kitchen is available for your catering needs. Our beautifully landscaped garden area includes a large pavilion tent, seating 100+ guests and is available for your wedding or reception. Our package price includes chairs, an oak podium, altar baskets, candelabras, and a brides' dressing room with a private balcony. Covered walkway and disabled access are provided as well as ample parking. A sound system is available or there is ample space for your own soloist or DJ. Easy access from I-205, take the Park Place exit (#10), continue south on highway 213 for approximately 7-1/2 miles, we are located on the left side of the highway just past Carus Road. Call for more information, we would be glad to schedule a tour of our facility.

CHRISTIAN LIFE CHURCH

Conveniently located five blocks off I-205,
Exit #12 (Clackamas/Estacada exit)
9215 S.E. Church Street
Clackamas, Oregon 97015
(503) 655-1224
Please call for an appointment to view

This delightfully quaint historic church provides the perfect atmosphere for a romantic wedding. Several brides have called Christian Life Church their "Little House on the Prairie" church. It is what many people think of when wanting a wedding in a historical church setting.

Built over 100 years ago, Christian Life Church is a registered historic landmark. It has recently been restored to its original character and charm. One Christian Life Church tradition is for the bride and groom to pause on the way out to ring the historic bell in celebration. The church seats up to 120 people and is available for those desiring a traditional or contemporary wedding. You may select your own Christian minister, or we will happily provide referrals.

We understand that your wedding day can be busy, but it need not be rushed. The modest fee includes four hours, giving ample time for the rehearsal, decorations, dressing, ceremony and keepsake portraits. Be a part of the legacy of happy memories in the oldest church in urban Clackamas County at Christian Life Church.

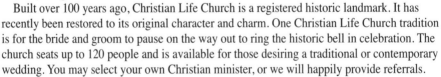

FIRST CONGREGATIONAL CHURCH

United Church of Christ

Rev. Patricia S. Ross
Rev. John Paul Davis III

1126 S.W. Park Avenue
Portland, Oregon 97205
(503) 228-7219
Business Hours: Mon–Fri by appointment

For more than a century, brides have selected First Congregational Church, United Church of Christ, as the perfect site for their wedding ceremony. A beautiful sanctuary, filled with handcarved woodwork and magnificent stained-glass windows, provides a special setting for a wedding of any size. A First Congregational Church minister will officiate at your ceremony, and our organist and wedding coordinator will assist you with your ceremony plans.

Located in the South Park Blocks in downtown Portland on the corner of S.W. Park and Madison, First Congregational Church is a Portland Historic Landmark and is listed on the National Register of Historic Places. The church is known for its Venetian Gothic architecture and the red-roofed bell tower that can be seen from many parts of the city. And yes, the church bell, obtained in 1871, will ring before and after your ceremony. For additional information, please call 228-7219, Monday through Friday.

316 E. Main St.
Battle Ground, Washington 98604
Contact: Susan Simonson (360) 687-7304
Web site: http://www.weloveweddings.com/weddingchapel

Located in the historic district of downtown Battle Ground, Washington, this chapel was originally constructed in 1928. The original charm and character of the building has been carefully maintained, creating a unique setting for your special day. The chapel can accommodate up to 100 guests and is a charming setting for your formal or informal wedding.

The downstairs reception area is a convenient place to hold an informal reception or is available for other occasions such as parties, anniversary celebrations, business meetings and dinner parties. We are available to help you with everything, from flowers to catering, to make your day special and worry-free.

Call for more information or an appointment to see Forever Yours. It is a truly special place for your memorable day.

Member of Wedding Link

MCLEAN HOUSE AND PARK

5350 River Street
West Linn, Oregon 97068
(503) 655-4268

The McLean House is a lovely 1920s home that borders the beautiful Willamette River in West Linn. The interior includes hand-crafted woodwork, charming fixtures, fireplace, spacious rooms, a sun-drenched conservatory, and a complete kitchen. The **2.4-acre park** surrounding the McLean House is a cornucopia of majestic evergreens, mighty deciduous trees, well-groomed gardens, large grassy expanses, winding trails, and secluded spots.

McLean
HOUSE & PARK

Through every season of the year, the McLean House and Park is the site of wedding and anniversary celebrations, family gatherings, class reunions, company meetings, seminars, formal and informal dinners, fund raisers, and religious services. **Guest capacity is 100.**

The McLean House and Park is owned by the City of West Linn and managed by the Friends of McLean House, a nonprofit organization dedicated to preserving the McLean House and grounds as well as making it a useful part of the surrounding communities.

For a special tour of the house, please call for an appointment Monday through Friday.

"THE GROVE"
AT
OAKS AMUSEMENT PARK

Portland, Oregon 97202
Contact: Volanne Stephens
(503) 233-5777
Business Hours: Mon–Fri 8am–5pm

"The Grove" located within historic Oaks Amusement Park, offers a unique, beautiful, quiet, wooded ceremony and reception site. The lovely, lacy outdoor gazebo provides the perfect setting in which to create special memories of your important occasion. "The Grove" is ideal for weddings, family receptions, anniversary celebrations and more. It is our policy to work closely with you, offering exemplary step-by-step service, allowing you to relax and enjoy the day.

Menus, all created by our in-house catering staff, are individually designed to meet your expectations, style, and tastes.

No surprises, just fun and best wishes!

See page 171 under Banquet & Reception Sites.

OAKS PIONEER CHURCH

455 S.E. Spokane
Portland, Oregon 97202
Contact: (503) 233-1497; Fax (503) 236-8402
Call for an appointment to view
our newly refurbished chapel.

Oaks Pioneer Church is located on the southern edge of Sellwood Park. The non-denominational church is managed by the Sellwood-Moreland Neighborhood Association. With seating for 75 guests plus the wedding party, it has been Portland's most popular intimate wedding chapel for many years. Prices start at $150.

Designated a national historic landmark, the church was built in 1851. The interior is finished in diagonal strips of natural wood. Two original pews are still in use and a carefully restored antique pump organ is available for the "Wedding March"–or more contemporary selections–as the bride comes down the aisle. An intricate stained glass window located above the altar is everyone's favorite photo backdrop! Newly installed air conditioning keeps the chapel comfortable in hot weather. An added wing houses modern dressing rooms for the bridal party.

Overlooking the Willamette River, the location of Oaks Pioneer Church provides an attractive natural setting as well as numerous excellent sites for outdoor photographs. The nearby S.M.I.L.E. Station, also a project of the neighborhood association, (234-3570) is available for receptions. Both the church and station are disabled accessible.

THE OLD CHURCH
THE OLD CHURCH SOCIETY, INC.

1422 S.W. 11th Avenue • Portland, Oregon 97201
Contact: Trish Augustin
(503) 222-2031; Fax (503) 222-2981
Office Hours: Mon–Fri 11am–3pm; Sat by appointment

The Old Church, located at S.W. 11th and Clay streets, has been a Portland landmark since its completion in 1883. On the National Register of Historic Places since 1972, it no longer serves Portland as a dedicated church but as an independent historical society. As a non-religiously affiliated church building, it allows each couple the opportunity to bring in the officiator of their choice. The Old Church stands as a striking example of Carpenter Gothic architecture with its Corinthian columns supporting a cathedral ceiling. The original ornate stained-glass windows filter the afternoon light into the chapel. Hand-carved pews surround the center aisle and slope to the altar area, giving an intimacy to the chapel that belies its 300-person capacity. A historic Hook & Hastings tracker pipe organ adds a warm ambiance to your wedding. Kinsman Hall, adjacent to the chapel, holds 200 for a standing buffet. Experienced wedding coordinators will assist you during your rehearsal and ceremony. Call The Old Church to schedule an appointment to discuss your wedding plans.

Your
Garden Wedding
at
The Quello House

16445 S.W. 92nd Avenue
Tigard, Oregon 97224
(503) 684-5456

Some people dream of a garden wedding...
A special few live their dream!

In Oregon's beautiful Tualatin Valley, 15 minutes from downtown Portland, amidst towering cedar and fir, with a view of Mount Hood, stands one of the Pacific Northwest's most beautiful houses.

Recipient of the prestigious 1995 "Great American Home Award," The Quello House, with its award-winning gardens, is ready to turn your dream into a reality.

You and your guests will love the idea of having your wedding and *reception* at one spectacular location. Owners and wedding consultants, Dan and Jacque Quello, will take the worry out of your wedding. By providing everything from flowers to music, minister to dance floor, catering to cleanup—you are left with little to do but enjoy your wedding day!

The Quello House, listed on the National Register of Historic Places... a "once upon a time" place... where dreams do come true!

Call for information or an appointment and we will send you one of our lovely brochures.

TIGARD UNITED METHODIST CHURCH

9845 S.W. Walnut Place
Tigard, Oregon 97223
(503) 639-3181
Contact: Pastor Wesley Taylor

Our fully remodeled and expanded sanctuary, equipped with a state-or-the-art sound system, seats up to 500 people. Warm, cheery colors, flexible seating, a grand piano and organ highlight the Tigard United Methodist Church. A large bridal dressing room is available. In addition, a chapel is available for small weddings.

Our three reception areas, including the main hall, can handle upwards of 400 guests, depending upon your needs (full dinner buffet planned, dance floor).

Please call the church office for more information or to request a wedding information book (503) 639-3181. Our church staff and wedding coordinator are ready to help with your plans.

UNITY OF BEAVERTON

12650 S.W. Fifth Street
Beaverton, Oregon 97005
(503) 646-3364
Office Hours: Tues–Fri 10am–5pm

Congratulations on your engagement! Unity of Beaverton invites you to visit our sanctuary and feel the warmth and serenity that make our church the ideal setting for your wedding. The sanctuary comfortably seats 140 people and features oak floors, contemporary lighting and soft upholstered chairs. We also have a piano and electronic keyboard available for your use.

You may select your own minister or ask for a referral list of ministers who are familiar with the setting and can tailor a ceremony to your special needs. Our reasonable standard fee for the facility includes three hours for the wedding plus one hour for a rehearsal prior to the ceremony.

Unity of Beaverton is centrally located near downtown Beaverton on the corner of Fifth and Angel, one block west of Watson (which runs parallel to Hall Boulevard). For further information or to schedule a tour of the facility, please call (503) 646-3364. If your call is answered by voice mail, be sure to leave a message and we will get back to you as soon as possible.

We look forward to helping you make your wedding day a joy-filled, memorable occasion. Let us know how we can help. Blessings!

The Wedding Place

♥

908 Esther Street • Vancouver, Washington 98661
Contact: Bobbee Sapp, Minister & Wedding Coordinator
(360) 693-1798
Office Hours: Mon–Fri 10am–4:30pm;
Evening tours by appointment
E-mail: WeddingPlace@WeLoveWeddings.com
Web site: www.weloveweddings.com/weddingplace

The Wedding Place is the perfect site for the small, intimate yet elegantly affordable wedding. The 1903 house is decorated throughout with florals and Victorian furnishings and antiques. It is fully air-conditioned. The tasteful, elegant living room is the perfect backdrop for an informal or formal wedding. It features a gas burning fireplace for an at-home feel. There are dressing rooms for the bride and groom. Whether you want an alternative from the courthouse atmosphere with a simple non-denominational Christian ceremony for the bride, groom and two witnesses; or are planning on a guest list for five to 50, The Wedding Place is the perfect place for your wedding and or/reception. Ministers are also available for ceremonies at your site of choice.

The Wedding Place is a convenient place to hold small receptions and is available for parties, bridal showers, anniversaries, and morning business meetings. We will help with all aspects of your wedding or event to make it a wonderful memory. There are florals, unity candles and bridal accessories available for those added touches that make your day special.

Woodland Chapel
"A Tradition"

582 High Street S.E.
Salem, Oregon 97301
Contact: Office coordinator (503) 362-4139
Business Hours: Tues–Fri 10am–3pm

Woodland Chapel features a tree-shaded private park and intimate creekside setting. Our wedding chapel facility includes a lovely sanctuary featuring an unusual stained glass window and an arboretum. Our chapel and grounds are the perfect place for your wedding day photographs. The Chapel seats 125 guests in air-conditioned comfort.

The Rev. Manon Hamile will custom tailor your wedding to suit you. Our wedding staff consists of wedding coordinators, organists and sound technicians available to respond to all your wedding questions and desires. For your convenience, a reception hall with a fully equipped kitchen is located downstairs. Larger reception facilities are located nearby. Conveniently located in downtown Salem with plenty of free parking available.

Woodland Chapel is a non-denominational church that promotes successful living based on the truth that each person is an expression of God. It provides a center for learning and practicing the recognition of self-worth in an atmosphere of love and fellowship. It teaches that there is a power of Good in the Universe, available to all.

MARRIAGE

My most brilliant

achievement was my ability

to be able to persuade my

wife to marry me.

Winston Churchill

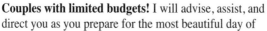

An Angelic Time

REV. D. DOUGLAS WHINERY

North Willamette Valley • Portland, Oregon
(503) 245-8281

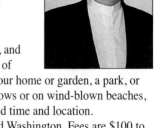

Couples with limited budgets! I will advise, assist, and direct you as you prepare for the most beautiful day of your lives. Whether your ceremony takes place at your home or garden, a park, or your "private dream place," in high mountain meadows or on wind-blown beaches, I will perform your wedding service at your specified time and location. Nondenominational. Registered for both Oregon and Washington. Fees are $100 to $125. We must have a no-obligation coffee call for planning the ceremony portion of your great celebration.

REV. SHARON K. BIEHL

(503) 653-2013

Creative, personalized wedding ceremonies. It's your day, so it should be your way! I specialize in traditional, nontraditional, religious, or nonreligious ceremonies tailored to fit your wishes and beliefs. As a nondenominational minister, I can be flexible to the situation, and I'll be glad to perform the ceremony at a site of your choice. There is no charge for an initial meeting to discuss your plans for the ceremony. At that time we'll be able to determine exactly what you want and discuss the costs. Call for an appointment anytime between 8am and 10pm. **Licensed to perform weddings in Oregon and Washington.**

CHAPEL OF THE HEART

A delightful setting for Special Occasions
P.O. Box 223 • Hillsboro, Oregon 97123
(503) 648-5160; Fax (503) 640-6766
The Reverends: Fran Lancaster, Lisa Neves and Fama Partlow

Our wedding ceremony is sure to delight and inspire you! It is nondenominational and written to honor the spiritual essence of your love. If you would like to create a more personal expression, we can adapt your own vows or special readings into your ceremony.

Together, we represent a personal history of commitment to the joy of strong family values. We know the worth of creating heartfelt memories that last a lifetime. Helping you create them is our delight! Let's begin a beautiful journey together soon. Recognition for blended families and step-children can also be made upon request.

We will perform the ceremony at our chapel or the location of your choice-at the beach, park, mountains...

REV. GARY CONKEY
REV. CATHERINE CONKEY
Heart-Centered Ceremonies
(503) 234-6851

Lovingly personalized wedding ceremonies. We specialize in creating a wedding ceremony that is unique to you and to your relationship, one that will become a moving and memorable experience for you and for your guests. Our goal is to have your guests tell us the ceremony sounds as though we wrote it just for you.

As nondenominational ministers, we are both open to performing a variety of ceremony styles and we have creative ideas to make your day extra special. We are licensed to perform weddings in Oregon and Washington at the location of your choice. Our fee is $100 and includes a planning session and officiating your wedding. Rehearsal time additional.

REV. GLORIA DAILY
(360) 574-2046

Licensed to perform weddings in either Oregon or Washington. I offer a traditional ceremony. I am a nondenominational minister, therefore able to be flexible and work with the bride and groom to personalize their ceremony. I am flexible to their ceremony site, whether it be at a church, home, park, or garden. Attire is always appropriate to the occasion. A meeting prior to the wedding is suggested but not required. There is no charge for the initial consultation. Fees begin at $75. Call for an appointment.

REV. KENNETH F. GUINN
affiliated with The Hostess House
(360) 574-3284

Licensed to perform weddings in both Washington and Oregon.
Your wedding ceremony is one of the most exciting and thrilling times of your life. It should be the way you want it to be. I work with you to design a personal and romantic ceremony and will travel to the site of your choice. A fee of $100 is charged for most weddings in Vancouver or Portland. If you would like me to attend the rehearsal, an additional fee for time will be charged. Nondenominational. Available seven days and nights a week.

Heartfelt Expressions
REV. LYNNE YON-STARK
4610 Fuhrer Street NE • Salem, Oregon 97305
(503) 390-9056 or (800) 779-7167

I believe this is your day, your once in a lifetime dream, an opportunity to share an intimate expression of your union. My goal is to help your unique vision of this special day become reality. Some weddings are elaborate and very formal, some simple and private. Each couple's needs are unique, which is why my motto is Your Wedding-Your Way. Together we can compose your vows and create your very personal wedding ceremony. I also offer prepared vows to couples who prefer to have theirs created for them. You choose your own special setting, backyard–beach–forest–park–hot air balloon–church. Prices, gladly discussed, vary according to services provided. Please call and let's work together to create your wedding-your way.

REV. GEORGIE HUSTEAD
Global Peace Center, Founder
Ordained Nondenominational Minister
(503) 643-2718

Personalized wedding ceremonies. I will work with you to help create the wedding ceremony that you want. Each beautiful and heartfelt ceremony is written individually for each bride and groom.

I do both traditional and nontraditional weddings, renewal of vows, within your budget, at the site of your choice. Family mem-bers or friends can participate by reading a special piece of poetry, singing, or playing an instrument. There is no charge for the initial meeting. Please phone for an appointment between 8am and 10pm.

"PASTOR BOB" HUTCHINSON
(503) 537-9726
Fax (503) 537-9726

Pastor Bob and his wife, Lois, share in planning your wedding ceremony. Pastor Bob is the creator of "The Family Blending Ceremony." Couples being married who have children from a previous marriage take vows focusing on loving and caring for one another's children. Inside weddings include the lighting of "The Unity Candle," while outdoor weddings include "The Communal Drink," a ceremony created by Pastor Bob. For a beautiful wedding ceremony by a minister with a wonderful sense of humor, call Pastor Bob.

JOHN L. RIGGS, JR.

(503) 656-3893 message phone; (503) 557-8557
Located in Oregon City-Portland area

Nondenominational minister with a sense of humor and the ability to ease your worries. Licensed to perform in Oregon and Washington. Available for weddings during weekdays too. Formality of the ceremony can be varied according to your wishes and beliefs. Meeting with the bride and groom is recommended to discuss standard or personalized marriage vows. References from happy brides and grooms provided on request. Prices vary according to services provided and are discussed gladly. Will be happy to perform ceremony in a park, your home or a church. Ceremonies performed in the past include those for ordinary hard-working couples, professionals and celebrities. All receive the same treatment for a realistic fee.

REV. ROBERT H. THOMAS

UNITED METHODIST CHURCH
12820 N.W. 33rd Avenue • Vancouver, Washington 98685
(360) 573-7725

Licensed to perform weddings in Oregon and Washington, I will be happy to perform your wedding at the location of your choice. At our initial meeting, we will discuss whether you want a traditional Christian service or if you would prefer to create your own. Each wedding is personalized to suit the couple. Premarriage counseling is available but not required. My fee for planning, rehearsal and officiating at your wedding ceremony is $125.

REV. KATE MCKERN VERIGIN

(503) 256-9833

Kate McKern Verigin, a licensed nondenominational minister, creates ceremonies that celebrate all aspects of life—marriage, family blessings, baptisms, retirement, landmark birthdays and anniversaries, and memorial services. Weddings are her specialty.

   *"A wedding ceremony is the ultimate ritual, a true rite of passage ceremony. My wedding ceremony is an intricately designed tapestry, interwoven with a variety of spiritual philosophies and cultural traditions. It creates a soulful expression of love and celebration for **everyone** in attendance."*   ~Rev. Kate Verigin

   A fee of $150 is charged for the wedding ceremony, plus one premarital planning session. Your personal needs and desires will be incorporated into her highly praised marriage ceremony. Kate also is an EMMY Award-winning television writer/producer, publicist, author, inspirational speaker, spiritual counselor and mentor, wife, step-mom and cat lover.

Notes

FACT

The bride and groom must make a public pronouncement that they want to marry this particular partner. By saying the words, "I, Mary, take thee, John" and vice versa, the wedding ceremony becomes legal.

Butterfly Magic

**Release Elegant Live Butterflies
At Your Wedding!**

For information or a brochure call (503) 774-9288

Add Fairytale Magic to Your Wedding!

A butterfly release is designed to make your special occasion enchanting and unforgettable. On that special day, we will deliver the butterflies to your event where you will distribute one box containing a butterfly to each guest. The guests will then release the butterflies at a specially designated moment and read time-honored "fortune cookie-type" passages about love, friendship, life or nature. A butterfly release occasion is great fun for all since it lets your guests participate in your wedding.

About the Butterflies

The butterflies are indoor-bred by the Northwest's most experienced butterfly company. The butterflies are well treated and are fed the day of the event, and there is no need to raise the butterflies yourself.

Samples of Messages Inside the Butterfly Boxes

♥ To find joy in another's joy: that is the secret of happiness.
♥ Real love begins when we expect nothing in return.
♥ A successful marriage requires falling in love many times with the same person.
♥ Of all the music that reaches farthest into heaven, is the beating of a loving heart.

Butterfly/Dove Combination Package

Now you can experience both butterflies and doves together at a very special price!

Reservations

To best ensure your reservation, it is recommended you order 6–8 weeks before your wedding. A 50% deposit is required at the time of the order and the balance is due 15 days before the event.

Availability

Butterflies: May–September
Doves: February–September (cages of doves are available throughout the year)

See Dove Magic, page 337.

DOVES AND BUTTERFLIES FOR RENT

MR. DOVELY

(503) 643-9730

Doves for Display and/or Release

With 12 years of experience Mr. Dovely is best known for his promptness, professional appearance—always arriving in a tuxedo and white gloves—and the attractiveness of his birds. The birds are clean, healthy and well-trained. Your guests will not soon forget the show of doves circling several times overhead before heading back to their home.

The release of doves at special events is an age-old tradition. The dove is a symbol of our love, our joy, and our hope. The release of doves (from gift wrapped boxes or cages) during a wedding or the display of doves in gilded cages at the church or reception makes a wonderful addition to any wedding.

A gentle butterfly release for a peaceful, quiet garden setting.

Availability and Cost

The doves fly from February to September, and cages of doves are available year 'round. Doves can fly up to 100 miles. Please call for a price quote.

Reservations

Please make your reservations early. The doves book quickly, particularly during the summer months. Gilded dove cages, and pictures of gift wrapped doves and doves in flight, are available at The Wedding Cottage at 4775 S.W. Watson Avenue, Beaverton, Oregon. Please call or stop by for more information.

DOVE TALES

"CREATING MEMORIES FOR YOU"

Contact: Alyce Dingler (503) 663-4229 or Rich Steele (503) 663-0123

Doves
Enhance your special day with the traditional and eternal symbol of
LOVE...DOVES.

During your wedding or reception, we can:
- Release white doves to fly
- Beautifully display live doves
- Send a special message to someone on the wings of a dove

Availability
Doves are available any time during the year for display. Doves released for flight
are available early spring through late fall (winter possible depending on severity of
weather). All doves are trained to return home after being released.

Reservations
Are required at least two weeks in advance. However, we recommend you reserve
early to ensure availability.

Cost
Price varies according to the number of birds, time of day, location, distance and
special arrangements required. Please call (503) 663-4229 or (503) 663-0123 for a
price quote based on your requirements. A 50% deposit is required at the time of
booking.

People Say
*"Your beautiful white doves made our wedding memorable and unique. Our guests
stood in awe as the birds took flight in honor of our special day. Thank you."* said
Kim Pascual (bride)

*"Your doves soaring above the thousands of women who came in support of finding
a cure for breast cancer set the stage for the 1997 Race for the Cure,"* said
Stephanie Koenig, Race for the Cure Marketing Chairperson. *"Our hearts and
minds flew on the wings of your birds as they lofted toward the sky. We look forward
to working with Dove Tales again in 1998."*

In our tradition of
"Creating Memories For You"©

Dove Magic

**Express Your Love
By Releasing Snow-white Birds**

For information or a brochure call (503) 774-9288

---

*"The Dove" — a strong but swift flyer;
yet, a gentle and devoted lover.
A perfect symbol for everlasting love.*

Doves for Display

Doves in gorgeous gilded cages can be placed by the entrance-way of your church or reception site to delight your incoming guests. Doves by the guest book or gift tables at your reception site will also set your guests a flutter.

Doves for Flight

Release two to twenty beautiful birds during or after the ceremony. Our doves are the healthiest and most spirited available.

Written Dove Introductions

Choose from many poetic ceremony introductions.

Butterfly/Dove Combination Package

Now you can experience both butterflies and doves together at a very special price!

Availability

The doves book on a first come, first serve basis from February through September. Yet, caged doves are available throughout the year.

See Butterfly Magic, page 334.

Notes

FLOWER
PETALS

*Flower petals strewn down
the aisle were used to put a
protective layer between
the floor and the bride's
feet, guarding her from the
evil ground monster.*

HELPFUL HINTS

- **Kinds of party supplies:** For the biggest party of your life, be sure to stop by a party supply shop. You will discover fun ways to decorate, from crepe paper to balloons in every color imaginable. A party-supply store can help you with special themes and ideas for decorating tables, walls, ceilings, and floors!

- **Wedding accessories and decorations:** If you're looking for wedding bells, streamers, banners, or car decorations, you'll be sure to find them at a party specialist shop. Matching tablecloths, napkins, paper plates, and cups will coordinate your reception. Some shops can provide imprinted napkins, matches, ribbons, and balloons.

- **Case or bulk discounts:** Be sure to inquire about discounts when buying large quantities of items. You may want to consider renting a tank of helium so you can coordinate your own balloon decorations for the reception and save money.

- **Bridal accessories:** Some party shops have bridal accessories including cake knives and servers, unity candles, toasting goblets, ring-bearer pillows, and gift ideas for bridesmaids and groomsmen.

- **Special-occasion decorations:** Party shops carry a large selection of party decorations and accessories for weddings, birthdays, anniversaries, etc.... Theme-coordinated decorations are very popular—matching plates, napkins, cups, invitations, and other accessories such as guest books and photo albums. Gift supplies include coordinated wrapping paper, ribbon, gift bags, tissue, cards, and more.

- **Balloon ideas:** Balloons are an inexpensive means of decorating while providing a dramatic visual effect. They can also be used to hide flaws in walls or ceilings. Balloons can be sculpted to create special effects—in heart shapes or any shape you desire. Arches made with helium balloons create a special effect over entrances, dance floors, and buffet tables. A fun idea is to have a balloon release with special notes inside. **NOTE:** Some reception facilities do not allow balloons. Check to be sure they are allowed before you place your balloon order.

- **Colors of balloons:** Your special wedding colors can be created by placing a balloon of one color inside another of a different color.

- **Imprinted balloons:** Balloons can be imprinted with your names and wedding date, or anything else you choose. One couple released balloons with their name, wedding date, and telephone number on them, and received calls from all over, wishing them well.

For more assistance with staying organized during the wedding planning process, check out the Bravo! Wedding Organizer. Detailed question worksheets double as contracts. This step-by-step system will keep every detail of your wedding organized. To order, refer to the order form on page 23 in this Guide.

THE PAPER TREE

2916 N.E. Broadway
Portland, Oregon 97232
Contact: Margo Alkema (503) 284-4741
Business Hours: Mon–Fri 9:30am–6pm; Sat 9:30am–5:30pm

Retail Party Supplies

The Paper Tree has a complete selection of party supplies at competitive prices. We have the widest selection of colors on the West Coast, numbering 37 at this time. Wedding designs featuring beautiful color combinations are our specialty.

Our products include the following:

- **Napkins:** solids, floral prints, and wedding patterns
- **Plates:** many colors and patterns
- **Cups** and drinkware in paper and plastic in various sizes
- **Table covers:** paper and plastic, round and rectangular
- **Flatware:** colored forks, spoons, and knives
- **Serving items:** plastic serving bowls and trays

Decorations

The Paper Tree has items to decorate your entire wedding within the theme. We carry these decorations:

- **Balloons:** festive balloons in many colors and sizes
- **Crêpe paper and streamers:** great for the reception in a variety of colors
- **Tissue bells** to decorate the reception site and car
- **Garlands** in numerous types and colors

Wedding Accessories

Our large stock of wedding accessories includes garters, guest books, feather pens, planning books, bride's memory books, picture albums, wedding knives and cake servers, toasting goblets, and cake tops. We also carry candles in a variety of colors.

Personalized Items

We can imprint napkins and matchbooks with less than one week's notice at a very competitive price.

ONE-STOP PARTY SHOP

The Paper Tree is truly a one-stop-shopping experience for all of your party needs from the bridal shower to the wedding reception. Our friendly, experienced staff is carefully chosen and trained to help plan your special occasion. We have served bridal needs in Portland for 41 years and have full-time bridal consultants on staff at all times to offer you assistance.

See page 395 under Invitations, Addressing & Calligraphy.

Beaverton • (503) 646-3145
Progress Plaza • 8620 S.W. Hall Blvd.
Portland • (503) 252-6032
205 Plaza • 10540 S.E. Washington
Salem • (503) 585-0292
Target Center • 3892 Center St. N.E.

Store Hours: Mon–Fri 9am–9pm; Sat 9am–7pm; Sun 10am–6pm

Party Depot is a locally-owned complete party supply and rental source with the largest selection of party goods in the Northwest. Imagine being able to get everything you need and expert advice to pull it all together in one visit.

HUGE SELECTION — COMPETITIVE PRICING
The largest and most complete selection of solid and patterned tableware.

- Tablecovers
- Table Skirts
- Plates
- Napkins
- Doilies
- Candles
- Serving Trays
- Tray Covers
- Serving Utensils
- Bowls
- Cake Toppers
- Cake Decorating Supplies
- Punch Bowls
- Champagne/Beverage Cups
- Hot/Cold Cups
- Tumblers
- Barware

DECORATIONS
Everything in every style and color for every occasion.

- Latex and Mylar Balloons
- Balloon Arches & Columns
- Tulle Netting and Circles
- Millinery Flowers
- Confetti
- Streamers
- Tissue Bells
- Centerpieces
- Party Favors
- Ribbons
- Potpourri
- Place Cards

WEDDING AND PARTY PROPS
Stop by our showroom to see our selection of arches, baskets, canopies, and more…

WEDDING ACCESSORIES

- Wedding Planners
- Photo Albums
- Guest Books
- Stationery
- Film
- Unity Candles
- Toasting Glasses
- Cake Servers
- Gift Wrap
- Cake Decorating Supplies
- Frames
- Baskets
- Ring Bearer Pillows
- Greeting Cards

INVITATIONS — 25–30% OFF CUSTOM INVITATIONS

- Orders can be ready in one–two weeks
- Printed Napkins
- Response and Thank-you Cards
- Matchbooks and Ribbons

YOUR COMPLETE PARTY SUPPLY
AND RENTAL STATION

1400 N.W. 15th Avenue
Portland, Oregon 97209
(503) 294-0412; Fax (503) 294-0616
Business Hours: Mon–Sat 8am–6pm
Appointments available any hour

Services

West Coast Event Productions is the Northwest's premier idea center for all events and special occasions. We specialize in the custom planning and design of event staging, lighting, sound, special effects, tabletop décor, and event and theme production. We are able to tailor your wedding to mirror your vision. We are here to help you make all your important event planning decisions. Please feel free to visit our newly designed showroom. Browse for ideas with our Photo Inventory Books. We have many of our specialty props, catering items and equipment displayed to aid in your event planning.

Rental Items Available

Table art: West Coast Event Productions features the Northwest's most outstanding selection of specialty linens and tabletop décor. Choose from designer florals, theme print linens, damasks, hand-painted tabletops and unique floral arrangements, along with a complete palette of solid colors with coordinating napkins and runners. Ask about our specialty chair covers and gold ballroom chairs.

Party rental supplies: West Coast Event Productions will also custom coordinate place settings, glassware and flatware with a variety of clever and innovative themes. Choose from a selection of 14 different china patterns. Our coordinating table accessories and centerpieces add excitement while complimenting your own individual style.

Custom themes: West Coast Event Production's visual department is deft in the handling and design of props for thematic events. We work with our clients to construct a concept that reflect our client's vision. The staff at West Coast Event Productions has the experience and creativity to produce events of any size or budget from small elegant gatherings to large elaborate weddings.

Wedding accessories: select from several styles of candelabras, brass and silver table candelabras, brass and contemporary full standing candelabras; wedding aisle and carpet runners; custom chuppahs; gazebos and arches; wood, ceramic, marble finish and Grecian columns; table accessories include urns, vases, hurricanes, votives, cherubs and table lamps.

New for this year: West Coast Event Production is the only event production company in Oregon to carry a full line of Kosher dishes. We also have a Chuppah complete with a canopy of two layers of linen and fabric adornments off each brass leg. Come see our new decorative gold and silver chargers; a perfect accent at any table setting. The gold chargers are ideal next to our beautifully crafted gold flatware.

West Coast Event Productions

We are dedicated in providing you with a service that is unmatched anywhere else. By providing a number of services in one location we are able to handle the all your special needs and requests. It is our personal attention to detail, client devotion and experience in the event rental and production field that has propelled West Coast Event Productions into one of the most celebrated "entertainment" companies in the Northwest.

Please let this business know that you heard about them from the Bravo! Bridal Resource Guide. **343**

Notes

THE BRIDE'S BOUQUET

The first flowers carried by

brides were a combination

of fragrant herbs whose

strong aromas were

purported to keep evil

spirits at bay.

As time passed, flowers

were added and came to

represent the bride's

virginity, femininity,

and fragility.

HELPFUL HINTS

- **Selecting a florist:** Most florists have a portfolio of their work. Choose a florist who will spend time with you. If the florist has not been to the site before, you may want them to do so to view the decor they will be working with. This ensures that they design your arrangements to match the surroundings and can be very helpful when you are discussing your ideas and needs with them. Ask for references to see what customers say about what was promised and what was actually delivered. Your florist can also inform you about what flowers will be in season and styles that will appropriately fit your theme and budget.

- **Develop a plan:** Think about your floral design and decorations and write it down. Determine what you will need for the various people involved, arrangements for the church, and decorations for the reception. Consider your budget. Ask several florists for formal bids based on your outline. Then determine which florist and budget you feel most comfortable with.

- **Meeting with the florist:** You should meet with your florist as soon as possible. A florist can only commit to a limited number of weddings or events, especially during the busy summer months. Be sure to bring color swatches of the exact colors you've selected.

- **Being prepared for your florist:** When meeting with your florist it is good to bring ideas to your first meeting. Although the florist may have photos of arrangements and bouquets or books, it is important to give a sense of what you are looking for. Take advantage of the florist's expertise. Be sure to tell the florist or designer if there are flower types that you absolutely do not like (i.e. carnations, baby's breath); also let them know what you love!

- **Flower shades and colors:** Colors and shades can be challenging when selecting flowers. If you select burgundy roses—beware, your burgundy may be the grower's "deep red". Always use a fabric swatch or ribbon sample to show your florist the exact color you are thinking of. The florist will help to tie the entire theme and mood of your wedding with the floral decorations and bouquets.

- **Throw-away bouquet:** Consider having a throw-away bouquet. When it comes time to throw the bouquet, many brides wish they had an alternative so that their own bridal bouquet could be preserved.

- **Mothers' corsages:** It is recommended that mothers and grandmothers wear wrist or purse corsages. This eliminates pin marks in a beautiful silk or chiffon dress. A shoulder corsage has a tendency to pull down on lightweight fabric, giving a beautiful dress an awkward look in photographs. Be sure to ask your florist to bring extra pins for corsages and boutonnieres.

- **Delivery and setup of flowers:** It is very important that your flowers be delivered at the right time. They shouldn't arrive earlier than necessary, since some facilities are not air conditioned and certain flowers deteriorate rapidly. If your flowers must be in place at a certain time, tell your florist what time they'll be needed. Always put the location and date on your contract, as well as the desired time of delivery so to prevent questions or last-minute problems. Check to see if the bid includes setup and delivery. If it doesn't, allow extra in your budget.

For more assistance with staying organized during the wedding planning process, check out the Bravo! Wedding Organizer. Detailed question worksheets double as contracts. This step-by-step system will keep every detail of your wedding organized. To order, refer to the order form on page 23 in this Guide.

BRIDAL BLOSSOMS

A Wedding Florist Who Also
Specializes in Flower Preservation
Contact: Shirley Keller
(503) 297-3042; Fax (503) 297-0459
Business Hours: Mon–Sat by appointment
E-mail: BriBlos@aol.com
Web site: www.citysearch.com/pdx/bridalblossoms

Throw Your Bouquet Our Way and Keep The Romance Forever!

There is one wedding memento you may not have realized you could save. It is your bouquet. Now, at Bridal Blossoms, you can capture the beauty and color of just-picked flowers for years to come. Preserve those floral memories beautifully arranged under glass with other keepsakes that you choose: a bit of lace, your grandmother's cameo, the groom's bow tie and boutonniere. Plan to include something with your names and the wedding date, which allows your special memories to live on as a romantic reminder of your wedding day. Bridal Blossoms offers a variety of designs in domes and hexagons to set on a table. They range from 4" x7" to 12" x23" and you have a choice of oak, fruitwood, or brass base. Or, you could choose the popular oval frame with convex glass and many choices of finishes, designs, colors, and sizes to enhance any floral arrangement and complement a wide variety of personal tastes. Custom-made rectangular frames are available in the size of your choice. Curio cabinets and tables with glass top and sides are also available. Each arrangement is one of a kind, personalized for you. Your flowers will be displayed in their three-dimensional beauty and entirety. Many brides choose to use the bridesmaids' dress fabric or fabric from their own gowns for the background.

Pre-planning

You will have to view a preserved bouquet to appreciate the beauty of this treasured keepsake. Call for an appointment before your wedding, so we can estimate the cost and give you instructions on the care of your bouquet. The fresher the flowers, the better the end results (NEVER FREEZE FLOWERS). For local weddings, designate someone to bring the flowers to Bridal Blossoms after the wedding (usually we receive the flowers from a Saturday wedding on the following Monday or Tuesday). Shirley Keller, designer at Bridal Blossoms, has been preserving bouquets since the early 1980s. Her specialty is wedding flowers, so the addition of preservation was a natural to follow.

   Bridal bouquet preservation is a great gift idea. Gift certificates are available.

COMPLETE WEDDING FLORIST

Bridal Blossoms designs fresh or silk flowers for the complete wedding, tailoring each package to each bride's needs and budget. Be sure to bring fabric swatches along with your ideas for the wedding you envision. No ideas? Then let us help you. We have a portfolio of photographs to help you choose which flowers and designs will best enhance your personality. This is your wedding, and our goal is to work with you to personalize your flowers. Bridal Blossoms recommends reserving your date as soon as possible as we do limit the number of weddings per weekend. The initial consultation is free. Let us help your wedding "Blossom."

Mention Bravo Bridal Guide and receive a 15% discount on preservation
when we do the wedding flowers. Not valid with any other offer.

From My Fathers Garden

Bridal flower preservation

212 W. 35th Street
Vancouver, Washington 98660
Contact: Michelle Bigelow
(360) 695-3212

The Everlasting Art of Floral Preservation

Let From My Father's Garden create for you a treasured heirloom using your bridal bouquet. We use the time tested Victorian technique of pressing the flowers. The flowers artistically embrace your invitation and chosen photo. Only acid-free materials will touch your flowers, photo and invitation. UV conservation glass is used in the framing process. We feel that by including your invitation, photo and flowers we can create a piece of art that you can cherish and adore for years to come!

Why this method? By pressing your flowers we are able to secure them so there will not be any accidental breakage. We also create an environment that deters deterioration by only using acid-free products and conservation glass.

We have several styles to choose from, creating for you a cherished heirloom—a lovely reminder of your special day!

A $70 deposit reserves your wedding date. Two free 8x10 pieces (framing not included, one offer per client) for booking your wedding date. These make a great gift for your mother and mother-in-law!

Helpful Hints

★ Call early for an appointment prior to your wedding date for a free consultation
★ The fresher the flowers, the lovelier the completed piece.
★ Refrigerate your flowers, preferably on the bottom rack (it's the farthest from the freezer!)
  *DO NOT FREEZE
★ DO NOT PLACE IN A PLASTIC BAG. DO NOT MIST OR WATER.

Gift Certificates Available

*"I am so pleased, not only with the piece, but with the memories
it invokes. It's taken the memory and made it an heirloom!"*
Wendy Justice, Bride

*"I love it. It is absolutely beautiful. It is much
lovelier than I thought it would be!"*
Leah Boyer, Bride

*"It's absolutely beautiful! I'll have my flowers, picture,
and invitation for the rest of my life"*
Rachel Meyer, Bride

BALLOON MANIA

1417 N.W. 138th Circle
Vancouver, Washington 98685
Contact: Rita Stromme
(360) 573-5465
Business Hours: day or evening appointments available

Design Ideas

Balloons are the perfect decorating alternative for any occasion or event. Arches, swags, columns and sculptures can highlight the focal points of your reception and give the room an air of festivity and elegance. Balloon centerpieces can be created for the dining, buffet and head tables with a special theme if desired.

Imagine how balloons can enhance your wedding photographs! They are available in an artist's palette of colors. Call for a free consultation and we can show you color samples. It is helpful to bring fabric and color swatches. You can browse through our extensive portfolio filled with design ideas and samples of Balloon Mania's work. We can then discuss ideas that will make your wedding just what you have envisioned. It is ideal to meet at the event site to determine the appropriate decor.

Cost and Terms

Appointments for a consultation should be made two to three months in advance if possible. Upon confirmation, a 50% deposit is required with the balance due two weeks prior to the event.

Experience

Enthusiasm and experience enable Balloon Mania to provide the personalized service you desire to make your wedding beautiful. Rita Stromme is a member of the Vancouver "Wedding Link", and the first Certified Balloon Artist in Southwest Washington.

Here are Some Quotes from our Satisfied Customers

"Thank you very much for all your help and creative ideas. It's been a pleasure working with you."

"I wanted to tell you how beautiful the balloons were for Kelly's wedding. She was thrilled. Thank you for your special touch to our celebration."

"I can't tell you how much it added to have such beautiful accents with your balloons—they really were perfect."

BALLOONS ADD FESTIVITY AND ELEGANCE

ARTISTRY IN FLOWERS

Contact: Jackie Ralphs
(503) 235-0079
(800) 843-0945

Wedding Flowers

Flowers create the mood and can transform any location into a romantic setting. Do you prefer rich classic traditional, the elegant simplicity of contemporary, or that fresh-from-the-garden look? Together we will design wedding flowers that reflect your own personal style.

Cost and Terms

Distinctive, innovative, one-of-a-kind designs are offered at affordable prices. Any design idea can be sized up or down to fit your location and budget. A $100 deposit reserves your date with the balance due two weeks prior to your event.

Specialties

Although I have extensive training in all areas of floral design, my specialty is weddings. You can expect fresh approaches to traditional themes and every detail given careful attention. Because I only schedule one wedding per day, you will have my undivided attention. Please call for a free consultation.

Atterbury's Wedding Flowers

A Natural Touch...

(503) 356-9071, (800) 499-8201

Niki Atterbury, owner of Atterbury's Wedding Flowers, is inspired by love… the love of the bride and groom, the love of the families helping with the wedding festivities, and her own love of the flowers themselves.

Niki's work brings her a lot of joy and satisfaction. She is awed by the fact that flowers add so much, not only to the most meaningful and important occasions of our lives, but also to the everyday activities… such as gardening at home or dressing up a family meal. There are few material things in life that are so versatile in their ability to express joy and love. Niki considers it an honor to share in the planning and be present at her clients' weddings.

Niki has found that some brides seek her out knowing exactly what they want, and hire her, as a professional to fulfill their version. However, part of Niki's service is helping the more common bride… the overwhelmed one. Many brides arrive discouraged because they don't know flowers well enough to make their own choices. Niki takes the time to sit down with them and guide them through their options… which can be as simple as just choosing a style and color so that Niki can then use her expertise and taste to fashion something the bride is sure to love.

Atterbury's Wedding Flowers has been a full-service florist for the past seven years and Niki Atterbury has more than 10 years experience as a floral designer. In 1998, Niki transformed Atterbury's Wedding Flowers into a "weddings only" florist, closing her retail shop after seven successful years in Beaverton. With a boutique attitude, Atterbury's maintains a small feel and only takes a limited number of weddings per weekend, so each bride can feel assured of receiving personalized attention.

Atterbury's offers both custom and package wedding flowers. To inspire your creativity, Niki would love to share the photo albums of her work with you. Niki maintains a library of wedding ideas that will inspire you both to create a floral attitude that is just right for your special day. Please call for an appointment.

Atterbury's Wedding Flowers offers delivery and setup for a small fee. This service includes assisting the wedding party with pinning on corsages and boutonnieres, placing arrangements in both the ceremony and reception venues, as well as instructing the ladies in the proper technique of carrying bouquets down the aisle.

The payment schedule requires a 25% deposit to reserve Atterbury's Wedding Flowers as your florist on your wedding day. The balance is due two weeks before the wedding date.

1924 S.E. Tanager Circle • Hillsboro, Oregon 97123
Contact: Balenda Weisskirchen
503.693.6086
Business Hours: Please call for an appointment
(days or evenings available)

A Wedding to Remember

With over 15 years of wedding floral design experience, Balenda's Flowers will provide the personal touch you so richly deserve. Our experienced staff will accommodate all of your needs so the wedding progresses flawlessly.

Whether you choose silk or fresh flowers, we will assist and advise you in your selection so your wedding turns out just the way you have always dreamed.

No matter what your budget, Balenda's Flowers can provide you with wedding memories that will last a lifetime.

Some of the services that we provide include:

Wedding Flowers

- Victorian, Contemporary or European
- Silk or fresh
- Your personal ideas or choose from many design books

Services Offered

- Set-up and delivery by an experienced designer
- Transporting flowers from wedding to reception site
- Pinning of corsages and boutonnieres at no extra charge

Cost and Terms

Costs vary with types of flowers and size of bouquets. A $50 deposit is required with the balance due 3 weeks prior to the wedding.

Free Floral Gift with booking if you mention this ad.

4201 N.E. Fremont • Portland, Oregon 97213
Contact: Pattie Scarpelli, Amy Walling, or Doug Lotz
(503) 281-5501
Business Hours: Mon–Fri 8am–5:30 pm; Sat 8am–3pm

Wedding Flowers

At Beaumont Florist we can do any wedding size from one simple bouquet to an extravagant affair.

Services Offered

- **Rehearsal dinner flowers:** centerpieces
- **Wedding-party flowers:** bridal and bridesmaid bouquets, flower-girl basket, headpieces, toss bouquet, boutonnieres, corsages
- **Ceremony flowers:** altar bouquets, pew decorations, garlands, and candelabra arrangements
- **Reception flowers:** buffet, serving and cake-table arrangements, guest book flowers, fresh flower decorations for the cake

Cost and Terms

We require a 25% deposit to book your wedding date with the balance due two weeks before the wedding. Delivery and setup are complimentary in the Portland metro area. Please call to make an appointment for consultation, so we can give you our undivided attention.

WE MAKE WEDDING DREAMS COME TRUE

Our design staff has a combined total of 55 years experience. We take great pride in meeting our customer's complete satisfaction. Feel free to bring in your fabric swatches, pictures, and dreams, and we will design a wedding to match your color scheme and budget.

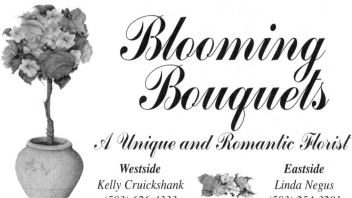

Blooming Bouquets

A Unique and Romantic Florist

Westside	Eastside
Kelly Cruickshank	*Linda Negus*
(503) 626-4333	*(503) 254-3281*

Elegant Wedding and Special Occasion Florist!

❀ **Complete Wedding Party** ❀ **Ceremony** ❀ **Reception** ❀ **Cake** ❀
❀ **Event and Rehearsal Dinner Flowers** ❀

❀ **Bridal Party Flowers:** bridal bouquets that are unique and one of a kind. Bridesmaids, flower girl bouquets, hair flowers, corsages and boutonniere

❀ **Ceremony Flowers:** altar bouquets, pew decorations, candelabras, gazebos, unity candles, garlands, arbor arches, topiaries, chuppas and pagalla decorations

❀ **Reception Flowers:** fresh floral cake decorations, cake table, buffet, serving and guest table bouquets

Costs and Terms

We are very conscientious about working with a budget and are able to give you more flowers at a more comfortable price. Every stem we purchase is used for your wedding only, giving you full and gorgeous bouquets. We never skimp. A nonrefundable deposit of $50 holds the date of your wedding.

Consultations

We have an extensive portfolio for you to look at during a free consultation. We have many creative, fresh and original ideas to make your wedding and reception one of a kind.

WEDDINGS ARE OUR AREA OF EXPERTISE

Blooming Bouquets has more than 15 years of design experience with a unique and romantic style. We can create any design you want, from romantic to contemporary wildflowers to orchids. We offer very personal attention in a comfortable atmosphere with attention to every detail. We take extra time to listen to your needs and fit your flowers to your style. We have done flowers for Portland's Rose Festival and have appeared on *AM Northwest!*

Please call for a free consultation.

"for Wedding Bouquets that are as beautiful and
timeless as the love that you have for each other."

Mention this ad and receive a free toss bouquet with order!

1256 N.W. 175th Place • Beaverton, Oregon 97006
Contact: Cheryl Skoric, CBA (503) 629-5827; Fax (503) 645-9404
Oregon's first Certified Balloon Artist
Business Hours: to suit your schedule,
day or evening by appointment

Bouquets & Balloons

Let Bouquets & Balloons Make Your Dreams Come True!

Being a freelance designer, Cheryl is able to focus her attention on you. Her creativity and experience enable her to help you plan custom floral and/or balloon designs that will beautifully reflect the theme and feel of the wedding or special event on any budget. Cheryl has 11 years experience as a florist and seven years experience in balloon design. She is a staff member of the International Balloon Arts Convention, and she continues to educate herself by attending conventions nationwide. Come in for a FREE consultation and review samples and portfolios of her work.

The personal consultation, visiting the church and reception sites, and pinning on the corsages and boutonnieres are all complimentary. Cheryl is there to make sure all the finishing touches are perfect.

Cost and Terms

Flowers: Costs vary with types of flowers and size of arrangement. Starting Prices:

Bouquets	$25	Boutonnieres	$3.50
Flower Girl Baskets	$15	Corsages	$4
Altar Arrangements	$80	Candelabra Arrangements	$35

Balloons: Costs vary due to size and type of balloon used
Arches: spiral, pearl, fishbone
Sculptures: bride, groom, swans, rings, hearts, wreaths and anything else you can dream up
Canopies: full balloon canopy, heart of tulle canopy, Cinderella canopy
Special effects: exploding balloons, exploding walls, confetti cannons and more!

Upon confirmation, a 25% deposit is required, with the balance due two weeks prior to your event.

Quotes From Our Satisfied Customers

Seen in March/April '98 *Bridal Connection* page 33: *"Cheryl did a fantastic job. I have really high expectations-and I've never seen flowers as beautiful."* — Jennifer (Kosta) Walsdorf

"Wow! I guess the delivery made a huge impression. I know we settled on $60, but due to the overwhelming reaction, I think it's worth a few more dollars. Thank you for such a terrific job on such short notice." — Scott Gee, ABC

BURLINGAME *Flower Shop*

246-1311

FLOWERS TO SUIT THE OCCASION

8605 S.W. Terwilliger Blvd.
Portland, Oregon 97219
Contact: Violet or Jan Patella (503) 246-1311
Business Hours: Mon–Fri 8am–6:15pm; Sat 8am–5:30pm

Wedding Flowers

Our wedding flowers are created to fit the individual and her unique personality. Selected staff will work personally with each bride, designing everything to fit her and her needs. For over 40 years, we've worked with all kinds of budgets from small to large, and we'll be happy to show you how to get the most from your wedding or event flower budget. Come in for a consultation and to review samples and portfolios of our work.

Services Offered

- **Rehearsal-party flowers:** table arrangements, garden baskets, and more
- **Wedding-party flowers:** bridal and bridesmaid bouquets and headpieces, flower-girl bouquets and baskets, men's boutonnieres, corsages
- **Ceremony flowers:** altar bouquets, candelabra arrangements, pew bows, etc.
- **Reception flowers:** buffet, serving, and cake-table arrangements; guest-table arrangements; fresh cake flowers

We recommend you provide us with color and fabric swatches so that the floral arrangements we design for you will complement, blend, and accent your wedding and reception settings as well as you and your attendants' attire.

Cost and Terms

Burlingame Flower Shop requires a 25% deposit when placing the wedding order, with the balance due one week prior to the wedding date. We ask our brides to schedule an appointment for a comprehensive consultation to discuss her floral needs. We feel you deserve our full attention without interruptions. Our services should be reserved as soon as possible.

Specialties, Rental Items and Decorations

Burlingame Flower Shop carries a large selection of unique flowers for you to choose from for your event. Trained, experienced personnel are available to work with you personally to provide you with the European to traditional styles you prefer. We pay special attention to flowers, plants, and natural materials to enhance your worship settings. For the finishing touches at your ceremony and reception sites, Burlingame Flower Shop has candelabra and other wedding props available for rent. We work with each bride to make sure she has just what she'll need.

WE DESIGN FLOWERS TO FIT YOU AND YOUR NEEDS

Burlingame Flower Shop has been serving the needs of bridal couples in the Portland metropolitan area for over 44 years. Because each customer is unique and special to us, we work hard to ensure they always get the kind of service and craftsmanship they deserve. Your flowers for this very special day should reflect your style and personality. We'll take the time and care to make sure they do!

© Raleigh Studios

Country Gardens Florist & Gifts

Hillsboro, Oregon • Easy access Hwy. 26
Contact: Carol Haag, owner; Joy, Sherri, Lynette, designers (503) 648-1508
Business hours: Mon–Sat 9am–6pm, Sun 1pm–5pm

Flowers assist in capturing the moments of romance on your wedding day. When you lovingly reminisce about your wedding and view photos, you will see images of happy people in love surrounded by family, friends and flowers. We at *Country Gardens* wish to help establish the ambiance of this romantic time—the boutonnieres, corsages, candelabra, petals, cake flowers, pew decorations, arrangements and bridal bouquet all support and convey the beauty of the occasion. The colors and fragrances help promote the joyous atmosphere unique to your wedding.

Country Gardens Florist and Gifts is an established, experienced full-time florist. Creatively, we arrange flowers on a daily basis. We have the facilities, the equipment/supplies and staff to do your wedding the way you want…any size…any place. We have arranged weddings at places of worship, vineyards, parks, yachts, private gardens, homes, chapels, the zoo and the Forestry Center.

You will enjoy working with us. Visit with us, look at our photographs, see samples of our floral work, and let us share creative ideas with you. Country Gardens is known for its friendly, caring service. We are confident that we can create the floral arrangement to fulfill your dreams. We are professionals ready to provide quality at a reasonable price.

From our customers

"Thank you again for all your work, planning and sweat that went into those beautiful wedding flowers."   ~J.S. 1985

"The special thought and generous effort is certainly appreciated and will always be remembered."   ~K & H 1990

"We received dozens of compliments on our flowers. Many people said they had never seen such beautiful flowers at a wedding before."   ~ C & J 1992

"Thank you so much for the beautiful flowers! They were my favorite part of the wedding."
                                                                                     ~M.H. 1993

"We delayed our honeymoon so we were able to enjoy all the flowers long after our wedding. They were perfect."   ~E & S 1995

CRYSTAL LILIES
Exquisite Floral Artistry

at Embassy Suites Hotel Downtown
337 S.W. Pine Street
Portland, Oregon 97204
(503) 221-7701

Studio
2607 S.E. Hawthorne Boulevard, Suite A
Portland, Oregon 97214
(503) 239-4553; Fax (503) 242-2563

© Holland Studios

Exclusively Weddings

Personal Consultations

Let the excitement of planning your wedding begin as you step into the old world charm of my studio at historic "Buschong House." As a Floral Specialist dedicated exclusively to the art of creating floral enchantment for weddings, my highest priority is for my artistry to reflect your unique style and taste.

We offer ideas suited to your own distinctive personality, and we will help you visualize the floral magic that will transform your chosen date into one that is truly yours alone. More than any other single element of your wedding, your flowers can elevate the ambiance from the everyday to the extraordinary.

Premiere Service

With more than 15 years experience in floral artistry for weddings, Crystal Lilies has earned a reputation for outstanding personal attention to each couple's special needs, including on-site floral analysis of your chosen location(s). Every detail of our floral artistry will be customized to coordinate perfectly to the mood, season and setting of your wedding.

Extraordinary Artistry

Staying in the fore of emerging floral trends and innovations, we take special pride in the accolades we continually receive for the stunning originality of our work. Along with breathtaking beauty, our talent for creating original masterpieces in floral design is the hallmark of our signature style.

We are skilled in a wide range of motifs, from European to contemporary, from understated elegance to baroque opulence, including hand-tied bouquets, altar arrangements flowing from Grecian style urns, ornate cake decorations, English countryside garlands and indoor and outdoor arches, gazebos and topiaries. The possibilities are as unlimited as your imagination.

Terms

A 20% deposit is requested to reserve our time for your special day, with the balance due three weeks in advance of the wedding date.

For a personal consultation, contact Kimberly for an appointment.

EDEN FLORIST & WEDDINGS

1037 N.W. 23rd Avenue
Portland, Oregon 97210
(503) 221-1847
Fax (503) 223-8931

CLACKAMAS FLORIST & WEDDING

10117 S.E. Sunnyside Road Suite L-1
Clackamas, Oregon 97015
(503) 652-9991
Fax (503) 652-9998

Our wedding packages are as unique as the couples who walk through our doors. We strive to meet the needs of all our clients. With over 30 years experience we are able to guarantee that from beginning to end, from the rehearsal to the reception, you will have the wedding flowers of your dreams.

Consultation
Please call to set up an appointment to meet with our floral design staff and plan out your special day.

Wedding Party Flowers
From the bride and groom, to the bridesmaids and flower girls—we can provide all the flowers for the wedding party. We also provide headpieces, boutonnieres, corsages, and many other accessories needed to walk down the aisle.

Ceremony Flowers
Whether you are having an indoor wedding with altar flowers and pew bows, or an outdoor garden wedding with an arch, we can make it the experience of a lifetime.

For Your Reception
We love to do table centerpieces, balloon decorations, flowers for the bride and groom's table, and let's not forget the decorations for the cake and buffet table.

Cost and Terms
To have the wedding flowers of your dreams, we invite you to come in for a consultation and meet with our design staff. We require is a 20% deposit to reserve the time and date of your special day. Your deposit will be applied to the balance of your wedding flowers.

Rental options are available to those couples choosing to have silk flowers, wedding arches, a fabulous spiraling candelabra holding 24 candles on each stand. Come in to see our fabulous selection.

We look forward to meeting with you and planning out your special day!

FLORISTS

© Stewart Harvey

FABULOUS WEDDING FLOWERS LTD.

6010 S.W. Corbett • Portland, Oregon 97201
Contact: Cydne Pidgeon, AIFD (503) 246-6522; Fax (503) 768-9163
By appointment; days or evenings

Your Flowers

If you feel you are too individual to be put into a package, we need to talk. As a member of the prestigious American Institute of Floral Design, I believe every bride deserves an original creation, and over a cup of tea in our elegant new studio, you can pore over our extensive portfolios of photos and references while we plan all the special details that will make your wedding unique. As Portland's premiere wedding florist, our creativity and exceptional flair for color and proportion will surround you with outstandingly photogenic arrangements that will complement your gown, the season, and the wedding and reception sites. From custom veils with fresh flowers to gazebos that drip with fresh wisteria, accomplishing your dreams is our mission. Even Valentine's and Mother's Day weddings are always available if you book early.

Services and Specialties

We have Portland's largest collection of exclusive props and rentals, from coordinating suites of ornate or classic pillars, urns, and cherubs in old garden cement, antique ivory, verdigris and gold-leaf finishes, custom-designed aisle and altar candelabra, lighted topiaries, garden arbors, fountains and French-wired aisle ribbons. Unforgettable cakes, adorned with fresh flowers, are presented on special tables draped in antique French lace, silk, moiré, brocades, even galax leaves for a garden setting, or under our wrought-iron cake arbor.

Our two extensive cutting gardens are overflowing with fragrant antique and English roses, lavender, rare and beautiful perennials, and foliage grown especially for your wedding. If your budget is limited, ask about our Elegant Simplicity plan—you can still have a lush and imaginative presentation of top-quality fresh flowers!

Terms

A 25% deposit is required with the balance due two weeks before the wedding. We recommend securing our services as soon as possible as we will not overbook a weekend. Delivery and setup charges vary with the complexity of the setup and distance travelled and always include a designer—your guarantee of perfection!

THE WEDDING OF YOUR DREAMS

Your wedding is the culmination of all your hopes and dreams and probably the biggest party you will ever throw. We would love to enhance the passion and perfection of your day by surrounding you in the magic of Fabulous Wedding Flowers.

Member, Gala Events Group, Inc.

360   *Please let this business know that you heard about them from the Bravo! Bridal Resource Guide.*

© Photography By Craig

Flowers & Stuff

Milwaukie, Oregon
Contact: Craig or Stacey McCollam
(503) 786-7231
Business Hours: Please call for an appointment

About Us

As Husband and Wife, we work together to create a wedding day to remember. Filled with the soft, fresh beauty of flowers, we capture those treasured moments forever with photographs that reflect your personality. We bring an artistic elegance to your custom flowers and photography. We love working together and truly enjoy helping you create a spectacular day.

What We Do

In a relaxed and quiet atmosphere, both Craig and Stacey will meet with you at a time convenient for you. Weekend and evening consultations are available for your busy schedules.

Stacey will spend time getting to know what you envision for your wedding flowers. From that vision, she will help you choose the flowers that fulfill your dreams and create a wedding day filled with the romance of flowers. Everything from a tulle draped aisle, to your custom bridal bouquet, to a handmade head piece for the littlest of flower girls, is created with artistic and loving attention to the smallest of details.

Craig will also take the time to help you choose a photography package that is right for you. Your wedding portraits will reflect the love and warmth of your special day. Whether you are planning a formal affair or a casual garden wedding, Craig's relaxed, casual style will capture your personality in portraits that you and your family will cherish for a lifetime.

About You

It is a wonderful time for you...filled with the excitement and anticipation of your wedding day. Let us help you create a day to cherish forever. Consultations are complimentary. To make an appointment to meet with us and view our portfolio of work, give us a call at (503) 786-7231.

As Husband and Wife we love working together and
look forward to being a part of your Wedding Day!

Flowers by

Jacobsens

"The Northwest's Family-owned
Wedding Specialist for Over 25 Years"

435 N.W. Sixth Avenue
Portland, Oregon 97209
(503) 464-1234, (800) 343-1235
Fax (503) 464-1218
E-mail: info@jacobsens.com
Web site: www.jacobsens.com

◆ **Flowers ◆ Photography ◆ Videography ◆**
◆ **Music ◆ Event Rentals ◆ Open 7 Days a Week ◆**

Wedding Flowers
Exquisite bridal bouquets, attendant and flower-girl designs, candelabra designs, pew decorations, boutonnieres, corsages, and specialty pieces. We are well known for our international flowers and designers, including European, Oriental, Hawaiian, and contemporary.

Reception Flowers
Centerpieces, garlands, arches, topiaries, buffet and table designs.

Rental Services
We offer a complete line of wedding and reception accessories such as Roman pillars, candelabra, and arches.

Costs
We will tailor our services to fit your needs. Call and make an appointment with one of our consultants. We provide exceptional references.

Some Extra Services We Provide
- Open 7 days a week with real people on weekends
- Fabulous gourmet baskets
- We have a liquor license
- Daily Portland and Vancouver metro area delivery

designs by
PATRICE NEWHOUSE
617 N.W. 94th Street
Vancouver, Washington 98665
(360) 576-3835, (800) 280-4783
Web site: http://www.weloveweddings.com/vango

Your Wedding Flowers

As a wedding specialist, Flowers by Van Go offers a unique talent for interpreting the needs and desires of the bride and turning it into the wedding of her dreams. My extensive experience with weddings enables me to assist you in designing your wedding so that no detail is overlooked. My goal is to design each arrangement to enhance and complete the look of your wedding.

You will be working with someone who is passionate about what she does, and my enthusiasm and dedication will give you the confidence that everything possible will be done to make your day perfect.

Personalized Services

- Free consultation—uninterrupted and focused only on you and your wedding party.
- On-site consultation after booking (wedding and reception site).
- Extensive resources of wedding props, tents, tables, chairs and an array of plants and waterfalls.

Free Toss Bouquet

A toss bouquet designed as a topiary of your wedding flowers. This piece alone is a work of art and it is my gift to you as a thank you.

I stand by my work and use only the finest of quality of flowers, ribbons and all other products used for your wedding. My goal is to give you the best value for your money.

Cost and Terms

A 25% deposit is required at the time of booking with the balance due three weeks before the wedding.

Visit our Web site:
www.weloveweddings.com/vango

Flowers of Romance

Contact: Diane Tiller AIFD (503) 232-4973
By Appointment

Your Wedding Flowers

At Flowers of Romance, my first concern is that the bride has the flowers and style that she desires for her wedding. To accomplish this, we listen to the bride to learn just what atmosphere she wishes to create for her wedding. And then we suggest the flowers and designs that will create that mood for her dream wedding. This also means we listen to whatever price considerations she may have. We can create her wedding design with the same feeling in a variety of price ranges.

We invite you to contact us for a complimentary consultation and to review our portfolios and wedding books. We do ask that you make an appointment so that we may give you the attention you deserve.

Our Services, Terms, and Rentals

We design your wedding as a whole, with each individual arrangement supporting and enhancing that whole. Each detail is given our most careful attention. Starting with the rehearsal-party flowers and continuing on with the wedding party, ceremony, reception, and honeymoon, we can create floral arrangements that will make your dream wedding come true.

Once your floral arrangements have been custom designed, we will deliver and place your flowers. We will also pin corsages and boutonnieres on the wedding party as well as handle any last-minute changes. The charge for this service varies depending on the size of your wedding. A deposit is required to hold your date, with the full payment due by two weeks prior to the wedding. Rental of a wide variety of items can be arranged. **Mention this ad and receive the groom's boutonniere free.**

THE MEMORY MAKERS

Our personalized service will help to create wonderful memories of your special day. Flowers are the magic that gives your wedding its own unique quality and makes your special day truly your own. Our trained, professional staff has the experience that is needed to create a wide range of styles—be it traditional, European, country, or contemporary—for your dream wedding. Let us help you.

Flowers
TOMMY LUKE

1701 S.W. Jefferson Street
Portland, Oregon

625A S.W. Morrison Street
Portland, Oregon

Contact: Dick Stetson
(503) 228-3140, (800) 775-3140;
Fax (503) 778-5544
Business Hours:
Mon–Fri 7:30am–5:30pm;
Sat 8am–4pm

SERVING PORTLAND SINCE 1907

Wedding Flowers

Flowers Tommy Luke takes great interest in making your wedding day the most memorable day of your life. We listen to your desires, take what we hear, and combine it with our ingenuity to create this important day. We have no wedding packages, but instead design a beautiful floral package that fits your needs and budget. Your flowers are created for you with your desires in mind. We take pride in our work and offer a 100% guarantee. Come in and view a portfolio of our work. Our services include all floral designs needed for the bridal party, ceremony, and reception locations.

Cost and Terms

Our costs vary since each wedding and event is individually created. A 25% deposit is required at the time of booking, with the balance due 10 days prior to the event. We deliver and set up at your event location. These fees are included in your estimate.

Rental Items and Decorations

We have the following items available for rent: aisle carpet, candelabra (in brass, wrought iron, or silver), wedding arches, chuppa, kneeling benches, centerpiece containers, and silver bowls. Silk flowers for wedding decorations are also available.

SERVING PORTLAND FOR OVER 90 YEARS

Flowers Tommy Luke has been serving the Portland area since 1907. We at Flowers Tommy Luke believe that customer satisfaction is the key to our success. To achieve that goal, we feel that quality, creativity, and cooperation must be incorporated into each job. Because of our size, we can pass on substantial savings to our customer. While savings is important, we never sacrifice creativity and quality.

FRANÇOISE WEEKS
FLORIST
503.236.5829

What is European Floral Design?

In recent years European Floral Design has received a warm reception in the Pacific Northwest. The style is characterized by simple and harmonious floral compositions using a wide variety of flowers and foliage. The look is natural, yet vivid and exciting.

Françoise Weeks Florist

Françoise Weeks was born and raised in Belgium, where flowers are a part of everyday life. Her passion and enthusiasm for flowers were nurtured from an early age - Françoise has over 20 years of training and experience as a European floral designer. Since she opened her business here in Portland three years ago, her elegant and pleasing designs have attracted attention from wedding consultants, caterers, and photographers. And brides appreciate her personalized and artistic attention to detail.

Terms

Consultations are by appointment only. A 20% deposit is requested to reserve your wedding day, with the balance due two weeks in advance of the wedding date.

Inspired by Flowers

I visited Françoise in her studio early one morning in April. She was in the middle of preparing for a wedding and the delicate fragrance of sweet peas and lily of the valley, combined with the intoxicating scent of lilacs and oriental lilies filled the room. Vases with soft colored spring blooms brightened the workbench, while buckets of tall stems of cherry blossoms and stunning delphiniums lined the floor. As she lead me around tables brimming with hand-tied bouquets, altar arrangements, garlands and centerpieces she explained, "Every wedding is unique. And working with a bride to choose the right arrangements for her wedding is really exciting!"

As I left, we stepped out into a colorful spring garden, which seemed like an extension of her studio. A worn brick path meandered through the flower beds. "The garden is a constant source of inspiration," said Françoise. "I love the process of arranging interesting shapes, different textures and complementary colors to satisfy every bride's dream."

~ Shannon Spence

GERANIUM LAKE FLOWERS

U.S. Bancorp Plaza
555 S.W. Oak St.
Portland, Oregon 97204
(503) 228-1920, (800) 228-1920; Fax 240-6362
Business Hours: Mon–Fri 8am–5:30pm

The Flowers

At Geranium Lake Flowers, we love flowers. We love the color, the textures, the scents and romance and the beauty they create. We specialize in weddings that have the unfussy simple beauty of the garden arranged with natural elegance. We pick from our own gardens that are filled with old fashioned garden roses, a wide variety of perennials and lavenders, lilies, wildflowers, fruit branches and a large selection of native ferns and other herbs. We also use a variety of locally grown flowers that are fresh and seasonal.

We have lots of props from garden arches made from birch and willow twigs to urns, silk ribbons and unusual containers.

Just for You

Another focus of ours is providing the most professional, complete service available. We start with consultations at your convenience. Centrally located in the U.S. Bank Tower in downtown Portland, we welcome you to make an appointment.

Of course, we can design your flowers with any style in mind. We are full of creative ideas, paying attention to all the details of your wedding. We welcome all faiths and lifestyles. Our flowers have adorned elegant halls, many backyards, sunrises at the beach, art galleries and of course many churches and synagogues.

Costs and Terms

We can provide you with wedding flowers to fit any budget. At Geranium Lake Flowers, we love to do weddings. Our enthusiasm comes through in providing you with a truly unique and creative product with outstanding service to match. We have an unconditional guarantee that everything that leaves our shop will be fresh, creative and beyond your expectations or we will replace it. We ask for a 25% deposit to reserve your date with the entire balance due two weeks before your event.

WE LOOK FORWARD TO MEETING YOU.

J & J Flowers

Jo (503) 694-2462 or
Juana (503) 245-0755

Attention to Detail

Whether you are having a simple or elaborate ceremony, the flowers will reflect the overall feel of the wedding. We pay particular attention to each and every detail of your floral arrangements, bouquets, altar pieces, pew decorations, and cake flowers. It is very important to us that your day be extra ordinary.

We Listen to Your Ideas

During our consultation, we listen carefully to your requests, likes and dislikes. It is our goal to make your flower selection process as fun and exciting as possible. Also, we encourage you to look through our portfolio and photographs for ideas of colors and designs.

Cost and Terms

It is our policy to request a $50 deposit to hold the date. The balance is due two weeks prior to the wedding day.

WE LOVE WHAT WE DO

Let us at J & J Flowers help you to design the flowers for the most beautiful event of your life.

"We love what we do and it shows."

PLEASE CALL FOR
AN APPOINTMENT

JO	JUANA
(503) 694-2462	(503) 245-0755

15630 S.W. Boones Ferry Road
Lake Oswego, Oregon 97035
Contact: Kumiko Jones (503) 635-2094; Fax (503) 635-0090
Business Hours: Mon–Fri 8am–6pm; Sat 8am–4pm; closed Sunday

At Lake Grove Flowers, our philosophy is, "Flowers to touch the heart." Getting married is one of the most important days of our lives and we would feel honored to be a part of your day.

Specialties and Services

Lake Grove Flowers has been open for 20 years and the owner, Kumiko Jones, has more than 30 years experience. Kumiko has many years of education in "Ikabana," the Japanese flower art. The staff at Lake Grove Flowers is a very experienced and talented group. We invite you to visit our shop to share our portfolio and ideas with you.

Everyone at Lake Grove Flowers feels strongly about quality and professionalism-we strive to help you make your day unique and give that personal touch. We take pride in staying educated in the trends, but we have a firm knowledge of tradition. Therefore, we are able to design anything from the contemporary to a European garden look..

Terms

Lake Grove Flower's complimentary, comprehensive consultation recommends that you bring swatches and any magazine clippings that have caught your eye. Our terms our 25% down with the balance due two weeks before the wedding. Please reserve your day as soon as possible in order for us to better serve you.

Sharon's
Nostalgia

Contact: Sharon Cochran
(503) 641-6396

11400 S.W. Bel Aire Lane
Beaverton, Oregon 97008

Wedding Flowers

You are special and your day should be as unique as you want it to be. With over nine years as a licensed designer specializing in color, contrast, imagination, creativity and how these relate to the total feel you would like. This can be created from your own ideas or from the pages and pages of designs and settings we have personally done and have available for you to view. YOUR dress, YOUR colors, YOUR ideas…not someone else's.

Specialties and Services…You

English settings, romantic designs. We have arbors, arches, urns, french and wired specialty ribbons, isle designs from simple to draped elegance, altar settings and pillars. (If we don't have it, we know where to get it.) We are happy to move your flowers from the church to the reception.

We will be glad to work with you and your family to incorporate your bridal shower, bridesmaids luncheon, rehearsal dinner or whatever events surround your special day. We can do this in one theme, or vary it as you desire.

Consultation

Initial consultation is at no cost. Once your wedding is booked, and our small fee is taken, further consultations are scheduled as often as necessary.

Cost and Terms

Cost is determined by type of flowers, as well as size and number of arrangements. As stated above, each bride is individually cared for. A small booking and delivery fee is taken, with final payment due the Monday before the wedding.

I LOVE WHAT I DO AND I CARE ABOUT YOU

We cater to the smallest, simplest of weddings, or can present the biggest party you want to give. We are a family-owned and -operated small business. Our goal is to help you be elated on this day that is so special.

(503) 641-6396

FLINGING THE STOCKING

A custom passed down by the British started when guests would invade the bridal chamber and vie for the bride's and groom's stockings. They then took turns flinging the stockings at the newlyweds, with the belief that whoever landed the stocking on the bride or groom's nose would be the next person to marry.

HELPFUL HINTS

- **Accommodations for wedding attendants and guests:** Attendants and guests who come from out of town can often stay with relatives or friends, but this is not always possible. Hotel accommodations may be more comfortable for everyone. It is not advised to have attendants or relatives stay with you before the wedding.

- **Who pays for accommodations?** The accommodations for wedding attendants are usually paid for by the bride and groom. Out-of-town guests, both relatives and friends, pay for their own accommodations. As a courtesy to these guests, facilities and costs should be researched by the bride and her mother to ensure comfort, convenient location, and reasonable price.

- **Special group rates:** Most hotels offer a special group rate for your guests. Many have information and special cards that you can send to your guests in the invitations or separately.

- **Transportation:** Inquire about transportation from the airport to the hotel. Some hotels provide this for your guests' convenience.

- **Honeymoon suites:** Your first night as newlyweds will often be more relaxed and comfortable if you don't try to leave town immediately after your reception. Find a honeymoon suite close to your reception site or the airport, depending on your travel plans. Most hotels will arrange for champagne and other special amenities as well as transportation to the airport.

- **Honeymoon destinations:** A walk on the beach hand-in-hand in Seaside or in St. Thomas—no matter what your honeymoon destination, the goal is that you spend time enjoying each other. Travel specialists can help you with honeymoon ideas and options that both of you will enjoy. They can make arrangements for any type of honeymoon, anywhere, and can work within your budget specifications. Travel agencies can offer you special packages that might not be available if you make airline, transportation, and accommodations reservations separately.

- **Compromise:** When planning your honeymoon, you must be willing to compromise. If one wants to go to a plush resort and the other wants to go camping, try to pick a spot that will meet both of your expectations for an ideal honeymoon destination.

- **Reservations and deposits:** Start planning your honeymoon early! Popular honeymoon sites are reserved six months to a year in advance, depending on the season. A deposit is required in order to make reservations, with the balance due in full 30 days to three months before your departure. The sooner you make your reservations, the better your choices are; in some instances early reservations on an airline will save you money.

- **Group rates or discounts:** Check with your travel agent about group rates or discounts on air fare and hotel accommodations.

For more assistance with staying organized during the wedding planning process, check out the Bravo! Wedding Organizer. Detailed question worksheets double as contracts. This step-by-step system will keep every detail of your wedding organized. To order, refer to the order form on page 23 in this Guide.

Unforgettable
HONEYMOONS
Romantic Travel for Couples

Located at the Alameda Bridal Faire
5707 N.E. Fremont Street • Portland, Oregon 97213
Contact: Reneé Duane
(503) 249-8444, Toll Free (888) 343-6413

Hundreds of Romantic Honeymoon Packages...to fit every budget!
Local to worldwide. We offer the widest range of honeymoon travel packages available. Our clients have honeymooned in quaint Northwest inns to exclusive private island hideaways in the South Pacific.

Our Service...a step beyond the ordinary
Informative Consultations—Honeymoon Consultant Renee Duane works closely with each couple, personally meeting and consulting with them several times before plans are finalized. She offers a lifetime of travel experience and first-hand knowledge of many of the destinations that couples most often choose for their honeymoon. Renee provides each couple with tips and suggestions on what to see, where to dine and what to pack.

Free Honeymoon—bridal registry
Your dream honeymoon becomes reality with our fabulous new registry program. We provide elegantly designed cards to be distributed to your wedding guests. Well-wishers can contribute to your honeymoon by ordering travel gift certificates.

Couples Only—All-inclusive Resorts...everything is included!
Honeymoon couples love the all-inclusive resorts that allow them to completely relax in a beautiful resort that includes all meals, drinks, activities and even tips! Just listen to their comments: Couples resort–Jamaica *"An amazing resort...had the time of our lives."* Gary and Christy; Sandals—Dunns River *"An awesome place...we had a blast!"* Tim and Brandi

HONEYMOON CRUISES AND CRUISE SHIP WEDDINGS
As members of the **Cruise Lines International Association** we represent every cruise line in the world. By working closely with major cruise lines, we are able to provide and offer special discounts, free upgrades, on-board credits and gifts to honeymoon couples. We also can arrange cruise ship weddings.

<u>Worldwide wedding arrangements.</u> We assist in arranging intimate or extravagant weddings just about anywhere in the world. We can also arrange for group travel discounts for all of your guests and loved ones.

Call for a free "Ideal Destination Planner"
See page 275 under Bridal Registry & Gifts.

Honeymoon Specialists

8285 S.W. Nimbus Avenue, Suite 140
Beaverton, Oregon 97008
(503) 626-4766, (800) 288-8646

Travel Services—Consultation and Reservations with a Personal Touch

We make it our priority to listen to your needs—*your dreams*—to give ideas and suggestions to guide in planning your special honeymoon. Rest assured that all the details of your important travel plans are in the hands of experienced and caring travel professionals. We welcome appointments—call us for a complimentary travel consultation for your wedding party travel needs and honeymoon. **Let us know you found us in the** *Bravo! Bridal Resource Guide* **and receive $50 credit on your honeymoon package.** (Some restrictions apply; available only at this Nimbus Avenue office.)

Honeymoon Destination Ideas

- ♥ **Cruises:** *The perfect honeymoon*—exotic ports of call and romantic nights at sea! Three, four or seven night cruises to the Caribbean, Mexico, Alaska, Hawaii or Tahiti. Extend your stay with a pre- or post-land tour. Invite the whole wedding party along!
- ♥ **Hawaii:** Paradise can be found in Hawaii. Non-stop service from Portland makes this a convenient choice with a variety of packages to fit any budget. Dreamed of getting married on the beach? We can help you arrange a wedding in Hawaii!
- ♥ **Islands of the South Pacific:** Experience unspoiled islands, deserted beaches and crystal clear water—a place where stars seem more like diamonds tossed across the sky. We know the South Pacific—let us find your island escape.
- ♥ **Caribbean:** Adventure and beauty await you on every island. Ask about our "All Inclusive" packages for <u>couples only</u>—these resorts were made for romance! Free weddings offered at select resorts with minimum six-night stay. We have two certified Sandals specialists.
- ♥ **Club Med:** "Special Honeymoon Packages" at incredibly beautiful destinations around the world. Everything included—active sports, delicious food, entertainment—we can help you select the perfect Club Med Village filled with the things you like to do.
- ♥ **Adventure Travel:** Providing a unique vacation environment where the two of you can share activities you enjoy while on your honeymoon. Hiking, skiing, biking, whitewater rafting, horseback riding, scuba diving, nature and wildlife viewing. From every corner of the world—we can help you plan your honeymoon adventure.
- ♥ **Wedding Night Hotel Reservations and Limousine Service:** Flight arrangements for you as well as your friends and family attending your wedding.

Honeymoon Registry

Register your honeymoon with **Morris Travels'** *Honeymoon Registry*. Your friends and family can purchase gift certificates which are applied towards your honeymoon as their wedding gift to you.

Honeymoons are as individual and personal as your wedding.
Morris Travel can help you plan just what you've been dreaming of…

MY TRAVEL AGENT, INC.

1588 Lancaster Drive, N.E.
Salem, Oregon 97301
(503) 371-0999, (888) 224-0110
Fax (503) 371-2850

and

1286 N. First Street
Stayton, Oregon 97383
(503) 769-6100, (800) 882-5240
Fax (503) 769-7801
E-mail: Mytvl@aol.com

YOUR HONEYMOON HEADQUARTERS
IN THE MID-WILLAMETTE VALLEY!

We know how hectic it is planning your wedding, let alone all the details of a perfect honeymoon. You tell us your "dream"—we'll find the ideal destination at a price that fits your budget. We'll plan your honeymoon from beginning to end—whether it's a once-in-a-lifetime journey to some exotic destination or a romantic getaway in Oregon.

- ❤ **Hawaii**—From the beaches of Waikiki to the clouds of Haleakala, the Hawaii Islands are a tropical paradise for honeymooners!

- ❤ **Mexico**—From the new Cancun to the old cities of Puerto Vallarta and Ixtapa, Mexico offers romantic moonlight strolls and fun shopping!

- ❤ **Caribbean**—From the Reggae in Jamaica to the waters of the Bahamas, the Caribbean delights honeymooners with the diverse activities available.

- ❤ **Las Vegas and Reno**—From the lights on the "Strip" to the operating oil rig in a casino, you'll find excitement and entertainment galore.

- ❤ **The Pacific Northwest**—From the mountains of Central Oregon to the beaches, from lively Seattle to serene Victoria, Canada, the Pacific Northwest has many excellent destinations for a quick romantic getaway.

- ❤ **Cruises**—From a short cruise to Mexico to one around the world, a cruise is a wonderful way to begin your life together.

- ❤ **All-Inclusive Resorts**—From the Caribbean to the Mexican Riviera, all-inclusive resorts will make your honeymoon memorable.

Open 7 days a week so we're here when you need us!

2126 S.W. Halsey
Troutdale, Oregon 97060
Contact: Sales Office (503) 492-2777
Business Hours: Mon–Fri 9am–5pm; Sat–Sun 10am–5pm; tours by appointment
E-mail: edge@mcmenamins.com; Web site: www.mcmenamins.com

McMenamins Edgefield is an unforgettable Northwest experience offering the best in food, beverage and relaxation. Originally built in 1911 as a Multnomah County Poor Farm, it is now on the National Register of Historic Places. The historical Main Lodge building is surrounded by auxiliary buildings and spectacular gardens and landscaping.

Accommodations

Edgefield offers over 100 bed and breakfast rooms furnished with cozy and inviting decor from the turn of the century. Televisions and telephones are absent from rooms, encouraging a tranquil retreat atmosphere. Romance package available: bottle of Edgefield Sparkling Riesling and two champagne flutes; massage oil, candles and chocolates.

Amenities

• Room rates include a full breakfast in the Black Rabbit Restaurant.
• Licensed massage therapist on site; aromatherapy baths
• 18 hole, 3-par golf course surrounding the property
• Winery with tasting room
• Brewery
• The Power Station Pub & Theater (classic English pub)
• Spectacular grounds and gardens on 25 acres
• Artwork painted by 15 different artists
• Amphitheater
• Distillery

Location

Edgefield is located 20 minutes from downtown Portland, five minutes from the Columbia River Gorge National Scenic Area and 15 minutes from Portland International Airport.

See page 162 under Banquet & Reception Sites.

Brickhaven

Bed & Breakfast

38717 E. Historic Columbia River Highway
Corbett, Oregon 97019
Contact: Ed and Phyllis Thiemann (503) 695-5126

Watch the sunrises and sunsets from the same location. See the city lights and follow the river traffic up and down the mighty Columbia…

Description

Designed and built in the 1950s by Portland's Commercial Cartoonist, Ernie Hager, Brickhaven is a design before its time. An eclectic combination of Frank Lloyd Wright architectural design, decorated in English Country décor.

Each room has its own view, either east toward Bonneville Dam or west toward Portland and surrounding area. To drive the view would require more than an hour.

Location

Experience the peace and tranquility of the country with all the comforts of home and only minutes from downtown Portland and Portland International Airport. Situated on approximately three acres overlooking the scenic Columbia River Gorge, Brickhaven proves to be one of the most unique settings to be found.

Brightwood Guest House

BED & BREAKFAST
Mount Hood, Oregon 97011
Your Host: Jan Colgan
(503) 622-5783, (888) 503-5783

"THE PERFECT PLACE TO SPEND THE FIRST NIGHTS OF THE REST OF YOUR LIFE TOGETHER"

"Peaceful, Private, Romantic…"

Situated on a two-acre portion of the historic Barlow Trail, surrounded by a clear mountain stream and tall firs, The Brightwood Guesthouse works magic to soothe the wedding weary. A Japanese garden harmonizes pleasantly with the cedar paneled oriental-furnished interior. Carpeted and comfortable living room, full kitchen, large bath, and sleeping loft with full-sized featherbed (audio provided by the waterfall outside) are yours to enjoy. Complimentary gourmet breakfast can be served on the private deck beside the koi pond or inside while watching wedding videos. Bikes and helmets are supplied as are washer/dryer, watercolors, bird and fish food, your daily *Oregonian*, and much more.

Special Services and Honeymoon Packages

Mount Hood offers secluded hikes, golf, tennis, skiing, and great restaurants. Limo service is available to airport; van shuttle to skiing. Honeymoon lodging packages begin at $135. Keepsake Basket begins at $40. Please call for details.

MT. HOOD BED & BREAKFAST

8885 Cooper Spur Road • Parkdale, Oregon 97041
Contact: Jackie Rice (541) 352-6885
Office Hours: Mon–Fri 8am–7pm

Description
Mt. Hood B&B provides breathtaking views of Mount Hood, Adams, Rainier. Our four guest rooms are decorated with antiques and period furnishings. We're a real working ranch and proudly serve a huge ranch breakfast daily.

Location
Nestled above Parkdale in the picturesque Hood River Valley. Close to skiing, sailboarding, hiking, golfing, rafting, biking, shopping and many other activities.

Honeymoon Packages and Prices
From romantic, quiet and intimate to active, to active on-the-go outdoor activities.

Special Packages and Prices
Rooms from $95. We do weddings, retreats, reunions, and much, much more.

Other Amenities
TV/VCR, video library, hiking trails, indoor basketball area, pool table, sauna, whirlpool, available for reunions, retreats, conferences, dances, anniversaries, weddings, graduation parties, and ski camps. Stargazing, fishing and mountain biking all are nearby.

See page 167 under Banquet & Reception Sites.

Pacific Rest Bed & Breakfast

. . . where relaxation is just the beginning

1611 N.E. 11th
Lincoln City, Oregon 97367
Contact: Ray and Judy Waetjen (541) 994-Beds (2337)
E-mail: jwaetjen@wcn.net
Web site: http://pacificrestbb.hypermart.net

Located on a peaceful hillside just off Highway 101

Take a Journey Back to Simpler Times…
At Pacific Rest Bed & Breakfast, located four short blocks from the beautiful Oregon Coast, you'll find respite for the spirit as well as for the body. Two unique suites, both with private baths and sun decks, make Pacific Rest ideal for a romantic getaway or honeymoon. Built especially for a bed and breakfast, Pacific Rest is a newer home with a "coming home" feeling.

Restaurants, antique shops, and outlet malls are within walking distance. Seven miles of wonderful beach and beautiful Devil's Lake are just a short stroll away.

Special Services and Honeymoon Packages
Suites begin at $85, including a full, gourmet breakfast by candlelight. Honeymoon packages are available—please call for details.

Pacific Rest Cottage, located across the street, sleeps up to eight and features a Jacuzzi, wood stove, and all the amenities of home (fully equipped kitchen). Gift certificates available.

Come and be pampered ~ Escape to Pacific Rest

102 Oak Avenue
Hood River, Oregon
97031

HOOD RIVER HOTEL & *Pasquale's* ristorante

Reservations
(800) 386-1859

Sales
(541) 386-1900

E-mail: HRHotel@gorge.net; Web site: www.hoodriverhotel.com

Description of Hotel

This charming European-style 1913 hotel is listed on the National Register of Historic Places. After complete restoration in 1989, the hotel has retained its turn-of-the-century character, yet offers the conveniences of a modern inn. One might choose from a lace canopy or brass bed, a view of the Columbia River, or one of our larger suites. Amenities include our wine cellar and meeting and event space for up to 200+ guests. You will want to make time to visit our fitness, Jacuzzi, and sauna facility. Pasquale's Ristorante offers breakfast, lunch, and dinner. We specialize in fine Italian and Pacific Northwest cuisine with menu items from pastas to wild game. After dinner, enjoy a cappuccino or cocktail by the fireplace. Pasquale's is the perfect place to relax after a day's adventure. The Hood River Hotel provides you and your guests a unique establishment, staffed to cater with a personal touch and offering wonderful food to remember us by.

Location

Conveniently located in historic downtown Hood River in the heart of the Columbia River Gorge National Scenic Area, the Hotel offers easy access to movie theaters, restaurants, and shopping. For those looking for outdoor adventure, the area offers windsurfing, white water rafting, skiing, swimming, golfing, and more.

Honeymoon Packages and Pricing

Enjoy a romantic evening in a lace canopy bed or suites. Custom-designed honeymoon packages to suit your budget and needs. Packages can include a chilled bottle of champagne or breakfast in your room, floral bouquet, movie for two, late checkout and a romance basket of massage oils, bath bubbles, customized glasses, and more.

Other Amenities

- 32 guest rooms
- Jacuzzi, sauna, and exercise facility
- Full-service restaurant and bar
- Banquet room accommodating up to 200+ people
- 9 suites with kitchen
- Wine cellar
- Air conditioning

Special Services

For your convenience, the Hood River Hotel offers free transportation to the Hood River Airport.

See page 74 under Rehearsal Dinner Sites.
See page 153 under Banquet & Reception Sites.

7025 N.E. Alderwood Road
Portland, Oregon 97218
Contact: Victoria Lessley
(503) 255-2700 or (888) 987-2700;
Fax (503) 255-4700
E-mail: reservations@alderwoodinn.com
Visit us at: www.alderwoodinn.com

Description of Hotel

Comfort and friendly hospitality await the newly married and their families in the newest hotel at the Portland International Airport, the Alderwood Inn. This four-story building, trimmed with river rock, features 154 spacious guest rooms and suites along with a restaurant, bar and banquet facilities. The perfect location for that "special day."

Location

Located only minutes from the Portland Airport and 15 minutes from downtown Portland.

Banquet and Meeting Facilities

The Alderwood Inn offers banquet facilities for up to 70 people. Picturesque windows provide an abundance of natural lighting. The finest in food and beverage is provided by Brenners Restaurant, owned and operated by the hotel. Our sales and catering department will attend to every detail to make your special day a success!

Honeymoon Packages and Price

The Inn will offer packages for honeymoon guests. Prices will vary depending on room or suite selection and number of nights stay. Call our reservation office for details.

Other Amenities

- Free airport shuttle
- Free breakfast
- Microwaves
- Refrigerators
- Hair dryers
- Iron/ironing boards (available at front desk)
- Free local telephone calls
- Fitness center
- Indoor swimming pool and spa
- Golf at adjacent golf course
- Special group rates
- Park-N-Fly program

© Dick Busher

309 S.W. Broadway
Portland, Oregon 97205
(503) 228-2000; Fax (503) 226-4603
Office Hours: Mon–Fri 8am–6pm
Available all other times by appointment
Web site: http://www.westcoasthotels.com

Description of Hotel

The Benson Hotel has long set the standard for elegance and service in Portland. This classic building in the style of the French Second Empire has undergone restoration, is registered as a national historic site, and is a Portland landmark. The look of the lobby features the cool tones of marble in handsome accord with smooth circassian walnut highlighted by the glimmer of crystal accents.

Location

The Benson Hotel is located in the heart of Portland's retail, financial, and arts district.

Special Honeymoon Packages

We have great things in store for your honeymoon. Call us for information on our "Champagne Kisses" package.

Other Amenities

The Benson is unparalleled in service and atmosphere. Our luxuriously appointed deluxe accommodations are in classic style in anticipation of your total comfort. We are here to cater to every your wish, be it for the bride and groom, out-of-town guests, or clients. You need only call us for a wide array of special services, including in-house exercise room, 24-hour room service, and clef d'or concierge. The Benson Hotel staff will delight in assuring that your stay is a memorable one.

Of course, no stay would be complete without a visit to our famed London Grill. In addition, the handsome Lobby Court features the soothing sounds of local jazz talent. We are fully equipped for large gatherings, with classic facilities for up to 400 people. Our experienced catering and banquet staff are prepared to help you with everything from planning to presentation, serving in style to your exact specifications.

CREATING NEW TRADITIONS

The Benson Hotel summons together the grandeur of times past with a freshly appointed ambiance that is in perfect harmony with contemporary lifestyles. Call us for details, we'll be happy to make all the arrangements for a most relaxing stay.

See page 109 under Banquet & Reception Sites.

TIGARD	HILLSBORO
COURTYARD	**COURTYARD**
BY MARRIOTT	**BY MARRIOTT**
15686 S.W. Sequoia Parkway	*3050 N.W. Stucki Place*
Tigard, Oregon 97224	*Hillsboro, Oregon 97124*
(503) 684-7900	*(503) 690-1800*
Fax (503) 620-3142	*Fax (503) 690-0236*

Courtyard by Marriott offers the finest service and accommodations for both business and leisure travelers at affordable rates. Exceeding our guests' expectations and fulfilling their needs is the standard for our success.

Locations

Tigard: *Courtyard by Marriott—Tigard* is conveniently located right off I-5, exit 291, on the corner of Upper Boones Ferry and Sequoia Parkway. The hotel is a short distance from shopping at Washington Square Mall and local restaurants.

Hillsboro: *Courtyard by Marriott—Hillsboro* is conveniently located off Highway 26, exit 64, nine miles west of downtown Portland. A 13-screen movie theater is across the street and just a block away from Tanasbourne Shopping Center and restaurants.

Amenities

- voice mail
- phones with dataport
- indoor pool and whirlpool
- coffee makers in every room
- daily housekeeping
- remote control cable television
- weekday valet and coin-operated laundry service
- full-service restaurant and lounge
- complimentary corporate shuttle (2-mile radius)
- exercise facility
- full-size irons and ironing boards in every room
- meeting rooms with in-house catering
- in-room hairdryers
- ergonomic desk chairs

(Ask us about group discounts for 10 or more rooms)

**For reservations
call (800) 321-2211**

14811 Kruse Oaks Boulevard
Lake Oswego, Oregon 97035
For banquet information:
Linda Goss (503) 624-8400 ext. 253
Special group rates:
Mandy Marsh (503) 624-8400 ext. 251

Description of Hotel

The luxurious and elegant Crowne Plaza features a six-story waterfall in the atrium and 161 tastefully decorated rooms. Other amenities include a concierge level, an indoor-outdoor pool, spa, sauna, exercise facility, and gift shop. This hotel is ideal for your rehearsal dinner, wedding reception, wedding, bridal shower or for your guests' sleeping rooms. The director of catering, Linda, has extensive experience in planning and helping to coordinate weddings and wedding receptions. Call for a complimentary consultation and tour of our facility.

Location

The Crowne Plaza is conveniently located at the intersection of Interstate 5 and Highway 217. Accessibility to Portland, Beaverton, Tigard, and Lake Oswego makes it ideally located for any of your wedding functions.

Special Romance Packages

The Grand Romance Package includes accommodations for two in a luxurious Jacuzzi suite, a tray of hors d'oeuvres in your room upon arrival, a bottle of champagne, roses, and breakfast in bed or…have us customize a package just for you!

Amenities

- Concierge level
- Full-service restaurant, lounge, and room service
- Full-time Guest Services Manager
- Irons and full size ironing boards in each room
- Full exercise facility on premises with sauna, Jacuzzi, and indoor/outdoor pool
- Free use of the Griffith Park Athletic Club
- Coffee makers in each room
- Nearby jogging and biking trails, with bikes available for guests
- Luxurious two-room suites (Jacuzzis available)
- Complimentary van transportation to local destinations (scheduled)

See page 124 under Banquet & Reception Sites.

S.W. Tenth at Alder
Portland, Oregon 97205
(503) 224-3400 or (800) 554-3456; Fax (503) 224-9426
E-mail: governor@transport.com; Web site: http://www.govhotel.com

Romantic, Boutique Hotel In The Heart Of It All

Discreet luxury awaits the newly married and their families in the elegant, turn-of-the-century Governor Hotel. Featuring 100 rooms, including 28 suites, this centrally located hotel offers lodging options that may include jet spa baths, terraces with city-scape views, or fireplaces. Combining services such as 24-hour room service, concierge services, twice-daily maid service with evening turndown, laundry and dry cleaning services, shoe shine, morning newspaper, and coffee in the lobby, The Governor offers a place of charm and style in which to prepare for and unwind from the event of a lifetime.

Special Packages and Pricing

The Governor Hotel's Romance Package is available for honeymoon or anniversary guests. Package prices vary depending on room selection and number of nights. Call (503) 224-3400 for pricing and details.

The Hotel also offers group rates for wedding parties. Families and friends will enjoy the downtown location close to shopping, city attractions, dining, the arts, and entertainment. Group rates vary. Call (503) 241-2106 for details.

Banquets and Catering

The Governor's West Wing is the former historic Elk's Lodge building. Here guests may create banquets and catering events that complement the love and magic of the wedding day. Superbly hand-crafted rooms serve from 6 to 600 for elegant seated meals or energizing standing receptions. Jake's Catering at The Governor will assist in all phases of planning and preparation, and will also accommodate off-site catering plans. Call (503) 241-2125 for information and details.

Hotel Ambiance and Services

Built in 1909, and fully restored to its original grandeur, The Governor Hotel is listed on the National Register of Historic Places. The striking exterior of terra cotta and white brick is an architectural beauty. A wood-burning fireplace, hand-painted sepia-colored murals, and traditional furnishings create a warm Northwest impression in the lobby. The restaurant and bar, Jake's Grill, is located off the main lobby. Offering traditional American cuisine, the restaurant has been named "one of the city's best" by *Condé Nast Traveler* magazine.

Historically tailored guest rooms and suites create a residential feel where guests may graze from private bars and relax with movies or cable TV. For a small fee, fitness-minded guests may enjoy privileges at the hotel's on-site, full-service, adult-only athletic club.

HOTEL VINTAGE PLAZA
Pazzo Ristorante

422 S.W. Broadway
Portland, Oregon 97205
For reservations call:
(503) 228-1212, (800) 243-0555

Description of Hotel

Hotel Vintage Plaza brings warmth and romance to downtown Portland with its European style. Each evening guests are invited to attend our Oregon Wine Reception fireside in the living room. In the morning, guests may enjoy fresh squeezed juices, gourmet coffee and muffins with the morning newspaper, which is arranged in our living room.

Location

Hotel Vintage Plaza is conveniently located in the heart of downtown Portland, on the corner of Broadway and Washington. A short walk to shopping, theatres and restaurants.

Special Honeymoon Packages

- **Nights in White Satin** in the two-level Townhouse Suite or our Hospitality Suite. This luxurious package includes rose petals scattered over the sheets at turn-down, scented bath salts for the two-person Jacuzzi, a chilled bottle of champagne, continental breakfast in bed, a keepsake white satin nightgown from Victoria's Secret, and valet parking. For reservations, call (503) 228-1212.
- **Romance Package** in our Starlight Room. This package includes rose petals scattered over sheets at turn-down, scented bath salts for tub, a chilled bottle of champagne, continental breakfast in bed, and valet parking. For reservations, call (503) 228-1212.

Out-of-Town Guest Rooms

If you need to book ten (10) or more guest rooms for your family and friends, we would be delighted to negotiate a special group rate for you. For group reservations, call (503) 412-6313.

Other Amenities

The Hotel Vintage Plaza has once again received the coveted 4-Star, 4-Diamond Award for excellence in service. The guestrooms in our 10-story boutique hotel are stylishly appointed in a traditional jewel-toned color scheme.

For memorable rehearsal dinners, our Pazzo Wine Cellar can create the perfect atmosphere. The Cellar will accommodate up to 80 guests for a sit-down dinner. We also have a variety of banquet rooms available for intimate wedding receptions for 100 guests. Banquets are catered exclusively by Pazzo Ristorante. For reservations, call (503) 412-6316.

"THE LUXURY HOTEL OF DOWNTOWN PORTLAND"

Come enjoy personalized service and European elegance. Experience surprises such as our complimentary Oregon Wine Reception, daily continental breakfast and shoe shine. Explore the friendly atmosphere of our "City of Roses" downtown shopping and restaurants, and the magnificent landscapes of our Northwest terrain. Of course, a visit to the Hotel Vintage Plaza would not be complete without a sumptuous dining experience at Pazzo Ristorante, our Northern Italian restaurant.

See page 178 under Banquet & Reception Sites.

Notes

Becoming Engaged

*The act of engagement has
been symbolized in many
different ways. During the
Middle Ages, an
engagement was assumed if
a woman drank wine or
another alcoholic beverage
with a member of the
opposite sex. In American
colonial times, a couple
who shared food in a
kitchen were thought to be
engaged.*

HELPFUL HINTS

- **Where do you draw the line with the guest list:** The bride's family, groom's family and bride and groom generally each develop a "wish list". Then the list is narrowed down closer to the attendance you have budgeted for. Usually the attendance will be between 60-75% based on if family and friends live in town or not. A good rule of thumb to narrow down the list—if you haven't made contact with the person in the last year, leave them off.

- **Single Friends and Guests:** If friends are single, you are not obliged to invite their guest or escort. If you do decide to invite their guest, find out the name and address and send them an invitation separately. It is recommended to not write "and Guest" on an invitation. If a couple is living together, then you can send one invitation with both their names listed alphabetically.

- **Don't forget to send invitations to:** Remember, even though special people are playing a role in your wedding you do need to send invitations to them: parents, grandparents, clergy, attendants and immediate family. A good idea is to even send an invitation to yourself to track the date guests will receive the invitation.

- **Number of invitations needed:** When figuring the number of invitations to order, combine the lists from the bride's parents, the groom's parents, the bride, and the groom. The mother of the bride or the bride should discuss with the groom's mother the number of invitations available to the groom's family. When the lists are compiled, any additions, deletions, and corrections can be made by everyone.

- **Invitation styles:** Thousands of invitation styles are available: traditional, contemporary, custom designs, some with double envelopes or a folding invitation sealed with a sticker. When it comes time to select your invitations, pick the one that best suits your tastes, personal style, and budget. This is the first presentation of your wedding to both your family and guests.

- **Ordering your invitations:** Ideally, you should order your invitations three to four months before the wedding to allow enough time for delivery. Some shops offer quick-print service in one day to one week. Invitations should be sent three to four weeks before the wedding. Ask if you can get the envelopes in advance for addressing. It's fun and time-saving to have an addressing and stuffing party.

- **Wording the invitation:** When you order, be sure to work with a shop that specializes in invitations. These experts can help you fill out the complicated order forms, and will help you with correct wording for the invitation.

- **Correct spelling of names:** Etiquette books cover proper addressing of both inner and outer envelopes. Before addressing your envelopes, make sure you double check on your master list for the CORRECT spelling of names.

- **Engagement announcements:** They are always a good idea to send, especially for out-of-town guests.

- **Calligraphy and addressing:** Invitations can be hand calligraphed or by machine. This adds a very personal touch to your invitations.

- **Custom hand-crafted and graphic designed invitations:** Invitations can tie in with the decor. Unique ideas include your own wedding wine and/or beer labels.

For more assistance with staying organized during the wedding planning process, check out the Bravo! Wedding Organizer. Detailed question worksheets double as contracts. This step-by-step system will keep every detail of your wedding organized. To order, refer to the order form on page 23 in this Guide.

Calligraphy by Jennifer

503-658-4211

Calligraphy Styles

Choose from a variety of styles for your special day including italic, uncial, foundational, and black letter. My calligraphy is always handcrafted and never computer generated.

Custom Services

My services include:
- Invitation and announcement addressing for all occasions
- Original invitation design
- Thank you notes
- Place cards, menu cards, wedding programs
- Wedding album fill-ins
- Poems, songs and quotations
- Certificates and awards
- Your choice of paper and ink color

I can coordinate the design and lettering of your complete wedding set, beginning with the invitations and ending with the thank you notes. Coordination of printing services is available, if necessary. Calligraphy adds sophistication, grace, and elegance to your special occasion.

Cost and Ordering

I offer unique, customized wedding invitations to fit your style and budget. Generally, you should place your order four to five months in advance, although rush jobs can be accommodated. I require a 50% deposit with the balance due upon delivery.

For one-on-one service and extra attention to details, please give me a call today to set up an appointment and to view samples! Add a touch of elegance to your special occasion... Calligraphy by Jennifer.

**Mention the *Bravo! Bridal Resource Guide*
and receive a $10 gift certificate toward your purchase!**

INVITATIONS AND ANNOUNCEMENTS

390

Please let this business know that you heard about them from the Bravo! Bridal Resource Guide.

ANDREW'S

Fisher's Landing Market Place
2100 S.E. 164th Avenue
Vancouver, Washington 98683
(360) 892-7773

11505 N.E. Fourth Plain Road
Vancouver, Washington 98662
(360) 254-5885

Selection and Styles of Invitations

Your wedding is a personal expression of your personality, style and dreams. Whether you select a traditional or contemporary style ... one with your photograph ... or something in between, we have a multitude of invitation choices in a variety of price ranges from several companies including Carlson Craft, Regency, Stylart and Hallmark's Wedding Collection featuring Precious Moments and exclusive Crown Collection designs. These albums also offer a wide selection of invitations suitable for special events and parties.

Wedding Accessories

Andrew's Hallmark can help you select your accessories — cake servers, toasting glasses, albums, frames, guest books, garters, ring bearer pillows, gifts for attendants, thank yous, napkins, cake tops, programs, plume pens, unity candles, map cards, scrolls, envelope seals, decorations and even a variety of items that can be personalized.

Personal Service

"Discover the Difference" is the motto for the Andrew's Hallmark stores. Our fully trained staff of Wedding Consultants guarantees excellent service and a personal touch second to none. We'll assist you as you choose your invitations and help you select your wording. Before you leave, we'll make sure we've helped you meet all your needs. We carefully double check all orders before they leave the store. When your order arrives, it is checked again and counted to make sure everything is perfect.

Additional Services

IN A HURRY? That's not a problem. With our in-store computer, we can create professional invitations for all occasions while you wait. RUSH service also is available for orders from our albums. We offer local imprinting on album covers and napkins purchased at our stores. With your Hallmark Gold Crown Card, your purchase earns you points toward FREE Hallmark merchandise.

Complete Wedding Printing, Inc.

Portland
2236 N.E. 82nd Avenue
(503) 252-6222

Beaverton
117th and S.W. Canyon Road, Suite E
(503) 646-0821

Open Mon–Fri and Sun;
evenings by appointment

For **Stress Free** ordering and **Quick** turnaround come to
Complete Wedding Printing.

Personal Service A Part Of Our Tradition!

All Major Books • Custom Designs • Your Design

The Personal Touch

Complete Wedding Printing is a locally-owned, specialty print shop. We are proud to offer an in-house printing facility along with one of the largest selections of wedding invitations from associated suppliers. The hallmark of our business is the "personal touch." If a bride wants a unique invitation with her artwork or calligraphy, we are glad to create the invitation she wants.

Competitive Prices

Shop and compare Complete Wedding Printing's personally printed invitations, prices and services, or choose from all the major books. We will work within your budget!

Personalized Printing

It's your wedding and we encourage you to do it your way, by creating the perfect wedding invitation. Our professional consultants are able to work with you to create your own special invitation. Using your design, ideas, artwork or photo our skilled printers can produce that unique image that is you. Whether printed personally or printed from a supplier, invitations with a rich appearance, raised lettering and a wide selection of designs are available.

Accessories

Many different accessories are available to personalize your wedding. These range from custom printed wedding programs, matches, napkins, ribbons, thank-you's, photo tissues to toasting glasses or unity candles. We are glad to provide that special accessory you need.

> **When placing your order, please mention that you saw**
> **this listing to receive 20% off on your invitations,**
> **and 50 FREE Thank-you's.**

MARK'S Hallmark

GOLD CROWN STORES

Clackamas Town Center	*Clackamas Towne Square*	*Washington Square II*
Lower Level/Next to Sears	*Upper Level/Near JCPenney*	*Near JCPenney*
(503) 653-5442	*(503) 659-4523*	*(503) 684-3982*
Lloyd Center	**Peterkort Towne Square**	**Washington Square**
(503) 288-6235	*(503) 643-3118*	*(503) 639-5481*
Downtown Portland	**Oregon City Shopping Center**	**Beaverton Mall**
(503) 295-3711	*(503) 655-7311*	*(503) 646-7613*
Hillsboro	**Hood Center Gresham**	**Tanasbourne Village**
(503) 648-3620	*(503) 666-2761*	*(503) 645-6121*

Salem Centre
(503) 363-5956

Lancaster Mall
(503) 363-1790

Invitations

Mark's Hallmark offers a large selection of invitations from the affordable traditional to the more expensive and elaborate. They also offer a "rush order" service. A consultant is available to help you.

Thank you's or Informals

We can match your invitations and personalize with your names.

Wedding Accessories

Mark's Hallmark has a large selection of keepsake wedding albums and accessories, including toasting glasses, cake knives and servers, and guest books.

Keepsake Albums

Large selection of wedding albums and photo albums to keep those treasured memories in.

Guest Books

Some with space for over 1,000 names and some complete with attached pen. Choices include designs that match keepsake albums.

Anniversary Accessories

All the needed items to plan a special anniversary celebration as well.

SPECIAL OFFER!
$10 Gift Certificate with Invitation Order

Bring your *Bravo Resource Guide* with you when placing
invitation order and receive a $10 gift certificate
redeemable for merchandise in the store.
Minimum order of $50 to receive certificate.
One certificate per order.

TIGARD	PORTLAND	EUGENE
11105 S.W. Greenburg Rd.	*835 E. Burnside*	*1090 Bailey Hill Rd.*
(503) 684-1892	*(503) 238-3607*	*(503) 345-3223*

Business Hours: Mon–Fri 7:30am–5:30pm; Saturdays 9am–2pm

Why Ready-to-Print Invitations and Announcements?

- **You Get Selection!**
  Paper Plus has over 200 designs and formats in stock and ready to print. Choose from formal, romantic, elegant, or plain and simple styles.
- **You Get Uniqueness!**
  When you pick the design and the printer, you have the ability to customize your invitation.
- **You Save Time!**
  By dealing with a local printer you can have your invitations in as little as a day or two.
- **You Save Money!**
  You only pay for the stock, the printing, and production cost. No sales agent mark-up and no shipping!

SHARING A SECRET...

Paper Plus is well-known for their printing and office supplies but their great selection and low prices on wedding supplies may be one of Oregon's best kept secrets.

THE PAPER TREE

2916 N.E. Broadway • Portland, Oregon 97232
Contact: Margo Alkema (503) 284-4741
Hours: Mon–Fri 9:30am–6pm; Sat 9:30am–5:30pm;
early evening by appointment

Selections and Styles of Invitations

Our name says it all. We're in the business of selling every kind of paper product imaginable. Come see our large selection of wedding invitations. The Paper Tree carries every style from traditional engraved invitations to modern, floral, cute, or elegant styles. Select from brands like Crane, Stylart, Regency, Classic, and many others. There are always lots of sample books on hand for you to go through to find the perfect invitation for your special day.

Special Services

Consultants are always available to help you select and order just the right invitation. They can assist you with ideas and wording or answer any questions you may have. Our consultants can also offer creative solutions for your business needs as well.

Cost

- **Price range:** about $45 per hundred and up
- **Price includes** raised print, two envelopes, tissue, and invitation
- **Additional costs:** reception footnote, return address, and colored inks
- **Minimum order:** 25
- **Wording:** a consultant will work with you, or select your own wording if you desire

Ordering Your Invitations

It's best to order your invitations three months before your wedding, no later than two months. Delivery usually takes less than two weeks, but arrangements can be made for faster delivery if necessary. A deposit is required when you order.

Other Services

Select from a variety of thank yous, ceremony programs, napkins, matchbooks, scrolls, personal stationery, ribbons, and personalized toasting goblets.

Wedding Accessories and Gifts for Attendants

The Paper Tree has wedding accessories like grooms-cake boxes and toasting goblets. Personalized notes and stationery, address books and lovely journals make very nice gifts for all your attendants.

WE GUARANTEE OUR SERVICE AND PRODUCTS

The Paper Tree has served bridal and business needs for over 41 years. We guarantee our service and products. We have full-time consultants on staff at all times to offer help and advice. Come in to see all The Paper Tree has to offer.

See page 341 under Decorations & Party Supplies.

Snead's PARTY TIME Rentals & Decorations
"ONE STOP PARTY SHOP"

141st & Tualatin Valley Highway
Beaverton, Oregon 97005
(503) 641-6778
Mon–Sat 7:30am–6pm; Sun 8am–4:30pm

Selections and Styles of Invitations

Sit down and relax in the quiet of our wedding room and browse through 19 albums from traditional to contemporary designs. Our suppliers offer beautiful craftsmanship featuring embossing, engraving, and thermography on bristol, vellum, mirrorkote, parchment, linen, foil, and laid finish with many using recycled paper. You will have many choices in lettering style and ink color. If you prefer, you may design and compose your own to make your wedding more personal.

Special Services

Our experienced wedding consultants check to make sure every detail is correct and that you are communicating with your family and guests in the mood you want for your wedding—all the while remaining within your budget. We can also assist by suggesting compatible wedding accessories and gifts for attendants along with an extensive selection of church and reception rental items and decorations.

Ordering and Cost

Allow ample time to receive and address your invitations. You need to mail them four to six weeks prior to the wedding. Although we can provide emergency three-day service, the average time is two weeks. Prices range from economical to upper moderate. We require a 50% deposit with the balance due on delivery.

Other Services

- **Imprinting is our specialty!!** We provide in-house quality imprinting of your napkins, ribbon, etc. Assorted type styles and colors, wedding symbols and emblems. Our selection of bulk-pack napkins is extensive.
- **Memories book:** an album of anniversaries from 10 to 60 featuring invitations, thank yous, beverage napkins, place cards, and ribbons.
- **Occasion book:** an album for holidays, religious celebrations, new baby, schools, sports, recitals, birthdays, retirements, galas, bon voyage, open house, picnics, and fund raisers, featuring regular and photo invitations, napkins, guest towels, coasters, matches, place cards, and ribbons.
- **Professional images:** an album for business stationery, office and specialty products, featuring business cards, letterhead, envelopes, statements and other forms, computer laser paper, announcements, folders, labels, signs, and specialty advertising.

CUSTOMER SERVICE AND SATISFACTION

Established in 1964, we pride ourselves on customer service and satisfaction. Please give us the opportunity to serve you!

See page 524 under Rental Items & Equipment.

Westside
4775 S.W. Watson Avenue
Beaverton, Oregon 97005
(503) 643-9730

Downtown
423 S.W. Fourth Avenue
Portland, Oregon 97204
(503) 827-4578

The most enormous selection of elegant accessories from economical to extravagant.

The Wedding Cottage is known for having the most beautiful invitations as well as the largest selection in the Portland area. With over 12 years of experience, The Wedding Cottage is able to help brides with those tough etiquette questions, and wording for traditional and contemporary invitations, announcements and receptions.

Selections and Styles

The selection of paper is enormous, with over 50 books containing hundreds of invitations from which to choose. Handmade papers, vellum overlays, tea length, and of course 100% cotton papers are just some of the choices. All can be printed in a variety of fonts and ink colors.

Personalized napkins and ribbons are printed in-house with a large selection of colors available. Rehearsal dinner and shower invitations along with thank you notes, place cards, and table cards are all in stock. We also offer blank invitation and ceremony program stock.

Ordering

Our knowledgeable staff provides excellent customer service and individual help in writing your invitations. Printed orders are generally back within two to three weeks, depending on the invitation. However, some can be received within two to three days, if needed. Of course allowing plenty of time is always best—three to four months prior to the wedding is recommended. Invitations are mailed out four to eight weeks before the wedding, depending on the situation.

Our main store is located in Beaverton, with a second location in downtown Portland, inside of the Ania Collection

Mention the Bravo! Resource Guide and receive a free packet of thank you notes.

See page 222 under Bridal Accessories & Attire.

Notes

ORIGINS OF THE ENGAGEMENT RING

The giving of an

engagement ring was

considered to show

commitment on the groom's

part to purchase the bride.

The use of rings within the

wedding ceremony can be

traced back to the ancient

Egyptians and Romans.

YOUR GUIDE TO GEMSTONE VALUE AND QUALITY

For most couples, the bride's engagement ring is the first major piece of jewelry that they have ever purchased. When you're making a purchase of this size and for something that the bride will wear for the rest of her life, it's nice to know what the jeweler is describing and what exactly you're getting.

The stone you select as the centerpiece of your engagement ring is judged by four distinct factors that combine in a number of ways to arrive at its value. These factors are commonly referred to as the Four Cs.

CARAT WEIGHT: The weight of all precious stones is expressed in carats. Originally, the word carat was derived from a natural unit of weight, the seeds of the carob tree. Traditionally, gemstones were weighed against these seeds, but in more recent times, a standardized system has been developed by which one carat equals 0.2 grams, or one-fifth of a gram. The carat is then divided into 100 "points," so that a gemstone of 25 points equals a quarter carat, or a gemstone of 50 points equals a half carat, etc.

CLARITY: Virtually every diamond (the most common stone selected for an engagement ring) has some minute traces of noncrystalized carbon, the element from which they were formed. In most cases, these traces of carbon are not visible to the human eye but become apparent under magnification and are referred to as "inclusions." These inclusions are actually nature's fingerprint and are what make every diamond different from another. Therefore, the freer the diamond or other gemstone is of inclusions, the rarer the stone will be, causing a higher value to be placed on the stone.

There are three major international grading systems for classifying diamonds— GIA, CIBJO, and HRD. A stone is termed flawless by the GIA if it is without inclusions internally or externally. The other systems use the term "loupe clean," or internally flawless.

COLOR: When it comes to diamonds, most of us don't think in terms of colors available, but diamonds do cover the spectrum of colors. While the majority range in color from a barely perceptible yellow or brownish tint, the really rare stones are described as "colorless." Even rarer diamonds, which are sometimes referred to as "fancies," can be found in shades of green, red, blue, or amber.

CUT: Of all the ways diamonds are rated, this is the one that man directly has an impact on. How each diamond is cut will directly affect its fire and sparkle, since it is the cutter's skill that ultimately releases the beauty of each stone. It is the talent, artistry, and years of experience of this person that enable the stone to make the best use of the light by allowing it to reflect from one facet to another and then disperse through the top of the stone. The better the cut, the more brilliance and sparkle you will see in the stone you select.

For more assistance with staying organized during the wedding planning process, check out the Bravo! Wedding Organizer. Detailed question worksheets double as contracts. This step-by-step system will keep every detail of your wedding organized. To order, refer to the order form on page 23 in this Guide.

D E S I G N E R J E W E L R Y
S H O W C A S E

One S.W. Columbia Street, Suite 0002
Portland, Oregon 97258
(503) 241-9389; Fax (503) 222-1310

Designer Jewelry specializes in platinum/18kt custom wedding sets also in ideal cut diamonds A.G.S.–G.I.A. certified. Our emphasis is on finer quality, color, clarity and cut. We help our clients to become informed buyers. We show diamonds unmounted and in the proper lighting so that their 4 Cs can be determined accurately.

Cut

Designer Jewelry feels that the cut is the most important and overlooked factor in determining a diamond's value and beauty. As Master Diamond Cutters, we are especially qualified to educate you in the finer details of cut.

The Ideal Cut: When a round brilliant diamond has been cut to "ideal" proportions by a master cutter, it is a splendor to behold.

The Ideal Cut Diamond describes a round brilliant diamond that has been cut to exact and mathematically proven proportions. Its symmetry, with 58 exactly placed facets, produces the ultimate in lustre and beauty. When a diamond is cut to the ideal proportions, all of the light entering from any direction is totally reflected through the top and is dispersed into a display of sparkling flashes and rainbow colors.

Cost

As a direct importer, Designer Jewelry is especially qualified to select the finest cut diamonds at the most competitive price. Cost is relative to quality, size and cut. Diamond prices will start to compound with increases in size. Our international experience gives us the ability to draw upon worldwide resources in locating rare and important diamonds. As a result, we have enjoyed a high rate of repeat and referral business.

Fred Meyer JEWELERS

"For All Those Special Times"

Now in most major malls!
Call for a location near you.
(800) 858-9202

For Your Wedding

Fred Meyer Jewelers goes to more weddings in the Northwest because you choose from one of the largest wedding ring collections, you will discover an impressive selection of classic and contemporary engagement rings, wedding sets and solitaires. A collection of unmounted diamonds in all shapes and sizes with an unrivaled selection of 14kt. and 18kt. gold settings. Fred Meyer Jewelers also offers the reassurance and protection of an independent appraisal on unmounted diamonds 1/4 carat or larger.

Custom Design and Jewelry Restoration

Fred Meyer Jewelers have custom design specialists on staff. Our in-store goldsmiths specialize in restoring keepsake jewelry or transforming an old treasure into a new beautiful creation.

Gifts for Wedding Attendants

- **Groomsmen:** men's accessory jewelry
- **Bridesmaids:** ladies fashion accessories, earrings, pendants and bracelets

Other Jewelry

Helpful gift hints for the bride or groom: diamond earrings, bracelets and neckwear for her; men's accessory jewelry, 14kt gold chains and bracelets, or quality watches from Seiko, Citizen, and Pulsar for him. Don't forget Mom, Dad, friends, and relatives who especially helped to make your wedding day perfect. Thank them with specially selected gifts.

Service: Financing and Guarantee

Fred Meyer Jewelers 30-day money back guarantee ensures your complete satisfaction with every purchase, and your diamond is protected against loss for as long as you own it (see our store for complete details). Our "Diamond Standard" includes free inspection, free cleaning, trade-in value, and guarantee against diamond loss. You can pay for your jewelry the easy way with our convenient revolving charge card.

Quality and Affordability

We're committed to quality and affordability. The selection of a wedding set is the ultimate expression of your hopes, dreams and promises. Fred Meyer Jewelers makes your selection easy with the Northwest's largest collection of exquisitely designed wedding rings in classic or contemporary designs. Or have our master goldsmith design a unique ring especially for you. We believe no sale is ever final until you, our customer, is completely happy. So come to Fred Meyer Jewelers and celebrate all those special times!

HAIMOFF

INTERNATIONAL JEWELERS

Tanasbourne Town Center
2711 N.W. Town Center Drive, Suite 104
Beaverton, Oregon 97006
(503) 533-9800
www.internationaljewelers.com

Diamonds at the Guaranteed Lowest Prices

Haimoff International Jewelers carries the largest selection of certified loose diamonds at the guaranteed lowest prices of any retail jeweler. Every loose diamond, from round to marquise, oval to princess shapes, is certified by an independent gemological laboratory. The certification provides you with the details of the diamond you choose, including cut, color, clarity, and carat weight.

Largest Selection of Wedding Sets and Bands

Haimoff International Jewelers' selection of wedding sets and bands is the largest in the Northwest. Weddings sets and bands are available in 14k and 18k gold and platinum, with or without side stones. From a traditional gold band to the ring of your dreams, Haimoff International Jewelers has something for everyone.

Haimoff International Jewelers is More than Diamonds

In addition to diamonds, Haimoff International Jewelers carries a wide selection of fine jewelry including:

- Sapphires
- Rubies
- Emerald
- Pearls
- Semi-precious Gemstones
- Earrings
- Gold chains
- Men's accessories
- Pendants
- Watches
- Tennis Bracelets

The Haimoff International Jewelers Advantage

- Lifetime guarantee against loss from mounting
- Lifetime trade-in value
- Free cleaning and inspection of all jewelry
- Certificate on each loose diamond
- Guaranteed lowest prices of any retail jeweler
- Financing available

A Better Way To Buy
HAIMOFF INTERNATIONAL JEWELERS

DOWNTOWN
901 S.W. Yamhill • Portland, Oregon 97205
(503) 223-9510

WASHINGTON SQUARE
9610 Washington Square • Portland, Oregon 97223
(503) 620-2243

Also located in the Oregon Market at the Portland Airport

Specialty Wedding Sets
We represent more than 25 jewelry designers with custom design service available at our downtown location. Engagement rings and wedding sets can be created in 14K or 18K yellow, rose or white gold and platinum. Large selection of original designs available and a friendly, knowledgeable staff to assist you. Loose diamonds and gemstones can be matched with designs in stock, or our on-staff designer can design something especially for you. Wedding rings from $250, plain bands from $65.

Gift Ideas for Bride, Groom and Attendants
Extensive collection of original and handcrafted fine jewelry, ceramics, art glass and exotic wood accessories that the wedding party will love to receive.

Services/Policies
- Layaway Available
- Gift Registry and Gift Certificates
- Packing and Shipping
- Gift wrap available for small fee

See page 272 under Bridal Registry & Gifts.

ZELL BROS
Jewelers ∴ Platinumsmiths

800 S.W. Morrison Street • Portland, Oregon 97205
(503) 227-8471 or (800) 444-8979; Fax (503) 223-8546
Business Hours: Mon–Fri 10am–5:30pm; Sat 10am–5pm

WE'VE HELPED PORTLAND KEEP
87 YEARS OF WEDDING PROMISES

Zell Bros, the Largest Full-service Jewelry and Tabletop Store in the West

Zell Bros is a wedding tradition. When we opened in 1912 in a small storefront near Union Station, Zell Bros made a promise: to consistently offer the most beautiful jewelry and the highest quality diamonds available. Choose from our large selection and let one of our expert on-staff designers create unique rings just for you. We've helped generation after generation of Portland brides and grooms keep their promises of finding "just the right" rings.

Shapes and Kinds of Stones Available

You name it, we have it. From the most brilliant diamonds, to lustrous pearls, rubies, and sapphires. All birthstones are available, too.

Custom Design and Jewelry Restoration

Our extensive, in-store manufacturing department is staffed with expert jewelers, designers, diamond setters, platinumsmiths, and watchmakers. We will create anything you can imagine, or restore, remodel and repair your treasured heirloom pieces.

Gift Ideas for Bride, Groom, and Attendants

Let our staff of expert gift consultants guide you throughout three floors in your quest for excellence.

Service is our Most Important Product

Here are a few things we offer:

- Our famous gift wrap
- Free diamond inspection
- Free jewelry cleaning
- Credit options

- Bridal gift registry
- Full-service Stationery Department
- Exchanges gladly within 180 days
- Parking validation with purchase

LET US HELP YOU KEEP YOUR PROMISE

See page 274 under Bridal Registry & Gifts.

Notes

ENSURE GOOD LUCK

During the Elizabethan era, to ensure good luck, the bride and groom were encouraged to kiss over a stack of small sweet buns that formed a centerpiece on a table. It was the French who, in the 17th century, started to frost the stack of cakes with a white sugar frosting so that they would stay upright. Thus was born the tiered wedding cake that brides use today.

Northwest Artist Management

Musicians, Concerts & Fine Events

6210 S.E. 41st Avenue
Portland, Oregon 97202
Contact: Nancy Anne Tice • Phone/Fax (503) 774-2511
Business Hours: Mon–Fri 9am–6pm
E-mail: nwartmtg@teleport.com

Entertainment Consultant Services

Northwest Artist Management is proud to offer the finest in classical, jazz, and international music for weddings and all fine occasions. From Arias to Zydeco, soloists to elegant dance bands and hot jazz ensembles, we can accommodate just about any entertainment need or musical preference, including assistance with technical details.

Specialty

We represent only the finest Northwest artists whom you can select with complete confidence, knowing they are as dedicated to creating special memories as you are! We offer string quartets, brass ensembles, classical soloists, and vocalists of all kinds, a wide variety of dance bands, jazz ensembles, and international music such as Italian, Irish, Mediterranean, Middle Eastern, Flamenco, Mariachi, Reggae, the Blues, Latin Salsa, Caribbean, and Cajun/Zydeco to suit most budgets.

Budget and Terms

Northwest Artist Management can accommodate any budget, ranging from $150 soloists to a large big band or orchestra. Reception bands and ensembles average between $350 and $1,500, depending on size, type, and reputation of the group.

How Much Can We Save?

Our commission is built into the artist's fee. We consult with you to determine just exactly what your preferences are, and can usually offer several choices from which to choose. We provide complete promotional materials, photos, demo tapes, references, and frequently, live performance observation possibilities so you can be assured of making an informed and confident decision.

How Far In Advance Should We Meet?

We have provided musicians as late as the day of the wedding, but usually prefer to consult with you six to nine months in advance. To engage certain groups, a one-year-in-advance reservation is advisable so you won't be disappointed.

Experience

All of the artists on our roster are gifted, polished professionals with years of experience in helping couples "custom-design" every detail of their wedding music. We are knowledgeable about all music from the grand Baroque period to the hottest Top 40. We are available to consult with you personally to help you select the perfect repertoire that will create and enhance the romance and magic of your special day, and accommodate the needs of your guests. We offer only the best, because you deserve nothing less!

Member of:

Weddings of Distinction, Jazz Society of Oregon,
Portland Oregon Visitors Association, Washington County Visitors Association

THE FIRST DANCE

The traditional bride and groom's first dance represents the start of their new life together. After the first dance together, the bride dances with her father and the groom with his mother.

HELPFUL HINTS

- **Deciding on a band:** Every band should have a music list available for you to review. This will be helpful in deciding on a band. You may want to ask if the band is currently playing somewhere, then you can listen to their music style live and see their stage presence before you make a final decision.

- **Reserving a band:** Reserve a band or orchestra for your reception immediately. There are only a limited amount of Saturdays available, especially in peak wedding seasons. Popular bands and orchestras are often reserved up to a year in advance.

- **Setup requirements:** The formality, facility, and size of your event will determine the type of music that is appropriate. Inquire about whether the site can accommodate dancing and has the area necessary for the musicians to set up and perform. Be very specific about getting the space and electrical requirements from the band so that you can accurately relay the information to your contact person at the facility.

- **Cut-off hours:** When you make all the final arrangements with your facility, be sure to ask if they have any specified time cut-offs for music. Some facilities require that music be stopped as early as 10pm for the comfort of neighboring homes, businesses, or other guests.

- **Background music and dancing music:** Remember when reserving your music that the first hour of your reception or event is a time for introductions and mingling with guests. If your band begins playing immediately, you'll want to make sure that the music is background-type music that doesn't overwhelm and interfere with mingling. The band can be instructed at a certain time or by signal to pick up the pace of the music for dancing.

- **Keeping the flow going at the reception:** It is a good idea to have a liaison between the bride and groom and the band. This person can instruct the band when it's time to play the "first dance" song. Many times the band leader will act as master of ceremonies, announce the cake cutting, throwing of the bouquet, and the garter toss. The best man may be the person to do this since he will be close at hand to coordinate the order of events with the bride, groom, and parents. This will help the day to flow smoothly for the bride and groom.

- **Band breaks:** How many breaks will the band be taking and for how long? Will there be music provided during this downtime? Will the musicians require food and/or beverages? This could effect your total count to the caterer.

- **What kind of band is appropriate:** for a wedding with 50-75 guests, a three-piece band is appropriate; for 75-200, a four- to six-piece band works well.

- **Saving on music:** The best way to cut music costs is to have your wedding in off-season: January through March, Sundays, early in the day. Musicians will be more willing to negotiate prices if it doesn't conflict with another high paying booking.

- **NOTE:** Make sure your contract is sound, and that your event won't be bumped for a larger engagement. A deposit is usually required.

For more assistance with staying organized during the wedding planning process, check out the Bravo! Wedding Organizer. Detailed question worksheets double as contracts. This step-by-step system will keep every detail of your wedding organized. To order, refer to the order form on page 23 in this Guide.

Another Night with

Johnny Martin

(503) 255-0974

Sinatra Swing, Inc.
From supper-club swing to dance floor romance.

"...STYLE AND PANACHE..."
—Jenni Minner, Performing Arts Coordinator, Portland Saturday Market

"...EXCELLENT..."
—Al Kendall, Entertainment Chairman, BPOE

"...COURTEOUS AND RELIABLE...COVERS SINATRA BEAUTIFULLY..."
—Eric B. Allen, Restaurant Manager, Willamette Athletic Club

"...TOP OF THE LINE..."
—Carmen Eastman, President/CEO, Eastman Entertainment

Make Your Wedding Swing!
Entertainer Johnny Martin brings 20 years of experience to the stage. He's made quite a splash at the Multnomah Athletic Club, Columbia Edgewater Country Club, Waverley Country Club, Queen of the West Cruise Line, and various Oregon casinos—to name a few.
   Widely recognized as an emerging vocal talent in Portland.

Something Old, Something Borrowed, Something Blue-eyed
Sinatra swing as performed by Johnny and backed up by the finest musicians in town.
   Not a variety act. Highly specialized swing music made popular by great artists such as Nelson Riddle, Billy May, Cole Porter, and Sammy Cahn. Brings all generations to the dance floor.

A Day Like This Should Be Special
Make your reservations now. Advanced booking recommended. Whenever there's a need for highly specialized music and entertainment.

**SUMMER WIND • LET'S FALL IN LOVE
HELLO YOUNG LOVERS • SOUTH OF THE BORDER
COME FLY WITH ME • OLD BLACK MAGIC
NIGHT AND DAY • UNDER MY SKIN
WITCHCRAFT • LADY IS A TRAMP**

Call for a free demo tape or live performance video.

BYLL DAVIS & FRIENDS
(503) 644-3493

WE BE A FUN BAND!
TRY US AT YOUR NEXT PARTY!

Type of Music

Byll Davis & Friends offers complete flexibility in all styles and eras of music, including ethnic, Big Band, good time rock 'n' roll and Top 40.

Instrumentation

Byll Davis can accommodate your needs with one to eight musicians. Dress is usually formal, but we'll dress to suit the occasion. Call for more details.

Experience

Byll Davis has a master's degree in music, has participated in several successful road tours and has led and performed in bands that specialize in Big Band, rock 'n' roll, Top 40 and variety and society musical styles. The Byll Davis & Friends ensemble has performed in literally thousands of engagements locally for a wide variety of events and audiences.

Musical Style and Audience Rapport

The following comments represent the kind of feedback Byll Davis & Friends receives:

"Byll, you were fabulous as always and a delight to work with."

"It was the perfect band for the evening…many, many compliments from our guests."

"Your selections for our event were based on your ability to adjust and come through with what people like."

"Your music was so good it made it difficult to keep the outsiders from crashing in."

Free Consultation

If hiring a band is new to you, or if you want to find out more about Byll Davis & Friends, make an appointment to meet with Byll. The service is free, the information invaluable.

Cost and Terms

Prices, space and electrical requirements will vary depending on the size of the band and location of engagement. Please call for additional information.

RELIABLE
APPROPRIATE
PRICED RIGHT
FUN ! ! ! !

(503) 644-3493

Cúl an Tí

505 S.E. 27th Avenue
Portland, Oregon 97214
Contact: Cary Novotny (503) 236-9781
E-mail: culanti@aol.com
Web site: http://members.aol.com/culanti/

ROUSING IRISH AND CONTEMPORARY FOLK MUSIC

Three strong instrumentalists make up this compelling ensemble, which combines the best elements of traditional Irish dance music with exciting, modern Celtic stylings. Bass and acoustic guitars blend with vocals, accordion and red-hot fiddle in fresh arrangements of traditional Irish music, perfect for dancing and celebration. Cúl an Tí—"cool ahn tee"— performs a broad range of music, including slow ballads and waltzes, lightning fast jigs, reels, polkas, bluegrass, American folk music, and a modest selection of classic rock. The band plays throughout the Pacific Northwest; appearances include the 1998 Portland Celtic Festival, the Portland Celtic Minifest, The Bite festival of Portland as well as countless dates in venues such as Kells and Biddy McGraw's in Portland, and Conor Byrne's Pub and Kells in Seattle.

Reception Options

Cúl an Tí is well connected in Portland's folk-music community, allowing them to invite additional top-notch musicians into the line-up if requested. Instrumentalists, singers, even Irish dancers and callers (to teach dance steps to your guests) are available to help create an even more spectacular performance. Scaled-down versions of the band (solo or duo format) are also available, for those on a thrifty budget.

Ceremony Options

Cúl an Tí can provide the soft and subtle melodies to help make your ceremony a moving and memorable event. They offer a wide variety of beautiful musical combinations, including classical and fingerstyle guitar, violin, male and/or female vocals, bass and Irish tin-whistle. Special requests for the processional/recessional are encouraged.

Special Services, Costs and Terms

Cúl an Tí's P.A. system is available for toasts and announcements; recorded music can be provided during breaks. Fees are determined on an individual basis, according to length of performance, location, and amplification requirements. All necessary details are included in contract. Demo tape and references are available upon request.

LIVELY, UPLIFTING MUSIC IN THE SPIRIT OF CELEBRATION

Give Cúl an Tí a call—they will help you find the right combination of ceremony and reception music to help make your wedding day a joyous and successful event.

DAVID COOLEY &
THE HARD SWING BAND

P.O. Box 2086
Vancouver, Washington 98668
PORTLAND (503) 227-1866
VANCOUVER (360) 693-1707
Fax (360) 693-4057

Type of Music

Referred to as "the Frank Sinatra of Portland," (Phil Smith, Oregonian) David Cooley's brand of Swing and Big Band vocals are the Northwest's finest. His recent release, "Fly Me To The Moon," on CD and cassette, is an impressive collection of popular Swing standards. In addition to Swing music, the band's repertoire also includes Rock 'n' Roll, Rhythm and Blues. The group provides background music, dance music and ceremony music. Special requests are welcome. Please call for more information.

Experience

David's 15 years as a singer and band leader guarantees you the perfect sound, style and pace for your reception. He understands what an important effect the band has on a successful reception. His performance credits include venues in Europe, Asia, Hawaii, Canada and the United States.

Instruments

The group may be booked in several different ways: from a trio, quartet, five or six-piece, all the way to the renowned 11-piece band featuring the Hard Swing Horn section. These variations allow great flexibility in choosing the appropriate sound, style and price range for your reception music.

Special Services

David Cooley is an excellent MC. He will help coordinate announcements, first dance, bouquet toss and other special activities. David will be at your service to help in every way possible.

Cost and Terms

Pricing is flexible according to the size of the band, venue and location. Please call for an estimate and more information.

Commitment

David Cooley's commitment to excellence in musical services extends beyond the reception itself. Advance planning and last-minute changes are accommodated with every means possible—no detail is too small.

Credits

OREGON SYMPHONY • OMSI • PORTLAND CENTER FOR PERFORMING ARTS MULTNOMAH ATHLETIC CLUB • MUSEUM AFTER HOURS • UNIVERSITY CLUB SALISHAN LODGE • PORTLAND HILTON • SEATTLE SHERATON • FOUR SEASONS OLYMPIC, SEATTLE • WASHINGTON ATHLETIC CLUB • GOVERNOR HOTEL • THE RACQUET CLUB • BENSON HOTEL • PORTLAND MARRIOTT • WAVERLEY COUNTRY CLUB • PORTLAND GOLF CLUB • SKAMANIA LODGE

If you're looking for a very special accent at your wedding, call now.
David Cooley & The Hard Swing Band *offers a classic musical atmosphere*
with all the style, charm and spirit to make your celebration unforgettable.

JANICE SCROGGINS/GARY HARRIS QUARTET

Contact: Nancy Anne Tice
Phone/Fax (503) 774-2511
E-mail: nwartmtg@teleport.com

Types of Music and Demo

Celebrated jazz, blues and gospel pianist, **Janice Scroggins** has teamed up with **Gary Harris** on sax and flute to form a lively and sophisticated instrumental quartet that plays jazz, blues, rhythm and blues and funk favorites for listening and dancing. If groovin' to the hits of Duke Ellington, Cole Porter, Marvin Gaye, Otis Redding, The Temptations, Glenn Miller, Kenny G., Stevie Wonder or Gershwin is your idea of a great time, please call for a free demo, promotional kit and references.

Instruments

The instrumental quartet consists of keyboards/synthesizer, bass, drums, saxophones and flute. A vocalist may be added as the budget allows.

Experience

Janice Scroggins and **Gary Harris** have dazzled audiences at concerts and festivals in Russia, Europe, Japan, Mexico, Hawaii, Africa and all over the United States and Canada. Janice has opened for Bill Cosby, BB King, Ray Charles and Taj Mahal. Gary has played with The Temptations, Four Tops, Lou Rawls, Manhattan Transfer, and George Benson. Janice's *Scott Joplin* album was nominated for a Grammy Award in 1988, and she has been the recipient of the Cascade Blues Society, Muddy Waters Award three times. Locally, Janice has played with Linda Hornbuckle, Lloyd Jones, Curtis Salgado and Norman Sylvester; Gary plays with Leroy Vinnegar's Quartet, and several big bands, and they both play and tour with Obo Addy. Gary has recorded the California Raisins theme for Will Vinton Studios on Atlantic Records. Both have played for countless weddings and private parties. Their quartet blends and combines all of their respective experience into a tight and polished ensemble that is sure to get you up and dancing!

Cost, Terms and Special Services

Competitive prices based on date, time, length of engagement and size of group. All details outlined in contract. Call for quote. They welcome your requests including ethnic favorites. They are happy to serve as MC if you wish. Tuxedo is standard attire for weddings, unless otherwise specified.

ELEGANT, SMOOTH AND SOPHISTICATED.
STYLISH, HIP AND GREAT FUN

This band knows exactly what to do to ensure the music will be the best it can be!

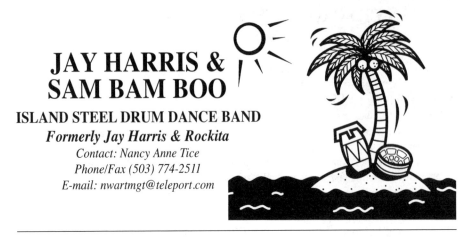

JAY HARRIS & SAM BAM BOO

ISLAND STEEL DRUM DANCE BAND

Formerly Jay Harris & Rockita

Contact: Nancy Anne Tice
Phone/Fax (503) 774-2511
E-mail: nwartmgt@teleport.com

Type of Music and Demo

Sam Bam Boo plays a unique blend of calypso, reggae, and island-style renditions of many types of popular music (blues, jazz, rock, even classical!), which they call "Rockalypso"! Much more than just a "steel drum band"—imagine your favorite Beatles, Elton John, Santana, Billy Joel, James Taylor, Sting or Van Morrison tunes played with that distinctive Caribbean flavor that makes you think of bright colors, steamy tropical nights, palm trees and exciting times on the dance floor. They also play all of your favorite island hits from "Jamaica Farewell" to "Day-O." Bob Marley, The Beach Boys, and Jimmy Buffett are well represented. Think of a festive "Island Carnival" and you have Sam Bam Boo. They also have a Limbo Stick and will teach you how to "Do the Limbo", an activity guaranteed to enliven any event! Call for free promotional package, demo, references, and song list.

Instruments

Sam Bam Boo is a trio that blends the bright, captivating tones of the steel drum with percussion, and bass and guitar. They frequently add a sax player when the budget permits. They are a surprisingly versatile ensemble with a full, rich sound. All the players also sing and wear tropical attire to complete the island look.

Experience and Special Services

Sam Bam Boo band members have played for hundreds of private parties, weddings, and corporate events in their many years on the band stand. They have played in every conceivable setting from boats, barns, and beaches, to parks, festivals, gardens, museums, wineries, mountain resorts, and all manner of commercial establishment…always with rave reviews and consistent invitations to return. They are pleased to serve as master of ceremonies and to play as many of your requests as possible. You are welcome to use their PA system for announcements. All ensemble members are talented, professional musicians, who are easy and fun to work with. You can trust your special day to Sam Bam Boo.

Cost

Sam Bam Boo is a highly affordable ensemble. Rates based on location, ensemble size, playing time, and season of year. Call for price quotation. We always use contracts.

KIM RALPHS & COMPANY

(503) 282-3421

Sinatra, Swing & More!

Imagine the lush soundtrack to *Sleepless in Seattle!* Classic and timeless. Band leader, **Kim Ralphs**, has assembled a fine group of professional musicians that specialize in the elegant and sophisticated music of the 1930s and '40s. They play quiet and tasty jazz instrumentals and the romantic love songs of Tony Bennett, Frank Sinatra, and Glenn Miller. For your dancing pleasure, they offer Big Band Swing and smooth Latin and Bossa Nova favorites.

In a more contemporary vein, they know all of Kenny G's most memorable hits. When you really want to take the temperature up, they can pump out some '50s and '60s rock. Kim Ralphs & Company are polished and versatile professionals who offer a wide variety of musical styles. They are always happy to accommodate your special requests to ensure your event is a success.

Kim plays **piano**, key-bass and various electric keyboard sounds such as **vibes** and **marimbas**. **Sax and flute, drums and vocals** complete the sound. The size of the group can expand to fit your budget. Both male and female vocalists are available, or the band can play only instrumentals, if you prefer.

Since 1985, Kim and his group have performed at the finest hotels and country clubs, and have been recommended by the best event planners and booking agencies. They are always happy to make announcements for you and help coordinate your party. Standard attire is black tuxedos. Let Kim Ralphs & Company create a warm and sparkling atmosphere for your next special event!

LISTEN TO WHAT THE PROFESSIONALS SAY:

"Kim is a fine pianist…and I always enjoy seeing him here."
Dennis Yamnitsky, F&B Manager, **Oswego Lake Country Club**

"Kim plays here often, and always does a great job..highly recommended."
Susan O'Neil, **Waverley Country Club**

*"All the music that I have listened to over the years and all the conventions
that I have gone to, I can truly say that this band was the best!"*
Colleen Greenen, Convention Sales Manager, **Portland Oregon Visitors Association**

"Impeccably professional and experienced…a pleasure to work with."
Nancy Tice, **Northwest Artist Management**

1035 S.W. Carson Street
Portland, Oregon 97219
Contact: Fritz or Julie Weber (503) 245-5055
E-mail: luminos@pacinter.net

Types of Music

Luminos is the musical group of Fritz and Julie Weber. They have over 16 hours of music in their repertoire. Much of that is jazz and classic rock, with several other areas of specialty: (1) New Orleans, including piano boogie, Cajun and zydeco, (2) tropical-style including Jimmy Buffett and (3) Brazilian jazz and bossa nova. They can play a cocktail hour as a strolling band, return to the stage for light jazz during dinner and play rock for dancing after dinner. A custom song list is created for every engagement after consulting with each client.

Instruments

Fritz plays piano, electric keyboards, keyboard bass, and rhythm synthesizer. Julie plays flute, alto flute, piccolo, conga drums and various other percussion instruments. Both of them are vocalists, and Julie also sings in French, Spanish and Portuguese.

The other band members play (1) flute and saxophones, (2) guitar and bass, and (3) drums. They include as many band members as appropriate, but even as a duo they have the sound of a full band.

As the sound engineer, Fritz sees that their volume level is always matched to the occasion. Their musical instruments, sound system and stage lights are of the best quality and never out of place, even in the most elegant surroundings.

Experience

They've played music together since 1973, performing in public clubs, at company parties, wedding services, receptions and many special events. They've played on the West Coast and Hawaii, in the Caribbean and in Europe. They are both classical percussionists and past members of the Marylhurst Symphony and the Portland Chamber Orchestra. Fritz is the Director of Music Ministries at St. James Episcopal Church in Tigard, Oregon. They're both members of the group, Carl Smith & the Natural Gas Co., a 12-piece band.

Cost

Their fee ranges from $225 to $1,200 and is affected by a number of factors.

"On your wedding day you should feel like royalty. As your Personal Music Director, I will see to it that the music ties your reception together as a unique celebration and a reflection of the two of you. I welcome you, or your musical friends, to prepare and perform special songs with us."
                                                                                            ~Fritz

LARRY NATWICK TRIO

Contact: Nancy Anne Tice
Phone/Fax (503) 774-2511
E-mail: nwartmgt@teleport.com

Types of Music and Demo

The Larry Natwick Trio specializes in the elegant and sophisticated favorites of the big band and swing era of the 1940s, the World War II years, jazz and pop standards, and bossa nova melodies that are so much fun to dance to. They play all the wonderful hits by Duke Ellington, George Gershwin, Cole Porter, Henry Mancini, Harold Arlen, Jerome Kern, Michel LaGrand, and Frank Loesser, to name a few. Whether you prefer the lush, romantic ballads, or if the high-energy swing tunes are more your style, Larry Natwick and Company have a vast repertoire from which to choose. If you want tasteful, background music, you can expect to hear many of the compositions of the greatest jazz artists of all time. Call for free promotional package, demo tape, references, and selected tune list.

Instruments

The Larry Natwick Trio consists of piano, stand-up string bass, and drums. They frequently work with vocalists, and can add horn players as the budget allows. They usually play totally acoustically, but sound reinforcement can easily be added for larger functions. Tuxedo, semiformal, or casual attire available to suit your needs.

Experience

Originally from the San Francisco Bay area, Larry Natwick began his career playing in many of the prestigious hotels including the famed Fairmount, The Lodge at Pebble Beach, the Highland's Inn in Carmel, and The River Inn in Big Sur. Since moving to the Northwest in 1979, he and ensemble members have played for countless private parties and weddings, every major Northwest festival, numerous concert series, and all the hottest jazz venues. They have also appeared at charity fund raisers, wineries, open houses, dinner dances, and conventions. Ensemble members include André St. James, bass and Donny Osbourne, drums —who worked with Mel Tormé for 22 years. They are 100% dependable, sensitive, professional musicians, ready to create a warm and sparkling atmosphere for your next special event. This band knows exactly what to do so you can relax and enjoy the party and your guests.

Cost and Special Services

Part of this wonderfully affordable ensemble, Larry Natwick also plays piano solo or in a duo with the bassist. Duos are a cost-effective way to go if you want background music. A keyboard system is always available, or you provide an acoustic piano. A microphone is available for toasts and announcements. Call for price quote. All details in contract.

c/o Berkshire Snow Productions
P.O. Box 14159
Portland, Oregon 97293-0159
(503) 235-3071, (503) 284-1186
E-mail: berksnow@teleport.com

T_{HE} MILLIONAIRE$

Good Time R&R, R&B, Blues,
Oldies and more, 40's thru 90's

Types of Music and Demo

The Millionaires bring a wealth of musical experience to your wedding reception or special event. With a repertoire that covers the history of rock 'n' roll, The Millionaires let the music speak for itself and the fun begin. From the days of Big Joe Turner and Howlin' Wolf, when the blues began to rock, through the hits of Elvis Presley, Roy Orbison and Chuck Berry and on to the British Invasion with the Rolling Stones and Beatles.

The Millionaires play the best of rock 'n' roll, rhythm and blues, blues, country and more — familiar songs from the '40s to the '90s. Our demo is available upon request.

Instrumentation and Personnel

We feature three male lead vocalists, accompanied by the classic four-piece format of electric guitar, Fender bass, electric piano/synthesizer/Hammond organ and drums.

Experience

Michael Kearsey, Don Heistuman and Jim Stein are backed by drummer Fred Ingram. These musicians have been members of some of the best loved groups in Oregon including Nu Shooz, Upepo, Diamond Hill, Razorbacks, the Larry Mahan Band, Saint Champagne, the Blue Devils and the Brothers of the Baladi. The Millionaires have played weddings, corporate events and club dates since 1992.

Musical Style and Audience Rapport

The Millionaires love to entertain and deliver songs that you love to hear. We will work with you to customize our sets to please the wide-range of ages that may be at your event and include styles from decades of great popular music. We are always happy to provide specialty songs that are most important to our clients. The bottom line for The Millionaires is to create the best musical memories for your needs.

Cost and Terms

Our prices will vary based on location, season, availability, length of engagement and special services you may need. We are flexible because we are The Millionaires!!

6210 S.E. 41st Avenue
Portland, Oregon 97202
Contact: Nancy Anne Tice at
Northwest Artist Management
Phone/Fax (503) 774-2511
E-mail: nwartmtg@teleport.com

Type of Music and Demo

OPUS 5 members combine many years of national and international touring and performing experience into a versatile, polished, and sophisticated dance band perfect for weddings, receptions, dinner and dancing, corporate entertaining, and elegant celebrations of all kinds. They are equally at home with Jazz, Pop, R&B, Country, Rock 'n' Roll, and the romantic, sentimental favorites of the past. Call for demo tape, photos, group résumé, play list, and references.

Instruments

OPUS 5 is a five-piece group with an extremely talented female lead vocalist. Instruments include keyboard/synthesizer, bass, drum, and guitar. Band members provide terrific lead vocals and smooth harmonies. They dress in formal attire unless you request otherwise to suit the occasion.

Experience, Music Style, and Audience Rapport

The members of OPUS 5 have played for hundreds of weddings over the years and know just what to do to keep your guests happy. They have played in places such as Oregon Symphony Gala, Atwater's, Oswego Lake Country Club, Columbia Gorge Hotel, The Governor Hotel and Benson Hotel, and at many local wineries and festivals. OPUS 5 is as dedicated to making special memories as you are. Accordingly, their play list is designed to perfectly suit the ambience of your special event, making sure the volume is just right and you and your guests have the time of your lives!

Special Services, Cost, and Terms

OPUS 5 encourages your special requests, including ethnic favorites. You are welcome to use their PA system for announcements and toasts. They will also serve as Master of Ceremonies for all dance traditions, bouquet and garter toss, etc. Taped music is provided for breaks. OPUS 5's prices are highly competitive and quoted individually, based on playing time, location, and season of the year. Details such as deposits, overtime, and cancellation charges are explained in their contract. Call for quotation.

Setting Requirements

Whether indoor or out, the band needs two 110-volt electrical outlets. Any outdoor engagements must have an awning or tent to cover the band. OPUS 5 prefers to set up several hours before the event if possible.

EXPERIENCE AND FLEXIBILITY

A thoroughly professional attitude helps ensure OPUS 5's success and popularity with its clients. The energy, elegance, and sparkle they bring to the bandstand are sure to enhance the mood and festive atmosphere of your next special event.

Patrick Lamb
PRODUCTIONS

544 N.E. Thompson, Suite A
Portland, Oregon 97212
Contact: Amy Maxwell
(503) 335-0790; Fax (503) 335-9074
Sax Line (503) 650-7138
E-mail: lamb@teleport.com

VISA MasterCard

© Rodolfo Hernandez

Types of Music and Demo

Imagine the sound of sweet saxophone permeating the atmosphere of your wedding. Patrick is versatile and plays music appropriate for the occasion including jazz, blues, motown, 70s retro, disco and original music of his own. His recent invitation to play at the White House and appearances at major festivals around the U.S. have given his career momentum. His new release, *For the Love* CD, is commercially available, and recently made "Top 10 in the Northwest" for Northwest bands. Patrick has a funky, versatile group which can tune itself for the needs of almost *any occasion*. From the traditional, relaxed background jazz which is needed for a dinner party, to the 70s party down retro and motown, Patrick's band is a consistent crowd-pleaser. Please call for a promotional package, demo tape and/or more information.

Instrumentation and Personnel

High quality professional musicians including saxophone, vocals, bass, drums, guitar, percussion, piano/organ as appropriate for the size and intimacy of the occasion.

Experience

You might be familiar with Patrick's music from his many appearances which include: The Mount Hood Festival of Jazz, The Bite, The Newport Jazz Festival, Hillsboro Concert in the Park, Lake Oswego Concert Series, Nordstrom, or the private parties he has played including one for FOX 49. Or you might have heard his new "Top 10 in the Northwest" release on KKJZ and KINK. Patrick has also toured and recorded with recording artists Tom Grant and Grammy recipient Diane Schuur, opening at festivals for people like Kenny G., Wynton Marseilles, Branford Marseilles, B.B. King, and many others. Patrick has experience in all aspects of the music business form touring, recording, and playing for all kinds of different occasions.

Cost and Terms

Prices are competitive and computed on an individual basis depending on month, day, time, and length of engagement. Our PA and lighting systems are always available for your use. Call for quotations.

Testimonials

"It certainly is a treat to hear Patrick Lamb perform! He is hot and he's in increasing demand to perform at events, concerts and functions around town... he instantly draws a crowd where ever he goes..."

—Hal Murray, on-air personality, 106.7 KKJZ, Portland, OR

"I want to thank you for your beautiful holiday performance at the White House. Your appearance helped to make our 1996 Christmas holiday program truly memorable."

—Ann Stock, social secretary, White House, Washington, D.C.

STAGE III

Contact: Nancy Tice
Phone/Fax (503) 774-2511
E-mail: nwartmgt@teleport.com

Type of Music and Demo

Stage III is an incredibly versatile trio of experienced, talented musicians that play all styles of music from the marvelous Big Band Swing Era of the '40s and '50s, to the exciting contemporary hits of the '90s. This includes '50s and '60s nostalgia favorites, classic rock, country, Latin and jazz standards, rock 'n roll, blues, and plenty of romantic ballads, perfect for listening and dancing the night away. They provide rich vocal harmonies and a solid sense of fun sure to keep the dance floor full. STAGE III welcomes your requests. Call for a free promotional package, song list and demo tape.

Instruments

STAGE III is a trio of two men and a female who provide superb lead and harmony vocals, as well as playing live on stage, keyboards, soprano, alto and tenor saxophones, trumpet, flute, conga with full percussion accompaniment, lead and acoustic guitar, along with all digital sound and lighting. It is hard to believe that such a full and complete sound comes from only three musicians!

Experience

Band leader, Ron Barnes, has performed nationally and locally for over 20 years. From the Grand Ole Opry to Disneyland, Ron has worked with entertainers such as Three Dog Night, Hank Williams Jr., the Osmond Brothers, the Kingsmen (Louie Louie), and Del Shannon (Runaway). He has performed for countless fairs, festivals, weddings and special events. Mike Reif, guitarist, has also performed for over 20 years in casual, Big Band and blues bands, and Jann-Marie has toured and worked with the gospel rock group, New Life, as well as with casual bands specializing in Classic Rock and R&B styles. She has also appeared with national artists such as Pat Boone and Andrea Crouch. You can feel confident trusting the music on your special day to STAGE III. They will work closely with you to play the kind of music that will make your event truly unique, special, and memorable in every way. STAGE III knows how to "read the crowd" and adjust the tunes and volume to suit the needs of you and your guests.

Special Services

STAGE III will provide taped music for breaks and serve as Master of Ceremonies if you wish. You are welcome to use their microphones for toasts and announcements. Tuxedo or less formal attire as requested.

Costs, Terms and Setting Requirements

STAGE III provides a full band sound without the full band price. Price is highly competitive depending on date, time and location of the event. All terms specified in contract. Please call for quotation. STAGE III prefers to set up at least three hours before the event. Two 20 amp power outlets and a stage area of 20' x 10' preferred.

STAGE III provides the sizzle, energy, romance and
sophistication that assures your next special event will be a smashing success!

SWINGLINE CUBS

0755 S.W. Miles Street
Portland, Oregon 97219
Contact: Teddy Deane (503) 246-4739
E-mail: swingcub@teleport.com
http://www.teleport.com/~swingcub/

Types of Music

We play all types of swing (especially the new high-energy variety), '60s Motown, '70s hits, rhythm & blues, awesome renditions of standards and ballads, and all varieties of rock 'n' roll as well as contemporary pop and jazz. We also have CDs commercially available.

Instrumentation and Personnel

Exceptional lead female and male vocals with vocal backups accompanied by sax/clarinet/flute, piano/organ/synthesizer, guitar, bass, drums and percussion.

Experience

In the last 15 years, we have played for well over 1,000 events of all kinds. Our client list includes: Portland Trail Blazers, Peter Jacobsen Productions, Oregon Symphony, Hewlett Packard, NIKE, Intel, Jantzen, Boys and Girls Aid Society, American Cancer Society, Doernbecher Children's Hospital, Komen Foundation, University of Oregon, Oregon Health Sciences University, University of Portland, Mayor Vera Katz, Portland Oregon Visitors Association, Reed College, The Bite, Rose Festival, Fort Vancouver Fourth of July, USA network movie, "The Haunting of Sarah Hardy"... and hundreds more.

Musical Style and Audience Rapport

The primary goal of the Cubs is to make your reception or event as enjoyable and memorable as possible. We are especially responsive to volume considerations. We will provide you with soft music for conversation and enthusiastic, energetic music for dancing.

Special Services

Ethnic music and special requests are gladly accepted. We can MC any activity from bouquet toss to door prizes. Our PA and lighting systems are always available for your use.

Cost and Terms

Prices are competitive and computed on an individual basis depending on month, day, place, time, and length of engagement. Call for quotations.

LOVE OF FESTIVITY

The "Cubs" are composed of personnel with a flair for elegance and a love of spontaneity and festivity. We cherish playing standards from the heart, but we absolutely love playing music that gets people moving, dancing, and celebrating.

WE'RE REALLY SERIOUS ABOUT THIS
WHOLE BUSINESS OF HAVING A GOOD TIME!

Member of Gala Events Group, Inc.

TRUE FRIENDS, FEATURING MARILYN KELLER

Contact: Nancy Anne Tice
Phone/Fax (503) 774-2511
E-mail: nwartmtg@teleport.com

Types of Music and Demo

Vocalist, **Marilyn Keller** brings sparkle, grace, excitement, and a wealth of experience to the bandstand. Known for her "riveting stage presence, and killer renditions of gospel/blues," her repertoire also includes jazz, big band hits, rhythm and blues, Motown, rock 'n' roll, funk and contemporary pop favorites. Her ballads are haunting, soulful and tender, but she "gets down" with the best of them in all kinds of high energy tunes that are so much fun to dance to. Call for free promotional package, demo, song list and references.

Instruments

True Friends is a five-piece band consisting of keyboard/synthesizer, bass, drums, guitar and Marilyn on lead vocals. Band members add great harmonies. For smaller events, they can perform as a quartet, or add horns as the budget allows. Her exquisite vocals are frequently requested for wedding ceremonies.

Experience, Style and Audience Rapport

Marilyn Keller has performed for countless weddings, corporate parties, music festivals, at wineries and with many of Portland's finest musicians, including, Tall Jazz, Ron Steen, Tom Grant, The Swingline Cubs, Don Latarski, and Michael Allen Harrison. She and her band have played for a weekly jazz church service at Augustana Lutheran Church for six years. She has opened for the legendary Ray Charles, sung the National Anthem at a Portland Trail Blazer game, and has been guest soloist with the Eugene Symphony Orchestra. Her warm, confident and easy-going style enables her clients to relax and have a wonderful time whenever she and her band perform.

Special Services

Marilyn Keller welcomes your special requests, invites you to use the microphone for toasts and announcements, and is happy to serve as MC for all of the special wedding traditions, including first dance and bouquet toss.

Cost and Terms

Price is highly competitive, and based on date, time, location and length of engagement. All terms are outlined in contract. Tuxedo is standard attire for weddings, unless you specify otherwise. Call for quote.

ADD SOME MAGIC...

Marilyn Keller is at ease in any setting from intimate piano bar to large concert hall or festival stage. Let her add some magic to your next special event.

Notes

ANCIENT GREEK TRADITION

Instead of figuring their

ages from their birthdates,

ancient Greek women

determined their ages from

their dates of marriage.

HELPFUL HINTS

- **Deciding on a disc jockey:** Be sure to meet with disc jockeys in person. Make sure the person you meet is the one you are hiring for your event. Ask to see the equipment and portfolios or presentations of their shows so you know what to expect. If they do more than one show per day, check to make sure they have the appropriate equipment setups for two or more shows. The disc jockey should be able to provide you with a list of music available so that you can preselect favorites you would like played. Be sure there is a good mix of music so that people of all ages can enjoy and participate.

- **Written contract:** It is advisable to get a written contract stating exactly what you have agreed upon: date, number of hours, types of equipment, who will be doing the show, the total cost, what is included, and so on.

- **Master of ceremonies:** Be sure to ask whether your disc jockey can act as master of ceremonies at your reception. This will help the flow of events like cake cutting, throwing of the bouquet, garter toss, and announcing the first dance. One disc jockey recommends that the toast to the bride and groom should immediately be followed by the "first dance." This breaks the ice and gets the party going, especially when the rest of the wedding party is invited to the dance floor during or after the first dance.

- **Volume of music:** Discuss with your disc jockey the volume you wish and the selection of music. Keep the volume of music low for the first hour of your reception, allowing guests to mingle and ensuring that the level is comfortable for older guests. Then when the dancing begins, the volume can be raised.

- **Setup requirements:** Inquire about whether the site can accommodate dancing. Find out whether your disc jockey needs early access to the room and what the space and electrical requirements are. Make sure your facility contact knows about these needs and that they can be met.

- **Cut-off hours:** When you make all the final arrangements with your facility, be sure to ask if they have any specified time cut-offs for music. Some facilities require that music be stopped as early as 10pm for the comfort of neighboring homes, businesses, or other guests.

- **Special effects and requests:** Most disc jockeys are glad to play special songs if they are requested. Also inquire about any special effects they can supply, such as lighting, strobes, mirror balls, and fog.

For more assistance with staying organized during the wedding planning process, check out the Bravo! Wedding Organizer. Detailed question worksheets double as contracts. This step-by-step system will keep every detail of your wedding organized. To order, refer to the order form on page 23 in this Guide.

A.A. TWO'S COMPANY
DJ SERVICE

P.O. Box 68211 • Portland, Oregon 97268
Contact: Chris Tjaden
(503) 786-9090

Type of Music

We supply your event with a wide range of music. You may choose from the '50s, '60s, '70s and '80s. big band, ballroom, jazz, country and Top 40. Our collection contains over 15,000 title songs, all on compact discs. We play to you and your guests.

Demo and Equipment

Our equipment is state-of-the-art with a clean professional look. We will give you a full, high-quality sound at a level you want. Our computerized lighting adds a special effect to your event. Upon request, we will mail you a promotional package, including photo, that will answer all of your questions.

Experience and Attire

With over 20 years experience in the entertainment industry, A.A. Two's Company knows what it takes to make your event a success. We always dress in appropriate attire for your occasion.

Cost and Terms

We prefer to speak with each client and ask a few questions about their plans for the event. We then describe our service and quote a price. A deposit is required with the signing of the agreement. As always with any special event, it is best to book as early as possible.

Special Services

We help coordinate all the events during your wedding reception. We will make any special announcements during the event. Our cordless microphone is always available to you and your guests. Special requests are always welcome before and during the event. For the adventurous group, we are happy to get out on the dance floor and teach your guests the "Macarena", "Electric Slide" or even the "Octoberfest Chicken Dance."

QUALITY SERVICE IS OUR GOAL

A.A. Two's Company is a unique husband-and-wife team who pride themselves on providing quality service. We feel every event deserves our focused attention, so we only book one event per day. Our goal is to make your event a total musical success.

A DANCING PENGUIN MUSIC

LIVE MUSIC & DJ

(503) 282-3421

A Dancing Penguin Music owner, Kim Ralphs, is a professional pianist and DJ with over 15 years of experience entertaining Northwest audiences. His company is very well known and respected in Portland. This outstanding reputation was built with great customer service and attention to detail. He listens to you!

Playing the right song at the right time keeps the dance floor full and your guests happy. Top 40/dance club, rock, oldies, country, jazz…It's up to you!

You'll have total control of music style and volume.

You'll hear your favorites and special requests.

Master of ceremonies and help coordinating your event are included.

Black tuxedo is standard attire.

Live piano with a DJ will make your event special!

LISTEN TO WHAT THE PROFESSIONALS SAY:

"Kim plays here often, and always does a great job…highly recommended."
Susan O'Neil, **Waverley Country Club**

"Kim is a fine pianist…and I always enjoy seeing him here."
Dennis Yamnitsky, F&B Manager, **Oswego Lake Country Club**

"Whenever I need a DJ, A Dancing Penguin Music is the first company I call."
Nancy Tice, **Northwest Artist Management**

"I've recommended Dancing Penguin Music for years. Real professionals."
Diane Parke, event planner, **Occasions Etc. Inc.**

"Kim's piano and DJ combination really adds a touch of class to your event."
Charlotte Seybold, event planner, **Special Occasion Consulting**

A.D.S. PROFESSIONAL

15010 S.E. McLoughlin Boulevard
Milwaukie, Oregon 97267
Contact: David B. Patterson
(503) 659-7808

Type of Music

Our disc jockeys are specialists in music from light jazz, big band, '50s, '60s, '70s, '80s, country, and the latest current hits. Special arrangements can be made for a variety of different ethnic music. As our customer, you will have total control over the style of music and the volume at which it is played.

Demo and Equipment

A.D.S., Inc. uses only professional sound equipment to ensure reliability and the highest sound quality. Our systems are built into custom cabinets and can accommodate most situations indoor and outdoor. Our music sources include CDs, tapes, and records.

Experience

A.D.S., Inc. has been a full-time disc jockey service for over 20 years. We have been a member of the Disc Jockey Association of America and are currently instrumental in forming the Northwest Professional D.J. Association. We are dedicated to providing our customers with the most outstanding and professional service available. Each year we are honored with the privilege of supplying music for over 350 wedding receptions, company functions, and special occasions. Our clients include Red Lion Hotel, Multnomah Athletic Club, Nabisco, Intel, Nike, Yoshida Group, and Weiden and Kennedy Agency. A.D.S. has also been on the entertainment board of directors for the March of Dimes Walk-a-thon for 1990-1997.

Cost and Terms

Prices vary according to month, day, time, and location of your event. A deposit is required to hold date, with the balance due the day of your function.

Special Services

Our special service includes custom lighting packages, karaoke, and laser light shows. A.D.S. can arrange other forms of entertainment to enhance your function such as magicians, impersonators, comedians, and dance instructors. Please call to make an appointment for a free consultation to discuss our special services.

EXPERIENCE AND DEDICATION TO EXCELLENCE

Our goal is to make your event a total musical success. Our strategy is to be the navigator for your party, leading your guests through a smooth blend of music, lights, and communication of all the special events at your function.

P.O. Box 3282
Portland, Oregon 97208
Contact: Eric Wright
(503) 452-0040
Web site:
http://www.bravowedding.com/pdxallwrightmusic

All Wright Music!

We love music! AWM DJs mix music from every era—Big Band to '90s top dance hits. Our collection also includes ballroom, disco, club hits, Latin and Top 40. We send out a detailed questionnaire to find YOUR wants and needs because every reception is unique. We also encourage all guests to make requests.

Sound and Lighting

Our sound and lighting systems are custom-built in Portland. The systems are compact and detail-finished for professional appearance. Lighting systems are designed for each reception and are always included in the wedding package!

Experience

All Wright Music Disc Jockeys have performed at over 3,500 events. Weddings are our favorite because they are true celebrations! We have also performed at private celebrations for celebrities, including Kevin Costner and Sylvester Stallone. AWM has been flown all over the world to create magical, festive receptions. Our résumé speaks for itself!

Cost and Terms

We speak with each client to find out the specific wishes and needs for their event. Please call me for a free personal consultation—brochures and information will always be mailed upon request.

Our Guests Have Spoken

"It has been over two years, and people still remember our reception as the best they've ever attended!"
—Mrs. R. Roake

"For the fifth year, you've made our annual event a true success! You are our 'Mr. Music!'"
—Julie Papen/Special Events, NIKE

"Thanks for the GREAT job! My daughter's night was truly memorable. Best wishes for success!"
—Former Governor Neil Goldschmidt

"Thank you for a fabulous evening! Our night was pure magic! Your music was outstanding!"
—Audrey Stewart, *Bridal Magazine*

It is your day!
Let us help you turn your reception into
a party of elegance, excitement, and lots of fun!

AM Productions

Disk Jockey Service
Since 1988

Contact: *Leland Moyers*
Portland: *(503) 233-9077*

Type of Music

AM Productions will make available for you and your guests their exclusive *Song Title Catalog*. The catalog contains thousands of danceable requests from the roaring '40s to Top 40s, Country and Western to the Bunny Hop. We can also perform ceremonies and provide live musicians for your event.

Demo and Equipment

Our brochure will answer all your questions. We use only state-of-the-art rack-mounted components from the leaders in sound equipment: Sony, EV, Ross, Peavey, Crest, Gemini and QSC.

Experience

We love doing what we do! Whether the situation calls for informal attire, a tuxedo, or anything in between, we will be appropriate. The key to disc jockeying is the ability to respond to all age groups and to have the backup resources to do it well. We have this and more.

Cost and Terms

Disc jockey package prices begin at $295. A $100 deposit is required to hold your date. Our event schedule fills quickly, so please call as soon as you know your date.

Special Services

Our disc jockeys are happy to make any special announcements and encourage song requests from you and your guests. Karaoke and lighting also available.

Setting and Requirements

One 110-volt power outlet and 4'x6' of space are all we require.

CUSTOM-TAILORED MUSIC FOR EACH EVENT

AM Productions specializes in *"Custom tailoring music for each event."* We pride ourselves on playing the music that you request as well as having extensive use of compact discs. From the day you inquire to the day of your wedding, we will be available to help make your event as special and memorable as we possibly can. Call us today!

AM Productions is a participant of the Better Business Bureau Mediation/Arbitration Program and a member of the Northwest Professional DJ Association.

Visit our Web site:
www.ampcenter.com

Anthony Wedin Productions, Inc.

DJ Entertainment • Slide Show Presentations • Audio/Visual Support

15044 S.E. Greenview Avenue
Milwaukie, Oregon 97267
Contact: Anthony Wedin
(503) 557-8554
Visit our Web sites:
http://www.citysearch.com/pdx/awp
http://www.bravowedding.com/pdxanthonywedin

Member of the

WHY HIRE A DISC JOCKEY WHEN YOU CAN HIRE AN ENTERTAINER?

Type of Music

Anthony Wedin Productions provides a wide variety of music from the '40s to the '90s. All music is on compact disc or mini disc to provide clear quality sound with a quick request time for you and your guests. A song list is also provided so you can pick out your favorite dance music months before your wedding.

Demo and Equipment

Just as you have high standards for your wedding day, Anthony Wedin Productions has high standards for its sound equipment. Professional sound equipment is always used to ensure a day of stress-free fun and enjoyment. Each sound system comes with a wireless microphone and optional dance lighting at no charge.

Experience

Anthony Wedin and his staff are trained to be an interactive part of your special event. We have the music and the music knowledge to make your wedding day exciting and one to remember. We have been creating fun and successful receptions for brides and grooms since 1988. Dress is always tuxedo, unless you request casual attire. Anthony Wedin and his staff are also members of the Northwest Professional Disc Jockey Association, Gala Events Group, and the Association for Catering and Event Professionals.

Cost and Terms

Prices start at $300 and vary depending on date and time of the function. Disc jockey and slide show presentation packages also available.

Slide Show Presentations

Anthony Wedin Productions can also compose a slide show presentation for your reception that will be the envy of all and create a lasting and unforgettable memory. The presentation is shown live at your reception, and you are given a video to cherish through the years. Packages available. Call for details.

Setting and Requirements

Music for both the ceremony and reception can be provided either indoors or outdoors. All that is needed is a banquet table and a standard outlet.

WHY ANTHONY WEDIN PRODUCTIONS?

Anthony Wedin and his staff's professionalism and attention to detail will make your wedding day worry-free. Acting as master of ceremonies and coordination of the day's activities are all part of the services provided. The enthusiasm is contagious and your guests will remember your wonderful day as one of fun, laughter and lively entertainment.

Fantastic Weddings by
AUDIO EXPRESS
Professional Disc Jockeys
P.O. Box 33096
Portland, Oregon 97292
(503) 232-6979

For nearly nine years *Audio Express* has helped make parties fun and exciting for many people. Not only do we play great music, but we also get involved with the crowd to ensure your event is enjoyable for everyone.

Outstanding Music Variety

It is very important to us at *Audio Express* that everyone at your event has a good time. For that reason we carry a huge variety of music to every show. Our music library consists of *Big Band, hits from the '50s through the '90s, Rock 'n' Roll, Motown, Country and today's top hits*.

Experienced Professionals

All *Audio Express* disc jockeys are experienced and trained to our high standards to provide the best disc jockey entertainment for your party. Your *Audio Express* disc jockey can make announcements, take requests, do dedications and select music that will keep everyone dancing and having fun. Your *Audio Express* disc jockey will do everything in his or her power to ensure that everyone has a good time.

Superior Sound and Lighting

At *Audio Express* we use some of the finest commercial sound and lighting equipment available. We service our equipment before every show and keep it looking nice for everyone to enjoy. With our top-of-the-line commercial sound system and lighting equipment, a clear sounding, dependable performance is guaranteed.

When planning your wedding reception, remember *Audio Express*. The DJ Service that can provide the entertainment necessary to ensure the success of your event.

Cost and Terms

Prices start at $325 for three event hours. A $100 deposit is required to secure date. Prices can vary, so please call today for an official price quote.

Package includes

Experienced disc jockey, sound system, special effect lighting (*optional*), music list, wireless mic and a fantastic time! *Free consultation.*

Audio Express (503) 232-6979

Celebrate with... **Big Mo**™ Productions

Custom DJ Services

(503) 492-2851; (888) 449-5099 toll free
E-mail: DJExtra@aol.com
http://www.weloveweddings.com/bigmo

Type of Music

Vast collection of danceable romantic and fun music for all ages from the 20s to the 90s current hits. Your selected music styles, your chosen dedications and requests are brought to your reception. Our music library has over 18,000 titles. Music styles include, but are not limited to: Contemporary and Traditional Wedding Ceremony, Rock, Country, Cajun, Big Band/Swing, Ballroom, Reggae, 50-60s, 70s, 80s, 90s, Classical, Early Americana, House, Disco, R&B, Motown, New Age, Jazz, Top 40, Holiday, Cultural and Ethnic Specialties.

Equipment

Only state-of-the-art professional 3-way Concert Quality Speakers, Digital Compact Disc and Mini-Disc Technology ensuring CLEAR AND SUPERIOR music for any size hall or facility.

Experience and Attire

Tuxedo, Cut-Away Tuxedo, Western, Casual or Theme attire as you desire. Big Mo Productions is solely owned and operated by Mel "Big Mo" O'Brien. Allow Big Mo to send recent references to answer all your questions about experience, professionalism and meeting his client's and guests' needs and desires with elegance and panache.

Here is a sampling of what our clients have written recently about our services:
•"I can't thank you enough. Everything was PERFECT." • "You (Big Mo) fulfilled your contract above and beyond." • "Everyone had a GREAT time!" • "I am recommending Big Mo to family, friends and EVERYONE!" • "The evening was wonderful! Thank you Big Mo!" • "The most memorable parts of our reception occurred on the dance floor." • **Member of National Association of Mobile Entertainers and O.D.J.A.**

Cost and Terms

Very competitive rates. Only $75 books your date. Booking deposits are conditionally refundable. Special discounts for non-Saturday receptions. We do not charge a full hour rate for partial hours of service, we offer half-hour rates. No "hidden charges." No "up selling." No charge for travel, setup or breakdown time. CREDIT CARDS ACCEPTED.

Special Services

Big Mo Productions recognizes that YOU are "the STARS" of your reception, NOT the DJ. FREE personalized 9" x 11" framed Custom Labeled Golden Record on Velvet of your First Dance as husband and wife. FREE give-aways for "the little ones" at your reception. Four-plus hour receptions: FREE Effects Lighting for evening and indoor receptions. New high-tech "non-smoke"—no heat or odor—hazer/fogger available.

"Quality, Value, Service...and Fun"

The Cadillac Music Company

2660 S.E. Park Avenue
Portland, Oregon 97222
Contact: Roy Wilkerson
(503) 786-9493

Experience

The Cadillac Music Company has been in business since 1979, and perform at over 500 events annually. Our experience speaks for itself. We have experience in live music productions, and have supplied and operated equipment for The Tiger Woods Foundation (3,000 spectators), The LDS Dance Festival (17,000 spectators), and Oregon DECA (1,200 spectators). We have performed for over 12,000 weddings and 500 ceremonies. We are very reputable.

Music

Your DJ will meet with you prior to your event to go over the music and any special needs that you may have. You may look at the equipment we provide for your event. We have a music list you may pre-select your favorite songs from. We have a wide music selection from the '30s to the '90s covering all types of dance music.

The DJ

Our DJs are trained to be the master of ceremonies for receptions. The DJ can announce the cake cutting, the bouquet toss, garter toss, and the first dance to help the event run very smooth.

Your DJ will dress appropriately for your event.

The first hour while your guests are dining we keep the music soft. As the evening progresses we bring the volume to an appropriate level.

Cadillac Music requires an 8' banquet table and one AC socket to power the necessary equipment. We prefer to be at your event 1-1/2 hours prior to the guests arriving.

We want you to have a lot of fun when we perform at your event.

Additional Information for the Ceremony and Reception

We can supply you with special effect lighting to decorate the walls and ceiling with gobo patterns — flowers, hearts, stars, etc. We can provide additional sound systems for the ceremony; wireless microphones so the bride, groom and minister can be amplified to the audience. We can provide outside lighting and generators.

Criteria

A contract will be provided by The Cadillac Music Company for you to sign. It will contain information on the date, number of hours to be performed, type of music, equipment needed, the name of the DJ, and any special needs you may have for your event. We have a wedding flow chart form for you to fill out when you meet with the DJ.

Please call for your event price.

Call to reserve The Cadillac Music Company for your next event.

COMPLETE MUSIC®

DISC JOCKEY SERVICE

Need a Great DJ?®
Call the Professionals.
Contact: David Gard
Portland (503) 223-1736 • Salem (503) 378-7975
http://www.cmusic.com

Ceremonies ⊗ Receptions

Type of Music

Complete Music takes great pride in being the finest and largest entertainment service in the nation. We are here to please our customers so they can be certain that their event will be cherished by everyone who attends. We bring to every event selections of the most popular music from the Big Band Era through today's Top 40 hits. Every song listed in your music catalog will be brought to your event, including the most recent hits. Call for a FREE catalog and video showing all your entertainment options.

Equipment

Our service includes Complete Music's professional sound system, our entire music library, a wireless microphone and our computerized lighting effects. Your DJ will act as the Master of Ceremonies for all your important events and will perform many audience participation dances at your request.

Experience

Complete Music was established in 1973 and has become the nation's largest due to the personal care taken in tailoring each reception to each bride and groom's wishes. We customize our service to fit your expectations and guarantee the results to your satisfaction.

Cost and Terms

Complete Music's fees are based on a five-hour program, which includes dinner music, background music and dance music along with a FREE computerized light package, which add to the smooth flow of your reception. Complete Music can also provide the music and/or equipment for your ceremony. Call us for our cost and deposit requirements.

Setup

Your DJ will arrive at least one hour prior to your event for setup. This allows the DJ time to prepare for your special event. All that we require is a standard six-foot banquet table and one electrical outlet.

Complete Music's Goals

Our first goal is to ensure that everything runs smoothly and according to your plans. Our second goal is to make certain that all your guests have a good time. Call Complete Music and allow us to find out what your needs are, so that we can combine your ideas with our experience to provide you with a unique reception.

Decades Mobile Music

6312 N. Willamette Lane
Portland, Oregon 97203
Contact: Brian Darby or Loretta Korsun
(503) 283-4886; Fax (503) 283-4857

Type of Music

The act of celebration has been associated with dancing since the dawn of time. When you invite Decades Mobile Music to your event, you and your guests can relax and celebrate as we play favorites for everyone— from the youngsters to the young-at-heart! We stock popular dance music and Top 40 for every decade: from the '40s, '50s, '60s, '70s, '80s, and '90s.

We will also act as Master of Ceremonies, if you request, so that every part of your special event flows smoothly.

Song List and Equipment

We provide a song list to help you select your favorite music. Our equipment is the latest professional gear, and all recordings are on compact disk. This assures the clarity that makes music enjoyable at any volume level you and your guests prefer.

Experience and Attire

Others talk… WE LISTEN! We tailor our services to meet your specific needs; your agenda is ours! Our skilled people and people skills make the difference! In addition to drawing on a great depth of knowledge for appropriate music selections, our DJs will play requests (can't remember the name?… hum a few bars!) and dedications, make announcements and keep the celebration going! Attire is normally a jacket and tie. We are happy to wear whatever is appropriate for your event.

Cost and Terms

A three-hour show starts at $350. A $100 deposit is required. Additional hours are $75. Lighting and props can be added to make your event more memorable. Special music requests, made in advance, are always free. You are given a written agreement to assure our services will match your expectations.

Setting and Requirements

We arrive at least an hour before the show to setup and test. This allows us ample time to adjust for local conditions. We require two standard 120v outlets, more if lighting is used. A space of 10' x 8' is necessary, indoors or out.

A Party in Every Package

OK

DeeJay Entertainment

Specializing in Weddings

503/460-2828 ▪ Toll Free 1-800/963-6968

Visit our Website:
www.deejayentertainment.com

Featuring Portland Radio DJs:

**RICH ELLIS ▪ CHRIS TAYLOR ▪ SCOTT LANDER
ROD KRAUSE ▪ DAN DUBAY**

Type of Music
DeeJay Entertainment can play a variety of hit music at your wedding reception, including top 40, country, 70s/80s retro, classic rock and oldies. Every crowd is different and DeeJay Entertainment reacts with the appropriate selections.

Experience
Featuring Portland Radio DJs, DeeJay Entertainment is fortunate to represent some of the most experienced and professional disc jockeys available in the Portland-metro area.

Demo
Call today and we will mail or fax you a brochure that includes references and a sample song list. Prior to scheduling your event with DeeJay Entertainment, we will discuss the range of music you like, and the presentation style. This will help us create the mood you desire for your reception. We set up our own state-of-the-art sound equipment and make announcements to keep your guests informed. We eliminate all hassles so you can focus on your special day! DeeJay Entertainment can also provide music at your wedding ceremony.

Costs and Terms
Saturday events scheduled between May 1–September 30, and December 1–31 are $400 (4 hours or less). All other dates are $350 (4 hours or less). Each additional hour is $50.

Thirty percent deposit is required to hold your date with the balance due prior to the start of the reception. VISA, MasterCard, and American Express gladly accepted.

PROFESSIONAL...

EXPERIENCED...

RECOMMENDED...

Eighty percent of the events scheduled with DeeJay Entertainment are referrals, so we encourage you to check on availability as soon as you have set a date. We hope to have the opportunity to serve you and invite you to call anytime with questions or to schedule an appointment with one of our representatives.

**Find out why so many of our past clients
refer other people to DeeJay Entertainment!**

Portland, Oregon
(503) 255-8047
E-mail: Encore@ethergate.com
Web site: http://www.bravowedding.com/pdxencore-dj

◆ Photography ◆ Videography ◆ Music

Music sets the mood for any occasion and is particularly important during your ceremony or wedding reception. Whether you need disc jockeys or musicians, let us assist you in providing the music you want for your wedding ceremony and/or reception.

Type of Music

For your listening pleasure and convenience, we provide music of all styles and have a huge library of music from the 20s to the 90s in all eras: Top 40, Country/Western, Jazz, Classical, Rock 'n' Roll, Motown, Rhythm & Blues, Swing, Ballroom, Big Band, Rap, Reggae, Disco and Ethnic. Your favorites are always welcome!

Equipment and Demo

We have state-of-the-art mobile equipment which sets up quickly in a 6' x 6' area with a standard 110-volt outlet. You are welcome to a private or live viewing.

Experience and Attire

With over 20 years of experience, you are assured of knowledgeable service with our professional and fun disc jockeys. We are not only disc jockeys but masters of ceremony as well, ensuring your wedding runs smoothly and successfully. We play the music you want to hear, and our packages are designed for every budget and musical preference. Casual or theme attire, tuxedos or suits and ties are available.

Cost and Terms

Wedding packages are $395, with no hidden or extra costs. Ceremony music only is $100. Corporate and private functions are customized to needs as well as budget. Packages include consultation, four hours of professional disc jockey time (additional beyond package at $25 per hour), and travel. Travel time nominal outside Portland/Metro and Vancouver areas.

Special Services

Special lighting, strobes, spots, mirror balls, ropes, and fog available for special effects.

Should you prefer live music for your entertainment needs, please ask one of our consultants for assistance.

Among our professional services we offer photography and videography services as well. Call Encore Studios today for more information and assistance. Consultants are available any time by appointment.

See page 490 under Photographers.
See page 541 under Videographers.

4949 S.W. Macadam Avenue
Portland, OR 97201
(503) 295-2212

Type of Music
Instant Parties is about energy and music. Our music library is one of the most extensive in the Northwest, ranging from today's hits, retro, classic rock, modern alternative, hip-hop, techno and even oldies. Instant Parties has it all for your celebration!

Equipment
Instant Parties features High Command Digital Sound Systems emancipating state-of-the-art sound with maximum clarity. We have an incredible mix of robotics, laser and strobe effects, all to inspire the appropriate mood. Instant Parties can even supply the mirror ball, fog machine and any other special effect desired to enhance your party or reception.

Experience
Instant Parties is supported by Z100 radio, Portland's hottest music station, winning numerous awards including Gavin's program director, music director and station of the year. Instant Parties represent positive high energy appropriate for all settings.

Cost and Terms
Our base price is $495 for a full show with lights, mirror ball and customized music. Rates can vary depending on date and time of event. There also is an additional investment for celebrity appearances. Instant Parties requires a 40% deposit to hold-the-date and balance is due prior to set-up on the day of the event.

Special Services
An Instant Parties disc jockey will be your emcee for the event, assisting with the traditions of weddings such as the bride and groom's first dance, cutting of the bridal cake and the tossing of the bride's bouquet and garter. A written event planner is provided compliments of Instant Parties to ensure your wishes are met prior to the event of your lifetime.

Setting and Requirements
Instant Parties arrives about one-hour before your event and can set-up easily in most locations, indoors or outdoors.

For the best music, energy and professionalism—
call Instant Parties today!

CorEvents

Experts in events marketing, comprehensive planning,
production and corporate sponsorship sales.

PORTLAND RADIO PERSONALITY
KEN O'BRIEN

KEN O'BRIEN PRODUCTIONS

P.O. Box 69541
Portland, Oregon 97201
(503) 648-3836

As a radio personality for years I've worked with and entertained thousands of people. Anyone can play a CD player and pretend to be a DJ. **Ken O'Brien Productions** has earned the respect and admiration of hundreds of brides, grooms and their families for years. If you take a highly experienced radio personality, nightclub DJ, a master of ceremonies, and mix in a lot of personality and energy, you get an **Entertainer**.

We will coordinate and choreograph your wedding ceremony (no matter what your religion). We personalize this special moment to fit your family. Your reception is meant to be the party of the year. **Ken O'Brien Productions** will make it just that.

Ken O'Brien Productions is very well known for their hands on, get involved personalities. But remember, you are the show and everyone will know it.

Type of Music
Ken O'Brien Productions provides music from the hit parade era of the '40s, to the sock-hop-doo-wop jitterbuggin' of the '50s, to the Motown and British invasion of the '60s, to the classic rock-disco and funk era of the '70s, and up through the '80s rock and top 40 and country hits of the '90s.

Experience
Ken O'Brien Productions has 16 years of master of ceremony and DJ experience. His DJs and MCs are the most energetic, mature **Entertainers** in the business.

Special Care
Ken O'Brien Productions takes all the stress and confusion away from you and your family on this special day as your master of ceremony and DJ with attention to detail.

Appointments
Ken O'Brien always meets with clients at their place of choice. It is important to get to know your DJ/MC before booking your date. Call to setup your appointment with **Ken O'Brien Productions**.

MOBILE MUSIC ENTERTAINMENT SERVICES

Since 1978

Professional DJ Services...

Contact: David Efaw
(503) 692-4498; Fax (503) 612-9433

Type of Music

Mobile Music has over 300 hours of music we bring to each event. Music selection ranges from big band, '50s, '60s, '70s, '80s, country, Top 40, rock, and jazz. We always play the music you want, and of course we play requests.

Equipment

The sound systems Mobile Music uses are custom built for mobile use. You won't find any home gear in our systems. The systems are compact and can be set up in 10 minutes. We do have larger setups for functions up to 5,000 people.

Experience

Mobile Music has been in business since 1978. We provide music and entertainment at over 1,000 events each year. We base our business on providing friendly, professional service to our clients. What you want comes first with us.

Cost and Terms

The basic package starts at $325 for three hours and $50 for each additional hour. Mobile Music also has light shows and other special effects available for rent. A 20% deposit and a signed contract hold your date for you.

Corporate Events

For corporate events, Mobile Music has a wide variety of activities, including **karaoke, contests and games**—all hosted by a professional master of ceremonies. Please call for more information and rates on packages.

Special Services

Mobile Music uses only professional mobile disc jockeys and club DJs from around the Portland area. Whether you want a life-of-the-party DJ or just music, we have the disc jockey for your event. Band packages also available.

Setting and Requirements

The standard setup requires a 10' x 4' space. Larger systems and lights require additional space. A 110-volt AC outlet is needed for power.

MUSIC THE WAY YOU WANT IT

We at Mobile Music pride ourselves on providing quality music the way you want it played. We use only professional disc jockeys with experience, who will help make your event everything you want it to be. If you have any questions or special requirements, feel free to call.

David Efaw

FOR THE PARTY YOU WISH WOULD NEVER END!

Music Express

Music Express

Mobile Disc Jockey Service

PORTLAND • SALEM • EUGENE

P.O. Box 4240
Salem Oregon 97302
Contact: Eric or Sheila Mousel
(503) 362-7216, (800) 222-7216
Web site: http://www.musicexpressdjs.com
E-mail: Fun@musicexpressdjs.com

As the Willamette Valley's premiere mobile disc jockey service, Music Express is dedicated to making your wedding reception the one that everyone wishes would never end! Your DJ plays an important role in setting the mood for your reception. Whether you are looking for something light and classy or you want a party that everyone will remember, Music Express has what you're looking for.

Experience and Attire

Music Express DJs are trained wedding specialists who are familiar with all types of music and are fully capable of acting as your Master of Ceremonies. Music Express will provide you with two of the best disc jockeys in the area. Having two experienced professionals at your reception allows a much smoother event and offers a greater level of guest interaction. The attire will be formal unless otherwise requested.

Types of Music

We have the music to satisfy almost any request. However, the music played at your reception will be customized for your tastes and desires. We like to get to know you a little bit and will determine our playlist based on your requests. You set the mood.

Equipment

We use only professional mobile DJ equipment that looks and sounds great! The equipment is customized to fit the needs of the event and is presented tastefully. Minimum setup requires one 6' or 8' banquet table and a standard 110-volt outlet.

Cost and Terms

Our prices are competitive. Prices start at $300 for a three-hour package and are based on your needs. A $100 retainer is required with signing of the reservation agreement. Credit cards are accepted.

Call Music Express for
the party you wish would never end!

NOTE WORTHY MUSIC

2233 N.E. Mason
Portland, Oregon 97211
Contact: John Mears (503) 284-3961

Types of Music

At Note Worthy Music we offer the music you want—and at a price that is affordable. We draw from any era of music that you desire! Whether you want Big Band, jazz, country, classic rock or Top 40, we will meet your needs. Because this is your event we will do everything to make it special. Our disc jockeys will meet with you to discuss any special needs.

Equipment

Note Worthy Music uses top of the line equipment to provide you with crystal clear music from our vast CD collection. Music volume is constantly monitored for your listening pleasure.

Services

Our disc jockeys will serve as your master of ceremonies if you desire and will dress according to your theme. With 15 years in the music industry, we will help make your special day a truly wonderful experience.

To enhance your special day we usually have soft background music provided as your guests enter your reception. As the party progresses we will announce special moments such as cutting of the cake, throwing of the bridal bouquet, shooting of the garter and the couple's first dance. As the reception continues the music is constantly monitored for both volume and style that you desire. From soft jazz to rock 'n' roll, it's all for you!

Our disc jockey services are provided for either indoors or outdoors. All that is needed is a standard wall plug and one banquet table.

Satisfied Customers are Saying

"Thank you for making our 50th wedding anniversary party such a wonderful occasion. Everyone enjoyed your musical selections which made for great dancing as well."
~Jo and Slats Austin, Forestry Center

"Thank you for the great music at Bob's birthday, and for the music you have provided for our Optimist dances. Everyone always enjoys your wide selection of music."
~Adele Hemstreet, President, The Optimist Club of Lloyd Center

"Our wedding would not have been the same without your services—Thanks again!"
~Robert Heinrich

"John, not only were you easy to work with but very accommodating to all our special needs for our wedding reception."
~Shelly Vanness

BRAVO! SPECIAL **$75 off**

Three hours for $275
$30 each additional hour

Mobile Disc Jockey Services
1332 S.E. Carlton
Portland, Oregon 97202
Contact: Earl Forster, Owner
(503) 235-2743
E-mail: OmegaAudio@aol.com

"We needed more than just music for our ceremony and reception, we wanted a party to remember. We got that—thanks to Omega Audio." —Steve & Rene Anderson

Experience

Omega Audio has been providing reasonably priced, top quality mobile music and lighting services for over 18 years. Our disc jockeys are professional in both attitude and appearance. We are ready to work with you to ensure that your event is everything you want it to be.

Type of Music

Omega Audio brings a tremendous selection of the most loved songs in America to your event. From hits of the '20s right up to today's chart-busters, we play the music you want to hear. Requests from your guests are always welcome, and our disc jockeys are happy to act as master of ceremonies.

Equipment

Our disc jockeys use systems with professional grade equipment to provide a state-of-the-art experience. We have sound systems to suit whatever size room your event requires. Thinking about an outdoor event? Omega Audio can accommodate!

Special Services

We can bring any room to life with lighting and special effects such as intelligent lighting, mirror balls, strobes, fog and much more. For added excitement, we have **Karaoke, Dance Lessons, and Casino Gaming,** as well as outdoor inflatable games for kids.

Cost and Terms

Packages start at $395 for four hours of uninterrupted music; no charge for set-up time. The rate for each additional hour is $50. A minimum deposit of $75 is required upon signing the contract. Be sure to reserve your date as far in advance as possible—it's never too soon to hire the best.

MAKE YOUR DREAMS COME TRUE

Everything you choose for your wedding day is a reflection of your dreams. We at Omega Audio would like to make those dreams come true!

On The Go!
Productions

6611 N.E. Wygant Street
Portland, Oregon 97218
Contact: Rudie Kerchal
(503) 358-6611
Web site: www.triax.com/onthego

Type of Music

On The Go! Productions' library covers music from the '40s Big Band era to the '50s, '60s, '70s, and '80s dance music, and the best country and current top 40 hits.

Equipment

We use commercial veritable pitch CD players, live music mixing consoles, Technique's turntables, Pro Audio speakers and amplifiers, full service lighting, and dance floors.

Experience

On The Go! Productions was established in 1976. We have performed at over 5,000 receptions and corporate events in the last 23 years. References and personal DJ information is available.

Cost and Terms

Our standard package starts at $275 for three hours of continuous music and lighting. Additional hours are $50. You may add karaoke to any package for an additional $100. A variety of packages are available—please call for additional information and a free brochure.

Special Services

Our disc jockeys are employees of On The Go! Productions. They are trained to be high-energy master of ceremonies. We meet every bride and groom in order to tailor our services to their personal requirements.

We furnish everything needed to perform for your event. All tables are draped and skirted to give a classy appearance at your event.

WHEN IT SOUNDS AND LOOKS THE BEST...
IT'S *ON THE GO!*

On The Go! Productions is a high quality professional disc jockey service, which will stop at nothing to provide you with the show of your lifetime. We take pride in what we do and that is reflected in how we dress, our equipment, and our attitudes.

Professional Design Entertainment

P.O. Box 1246
Gresham, Oregon 97030-0261
Contact: Jayson Yates
Office (503) 674-5890; Mobile (503) 380-6319
E-mail: JYates5539@aol.com

"WE DESIGN CUSTOMIZED MUSIC PACKAGES THAT PROVIDE YOU WITH CONFIDENT, WORRY-FREE SERVICES WHICH ALLOWS YOU THE FREEDOM TO FULLY ENJOY YOUR SPECIAL EVENT OF A LIFETIME."

Providing Specialty Services

Professional Design Entertainment specializes in weddings and receptions, company events, school functions, holiday parties, parties and karaoke.

Types of Music

We feature music from the '50s–'80s, top 40, country, jazz, big band and classical. Custom music ordering is also available.

Formal Attire

Tuxedos/suits worn at all events unless otherwise requested by the customer.

Equipment

Professional Design Entertainment operates with current state-of-the-art equipment.

Cost and Terms

Basic music packages start as low as $100 per hour up to four hours. Light packages, games and prizes also available!

Professional, Courteous DJs

Our DJs are experienced in providing music and MC services for a variety of occasions. Professional Design Entertainment is a member of the American DJ Association.

Please call about our free DJ wedding package.

"Let us design the music memories are made of."

"The Wedding Reception Specialists"

(One block west of I-5)
601 Main Street, Suite 210 • P.O. Box 65616
Vancouver, Washington 98665
(800) 903-3830; Fax (800) 328-3930
E-mail: info@ssdj.com
Check out our Web site at: www.ssdj.com

Type of Music

Our high-quality digital music library contains a huge selection of music, enjoyable to all ages. Special requests are always welcome. This will ensure that you and your guests have a fantastic wedding-day experience.

Demo and Equipment

We invite you to call our office for a complimentary consultation. At this time, you can meet your prospective disc jockey, go over our extensive music lists, and arrange any extra details for your special day. You can rest assured that our sound and lighting systems use only the finest professional gear. And our setup appears tasteful, without unsightly cords everywhere.

Experience

Signature Sound disc jockeys have performed from coast to coast, and have an extensive background entertaining all types of people. Our references include the Portland Trail Blazers, Intel and more. From traditional to modern, extravagant to simple, we can make your wedding reception uniquely yours.

Cost and Terms

Our wedding packages range in price from $299 to $999. We offer many options, including exciting lighting packages, bubble machines, extra hours of dance music, and ceremony music and sound systems. A 10% deposit and a signed contract are the only requirements to reserve your date.

Setting and Requirements

We can perform at any location, anytime. From the Benson Hotel to your backyard, we've "been there…done that." A typical wedding reception requires a normal 110-volt outlet, and a table at least six feet in length, with tablecloth and skirting to match the other tables. If we need to provide our own table, just let us know!

Why Choose Signature Sound?

It's your wedding day, and you're the center of attention, not us! All DJ advertisements may look alike, but all DJs don't necessarily perform the same. Our full-time office staff, experienced and talented disc jockeys, large music library, and premier sound and lighting equipment make the difference between an extraordinary day and "just another wedding."

"SoundChoice" Mobile Music

Kimberly Fogg
Professional DJ/MC, Line Dance Instructor, Vocalist
Office (503) 408-5728; Cell phone (503) 449-4362
E-mail: scmmkf@aol.com

"SoundChoice" offers the ultimate in a DJ service. I include many extras to make your event a big hit and stress-free! With over 15 years experience as a performer, I am very able to MC the activities so *all you have to do is enjoy yourself!* You can count on me to be *professional, interactive, reliable and fun.* Please call for a list of current references. I am proud to be able to offer so much to my clients at such a reasonable price!

♪ **900+ CD Albums** ranging from the roaring '50s & '60s, to swing, today's chart toppers of country, rock 'n' roll, dance, alternative, blues, R&B and **wedding ceremony music.** A **current song list** is available to your party for requests. This is your event—I play it any way you like!

♪ SoundChoice uses **only professional rack-mounted equipment** in a slick stand-alone unit. To ensure a quality sound, the heart of my system is a 550 watt Crest amp and a large Eminence speaker system. Only a standard outlet and a 4' x 6' area is needed.

♪ *Special Options:* **Demo tape of wedding songs, lighting, a fog machine,** and a **quality cordless mic** is offered at *no extra cost to you!* **Karaoke services** available for a *small* additional fee.

♪ **Six years of experience giving line dance lessons**, and I can teach any "two left feet" anything from the Boot Scootin' Boogie to the Macarena.

♪ SoundChoice would be happy to **meet with you for a free, no obligation consultation**. I feel it is important to *meet any DJ before you book a date*. To ensure that you receive top-notch quality, all meetings and performances are done by myself and I only book one event a day.

♪ Packages begin at **$380 for four hours, and $30 each additional hour**. It is straightforward, and there are no hidden costs. All booked dates are contracted. (Setup and tear down are not part of the four hours.)

References Speak for Themselves

"Kim DJ'd my daughter's graduation party with over one hundred graduating seniors in attendance. She handled the requests with compassionate efficiency. She partied with the guests and made them feel a part of the event. Many of them stopped at the end of the night to comment just how at home Kim made them feel. It is my most heartfelt feeling that Kim made the party into a lifetime memory."

—Dr. Michael Booth, DVM

"Kim is our house DJ/Promotional Manager and is a multi-talented entertainer...A genuine asset to our business."

—Jim O'Hollaren/Owner, The Candy Store

ULTIMATE ENTERTAINMENT
Portland's Premier
Full Service DJ Company
916 S.E. 29th Avenue
Portland, Oregon 97214
(503) 234-3055, (888) 332-6246
E-mail: Claraswe@Sprynet.com

Clara's Wedding Establishment's Own:

Type of Music

We feel strongly about giving you the right music. Songs that are proven to get your guests up and dancing. That's why we provide you with a catalog of the biggest party songs of all time. Choose from any era...Big Band, Country, 50s & 60s, 70s & 80s, R&B, Top 40, Classic Rock and more! All music is on compact disc to provide clear digital sound. Special requests are always welcome.

Equipment

What's great music without great sound? At Ultimate Entertainment, we use sound systems that contain the finest audio components available. Sound checks are made before guests arrive to ensure excellent sound at every location, both indoors and out. We have a wireless microphone at every event for your convenience. For nighttime functions, a dazzling array of lighting is an option you may choose to enhance your celebration. From the smallest backyard to the largest banquet hall, Ultimate Entertainment has the equipment to handle any situation effectively and efficiently.

Experience

Music and entertainment is the most important factor to the success of any event. When you choose Ultimate Entertainment, you get more than a DJ, you get our experience, quality, and professionalism. We are actively involved before, during, and after your event. This is why we stand by our reputation as "Portland's Premier Full Service DJ Company."

Cost and Terms

Ultimate Entertainment offers two different packages to choose from:
- **Package A includes**: four hours of entertainment, Disc Jockey in formal attire, all of your announcements, and a bubble machine. Our price to you… $350.
- **Package B includes:** All of the above, plus a dazzling light show, and a FREE hour of limousine service compliments of Clara's Limousine Service. Our price to you… $450.

Only a $50 deposit holds your date. Additional entertainment hours are available for only $50 per hour. We also provide music for ceremonies starting at $100. Please call for your free hour consultation with video presentation.

Special Services

Our disc jockeys are trained event coordinators and will handle your special activities during your reception. Whether you are looking for an "interactive DJ" or a "low key DJ," our DJs can help you with your event. Ultimate Entertainment also has: karaoke, special effect lighting, fog machines, snow machines, and party kits (novelty items...leis, sunglasses, inflatable guitars, saxophones, and beach balls).

OUR CUSTOMERS SAY IT BEST

"Thank you Ultimate Entertainment for making our wedding day such a success! We could not have asked for a more perfect selection of music. Everything was truly superb!"
~ Mary and John Caruthers

"Our DJ was extremely professional and was enjoyed by all. Your company knows how to throw a party!"
~ Angela and Steve Barnette

SWEET DREAMS

*Legend has it that
unmarried guests who sleep
with a piece of the grooms
cake under their pillows
will dream of their future
spouses.*

HELPFUL HINTS

- **Live music sets the stage:** Live music adds to the ceremony and can be as soft or dramatic as you choose. There are a variety of musicians to select from: individual pianists, harpists, trumpeters, mandolin trios, string quartets, and brass quartets—just about any combination you would like. Most musicians are very affordable and will accommodate your requests.

- **Be creative with your selection of musicians and songs:** You'll enjoy selecting music with special meaning for you and your groom. If you can't decide, talk with some of the musicians, listen to their demo tapes, and view their song lists. Musicians are usually very helpful and will gladly offer ideas and suggestions to make your wedding special and meaningful.

- **Approve your music selections with clergy:** Make sure your clergyman is aware of your music selections. Ask whether there are any restrictions on music. Some ministers insist on approving all the music prior to the ceremony. Your favorite love song may seem offensive to the clergyman; neither you nor your musicians will enjoy any last-minute confrontations.

- **Be sure to find out about the musicians' requirements:** They may need to set up and warm up before the event begins. Make sure the ceremony or event site is open at least one to two hours earlier. A music rehearsal may conflict with your photographs, but the solution is to plan ahead and inform the musicians and the photographer of each other's needs.

- **Amplification equipment:** Help the musicians coordinate any necessary amplification equipment. Find out ahead of time if the church or hall has a PA system. If so, ask whether the church will permit you to use the system for your wedding. Find out whether it is compatible with the musicians' equipment (many churches have older systems with incompatible microphones).

- **Plan how to start the music:** Prelude music is a nice touch as the guests are being escorted into the church. To start the processional music, have someone signal the musicians at the appropriate time. Setting a specific time doesn't always work because guests are still coming in, or delays get in the way of starting the ceremony on time. One way to handle this is to have your clergyman signal the musicians to start the processional music after a nod from the father of the bride. Also provide your priest, judge, or pastor and the musicians with a cue sheet. The person officiating can unknowingly cut your well-planned music.

- **Saving on music:** The best way to cut music costs is to have your wedding in off-season: January through March, Sundays, early in the day. Musicians will be more willing to negotiate prices if it doesn't conflict with another high paying booking.

- **Hire for both ceremony and reception:** Most musicians can perform both at the ceremony and reception. For instance a string quartet can be hired for the one-hour ceremony for $325 and then each additional hour at the reception would be $75 per hour. This would be nice for greeting guests, mingling and dinner music. Ask your musician if he can do both; some individual musicians have pieces that they can add on to make a trio.

For more assistance with staying organized during the wedding planning process, check out the Bravo! Wedding Organizer. Detailed question worksheets double as contracts. This step-by-step system will keep every detail of your wedding organized. To order, refer to the order form on page 23 in this Guide.

Michael Allen Harrison

P.O. Box 30448
Portland, Oregon 97294
(503) 255-0747

Types of Music

Composer/pianist Michael Allen Harrison is an international recording artist who resides in his hometown of Portland, Oregon. Over the last 15 years Michael has released 20 albums of his signature adult contemporary style of new age, classical, pop and jazz, four Christmas albums and an album dedicated to Gershwin and other artists of that era. His music is heard around the world and locally on KINK FM 102, KKJZ, KMHD, K103, and regularly as the leader of the Good Day Oregon Band on KPTV Channel 12 Good Day Oregon Show. Michael has written and performed his music with orchestras, ballet companies, motion pictures, short films, commercials, and is the featured guest artist for the Celebrity Forum lecture series where he has opened for Walter Cronkite, Jerry Lewis, Collin Powell, Margaret Thatcher, Jerry Spence, Cokie Roberts and James Whitmore.

Experience and Demo

Michael has been performing professionally for 15 years. One of the Northwest's favorite pianists, he regularly plays weddings and many other kinds of special events. Fees vary depending on whether he plays piano solo or is joined by part or all of his band. Michael loves to play his original music as well as the favorites and wishes of many clients. He also loves to sing and write new original music for the bride and groom and asks the couple to each write a letter or poem on how they feel about their beloved. Michael then puts the words together into one song and performs it at the wedding ceremony or reception where the couple hears their song for the first time. Photos, demos, and promo material are available upon request.

© Adams & Faith Photography

Harpist
Ellen Lindquist

(503) 626-4277
Web site:
http://www.bravoevent.com/pdx/ellenlindquist

DISCOVER THE AMBIANCE AND ELEGANCE OF HARP MUSIC AT YOUR WEDDING AND RECEPTION

Types of Music

Harp music adds elegance and magic to any wedding and reception. Ellen's repertoire spans many decades to include Classical, Love Songs, Movie Themes, Show Tunes, Oldies and New Age. Her repertoire ensures each wedding and reception is personal and unique.

Harp Music is Perfect for

- Ceremonies
  - Receptions
    - Rehearsal Dinners
- Engagement Parties
  - Bridal Showers
    - Bridal Luncheons

Experience

With over 18 years of professional experience, Ellen knows what her clients want and expect. She has played at hundreds of weddings and receptions. She has played at most of the bridal sites in Portland/Vancouver and can make suggestions to the bride/groom to enhance their wedding day. She has played with the Columbia Symphony, Portland Chamber Orchestra, Eugene Symphony, Oregon Festival of American Music, Ernest Bloch Music Fest and Peter Britt. Her experience includes working on cruise ships, hotels in Japan and she has played with celebrities from Kenny Rogers to the Moody Blues. She was trained at the Music Academy of the West, Julliard School of Music in New York and California State University Northridge.

LET HARP MUSIC CREATE
THAT EVERLASTING MEMORY

Call for a free brochure, references and prices. Harp/flute also available.

Musical Elegance
Elaine Seeley
·HARPIST·

(503) 636-0349

Types of Music
No musical instrument compares to the harp when it comes to bringing style and beauty to complement your special occasion. Elaine Seeley has played for many types of events and locations including:

- Weddings and Receptions
- Open Houses
- Corporate Events
- Restaurants and Hotels
- Banquets
- Private Parties

Ms. Seeley's varied and extensive solo repertoire includes classical music, rhythmical arrangements, and popular show tunes. Also available are duo combinations—harp and flute, harp and violin, and harp and voice.

Experience
Ms. Seeley is a harp instructor at Lewis & Clark College and former music specialist at Oregon Episcopal School. Her professional background is impressive. Her affiliations include the following orchestras:

- Portland Opera
- Oregon Symphony
- Vancouver Symphony
- The Musical Theater Company
- Ballet West
- Chamber Music Northwest
- Sunriver Music Festival

Education
Ms. Seeley acquired her B.A. degree in music education at the University of Southern California. She has an M.F.A. in harp performance from California Institute of the Arts.

Cost
For a personal quotation and consultation regarding music for your event, please call Elaine Seeley at (503) 636-0349.

AN ELEGANT ACCOMPANIMENT
TO YOUR EVENT

STRING QUARTET

For that perfect wedding...

The Stradivari String Quartet

Winchester Enterprises
(503) 232-3684
Fax (503) 236-2920
Hugh Ewart, Concertmaster
Oregon Symphony Pops

Types of Music

For that perfect wedding or event...perfect music by The Stradivari String Quartet for ceremonies and receptions in your church, synagogue, private club, residence, or garden. The style is elegant, distinctive, and affordable. Information packet including music list available upon request.

Experience

Distinguished wedding music since 1961. Our clientele has included prominent Northwest social and business leaders. In 1980 Stradivari String Quartet appeared in the Paramount motion picture "First Love" filmed on location in Portland.

Cost

Call for current prices and availability.

CHARMING AMBIANCE

"The Stradivari String Quartet added a charming ambiance to the event."
Barbara Jordan
The Oregonian

Call for your FREE demo cassette.

QUARTET • TRIO • DUO

Alderwood Strings

1830 N.E. 13th Avenue
Portland, Oregon 97212
Contact: Dieter Ratzlaf
(503) 288-6577

Types of Music

Let the Alderwood String Ensemble add elegance and sophistication to your event. We offer exquisite performances of the classics as well as charming melodies from contemporary literature. We cater to your requests.

Experience

The ensemble coordinator has won numerous musical awards and has performed extensively as soloist, recitalist and chamber musician. Alderwood musicians hold musical degrees from prestigious institutions including the San Francisco Conservatory of Music and Indiana University–Bloomington. The ensemble has enhanced dozens of weddings, banquets and special events all along the West Coast.

Cost

The Alderwood Strings are committed to affordable excellence. Cost depends on time and place of the event. Demo tape available upon request.

AMERICAN FEDERATION OF MUSICIANS

Local 99

325 N.E. 20th Avenue
Portland, Oregon 97232
(503) 235-8791

Experience

Founded in 1899, the A.F. of M. Local 99 is a nonprofit organization established by professional musicians <u>for</u> musicians. We represent the finest musicians from Portland to Central Oregon, the Coast and up through Southern Washington. With a membership of over 700, we can offer a wide variety of musical styles:

- Chamber groups of all sizes and styles, from a strolling violinist to a string quartet or symphony orchestra!
- Pianists, organists, harpsichordists, classical guitar, flute, harp;
- Jazz ensembles to big band, bagpipes to dulcimer;
- New Age, fusion, Latin salsa, light rock, blues, country and Top 40!

No Agency Fees…Free Referral Service

Many of our artists have tapes, song lists, and photos to make it easier for you to decide exactly what music you want and how you would like it to be presented. We will gladly put you in touch with the musicians of your choice. Local 99 charges you nothing…this is a free referral service! **Call for a free video showcasing the variety of musicians we represent.**

Please let these businesses know that you heard about them from the Bravo! Bridal Resource Guide. **459**

STRING QUARTET
BRIDGEPORT STRING QUARTET

Karen Hilley (503) 230-7116
Kim Lorati (503) 244-5208

Types of Music

Bridgeport String Quartet provides the finest quality classical and popular music for wedding ceremonies, receptions, or special events. A demo tape is available.

Experience

Members of the Bridgeport Quartet are experienced, professional musicians who have provided music for weddings, receptions, and other special events for many years. Dress is formal or semiformal. References available upon request.

Cost

Fees are determined by the duration and location of the event. A contract is provided that explains our services and requirements.

A MEMORABLE OCCASION

A representative from the quartet can help you plan special music to make your event a memorable occasion.

PIANIST AND VOCALIST
JO ANNA BURNS-MILLER

P.O. Box 20594 • Portland, Oregon 97294
(503) 254-5776, (800) 893-5776
E-mail: lilpond@internetcds.com

Types of Music

Uplifting, versatile, and professional are just a few words to describe Jo Anna Burns-Miller's music for weddings and receptions. Accomplished on vocals and piano, she will give you an occasion to remember with a variety of stylings and repertoire. Demo tape and music list available on request.

Experience and Cost

With over 25 years of experience in the music business, Jo Anna's performances include nightclubs, resorts, churches, concerts, corporate and private functions, with over 500 weddings and receptions to her credit. Dress is color-coordinated to your colors. Her fee for most weddings is $175, and for most receptions, $250 for the first two hours (prices are negotiable for corporate and private events). She provides a sound system when necessary, and an electric piano for a cartage fee of $50, if none is available. A consultation in her home to discuss music for your event is included.

MUSIC FROM MANY ERAS

Vocals and piano include soft pop, soft jazz, new age, semiclassical, old standards, and some originals. She can also provide your prelude and postlude music, as well as the processional and recessional music.

TRADITIONAL IRISH MUSIC

CELTIC WEDDING MUSIC
by INNISFREE

Contact: Brenda or Jim (503) 282-3265

Types of Music

We specialize in heartfelt Irish/folk instrumentals and songs for wedding ceremonies, receptions and other joyful events. Our strength lies in adapting this gorgeous music to each unique ceremony, calling on our long wedding experience and drawing from the rich storehouse of airs, songs, jigs and reels in the tradition. At receptions we play sweet waltzes and great dances to encourage brides, grooms and loving fathers to step out in dances you'll always remember! Multi-instrumentalists, we perform on whistle, guitar, Irish drum, button accordion and mandolin. We can perform non-Irish standards and are happy to learn requests (songs and instrumentals) as well. And, of course, our top-quality sound system is yours to use. Please call for a demo!

UNFORGETTABLE MUSIC

We've found that couples are thrilled to use the Irish music they love, tailored to fit their own wedding. A husband-and-wife duo ourselves, we will bring all the warmth we can to your special day.

TRADITIONAL IRISH MUSIC

THE CLINTON STREET CEILI BAND

Contact: Mr. Jan DeWeese (503) 236-6752

Although the Gaelic word "ceili" now refers to any social gathering with music and dance, in the old days ceili bands played mainly for wedding parties. In addition to our quartet's extensive experience at such spirited occasions, we've been to numerous festivals, colleges and pubs—its founding members formed the first house band for Kells Irish Pub in downtown Portland—as well as to Ireland for traditional dance studies. Our instruments include fiddle, wooden flute, mandolin, cittern, guitar and bodhran (Irish drum). For the wedding service, we have a repertoire of settings from the Irish Baroque and for the reception, a wealthy reserve of traditional tunes to which the party guests can be taught dance steps. A singer of traditional and contemporary Celtic songs (including any special ones you wish to hear) is also available upon request. Please call for demo and price quote.

RENEW THE OLD WAYS

Treat your guests to a timeless form of expression that lifts the feet and moves the heart with simple means, well crafted and finely seasoned! The Irish in all of us awaits.

SOLO TRUMPET/BRASS ENSEMBLE

CRAIG GIBSON, TRUMPET
COLUMBIA BRASS, BRASS ENSEMBLE

4107 S.E. Knapp • Portland, Oregon 97202
Contact: Craig Gibson (503) 775-1126
E-mail: CGibsonTpt@aol.com

Music for Your Ceremony

Your wedding music is an important part of your special day! The majestic sound of brass offers an unequaled touch of class for your ceremony. Whether it is a Solo Trumpeter playing with your Organist or String Quartet, or a Brass Ensemble providing a rich, full sound, you and your guests will be certain to enjoy that "something special" which brass music provides.

Experience and Other Important Details

Over 17 years of wedding experience throughout the Northwest. References provided on request. A demo tape and play list are available. Attire can be either Coat and Tie or Tuxedo.

Cost

Cost is primarily based on the number of musicians—please call for more details. A contract is always used.

Reception music

In addition to your ceremony, the Columbia Brass can provide reception music from a variety of styles. Please call for a free consultation.

"FOR A TOUCH OF CLASS, THINK COLUMBIA BRASS"

For all your music needs!
(503) 533-5382 or (503) 682-2851

• Soloists • Duets • String Quartets • Bands • DJ Service

The Musicians

DyAnne—She makes every song her own and presents it with grace and energy. From love songs and ballads to modern rock, you're sure to be pleased with the perfect blend of energy and gentleness.

Don—Often working with DyAnne, Don Wood provides accompaniment and harmonies. Also a writer, Don has many spiritual and love ballads—he can even write a song just for your special occasion!

Sarah—A professional vocalist for many years, her charismatic personality and energy are expressed through a wide variety of vocal styles. Her repertoire includes classical, soft pop, contemporary, country and the ever popular, modern rock.

Full Service

Having been in the music business for some time now, we also have String Quartets, Rock 'n' Roll bands and DJs, completing the package for any special occasion which you have planned.

Personalized Wedding Packages Starting at $125

VIOLIN & CELLO/STRING QUARTET

Duo con Brio

10900 S.W. 76th Place, Suite 55
Tigard, Oregon 97223
Corey Averill (503) 297-6695

Types of Music
Duo con Brio is a professional ensemble consisting of cellist Corey Averill and violinist George Shiolas. The duo may be augmented to a string trio or quartet. We have a large repertoire, from Baroque through Contemporary, as well as seasonal music.

Experience and Cost
Formed in 1989, the duo's members have performed with the Portland Opera, Oregon Ballet, and appeared as soloist with the Oregon Symphony and other orchestras in North America. We have also performed extensively in Europe and the Orient. Duo con Brio supplies a wide range of services, including free consultations and a demo cassette. We look forward to assisting you with your wedding, reception or other special event.
- **Duo** $225 first hour ($100 each additional hour)
- **Trio** $325 first hour ($100 each additional hour)
- **Quartet** $395 first hour ($125 each additional hour)
- **DAT Digital Recording** $65
- **Amplification** $50

Todd Gang

Singer, Guitarist, Songwriter, Recording Artist
(503) 579-3901

Todd Gang

Type of Music
Todd Gang is one of Portland's most versatile vocalists and musicians. His talents range from straightforward jazz, to pop, soft rock, blues and Latin. Photos, demos, and promotional material are available upon request.

Experience
Todd Gang has been singing and performing professionally since he was 16. He is suited for anything from a casual party to the most formal wedding reception. Todd has appeared internationally, and on television and radio in the United States, Mexico, and the Caribbean.

Cost and Terms
Cost varies according to the number of musicians required, hours and distance traveled. He specializes in romantic love songs, and has a large repertory—he is able to mold the music to the specific desires of couples on their wedding day.

Services
Todd Gang is a singer, songwriter, guitarist and recording artist. He is available for weddings or private parties, from a solo act (guitar only), to a jazz duo, trio, quartet, or even a 12-piece Latin band. Todd writes equally well in Spanish and English. Whatever your wedding or party musical needs, Todd Gang's smooth voice and classy delivery will be the perfect complement to your special occasion.

P.O. Box 25711 • Portland, Oregon 97225
(503) 297-6304

Types of Music

Tom Grant is an international recording artist who resides in his native Oregon. He has 15 albums to his credit and has toured the world playing his own special blend of pop and jazz. His records have regularly topped the charts in *Billboard* and the other major music industry publications. He recently appeared on the Jay Leno show and his music can be heard on the syndicated "Fishing the West" show as well as on many daytime soaps, Olympic games and other sports telecasts. In Portland, his music is a staple of KKJZ and KMHD radio and he has his own show on KKJZ.

Experience and Demo

Tom has over 20 years experience as a performing musician. He is a pianist, singer, and songwriter. He regularly plays weddings and other types of private events. The cost is variable depending on whether Tom plays solo piano or provides a band. He often provides a high quality grand piano and a sound system as part of the package and his repertoire usually includes his own music as well as other favorites as per the wishes of his client. Photos, demos, and promo material are available upon request.

PIANO
DARLENE HARKINS
(503) 357-9037

Types of Music

Darlene has an easy-listening style enjoyed by all ages. She performs your requests for music from all eras, including contemporary love songs, country, sacred and light classics, Broadway show tunes, New Age, and current favorites.

Experience

Darlene has studied piano from age five. She received a music scholarship to and graduated from Pacific University. An accomplished pianist, she can hear a tune and adapt it to the piano to fulfill special requests. Her personality is reflected in the warmth and charm of her playing, setting whatever mood you desire for your event.

Free consultation and Planning

Call Darlene to play for you over the phone–"a neat idea and real time saver," say many brides and grooms. She will play your choices and, if you wish, offer suggestions based on her extensive experience.

For your ceremony, she carefully correlates music to the proceedings, timing your selections to the entrances of parents, candlelighters, and the wedding party.

For your reception, her ability to play requests from your guests can contribute greatly to creating the happy, upbeat atmosphere for a festive celebration.

FLUTE/SAX AND GUITAR DUO

GARY HARRIS AND MATT SCHIFF

Contact: Nancy Anne Tice, Phone/Fax (503) 774-2511
E-mail: nwartmgt@teleport.com

Types of Music

Gary Harris and Matt Schiff blend a vast knowledge of musical styles ranging from classical to jazz and the popular music of the 20th century into a polished, versatile ensemble perfect for weddings, receptions and elegant celebrations of all kinds. For weddings they play all the most beloved and requested traditional pieces. For receptions, they offer lighter, more upbeat jazz and contemporary favorites played on flute as well as tenor and soprano saxophone with guitar. Call for free promotional packages, demo tape, play list, references and price quote.

Experience

Their many years of national and international touring and performing experiences enable them to create a perfect mood and sparkling atmosphere for your next special occasion. Either as a duo or with added rhythm selection, their music is appropriate for listening and dancing. They are always happy to play your requests.

Cost

Highly cost-effective, professional ensemble. All details in contract. Tuxedo, semi-formal or casual attire.

PIANO

DAVE LEE

(503) 648-1796

Your Wedding Is Special

Your wedding should be unique and special. Dave Lee can help you make it that way. Hear Dave at Nordstrom Washington Square, at the Airport Shilo, on Dave's recordings *After the Storm* and *When Your Eyes Met Mine* or on the Internet at http://www.biojazz.com/~dleegp/.

Experience

Dave Lee has played keyboards for 33 years—23 in a professional capacity. Fees depend on your event's requirements. A **free** consultation is offered to plan your musical needs. Attire is coordinated to your event.

Recordings

Dave Lee's first recording *After the Storm* (December 1995) and *When Your Eyes Met Mine* (June 1997) have been heard on the radio from San Francisco to Anchorage to Portland's KINK, KKJZ and KMHD. Dave's third project *Jukebox* was released Fall 1998.

Media Reaction

The Oregonian A&E states, "Lee is a fine pianist whose musicianship elevates the CD over many run-of-the-mill jazz artists." KKJZ says, "Your album has the melodies and hooks we look for in any release—local or national."

More Than Piano

Dave's work on piano is supplemented with electronic keyboards. The **Dave Lee Band** is available as well in various configurations.

MANDOLIN, GUITAR AND MANDOBASS

MANDOPHONIC TRIO

Ken Culver (503) 232-0976

Types of Music and Demo

This three-member band plays mandolin, guitar and mandobass. Piano and accordion can be added upon request. The unique style is Mediterranean, European and classical music with a Spanish flavor. Valentine's week or your special holiday, send the Mandophonic Trio to your sweetheart for a 15- to 20-minute Valentine at work, home or your favorite rendezvous.

Experience and Cost

Since 1975, Mandophonic Trio has played concerts, weddings, receptions, conventions and many other events, including Portland's first Festa Italia, Street of Dreams and Art Quake. Please call for current rates.

Setup and Requirements

The Mandophonic Trio can play indoors or out with small space requirements.

SPARKLING AND FESTIVE MUSIC

The strolling Mandophonic Trio brings sparkling and festive music to your special day. This delightful music is pleasing to all ages and will bring a smile to everyone's face. Our trio is perfect for any occasion and will add to the ambiance and celebration of the day.

VIOLINIST

AARON MEYER

(503) 221-4266

Type of Music

Aaron Meyer's music ranges from traditional, classical music and jazz standards, to his own unique blend of original, pop, and world music. He can perform solo or with accomplished singers and guitarists Tim Ellis and Jeroan Van Aichen in a band format. Percussion and bass can easily be added to complete the band.

Experience

As a previous soloist with the Philadelphia Orchestra, former member of the band Pink Martini, guest artist on Cunard Cruise Line, and current member of the Michael Allen Harrison band, Aaron has gained the experience to entertain at wedding ceremonies, wedding receptions, corporate functions, and other events. Photos, demos, and references are available upon requests.

Cost

The cost is variable upon Aaron playing solo, in a duo with guitar, or with his complete band. Please call for more details.

Mezzanotte Strings

Quartets, Trios, Duos and Soloists
Contact: (503) 788-7709
Northwest Artist Management (503) 774-2511

Type of Music

Portland's premiere wedding quartet, The Mezzanotte Strings, combines musical excellence and personalized attention to create an enchanting atmosphere for your ceremony and reception.

While the group specializes in classical music, our extensive repertoire also includes romantic favorites, jazz standards, swing, ragtime, pop songs, waltzes, and Broadway hits. From Bach to The Beatles, we continuously update our repertoire in order to bring you the finest music possible.

Experience and Cost

The Mezzanotte Strings are gifted, experienced professional musicians who perform with many of Portland's finest orchestras. We have played for countless weddings, receptions, and special events in the area's most prestigious locales, and we combine our wealth of experience with a commitment to personalized service. We will be responsive to your suggestions, sensitive to your needs, and provide consultations at no extra fee.

Quotes given include musicians in formal attire, music for your entire event, and travel allowance if applicable. Call for a free demo tape, promotional package and repertoire list.

JOHN O'BRIEN

guitarist

Contact: Nancy Anne Tice
Phone/Fax (503) 774-2511; E-mail: nwartmtg@teleport.com

Types of Music

John O'Brien is a guitarist in the Romantic tradition of Andres Segovia. He is known for his unique arrangements of Irish harp music from the Baroque period, as well as many of the virtuoso works of J.S. Bach, Sor, and F. Tarrega, and works for Renaissance lute. Mr. O'Brien is equally at home with light jazz and bossa nova. His music lends itself beautifully to the wedding ceremony, where he is pleased to design the music program to accommodate your requests, whether you want traditional pieces or something truly out-of-the-ordinary.

Experience and Cost

John O'Brien is a 20-year veteran of the musical stage. He has played solo concerts, private parties, weddings, fund-raisers, open houses, club dates, and has toured internationally. Selected corporate clients include Timberline Lodge, Atwater's, The Heathman Hotel (where he plays for High Tea during the holidays), AT&T, Pioneer Place, and OMSI. Call for free promotional package, demo, references, and price quote. Tuxedo, coat and tie, or casual attire available. All details outlined in contract.

CRITICAL ACCLAIM

"O'Brien captures the true spirit of chamber music" ~The Oregonian

PROFESSIONAL MUSICIANS AGENCY

325 N.E. 20th
Portland, Oregon 97232
Contact: Calvin J. Walker
(503) 235-8379
Fax (503) 235-2488
E-mail: cwalker.afm99@juno.com

The Perfect Event

When you're planning the perfect event you'll need the perfect music and that's just what you'll get when you use the Professional Musician's Agency. We specialize in making sure everyone has a great time.

Events and Occasions

Weddings, Birthdays, Bar/Bat Mitzvahs, Grand Opening Presentations, Fund Raisers, Conventions, Corporate Parties, Company Picnics, Anniversaries.

No Hidden Costs

The right music for the right occasion that's exactly what you'll get with the Professional Musicians Agency and no hidden costs!!! Call today for your free consultation and be on your way to a great event.

SAXOPHONE QUARTET

QUARTETTE BARBETTE
Four Well-tuned Saxophones

317 N.E. 27th Avenue
Portland, Oregon 97232-3142
Contact: Barbette Falk (503) 232-8862

Types of Music

Our extensive repertoire contains many varieties of music ranging from classical favorites to elegant jazz. The beautiful blending of soprano, alto, tenor and baritone saxophones played together create a unique expression of sound that can be tailored to fit your wedding ceremony and/or reception.

Experience

Quartette Barbette personnel have over 20 years of performing experience, appearing in concert and on local television. We have performed many well-known classical pieces as well as swinging jazz and ragtime for weddings and receptions. Outdoor concerts have included the urban settings of Artquake and the Hawthorne Street Fair, to the lush tranquillity of Tryon Creek State Park.

Cost

Fees are on an hourly basis or per service. In addition to a demo, we can provide you with a free consultation detailing a set list custom-designed to suit your event.

RUSLAN STRING QUARTET

Kirsten Hisatomi, violin • Neil Hollister, violin • Shauna Keyes, viola • James Smith, cello
Contact: Lisa Comer, Manager (503) 233-3992

Types of Music

Performing for weddings, receptions, dinner parties, and corporate events, the Ruslan String Quartet has provided friendly, professional service since 1991. As experienced artists, the members of Ruslan are happy to work with you to find music that will enhance your wedding. Besides an extensive knowledge of the standard Classical and Romantic faire, Ruslan's repertoire also includes Irish melodies and music from the Renaissance. Jim Smith, Ruslan's cellist and a published transcriber, can also provide arrangements of special requests. Ruslan can also provide accompaniment for vocalists or other instrumentalists.

Experience

The members of Ruslan have performed with the Oregon Symphony, Eugene Symphony, Vancouver Symphony, Oregon Ballet Orchestra, and Portland Opera Orchestra. They have also performed at many chamber music festivals throughout the United States and Europe including Curse International de Musica Estiu and the Tanglewood Music Festival. As a group, Ruslan has played for numerous weddings, corporate parties, and special events. They have performed many recitals at the University of Portland, Multnomah Athletic Club, and Collins Gallery in the Portland Central Library.

Contracting Information

Please call for a demo tape, a guide to selecting ceremony music, Ruslan's brochure and rates.

SERENDIPITY MUSIC

Ceremony & Reception/Party Specialists
Contact: Patty Vinikow (503) 646-5086

The Combination of Instruments Just Right for Your Event
• Solo • Duo • Trio
Quartet or Dance Band

Exclusively weddings, ceremonies and receptions, parties, anniversaries, bar mitzvahs, dancing or background music for any occasion—over 15 years experience!

I meet with you and customize your special day. Traditional, jazz, swing, classical, ethnic or non-traditional—I'll help you plan your musical needs suited to the occasion and budget.

" Patty worked with us all the way—the music was perfect and our guests still comment about it!"
~ Jeff and Sandra Walker

Vice President, American Federation of Musicians, Local #99

Brochure, CD, References Available.

Please let these businesses know that you heard about them from the Bravo! Bridal Resource Guide. **469**

PIANO & ORGAN

THEO

Steven Theodore Burke
2014 S.E. 12th, Suite 102 • Portland, Oregon 97214
(503) 284-1960

Types of Music and Demo

Theo offers a *wide* authentic range of styles, due to his experience with classical, jazz, pop, rock, blues, and gospel. His lively style of playing is unobtrusive, yet spirited and perfect for your wedding. Hear him live at his studio, over the phone, or on his demo tape.

Services and Cost

"My clients quickly see the benefit of my enthusiasm, and my offer to do 'any song in the world.' If I don't already know your favorites, I quickly learn them from tape, CD, or sheet music. I've performed everything from Pachabel's Canon to Tesla, at weddings!"

"My enthusiasm rubs off. Clients often come unsure of their music plans, but leave with lots of ideas! I offer all ceremony music, plus any new songs requested, plus consultation time for $175. And I will play as long as you need me."

When a piano is not available, Theo can bring his very realistic ivory digital piano for only $40. He rehearses additional singers or musicians for a $45 fee.

Experience

"After 60 weddings, I'm knowledgeable and still excited. I majored in composition/jazz at Arizona State School of Music. My style evolves from 18 years experience in weddings, receptions, gospel choirs, rock bands, and night clubs (www.audiophile.com/noir)."

VOCALIST

TERRIE SERVICE

(503) 784-9179
E-mail: tservice@pacifier.com

Vocalist

Terrie Service's repertoire focuses on Jazz Standards, singing sometimes romantic, sometimes sassy tunes in a lovely mezzo tone. A versatile vocalist, she can move easily into pop or R&B tunes and throw in a country classic as well.

She performs with top well-known Northwest jazz musicians accompanying her on piano/keyboard, bass, drums as a duo, trio or quartet.

Weddings • Receptions • Private Parties
Banquets • Conferences • Resorts • Festivals • Fund-raisers
Holiday Events • Corporate Events & Parties • Concerts • Nightclubs

Terrie provides a high quality sound system and state-of-the-art portable equipment. Demo cassette, promotional material and fees upon request.

THE WEDDING MUSICIANS
LOIS BACHHUBER
(503) 246-4464

Organ (strings)
String Duo/Trio
Violin – Viola – Cello
Piano (strings)

Quality custom tailored music for your
wedding ceremony and reception

PIANO • KEYBOARDS • VOCALS
SUSY WOLFSON
(503) 244-9607

Solo Background
Susy Wolfson is a musician of uncommon versatility. She is equally
comfortable as a solo pianist or accompanying her own vocals, moving
smoothly from contemporary styles, jazz standards, rock 'n' roll or
rhythm & blues to classical music. Her background includes a magna
cum laude performance degree from the prestigious Indiana University School of Music and
performances at numerous festivals and engagements including the Spoleto Festival in Italy as
well as many years as a freelance musician.

Trio/Quartet/Quintet
Using the classic format of the piano trio plus guitar (with vocals or instrumental only), these
musicians are in constant demand for receptions, corporate events, country clubs and winery
festivals. From black tie and smooth jazz one night to a kick-off-your shoes rock 'n' roll
dance the next, this group will keep 'em dancing! Their song list ranges from Duke Ellington
to Sheryl Crow to Stevie Ray Vaughn… and all points in between!

Performance Combinations
- **Solo Piano or Keyboard**
- **Trio/Quartet/Quintet** (vocals, keyboard,
  guitar, bass, drums—optional saxophone or flute)
- **Vocals and Piano/Keyboard**
- **Flute and Piano Duo** (vocals optional)

Demos, song lists and references for all musical combinations are available upon request.

Please let these businesses know that you heard about them from the Bravo! Bridal Resource Guide. **471**

Notes

TRADITIONS

Gifts to the bride's parents:
The groom would indicate
how much he thought the
bride was worth by giving
farm animals, weapons or
crops to the bride's family.
The more gifts, the more
valuable the bride.

HELPFUL HINTS

- **Why are photographs important?** After the cake's been eaten, the tuxes returned, the flowers wilted, and you've shaken the last grains of sand off from the honeymoon, what's left of the wedding? Those treasured glimpses captured in photographs can in a moment rekindle the joy for both of you, bring back the friends, and show the love within families.

- **Selecting a photographer:** Find a photographer whose style you feel comfortable with. Look closely at his or her sample albums, and don't be afraid to ask for references. A contract is important to reserve the date and should confirm that the estimate given will be the total cost excluding extra prints or specialty photographs ordered. Within this section you will find pages of photographers; compare the information listed and make sure they meet your needs. The prices vary from one photographer to another; make sure you understand what the "package price" is and what the extras are.

- **Consulting with your photographer:** When you finally select your photographer, sit down together so you can communicate what you imagine your pictures to be. Get specific about formal and candid photographs. Be sure you let the photographer know what you are expecting. Some provide a checklist for you to fill out.

- **Assigning a photographer's helper:** You should submit a list of photographic requests to both the photographer and helper so that your helper can guide the photographer to the right people.

- **Have formal portraits taken before the ceremony:** More brides and grooms are deciding to have formal portraits taken before the ceremony to maximize time with their guests. If you do choose to have formals done before the ceremony, make sure everyone is dressed and ready for pictures at the time designated.

- **Black and white photos:** The traditional formal wedding photos are taking on some new and exciting looks, such as the photojournalist style, which is a more candid documentation of the day. Black and whites are timeless and classic, and handpainting will make the photos an original piece of artwork.

- **View your wedding photos on computer:** This relatively new technology allows you to see your photos very quickly after the wedding. You can see photos in different sizes and shapes, and lay out your entire wedding album before making those expensive decisions on which photos to choose. Some photographers will set it up so your entire family and friends can attend the viewing and order photos.

- **Store your wedding photos on CD:** Ask your photographer if he or she can help you store your photos on CD for safe-keeping.

- **Storing your photos:** Store your wedding photos in a safe place; it is recommended to keep them in the box provided with the wedding album. If you just ordered the photos and no album, make sure to put them in an album soon after receiving them. Keep them out of a damp area.

- **Engagement photo guest book:** A fun idea is to use your engagement photo with a large matte area around it for your guest book. This way family and friends can sign around your photo with well wishes. This is a wonderful keepsake to frame and display on your wall. Rarely do you pull out your guest book and think about all who were there to celebrate your wedding day with you.

A Special Day Photography
(503) 639-6666

Your wedding day can be perfect! The splendor of your dress, the fragrance of your flowers, walking down the aisle to the man of your dreams, the joy of sharing your happiness with your friends and family at the reception…can all be captured in the timeless beauty of your photographs. **A SPECIAL DAY PHOTOGRAPHY** will be there to capture your unforgettable day in priceless photographs that you can return to again and again.

- **Two photographers at every wedding.** The husband and wife team of Daniel Bernath and Martha Wong photographs every wedding. Dan has been a TV/radio newscaster and a lawyer, *"but most of all, I like capturing special moments for a memory book that I know the bride will love forever."* Dan creates in the classical style. *"I love the pictures of Ross and myself, the misty and romantic look. It's light, romantic, warm, fuzzy…gives you a good feeling when you look at it."* **Verna S.**

  Martha is an architect and believes, *"nothing is more enjoyable than capturing the joys and emotions of people in love on their wedding day."* Martha's style is photojournalistic.

- **We bring an entire photo studio to your wedding** to create studio-quality portraits of all your family members, you and your new husband and special friends. *"When I look at my pictures I get the same feelings of the closeness of my husband and I. My mother showed my pictures and everybody came to tears because they really brought out the feelings of us and the day."* **Lisa G.** *"You definitely captured the 'romance of the day.' You made us feel comfortable enough that we both looked natural. The pictures captured our enjoyment of the day and our feelings for each other."* **Lisa M.**

- **Exclusive Panorama Montage Album.** You can put large photographs up to two feet by two feet of your wedding ceremony into the same album with tons of candid photographs. *"Looking at my panorama album, I get the same feelings I got on my wedding day, over and over again. Martha captured little moments all day long."* **Laura B.**

- **Reflections of Love Video.** We start by combining pictures of you growing up and dating your fiance. Then we capture new romance pictures of the two of you. We blend your voices as you talk about your lives before your biggest romance, how you met, how you fell in love and how he proposed! It's all set to music and played for your family and friends at the reception. *"It was definitely one of the highlights of our reception—it was a lot of fun!"* **Adrienne C.** *"Everybody loved it. It made me feel good."* **Verna S.**

- **Don't hire a photographer!** Instead, invite two artists, Dan and Martha, to capture your wedding memories. *"It's not just a job or income to you. I do believe you really want to give your customers those memories for a lifetime…"* **Samantha B.**

  A craftsman creates with his eyes and hand. An artist with his heart. **A SPECIAL DAY** has the uncommon gift of capturing your wedding day by hand, eyes and heart.

Adams & Faith Photography

800 N.W. 6th Avenue, Suite 211
Portland Oregon 97209
Contact: Tony or Lori
(503) 227-7850;
Fax (503) 227-1863

Adams & Faith Photography is undoubtedly the Northwest's premier photography studio...

Located in the glorious (and convenient) Union Station in downtown Portland since 1976, they have made style and creativity coupled with superb professional service their hallmark.

As Tony and his wife, Lori, owners of the prestigious Adams & Faith, along with their staff go about their daily business of managing the studio, they are humbled again and again as their work gains an ever-expanding audience...a photo in *Bride's Magazine*, an image in Beverly Clark's book, "Weddings: A Celebration," one prize-winning photograph after another.

Just recently, Tony received one of the highest honors possible for a photographer. Kodak chose him for their elite International Pro Team and included his story in their book, Promise of Excellence Pro Team.

The recognition of their work has brought national attention, accolades from a state senator and acknowledgment from business leaders throughout the community, but none of that compares to the pride Tony, Lori and their photographers take in capturing wedding images for brides and grooms.

Adams & Faith offers a service that is practically unheard of in the photography business... To determine which photographer best suits their own style, brides and grooms look through the outstanding display of wedding albums and the unique photographs that surround the consultation room at Adams & Faith. There they are met by Tony, Lori or one or their knowledgeable staff who introduce them to the philosophy of Adams & Faith and the creative styles of their extraordinary photographers.

Once the bride and groom make their selection, they meet with their chosen photographer before the wedding for a "details meeting." This enables everyone to familiarize themselves with each other and go over all the necessary details, eliminating any last-minute questions and ensuring that every aspect of the day shall be captured... from the superb images that add extra meaning to your special day, to the formals, and party candids.

After the wedding, Adams & Faith puts your story together with photographs of your choosing in an exquisite album featuring the highest quality professional prints that are backed by Kodak's lifetime warranty.

Because Adams & Faith focuses on you and your story, your photographs will be simply spectacular... a tender moment, a gentle nudge, the essence of true love will be forever captured and then turned into your own Adams & Faith trademark image.

Visit Adams & Faith... they'll capture your memories in style!

Keith Aden

P H O T O G R A P H Y & V I D E O P R O D U C T I O N S

1613 SE 7th Avenue • Portland, Oregon 97214

503 230-0325

Web Addresses:
www.bravowedding.com/pdxkeithadenphoto
www.bravowedding.com/pdxkeithadenvideo
www.bravoevent.com/pdxkeithaden

Wedding Packages

Packages are designed to suit weddings of all sizes and start at $450. Wedding coverages from one hour to unlimited time, as needed. Brochures listing services and prices can be sent to you upon request. Call for an appointment at the studio to see samples of photography and video.

Services and Equipment

Only the finest camera equipment is used, Hasselblad *medium-format* cameras with backup Hasselblads, not 35mm cameras.

* We can shoot in available light or will provide light as needed
* Formals may be done either before or after the ceremony; it's your choice
* Photo requests gladly accepted—after all, it's your wedding
* Video Coverage (3-Chip S-VHS Cameras and a state of the art Digital Editing Suite)
* Wedding Invitations, Photo Christmas/Thank-You Cards, Gift Albums
* Wedding announcement photographs for the newspaper are $15 each.

Original Prints and Reprints

Original prints are available in approximately three to four weeks after the wedding. Reprint sizes are 5x5 to 40x60, and start at $10. Original photographs are included in the package price. Art Leather albums are included in all plans. No minimum order required.

Terms and Payment

Reserve our services as soon as possible or six months or more in advance of your wedding. A $100 deposit is required, with the balance due 10 days before the wedding. A full refund is given for cancellations if the date and time can be filled. Travel outside the metro area may require an additional charge. Discover, Visa or Mastercard accepted.

SENSITIVE, CREATIVE AND EXPERIENCED PHOTOGRAPHY!

It's your special wedding day, a day to be remembered for the rest of your life. Through the years, your memories will become even more special, as will your wedding album and videotape. Your choice of a photographer is an important one. Since 1968, Keith Aden has been specializing in wedding and commercial advertising photography, including video production. His 31 years of experience and knowledge of the very special art of wedding photography makes him sensitive to your needs and requests. Keith is a photographer who actually cares about you and your wedding.

ASPEN PHOTOGRAPHY & VIDEO STUDIO

14120 S.W. Stallion Drive
Beaverton, Oregon 97008
Contact Gregg & Lee Ann Childs
(503) 524-8230
Business hours: by appointment

Selecting a Professional Wedding Photographer

There are two important areas to consider: the professional abilities of the photographer and the pricing structure. At *Aspen Photography & Video*, Gregg Childs is an educated, trained and licensed professional photographer. He has been a professional studio and wedding photographer for 16 years and he uses the same lighting techniques at weddings that are used in the studio. Many of the photographs that Gregg sets up with natural lighting have won awards and honors.

With respect to pricing, *Aspen Photography* has made it very simple. First, we have a photographer's fee of $195. There is no time limit. (Aspen does only one wedding per day), and there are no add-on fees for going to a different location for the reception. We do not have packages that constrain you to purchase a certain selection and number of pictures. Instead, we offer deluxe previews and reprints at specified prices and let you select what you desire. **Price structure:** 4x5 $12; 5x7 $18; 8x10 $22.

"Thanks, Gregg, for the outstanding photographs. You're definitely one of the top three wedding photographers in the metro area." M.L. — 1993

What Makes a Professional Photographer a GREAT Photographer?

Even if you find a photographer with professional capabilities and a pricing structure that matches your budget, you will also want to make sure it is a person with whom you feel comfortable. A GREAT photographer is one who is compatible with you and your needs, and one who helps you feel at ease. After all, if you're not relaxed, it will show in your photographs. Aspen excels at making people feel comfortable and relaxed in front of our cameras.

"Thanks for making me feel so relaxed. I have always hated having my picture taken, but you make everything so natural… You're the greatest." S.L. — 1994

Why Should your *Videographer* be a Professional *Photographer*?

Videographers, traditionally, are not trained to be concerned with good lighting and composition (we know, because we have taken the same classes with other professional videographers). On the other hand, professional photographers have been trained to use good lighting techniques and see good composition.

Aspen Photography & Video is the only studio with photographers who are technically trained and expert in both photography and videography. We are professionals in both fields; we do not use outside sources for our video. The artistic lighting and composition talents we have developed as photographers transfer very well to the discipline of video. It is all very evident when you see our videos and how well they complement our still photographs. Our wedding videos are vibrant, colorful and artistically beautiful!!

"We're so happy that we decided to have you do our video also. It's a beautiful package."
B.B — 1994

"Your video of our wedding has been edited in a very sensitive manner. Thanks for your artistic touch." L.Z. — 1993

Ray Bidegain Photography

17 S.E. Third Ave., Suite 43 • Portland, Oregon 97214
(503) 289-5998

I have been a professional photographer for 17 years and have photographed hundreds of weddings. I know from experience that each couple, each ceremony and each reception are unique. I 'd like to meet with you, show you my work and discuss your ideas and vision for your wedding day. I usually take a few formal group portraits, in combinations that you specify. However, the majority of my time is spent capturing those lyrical moments that will spark your memories of the event. I am particularly talented at catching those candid, fleeting moments and at recording the unique story of your wedding day as it unfolds. I find that my friendly, easygoing style helps the bridal couple and their guests relax so that photos truly reflect their personalities and the joy that they share, rather than looking stiff or posed.

I am very experienced in both color and black and white photography, and I especially enjoy creating fine art black & white and hand-tinted photos. I do my own darkroom work with the black and white photography to ensure flawless prints, and many couples choose to combine the timeless look of black and white prints with the traditional color prints for their wedding album. There are many wedding package options, and all can be customized to meet your specific needs. I only book one wedding per day so that I have no time constraints and am able to arrive early to record your preparations and take some group photos, and to stay at your reception until the last guest says good-bye.

Please call and set up an appointment to view my portfolio and discuss your wedding plans. I will gladly put you in touch with any of my past clients. They will tell you I am friendly, flexible and professional and that the wedding photos I created record the memories of their wedding day perfectly.

JAMIE BOSWORTH
PHOTOGRAPHER

503 · 246 · 5378

I will spend the day with you, usually about seven or eight hours, trying to tell the story of your wedding on film… I'm not there to create the day, I'm there to record it as it happens. Many of my clients have thanked me for my unobtrusive presence, always surprised at the variety of photographs. You will see happy, relaxed people in my pictures, the same happy people you saw around you at your party. The only part of the day that requires organization is the time we set aside for the formal group photographs… the rest of the day should be yours to enjoy with your family and friends.

I hear from a lot of my brides and grooms that the day was almost a blur… when they look through my photographs, they truly get to see the special details, all the lovely things that they spent so much time designing.

Plan on spending an hour or so with me… I will show you many photographs. While you look, we will talk about your wedding ideas and how you see the day unfolding. As we talk and I get a feel for what you like, I can start to tailor my working approach to suit you. I use a mix of 35mm and medium format cameras… I shoot color, black and white and infrared films. There are also some special things we can do after the fact, like Polaroid transfers and toned photographs.

After thirty two years of photography, twelve as a professional, I feel like I can bring a lot of heart and experience to your wedding.

Let me show you what I can do.

Jamie Bosworth Photographer
by appointment, please
(503) 246-5378

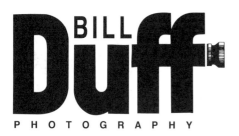

P H O T O G R A P H Y

4206 S.E. 72nd Avenue • Portland, Oregon 97206
Contact: Bill Duff
(503) 775-8589 • Fax (503) 775-2126
Business Hours: Mon–Fri 9am–5pm; please call first

—— *Your Photographer* ——————————————————

Wedding Packages and Prices $595–$1,595

Various packages are available for you to choose from, depending on the services you request. Packages include photographer's time, completed photographs, and your choice of two styles of albums. The number of photographs taken will depend on the package you select. Albums, folios, and wedding portraits are available for your review. Firm bids in writing are given from a price list provided upon request. Special packages include flexible combinations and photographs for the parents. May through September weddings should be booked one year in advance. I have 27 years experience in photographing people and events. Please call for additional information on convention, corporate identity, awards, and advertising photography.

Services and Equipment

Photo-session planning, portraits and news releases, studio sessions, and album planning are all part of the services available to each bride.

- Medium-format 2 1/4" cameras and professional lighting are used.
- A new studio and an outdoor garden setting are available for portrait shots.
- Bridal announcement pictures for the newspaper are $25 per session.
- The bride chooses when to take pictures, before or after the wedding ceremony.
- The bride's input and photo requests are greatly appreciated.

Proofs and Reprints

Single or multiple proof sets can be purchased at a discounted rate. There is no minimum order. An example of costs of reprints is an 8x10 for $19. All sizes of prints and reprints are available. Proofs are available two weeks after the wedding.

Terms and Payment

A deposit of $295 is required on booking. Visa, MasterCard and American Express are accepted, and 90-day payment plans are available. Credit is given for cancellations made 30 days in advance of the event. Within the Portland area, all travel charges are included in the package price.

Additional Services

Black and white images, thank-you cards, gift albums for relatives, retouching services and more. For an evening appointment call (503) 775-8589.

BRIAN FOULKES PHOTOGRAPHY

5711 S.W. Boundary Street
Portland, Oregon 97221
Contact: Brian Foulkes (503) 245-2697
Business Hours: by appointment

Wedding Packages and Prices

Brian Foulkes Photography specializes in candid photographs of weddings and wedding-related parties like your wedding rehearsal and dinner. We focus on all the fun, candid photos of family and friends. There are no packages as such, because we just charge a flat rate for time plus film costs, then hand the film over to you so you can handle the processing and place the print order yourself. Call for an appointment to see samples of our work.

Services and Equipment

- Use medium format and 35 mm cameras
- Can shoot in available light or use flash as needed
- Will work with you or a person of your choice to make sure you get the photographs you want of family and friends
- You keep the negatives

Proofs and Reprints

For most couples, after the wedding we drop off their film at the lab we recommend, in the couple's name. Those who wish can also keep the film to take to a lab of their choice. All prints and reprints are thus purchased at cost with no mark-up. Those who wish to go digital can easily have their negatives scanned onto a photo CD.

Terms and Payment

Fees are based on a flat rate of $325 to $450 and include up to six hours of on-site photography. A $25 deposit is required to hold the date, with the balance due on delivery of the film. Travel time is included in the flat rate unless the site is more than 25 miles away. Overtime is negotiable.

WONDERFUL, NATURAL PHOTOS

This service is for people who want candid photographs of their wedding and party. All of the traditional portraits are taken; however, the idea is to include pictures of the preparations, the setting, your friends, and the party. For those who are getting married at a private home or outdoors, perhaps in a small ceremony followed by a reception, here is a way of getting wonderful, natural photos that record the day. Brian Foulkes is sensitive to your wishes and will fit in comfortably with your family and guests. Charges are based on a reasonable flat rate plus the cost of film used. The exposed film then is either left with you, or we will arrange processing. Either way, you keep the negatives.

Contact: Kirby & Pam Harris
(800) 362-8796 or (360) 574-7195

Brides' Choice

Business Hours: appointment available in your home; days and evenings
Web site: http://www.weloveweddings.com/brideschoice

Your wedding photography is too important to entrust to anyone but a professional. We have over 20 years experience photographing weddings, as well as five years teaching photography at the college level. Photography is our full-time occupation.

As a husband and wife team, we are committed to giving you superior quality photographs, creatively capturing the mood and joy of your special day. We use medium format film and equipment, and professional labs for processing and printing.

This Day Belongs To You

By maintaining a low profile, remaining flexible, and flowing with events as they occur, we do our part to make your day memorable and enjoyable. Brides consistently thank us for helping them feel relaxed and at ease.

Thorough preparation for your wedding photography is our priority. We welcome and encourage your participation in pre-planning the type of photographic services that most completely meet your needs and desires. A pre-wedding consultation is scheduled three to four weeks prior to your wedding date. In addition, we usually attend your rehearsal so that we will have the opportunity to meet your family and attendants.

Our Brides Tell It Like It Is

"…and as soon as you walked in the room, Pam, we could feel the stress drain out of us. You're a calming influence. Thank you for that."   ~Sally, a bride's mother

"You were so patient and helped us to relax and enjoy the day."   ~Shelly and Charlie

"…we feel that you have become part of our family."   ~Gabriela and Ian

"How did you get all those great shots? We didn't even know you were taking them!"
                    ~Pete and Debbie

Pricing Information

- Pre-selected packages are available; however, we will be glad to custom-tailor a package to meet your specific requirements and budget.
- Pre-selected wedding packages are priced from $595 to $2,295.
- Color preview originals are included in all packages. They are yours to keep.
- You are not required to make a package selection at the time you reserve your wedding date. After you receive your preview album, you can curl up on your sofa, in front of a fire, and leisurely make your selection.

Studio C
professional photographers

Located in The Fountains Ballroom
223 S.E. 122nd Avenue • Portland, Oregon 97233
Contact: Denise or Becky (503) 261-9424
Web site: http://www.lum.com/fountainsballroom

With over 20 years of wedding photography experience, C Studio has formed a way to keep your special day fun and relaxing. We keep everything simple, affordable and best of all, we capture your wedding style and creativity.

Customize Your Own Package
- **negatives**
- **proofs**
- proof albums
- custom wedding and parent albums
- beautiful enlargements
- studio portraits
- black and white; custom hand coloring
- basic to complete coverage (2–8 hours)
- newspaper photos

Packages Ranging from $645–$1,995

Our Offices Also Provide *A Complete Wedding Package Like No Other in the Entire Portland Area!*
- elegant ballroom facility—up to 300 guests
- wedding catering
- bridal flowers
- decorating
- wedding cakes
- espresso bar service
- ice carvings
- video, DJ, limousine and formal wear referrals

See page 140 under Banquet & Reception Sites.
See page 296 under Caterers & Ice Carvings.

CAMERA ART

5285 N.W. 253rd
Hillsboro, Oregon 97124
(503) 648-0851

Weddings are supposed to be one of the highlights of a couple's life, but all too often the planning—choosing a dress, selecting a florist, a bakery, or even the invitations—can become a blur.

Have you reached the frustration stage in trying to choose your photographer? Are you having trouble comparing the Gold Edition package from one photographer to the Prestige Album set from another? Or maybe three 8x10s and 40 4x5s just don't meet your needs. Well, Camera Art has a better way.

Our goal is to take all the confusion out of pricing a wedding, and at the same time, allow the bride and groom to control their own budget and what they order.

Here is How it Works

We charge a $195 camera fee to shoot your wedding. That covers the photographer's time regardless of how long it takes to cover your wedding from start to finish. We'll follow you from dressing shots beforehand until you leave your reception. The camera fee also covers all travel fees and location changes.

After you receive your proofs, you simply order what **you** want. You order what meets your needs and budget. If your order consists of three 8x10s and 40 4x5s, that's fine, but if your order is one 8x10, nine 5x7s, and 17 4x5s, that's fine, too. The cost of your "package" is simply the cost of your individual prints.

No extra fees, no hidden costs. Simple–YES. Confusing–NO, and we like it that way. So do our customers—8x10s are $22, 5x7s are $18, and 4x5s are $12.

Services and Equipment

- Professional medium-format cameras (including backup equipment) are used
- Portable studio backdrop and lighting are used at each wedding
- Special effects include soft focus
- Available-light photographs are a specialty

Terms and Payment

A $95 deposit reserves the day. The remainder of the $195 camera fee is due 30 days prior to the wedding.

NATIONAL AWARD-WINNING PHOTOGRAPHY
AT SENSIBLE PRICES

by Michael Bickler, Robert Kuhn and Matt Furcron

CLASSIC PORTRAITS

in Salem
Contact: Neal White
(503) 399-1994, (800) 290-1994
Business Hours: Mon–Sat 9am–9pm
E-mail: CP2901994@aol.com

Visa and MasterCard accepted

Wedding Packages and Prices

- **Keepsake $780:** Hinge-style wedding album
  36 — 5 x 7
  2 — 8 x 10
  four-hour coverage

- **Silver $880:** Hinge-style wedding album
  48 — 5 x 7
  4 — 8 x 10
  six-hour coverage

- **Gold $1,080:** Deluxe "Florentina" album
  60 — 5 x 7
  16 — 8 x 10
  unlimited time coverage; engagement portrait session;
  Signature wall portrait

- **Diamond $1,480:** Deluxe "Florentina" album
  68 — 8 x 10
  64 wallet portraits
  unlimited time coverage; engagement portrait session;
  Signature wall portrait; 2 — deluxe leather parent albums

- Every package includes studio style portraits of the bride and groom, formal portraits of the bride, groom, entire wedding party, immediate and extended family, ceremony and reception. Photographs for the newspapers are also included.

Services and Equipment

Classic Portraits carefully blends formal posed portraits with special candid photographs that tell a love story about you on your wedding day. Because your wedding memories are so valuable, we photograph only one wedding per day. This enables us to capture all the love and emotion of this very special occasion.

Terms and Payment

- You will receive an agreement of complete wedding coverage.
- A $100 deposit is required to reserve your wedding date.
- Interest-free accounts are available.

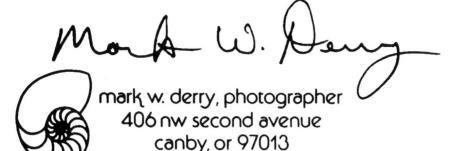

mark w. derry, photographer
406 nw second avenue
canby, or 97013
(503) 266-9393
Business Hours: Tues–Fri 9am–5:30pm; Sat by appointment

Wedding Packages and Prices

The most popular full-coverage package starts at $999, and includes four-and-one-half hours of time, prints in the sizes of your choice, lacquer finish of prints, an album, pages, engraving, and thank-you cards. The average number of wedding pictures taken ranges from 120 to 200. Please reserve your date from four months to a year in advance.

Experience, Services, and Equipment

Mark Derry graduated from Brooks Institute of Photography, one of the best-known schools for professional photographers, and is one of 20 Certified Professional Photographers in the state of Oregon. He is a past President of Professional Photographers of Oregon. Mark is trained in commercial photography and has corporate clients such as Johnson Controls, Chiquita Bananas, and Super 8 Motels. He has 16 years of experience in his full-service portrait studio and enjoys giving people a visual record of their wedding day. A list of references is available upon request. Mark works with medium-format Hasselblad cameras and can provide images up to 40x50 in size. Brides and their families may choose from a variety of styles and extra effects, including double exposures and misties. Mark will be happy to work with your preference of background, be it a formal portrait, beach location, etc. We recommend formal photos be taken before the ceremony, but scheduling is completely your choice.

Proofs and Reprints

The choice is yours regarding what portraits to print, in what quantities, and at what sizes. Prices range from $15 for a 4x5 and up.

Terms and Payment

A down payment of one half the total is required to reserve your date, with the balance due before the wedding. The reservation fee is nonrefundable, but may be credited toward other services. Overtime hours will be charged at $50 per half hour.

Additional Services

Mark offers a Complimentary Engagement Sitting for all wedding couples. Invitations, newspaper black-and-whites, wallets, folios, parents' albums, and wall-decor portraits are all available. Mark generally wears a tuxedo to the wedding.

PHOTOS CAN EXPRESS ALL YOUR LOVE AND JOY

Mark has a real gift for understanding people through the lens, and is able to capture the love and joy that make weddings so special. Above all, Mark is flexible to the needs of the bride, groom, and their families, so that final pictures reflect the spirit of the event.

DEBORAH DOMBROWSKI PHOTOGRAPHY

4631 N.E. Ainsworth St.
Portland, Oregon 97218
Contact: (503) 282-5511
Business Hours: by appointment

I Take Wonderful Photographs; Come See My Portfolio!

You'll find pictures that shine with the tenderness, humor, excitement, and love that fill a wedding day. Although I am happy to take formal portraits and group pictures, I am especially skilled in making affectionate, candid portraits of you and your guests. It's important to be sensitive to the small moments that make up the day—reunions between old friends, nervous laughter, shared secrets and jokes. I'll take the photographs that your best friend would take if she had 10 years of training in art and photography. From dressing up to cutting the cake and dancing all night, there will be pictures of the two of you that will capture the joy of your celebration. I'll consult with you before the wedding to find out what photographs are especially significant to you. Are your grandparents visiting from England? Does your sister have a new baby? We can fit these pictures into your plans for the day. Working with you, I'll create a beautiful and spontaneous record of your wedding.

Services and Proofs

I offer a flexible range of photographic services. I have recorded formal weddings in cathedrals and small family gatherings in the backyard. Both black and white and color photography are available. We can design a plan together that will fit your needs and desires. You will receive from 200 to 300 proofs that are yours to keep. Proofs are available approximately six weeks after the wedding. Beautiful custom albums are available upon request, and enlargements may be ordered separately. Enlargements may be ordered separately. Black and white photos are available for newspaper announcements.

Equipment

I use all Nikon equipment for candid shots, and I am equally adept at working with natural or artificial light. I use a medium format camera for detailed portraits in both black and white and color.

Cost and Terms

I'll work with you to plan the perfect coverage of your entire wedding day. I've been photographing people for 15 years, and it shows! It's a good idea to reserve your wedding date a few months in advance. I look forward to talking with you in person.

920 S.W. 13th Avenue • Portland, Oregon 97205
(503) 224-4410; Fax (503) 224-4429
Business Hours: Mon–Fri 9:30am–5:30pm;
other hours by appointment

Photographing Portland's important events since 1968.

Q. Why should I hire a professional photographer?

A. Photography is the only way to remember all the details of the most exciting times in your life. After nearly every wedding, we are told, "The day seemed to go by in a blur–I don't remember this. I'm so glad you got the picture." Only a trained, experienced photographer knows the difference between a "snapshot" and an image that becomes a lasting MEMORY of your most valued moments.

Q. But isn't good photography expensive?

A. Our prices are as varied as the individuals we serve. This is why we have so many options on the number of photographs and the amount of time for photography coverage. The old saying "you get what you pay for" is especially true in this instance. Our prices have always represented exceptional value. You cannot buy equivalent quality for less money anywhere.

Q. Why choose Edmund Keene Photographers?

A. Because your photographs mean as much to us as they do to you. Our aim is to make you so happy with your photographs that you'll be able to relive the day over and over again five, ten, or fifty years from now as you look through the memories kept in your wedding album.

If you're planning a **corporate event such as a holiday party, awards banquet, or seminar** that needs the careful attention and unobtrusive approach of an experienced professional ... WE CAN HANDLE THE ASSIGNMENT.

SO GIVE US A CALL. WE WOULD LOVE TO MEET YOU.
(503) 224-4410

ENCORE
S T U D I O S

Portland, Oregon
(503) 255-8047
E-mail: Encore@ethergate.com
Web site:
http://www.bravowedding.com/pdxencore-photo

◆ Photography ◆ Videography ◆ Music

Encore Studios offers a wide selection of packages designed to fit your budget and customized to your special needs. We pride ourselves on helping coordinate your wedding so it runs smoothly, allowing you to enjoy this very special time in your lives. You'll meet with your photographer to go over all the details and what photographs are the most important to you. On the day of your wedding, we help you relax in a friendly atmosphere, creating beautiful photographs you'll cherish forever!

Additional Services

- Studio portraits
- Multiple location photography
- Black and white photographs
- Invitations
- Newspaper photographs
- Custom mounting, spraying, retouching, texturing
- Frames and framing services
- Huge variety of albums, parent albums and folios

Photography Packages and Prices

Encore Studios offers you selections to preserve your wedding memories in a variety of ways. Several affordable packages are available as well as the opportunity to purchase your photographs at individual prices. Whichever method you choose to tell the story of your wedding day, we will be there to help you design a package that shows every wonderful moment you will want to remember. Most packages include consultation, a standard album and maximum professional photographer time. Options include original prints, folios, deluxe leather albums of your choice, customized prints and travel time. Travel time nominal outside Portland/Metro and Vancouver areas. Medium and 35mm formats are available. Ask about our popular Signature Packages. Individuals, children, seniors, family, glamour and group portraits in our studio or on location also available.

   Among our professional services we offer videography as well as music (disc jockey and live entertainment). Call Encore Studios today for more information and assistance. Consultants are available any time by appointment.

See page 441 under Disc Jockeys.
See page 541 under Video Services.

E X C E P T I O N A L   P H O T O G R A P H S   B Y

STEWART HARVEY & ASSOCIATES

2405 NW THURMAN • PORTLAND, OR 97210 • (503) 274-9711

Storybook Weddings

"There's magic in the smallest things: The quiet touch of hands, or a moment of joyful abandon…" Your wedding is a statement about your personal artistic style, and your wedding photographs should be as individual and expressive as you. Whether your wedding is fancy and formal or candid and spontaneous, Stewart Harvey discovers the personal moments that are unique to your wedding day. From his studio in a charming turn-of-the-century theater building, Stewart has gathered together a talented group of photographers who share his commitment to capturing each wedding story in a visual style that is the most appropriate and authentic to the occasion.

Why Choose Stewart Harvey Photography?

The reasons are many: state-of-the-art studio cameras and equipment, a commitment to medium format, the best wedding products available, and multiple service options. You may choose between A La Carte, Create-A-Story and limited or unlimited Storybook Packages. **There is also the Stewart Harvey attitude.** After 25 years of photographing some of Portland's most distinctive couples, he doesn't believe in generic weddings or generic wedding photographers. Each photographer is an individual artist chosen for their talent and personality, and you book the person whose style and vision fits with your wedding and budget.

These are many great reasons for choosing Stewart Harvey, but the most compelling reasons of all are best expressed by some of the hundreds of delighted couples who have selected Stewart Harvey and Associates as their wedding photographers:

"…we were nothing less than totally, emotionally overwhelmed! All the photographs are absolutely stunning. And from the very beginning in the church to the cutting of the cake, the photographs capture the spirit of our state of mind, the emotions of our family and friends and the beauty of the day."
~ Sarah Baker Morgan

"Thanks for making our wedding special with your beautiful photographs. Your attitude and friendly personality helped make the picture taking lighthearted and fun!"
~ Frank and Alaina

"Gary and I would like to thank you for helping to make Kristin and Matt's wedding day go so smoothly. You made it so easy for us!… We are all thrilled. Your kind attentions are very much appreciated!"
~ Karen Genzer

Member, Gala Events Group, Inc.

HOLLAND STUDIOS

SPECIAL OCCASION PHOTOGRAPHY

Professional • Relaxed • Creative

134 S.E. Taylor
Portland, Oregon 97214
Contact: Eric Holen (503) 706-5763
Business Hours: By appointment

Portraits that will give you goose bumps and capture a memory for a lifetime...this is what I strive to shoot for you at **Holland Studios**. The images of your special day should portray a complete story—from the engagement sitting on Cannon Beach, to the last kiss before the door closes on your honeymoon suite. My desire as a wedding photographer is to be involved from the very first phone call, to perhaps photographing your family in a few years time...

It's imperative to me that I know my clients before the wedding day—most of my packages include an engagement session, and *all* require a details meeting.

> *"We are excited to work with you on our special day, especially after seeing the finished work at our engagement session."* — Jean, bride

As you know, before booking a photographer, first meet with him or her. Discuss your ideas and visions for your wedding day; ask for references, and observe samples of their more recent work. Most importantly, see how your personalities complement one another. I go out of my way to ensure that things are not rushed; I want you to relax and enjoy your day.

> *"Eric is an incredibly talented photographer and also has a natural talent for putting people at ease,"* — Carol, mother of the bride

My assistant and I will dress for the occasion. As professionals, our goal as a team is to make sure your day is a special day for everyone, especially *you*.

I only shoot one wedding a day, allowing for unlimited time. The packages will fit everyone's budget, ranging from $695 to $2,795. Whether it's a black tie affair or an intimate gathering on the beach, I will be there to capture those special moments.

> *"Thank you so much, each picture is better than the last."* — Lisa, bride

I look forward to helping you create and document your wedding day. Please call me to schedule an appointment to view my portfolio, or with any questions you may have. Remember, *you* are unique and deserve only the best.

"This is your time.
And with a classic image from
Holland Studios,
Your time is Forever."

IMAGES
By Floom

(in Multnomah Village)
7843 S.W. Capitol Highway
Portland, Oregon 97219
(503) 245-3676

• Beautiful Formals
• Spectacular Candids
• Reprints starting as low as $7
• Superior customer service second to none

These are just a few of the fantastic features *Images by Floom* has to offer. You've probably already heard our name. It is commonly becoming a "buzz" word among brides, wedding and church coordinators who all want the perfect photographer to capture those treasured moments, without being pushy or controlling the event. Our job is to make your special day go as smoothly as possible, without any glitches. Our highly professional and trained staff are committed to this. Our packages start as low as $295 and go up to $1,795. Reprints at $7 per 4x6 photograph are almost unheard of in the wedding business. This is fantastic for parents, friends and relatives who want extra pictures—which we all know are usually too expensive to buy.

When we photograph your wedding it does not stop there; we will photograph your first anniversary, children's pictures, and so on. In our full-service studio, conveniently located in the heart of SW Portland, we know you'll be so pleased with the quality and customer service you'll receive at your wedding that we really will be your photographers for life!

- **$150 deposit books us for your day**–make no other package decisions until one month prior to the wedding.

- **There are no hidden costs**–at our initial meeting we will go over everything so you know exactly what you are paying.

- **We have packages for every budget.**

LOOK FOR US AT EVERY BRIDAL SHOW
OR
CALL TODAY FOR AN APPOINTMENT
(503) 245-3676

"They photographed three of my children's weddings beautifully.
Don't bother going anywhere else."   Mrs. Pat Reser, Reser's Fine Foods

---

Please let this business know that you heard about them from the Bravo! Bridal Resource Guide.   **493**

Images Forever Studio
Artistry in Portraiture
(503) 626-2738

Realizing your Dream ...
Since you were a little girl you have dreamed of the wonder of your wedding day.

Capturing the Glow ...
The magic of this day must be something to hold in your heart and share with your loved ones through your fabulous photographs.

Warming the Heart ...
with images to treasure for a lifetime. *Images Forever* has been creating cherished wedding storybooks for 20 years. After the day has ended your photographs will keep the memories fresh and vibrant.

About *Images Forever Studio* and *Kyle Saunders'* philosophy

Flexibility
Images Forever is committed to excellence in wedding photography...**your way!** Whether you prefer a traditional coverage or have special considerations, Kyle will cover your event as you request. Kyle is an expert at combining elegant, relaxed portraits with romantic wedding illustration and delightfully fun candids.

Romance
Images Forever takes romance seriously and strives to create images that show genuine emotion. Your photographs will bring back exquisite, tender memories and remind you of your lifelong promise to each other.

Experience
Kyle Saunders has worked for 20 years and personally photographs each wedding. Count on Kyle's expertise in planning and coordinating so that your day will flow perfectly and be relaxed and fun.

**If your wedding portraits are important to you,
you need to talk with Kyle today.
For an appointment call:
(503) 626-2738**

Professional Photographers of America
THE WORLD'S GREAT STORYTELLERS℠

Jak Tanenbaum
PHOTOGRAPHY ASSOCIATES

P. O. Box 82758
Portland, Oregon 97282
Contact: Lynden or Jak Tanenbaum
(503) 232-1455
Available By Appointment
Web site: http://www.photographyassociates.com

Wedding Packages and Prices

Our unique photographic documentaries are tailored to meet the needs of all sizes and styles of weddings. Our basic coverage starts at $399 and includes up to two hours of photography time and 20 deluxe color prints bound in a quality presentation album. We also offer unlimited wedding coverage, reception coverage, studio portraiture and classic black and white fine art wedding portfolios. Please call for additional information, our brochure and price lists, or an appointment in our conveniently located Westmoreland-Sellwood studio.

Services and Equipment

We use medium-format Hasselblad cameras, the best portable studio-style lighting available, and never go on location without carrying backup cameras and strobelights.

Proofs and Reprints

Our photography contract includes a specific number of deluxe 5"x5" color photographs displayed in a quality presentation album. Additional 5"x5" preview photographs can be purchased for as little as $4 each. Our quality reprints and enlargements are reasonably priced, and with our *"Punctuality Plus"* discount you can save 15% off our published prices when ordering reprints or enlargements within 30 days of the delivery of your presentation album.

Terms and Payment

In order to guarantee our availability for your wedding date, we require a $150 deposit upon the receipt of our signed *Contract for Photography*. The balance is payable on or before the day of the wedding. We accept all major credit cards.

FINE ARTISTS! PROFESSIONAL TRAINING! EXPERIENCE!

For over 20 years Jak Tanenbaum PHOTOGRAPHY ASSOCIATES has been providing individuals, families, galleries, museums, publications, collectors and corporations with the finest in photographic portraiture. We tailor each job to your desires, and we listen. We offer sensitive informed advice gained from years of experience and provide a variety of unique photographic services.

Jak Tanenbaum received a B.F.A. in photography and design from the University of North Carolina and an M.F.A. in photography from the Academy of Art College in San Francisco. He has been an active exhibiting artist for 25 years. His wife and partner, Lynden Tanenbaum received her B.F.A. in photography from Humboldt State University and is also actively involved in exploring the creative, fine-art aspect of the medium. Jak and Lynden often work as a team, and when they put their minds together, amazing things can happen. WOW!

PHOTOGRAPHER

5500 S.W. Ames Way
Portland, Oregon 97225
(503) 246-7911
Businesss Hours: by appointment please

He simply goes by "Joseph," not "Joseph, the country's best wedding photographer."

This is, however, the consensus label a number of hot bridal publications are giving this Portland-based photographer. "Great images," *claims Bridal Guide,* "The right photographer." "Storybook photographer...really special," according to *Bridal Connection.*

Having shunned the predictable series of canned wedding photos, Joseph Grimes has virtually changed the face of wedding photography with his journalistic approach. Accepting only 52 assignments a year, he's taken his Rolleiflex and Nikon from Vancouver to Venice for society brides. Thirty percent of his clients are "high profile," a term he gives such notables as Michelle and Brad Tonkin, Jennifer and Harry Glickman, French covergirl Gisell Meca, Lorraine and Rabbi Emanuel Rose, and Laurie and Neil Lomax. With an average of seven requests per weekend, he typically is able to accept only one.

Regardless of who his subjects are (booking is strictly egalitarian—first come, first served), Joseph works his documentary magic to capture what he describes as the "decisive moment" for each situation. "If human emotions could be charted on a graph, each interaction would build to its highest point before declining." He aims his camera, and his art, for "the apex of the curve...that split-second thrill!"

People look their best when not posing," Joseph believes. As a guest at friends' weddings, he finds it annoying "when photographers take over and direct people to tip, turn, twist, and hold it. Or manipulate the bride into some awkward Kung-fu pose staring at her bouquet, resulting in a horrendously concocted bit of melodrama. It's pure fiction!" (If Joseph had asked Neil Lomax to gaze at a Super Bowl ring, with his coach holding a whistle softly out of focus in the background, would *Sports Illustrated* be interested?)

"Of course brides will allow a few minutes for beautiful family portraits," Joseph says, "but documenting the event and conveying the mood is what today's bride really wants." For instance, one of his widely recognized photos shows a gust of wind catching Gisell Meca's long wedding veil, temporary ensnarling a line of bridesmaids and garden roses. Joseph only had a split second to capture all the women laughing and rushing to rescue the veil.

As he talks, Joseph gestures toward another shot from the much-publicized wedding of Malibu's Heidi Brusco. "It's of her dad, relaxing at the reception, not grinning into the camera, but just head and shoulders from behind. He's sitting, right arm resting on a chair, hand casually holding his trademark Cuban cigar, smoke swirling up and away as he shares a father-of-the-bride story with is friends. Their faces show it to be great story. His face is unseen, but Heidi loved it because she knows the story he's telling."

Since 1970, Joseph Photographer, Raleigh Hills.

JP'S PHOTO EXPRESSIONS

"We Love Weddings"

Contact: John and Amy Prutch (360) 694-6684
By appointment

A wedding is a wonderful event that evokes once-in-a-lifetime memories—a time you will want to capture with quality, sensitive, professional photography. We specialize in capturing the mood, style, and fun of your special event. **We love weddings!**

A deposit of $200 is required upon booking your wedding date. This covers the photographer's time regardless of the amount of coverage you choose. The remainder of your cost will be your print credit.

Why print credit? We realize that you are unique and so are your needs. By using print credit, you do not have to settle for a package that fits the photographer's needs, but one that meets your own. We personally assemble your wedding album to your specification of portraits.

Take, for example, our four-hour wedding coverage, the price of which is $750. Subtract the $200 photographer's fee, and your print credit will be $550. You may use this credit towards your selections of portraits, albums, and accessories. Our prices range from $450 to $950.

We Love Weddings

Don't choose your wedding photographer by price alone! Choose them on the quality of their work and their enthusiasm about the weddings they cover. A husband and wife team, our photography studio is devoted exclusively to wedding photography. We use medium-format Bronica and Hasselblad cameras for all formals. You will have **two photographers** at your wedding regardless of the coverage you choose. At your request, we will attend your rehearsal to meet wedding party and family as well as review your photography schedule. We welcome special requests. There are no additional fees for your rehearsal consultation, travel time, mileage, or different locations. We accept only one wedding per day so we don't watch the clock. We never forget—it's your wedding!

Thank you for considering us to photograph your wedding. We can make your day come alive in photographs—yours to enjoy forever. We love weddings!

See our portraits on our Web site:
www.WeLoveWeddings.com

PHOTOGRAPHY
in the Northwest Tradition
TERESA KOHL
9150 S.W. Whispering Fir
Beaverton, Oregon 97007
(503) 848-4631; Fax (503) 848-5728

Personal Attention

Bridal consultations are fun and informative. Brides and grooms are welcome to bring family members or anyone from their wedding party. Relax with refreshments while viewing sample albums, actual proof books, and large images from many of the key locations around Portland. Budgets are reviewed and a personalized plan is formed to suit my couple's individual needs. This is followed up by a detailed, time frame itinerary. My average booking is around $1000, however, there are many options to fit every budget.

Quality and Professionalism

Hasselblad cameras are used exclusively for all formals. Use of the available site is combined with imagination and creativity for unique coverage or, for an additional fee, a fully equipped, portable studio is available. Photojournalistic coverage is an option for those wanting bolder, non-traditional coverage. All coverage is fun, exciting, and personalized for your special day!

Proofs and Reprints

Your original prints that tell the story of your wedding day are ready usually by the time you return from your honeymoon. You may order any additional sizes for very reasonable rates ranging from $3 to $45 for sizes 2x3 to 10x10 standard prints. I encourage couples to wait until their first anniversary to build their storybook album when all of the excitement has ebbed a bit. It is the best gift you can give each other for that very important first anniversary.

Terms and Payment

A deposit of $200 is required to secure your date, and is applied to the total price of your coverage. Usually by the time of your wedding, 80% of the total has been paid.

Let's Make a Deal!

I offer incentives and discounts for January to April weddings, and also for creative, fun or theme coverage. I love the unusual as well as the timeless, traditional coverage. Barter and service trades are also welcome for 1999!

LAKE OSWEGO PHOTOGRAPHERS

15830 S.W. Upper Boones Ferry Road
Lake Oswego, Oregon 97035-4066
Contact: Dan or Teresa Poush
(503) 624-1515, (888) 269-4000
Call for an appointment

Making The Right Choice...

We know it is a difficult task for you to select your wedding photographer. To convince you to meet us and see our work is equally difficult, but once you do, you will understand why we have a real advantage.

It's A Gift

Our husband-and-wife team combines photographic talent with a special gift for working with people. We feel it's our most important service. All photographers in this book will most likely produce nice photographs. Our value is measured in the quality of service. Throughout your day, we try to capture all the beauty of your wedding, while at the same time making the photography a very positive and pleasant activity.

We work with you and your family to individualize your coverage while producing elegant photographs in a relaxed atmosphere.

Everything You've Always Wanted

Our service is intended to be simple. You select the package you desire, and we do the rest. All packages include our time, the selected color enlargements, and a beautiful album of your choice.

One price, no surprises.

The Finest Quality

Our beautiful wedding prints are produced by the finest color lab in the Pacific Northwest. This allows our studio to "guarantee your photographs for a lifetime." So, give us a call. Our showroom is a relaxed place to view sample albums and wall prints.

Invest In Friends

Once you meet us, you will see why so many of our couples consider us friends, long after the wedding photographs are delivered.

DELIVERING A LIFETIME OF PROFESSIONAL PHOTOGRAPHY

Call early for an appointment.
Dan & Teresa Poush
(503) 624-1515 or toll free (888) 269-4000

With over 20 years experience in photography, we can also handle any celebration, party, or corporate event with ease.

LASTING MEMORIES PHOTOGRAPHY

6235 E. Burnside
Portland, Oregon 97215
Contact: Ron or Mary Price
(503) 236-0174
Business Hours:
by appointment to accommodate your schedule

At Lasting Memories Photography we realize that your wedding day is the most important day of your life. Your wedding photographs will help make the memories of your day last forever. We cater to making your wedding photography as simple and stress-free as possible. Call us today for an appointment, then come in and discuss your wedding and we can show you our many samples, and our file of thank you notes from happy customers.

Wedding Packages

All packages start with a romantic engagement session. We start this session in our studio for some formal portraits, then after a clothes change we finish the session in a local park. You receive any eight prints in a folio to display at your wedding.

We photograph your wedding much like a photographic journal. We cover everything from last-minute touches to the bride, formal posed pictures, fun shots, wedding ceremony and all the traditional and fun events that happen at the reception. You receive all your proofs assembled in an album. You also receive a black and white photo for the newspaper.

Experience

Mary Price is a photographer with an eye for romance and a personality for fun. She has the experience and expertise to make your wedding memories all you want them to be. Working all weddings by her side is her husband, Ron, who also manages the business. They have worked hundreds of weddings together and their teamwork shows. We know that you will feel very comfortable working with Ron and Mary and that will be visible in your wedding photographs.

Mainlight Media, Inc.
642-1251

17900 S.W. Frances Street
Aloha, Oregon 97006
Contact: Gordy Teifel
(503) 642-1251
E-mail: teifel@pacifier.com

Event Packages and Prices

Mainlight Media album packages will fit your budget perfectly: $165 to $2,490. Our professional photography extends from appropriate films and exposure to print production and presentation. Most of all, our packages are good starting points to tailor to exactly what you want. We feature electronic previews—positive video images made from color negatives. Client may request color previews.

Photography and Video Services

The personality of the photographer is important on your special day. Gordy Teifel, our lead photographer, will easily guide you through the process of photographing your story. His assured style can be applied to creating your memories. Trust this assignment to Gordy Teifel, a veteran of hundreds of weddings. Call for an interview. **BONUS: If you sign up for both photography and video recording, we'll supply another video camera at your wedding service at no additional charge.**

Video Production Services

Relive the first day in your married life! Memories of a lifetime are captured through the imaginative direction of a video producer. Enjoy the treasured moments of getting ready, sharing your vows with each other, the rings, the cake cutting, the toasting and the expressive comments of guests and relatives.

Quality programming with the benefits of Digital Video and Hi8 industrial equipment. Audio is the foundation of successful videos. Audio sourcing includes wireless mics, a PZM and other microphone types with mixing techniques. Our cameras carry exceptionally low light capability. However, superior performance is attained with complimentary illumination. Editing with Adobe Premiere is performed on a computer loaded with video and photographic imaging tools.

Additional Benefits

Mainlight Media produces tape-slide and video programs that visually show family histories. This high-impact presentation is caringly created from old photographs. Background music is added to set the mood. The tape-slide format is excellent to share with an audience. The video version is ideal to enjoy at home. Call Mainlight Media to begin the planning of your Nostalgia Program. The Nostalgia Programs are often associated with grateful responses, heartfelt appreciation, and even inexpressible joy.

Michael's Weddings, Etc.

(503) 760-8979
"Portland's Most Unique"

From a Recent Interview:

JB Unique. An interesting word. Why do people, including other photographers around the country, call your pictures unique?

M Well, first of all I'm an artist. An artist that pre-visualizes what the actual picture will look like as I'm focusing each frame in the camera. This is done with concept ideas that have been discussed with each bride and groom, usually far in advance of the wedding date. These may be subject to change minute-to-minute at the actual wedding as each wedding takes on a life of its own as individual as the bride and groom.

JB I've been told you really get into your work. Is there something about weddings that really turns your mind on?

M I love to take pictures of people as much as life itself. God has given me a talent to work with people in the wedding environment so that the end product is a set of pictures that could become family treasures. Much in the same way we love to look at our parents' and grandparents' pictures. Weddings to me are a thrill, the same way some people like to ride the biggest, wildest adrenaline-rush roller coaster—except I start getting pumped days, if not weeks before the wedding!

JB Your pictures show so much passion, care and life. How can this happen when you usually have only one chance for a particular picture or a very short time to set up a group picture?

M Experience! I'm here to tell ya', you can't beat 24 years of wedding experience to size up a situation and make a picture that you know is a once-in-a-lifetime shot! You learn to expect the unexpected—or to make the unexpected happen. Cool! I love it!

Photography by Bob Welsh
Master Photog. Cr., PPA Certified, FP
5035 N.E. Elam Young Parkway
Hillsboro, Oregon 97124
(503) 648-0586; Fax (503) 640-1617
E-mail: mitp@teleport.com
Web site: www.mitstudio.com

Your Wedding...

is an expression of Love that you have spent much time and energy to create. You have chosen the perfect dress, colors and flowers for your wedding. Everything is in place and your wedding memories will be forever captured with portraits designed by **MIT**.

Moments in Time Photography...

is one of the premier studios in the Northwest. This reputation has been built through award-winning photography that shows the elements of personality and emotion. We also take pride in the quality of our service to you, our client.

When you call and reserve your wedding with us, you have started a relationship that goes beyond simply photographing your wedding. Bob Welsh, a Master Craftsman photographer and his staff truly care about the service they provide. The planning process is important and one of our specialties.

Exciting Pictorial Session

This sought after session, at a favorite location of your choice, has become one of the featured elements of our relationship with couples from Seattle to San Francisco. Artistic views showcased through black and white and architectural design make this an irreplaceable memory.

As you search for your photographer, take the time to visit our studio. We believe that once you visit us, your search will be over and you will feel assured your wedding portraits are photographed by wedding experts.

Do it right; memories will fade, but portraits by **MIT** become treasured testimonies of your LOVE.

COMMUNICATION
DESIGN
ART

Web site: www.mitstudio.com

MOSER
FINE PHOTOGRAPHY

*The Ultimate
Wedding Experience*

*319 E. Evergreen
Vancouver, Washington
(360) 699-6221, (888) 699-6221*

You Have Dreamed of This Day All of Your Life

You worked hard to make everything perfect. Preserve this day forever with the ultimate in wedding photography.

Imagine...

No rushing around, no confusion and no one to intrude on your intimate moments with your friends and loved ones. We'll create the Ultimate Wedding Experience for you. You will be pampered as we create breathtaking images that you will cherish for a lifetime.

The Ultimate Wedding Coverage

Designed to give you total control and flexibility of your wedding photography, your Ultimate Wedding Experience includes:

- Pre-wedding planning session
- Unlimited coverage of the wedding and reception
- Unlimited number of locations
- Unlimited number of images created
- Album design session using our unique album designing system
- Custom designed album selections to suit your needs

Custom Designed Albums

After the honeymoon, you will be blown away when you view your images in our surround sound mini theater. You will view these high impact images on a large screen set to music. After which, our album design specialist will assist you in designing your custom album as you view the album page by page on the screen.

"Thank you! Thank you! Our photos are absolutely beautiful. You captured our wedding day so perfectly. We are so glad we found you and you were able to do our wedding."

~Tina and Damon

"Thank you so much for helping our day go so smoothly. You really helped to coordinate things and keep us relaxed and enjoying the day. Thank you again."

~Kymberly and Brian

**Please give us a call and let's talk about your wedding dreams.
As this couple said, you'll be glad you did!
(888) 699-6221 • (360) 699-6221**

WILLIAM OCELLO
PHOTOGRAPHER

(503) 698-4262 or
(503) 222-4262

Web sites:
www.bravowedding.com/pdxwilliamocello
www.oregonlive.com

Are You Looking For...

A photographer whose signature photojournalist style includes excellent candids?

An accomplished black-and-white artist?

A photographer who captures beautiful photos of people who do not think they are photogenic?

An artist who treats your families with respect, and has a great sense of humor?

A photographer who places less emphasis on formals, with more candids at the reception?

An artist who wants you both to enjoy the experience and his believable formal and portrait shots?

... then call William

Hi, I'm William; and there are several things I want you to know about the way I'll photograph your wedding. I'll only shoot one wedding a day, so you'll have my complete attention. This helps you to enjoy a more carefree celebration, and allows me to shoot a balanced wedding. One where you both get what you want, while I use the time to photograph your families equally. I shoot light formals before the ceremony so that traditional formals will not dominate your day. This will ensure that you'll have more time to enjoy each other at the reception. I also shoot a strong ceremony in order to record the commitment you've made. And, if you wish, I'll shoot the traditional cake cutting, toast, etc., in between the many candids at the party.

If you're looking for a fun, unhurried style, then call me to set up a relaxed meeting. Please remember, I never book at the first meeting in order to give you time to compare styles.

Wedding Coverage and Prices
My coverage is designed to include most situations, and I also welcome custom coverage to suit your plans.

Location and studio shoots are always available, and you can secure my services for as little as $695.

Why call?
Because I'll be happy to be there.

Pearl Studios

Portland, Oregon
(503) 771-6409
Business Hours: by appointment please

Background

Gustav Knecht, owner of Pearl Studios, has worked in cosmopolitan cities in both Europe and North America. His pictures are fresh and original, reflecting his creativity while still capturing each couple's individual personality and style. Romantic, unique, and timeless images you will never tire of. Gus is the sole photographer, so the quality images you see are the images you will get, all captured by medium format camera in color and black and white.

> *"The pictures are fantastic! The composition of the shots including different shapes, colors and lighting are outstanding."* — Pat and Gary Ray

Service

At Pearl Studios, every wedding is unique and special to us, with customer service as our priority before, during and after the wedding day. With two consultations before the day, we can plan everything so you can be relaxed and therefore *enjoy* your wedding, which is the most important thing!

> *"Your kind, friendly, and caring way really helped us to have a fun and relaxing day! The pictures are absolutely wonderful. They are more than we could have ever hoped for."* — Shannon and Bret VanHorn

Quality

We will ensure that your finalized album will be of the highest quality. All photographs are studio prints with color correction, not proofs. We also offer handcrafted customized prints featuring specialized borders, textures and handtinting to enhance your album. All these are created and printed by Gus himself. He enjoys all aspects of the business, from the initial meeting to the assembly of the album. This results in a beautiful album, one that has been created especially for you by someone who takes pride in his work from start to finish.

> *"Thanks for taking the time to make our pictures special. Our families are so impressed with them, too. We actually felt like you were enjoying photographing us."* — Janene and Paul Tamborello

Price

Choose from our set Pearl packages or let us custom design something specific to fit your needs.

> *P.S. Thank-you for reading about us. We hope to work with you soon.*

PHOTO MEMORIES BY HARVEY

955 S.W. 193rd Court
Aloha, Oregon 97006 • Please Call for Directions
Harvey Thomas (503) 629-5605 or (800) 743-2905
Fax (503) 690-8537
Hours: Mon–Fri 8:30am–5:30pm; Sat 9am–2pm;
evenings by appointment

Wedding Packages and Prices

Our hundreds of happy customers are our best advertisement:

"We couldn't have done it without you. You knew just when to do things; never intrusive, but always getting the photo."   *~Eileen & Darrel Burt*

"Harvey did our daughter's wedding. We had as much fun, and Harvey did as great a job as he did 26 years ago at our wedding"   ~Jan & Darrel Mattoon

We offer couples a variety of choices from one to six hours of coverage, and from 24 to 120 originals. Package prices range from $325 to $1,375. We can also tailor any package to fit your needs. Come to our studio to review our work.

Services and Equipment

- 2 1/4 ideal-format cameras; professional lighting as needed.
- Full-service studio with controlled lighting and backgrounds.
- Photo requests encouraged. We'll provide you with a checklist of photo poses so you can determine all the important photos you want before the wedding day.
- We encourage formal wedding pictures be taken before the ceremony to make sure the bride and groom are thoroughly relaxed before they go down the aisle, and so there won't be any delays between the ceremony and the reception.

Previews and Reprints

We allow you to take your previews home so that you can select the photos you want in a relaxed and familiar environment. All standard sizes of reprints are available. Proofs and reprints are deluxe, professionally processed, and finished in a lab for the best quality and color. **SPECIAL INCENTIVE: if reprint orders are received within 21 days from the date the originals are delivered, you will receive a 10% discount on the reprint order. No exceptions please.**

Terms, Payment, and Additional Services

A 50% deposit is due to reserve your wedding date, with an additional 25% due by the wedding date. The balance is due upon receipt of your previews—usually two to three weeks after the wedding. We try to be flexible to your needs. In case of cancellation, your deposit may be applied to a later date. Moderate charges for travel outside of the metro area. We also do portraits for individuals, couples, families, and high school seniors. Invitations and accessories available at a discount.

WEDDING MEMORIES *To the bride and groom,*

Your wedding is a special day in your life. Our philosophy is to capture those memories on film. By getting to know the people involved in your wedding and putting you at ease, we are able to make your loving day become a cherished and captured memory. The all-important traditional formal poses will be recorded as well as contemporary and candid memories.

~Harvey

PHOTOGRAPHY BY
PETER PAUL RUBENS

(503) 293-0467

Visit us at: www.peterpaulrubens.com

If you pride yourself on researching carefully, consider closely Peter Paul Rubens. Discover:

- A personable, friendly, yet clearly professional approach
- An image style described by brides as, "*...distinctive, without comparison*"
- National award-winning, published photography

Peter is known as the "photographer's photographer" with coverages nationwide. The Chairman of Kodak wrote: "*The price seemed a small amount to pay. It was obvious that you were not only doing fine work in the overall wedding celebration, but there was evidence of true creative approaches. I thought the photographs were absolutely outstanding. You obviously are an accomplished artist.*"

Services and Equipment

Expect imaginatively composed images, blended with fresh, candid scenes. Count on a responsive approach to the look you like whether it's casual and fun, simple and elegant or stunningly grand. The most frequently chosen coverages range between $1,895 and $3,995.

- He cares—enough to learn the names of everyone in your wedding party and family.
- Quality equipment—superb, medium-format cameras, together with sophisticated candid systems. Multiple light approach for a dimensional, complimentary look.
- Highly skilled. Masters Degree: Professional Photographers of America.
- Appropriate. Peter adapts his attire from tux to jacket/tie to professionally casual.
- Special procedures to ease and clarify ordering if you or family live out of town.
- Black and White. Try a bit for a traditional or artistically different look.
- Way Fun. "*...such a character. Your sense of humor is priceless*" ~D. Nicolik
- Experienced. Professional over a dozen years. Reliable.
- Not a one-man show. Responsive office staff. Fast results.
- Skilled assistants provide technical support, enabling Peter to devote full attention to you.

"A lab of rare quality" best describes the facility that will craft your photographs. Perfectionists —each photograph is both machine optimized and operator fine-tuned. The resulting vivid color and vibrant skin tones are guaranteed by this lab for a lifetime.

This note arrived two years after the wedding: "*The wedding album is such an unbelievable hit with everyone who sees it! I'm embarrassed you made me look so beautiful.*" ~Angela Hart

THE HALLMARKS OF A RUBENS...
STYLE, WARMTH, EXCELLENCE

You can count on a photography session that, beyond being a vivid record, has its own joy—a session that delights in laughter and is naturally romantic.

ROB POWELL PHOTOGRAPHY

since 1975

Beaverton, Oregon
(503) 646-4710
Business Hours:
by appointment
E-mail: AnselRob@aol.com

"Thanks for doing such a nice job on our photos! It was great to have a photographer who was so polite to our friends and relatives." —David and Paula Lynn Olson

"Our wedding album looks so much better than others we've seen! You really helped us relax and have fun on our special day." —Paul and Chris Vincent

Honors
- National Master of Photography degree
- Oregon Fellow of Photography degree
- Numerous prints in the international traveling loan collection

Prices
My most popular plan is three hours of time with a leather-bonded album of 120 5x5 original prints and nine separate 8x10s for a total cost of $585. Other options are available. I can send you a complete list by mail or fax.

Reprints
Reorders are not required. If you would like additional photos, my prices are lower than most: 5x5=$7; 5x7=$9; 8x10=$14. I can make print sizes from wallets through 40x60. Complete retouching is available, including new digital techniques.

Free Studio Portrait
For any couple using three or more hours on their wedding day. Includes one-half hour of studio photography and eight 4x5 original prints, at no extra charge! A few friends or relatives may be photographed with you.

Experience and Qualifications
In the last 24 years, I have personally photographed over 750 weddings. In that time I have never failed to show up as scheduled for a wedding. I have never sent out a substitute photographer in my place, and I have never ruined or lost wedding film. You can depend on me.

I Believe in Marriage
My wife Roberta and I have been joyfully married since April 12th, 1980—19 happy years! We wish the same blessing for you. The vows you take will be sacred and permanent, and I will act in a supportive and respectful manner on your wedding day. I truly enjoy seeing a man and woman in love give their lives to each other. I would be honored to join your celebration.

May God bless your engagement… —Rob Powell, M. Photog.

Raleigh Bennett, Master Photographer
Lois Bennett, Consultant and Photographer
Call (503) 646-4624 for additional information

Who is Raleigh ?

Raleigh and Lois Bennett, owners of Raleigh Studios, have been creating visual magic from their home-studio for more than 22 years. In that time, Raleigh has specialized in beautiful story-telling weddings and elegant portraits wall decor. Raleigh and Lois are committed to photographic excellence and superior client service. Careful planning and attention to detail are a key to client satisfaction and are some of the many differences that separate Raleigh and Lois from all the others…

Your Love Story

The two of you met, fell in love, and that love has grown to the love you now share. Your Love Story, on the beach, in the mountains, or at the park is designed with you to reflect that special time and the feelings that are a part of it. With Raleigh's sensitive and artistic approach, your romance and the feelings you share will be captured forever…

Your Wedding Story

The most beautiful and elegant Wedding Stories are illustrated by Raleigh. The love you share, the special time spent with family and friends, the traditional and creative moments, as well as those spontaneous candids, will all be captured with a unique style and elegance. Your wedding story will be ready for your "album design session" on our Album Arranger Computer within five days of your wedding. With the very latest computer technology you will design and visualize your completed wedding album. Visit our studio today and see this fantastic process…

What You Can Expect From Raleigh

…Wedding photographs with a unique style and elegance.
…Beautiful portraits of loved ones.
…Photographs created in an informal, relaxed atmosphere.
…Sensitivity to your needs and desires.
…Meticulous planning and careful attention to detail.

Member:
Weddings of Distinction
Wedding Photographers International
Professional Photographers of Oregon
Professional Photographers of America
Portland Metro Photographers Association

red door studio
(360) 699-0604
Web site: www.reddoorstudio.com

"the truth about weddings"

No, this is not your typical wedding photography. We don't feel that it's our role to orchestrate the events of your day or ask the two of you to strike silly, contrived poses to create stiff, cheesy portraits. (Besides, grooms really hate that stuff!) We believe you want something a little more honest and artistic than that. Weddings are filled with so many visual and emotional nuances that there is no need to fictionalize them. We choose instead to use our skills as photographic storytellers to simply recognize and record those genuine moments on film, quietly capturing traditions, rituals and interpersonal relationships in their purest form. It's about telling the truth. What we offer you in the end is a full album, a fine-art photographic journal, filled with moving images that tell your own unique story.

"the essence of black and white"

Black and white is the signature look that defines the journalistic story of your wedding. Bold, crisp and infinitely detailed, the black and white image beholds a timeless, classic quality that ordinary color simply cannot match. Formals are photographed on color film, at your request. Our price is not based on number of hours, prints or rolls of film. We work on an all-inclusive fee that includes two photographers, all day. Complete, meticulous coverage.

"the book"

Designed exclusively by red door studio, the wedding journal is an art piece worthy of display. Each page bears a single image, leaving you to ponder and reflect on each precious moment individually. Custom printed by the artists, every photograph exudes an exquisite tonal quality that far surpasses that of even the most respected professional labs. Available in classic black and white, or warm brown sepia, both styles are bound in an album of the richest Napa leather we could find. Simple, yet classic styling. They're heirloom quality, as we want future generations to derive as much pleasure from them as you will.

"the sophisticated bride"

You made it possible for me to express my joy naturally…each picture is filled with so much life and emotion…this was the best wedding present we could have given ourselves.

Allison and Reuben Johnson, 8/16/97

We were thinking of the future when choosing red door studio. It was money well spent… a quality journal of life that we can share with our family for generations to come.

Nancy and Jamie Anderson, 7/18/98

Each time we open our book, we relive the most perfect day of our lives.

Chris and Eric Hubbard, 7/6/96

We invite you to experience the ***red door studio*** difference.

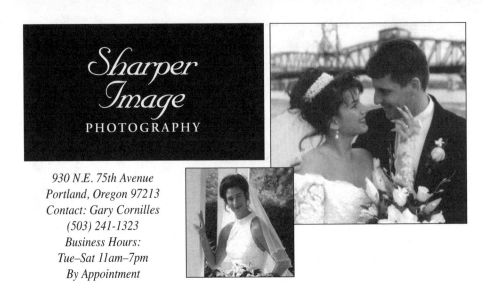

Sharper Image PHOTOGRAPHY

930 N.E. 75th Avenue
Portland, Oregon 97213
Contact: Gary Cornilles
(503) 241-1323
Business Hours:
Tue–Sat 11am–7pm
By Appointment

Flexible Coverage

We know that not every couple wants the same thing when it comes to wedding coverage. So, we offer several unique packages that allow you flexibility to create the perfect album. For small intimate ceremonies, coverage starts at just $395. For larger formal events, we offer several packages with combinations of prints, albums, wall portraits, and parent albums starting at $1,295. A private consultation is recommended to personally view our collection of sample albums and wall portraits. Consultations are available by appointment and can be arranged to fit your busy schedule.

Studio Information and Equipment

- Full-time professional photographer with 14 years of experience.
- Family-owned and -operated from comfortable home studio.
- Centrally located minutes from downtown Portland.
- All medium-format equipment/studio quality lighting.
- Computerized album design.
- Fine art custom black-and-white prints available.

Reserving your Wedding Date

Because dates fill up very quickly during the spring and summer months, we recommend booking your date as soon as you possibly can. Typically, six to nine months in advance is advised though not always necessary. Please call for availability. A deposit of $250 will reserve your exclusive date/time. All services are reserved by contract.

Capturing Memories

"On one of the most important days of your life, we want you to have it all! Let us capture these memories in a way that you will never forget! The love, the humor, the family, and all the little things are what we *focus* on."

www.sharperphoto.com
E-mail: garyc@teleport.com

2127 N. Albina, Suite 315
Portland, Oregon 97227
(503) 249-7575; Fax (503) 288-3751

Don't Say "Cheese."

There's no reason to spend your wedding day doing things you "have to do" instead of celebrating with those you love. Unfortunately, many brides and grooms (and photographers) miss out on some of the best moments of a wedding day because of an emphasis on posing for (and shooting) long lists of pre-planned photos—before, during, and after the ceremony and reception. Thankfully, there is another option that is becoming increasingly sought after: journalistic-style wedding photography that incorporates a modest number of portraits, yet stresses honest and genuine (not cheesy, frozen-grin) photographs. This style—including an emphasis on dramatic black-and-white, fine art images—is the focus of Strong Photography.

"We Didn't Want Any Stiffly Posed or Phony Pictures..."

"We were looking for a photographer who could capture the mood and spirit of our wedding," says Leslie Constans. "We didn't want any stiffly posed or phony pictures—we wanted real emotion and spontaneity. That's what was appealing about Craig Strong's photojournalistic style. We never felt nervous or on the spot, as people often do around professional photographers, because Craig blended into the background. In fact, we often didn't realize he was taking photos. The result: he captured some wonderful private moments and emotions that I don't think would have been possible otherwise."

Creative. Artistic. Honest. Different.

The most joyful weddings are the ones that allow the bride and groom time and freedom to experience, savor, and celebrate. These are the days best served by a photojournalist's touch. Strong Photography is not interested in shooting every wedding in town and won't take an assignment if it's not a good match. Craig Strong is dedicated to chronicling the stories of couples who share a vision for spontaneity, honesty, art, and beauty.

If that's you, give Strong Photography a call. Check out Craig Strong's portfolio and references. You just may decide to entrust your memories to an award-winning photojournalist. Then there's nothing left to do but relax, bask in the moment, and focus on the things that truly matter to you—your marriage, your family and friends... and each other.

Visa, MasterCard, American Express, and Discover accepted.

www.strongphotography.com

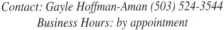

Contact: Gayle Hoffman-Aman (503) 524-3544
Business Hours: by appointment

...for photography that does much more than simply document your wedding; it helps you re-experience each unique moment.

It's part of wedding tradition to have a series of posed, formal photographs. But in order to remember your wedding with the warmth and spontaneity of that special day, you should have the creative touch of THROUGH A LOOKING GLASS...to remember the proud look on a father's face as he escorts his daughter down the aisle, or the gleeful smile of a child being asked to dance.

THROUGH A LOOKING GLASS provides a one-of-a-kind photographic memento of the entire wedding experience—literally from rehearsal to reception—or anything in-between. We work with the bride and groom ahead of time to make sure nothing is overlooked—neither traditional elements nor the creative, unique features you've added just for your wedding. Advance planning assures that the natural, spontaneous, personal moments you'll want to save will be captured forever.

Call THROUGH A LOOKING GLASS by Gayle to see photography that is special and unique...the kind of pictures you should have of your wedding.

Wedding Packages and Prices

Packages are tailored to fit your individual needs. Prices include consultation, photographer's time, all the processing, original proofs and negatives. *You own all the negatives and all the proofs!* You can do your own reprints and enlargements or we will gladly handle it for you. Complete packages begin at $600. If you want, additional time can be added, billed at half-hour increments. You can also add more film, charged at a flat per-roll rate which includes processing, *all your original proofs and negatives*. Travel time within the Portland/Vancouver area is included. A price list for enlargements, albums and gift folios is available upon request.

Terms and Payment

Services should be booked as far in advance as possible. A $300 deposit is required, with the balance due upon receipt of the proofs and negatives. At the time of booking you will be given a clearly written, signed agreement summarizing and guaranteeing services to be provided. Your deposit or booking fee is subtracted from the invoice and, in the case of cancellation, is fully refundable if the date and time can be rebooked.

AISLE RUNNER

The red carpet and white

aisle runner are vestiges of

the many fanciful ways that

brides were kept "walking

on air."

HELPFUL HINTS

- **Rental stores carry almost everything** from candelabra to coffee makers. They feature specialty wedding items for your ceremony and reception. You'll find such things as serviceware, portable bars, arches, tents, chairs, tables and all the tableware, dishes, glassware, flatware, and much more. Many shops also carry disposable paper products, decorations, and a selection of bridal accessories. For meetings, seminars, and conventions you will find audiovisual and sound equipment to meet your needs.

- **Visit a rental shop while planning:** Visit a showroom for ideas and to see the types and styles of merchandise and equipment available. They have brochures available that describe all the different items available for rent: style, colors, sizes and prices. They're also a terrific place to get ideas for decorations. Meet with one of the shop's consultants and go through your wedding plans step by step. You'll find they will help you select just the right wedding items to suit your style and taste, as well as help you determine quantities needed.

- **Decide on formality and budget:** Keep in mind the colors and decor of the site. Pick linens or paper products and tableware that will complement the room. Prices vary depending on the formality you choose; cloth linens will be more expensive than disposable tablecloths.

- **Rental items for all occasions:** Don't forget the rental store for all your wedding-related party needs—rehearsal dinner, showers, bachelor and bachelorette parties, birthdays, anniversaries and theme parties.

- **Deposits, delivery, and setup:** Reserve your items as far in advance as possible, especially during the summer months when outdoor weddings are popular. A deposit will secure the order for your date. There are only a certain number of heart-shaped candelabra available, and every item is reserved on a first-come, first-served basis. There is a charge on most items for delivery, setup, and pickup. Make sure to ask in advance how much those charges are so you can include them in your budget. You can also make arrangements to pick up and return the items yourself.

- **Returning items:** If you don't arrange delivery and pickup services with the rental company, you will want to put someone in charge of picking up and returning the rented items for you. You will be responsible and may forfeit any deposit for items that are damaged, broken, lost, or late. Make sure to inform your parents ahead of time or assign a reliable friend to keep track of rented items and return them safely to the place they were rented.

- **Theme wedding:** Theme weddings are very popular and can include Western, Mardigras, and Jazz. Props to enhance your decor are available at most rental shops. Couples can also personalize their wedding by including hobbies and personal passions as their theme.

For more assistance with staying organized during the wedding planning process, check out the Bravo! Wedding Organizer. Detailed question worksheets double as contracts. This step-by-step system will keep every detail of your wedding organized. To order, refer to the order form on page 23 in this Guide.

Custom Chair Covers

The Pacific Northwest's Original Chair Cover Rental Company
(800) 994-1055

AFFORDABLE ELEGANCE
for
"The Discriminating Bride"

We can bring your ideas to life...
Let us help you bring your ideas and party theme to life with chair covers that will make your special event extraordinary, not ordinary.

- Rehearsal Dinner
- Birthday
- Holiday Party
- Wedding Reception
- Anniversary
- Special Event

With Custom Chair Covers designed to match your colors and theme. Choose from
We work with you to coordinate all the decor with chair covers accented with flowers or decorative bows. Our chair covers are available in a variety of:

- Assorted Solid Colors
- Brocades

Accented with festive bows to finish the look...
At Custom Chair Covers, we provide you with a variety of matching or contrasting bows that will complement and enhance your wedding colors and theme. Match them to your flowers or table linens as well as the room decor.

Custom Chair Covers
Making Ordinary Chairs... Extraordinary

For Rental or Sales Information, Please Call:
(800) 994-1055

Custom Decor
Wedding & Party
Rentals

Reed Opera House Mall
189 Liberty N., Suite 208
Salem, Oregon 97301
Contact: Jane Huntley (503) 585-7522
Hours: Tues–Thurs 1:30pm–5:30pm;
or by appointment

Rental Items Available

We specialize in renting unique items for event decorating.

- **Specialty table linens:** excellent selection of round cloths in solid colors, florals, prints, damask, and moiré; square overlays in coordinating colors and florals; banquet cloths; lace cloths in several colors and sizes; napkins also available
- **Tabletop decor:** metal bird cages, hats, baskets, vases in all sizes, rose bowls, chimneys, candleholders, candles, wreaths, mirrored squares, etc.
- **Wedding baskets:** baskets in all shapes and sizes for floral arrangements or food service; pedestal baskets with or without silk-flower arrangements; large, antique, freestanding wicker baskets
- **Silk plants and dried flowers:** ficus and topiary trees, table arrangements, silk altar arrangements in freestanding white wicker baskets, garlands, and more
- **Other rental items** include a wonderful wrought iron bench and table and chair set perfect for the garden wedding; wicker settee, wrought iron candelabra, trellis, parasols, money trees, wall decor, pedestals, flower boxes, etc.

Bridal Accessories

We carry a selection of wedding planners, shower guides, guest books, pens, albums, garters, ring-bearer pillows, aisle runners, cake knives and servers, and toasting goblets.

Special Services

At Custom Decor Rentals we specialize in decorating for private parties, proms, class reunions, rehearsal dinners, weddings, receptions, and meetings. We can show you what to do, or do it for you! We are not limited to decorating, but can also offer individualized service in handling many of the details involved in coordinating your event.

THE PERSONAL TOUCH FOR YOUR SPECIAL OCCASION

If you have an idea, we will make it work. If you have a need, we will make it happen. We pay attention to every detail to make sure everything is just right.

A TO Z PARTY RENTAL

995 Commercial Street, S.E.
Salem, Oregon 97302
Business Hours: Mon–Sat 7:30am–5:30pm; Sun noon–4pm
(503) 585-7782; Fax (503) 362-8647

A to Z Party Rental is a
full-service, special event supplier.
Our large inventory of equipment and
supplies will ensure a successful event.

Knowledgeable Staff

Our staff will work with you to sort out the details for your event. Years of experience are at your disposal with proven success. You can count on receiving your rentals and purchases as ordered and ready for use with no worries or hassles. Our job is to make you a guest of your own party or event.

Ordering and Delivery

Our delivery rates are determined per zone and amount of time and man-power required.

Equipment and Accessories

- Tables and chairs
- Canopies
- Candelabras and pew abras
- Fencing and panels
- Audiovisuals
- Food preparation equipment
- Barbecues and crab pots
- Silk arrangements
- China and glassware
- Cutlery
- Arches
- Party lighting
- Chafers, trays, salad bars
- Stanchions, traffic cones
- Balloon bouquets
- *Please call for complete list*

Merchandise

- Items available in 23 colors:
  Plates, cups, napkins, cutlery, tablecovers, and tablerolls
- Balloons, balloon bouquets, candles, and arches also available

We Can Special Order Merchandise For You— Ask For Details!

DELIVERY SERVICE AVAILABLE

FOSTER RENTALS AND
THE PARTY PRO'S

5100 S.E. Foster Road • Portland, Oregon 97206
(503) 774-5508; Fax (503) 774-8563

2460 N.E. Griffin Oaks St., Suite 1500 • Hillsboro, Oregon 97124
(503) 844-9798; Fax (503) 844-2902

Business Hours: Mon–Sat 9am–5:30pm
E-mail: PARTYPRO1@juno.com

Rental Items Available

- **Wedding accessories:** gazebo; arbors, arches, lattice screens, guestbook stands, Grecian pillars, urns, wicker flower stands, kneeling benches, brass candelabra (several styles), candlelighters, silver tabletop candelabra, a wide selection of centerpiece bowls and decorations for floating flowers or candles.
- **Tents and canopies:** many sizes to fit your needs
- **Serving pieces:** punch bowls; chafing dishes; acrylic, stainless and silver: bowls, trays, tongs, spoons and servers; silver tea service; stainless flatware
- **Glassware:** champagne, punch, coffee, rocks, wine, water, or specialty
- **China:** sophisticated ivory with gold trim, or simple clear glass
- **Tables and chairs:** banquet and round tables; Samsonite folding chairs and white wood folding chairs
- **Linens:** fine-quality linens available in many different colors; banquet, 90" round, 120" round, napkins and skirting
- **Beverage service:** champagne fountains, coffee makers, insulated beverage dispensers, carafes, pitchers and beer taps

Specialty Wedding Retail Items

Custom silk flower bouquets, wishing wells, decorations, centerpieces and ideas galore. Wedding invitations, imprinted napkins, matchbooks and ribbons. Mylar and latex balloons in many colors as well as curling ribbons.

Retail Paper, Plastic and Disposable Items

Paper tableware: floral and solid plates, cups and napkins. Plastic cups, cutlery, glasses, tablecloths, skirting, bowls and trays. Dripless candles in many colors. Cake tops, plume pens, guest books, unity candles. Beautiful pew and flower bows.

Full-service, On-site Decorating Service

Were you wondering how to decorate your reception site, church, house or backyard to complete the feeling for your wedding? We will meet you at your location to design the decorations to best fit the location with the ambiance you would like to create. The day of the wedding we will take care of everything from setup to cleanup. References are available on request.

Ordering and Delivery

Reservations are highly recommended so that we can guarantee item availability for your special event. We are happy to deliver and pick up. Please call our party consultants for an estimate.

NO STANDARD IS TOO HIGH!

Our ultimate goal is total customer satisfaction during and after the hustle and bustle of your wedding or event planning. Large or small, we can make it happen for you!

INTERSTATE *Special Events*

5420 N. Interstate Avenue
Portland, Oregon 97217-4597
(503) 285-6685

Tents and Canopies

Whether rain or shine is predicted for your wedding day, our white canopies will dress up your wedding and reception. Sizes begin at 10'x10'. We have many accessories to help create an elegant and finished look for your special day. These include fabric pole sleeves, dance floor, white liner, cathedral window siding, lighting and much more.

Tables and Chairs

We offer banquet, round, half-round, umbrella, bistro, and even stylish serpentine tables. One of our experts will help you determine your size and quantity needs. Classic white wood chairs are available, as well as folding Samsonites, white patio and Bistro, and black, padded stacking chairs. And don't forget—we have one-of-a-kind wedding table linens!

Wedding Accessories

Select from different styles of floor brass candelabra, brass and white wood arches, white Grecian pillars, and white lattice panels. Some of our centerpieces include 14" hurricane lamps, glass floral bowls, and 29" five-branch candelabra. Dance floors available in oak or classic black and white.

Tableware

We offer linen tablecloths, napkins, and skirting in a wide variety of colors and sizes as well as ivory and white lace. China styles include classic white, elegant ivory with gold band, and clear glass. Glassware includes styles for any reception need. Stainless and silverplate flatware and serving accessories are available.

Serviceware

We have many silverplate items such as tea services, trays, punch bowls, chafing dishes, as well as vases and bowls in glass, stainless, acrylic, and silver.

Beverage Service

We offer porta bars, beermeisters, beverage fountains, kegtainers, coffeemakers and carafes, pitchers, and insulated dispensers.

Retail and Disposables

Over 20 solid colors to choose from in paper plates, napkins, table covers, table rolls, cups, and balloons.

Ordering and Delivery

Reservations are most definitely recommended to ensure availability and assist us in meeting your needs. A deposit and rental fee are due upon receipt of the equipment. Affordable and convenient delivery, as well as setup services, are available. Please call for a price quote.

❤ Member of Weddings of Distinction

Pacific Party Rental
Vancouver's Newest
Equipment for every event!
Holiday Parties ◆ Company Parties ◆ Weddings ◆ Birthdays

12814 N.E. Highway 99
Vancouver, Washington 98686
(360) 576-1907
Business Hours: Mon–Sat 8am–5pm

Wedding Decor
- ◆ Guest Book Stands
- ◆ Wishing wells
- ◆ Aisle runners
- ◆ Gazebo
- ◆ Columns & flower stands, panels
- ◆ Brass & white lattice arches (variety of styles)
- ◆ Table & floor candelabra

China
- ◆ Clear glass
- ◆ White
- ◆ Ivory with gold trim

Flatware
- ◆ Stainless
- ◆ Silver plated (service accessories available)

Glassware
- ◆ Champagne
- ◆ Margaritas
- ◆ Rock
- ◆ Water
- ◆ Wine

Beverage Service
- ◆ Portable bars
- ◆ Fountains
- ◆ Coffee makers
- ◆ Pitchers
- ◆ Punch bowels

Serviceware
- ◆ Tea services
- ◆ Tray
- ◆ Chafer dishes
- ◆ Bowels (glass, stainless, acrylic, silver)

Miscellaneous
- ◆ Tents & canopies
- ◆ Audiovisual equipment
- ◆ Golf carts

Linens
- ◆ All sizes

Tables & Chairs
- ◆ Banquet and conference
- ◆ Card & children's
- ◆ Round & serpentine
- ◆ Wood folding: white
- ◆ Resin: white
- ◆ Samsonite folding chairs (white, black, and brown)

Delivery and Setup Available
Located where I-5 & I-205 meet

Mention this ad and receive a special 10% discount package.

The Party Place

A DIVISION OF PORTLAND RENT ALL

Eastside: 10101 S.E. Stark, Portland, Oregon (503) 252-3466
Westside: 8904 S.W. Canyon Road, Portland, Oregon (503) 292-8875

Specializing in event rentals and merchandise.
Here is a sample of what we have to offer:

TENTS AND CANOPIES

Sizes range from 10'x10' to our new 60'x160' New Century Tent. Styled with futuristic elegance, this beautiful tent will provide the right atmosphere to your next event. Delivery and set-up included in the Portland/Vancouver metropolitan area. Also available: sidewall, liners, pole covers, lighting, heating, air conditioning and generators. Larger tent sizes available.

STAGING AND DANCE FLOOR

- Staging and stage skirting
- Dance floor available in wood parquet or black and white check.

TABLES AND CHAIRS

- 6' and 8' Banquet Tables
- 15"x72" Conference Tables
- 30", 36", 48", 60", 72" Round Tables
- Card and Serpentine Tables
- Childrens Tables
- White and Black Wood Folding Chairs
- Resin Black and White Bistro Chairs
- Brown, White or Ivory Samsonite Folding Chairs
- Black Stack Chairs (padded)
- Elegant Chivari Chairs
- Childrens Chairs

LINENS AND SERVICEWARE

- 29 colors available
- Banquet Cloths (60"x120")
- 90", 108", 120" Rounds
- Card Table Cloths
- Elegant Gathered Skirting or Box Skirts (prints also available)
- Chafers in Plain Stainless, Brass Trim
- Stainless or Silver Serviceware
- Stainless and Silver Trays (variety of sizes)
- Serving Bowls in Plastic, Glass or Silver
- Other Silver Pieces and Gold Holloware
- Coffee Makers and Insulated Dispensers

CHINA, GLASSWARE AND FLATWARE

Our china styles include Clear Glass, White, Ivory with a Gold Band and Black Octagonal. We also offer a wide variety of glassware options, such as Crystal, Cutglass or Black Stem and our standard glass barware. From Margaritas to Martinis, you'll find the glassware you're looking for. Flatware styles available are plain stainless, hammered stainless or silverplate.

WEDDING ACCESSORIES

- Kneeling Benches
- Pew Candelabras
- Guest Book Stands
- White Wishing Well
- Gazebo
- Aisle Runners
- Candle Holders
- Money Tree
- Table and Floor Candelabras
- Brass and White Wood Arbors
- Flower Bowls and Mirrors
- Columns and Flower Stands

WEDDING MERCHANDISE

- Paper Bells and Streamers
- Centerpieces
- Trays and Bowls
- Favor Ideas
- Balloons
- Invitations
- Doilies
- Wedding Organizers
- Wedding and Guest Books
- Paper Plates and Napkins
- Paper and Plastic Table Covers
- Plastic Flatware, Cups, Plates

141st & Tualatin Valley Highway
Beaverton, Oregon 97005
(503) 641-6778
Mon–Sat 7:30am–6pm; Sun 8am–4:30pm

Rental Items Available *(call for free brochure)*

- **Wedding accessories:** Arches, arbors, gazebos, flower stands, pillars, pedestals, and columns. Candelabra: brass in 12 styles, pew, spiral, and heart shapes (some styles in white, silver, and pewter), silver and brass table candelabra. Centerpieces: rose bowls, brandy snifters, champagne glasses for floating candles or flowers, marbles and mirrors, socialite votive holders with pastel candle rings.
- **Tableware:** Tables: banquet, round, heart, serpentine, card, and cocktail. Chairs: white wood, bistro and samsonite. China: ivory, white, and black. Flatware: stainless or silverplate. Glassware: stemware, lead crystal, black stem, and barware. Linens: 22 colors, banquet, round or cardtable. Napkins. Skirting: four styles.
- **Serviceware:** Trays, bowls, candy and nut dishes, and food servers. Chafers, food warmers, and prep. equipment, champagne or wine coolers. Cake knife and servers.
- **Beverage service:** Silver, gold, glass punch bowls, fountains, goblets, coffee and tea service. Coffee makers and servers. Bars, beer dispensers and taps.

Specialty Rental Items

- **For the wedding:** White heart-shaped arbor. Chuppa canopy. White and gray carpet aisle runners. Bride's full-length mirror. Guest-book stands. Kneeling benches. Ornate white bird cage. Silk flower church bouquets–11 colors. Lighted ficus trees, flowering trees, ivy and floral garlands. Sound systems. Camcorders.
- **For the reception:** Antique silver table items. Deluxe white canopies in many sizes and white, silky, linen canopy liners and leg drapes. 16' white market umbrella. Dance floors: outdoor and indoor, oak or white. Staging, lighting, and fountains. Umbrella tables and umbrellas, barbecues, and helium tanks.

Wedding Accessories, Invitations, Disposables, and Balloons

- Huge selection of **Paper Tableware**: 38 colors, 14 wedding patterns plus florals. **Plastic Tableware**: 12 colors: plates, trays, tablecovers, barware and more. **Favors–Ribbons–Candles–Books**: mini champagne glasses, floral ribbon and bows, ice sculpture molds, candelabra and unity candles, guest books, toasting glasses and more. **Wedding Decorations**: garlands, streamers, bells, confetti, signs, banners and more. **Balloons**: 45 colors in 2 sizes. We rent heart and column frames with lights. **Helium**: we rent 8 sizes. We teach you how to decorate with balloons. **Invitations**: large selection. See invitations in this book. **Imprinting is our specialty!** Quality imprinting in our store of your napkins, matches, ribbon etc. Assorted type styles and colors, wedding symbols, emblems. Fast service!

FOR A PERFECT WEDDING, VISIT SNEAD'S

Advance reservations and delivery available. Serving West Portland for 34 years. Our staff will make your event ours...by providing service and quality products at reasonable prices. Receive a 10% discount on wedding rental items with this book!

SPECIAL EVENTS CO.

79 S.W. Oak Street
Portland, Oregon 97204
(503) 222-1664
Fax: (503) 222-1047
Business Hours: Mon–Sat 8am–6pm
Since 1958

Tents and Canopies
- Canopies from sizes 10'x10' up to 100'x100'
- Chiffon canopy liners & pole sleeves
- Clear canopy tops
- Sidewall: clear, white & windows
- Lighting & generators
- Flooring
- Heating & air conditioning

Dance Floor/Staging
- Wood parquet dance floor
- Black & white checkered dance floor
- Stage risers
- Stage carpet & skirting

Tables and Chairs
- 4', 6' & 8' banquet tables
- 24", 30", 36", 48", 60", & 72" round tables
- Umbrella tables with umbrellas
- Bistro resin chairs: white or black
- Folding chairs: white, black or brown
- White wood folding chairs
- Black padded stack chairs
- Gold Chivari chairs, ivory cushion

Linen
- Various colors & sizes
- Banquet & round linens
- Cloth table skirting
- Table runners
- Napkins: solid & damask
- Patterns: fleur de leis, grape damask white rose damask, floral Monet
- Lace & gold lame cloths
- White linen chair covers
- Aisle runners

China, Glassware and Flatware
- China: ivory with gold rim, white, white lace & glass
- Flatware: silver & stainless
- Glassware & stemware: many styles

Serviceware
- Silver five-piece coffee service
- Champagne fountains & punch bowls
- Barware, blenders & bar accessories
- Silver serving trays & bowls
- Portable bars & beermeisters
- Coffee makers
- Silver or gold plate chargers
- Chafers: silver & stainless

Wedding Specialty Items
- Gazebos: lattice & wrought iron
- Arches: lattice & wrought iron
- Picket fencing & lattice panels
- Guest book stands
- Candelabras: floor, table, pew
- Water fountains
- Audiovisual, lighting, & sound systems
- Grecian columns
- Floral & candle stands
- Centerpieces & vases
- Ficus trees, floral garlands
- Market umbrellas
- Candle lighters & unity candles
- *and much, much more!*

Special Events Co. offers a spectacular variety of rental items. Our company is dedicated to quality service at affordable prices. We have 40 years of industry expertise and event planning to ensure a successful event. Our staff can assist you in design and implementation of your wedding needs. Delivery, pickup and decorating services are also available.

1400 N.W. 15th Avenue
Portland, Oregon 97209
(503) 294-0412; Fax (503) 294-0616
Business Hours: Mon–Sat 8am–6pm
Appointments available any hour

Services

West Coast Event Productions is the Northwest's premier idea center for all events and special occasions. We specialize in the custom planning and design of event staging, lighting, sound, special effects, audiovisual presentations, tabletop décor, and event and theme production. We are able to tailor your event or special occasion to mirror your vision. We are here to help you make all your important event planning decisions. Please feel free to visit our newly designed showroom. Browse for ideas with our Photo Inventory Books. We have many of our specialty props, catering items and equipment displayed to aid in your event planning.

Rental Items Available

Tents and canopies: Sizes range from 10' x 10' to 100' x 200'+ and vary in color from solid white to striped red, green, blue or yellow. Custom tent decorating includes elegant fabric liner, fabric tent pole covers in any color, floral garlands, ambient tent lighting and twinkle lights. French and Cathedral window sidewalls, heaters, air conditioning and flooring are also available.

Wedding accessories: Select from several styles of candelabras, brass and silver table candelabras, brass and contemporary full standing candelabras; wedding aisle and carpet runners; custom chuppah; gazebos and arches; wood, ceramic, marble finish and Grecian columns; table accessories include urns, vases, hurricanes, votives, cherubs and table lamps.

Tables and chairs: Choose from our complete selection of tables and chairs in a variety of sizes and styles: White wood garden chairs, black wood chairs, gold ballroom chairs, folding and stacking chairs. *Ask about our new specialty chair covers.*

China, flatware, glassware and serviceware: Impressive selection of china in 14 different patterns: ivory with gold, white, black octagon and clear octagon. Solid colors in red, yellow, blue and green, formal bone china, contemporary patterns. Stainless, silverplate and goldplate flatware. Glassware for every occasion. Catering items for food service and many other items available.

Sound system, lighting and audiovisual: Complete array of sound equipment from amplifiers, microphone and mixing counsels to high-end data projectors. We offer a variety of unique lighting fixtures and special effects for outdoor receptions.

Stage and dance floor: An assortment of floors from elegant oak parquet to black and white or colored checks. Elevated foundations for ceremony, head table riser and entertainment—all attractively carpeted and skirted.

New for this year: Portland now has *Skydancers! Skydancers* are 20-foot tall brightly colored tubular balloon people that dance and sway under a large turbine fan. As seen at the 1998 Super Bowl. Perfect for grand openings and high profile events.

WHEN TRAVELING

Newlyweds were thought to

be particularly vulnerable

while traveling, so tin cans,

horns and other

noisemakers were tied to

the carriage or wagon to

create such a racket that

evil spirits would be scared

away.

HELPFUL HINTS

- **Renting a limousine:** Everyone enjoys the experience of riding in a luxury limousine at least once in a lifetime. It can be the final touch that makes your wedding day or event complete, so be sure to include it in your budget. The bride and her parents ride to the ceremony site in a relaxed and stylish atmosphere, then the bride and groom make their grand exit as they leave for the reception.

- **Don't reserve a limousine over the phone:** Go to the limousine service and personally inspect the vehicle you are considering renting. Be sure you're dealing with an established, reputable company. These businesses will display or readily have available important information like a business license and liability insurance certificate. If you have any concerns or questions about the service, ask for references and check them out.

- **Be sure to get what you paid for:** Make sure the limousine will be cleaned and presentable when it arrives on your wedding day. Read the contract carefully before paying a deposit. Make sure the date, times, locations (addresses), and the specific limousine you want are spelled out in writing on your contract. Remember that gratuities are usually additional. If the vehicle is not presentable and the chauffeur isn't professional, you are under no obligation to pay a tip.

- **Many styles of luxury transportation:** Various styles of limousines are available: Presidential stretch, super-stretch, mega-stretch, stretch flagships, and vintage limousines (including Rolls Royces). Luxury vans for transporting wedding party members and guests are also available.

- **Transportation for wedding attendants:** The wedding attendants are usually responsible for providing their own transportation to and from the wedding and reception. Sometimes, however, arrangements are made by the bride and groom. Luxury vans are a convenient way to transport wedding attendants to the ceremony and reception sites and also ensure everyone arrives at once and on time.

- **Many uses for luxury vans:** Vans are also handy for transporting wedding gifts to their designated destination conveniently and safely. You may want to ask a responsible person to be in charge of supervising the moving of gifts to the place they will be stored until you return from your honeymoon. Other uses include carrying decorations, food, and out-of-town guests.

For more assistance with staying organized during the wedding planning process, check out the Bravo! Wedding Organizer. Detailed question worksheets double as contracts. This step-by-step system will keep every detail of your wedding organized. To order, refer to the order form on page 23 in this Guide.

LLC

(503) 244-7758

Have You Thought About Parking?

Let us do the thinking for you…When planning for your wedding day, selecting the right valet service will add a great first impression, as well as smooth, convenient parking accommodations.

Consider the unparalleled level of personalized service and professionalism that Premiere Valet Service, LLC ensures. Superior guest service and responsiveness to our clients' needs are our preeminent themes. From the relaxed, comfortable initial consultation to the graciously assisted departure of your last guest, Premiere Valet Service, LLC will make the impression that you and your guests will notice and appreciate.

With our experience and knowledge, we have the ability to solve any parking problem. Insurance, claim checks, and signs are provided.

Services

- Shuttle vans
- Lot attendants
- Parking consulting services
- Fully insured and licensed

Cost and Terms

Charges start as low as $100, but do vary according to parking circumstances and time duration. Please reserve your event date as far in advance as possible to ensure availability. A deposit of 50% of the total bill is required upon booking. Balance is due the day of the event.

LET PREMIERE VALET SERVICE, LLC
ENHANCE YOUR WEDDING OR EVENT

Premiere Valet Service, LLC has been giving Portland residents and restaurants quality valet service for more than two years. All valets are trained, screened and field tested to ensure that you will receive only the finest service available.

"Parking with a Personal Touch"

Clara's Limousine Service

916 S.E. 29th Ave.
Portland, Oregon 97214
(503) 234-3484
Fax (503) 234-0404

Every Bride Deserves The Best!
We Are Portland's Wedding Limousine Specialists.

Clara's Limousine Service is a division of Clara's Wedding Establishment Ltd. We specialize in providing the best service possible for your wedding day. All of our cars are white stretch Lincoln limousines. We cater to your every need for that special day with:

- Immaculate stretch limousines
- Professional, formally attired drivers
- Complimentary soft drinks
- All of the amenities necessary
- No minimum hours required for weddings

Our Customers Say

- "The end to a perfect wedding!"
- "The service was outstanding… we will recommend you to everyone."
- "The driver went out of her way to give us special treatment."
- "Just perfect."

Make an appointment today
to see one of our limousines?

Call **(503) 234-3484** to reserve a
limousine for your wedding day.

LET CLARA'S LIMOUSINE SERVICE PROVIDE YOUR CHARIOT FOR YOUR DREAM WEDDING!

See page 233 under Bridal Accessories & Attire.
See page 452 under Disc Jockeys.

PORTLAND LIMOUSINE COMPANY

730 N.E. Twenty-First Avenue
Portland, Oregon 97232
(503) 235-2221, (800) 826-1431;
Fax (503) 235-2821
Office Hours:
Mon–Fri 8am–7pm; Sat 10am–3pm

PORTLAND LIMOUSINE COMPANY:
YOUR COMPLETE GROUND TRANSPORTATION COMPANY

Portland Limousine Company has

- Sedans
- Limousines (six, eight and ten passenger)
- Fifteen passenger vans
- Sixteen and Nineteen passenger buses
- 1961 Bentley S2

All of the vehicles from Portland Limousine Company are driven by professionally trained, uniformed chauffeurs. Our limousines have all amenities including televisions, stereos, CD players, halo lighting, VCRs, cellular phones, moon roofs, champagne flutes, crystal glasses, and are stocked with ice. Our limousines and buses will accommodate from one to 19 people depending on vehicle type.

Cost and Terms

Some vehicles have a minimum of only one hour of service. Chargeable time in the Portland tri-county area begins upon arrival and ends at final destination. Various special wedding packages and tours are available. Please call for details.

Additional Information

Portland Limousine Company has provided the finest limousine service since 1983. We pride ourselves on efficient, professional, courteous service. Our trained staff and concierge are available to help plan your wedding event and will help you find those little extras that will make your special day "perfect."

SPECIAL ATTENTION

Portland Limousine Company has the largest fleet of limousines in the area. We have provided special-occasion service since 1983. We pride ourselves on efficient, professional, courteous service.

CALL PORTLAND LIMOUSINE COMPANY FOR
OREGON'S FINEST CHAUFFEURED VEHICLES
(503) 235-2221 OR (800) 826-1431
Web site: http://www.portlandlimousine.com
E-mail: Portlandlimo@juno.com

GOLDEN TIMES CARRIAGE SERVICE

Contact: Duane or Roberta Ogle
(503) 666-4647

Types of Horse-drawn Carriages
- **Vis-à-vis carriage:** single horse; driver; midnight blue; holds four people
- **Enclosed Cinderella coach:** white; team of horses; driver and doorman; holds up to six people; completely upholstered inside the coach

Service Fee
Fees are based on time. Carriage: $200 for up to one and a half hours, $100 for each additional hour. Coach: $300 for up to one and a half hours, $150 for each extra hour. There is an additional charge for transporting carriage/coach if location is outside of Portland area. Gratuities are extra and much appreciated.

Reservations
The carriage or coach should be reserved as soon as possible, especially during the summer months. A deposit is required on both the carriage and coach; $75 and $100 respectively. The deposit is applied to the total charge for the carriage or coach. In case of cancellation the deposit is nonrefundable. Prices are subject to change without notice.

Decorations
The carriage and coach may be decorated, but please, nothing that will damage the finish.

Portland's Oldest Carriage Service
Golden Times Carriage Service has been providing brides and grooms with the most professional and courteous service available for over 14 years.

AN AFFORDABLE REMEMBRANCE
Golden Times Carriage Service—carriage for hire. This is a special form of transportation on a day you will always cherish, an affordable remembrance for any occasion: weddings, birthdays, anniversaries, proms, and special events to make a grand entrance or departure.

MONARCH CARRIAGE CO.
(Formerly The Palmer House Carriage Co.)

P.O. Box 2633
Portland, Oregon 97208
Contact: Mary or Richard
(503) 284-5893, (800) 518-5893
E-mail: marysauter@aol.com

Wedding and Special Event Carriages

- **1895 State Coach** with coachman and two footmen: team of horses; blue watered-silk upholstered interior, five windows. Reportedly part of the British Royal Collection, this carriage has the British Royal Seals on the doors.
- **Landolet** with coachman and footman: team of horses; black with green upholstered interior. This carriage with windows can be totally enclosed or open; previously owned by Warner Brothers and seen in "Pride and Prejudice" with Sir Lawrence Olivier.
- **1880 Victoria:** burgundy; maroon wool upholstery; collapsible bonnet; single horse, seats two passengers; as seen in numerous Hollywood films
- **Vis-a-vis:** black with red velvet upholstery; burgundy undercarriage; collapsible bonnet, stereo system; single horse; driver

Taxi Service and Private Parties

- **Rockaway:** black with green velvet interior upholstery and undercarriage; eight windows provide high visibility and protection from the rain and cold during winter months; single horse; seats four; carried Teddy Roosevelt in Chicago
- **Western surrey:** cherry red with black fringed top; single horse; seats eight passengers
- **Vis-a-vis:** burgundy; red undercarriage; single or pairs; seats four to six passengers

Service Fee

In downtown Portland, rates are based on time and type of vehicle. The fee for a carriage-taxi tour of downtown Portland starts at $75 an hour for two to four people. Wedding carriages start at $250 per hour. Additional charges are based on distance and on the specific requirements necessary to provide both a safe and memorable service. The minimum rental time is one hour in city center and two hours outside the city. Gratuities are not included in rates.

Reservations

To avoid disappointment, we suggest that reservations be made as soon as your date is set. A nonrefundable deposit is required to hold the date.

DISTINCTIVE CARRIAGES
FOR THE DISCRIMINATING CLIENT

Owners Mary and Richard Sauter love horses, carriages and weddings, which is why after 10 years in the carriage business, they decided to specialize in weddings. While only two carriages are on the street at any given time, their fleet expands yearly to provide choices to fit different tastes and budgets. The greatest joy, they say, is being able to provide a remarkable carriage with beautiful horses and appropriately-attired driver and footman for a truly unforgettable event.

Flier, photos and
"How to Shop for a Wedding Carriage"
available upon request.

Notes

THE MARRIAGE SACRAMENT

In many parts of Sicily, Italy, the bride and groom did not take the marriage sacrament until the death of one of them. The reason for this is that until they had lived a life together they were not spiritually bound by the marriage tie.

HELPFUL HINTS

VIDEO SERVICES

- **Why videotape?** Videotaping your wedding or event is a wonderful way to bring the event to life. Extra copies of the wedding or special event make great gifts.

- **A good recommendation:** Store one copy of your video in a safe place. Many times the video is watched so much that it gets worn out or lost in a move. In years to come you will want to share your wedding day with your children.

- **Why hire a professional?** There are many reasons why it is important to hire a professional. They have the technical equipment and skills such as editing and sound variations to create a professional video. Ask what kind of equipment they have. Take the time to view video samples from other events they have done; it will be worth your time. Check the background of the company or individual; have they been professionally trained or are they self-taught?

  Don't take the chance of letting an amateur practice his or her video skills at your event. Your video might be out of focus, the shots will be all wrong, or it will be too dark. This is not to say that you can't have a friend or family member videotape, but just remember—there's only one chance to get it right.

- **Research the different packages:** Packages that offer two video cameras provide different perspectives. With only one camera, you can't tape the processional and get to the altar in time to set up and catch those special close-up shots. Two camera locations offer different views of the wedding that can be edited down using only the best shots. Many brides and grooms comment after the wedding is over, "the day went so fast, it was just a blur." A videotape can put the whole day back into focus. **NOTE:** You'll also want to coordinate their needs with those of your photographer to avoid confusion or bad feelings on the wedding day.

- **Traditions first, then have fun!:** After the meal, go right to the cake cutting, then immediately to the first dance, followed by throwing the bouquet and garter, etc. If these events are moved through one after another, then all the traditional duties will be done and the fun can begin. This way you will only need your photographer and video person for one to two hours at the reception instead of three to four.

- **Pay by the hour or the special package:** Figure out the prices for both hourly and special package rates. You may pay just as much with a package, and with hourly you might be able to custom design a package that better suits your needs.

- **What you ask is what you get:** Be sure to communicate with your video person what you expect your video to be like. Sentimental, glittery, romantic, story, interview style. Ask to view some different styles of videos he/she has done.

- **Interviewing guests:** A fun suggestion is to interview guests at the event or reception. It's enjoyable to hear what people have to say, and provides entertainment for the guests as well.

- **Low lighting:** The low light level of a candlelight ceremony makes it difficult for your videographer to work. He or she may need to bring in extra lights that could cancel out the candlelight atmosphere you were seeking. Be sure you discuss the lighting needs well in advance so everything meets your satisfaction.

For more assistance with staying organized during the wedding planning process, check out the Bravo! Wedding Organizer. Detailed question worksheets double as contracts. This step-by-step system will keep every detail of your wedding organized. To order, refer to the order form on page 23 in this Guide.

A VIDEO REFLECTION

Serving East, West and Vancouver Areas
Contact: John or Kris
(503) 631-7054

Description of Video Service

When you call A Video Reflection you will not hear a big sales pitch! What you will receive is a free wedding demo tape with all the information first. We want you to view our quality and style in your own home, on your own television. We let our video work from previous weddings speak for itself on our demo. Isn't the sight, sound, and most of all, the quality in a wedding video what you are really shopping for and not just talk? You then can make an appointment and meet with us or just call and we will answer any questions you might have. Being in the business seven years, we know how to create on film one of the most important days of your life. Call now for your free wedding demo tape and money saving specials.

Equipment Options and Techniques

- One or two professional videographers, depending on your package.
- Always two to three broadcast-quality cameras taping your ceremony.
- A professional diversity lapel microphone on groom for superb audio.
- Post-production editing in our studio, using computer graphics and special effects to polish off your wedding video.
- We try to attend every rehearsal to see how your ceremony will be performed.

Five Wedding Packages and Prices to Choose From

- **Corsage Package:** four hours, one videographer, two-camera ceremony coverage, plus your reception. **$699**
- **Bouquet Package:** six hours, one videographer, two-camera ceremony coverage, plus your reception. **$799**
- **Bridal Guide Package:** six hours, two videographers, two-camera ceremony coverage, plus your reception. **$899**
- **Black Tie Package:** seven hours, two videographers, two to three-camera ceremony coverage, plus your reception. **$999**
- **The Ultimate Wedding Day Package:** eight hour all-day wedding coverage, two videographers, three-camera ceremony coverage, plus two videographers at your reception. **$1,099**

Reservations

A $200 deposit is required at the time of booking with the balance due two weeks prior to the wedding. Visa or MasterCard are gladly accepted.

LOOK FIRST FOR THE VERY BEST QUALITY!
SECOND—THE BEST PRICE YOU CAN AFFORD.
WHY?...

Because when you watch your wedding video, price will no longer be the issue or concern, but the **quality** and **professionalism** of your tape will mean everything to you. First shop quality then shop price! **Call now for your free wedding demo tape and money saving specials. (503) 631-7054.**

Keith Aden
PHOTOGRAPHY &
VIDEO PRODUCTIONS

1613 SE 7th Avenue • Portland, Oregon 97214

503 230-0325

Web Addresses:
www.bravowedding.com/pdxkeithadenphoto
www.bravowedding.com/pdxkeithadenvideo
www.bravoevent.com/pdxkeithaden

Since 1968, Keith Aden Photography has been specializing in wedding photography. Our professional and unobtrusive style bends perfectly with even the most elegant of weddings. We feel that you are the most important part of the wedding and therefore we listen very carefully to your wants and needs. Every wedding is unique and must be recorded in a way that reflects your personality, not ours!

Equipment
We use professional 3-chip SVHS stereo Hi-Fi cameras with 700 lines of resolution for quality that surpasses most home video playback equipment, at 240 lines of resolution, even after editing and duplication. Also, we use wireless remote microphones for superb sound. In one plan we offer two-camera coverage of the ceremony and digital non-linear studio editing with special effects. In the edited versions we can include childhood, engagement, wedding, and honeymoon photographs, titles, music and interviews with family and friends.

Personalized Wedding Coverage
- **Basic coverage:** Four-hour coverage, one S-VHS camera, radio microphones, field editing, one VHS tape. **$525**
- **Standard coverage:** Four-hour coverage, one S-VHS camera, radio microphones, studio editing, one VHS tape. **$675**
- **Custom coverage:** Unlimited coverage, one S-VHS camera, radio microphones, studio editing, one VHS tape. **$825**
- **Masterpiece coverage:** Unlimited coverage, two S-VHS cameras/one videographer, radio microphones, digital non-linear studio editing, three VHS tapes. **$975**

Reservations and Overtime
You should make your reservation right away. Six months or more in advance would be wise during the peak summer season. A deposit of $100 will hold your date and the balance is due 10 days before the wedding. Duplicate VHS tapes are $25. Additional coverage time is $75 per hour. Corporate events, conventions, industrial, business, educational, and other special events by quotation, based on your specific needs. Discover, Visa or Mastercard accepted.

SOMEONE WHO CARES
Your choice of a videographer is an important one. It takes a special person who is sensitive enough to capture the emotion of the day, someone experienced in the very special art of wedding videography. In short, someone who actually cares about you and your wedding.

ASPEN PHOTOGRAPHY & VIDEO STUDIO

14120 S.W. Stallion Drive
Beaverton, Oregon 97008
Contact: Gregg and Lee Ann Childs
(503) 524-8230
Business Hours: by appointment

Selecting a Professional Wedding Videographer

Selecting a professional videographer for your wedding is a very difficult adventure. There are several factors to consider: 1) you want a professional that is an artist and enjoys what he/she is doing; 2) you want someone who is very personable, someone that can blend in with you and your guests; 3) yet you want someone who will be discreet and not attract attention; 4) you want a studio that uses top-of-the-line equipment; and 5) you want an editor that is sensitive and artistic.

Exceeding Your Expectations

Many brides and grooms, their families, and their friends have told us that Aspen Video & Photography meets and exceeds all these factors. We are professional videographers by trade and by training. And we go one big step further than all other video studios: we are also professional photographers. We have been professional wedding photographers and videographers in the Portland area for over 15 years. In fact, we are the only professional photographers who are also professional videographers in the metro area. The artistic lighting and composition talents we have developed as photographers transfer very well to the medium of video.

Experience

We are experienced with the needs and desires of brides and grooms, of families, and of friends. The experiences gained at over 600 weddings make us one of the best wedding service providers in the area.

Wedding Package

Our wedding package is awesome: edited highlights of wedding/reception, growing-up pictures with music, two-camera coverage at wedding and reception, honeymoon pictures, all with sensitive and artistic editing. Price: $795.

Please come and meet us, see our portfolios, and ask for references. We love working weddings, and our results show it.

"Your video of our wedding has been edited in a very sensitive manner. Thanks for your artistic touch." L.Z. — 1993

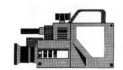 *Creative Video Productions*

3827 S.W. Hall Boulevard
Beaverton, Oregon 97005
Contact: Randy Stumman (503) 524-1780
Web site: http://www.cvpvideo.com

Premier Video Production Company

Creative Video Productions is a premier video production company. We will produce for you a grand and elegant wedding video that will amaze and astound you and your family. Our wedding productions rival the high standards and extreme perfection of broadcast television. We will bring our television commercial expertise and industrial equipment department on location to your ceremony and reception locations thus bringing to you the very finest in wedding picture quality and special effects. And doing all this in a way that our clients find incredibly unobtrusive. Then back in the studio, our editing department—utilizing only frame accurate computerized editing equipment complete with computer graphics, 3D motion animations and television graphic composer titling—will develop a wedding production that will leave you wanting to watch your wedding over and over again.

Production Tools

Ceremony: *Creative Video Productions* will use only industrial broadcast 3 Chip SVHS cameras producing over 750 lines of resolutions, multiple wireless microphones to capture all the audio, completely manned cameras with professional tripods for stability, 4 point star filters and Motorola 2-way communicators for planning truly unique videotaping.

Studio: *Creative Video Productions* utilizes computer editing, computer graphic programs, computer 3D animation, television graphics composers, computer non-linear editing, frame accurate editing, music composition capabilities, only Betacam SP mastering, digital transitions and Hollywood type special effects.

Production Prices

Bridal Production: ceremony and reception coverage, up to 4 hours—1 camera, 3D motion titling, slo-motion effects, interviews of guests and 3 copies **$675**

Ceremonial Production: complete coverage using up to 5 hours—2 cameras, all of the above plus photo montage, digital transitions, 4 point star filter, split screen effects, , 6—3D motion titles and more **$985**

Grand Elegance Production: wedding coverage up to 6 hours—2 cameras, includes all of the effects and editing from the first two productions, picture in picture effects, 60% digital transitional effects, 9—3D motion titles and more **$1,175**

Supreme Royale Production: all-day coverage, 2 cameras, includes all the effects and editing from the first three productions, plus TV graphics titling, unlimited music selections, leather type cassette case, special cleaning process of photos, non-linear editing, custom 3D titling using your names, engagement re-enactment, video analyzed and adjusted with vectorscope and waveform monitor, SHG 5 tape copies all in custom cases, 80% digital transitional effects, 3 stage morphing, 30 minute highlite tape, complete animated titling of all events and more **$1,895**

Creative Video Productions will help guide you through the video production process to ensure you acquire the highest quality wedding video on the market today. We have a price for all budgets but only 1 high level of quality. Call today for an appointment and then stop by for our free demo copy and a "no-hassle" exploration to see how *Creative Video Productions* can turn the most important day of your life into a loving and lasting memory.

VISA — MASTERCARD — WEVA MEMBER

ENCORE
S T U D I O S

Portland, Oregon
(503) 255-8047
E-mail: Encore@ethergate.com
Web site:
http://www.bravowedding.com/pdxencore-video

◆ Photography ◆ Videography ◆ Music

Our video professionals will help you create those precious moments to be cherished forever on film. Encore Studios offers a wide selection of packages designed to fit your special needs and budget. With over 19 years of video experience, we are one of the video pioneers, and since most of our work is from *personal* referrals, we are proud of our history.

Videography Packages and Prices

Videography takes you where no still camera can, capturing those special moments before, during, and after your ceremony, as well as at your reception, allowing you to relive them over and over again. Our videographers are courteous and subtle in their approach, making your day most enjoyable. Video packages include consultation, professional videographer time, travel time and studio editing. Options available include:

- History of bride and groom
- Pre-ceremony events
- Personal messages
- Cordless microphones
- Entire ceremony
- Entire reception
- Special digital effects
- Montages and music

Special Video Services

- Engagement scenic video
- Multiple camera angles
- Engagement party video
- Multiple locations
- Rehearsal dinner video
- Tape duplication

Description of Services and Equipment

We utilize Hi-8, Betacam SP, and S-VHS formats for ultimate picture quality; our equipment enables us to shoot even candlelight ceremonies without lighting. We also use wireless remote microphones for superior sound quality, especially during your ceremony. Our edit suite features complete editing services with music selections from all styles and eras, since we are a disc jockey service as well and have an extensive music library. Special effects include digital as well as studio audio dubbing and mixing. We welcome inclusion of photographs, invitations, programs, and other personalized memorabilia for your wedding video.

Among our professional services we offer photography as well as music (disc jockey and live entertainment). Call Encore Studios today for more information and assistance. Consultants are available any time by appointment.

See page 441 under Disc Jockeys.
See page 490 under Photographers.

VIDEO PRODUCTIONS

2580 N.W. Upshur Street
Portland, Oregon 97210
Contact: Eric Newland
(503) 295-1991 or (360) 993-1991
Web site: http://www.hybridmoon.com

What is so Different about Hybrid Moon?

We are the experts in helping you tell the story of the most important day of your life. We work with you to create a customized video production you will cherish forever. Our equipment is top-notch and our production team is second-to-none. Hybrid Moon was recently awarded a coveted 1998 Videographers Award of Excellence. But to us, every wedding video we produce is an award-winner. Our demo reel speaks for itself.

Program Features...

Our wedding video programs include coverage of the ceremony and reception with up to three video cameras. We will capture every special moment of your wedding day from the pre-ceremony activities to the bon voyage send off.

Hybrid Moon Video also features unique video services to help you tell your special story.

- **Photos-n-Motion:** a creative combination of your memorable photos and music.
- **Engagement Sitting:** an ensemble of special moments to create a living portfolio of your special relationship together.
- **Ceremony Switched Live:** when it comes to recording every thrilling moment of the ceremony, we don't miss a beat!
- **Male/Female Camera Crews:** we capture all the excitement and anticipation leading up to the main event!
- **Candid Interview:** a personalized interview that you will never forget.
- **Reception Projection:** a heart-warming production of your love story presented on a big screen during your reception.
- **Full Production Package:** we combine your wedding video with sound, music, graphics, titles, and EFX to create a finished product you will enjoy watching for years to come!

Hybrid Moon Video allows you to tell your own unique story in a way that will perfectly describe the excitement and rush of emotions during this once in a lifetime event. Catering to individual needs and styles is what we do best! Call us today and let us help you design your special video. When you see what we can do, you'll agree: *there's nothing like Hybrid Moon!*

Discover the Hybrid Moon advantage
(360) 993-1991 or (503) 295-1991

KTVA Productions

P.O. Box 22911
Milwaukie, Oregon 97269
(503) 659-4417, (800) 282-KTVA
Fax (503) 659-4438
Web site: www.ktvavideo.com
E-mail: sales@ktvavideo.com

YOU WON'T REMEMBER US!

You will cherish our award-winning work, though. We will not intrude upon the sanctity of your wedding with a grand production. We specialize in discretely preserving memories.

- **Wedding Memories Standard Package ($699).** Romantically edited, we capture the grand celebration of your union with up to six hours of coverage. All of the distinctive and carefully planned details of your ceremony and reception, the cherished thoughts and wishes of your guests, and of course the great fun, are now forever preserved.
- **Plus Package ($849).** Enhance your wedding day keepsake with a beautiful love story, artistically created from your childhood photographs, wedding day moments and personal music selections. Tasteful special effects and closing wedding party scroll complete this entertaining, yet respectful record of your day.
- **Classic Package ($999).** Compliment the Plus package with a second camera's vantage point of your ceremony, a heart-touching wedding vow reminiscence, one additional videotape and one 8"x10" videoprint. Our most popular package!
- **Ultimate Package ($1,699).** Embellish our Classic package with three cameras recording your ceremony, two professional videographers and up to eight full hours of coverage, capturing your very special day from start to finish. You receive four videotapes in handsome leather cases and two full-color 8"x10" videoprints.

All videography services include well-maintained primary and reserve equipment, appropriate attire, cooperative style and at least two videotapes. Should your reception be at a location different from that of your ceremony, please add $35.

- **Screening Party ($499)**. A most memorable evening awaits you at the classically romantic Mallory Hotel (near downtown Portland). This carefree, yet elegant celebration includes food and beverages for twenty people (no-host bar available). *Relive the memory* of your special day, surrounded by loved ones as you enjoy the premiere of your videotape, presented in movie theater style!
- **Bridal Gift Registry.** This traditional service, offered at no additional cost, provides your friends and family an opportunity to support the preservation of your wedding day (the perfect gift).

Just a $100 deposit holds your date. Our overtime rate is $75 per hour. We are one of the few full-time video production companies in the Portland/Vancouver area. We are members of the Portland Oregon Visitors Association (POVA), the Wedding and Event Videographers Association (WEVA) and the Gala Events Group, Inc. We are on the board of directors for the Association of Catering and Event Professionals (ACEP) and the Portland chapter of the International Television Association (ITVA). We are very serious about our commitment to you and our industry, but we still have fun!

"We love our work and so will you."

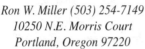

Ron W. Miller (503) 254-7149
10250 N.E. Morris Court
Portland, Oregon 97220

Description of Video Service

We will be there from start to finish. Final edited tapes average two hours in length. We pride ourselves on providing you with the highest quality wedding-video services available. We are experts in lighting, sound, and camera locations. Knowing where to be at the right time and having the creativity to make it special are where we excel. We are well versed in wedding etiquette and will blend in with your special occasion. Cheerful, courteous, and creative, we will take care of your memories. Your wedding video will be one you will cherish as a masterpiece forever.

Options and Techniques

- **440 lines of resolution:** using the Hi-8 Hi-Fi, stereo format—the "high resolution" tape that gives you the best possible picture and sound
- **Wireless microphones:** you have to hear the vows as well as see them
- **Studio editing special effects:** slow motion, multi-screen, mosaic, titling, strobe, paint solarization, audio dub. We incorporate your favorite songs, childhood pictures, and honeymoon shots into the final edited tape. A summary tape is also available.
- **Live to live dissolve** edits between two cameras for that professional touch.
- **Over 100 samples** can be viewed in the studio.
- **List of references** gladly supplied upon request.

Packages and Price Range

All editing is free and included in the package price. No extra charges.

- **$850**: Hi-8 and Super-VHS format, single camera, studio editing, one master SVHS edited tape, plus one VHS edited copy
- **$1,050**: Hi-8 and Super-VHS format, two cameras, studio editing, one master SVHS edited tape, plus one VHS edited copy
- **Copies:** $25 for edited tapes   • Rehearsal: $50   • Summary Video: $100
- **Deposit:** $150 required at the time of booking

Grand Prize Winner of the 1995 Wedding Video Competition at the MBA National Wedding Videographers Convention, held at the MGM Grand Hotel in Las Vegas, Nevada.

MEDIA F/X

VIDEO PRODUCTION

4584 SW 103RD AVENUE
BEAVERTON, OR 97005-3208

TEL (503) 646-9884
FAX (503) 245-1011

What Media F/X Can Offer You

Quality. Media FX makes quality our number one emphasis for your wedding video. We have over 15 years of experience shooting professional video, and we know what to look for. We capture all the details that you have worked hard putting into your wedding. But don't just take our word for it. We recommend that you look at our wedding demo, and also the demos other wedding videographers. Compare and see the difference. References gladly provided.

Tools of the Trade

Media FX utilizes the newest state-of-the-art, mini-digital video equipment. These cameras are professional broadcast-quality originally designed for commercial TV and news applications. We use UHF wireless microphones, and we edit on a non-linear editing system, originally designed to meet the needs of corporate and commercial clients. We master your wedding to DV-CAM, one of the newest high-definition digital video formats.

Packages and Prices

- The **Golden** package features four hours of single camera videography, complete with editing, 3-D animation and titles, twenty of your photographs converted to video stills and set to music, coverage of events at the reception and interviews with your guests, plus three copies in deluxe cases. Saturday price — **$695**
- The **Enchantment** package has all the features of the Golden, and more. You get six hours of coverage, with two cameras at the ceremony, and one at the reception. Forty photographs of your choice are set to music. Saturday price — **$995**
- The **Elegant** package adds to the Enchantment, providing you with seven hours of coverage, with two cameras at both the ceremony and the reception. Sixty photographs are included, as is a special wedding highlights sequence and video of your photo shoot.
  Saturday price — **$1,195**
- The **Royal** is our premier package, including all the features of our other packages, plus three days of videography. Day One we do a four hour shoot of your engagement/love story, edit it and then we show at your reception. Day Two we provide three hours of single camera coverage at the rehearsal or rehearsal dinner, then eight hours of coverage on the day of the wedding, with three cameras at the ceremony, and two at the reception. Eighty photographs are included, and your wedding is presented as a two-volume set, with a copy for you and for each pair of parents, all in deluxe cases. Saturday price — **$2,495**

Reservations

We offer discounts for off-peak bookings, and provide an array of other options and services. We require 1/3 the total cost of the package as a deposit at the time you make your reservation, with the remainder due at the rehearsal.

PRO 2000
VIDEO PRODUCTIONS
Boring, Oregon
Phone/Fax (503) 668-5140

E-mail: pro2000videopro@webtv.net

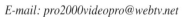

Your Wedding Video
Let Us Capture The Magic

A Bride's Dream Come True
We bring over 25 years of wedding experience to your special day… we are a husband and wife team who worked together for 20 years as wedding photographers and, since 1993, as wedding videographers. Weddings are our life! We will see your wedding through an artist's eye and the heart of a romanticist. The result is a masterpiece to be treasured the rest of your life. We are often told, by brides of yesteryear, that the emotions we captured, continue to touch their heart.

Equipment
We bring professional Super VHS and Digital cameras to record your special day. Very importantly, we also bring backup components and equipment to cover equipment failure. We use wireless remote microphones to record every word in superb high-quality audio. Always three cameras at your ceremony! Our professional cameras allow us to record your ceremony without adding glaring bright lights.

Post-Production
Our total attention is given to editing your wedding video in the days following your special day. The emotion of the day is still with us as we plan the editing and share our ideas for a personalized and unique wedding story. We include computer graphics, special effects, wipes, swipes, dissolves, scrolling, wedding and reception invitations, wedding program, reception scroll and any other special printed wedding or reception material.

Price
Full coverage: $675. No extra charges. Reserve your wedding date with a nonrefundable deposit of $250. Balance is due by your wedding date.

Optional Features
Duplicate video copies ordered and paid prior to wedding: $25 each. Copies ordered after delivery of edited videos: $30 each. Rehearsal coverage: $50. Rehearsal dinner coverage: $50.

"Pathways to A Love Story"
A 20-minute photo video for presentation at the rehearsal dinner, wedding ceremony or reception. Comprised of childhood photos, courtship and engagement photos, complete with computer graphics, special effects and music: $175.

Other Services
Bar/Bat Mitzvahs, anniversary receptions, family reunions, birthday celebrations, awards banquets… other special occasions.

"Through the music of our marriage, we will, together, wander through time."

ROYAL VIDEO AND ELECTRONICS

Formerly Computer Graphics Unlimited

224 Northridge Court, N.
Keizer, Oregon 97303
Contact: Wes Jensen
(503) 390-4220 or (800) 290-6584 PIN #4602
Web site: http://www2.ncn.com/~wesj
Business Hours: by appointment

Description of Video Service

Video for all special occasions; specializing in wedding photography, editing and copying service. Providing service since 1987.

Options and Techniques

- Hi-8 format for best picture quality
- Non-linear editing with dazzling 3-D transitions and digital effects
- True diversity; wireless mic available; direct connect to sound system when possible
- Studio editing providing special effects (as appropriate) such as mosaics, dissolves, paint, titles, slow motion and more
- Studio audio mixing to add music for viewing pleasure
- Tape copies available on VHS, or 8mm, S-VHS, or Hi-8 on request

Packages and Price Range

- **#1–$350:** Includes titles (scrolling names of everyone in wedding party), pre-ceremony family group pictures, ceremony, and reception. Still pictures such as engagement or baby pictures can be incorporated into your final video. A six minute "short" of entire video is standard. Music added in the studio for your viewing pleasure. Price includes three copies. The "edit master" is kept in my library for making additional copies on request, but can be purchased for $25. Additional copies may be purchased for $15 each.
- **#2–$520:** Two cameras and two camera operators, providing two angles for better coverage.
- **Ask about** other multi-camera options.
- **Additional cost:** Add $50 for tapings outside of Salem/Keizer area.

Reservations

Many weddings are booked six months in advance. Book your wedding early to reserve your date. A deposit of 50% is required at the time of booking, with the balance due on your wedding day.

RELIVE THE SIGHTS AND SOUNDS OF YOUR WEDDING DAY!

Sit back and relax with friends and relatives, and watch the beauty and excitement of your wedding unfold. See pictures and hear comments from your friends and relatives wishing you a life of happiness together.

What some of them are saying . . .

"We watch the tape every couple of weeks. It brings back so many fond memories."

"We watched the tape on our anniversary, and cried as we relived our day."

"Very professional . . ."

Notes

TRADITION

To symbolize family unity, three

candles are lit: first the bride's

parents light the candle on the

right, then the groom's parents

light the candle on the left, and

finally, the bride and groom

light the third candle, called the

unity candle, from the flames of

the other two candles.

ADDRESS	CAPACITY	CONTACT
Agnes Flanagan Chapel Lewis & Clark College 0615 S.W. Palatine Hill Rd. Portland, OR 97219-7899	Indoor: Up to 600 W/	Emi Jean Sakamoto (503) 768-7085 Fax (503) 768-7084
Albertina Kerr Centers' **Hood Memorial Chapel** 722 N.E. 162nd Portland, OR 97230 *See page 318*	Chapel: Up to 180 Fireside Room: Up to 55 W/M/S/	Chaplain Lee Lower (503) 255-4205
Atkinson Memorial 710 Sixth St. Oregon City, OR 97045	Ceremony: Up to 225 Reception: Up to 180 W/R/	Church Secretary (503) 66-7296
Baker Cabin Pioneer Church Corner Hattan & Gronlund Rd. Oregon City, OR 97045	Up to 90 W/R/ (outdoor)	Reservations Secretary (503) 631-8274
Beaverton Christian Church 13600 S.W. Allen Blvd. Beaverton, OR 97005	Chapel: 185 Worship Center: 1,400 W/R/	Rose (503) 646-2151 Fax (503) 627-0780
Canby Pioneer Chapel N.W. Third & Elm Canby, OR 97013 *See page 319*	Up to 120 W/	Darlene Key (503) 263-6126
Canterbury Falls **& English Gardens** P.O. Box 156 Molalla, OR 97038 *See page 114*	Outdoor: Up to 400 W/R/B/M/P/	Judy Hall (503) 829-8821
The Carus House **Wedding Chapel** 23200 S. Highway 213 Oregon City, OR 97045 *See page 320*	Up to 125 seated W/R/B/	Wedding Coordinator (503) 631-7078
Christian Life Church 9215 S.E. Church St. Clackamas, OR 97015 *See page 320*	Up to 120 W/R/	Wedding Coordinator (503) 655-1224
Crystal Springs **Rhododendron Garden** S.E. 28th & Hawthorne Portland, OR 97215 *See page 126*	Up to 150 W/R/P/	Event Coordinator (503) 256-2483
First Christian Church 1315 S.W. Broadway Portland, OR 97201	Up to 300 W/R/	Dorothy Pearce (503) 228-9211 Fax (503) 222-1313
First Congregational Church 1126 S.W. Park Ave. Portland, OR 97205 *See page 321*	Ceremony: 40-850 W/	Church Office (503) 228-7219

W=Wedding Ceremony   R=Reception   B=Banquet   S=Seminar   M=Meeting   P=Picnic

Please let these businesses know that you heard about them from the Bravo! Bridal Resource Guide.

PORTLAND AREA
CEREMONY SITE LISTINGS

ADDRESS	CAPACITY	CONTACT
First Pentacostal Church of God 6030 S.E. 136th Ave. Portland, OR 97236	Up to 175 W/R/S/M/	Rev. Lawrence Haddock (503) 761-1491
Gray Gables Estate 3009 S.E. Chestnut Milwaukie, OR 97222 *See page 144*	Indoor/Outdoor: Up to 275 W/R/B/S/M/P/	(503) 654-0470
The Grotto Catholic Church Sandy at N.E. 85th Portland, OR 97294	Indoor: up to 450 Outdoor: up to 700 *bride or groom must be a practicing Catholic and registered in a parish W/	Sr. Ruth Arnott (503) 254-7371
The Grove at Oaks Amusement Park Portland, OR 97202 *See page 322*	Up to 450 W/R/P/	Volanne Stephens (503) 233-5777
Hillsdale Community Church 6948 S.W. Capitol Hwy. Portland, OR 97219	Ceremony: Up to 325 Reception: Up to 325 W/R/B/	Secretary Day (503) 246-5474 Evening (503) 245-2960
McLean House 5350 River St. West Linn, Oregon 97068 *See page 322*	Indoor/Outdoor: Up to 100 W/R/B/S/M/P/	(503) 655-4268
Meridian United Church of Christ 6750 S.W. Boeckman Rd. Wilsonville, OR 97070	Up to 100 W/R/	Joyce Liden (503) 682-0339 Fax (503) 682-0339
New Hope Community Church 11731 S.E. Stevens Rd. Portland, OR 97226	Ceremony: Up to 2,500 Reception: Up to 500 W/R/B/S/M/	Gloria Leslie (503) 698-5095 or (503) 659-5683
Oaks Pioneer Church 455 S.E. Spokane St. Portland, OR 97202 *See page 323*	Up to 75 W/	Manager (503) 233-1497
The Old Church 1422 S.W. 11th Ave. Portland, OR 97201 *See page 323*	Ceremony: 300 Reception: 200 W/R/	Wedding Coordinator (503) 222-2031
Old Laurelhurst Church 3212 S.E. Ankeny Portland, OR 97214 *See page 317*	Ceremony: Up to 650 W/R/M/	Deborra Buckler (503) 231-0462
Open Bible Church 3223 S.E. 92nd Portland, OR 97266	Up to 300 W/R/	Wedding Coordinator (503) 775-1565

W=Wedding Ceremony   R=Reception   B=Banquet   S=Seminar   M=Meeting   P=Picnic

Please let these businesses know that you heard about them from the Bravo! Bridal Resource Guide.   **551**

PORTLAND AREA
CEREMONY SITE LISTINGS

ADDRESS	CAPACITY	CONTACT
The Quello House 16445 S.W. 92nd Ave. Tigard, OR 97224 *See page 324*	Up to 200 W/R/B/P/	Dan or Jacque Quello (503) 684-5456
Rivercrest Community Church 3201 N.E. 148th Portland, OR 97230	Ceremony: 300 Reception: 200 W/R/	Office (503) 254-4400 or (503) 661-3767
Scottish Rite Center 709 S.W. 15th Ave. Portland, OR 97205	Ceremony: up to 700 Reception: up to 400 W/R/B/S/M/	Bill Stanger (503) 226-7827
St. James Lutheran 1315 S.W. Park Portland, OR 97201	Up to 350 Small receptions W/	Pastor Smith (503) 227-2439
St. Mark Presbyterian 9750 S.W. Terwilliger Blvd. Portland, OR 97219	Up to 150 W/	Rev. David Lee (503) 244-8177
Sunnyside Centenary United Methodist Church 3520 S.E. Yamhill Portland, OR 97213	Up to 350 W/R/	(503) 235-8726
Tallina's Gardens & Conservatory 15790 S.E. Hwy 224 Clackamas, OR 97015 *See page 199*	Rose Garden: 200 Conservatory: 160 W/R/B/M/P/	Tallina or Tina (503) 658-6148
Tigard United Methodist 9845 S.W. Walnut Pl. Tigard, OR 97223 *See page 324*	Ceremony: Up to 500 seated Reception: Up to 400 R/B/M/	Pastor Wesley Taylor (503) 639-3181
Thunder Island at Cascade Locks Cascade Locks Marine Park Cascade Locks, OR 97014	Outdoor: Up to 4,000 Covered: Up to 400 W/R/B/M/P/	The Cascade Sternwheelers (503) 223-3928 Fax (503) 223-4013
Unity of Beaverton 12650 S.W. Fifth St. Beaverton, OR 97005 *See page 325*	Up to 140 W/	Wedding Coordinator (503) 646-3364
The Wedding House 2715 S.E. 39th St. Portland, OR 97202 *See page 204*	Ceremony: Up to 100 Reception: Up to 150 W/R/B/S/M/	Owner (503) 236-7353
YWCA 8010 N. Chalrleston St. Portland, OR 97203	Fireplace Rm: Up to 50 Auditorium: Up to 200 W/R/B/M/	Outreach Coordinator (503) 721-6777

W=Wedding Ceremony   R=Reception   B=Banquet   S=Seminar   M=Meeting   P=Picnic

ADDRESS	CAPACITY	GUEST ROOMS	CONTACT
ALOHA			
Aloha Odd Fellows Hall 3670 S.W. 185th Ave. Aloha, OR 97007	Up to 100 W/R/B/S/M/		Rental Manager (503) 292-3988
Jenkins Estate 8005 S.W. Grabhorn Rd. Aloha, OR 97007	Indoor: Up to 125 Outdoor: Up to 22 W/R/B/S/M/P/		Program Coordinator (503) 642-3855 Fax (503) 591-1028
The Keg Restaurant 18875 S.W. TV Hwy. Aloha, OR 97006	Up to 35 R/B/S/M/		Manager (503) 649-2092
The Reserve Vineyard & Golf Club 4747 S.W. 229th Ave. Aloha, OR 97007	Up to 175 W/R/B/M		Dennen Van Wegner (503) 649-2345
AURORA			
Aurora Colony Historical Society 21581 Main St., N.E. Aurora, OR 97002	Indoor/Outdoor: Up to 150 W/R/B/P/		Dan McElhinny (503) 678-1629 (503) 678-5754
Willamette Gables 10323 Schuler Rd. Aurora, OR 97002 *See page 206*	Outdoor: Up to 200 W/R/B/P/		Laurel Cookman (503) 678-2195
BEAVERTON			
Beaverton Community Center 12350 S.W. Fifth St. Beaverton, OR 97006	Small room: Up to 35 Large room: Up to 140 R/B/M/S/P/		(503) 526-2648
Chevys 8400 S.W. Nimbus Ave. Beaverton, OR 97005	Reception: Up to 75 R/B/M/		General Manager (503) 626-7667
Elsie J. Stuhr Adult Leisure Center 5550 S.W. Hall Blvd. Beaverton, OR 97005	Sit-down: Up to 150 Reception: Up to 200 *No alcohol W/R/B/S/M/		Center Supervisor (503) 643-9434
Elmer's Pancake & Steak House 3455 S.W. Cedar Hills Blvd. Beaverton, OR 97005	Up to 80 R/B/		Banquet Coordinator (503) 641-3455
The Greenwood Inn 10700 S.W. Allen Blvd. Beaverton, OR 97005 *See page 146*	Up to 500 W/R/B/S/M/	250	Catering Office (503) 643-7444 Ext. 726 or 727

W=Wedding Ceremony   R=Reception   B=Banquet   S=Seminar   M=Meeting   P=Picnic

Please let these businesses know that you heard about them from the Bravo! Bridal Resource Guide.

PORTLAND AREA
BANQUET SITE LISTINGS

ADDRESS	CAPACITY	GUEST ROOMS	CONTACT
Griffith Park Athletic Club 4925 S.W. Griffith Dr. Beaverton, OR 97005	Reception: Up to 300 R		Manager (503) 644-3900
Hall Street Bar & Grill 3775 S.W. Hall Blvd. Beaverton, OR 97005	Up to 40 W/B/M/		(503) 641-6161
McCormick & Schmick's Fishhouse & Bar 9945 S.W. Beaverton-Hillsdale Hwy. Beaverton, OR 97005	Up to 35 W/R/B/S/M/		General Manager (503) 643-1322
McMenamins— Cedar Hills 2927 S.W. Cedar Hills Blvd. Beaverton, OR 97005	Sit-down: Up to 64 Patio: Up to 48 R/B/M/		Management Team (503) 641-0151
Red Robin 4105 S.W. 117th Beaverton, OR 97005	Up to 75 R/B/M/		Manager (503) 641-3784 Fax (503) 626-1899
Sayler's Old Country Kitchen 4655 S.W. Griffith Dr. Beaverton, OR 97005 *See page 82*	Capacity: 10–300 R/B/M/		Sally Kanan (503) 644-1492 or (503) 252-4171
Stockpot Restaurant & Catering Co. 8200 S.W. Scholls Ferry Rd. Beaverton, OR 97005 *See page 197*	Indoor: Up to 350 Outdoor: Up to 600 W/R/B/S/M/P/		Gary (503) 643-5451 Fax (503) 641-3265

BRIDAL VEIL/CORBETT

ADDRESS	CAPACITY	GUEST ROOMS	CONTACT
Bridal Veil Lakes P.O. Box 5 Bridal Veil, OR 97010 *See page 111*	Indoor: Up to 150 Outdoor: Up to 1,000 W/R/B/M/S/		Jennifer Miller (503) 981-3695 (503) 982-0944
The Viewpoint Inn 40301 E. Larch Mountain Rd. Corbett, OR 97019 *See page 203*	Sit-down: 140 Reception: 160 Outdoor: Up to 350 W/R/M/S/	4	Geoff Thompson (503) 695-3256

CLACKAMAS

ADDRESS	CAPACITY	GUEST ROOMS	CONTACT
Clackamas Armory 10101 S.E. Clackamas Rd. Clackamas, OR 97015	Reception: Up to 750 Sit-down: Up to 450 W/R/S/M/B/		Facility Manager (503) 557-5368
Clackamas Community Club Dow Center 15711 S.E. 90th Ave. Clackamas, OR 97015	Sit-down: Up to 110 Reception: Up to 150 W/R/B/S/M/		Director (503) 653-7432

W=Wedding Ceremony   R=Reception   B=Banquet   S=Seminar   M=Meeting   P=Picnic

ADDRESS	CAPACITY	GUEST ROOMS	CONTACT
Clackamas County Fair & Event Center 694 N.E. Fourth Ave. Canby, OR 97013	Sit-down: Up to 450 Reception: Up to 500 R/B/P/S/M/		Events Coordinator (503) 266-1136 Fax (503) 266-2833
Monarch Hotel & Conference Center 12566 S.E. 93rd Ave. Clackamas, OR 97015	Up to 1,000 W/R/B/S/M/	193	Director of Catering (503) 652-1515 Fax (503) 652-5989
The Old Spaghetti Factory 12725 S.E. 93rd Ave. Clackamas, OR 97015 *See page 76*	Sit-down: Up to 75–150 R/B/S/M/		Banquet Manager (503) 653-7949
Tallina's Gardens & Conservatory 15791 S.E. Hwy. 224 Clackamas, OR 97015 *See page 199*	Indoor: 160 Outdoor: 300 W/R/B/M/P/		Tallina or Tina (503) 658-6148

COLUMBIA GORGE/HOOD RIVER

ADDRESS	CAPACITY	GUEST ROOMS	CONTACT
Big Horse Brewery & Pub 115 State St. Hood River, OR 97031	Sit-down: Up to 40 R/B/		Randy Orzeck (541) 386-4411
Charburger Restaurant 4100 Westcliff Dr. Hood River, OR 97031	Sit-down: Up to 95 R/B/		Steve or Blanch (541) 386-3101
Cherry Hill Bed & Breakfast 1550 Carroll Rd. Mosier, OR 97040 (Columbia River Gorge National Scenic Area) *See page 119*	Indoor: Up to 80 Garden: Up to 200 W/R/B/S/M/P/	3	Elizabeth Toscano (541) 478-4455 Fax (541) 478-4457
Columbia Gorge Hotel 4000 Westcliff Dr. Hood River, OR 97031 *See page 122*	Up to 200 W/R/B/S/M/	41	Wedding Consultant (541) 387-5405 (800) 345-0931
Hood River Hotel & Pasquale's Ristorante 102 Oak Ave. Hood River, OR 97031 *See page 153*	Up to 250 W/R/B/S/M/	41	Reservations (800) 386-1859 Sales Office (541) 386-1900
Hood River Inn 1108 E. Marina Way Hood River, OR 97031	Sit-down: Up to 225 Reception: Up to 300 W/R/B/S/M/	149	Sales & Catering (541) 386-2200 (800) 828-7873
Maryhill Museum of Art 35 Maryhill Museum Dr. Goldendale, WA 98620	Indoor: Up to 175 Outdoor: Up to 1,500 W/R/B/S/M/P/		Elizabeth Toscano at Cherry Hill (541) 478-4455

W=Wedding Ceremony   R=Reception   B=Banquet   S=Seminar   M=Meeting   P=Picnic

PORTLAND AREA
BANQUET SITE LISTINGS

ADDRESS	CAPACITY	GUEST ROOMS	CONTACT
Mt. Hood Bed & Breakfast 8885 Cooper Spur Rd. Parkdale, OR 97041 *See page 167*	Indoor/Outdoor: Up to 200 W/R/B/P/	4	Jackie Rice (541) 352-6885
Oregon Nat. Guard Armory 1590 12th St. Hood River, OR 97031	Reception: Up to 450 R/B/		David Arnold (541) 386-3161

CORNELIUS

Pumpkin Ridge Golf Course 12930 Old Pumpkin Ridge Rd. Cornelius, OR 97113-6147	Up to 250 W/R/B/S/M/		Event Coordinator (503) 647-4747

CORVALLIS/ALBANY

Bell Fountain Cellars 25041 Llewellyn Rd. Corvallis, OR 97333	Indoor: Up to 50 Outdoor: Up to 100 R/B/S/M/		Jeanne Mommsen (541) 929-3162
Linn County Fair & Expo Center 3700 Knox Butte Rd. Albany, OR 97321 *See page 158*	Up to 6,000 B/R/M/		Jill Henderson (541) 926-4314 (800) 858-2005
Salbasgeon Suites 1730 N.W. Ninth St. Corvallis, OR 97330	Up to 150 M/B/R/S/	105	Virginia Gillespie (800) 965-8808

FOREST GROVE

Elk Cove Vineyards 27751 N.W. Olson Rd. Gaston, OR 97119	Up to 200 W/R/B/S/M/P/		Ann Clayton (503) 985-7760
Laurel Ridge Winery 46350 N.W. David Hill Rd. Forest Grove, OR 97116	Sit-down: Up to 65 Reception: Up to 200 W/R/B/S/M/P/		David Teppola (503) 359-5436
Masonic Lodge 2019 Main St. Forest Grove, OR 97116	Reception: Up to 120 R/B/P/S/M/ *No alcohol		Harold Johnson (503) 357-6979
Oregon Nat'l Guard Armory 2950 Taylor Way Forest Grove, OR 97116	Reception: Up to 450 R/B/		Frank Wallace (503) 359-4632
Pacific University University Center 2043 College Way Forest Grove, OR 97116	Up to 50 R/B/S/M/W/		Director of Conferences (503) 359-2133

GRESHAM/BORING

Cascade Athletic Club 19201 S.E. Division St. Gresham, OR 97030	Up to 200 W/R/B/S/M/		Brian Ancheta (503) 665-4142 Fax (503) 667-4948

W=Wedding Ceremony   R=Reception   B=Banquet   S=Seminar   M=Meeting   P=Picnic

PORTLAND AREA
BANQUET SITE LISTINGS

ADDRESS	CAPACITY	GUEST ROOMS	CONTACT
Club Paesano 3800 W. Powell Loop Gresham, OR 97030	Up to 500 W/R/B/S/M/P/		Rose Sisson (503) 666-7636
East Fork Country Estate 9875 S.E. 222nd Gresham, OR 97080 *See page 132*	Indoor/Outdoor: Up to 250 W/R/B/S/M/P/		Karen Reed (503) 667-7069
Gresham Armory 500 N.E. Division St. Gresham, OR 97030	Up to 379 W/R/B/S/M/		State Employee (503) 665-2511
The Keg Restaurant 3150 N.E. Division St. Gresham, OR 97030	Up to 25 R/B/S/M/		General Manager (503) 667-5114
Mountain View Golf Course 27195 S.W. Kelso Rd. Boring, OR 97009 *See page 166*	Up to 350 R/B/S/M/		Sally Drew (503) 663-5350
Mt. Hood Community College 26000 S.E. Stark St. Gresham, OR 97030	Fireside Lounge: Reception: Up to 300 W/R/ Game Room: Sit-down: Up to 144 Reception: Up to 160 R/W/B/ Keg Lawn: Oudoor: Up to 300 W/R/ Vista Dining Center Sit-down: Up to 350 Reception: Up to 400 W/R/B. Coffee Shop: Sit-down: Up to 100 Reception: Up to 150 R/B/M/ Town & Gown Room: Sit-down: Up to 75 Reception: Up to 100 W/R/M/		Dee Ann Melland (503) 491-7449 Fax (503) 491-6011
Persimmon Country Club 500 S.E. Butler Rd. Gresham, OR 97080 *See page 179*	Up to 300 W/R/B/S/M/		Event Coordinator (503) 667-7500

HILLSBORO

ADDRESS	CAPACITY	GUEST ROOMS	CONTACT
The Brass Horn 4550 N.E. Cornell Rd. Hillsboro, OR 97124	Up to 200 W/R/B/S/M/P/		Janet Goodell or Kelly Probasco (503) 640-5527

W=Wedding Ceremony   R=Reception   B=Banquet   S=Seminar   M=Meeting   P=Picnic

Please let these businesses know that you heard about them from the Bravo! Bridal Resource Guide. **557**

PORTLAND AREA
BANQUET SITE LISTINGS

ADDRESS	CAPACITY	GUEST ROOMS	CONTACT
Cavanaugh's Hillsboro Hotel 3500 N.E. Cornell Rd. Hillsboro, OR 97124 *See page 116*	Reception: Up to 150 W/R/B/S/M/	124	Catering Office (503) 648-3500 ext. 507 (800) 325-4000
McMenamins— Cornelius Pass Roadhouse 4045 N.W. Cornelius Pass Rd. Hillsboro, OR 97214	Indoor: Up to 65 R/B/S/M/		Management Team (503) 640-6174
McCulloch Farms 6065 S.W. River Rd. Hillsboro, OR 97123	Indoor: Up to 150 Outdoor: 500+ W/R/B/S/M/P/		Sharon McCulloch-Gilson (503) 649-7117
Meriwether National Golf Course 5200 S.W. Rood Bridge Hillsboro, OR 97123	Up to 225 R/B/S/M/		Joyce Currie (503) 693-8707
The Old Spaghetti Factory 18925 N.W. Tanasbourne Dr. Hillsboro, OR 97124 *See page 76*	Sit-down: 75–150 R/B/S/M/		Banquet Manager (503) 617-7614
Tuality Health Education Center 334 S.E. Eighth Ave. Hillsboro, OR 97123 *See page 202*	Sit-down: Up to 250 Reception: Up to 400 R/B/S/M/		(503) 681-1700
Washington County Fair Complex 873 N.E. 28th St. Hillsboro, OR 97124	40 to 2,500 W/R/B/S/M/P/		Margaret Garza (503) 648-1416 Fax (503) 648-7208

JUNCTION CITY

ADDRESS	CAPACITY	GUEST ROOMS	CONTACT
Shadow Hills Country Club 92512 River Rd. Junction City, OR 97448	Up to 250 W/R/B/S/M/		Jennifer Brandt (541) 998-2365 Fax (541) 998-6779

LAKE OSWEGO

ADDRESS	CAPACITY	GUEST ROOMS	CONTACT
A Touch of Romance Ltd. 530 First St. Lake Oswego, OR 97034 *See page 89*	Up to 25 B/Showers		Stephanie (503) 636-0179
Amadeus 148 B. Avenue Lake Oswego, OR 97034	Up to 100 R/B/M/		General Manager (503) 636-7500
Crowne Plaza 14811 Kruse Oaks Blvd. Lake Oswego, OR 97035 *See page 124*	Up to 300 W/R/B/S/M/	161	Linda Goss (503) 624-8400

W=Wedding Ceremony   R=Reception   B=Banquet   S=Seminar   M=Meeting   P=Picnic

ADDRESS	CAPACITY	GUEST ROOMS	CONTACT
Celebrate Catering & Reception Facility 15555 S.W. Bangy Rd. Lake Oswego, OR 97035 *See page 117*	Sit-down: Up to 200 Reception: Up to 300 W/R/B/S/M/		Barb Chirgwin (503) 684-1880
Fuddruckers 17815 S.W. 65th Ave. Lake Oswego, OR 97035	Up to 75		Manager (503) 620-5119 (Fax) 639-1787
Hunan Pearl 15160 S.W. Bangy Rd. Lake Oswego, OR 97035	Sit-down: Up to 30 R/B/		Miles Shu (503) 968-6868
Lacey's in Lake Oswego 500 S.W. First St. Lake Oswego, OR 97034	Sit-down: Up to 60 Reception: Up to 100 R/B/P		Ed Lacey (503) 636-2024
Lakewood Center for the Arts 368 S. State St. Lake Oswego, OR 97034 *See page 157*	Sit-down: Up to 150 Reception: Up to 225 Theater: 200 W/R/B/S/M/		Executive Director (503) 635-6338
Ram Restaurant & Big Horn Brewery Co. 320 Oswego Point Blvd. Lake Oswego, OR 97034 *See page 184*	Up to 70 W/R/B/S/M/		(503) 697-8818
Sherwood Inn/Best Western 15700 S.W. Upper Boones Ferry Rd. Lake Oswego, OR 97035	Sit-down: Up to 80 Reception: Up to 100 W/R/B/S/M/	101	General Manager (503) 620-2980 Fax (503) 639-9010
A Taste of China 15450 Boones Ferry Rd. Lake Oswego, OR 97035	Up to 50 W/R/B/S/M/		Owner/Manager (503) 699-5056 Fax: (503) 699-0319

McMINNVILLE

ADDRESS	CAPACITY	GUEST ROOMS	CONTACT
Golden Valley Brewery & Pub 980 E. Fourth McMinnville, OR 97128	Sit-down: Up to 65 Reception: Up to 100 (Private room) R/B/S/M/		Doug Reed or Shannon Cullen (503) 472-2739 Fax (503) 434-8523
Youngberg Hill Vineyard 10660 Youngberg Hill Rd. McMinnville, OR 97128	Indoor: Up to 20 Outdoor: Up to 150 W/R/B/S/M/P/	6	Tasha and Kevin Byrd (503) 472-2727 (888) 657-8668

MILWAUKIE

ADDRESS	CAPACITY	GUEST ROOMS	CONTACT
Amadeus at the Fernwood 2122 S.E. Sparrow Milwaukie, OR 97222 *See page 102*	Up to 300 W/R/B/S/M/		Kristina Poppmeier (503) 659-1735

W=Wedding Ceremony   R=Reception   B=Banquet   S=Seminar   M=Meeting   P=Picnic

Please let these businesses know that you heard about them from the Bravo! Bridal Resource Guide.   **559**

PORTLAND AREA
BANQUET SITE LISTINGS

ADDRESS	CAPACITY	GUEST ROOMS	CONTACT
Broetje House, Historic 3101 S.E. Courtney Milwaukie, OR 97222 *See page 112*	Indoor/Outdoor: Up to 150 W/R/B/S/M/P/	3	Lorraine or Lois (503) 659-8860
Gray Gables Estate 3009 S.E. Chestnut Milwaukie, OR 97267 *See page 144*	Indoor: Up to 75 Indoor/Outdoor: Up to 275 W/R/B/S/M/P/	7	(503) 654-0470
Milwaukie Center (in North Clackamas Park) 5440 Kellogg Creek Dr. Milwaukie, OR 97222 *See page 164*	Sit-down:Up to 350 Reception: Up to 600 Two rooms W/R/B/S/M/P/		Community Use Scheduler (503) 653-8100
The Milwaukie Grange P.O. Box 220071 Milwaukie, OR 97269	Up to 150 W/R/B/S/M/		Carmelita Coats (503) 654-8771

MOLALLA

ADDRESS	CAPACITY	GUEST ROOMS	CONTACT
Canterbury Falls & English Gardens P.O. Box 156 Molalla, OR 97038 *See page 114*	Outdoor: Up to 400 W/R/B/M/P/S/		Judy Hall (503) 829-8821

MOUNT HOOD/SANDY

ADDRESS	CAPACITY	GUEST ROOMS	CONTACT
Best Western Sandy Inn 37465 Hwy 26 Sandy, OR 97055	Sit-down: Up to 50 B/R/P/	45	Kevin Ryan (503) 668-7100
Mt. Hood Bed & Breakfast 8885 Cooper Spur Rd. Parkdale, OR 97041 *See page 167*	Indoor/Outdoor Up to 200+ W/R/B/P/	4	Jackie Rice (541) 352-6885
Mt. Hood Meadows Ski Resort 1975 S.W. First Ave., Suite M Portland, OR 97201	Up to 400 W/R/B/S/M/P/		Marketing & Sales Office (503) 287-5438
Mt. Hood Village 65000 E. Hwy 26 Welches, OR 97067	Indoor: Up to 340 Outdoor: Up to 400+		Marilyn Peterson (503) 622-4011 ext. 215 Fax (503) 622-4881
Timberline Lodge Mount Hood, OR 97028 *See page 201*	Sit-down: Up to 200 Reception: Up to 400 W/R/B/S/M/P/	71	Catering (503) 622-0722 Fax (503) 272-3708

NEWBERG

ADDRESS	CAPACITY	GUEST ROOMS	CONTACT
The Calico Rose 117 N. Meridian St. Newberg, OR 97132	Sit-down: Up to 100 Reception: Up to 150 W/R/B/S/M/P		Kit Wheeler (503) 538-0718

W=Wedding Ceremony   R=Reception   B=Banquet   S=Seminar   M=Meeting   P=Picnic

ADDRESS	CAPACITY	GUEST ROOMS	CONTACT
Chehalem Armory 620 N. Morton St. Newberg, OR 97132	Reception: Up to 200 W/R/B/S/M/		Anna (503) 538-7454
Chehalem Community Center 502 E. Second St. Newberg, OR 97132	Up to 350 R/B/		Anna (503) 538-7454
Chehalem Community Senior Center 501 Foothills Dr. Newberg, OR 97132	Up to 225 W/R/B/S/M *No alcohol		Anna (503) 538-7454
Shilo Inn 501 Sitka Ave. Newberg, OR 97132	Up to 50 R/B/		Manager (503) 537-0303

OREGON CITY

ADDRESS	CAPACITY	GUEST ROOMS	CONTACT
Captain Ainsworth House Bed & Breakfast 19130 Lot Whitcomb Dr. Oregon City, OR 97045 *See page 115*	Sit-down: Up to 70 Reception: Up to 100 W/R/B/S/M/P/	4	Claire Met (503) 655-5172
Carpenter Hall 276 Warner Milne Rd. Oregon City, OR 97045	Up to 200 W/R/B/S/M/		Marcy Schram (503) 656-7716 Fax (503) 650-8051
The Carus House Wedding Chapel 23200 S. Highway 213 Oregon City, OR 97045 *See page 320*	Up to 125 seated W/R/B/		Wedding Coordinator (503) 631-7078
Edgewater Inn 1900 Clackamette Dr. Oregon City, OR 97045	Up to 125 R/B/S/M/		Banquet Coordinator (503) 655-5155
Environmental Learning Center (Clackamas Community College) 19600 S. Molalla Ave. Oregon City, OR 97045	Up to 110 P/R/B *No alcoholic beverages		Dawn Todd (503) 657-6958 ext. 2351 Fax (503) 650-6669
Grand Oregon Lodge 600 Seventh St. Oregon City, OR 97045 *See page 143*	Up to 299 W/R/B/S/M/		(503) 722-4190
Oregon City Golf Club 20124 S. Beavercreek Rd. Oregon City, OR 97045 *See page 173*	Sit-down: Up to 125 Reception: Up to 160 W/R/B/M/S/		Rose Holden (503) 656-2846 (503) 656-0038
Phelps Family Farm 22011 S. Penman Rd. Oregon City, OR 97045 *See page 96*	Up to 300+ W/R/B/S/M/P/		Sherri (503) 722-3267

W=Wedding Ceremony   R=Reception   B=Banquet   S=Seminar   M=Meeting   P=Picnic

Please let these businesses know that you heard about them from the Bravo! Bridal Resource Guide.   **561**

ADDRESS	CAPACITY	GUEST ROOMS	CONTACT
Pioneer Community Center 615 Fifth St. Oregon City, OR 97045	Up to 400		Susan Devecka (503) 657-8287 Fax (503) 657-9851

DOWNTOWN PORTLAND

ADDRESS	CAPACITY	GUEST ROOMS	CONTACT
The Adrianna Hill **Grand Ballroom** 918 S.W. Yamhill, 2nd Floor Portland, OR 97205 *See page 98*	Up to 300 W/R/B/S/M/		Philip Sword (503) 227-6285
Alexis Restaurant 215 W. Burnside Portland, OR 97209	Up to 100 W/R/B/S/M/		Gerry (503) 224-8577 Fax (503) 224-934
Arlene Schnitzer **Concert Hall** 1111 S.W. Broadway at Main Portland, OR 97205	Sit-down: Up to 200 Reception: Up to 400 Theatre: Up to 2,776 W/R/B/S/M/		Booking & Sales (503) 248-4335 (503) 274-7490
The Atrium 100 S.W. Market St. Portland, OR 97201 *See page 104*	Sit-down: Up to 150 Reception: Up to 250+ W/R/B/S/M/		Catering Director (503) 220-3929
Atwater's Restaurant **& Bar** 111 S.W. Fifth Ave., 30th Floor Portland, OR 97204 *See page 105*	Up to 300 W/R/B/S/M/		J.J. Fox (503) 275-3662
The Benson Hotel 309 S.W. Broadway at Oak Portland, OR 97205 *See page 109*	Sit-down: Up to 400 Reception: Up to 500 W/R/B/S/M/	286	Sales (503) 295-4140 Fax (503) 241-3757
Berbati Restaurant 19 S.W. Second Portland, OR 97204	Up to 350 W/R/B/S/M/		John (503) 226-2122
British Tea Garden 725 S.W. 10th Ave. Portland, OR 97205	Sit-down: Up to 60 Bridal teas, showers, luncheons		Judith (503) 221-7817
Cassidy's Restaurant 1331 S.W. Washington Portland, OR 97205 *See page 70*	Sit-down: Up to 36 Reception: Up to 200 W/R/B/S/M/		Christine, Bob or Mercedes (503) 223-0054
Central Library 801 S.W. 10th Ave. Portland, OR 97205 *See page 118*	Reception: Up to 1,200 Sit-down: 300 W/R/B/M/		Sandra Lahti (503) 306-5578
The Crown Ballroom **& Garden Court** 918 S.W. Yamhill, 5th Floor Portland, OR 97205 *See page 123*	Up to 400 W/R/M/S/B/		Manager (503) 227-8440

W=Wedding Ceremony   R=Reception   B=Banquet   S=Seminar   M=Meeting   P=Picnic

PORTLAND AREA
BANQUET SITE LISTINGS

ADDRESS	CAPACITY	GUEST ROOMS	CONTACT
The Crystal Ballroom 132 W. Burnside Portland, OR 97209 *See page 125*	Sit-down: Up to 350 W/R/B/S/M/		Sales Office (503) 472-2777
Days Inn City Center 1414 S.W. Sixth Ave. Portland, OR 97201	Up to 150 W/R/B/S/M/	173	Judy Kaski (503) 221-1611 (800) 899-0248 Fax (503) 226-0447
Demetri's Mediterranean Restaurant 1650 W. Burnside Portland, OR 97209	Up to 150 W/R/B/S/M/		Owner (503) 222-1507
DoubleTree Hotel Downtown 310 S.W. Lincoln Portland, OR 97201 *See page 128*	Up to 250 W/R/B/S/M/	235	Sales Office (503) 221-0450
Embassy Suites— Portland Downtown 319 S.W. Pine St. Portland, OR 97204 *See pages 135*	Sit-down: Up to 220 Reception: Up to 300 R/B/S/M/	276	Denise Fredlund (503) 279-9000 Fax (503) 497-9051
Fifth Avenue Suites Hotel/ Red Star Tavern & Roast House 506 S.W. Washington Portland, OR 97204 *See page 138*	Reception: Up to 200 R/B/S/M/C/	221	Margie Yager (503) 417-3377
First Christian Church 1315 S.W. Broadway Portland, OR 97201	Up to 300 W/R/		Dorothy Pearce (503) 228-9211 Fax (503) 222-1313
First Congregational Church 1126 S.W. Park Ave. Portland, OR 97205 *See page 321*	Ceremony: 40 to 850 Reception: Up to 175 W/R/		Church Office (503) 228-7219
The Georgian Restaurant at Meier & Frank Downtown 621 S.W. Fifth Avenue, 10th Fl Portland, OR 97204 *See page 141*	Sit-down: Up to 200 Reception: Up to 250 R/B/M/S/		Don Olson (503) 241-5163
Jake's Catering at The Governor Hotel 611 S.W. 10th St. Portland, OR 97205 *See page 142*	Sit-down: Up to 450 Reception: Up to 600 W/R/B/S/M/	100	Catering Sales (503) 241-2125 Fax (503) 220-1849
Greek Cusina Minoan Room 404 S.W. Washington Portland, OR 97204 *See page 145*	Up to 500 W/R/B/S/M/		Ted Papas (503) 224-2288

W=Wedding Ceremony   R=Reception   B=Banquet   S=Seminar   M=Meeting   P=Picnic

Please let these businesses know that you heard about them from the Bravo! Bridal Resource Guide.   **563**

PORTLAND AREA
BANQUET SITE LISTINGS

ADDRESS	CAPACITY	GUEST ROOMS	CONTACT
Harborside Restaurant 0309 S.W. Montgomery Portland, OR 97201	Sit-down: Up to 70 W/R/B/S/M/		Banquet Manager (503) 220-1865
The Heathman Hotel 1001 S.W. Broadway at Salmon St. Portland, OR 97205 *See page 148*	Sit-down: Up to 80 Reception: Up to 140 W/R/B/S/M/	75	Catering Manager (503) 790-7758
Hilton Portland 921 S.W. Sixth Ave. Portland, OR 97204 *See page 150*	Up to 1,200 W/R/B/S/M/	461	Catering (503) 220-2684 Fax (503) 220-2293
Huber's 411 S.W. Third Portland, OR 97204	Sit-down: Up to 164 Reception: Up to 164 R/B/		James or David Louie (503) 228-5686 Fax (503) 227-3922
Imperial Hotel 400 S.W. Broadway Portland, OR 97205	Sit-down: Up to 150 Reception: Up to 174 R/B/S/M/	136	Catering Manager (503) 228-7221 (503) 223-4551
The Irish Bank 409 S.W. Second Ave. Portland, OR 97204	Up to 45 R/B/M/		Todd Smith (503) 464-1122
Jake's Grill 611 S.W. 10th Portland, OR 97205	Up to 500 R/B/S/M		Dorcas Popp (503) 241-2125
Jasmine Tree 401 S.W. Harrison Portland, OR 97201	Up to 150 W/R/B/S/M/		Manager (503) 223-7956
Kells—Portland's Irish Restaurant & Pub 112 S.W. Second Ave. Portland, OR 97204 *See page 155*	Sit-down: Up to 80 Reception: Up to 100 W/R/B/S/M/		Banquet Manager (503) 227-4057 Fax (503) 227-5931
The Mallory Hotel 729 S.W. 15th Ave. Portland, OR 97205 *See page 159*	Sit-down: Up to 90 Reception: Up to 125 W/R/B/S/M/	150	Catering Department (503) 223-6311
Mandarin Cove Chinese Restaurant 111 S.W. Columbia Portland, OR 97201	Sit-down: Up to 250 Reception: Up to 250 W/R/B/S/M/		Jen Tsui (503) 222-0006
Marriott Hotel—Portland 1401 S.W. Naito Parkway Portland, OR 97201 *See page 160*	Up to 1,000 W/R/B/S/M/	503	Catering (503) 499-6361
McCormick & Schmick's Seafood Restaurant 235 S.W. First Ave. Portland, OR 97201	Up to 40 R/B/S/M/		General Manager (503) 224-7522 Fax (503) 220-1881

W=Wedding Ceremony   R=Reception   B=Banquet   S=Seminar   M=Meeting   P=Picnic

ADDRESS	CAPACITY	GUEST ROOMS	CONTACT
New Theatre Building at the Portland Center for the Performing Arts 1111 S.W. Broadway Portland, OR 97205	Sit-down: Up to 400 Reception: Up to 1,000 W/R/B/S/M/		Booking & Sales (503) 248-4335 (503) 274-7490
The Old Church 1422 S.W. 11th Ave. Portland, OR 97201 *See page 323*	Ceremony: Up to 300 Reception: Up to 300 W/R/B/S/M/		Trish Augustin (503) 222-2031 Fax (503) 222-2981
Oregon Sports Hall of Fame & Museum 321 S.W. Salmon St. Portland, OR 97204	Sit-down: Up to 150 Reception: Up to 300 R/B/S/M/C/P		Operations Director (503) 227-7466 Fax (503) 227-6925
Pazzo Ristorante Hotel Vintage Plaza 422 S.W. Broadway Portland, OR 97205 *See page 178*	Sit-down: Up to 80 Reception: Up to 100 W/R/B/S/M/	107	Catering (503) 412-6316
Piatti on Broadway 319 S.W. Broadway Portland, OR 97205 *See page 78*	Up to 110 R/B/S/M/		Ray Colvin (503) 525-0945
Portland Art Museum North Wing 1119 S.W. Park Ave. Portland, OR 97205 *See page 180*	Up to 1,500 W/R/B/S/M/		Event Coordinator (503) 226-2811 ext. 290
RiverPlace Hotel 1510 S.W. Harbor Way Portland, OR 97201 *See page 186*	Sit-down: Up to 200 Reception: Up to 400 W/R/B/S/M/	84	Sales & Catering (503) 423-3111
The Riverside 50 S.W. Morrison St. Portland, OR 97204	Sit-down: Up to 40 Reception: Up to 50 R/B/S/M/	140	Kelly Nestlen (503) 221-0711 Fax (503) 274-0312
Sandoval's Food & Cantina 133 S.W. Second Ave. Portland, OR 97204	Sit-down: Up to 200 Reception: Up to 250 P/R/B/M/C/		Danny Sandoval (503) 223-7020 Fax (503) 223-6883
Scottish Rite Temple 709 S.W. 15th Ave. Portland, OR 97205	Up to 400 W/R/B/S/M/		Building Manager (503) 226-7827 Fax (503) 223-3562
Tiffany Center 1410 S.W. Morrison Portland, OR 97205 *See page 200*	Up to 1,300 Theatre: Up to 975 W/R/B/S/M/		Events Manager (503) 222-0703 or (503) 248-9305
Wilf's Restaurant & Piano Bar N.W. Sixth & Irving Portland, OR 97209 *See page 85*	Sit-down: Up to 150 Reception: Up to 160 R/B/S/M/		Manager (503) 223-0070 Fax (503) 223-1386

W=Wedding Ceremony   R=Reception   B=Banquet   S=Seminar   M=Meeting   P=Picnic

Please let these businesses know that you heard about them from the Bravo! Bridal Resource Guide.   **565**

ADDRESS	CAPACITY	GUEST ROOMS	CONTACT
World Trade Center Two World Trade Center 25 S.W. Salmon St. Portland, OR 97204 *See page 209*	Sit-down: Up to 300 Reception: Up to 400 Outdoor: Sit-down: Up to 500 Reception: Up to 800 W/R/B/S/M/		Reservations (503) 464-8688

NORTH PORTLAND

ADDRESS	CAPACITY	GUEST ROOMS	CONTACT
Best Western Inn At The Meadows 1215 N. Hayden Meadows Dr. Portland, OR 97217	Up to 75 R/B/S/M/	146	Director of Sales: Chris (503) 286-9600 Fax (503) 286-8020
Cucina! Cucina! Italian Cafe One Center Court Portland, OR 97227	Up to 200 R/B/S/M/		Doreen Lowndes (503) 238-9800 Fax (206) 238-9749
DoubleTree Hotel— Columbia River 1401 N. Hayden Island Dr Portland, OR 97217 *See page 127*	Up to 1,200 W/R/B/S/M/	351	Sales Office (503) 283-2111
DoubleTree Hotel— Jantzen Beach 909 N. Hayden Island Dr. Portland, OR 97217 *See page 130*	Up to 1,200 W/R/B/S/M	320	Sales Office (503) 283-4466
Elmer's Pancake & Steak House 9848 N. Whitaker Rd. Portland, OR 97217	Up to 100 R/B/M/		Sandra Lewis (503) 289-9848 Fax (503) 289-1195
Friends of Columbia Park Columbia Cottage 4339 N. Lombard Portland, OR 97203	Up to 100 W/R/B/S/M/P/		Bill Minard (503) 735-1537 or (503) 289-0195
Hayden Island Yacht Club 12050 N. Jantzen Rd. Portland, OR 97217	Sit-down: Up to 150 Reception: Up to 200 W/R/B/M/		Terri Richen (503) 283-4369
Historic Kenton Firehouse Community Center 8105 N. Brandon Portland, OR 97217	Upstairs: Up to 20 Downstairs: Up to 100 R/M/S/B/W/		Coordinator (503) 285-7843
Interstate Firehouse Cultural Center 5340 N. Interstate Ave. Portland, OR 97217	Up to 400 Theater: Up to 110 R/S/M/W		Rental Coordinator (503) 823-2000 Fax (503) 823-2061
The John Palmer House 4314 N. Mississippi Ave. Portland, OR 97217	Indoor: Up to 50 Outdoor: Up to 200 W/R/B/S/M/P/	3	Marketing Representative (503) 284-5893 (503) 284-1239

W=Wedding Ceremony   R=Reception   B=Banquet   S=Seminar   M=Meeting   P=Picnic

ADDRESS	CAPACITY	GUEST ROOMS	CONTACT
McMenamins St. Johns Pub 8203 N. Ivanhoe Portland, OR 97203	Sit-down: Up to 100 Reception: Up to 200 Entire facility: Up to 300 *Includes bar W/R/B/S/M/		Sean Crieghton (503) 283-8520 Fax (503) 283-8609
North Star Ballroom 635 N. Killingsworth Court Portland, OR 97217 *See page 168*	Up to 375 R/B/S/M/		Harriet Fasenfest (503) 240-6088
The Overlook House 3839 N. Melrose Dr. Portland, OR 97227 *See page 176*	Indoor: Up to 75 Outdoor: Up to 150 W/R/S/M/P		Building Coordinator (503) 823-3188
Oxford Suites Hotel 12226 N. Jantzen Dr. Portland, OR 97217	Up to 120 R/S/M/	203 Suites	Sales (503) 283-3030 (503) 735-1661
Queen Anne Victorian Mansion 1441 N. McClellan Portland, OR 97217 *See page 183*	Sit-down: Up to 200 Reception: Up to 300 W/R/B/S/M/		Bridal Coordinator (503) 283-3224 Fax (503) 283-5605
Red Lion Inn—Coliseum 1225 N. Thunderbird Way Portland, OR 97227	Sit-down: Up to 150 Reception: Up to 300 W/R/B/S/M/	212	Catering Office (503) 235-8311
Shenanigans' on the Willamette 4575 N. Channel Portland, OR 97217 *See page 192*	Sit-down: Up to 400 Reception: Up to 800 W/R/B/S/M/		Orrin Johnston (503) 289-1597
University of Portland Chiles Center 5000 N. Willamette Blvd. Portland, OR 97203	Up to 5,000 R/B/S/M/		Director University Events (503) 283-7523 Fax (503) 283-7451
University of Portland Commons/Main Dining Rm 5000 N. Willamette Blvd. Portland, OR 97203	Up to 600 R/B/S/M/ *Dining room available summer breaks only		Director University Events (503) 283-7330 Fax (503) 283-7544
YMCA—St. Johns Center 8010 N. Charleston Portland, Oregon 97203	Large hall: Up to 100 Meeting room: Up to 30 W/R/M/S/B		Rental Coordinator (503) 721-6777 Fax (503) 721-6751

NORTHEAST PORTLAND

ADDRESS	CAPACITY	GUEST ROOMS	CONTACT
The Alberta Station Ballroom 1829 N.E. Alberta Portland, OR 97211 *See page 99*	Up to 570 (open floor) W/R/B/M/		Pat Goebel (503) 284-8666

W=Wedding Ceremony   R=Reception   B=Banquet   S=Seminar   M=Meeting   P=Picnic

PORTLAND AREA
BANQUET SITE LISTINGS

ADDRESS	CAPACITY	GUEST ROOMS	CONTACT
Albertina's Restaurant at The Old Kerr Nursery 424 N.E. 22nd Ave. Portland, OR 97232 *See page 100*	Up to 250 W/R/B/		Catering Coordinator (503) 231-3909
Amalfi's 4703 N.E. Fremont Portland, OR 97213	Up to 40 W/R/B/S/M/		Manager (503) 284-6747
Capers Cafe & Catering 12003 N.E. Ainsworth Circle, Suite A Portland, OR 97220 *See page 295*	Up to 150 R/B/S/M/		Christian or Annette Joly (503) 252-1718 Fax (503) 252-0178
Colwood National Golf Course 7313 N.E. Columbia Blvd. Portland, OR 97218	Up to 200 R/B/S/M/		Club Manager (503) 254-2567 Fax (503) 255-0504
Courtyard by Marriott— Portland Airport 11550 N.E. Airport Way Portland, OR 97220	Up to 125 R/B/S/M/	150	Dawna Anderson (503) 252-3200 Fax (503) 252-8921
DoubleTree Hotel— Lloyd Center 1000 N.E. Multnomah Portland, OR 97232 *See page 131*	Up to 1,100 W/R/B/S/M/	476	Catering Office (503) 249-3130
Embassy Suites— Portland Airport 9700 N.E. 82nd Ave. Portland, OR 97220 *See page 134*	Sit-down: Up to 563 Reception: Up to 1,127 W/R/B/S/M/	251	Peggy Gitts (503) 460-3000
Holiday Inn—Airport 8439 N.E. Columbia Blvd. Portland, OR 97220 *See page 151*	Up to 1,200 W/R/B/S/M/	286	Sales & Catering (503) 256-5000
Irvington Club 2131 N.E. Thompson Portland, OR 97212	Up to 175 W/R/B/S/M/		Heidi Kamm (503) 287-8749 Fax (503) 284-5308
Jag's Restaurant & Lounge 10 N. Weidler Portland, OR 97227	Up to 250 R/M/B/		Tony Klein (503) 287-9900
J.J. North's Grand Buffet 10520 N.E. Halsey Portland, OR 97220	Up to 125 R/B/S/M/		Manager (503) 254-5555 Fax (503) 254-8411
O'Callahan's at the Ramada Inn 6221 N.E. 82nd Ave. Portland, OR 97220 *See page 170*	Sit-down: Up to 300 Reception: Up to 500 W/R/B/S/M/	202	Ann Conger (503) 253-2400 Fax (503) 253-1635

W=Wedding Ceremony   R=Reception   B=Banquet   S=Seminar   M=Meeting   P=Picnic

PORTLAND AREA
BANQUET SITE LISTINGS

ADDRESS	CAPACITY	GUEST ROOMS	CONTACT
Oregon Convention Center (Fine Host) 777 N.E. Martin Luther King, Jr. Blvd. Portland, OR 97232 *See page 139*	Up to 1,200 W/R/B/S/M/		Fine Host Catering (503) 731-7851
The Oregon Square Courtyard between Seventh & Ninth on N.E. Holladay Portland, OR 97232	Up to 2,000+ W/R/B/S/M/P/		Property Manager (503) 233-4048 Fax (503) 231-3954
Portland Conference Center 300 N.E. Multnomah St. Portland, OR 97232 *See page 181*	Sit-down: Up to 400 Reception: Up to 600 12 rooms W/R/B/S/M/		Event Coordinator (503) 239-9921
Portland's White House 1914 N.E. 22nd Ave. Portland, OR 97212	Up to 100 W/R/S/M/	9	Owners: Steve and Lanning (503) 287-7131 (800) 272-7131
Ramada Plaza Hotel 1441 N.E. Second Ave. Portland, OR 97232 *See page 185*	Up to 200 R/B/S/M/	238	Lucy Mitchell (503) 233-2401 Fax (503) 238-7016
The Refectory Restaurant 1618 N.E. 122nd Ave. Portland, OR 97230	Indoor: Up to 300 R/B/S/M/		Brian or Rita (503) 255-8545 Fax (503) 255-8230
Rheinlander 5035 N.E. Sandy Blvd. Portland, OR 97213 *See page 80*	Sit-down: Up to 100 Reception: Up to 150 W/R/B/S/M/		Banquet Manager (503) 288-8410
The Ringside 14021 N.E. Glisan Portland, OR 97230	Up to 65 *Not weekends B/S/M/		Cathy/John/Michelle (503) 255-0750
Salty's on the Columbia 3839 N.E. Marine Dr. Portland, OR 97211 *See page 81*	Sit-down: Up to 80 Reception: Up to 200 W/R/B/S/M/		Dorothy Lane (503) 288-4444
Sheraton Portland Airport Hotel 8235 N.E. Airport Way Portland, OR 97220-1398 *See page 193*	Sit-down: Up to 450 Reception: Up to 750 W/R/B/S/M/	215	Catering Department (503) 249-7642 Fax (503) 249-7624
Shilo Inn Suites Hotel, Restaurant & Convention Center 11707 N.E. Airport Way Portland, OR 97220-1075 *See page 195*	Sit-down: Up to 350 Reception: Up to 500 W/R/B/S/M/	200	Catering Office (503) 252-7500 ext. 270

W=Wedding Ceremony   R=Reception   B=Banquet   S=Seminar   M=Meeting   P=Picnic

Please let these businesses know that you heard about them from the Bravo! Bridal Resource Guide.   **569**

PORTLAND AREA
BANQUET SITE LISTINGS

ADDRESS	CAPACITY	GUEST ROOMS	CONTACT
Sylvia's Italian Restaurant 5115 N.E. Sandy Blvd. Portland, OR 97213 *See page 83*	Up to 80 Theatre: Up to 100 W/R/B/S/M/		Norm Stone (503) 288-6828
Windows Sky Room & Terrace at the Holiday Inn 1021 N.E. Grand Ave Portland, OR 97232 *See page 208*	Up to 250 W/R/B/S/M/	160	Mary Baskerville (503) 820-4160 Fax (503) 235-0396
YWCA—N.E. Center 5630 N.E. MLK Blvd. Portland, OR 97211	Meeting Room 1: Up to 12 Meeting Room 2: Up to 25 M/S/		Rental Coordinator (503) 721-1750 Fax (503) 721-1751

NORTHWEST PORTLAND

ADDRESS	CAPACITY	GUEST ROOMS	CONTACT
BridgePort Brewery 1313 N.W. Marshall Portland, OR 97209	Sit-down: Up to 75 R/B/S/M/ *Non-smoking		Event Coordinator (503) 241-7179 Fax (503) 241-0625
Couch Street Fish House 105 N.W. Third Ave. Portland, OR 97209	Sit-down: Up to 20 R/B/M/		Manager (503) 223-6173 (503) 721-0802
Friendly House 1737 N.W. 26th Portland, OR 97210	Up to 300 R/B/S/M/P/		Vaune Albanese (503) 228-4391 Fax (503) 228-0085
The Gatelodge at Pittock Mansion 3229 N.W. Pittock Dr. Portland, OR 97210	Sit-down: Up to 50 B/M/P/S		Lisette Hollis (503) 823-3627
Il Fornaio 115 N.W. 22nd Ave. Portland, OR 97210 *See page 75*	Up to 150 R/B/S/M/		Faith Chhim (503) 248-9400 or (503) 248-4324
Montgomery Park 2701 N.W. Vaughn St. Portland, OR 97210 *See page 165*	Sit-down: Up to 400 Reception: Up to 1,200 W/R/B/S/M/		Event Coordinator (503) 228-7275
Northwest Neighborhood Cultural Center 1819 N.W. Everett St. Portland, OR 97209	Sit-down: Up to 200 Reception: Up to 200 W/R/B/S/M/		Scheduling Coordinator (503) 228-6972 Fax (503) 228-8368
Paragon Restaurant & Bar 1309 N.W. Hoyt Portland, OR 97209 *See page 77*	Up to 150 R/B/S/M/		Joseph Moreau (503) 833-5060
Rock Creek Country Club Clubhouse 5100 N.W. Neakahnie Ave. Portland, OR 97229-1964 *See page 187*	Indoor: Up to 250 Outdoor: no limit R/B/S/M/W/P/		Manager (503) 690-4826

W=Wedding Ceremony   R=Reception   B=Banquet   S=Seminar   M=Meeting   P=Picnic

ADDRESS	CAPACITY	GUEST ROOMS	CONTACT
The Screening Room 925 N.W. 19th Portland, OR 97209	Up to 120 R/M/S/		(503) 294-7153
Sunset Athletic Club 13939 N.W. Cornell Rd. Portland, OR 97229	Up to 150 W/R/B/S/M/		Kathi Marcus (503) 645-3535 Fax (503) 645-8259
SOUTHEAST PORTLAND			
Arnegards 1510 S.E. Ninth Portland, OR 97214 *See page 103*	Up to 450 R/B/S/M/		Robin Andersen (503) 236-2759
British Tea Garden/Tea Time 3439 S.E. Hawthorne Blvd. Portland, OR 97214	Indoor: Up to 50 Outdoor: Up to 60 W/R/B/S/M/		Sarah (503) 231-7750
Brentwood/Darlington Center 7211 S.E. 62nd Ave. Portland, OR 97206 *See page 110*	Up to 130 P/R/B/S/M/		Mary Davis (503) 306-5961 ext. 223
Chez Grill 2229 S.E. Hawthorne Portland, OR 97214 *See page 72*	Private room: Up to 40 Entire restaurant: Up to 120		Charlie Slate (503) 239-4002
Chief Obie Lodge 11300 S.E. 147th Ave. Portland, OR 97236 *See page 120*	Up to 250 *No alcohol W/R/B/S/M/P/	75	Sales Office (503) 225-5759
Crystal Springs Rhododendron Garden S.E. 28th N. of Woodstock Portland, OR 97202 *See page 126*	Indoor/Outdoor: Up to 150 W/R/P/B/S/M/		Event Coordinator (503) 256-2483
Eastmoreland Grill at the Eastmoreland Golf Course 2425 S.E. Bybee Blvd. Portland, OR 97202 *See page 133*	Sit-down: Up to 125 Reception: Up to 175 R/B/S/M/		Jerilyn Walker (503) 775-5910
The Fountains Ballroom 223 S.E. 122nd Ave. Portland, OR 97233 *See page 140*	Up to 300 W/R/B/S/M/		Denise or Becky (503) 261-9424 Fax (503) 261-2989
Lakeside Gardens 16211 S.E. Foster Rd. Portland, OR 97236 *See page 156*	Indoor: Up to 180 Indoor/Outdoor: Up to 300 W/R/B/S/M/P/		Consultant (503) 760-6044
Laurelhurst Club 3721 S.E. Ankeny St. Portland, OR 97214	Up to 200 W/R/B/S/M/P/		Manager (503) 235-0015

W=Wedding Ceremony   R=Reception   B=Banquet   S=Seminar   M=Meeting   P=Picnic

Please let these businesses know that you heard about them from the Bravo! Bridal Resource Guide. **571**

PORTLAND AREA
BANQUET SITE LISTINGS

ADDRESS	CAPACITY	GUEST ROOMS	CONTACT
Lucky Labrador Brewing Co. 915 S.E. Hawthorne Blvd. Portland, OR 97214	Up to 60 B/S/M/R		(503) 236-3555
The Melody Ballroom 615 S.E. Alder St. Portland, OR 97214 *See page 163*	Up to 1,100 W/R/B/S/M/		Kathleen Kaad (503) 232-2759
Metro Police Club 618 S.E. Alder Portland, OR 97214	Up to 350 W/R/B/S/M/		Manager (503) 235-0202
Monte Carlo 1016 S.E. Belmont St. Portland, OR 97214	Up to 150 R/B/M/		Linda (503) 238-7627 Fax (503) 235-9171
OMSI 1945 S.E. Water Ave. Portland, OR 97214 *See page 172*	Up to 4,000 R/B/S/		Event Sales (503) 797-4671
Oaks Park Historic Dance Pavilion At Oaks Park (Sellwood) Portland, OR 97202 *See page 171*	Indoor: Up to 500 Sit-down: Up to 275 Outdoor: Up to 1,000 W/R/B/S/M/P		Volanne Stephens (503) 233-5777
NCP Pantheon Banquet Hall 5942 S.E. 92nd Ave. Portland, OR 97266 *See page 177*	Up to 500 W/R/B/S/M/		Banquet Coordinator (503) 775-7431 Fax (503) 775-3068
Persimmon Country Club 500 S.E. Butler Rd. Gresham, OR 97080 *See page 179*	Sit-down: Up to 300 Reception: 300+ R/B/S/M/		Event Coordinator (503) 667-7500 Fax (503) 667-3885
Reed College 3203 S.E. Woodstock Blvd. Portland, OR 97202	Gray Center Lounge: 75 Auditorium: 760 Chapel: Up to 240 Banquet: Up to 400 W/R/B/S/M/P *Nondenominational		Helen Ivey Conference/Event Planner (503) 777-7289 Fax (503) 788-6688
Sayler's Old Country Kitchen 10519 S.E. Stark Portland, OR 97216 *See page 82*	Sit-down: Up to 300 R/B/S/M/		Sally Kanan (503) 252-4171 or (503) 644-1492
Scandia Hall 1125 S.E. Madison Portland, OR 97214	Up to 299 R/B/W/S/M/		Joan Olsen (503) 232-8262
Sellwood Community Center 1436 S.E. Spokane St. Portland, OR 97202	Sit-down: Up to 75 W/R/B/S/M/		Portland Parks & Rec. Building Director (503) 823-3195 Fax (503) 823-3139

W=Wedding Ceremony   R=Reception   B=Banquet   S=Seminar   M=Meeting   P=Picnic

PORTLAND AREA
BANQUET SITE LISTINGS

ADDRESS	CAPACITY	GUEST ROOMS	CONTACT
The S.M.I.L.E. Station 8210 S.E. 13th Ave. Portland, OR 97202	Sit-down: Up to 80 Reception: Up to 100 W/R/B/S/M/		Booking Director (503) 234-3570
The Wedding House 2715 S.E. 39th St. Portland, OR 97202 *See page 204*	Sit-down: Up to 100 Reception: Up to 150 W/R/B/S/M/		Owner (503) 236-7353
The Wild Berry Room 3220 S.E. Milwaukie Blvd. Portland, OR 97202 *See page 84*	Up to 50 W/R/B/		Charles Barker (503) 234-1978
The Woodshed 16015 S.E. Stark St. Portland, OR 97233	Up to 70 R/B/S/M/		Mary Tanaka (503) 256-2575

SOUTHWEST PORTLAND

ADDRESS	CAPACITY	GUEST ROOMS	CONTACT
Avalon Restaurant 4630 S.W. Macadam Ave. Portland, OR 97201 *See page 107*	Indoor: Up to 250 R/B/S/M/		Kimberly Lang (503) 227-4630 Fax (503) 796-2704
Buffalo Gap Saloon & Eatery 6835 S.W. Macadam Ave. Portland, OR 97219 *See page 69*	Up to 50 W/R/B/S/M/		Event Coordinator (503) 244-7111 Fax (503) 246-8848
Cal's Pacific Rim 5310 S.W. Macadam Ave. Portland, OR 97201	Up to 250 W/R/B/S/M/		Banquet Manager (503) 241-2971 Fax (503) 241-8329
Chart House 5700 S.W. Terwilliger Blvd. Portland, OR 97201 *See page 71*	Up to 200 W/R/B/S/M/		Banquet Manager (503) 246-6963
Ernesto's Italian Restaurant 8544 S.W. Apple Way Portland, OR 97225 *See page 73*	Sit-down: Up to 150 R/B/S/M/		Gwen Tiemeyer (503) 292-0119
Fuddruckers 10100 S.W. Washington Square Rd. Portland, OR 97223	Up to 75 R/B/S/M/		Manager (503) 620-1819
Henry Ford's Restaurant 9589 S.W. Barbur Blvd. Portland, OR 97219	Up to 300 W/R/B/S/M/		General Manager (503) 245-2434 Fax (503) 246-9901
The Melting Pot 4439 S.W. Beaverton- Hillsdale Hwy. Portland, OR 97221	Upstairs: Up to 50 R/B/M/		Wade Fee (503) 452-1096

W=Wedding Ceremony   R=Reception   B=Banquet   S=Seminar   M=Meeting   P=Picnic

Please let these businesses know that you heard about them from the Bravo! Bridal Resource Guide.   **573**

ADDRESS	CAPACITY	GUEST ROOMS	CONTACT
The Multnomah Center 7688 S.W. Capitol Hwy. Portland, OR 97219	Sit-down: Up to 200 Reception: Up to 450 W/R/B/S/M/		Rental Coordinator (503) 823-2787 Fax (503) 823-3161
The Old Spaghetti Factory 0715 S.W. Bancroft Portland, OR 97201 *See page 76*	Sit-down: 75–150 R/B/S/M/		Banquet Manager (503) 222-5375
Oregon Zoo 4001 S.W. Canyon Rd. Portland, OR 97221 *See page 175*	Indoor: Up to 800 Outdoor: Up to 6,000 W/R/B/S/M/P/		Kristen Backsen (503) 220-2789 Fax (503) 220-3689
Raccoon Lodge & Brew Pub 7424 S.W. Beaverton- Hillsdale Hwy. Portland, OR 97225 *See page 79*	Sit-down: Up to 100 Reception: Up to 150 B/M/S/R/		Tim Larrance (503) 296-0110
The Riverside 50 S.W. Morrision St. Portland, OR 97204	Sit-down: Up to 40 Reception: Up to 50 R/B/S/M/	140	Catering (503) 221-0711
Shilo Inns— **Portland/Beaverton** 9900 S.W. Canyon Rd. Portland, OR 97225 *See page 194*	Up to 160 W/R/B/S/M/	142	Catering Office (503) 297-1214 (800) 222-2244
The Sweetbrier Inn 7125 S.W. Nyberg Rd. Tualatin, OR 97062 *See page 198*	Sit-down: Up to 250 Reception: Up to 300 R/B/S/M/	131	Catering Office (503) 692-5800 Fax (503) 691-2894
Willamette Cafe **(Willamette Athletic Club)** 4949 S.W. Landing Dr. Portland, OR 97201 *See page 205*	Sit-down: Up to 100 Reception: Up to 250 R/B/S/M/		Catering Coordinator (503) 225-1068
World Forestry Center 4033 S.W. Canyon Rd. Portland, OR 97221	Sit-down: Up to 300 Reception: Up to 400 W/R/B/S/M/P/		Roxy Boyles (503) 228-1367 ext. 101

SOUTHWEST SUBURBAN

ADDRESS	CAPACITY	GUEST ROOMS	CONTACT
Alfie's Wayside Country Inn 1111 Hwy 99 W. Dundee, OR 97115 *See page 101*	Up to 400 W/R/B/		Alfie (503) 538-9407

SHERWOOD

ADDRESS	CAPACITY	GUEST ROOMS	CONTACT
Marjorie Stewart Senior **Community Center** 855 N. Sherwood Blvd. Sherwood, OR 97140	Sit-down: Up to 225 W/R/B/		Peggy Federspiel (503) 625-5644

W=Wedding Ceremony   R=Reception   B=Banquet   S=Seminar   M=Meeting   P=Picnic

Please let these businesses know that you heard about them from the Bravo! Bridal Resource Guide.

ADDRESS	CAPACITY	GUEST ROOMS	CONTACT
TIGARD/TUALATIN			
Century Hotel 8185 S.W. Tualatin- Sherwood Rd. Tualatin, OR 97062	Up to 50 R/B/S/M/	40	Manager (503) 692-3600 Fax (503) 691-9142
Cucina! Cucina! Italian Cafe 10205 S.W. Washington Sq. Rd. Tigard, OR 97223	Up to 30 R/B/S/M/		Banquet Manager (503) 968-2000 Fax (503) 968-2079
Dalton's Neighborhood Grill 17930 S.W. McEwan Rd. Tigard, OR 97224	Up to 50 R/B/		Dave Dalton (503) 639-7211
Embassy Suites Hotel— Washington Square 9000 S.W. Washington Sq. Rd. Tigard, OR 97223 *See page 136*	Up to 1,200 W/R/B/S/M/	354	Lisette Crepeaux (503) 644-4000
Hi Hat 11530 S.W. Pacific Hwy. Tigard, OR 97223	Up to 350-400 R/B/S/M/		Steve Louie (503) 246-4055
Rich's Restaurant 18810 S.W. Boones Ferry Rd. Tualatin, OR 97062	Up to 100 R/B/S/M/		Banquet Manager (503) 692-1460
The Quello House 16445 S.W. 92nd Ave. Tigard, OR 97224 *See page 324*	Up to 200 W/R/B/P/		Dan or Jacque Quello (503) 684-5456
The Sweetbrier Inn 7125 S.W. Nyberg Rd. Tualatin, OR 97062 *See page 198*	Sit-down: Up to 250 Reception: Up to 300 R/B/S/M/	132	Catering Office (503) 692-5800 (800) 551-9167 Fax (503) 691-2894
Tualatin/Durham Senior Ctr. 8513 S.W. Tualatin Rd. Tualatin, OR 97062	Sit-down: Up to 160 W/R/B/S/M/P		Parks Department (503) 692-2000
TROUTDALE			
The Lake House at Blue Lake 21160 N.E. Blue Lake Rd. Troutdale, OR 97060	Indoor: Up to 175 Outdoor: Up to 400 W/R/B/S/M/P/		Facility Manager (503) 667-3483
McMenamins Edgefield 2126 S.W. Halsey Troutdale, OR 97060 *See page 162*	Sit-down: Up to 200 Reception: Up to 250 Theater: Up to 125 W/R/B/S/M/P/	103	Sales Office (503) 492-2777

W=Wedding Ceremony   R=Reception   B=Banquet   S=Seminar   M=Meeting   P=Picnic

PORTLAND AREA BANQUET & EVENT SITES

ADDRESS	CAPACITY	GUEST ROOMS	CONTACT
WEST LINN			
McLean House & Park 5350 River St. West Linn, OR 97068 *See page 322*	Indoor/Outdoor: Up to 100 W/R/B/S/M/P/		(503) 655-4268
The Oregon Golf Club 25700 S.W. Pete's Mountain Rd. West Linn, OR 97068 *See page 174*	Up to 500 W/R/B/S/M/P/		Michelle Mahurin (503) 650-6900
WILSONVILLE			
Denny's 30175 S.W. Parkway Wilsonville, OR 97070	Up to 40 W/R/B/S/M/		Carl Henden (503) 682-1711 Fax (503) 682-0283
Holiday Inn Select 25425 S.W. 95th Ave. Wilsonville, OR 97070 *See page 152*	Sit-down: Up to 600 Reception: Up to 850 R/B/S/M/W	170	Catering Department (503) 682-2211
YAMHILL			
Flying M Ranch 23029 N.W. Flying M Rd. Yamhill, OR 97148	Indoor: Up to 200 Outdoor: Up to 1,500 W/R/B/S/M/P/	36	Kristen (503) 662-3222 Fax (503) 662-3202

W=Wedding Ceremony   R=Reception   B=Banquet   S=Seminar   M=Meeting   P=Picnic

Please let these businesses know that you heard about them from the Bravo! Bridal Resource Guide.

ADDRESS	CAPACITY	CONTACT
BOATS & YACHTS		
The Cascade Sternwheelers "Columbia Gorge" P.O. Box 307 Cascade Locks, OR 97014 *See page 91*	Sit-down: Up to 200 Reception: Up to 375 W/R/B/S/M/P/	Sales Department (503) 223-3928
Crystal Dolphin 1200 N.W. Front Ave., #120 Portland, OR 97209 *See page 92*	Apr-Sept: Up to 90 Oct-Mar: Up to 75 Outdoor: Up to 180 W/R/B/S/M/	General Manager (503) 226-2517 Fax (503) 226-2539
Portland Spirit 842 S.W. First Avenue Portland, OR 97204 *See page 93*	Sit-down: Up to 350 Reception: Up to 540 W/R/B/S/M/	Sales Office (503) 224-3900 (800) 224-3901 Fax (503) 286-7673
The Sternwheeler Rose 6211 N. Ensign Portland, OR 97217 *See page 94*	Up to 130 W/R/B/S/M/P/	Judy (503) 286-7673
Willamette Star 842 S.W. First Ave. Portland, OR 97204 *See page 93*	Sit-down: Up to 80 Reception: Up to 120 W/R/B/S/M/	Sales Office (503) 224-3900 (800) 224-3901 Fax (503) 286-7673
Yachts-O-Fun Cruises, Inc. Foot of S.E. Marion St. Portland, OR 97202	Sit-down: Up to 48 W/R/B/P/	Vikki Collie (503) 234-6665
TRAINS		
Mt. Hood Railroad 110 Railroad Ave. Hood River, OR 97031	Up to 330 W/R/S/M/	Passenger Service (541) 386-3556 (800) 872-4661 Fax (541) 386-2140
Vintage Trolley 115 N.W. First, Suite 200 Portland, OR 97209	Up to 70 W/R/M	Sarah Fuller (503) 323-7363

W=Wedding Ceremony   R=Reception   B=Banquet   S=Seminar   M=Meeting   P=Picnic

Please let these businesses know that you heard about them from the Bravo! Bridal Resource Guide.   **577**

PORTLAND AREA
PARK SITE LISTINGS

ADDRESS	CAPACITY	CONTACT
CASCADE LOCKS		
Marine Park **& Thunder Island** Port of Cascade Locks Cascade Locks, OR 97014	Outdoor: Up to 4,000 Covered: Up to 175 W/R/B/P/	Cascade Sternwheelers (503) 223-3928
ESTACADA		
McIver State Park 24101 S. Entrance Rd. Estacada, OR 97023	Up to 1,000 W/R/S/M/	Reservations Tryon Creek State Park (503) 630-7150 or (503) 636-9886
GRESHAM		
Oxbow Park 3010 S.E. Oxbow Park Way Gresham, OR 97080	Outdoor shelter (4): Up to 350 W/R/S/M/P/B	Metro Regional Parks (503) 797-1834
MILWAUKIE		
North Clackamas Park **The Milwaukie Center** 5440 S.E. Kellogg Creek Milwaukie, OR 97222 *See page 164*	Indoor: Up to 600 Outdoor (shelter): Up to1,200 W/R/S/M/P/	(503) 653-8100
PORTLAND		
Blue Lake Park 205000 N.E. Marine Drive Fairview, OR 97024	Outdoor: Up to 7,000 Covered (10): 50 to 125 Lake House: Up to 175 W/R/P/B/S/M/	Metro Regional Parks (503) 797-1834
Council Crest Park S.W. Council Crest Dr. Portland, OR 97201	Outdoor (no shelter): Up to 150 W/R/	Parks Permit Center (503) 823-2525
Crystal Springs **Rhododendron Garden** 7215 S.E. Hawthorne Portland, OR 97215 *See page 126*	Indoor: (shelter) Up to 150 Outdoor: 3 sites Up to 200 W/R/P/M/S/	Rita Knapp (503) 256-2483
Howell Territorial Park 13901 N.W. Howell Rd. Sauvie Island, OR	Outdoor : Up to 300 W/R/B/P/S/M/	James Metro Parks & Greenspaces (503) 797-1834
Hoyt Arboretum 4000 S.W. Fairview Blvd. Portland, OR 97221	Outdoor (shelter): Up to 140 W/R/P/	Parks Permit Center (503) 823-2514
Hoyt Wedding Meadow 4000 S.W. Fairview Blvd. Portland, OR 97221	Outdoor (no shelter): Up to 100 W/R/P/	Parks Permit Center (503) 823-2525

W=Wedding Ceremony   R=Reception   B=Banquet   S=Seminar   M=Meeting   P=Picnic

Please let these businesses know that you heard about them from the Bravo! Bridal Resource Guide.

ADDRESS	CAPACITY	CONTACT
Laurelhurst Park S.E. 39th & Oak Portland, OR 97214	Outdoor (no shelter): 100+ W/R/P/	Parks Permit Center (503) 823-2525
Leach Botanical Gardens 6704 S.E. 122nd Ave. Portland, OR 97236	Indoor: Up to 70 Outdoor: Up to 85 W/R/B/S/M/P/	Rental Coordinator (503) 761-9503
Mt. Tabor Park S.E. 60th & Salmon Portland, OR 97214	Outdoor (shelter): 100+ W/R/P/	Parks Permit Center (503) 823-2525
The Overlook House 3839 N. Melrose Dr. Portland, OR 97227 *See page 176*	Indoor: Up to 75 Outdoor: Up to 150 W/R/S/M/P/	Building Coordinator (503) 823-3188
Peninsula Park **Rose Garden** N. Albina & Portland Blvd. Portland, OR 97217	Outdoor: Up to 70 (shelter) W/R/P/	Parks Permit Center (503) 823-2525
Pier Park N. Seneca & St. John's Portland, OR 97203	Outdoor (shelter): 200+ W/R/P	Parks Permit Center (503) 823-2525
Pioneer Courthouse **Square** 701 S.W. Sixth Ave. Portland, OR 97204	Outdoor: Up to 15,000 W/R/B/M/P/	Program Director (503) 223-1613 Fax (503) 222-7425
Washington Park **Rose Garden Amphitheater** 400 S.W. Kingston Blvd. Portland, OR 97201	Outdoor: Up to 3,000 W/R/P/	Parks Permit Center (503) 823-2525

ST. PAUL

Champoeg Park 8239 Champoeg Rd., N.E. St. Paul, OR 97060	Indoor: Up to 49 Outdoor: Up to 200 W/R/P/	Reservation Information (503) 678-1251 (800) 452-5687

TROUTDALE

Glenn Otto Comm Park **& Sam Cox Bldg.** 1120 E. Historic Columbia River Hwy. Troutdale, OR 97060	Indoor: Up to 250 Outdoor: Up to 1,000 W/R/B/S/M/P/	Samantha (503) 665-5175 ext. 254 Fax (503) 665-1137

WASHINGTON COUNTY

Cedar Hills Park Cedar Hills Blvd. & Walker Rd. Beaverton, OR 97005	Outdoor only: Up to 100 W/R/P/	Tualatin Hills Park & Rec. (503) 645-3539 Fax (503) 614-9514
Jenkins Estate Grabhorn Rd. at S.W. 209th & Farmington Aloha, OR 97006	Indoor: Up to 125 Outdoor: Up to 175 Stable: Up to 250 W/R/B/S/M/P/	Program Supervisor (503) 642-3855 Fax (503) 591-1028

W=Wedding Ceremony   R=Reception   B=Banquet   S=Seminar   M=Meeting   P=Picnic

Please let these businesses know that you heard about them from the Bravo! Bridal Resource Guide.   **579**

PORTLAND AREA
PARK SITE LISTINGS

ADDRESS	CAPACITY	CONTACT
Metzger Park Hall 8400 S.W. Hemlock St. Portland, OR 97223	Indoor Facility Ceremony: Up to 100 Reception: Up to 200 W/R/B/S/M/P/	Administrative Assistant (503) 246-0998
Raleigh Park 3500 S.W. 78th Ave. Portland, OR 97225	Outdoor Only: Up to 100 W/R/P/	Tualatin Hills Park & Rec. (503) 645-3539 Fax (503) 614-9514
Scoggins Valley Park/ **Henry Hagg Lake** 111 S.E. Washington Hillsboro, OR 97124	"C" Ramp Pavilion: Up to 700 Sain Pavilion: Up to 300 2 additional sites: Up to 80 W/R/P/	Administrative Asst. (503) 648-8715
WEST LINN		
McLean House & Park 5350 River St. West Linn, OR 97068 *See page 322*	Indoor/Outdoor: Up to 100 W/R/B/S/M/P/	(503) 655-4268
Willamette Park 12th & Volpp St. West Linn, OR 97068	Gazebo: Up to 35 Willamette Shelter: Up to 64 Entire Park Area: Up to 200	Parks Department (503) 557-4700 Fax (503) 657-3237

W=Wedding Ceremony   R=Reception   B=Banquet   S=Seminar   M=Meeting   P=Picnic

ADDRESS	CAPACITY	CONTACT
Airlie Winery 15305 Dunn Forest Rd. Monmouth, OR 97361	Outdoor: Up to 200 W/R/B/P/	Owner (503) 838-6013
BeckenRidge Vineyard 300 Reuben-Boise Rd. Dallas, OR 97338 *See page 108*	Up to 120 W/R/B/S/M/	Becky Jacroux (503) 831-3652
Champoeg Wine Cellars 10375 Champoeg Rd. N.E. Aurora, OR 97002	Indoor: Up to 20 Outdoor: Up to 100 W/R/B/P	Manager (503) 678-2144
Chateau Bianca Winery 17485 Hwy 22 Dallas, OR 97338	Indoor: Up to 50 Outdoor: Up to 250 W/R/B/S/M/P/	Bianca Wetzel (503) 623-6181Era
Chateau Lorane 27415 Siuslaw River Rd. Lorane, OR 97451	Indoor: Up to 80 Outdoor: Up to 300 W/R/B/P/	Linde Kester (541) 942-8028 (541) 942-5830
Elk Cove Vineyards 27751 N.W. Olson Rd. Gaston, OR 97119	Indoor: Up to 200 Outdoor: limited W/R/B/S/M/P/	Hospitality Director (503) 985-7760
Eola Hills Wine Cellars 501 S. Pacific Hwy. W. Rickreall, OR 97371 *See page 137*	Indoors: Up to 250 Outdoors: Up to 250+ W/R/B/S/M/P/	L.J. Gunderson (503) 623-2405 Fax (503) 623-0350
Erath Vineyards 9409 N.E. Worden Hill Rd. Dundee, OR 97115	Indoor: Up to 25 Outdoor: Up to 50 P/M/S/	Mike Harris (800) 539-9463
Flerchinger Vineyards 4200 Post Canyon Dr. Hood River, OR 97301	Indoor: Up to 30 Outdoor: Up to 100 W/R/B/S/M/P/	Manager (800) 516-8710
Honeywood Winery 1350 Hines St. S.E. Salem, OR 97302	Indoor: Up to 150 W/R/B/S/M/P/	Marlene Gallick (503) 362-4111 Fax (503) 362-4112
Kramer Vineyards 26830 N.W. Olson Rd. Gaston, OR 97119	Indoor: Up to 30 Outdoor: Upt to 100 W/R/S/M/P/	Trudy Kramer (503) 662-4545
Laurel Ridge Winery 46350 N.W. David Hill Rd. P.O. Box 456 Forest Grove, OR 97116	Indoor: Up to 65 W/R/B/S/M/P/	David Teppola (503) 359-5436
Marquam Hill Vineyards 35803 S. Hwy. 213 Molalla, OR 97038	Indoor: Up to 20 Outdoor: Up to 2,000 W/R/M/P/	Marylee or Joe Dobbes (503) 829-6677
Rex Hill Winery 30835 N. Hwy 99W Newberg, OR 97132	Indoor: Up to 150 Outdoor: Up to 200 Amphitheater: Up to 300	Rochelle Tasting Room Manager (503) 538-0666

W=Wedding Ceremony   R=Reception   B=Banquet   S=Seminar   M=Meeting   P=Picnic

Please let these businesses know that you heard about them from the Bravo! Bridal Resource Guide.

OREGON
WINERY SITE LISTINGS

ADDRESS	CAPACITY	CONTACT
Stangeland Vineyards & Winery 8500 Hopewell Rd. N.W. Salem, OR 97304	Indoor: Up to 50 Outdoor: Up to 200 W/R/B/S/M/P/	Kinsley Miller (503) 581-0355
St. Josef's Wine Cellars 28836 S. Barlow Rd. Canby, OR 97013	Indoor: Up to 125 Indoor/Outdoor: Up to 250 W/R/B/S/M/P/	Lilly Fleischmann (503) 651-3190
Willamette Valley Vineyards 8800 Enchanted Way S.E. Turner, OR 97392 *See page 207*	Indoor/Outdoor: Up to 600 W/R/B/S/M/P/	Hospitality Coordinator (503) 588-9463 (800) 344-9463
Wine Country Farm 6855 Breyman Orchards Rd. Dayton, OR 97114	Indoor: Up to 80 Outdoor: Up to 250 W/R/B/P/S/M	Joan Davenport (503) 864-3446
Youngberg Hill Vineyard 10660 SW Youngberg Hill McMinnville, OR 97128	Indoor: Up to 20 Outdoor: Up to 120 W/R/B/P/M/	Kevin & Tasha Byrd (503) 472-2727 (888) 657-8668

W=Wedding Ceremony   R=Reception   B=Banquet   S=Seminar   M=Meeting   P=Picnic

THE
WEDDING SLIP

A law was passed in 1547

stating that if a woman wore

only a slip at her wedding, it

would be considered a public

announcement that any debts

she or a previous husband may

have incurred were not her new

husband's responsibility.

ADDRESS	CAPACITY	GUEST ROOMS	CONTACT
BATTLE GROUND			
Battle Ground Senior Center 116 N.E. Third Ave. Battle Ground, WA 98604	Up to 100 *No alcohol		Battle Ground City Hall (360) 687-7131
The Burdoin Mansion 18609 N.E. Cramer Rd. Battle Ground, WA 98604 *See page 113*	Indoor: Up to 65 Outdoor: Up to 200 R/B/S/M/P/		Rob and Becky Neuschwander (360) 666-4828
Forever Yours Wedding Chapel 316 E. Main St./P.O. Box 475 Battle Ground, WA 98604 *See page 321*	Ceremony: Up to 100 Reception: Up to 75 W/R/M/		Sue Simonson (360) 687-7304
BRUSH PRAIRIE			
The Cedars Golf Club 15001 N.E. 181st St. Brush Prairie, WA 98606	Sit-down: Up to 175 Reception: Up to 250 R/B/S/M/		Vickie Hernandez (360) 687-6092 (503) 285-7548
CAMAS			
Camas Community Center 1718 S.E. Seventh Camas, WA 98607	Up to 300 R/B/S/M		Parks & Recreation Dept. (360) 834-7092
Crown Park N.E. 15th Ave. & Everett St. Camas, WA 98607	20' x 20' Picnic Shelter *No alcohol P/		Parks & Recreation Dept. (360) 834-7092
Rocket City Neon Advertising Museum & Reception Hall 1554 N.E. Third Ave., Suite 2 Camas, WA 98607 *See page 188*	Up to 300 W/R/B/S/M/		Kirsten Benko (360) 834-9467
GOLDENDALE			
Maryhill Museum of Art 35 Maryhill Museum Dr. Goldendale, WA 98620	Indoor: Up to 75 Outdoor: Up to 1,500 W/R/B/S/M/P/		Elizabeth Toscano at Cherry Hill (541) 478-4455
KALAMA			
Columbia Inn Restaurant 698 Frontage Rd. Kalama, WA 98625	Up to 100 W/R/B/S/M/		General Manager (360) 673-2800

W=Wedding Ceremony   R=Reception   B=Banquet   S=Seminar   M=Meeting   P=Picnic

Please let these businesses know that you heard about them from the Bravo! Bridal Resource Guide.

ADDRESS	CAPACITY	GUEST ROOMS	CONTACT
RIDGEFIELD			
Clark County Fair Association 17402 N.E. Delfel Rd. Ridgefield, WA 98642	Indoor: Up to 200 Outdoor: 100+ Grandstand: Up to 7,200 W/R/B/S/M/P/		Cathie Garner Events Coordinator (360) 737-6180
STEVENSON			
Columbia Gorge Interpretive Center 990 S.W. Rock Creek Dr. Stevenson, WA 98648	Reception: Up to 400 Theatre: Up to 48 R/B/		Pamela Robinson (509) 427-8211 Fax (509) 427-7429
VANCOUVER			
The Academy Chapel & Ballroom 400 E. Evergreen Blvd. Vancouver, WA 98660 *See page 97*	Ceremony: 225 Reception: Up to 300 Sit-down: Up to 250 W/R/B/S/M/		Windsor Consultants (360) 696-4884
American Legion/Post 14 710 Esther St. Vancouver, WA 98660	Up to 350 R/B/S/M/		Howard Rice (360) 696-2579
American Legion/Post 176 14011 N.E. 20th Ave. Vancouver, WA 98686	Up to 200 R/B/S/M/		Andrea Bouchard (360) 573-2331 Fax (360) 573-1475
A Night in Shining Amour 115 W. Ninth St. Vancouver, WA 98660 *See page 95*	Ceremony: Up to 125 Reception: Up to 150 R/B/S/M/		Pam and Joe Thielman (360) 750-7891
Avalon at St. James Place 4607 N.E. St. James Rd. Vancouver, WA 98663 *See page 106*	Chapel seated: Up to 220 Reception: Up to 300 W/R/S/M/		Chérie Ronning (360) 906-0960 or (888) 806-0960
Bagley Center 4100 Plomondon Vancouver, WA 98661	Reception: Up to 350 Sit-down: Up to 300 W/R/B/S/M/ *No alcohol		Bill Grantz Facilities Coordinator (360) 696-8219
Best Western Ferryman's Inn 7901 N.E. Sixth Ave. Vancouver, WA 98665	Up to 200 R/B/S/M/	134	Tonya Kelly Manager (360) 574-2151
Bill's Chicken & Steak House 2200 St. John's Blvd. Vancouver, WA 98661	Up to 120 W/R/B/S/M/		Manager (360) 695-1591
Chart House 101 E. Columbia Wy. Vancouver, WA 98661	Up to 200 W/R/B/S/M/		General Manager (360) 693-9211

W=Wedding Ceremony   R=Reception   B=Banquet   S=Seminar   M=Meeting   P=Picnic

Please let these businesses know that you heard about them from the Bravo! Bridal Resource Guide.   **585**

ADDRESS	CAPACITY	GUEST ROOMS	CONTACT
City Grill—Northeast 605 N.E. 78th St. Vancouver, WA 98605 *See page 121*	Up to 125 W/R/B/S/M/		Leslie Walls (360) 574-2270
City Grill—Southeast 916 S.E. 164th Ave. Vancouver, WA 98683 *See page 121*	Up to 125 W/R/B/S/M/		Dave Walls (360) 253-5399
Clark County Saddle Club 10505 N.E. 117th Ave. Vancouver, WA 98662	Up to 150 R/B/S/M/		Rental Coordinator (360) 574-9000
Clark County Square Dance Center 10713 N.E. 117th Ave. Vancouver, WA 98662	Up to 500 W/R/B/S/M/		Rental Coordinator (360) 256-5049
Club Green Meadows 7703 N.E. 72nd Ave. Vancouver, WA 98661	Indoor: Up to 275 W/R/B/S/M/		Ray Weldon (360) 256-1510
Covington House 4201 Main St. Vancouver, WA 98660	Up to 75 W/R/B/S/M/		Owner (360) 695-6750
The Crossing Restaurant 900 W. Seventh St. Vancouver, WA 98660	Sit-down: Up to 100 W/R/B/S/M/		Catering Manager (360) 695-8220 Fax (360) 695-8626
DoubleTree at the Quay 100 Columbia St. Vancouver, WA 98660 *See page 129*	Up to 600 W/R/B/S/M/	160	Director of Catering (360) 694-8341
First Evangelical Church 4120 N.E. St. Johns Rd. Vancouver, WA 98661	Auditorium: Up to 300 Reception: Up to 200 W/R/S/M/		(360) 694-2525
Fruit Valley Community Center 3203 Unander St. Vancouver, WA 98660	Up to 100 *No alcohol W/R/		Karen McCallister (360) 695-5647
The Heathman Lodge 7801 N.E. Greenwood Dr. Vancouver, WA 98662 *See page 149*	Indoor: Up to 400 R/B/M/S/	143	Catering Office (360) 254-3100 or (888) 475-3100
Hidden House Restaurant 100 W. 13th St. Vancouver, WA 98660	Indoor: Up to 80 Indoor/Outdoor: Up to 125 W/R/B/S/M/		Susan Courtney Manager (360) 696-2847
The Holland Restaurant 1708 Main St. Vancouver, WA 98660	Up to 50 R/B/S/M/		Manager (360) 694-7842

W=Wedding Ceremony   R=Reception   B=Banquet   S=Seminar   M=Meeting   P=Picnic

VANCOUVER AREA
CEREMONY & BANQUET SITE LISTINGS

ADDRESS	CAPACITY	GUEST ROOMS	CONTACT
The Hostess House Wedding Chapel & & Reception Center 10017 N.E. Sixth Ave. Vancouver, WA 98685 *See page 154*	Ceremony: Up to 200 Reception: Up to 300 Sit-down: Up to 175 W/R/B/S/M/		Julie or Tom (360) 574-3284
Leverich Park 39th & Main St. Vancouver, WA	Sit-down: Up to 100 W/R/B/S/M/P/		Facilities Coordinator Bagley Center (360) 696-8236
Life Center Church 10709 S.E. 10th St. Vancouver, WA 98664	Reception: Up to 150 (only if using chapel) *Kitchen available		Rev. Thurston (360) 892-6020
Luepke Senior Center 1009 E. McLoughlin Blvd. Vancouver, WA 98663	Up to 300 *No alcohol W/R/B/S/M/		Facilities Coordinator (360) 696-8219
Magnolia Gardens 9113 N.E. 117th Ave. Vancouver, WA 98662	Outdoor: Up to 175 *No alcohol W/D/R/B/		Kel Crafton (360) 256-4753
The Rodeway Inn Cascade Park 221 N.E. Chkalov Dr. Vancouver, WA 98684	Sit-down: Up to 300 R/B/S/M/	118	Sales Office (360) 256-7044 (800) 426-5110
Marshall Center 1009 E. McLoughlin Blvd. Vancouver, WA 98663	Up to 125 R/B/S/M/ *No alcohol		Facility Coordinator (360) 696-8219
The Marshall House 1301 Officers' Row Vancouver, WA 98661 *See page 161*	Indoor: Up to 225 W/R/S/M/		Frances Anderson (360) 693-3103
Vancouver Masonic Temple 2500 N.E. 78th Vancouver, WA 98665	Up to 200 R/B/S/M/		Event Scheduler (360) 693-1051
My Sister & I 116 E. Evergreen Blvd. Vancouver, WA 98660	Up to 50 W/R/B/S/M/		Owner (360) 695-2164
Old Country Buffet 7809-B N.E. Vancouver Plaza Dr. Vancouver, WA 98662	Up to 60 R/B/S/M/		General Manager (360) 256-9420 Corp. Office (360) 694-6124
Pearson Air Museum 1115 E. Fifth St. Vancouver, WA 98661	Up to 500 W/R/B/		Tom Clark (360) 694-7026
Pied Piper Pizza 12300 N.E. Fourth Plain Rd. Vancouver, WA 98682	15-80 4 rooms R/B/M/		Manager (360) 892-6430
Prairie Community Church 10702 N.E. 117th Ave. Vancouver, WA 98662	Up to 600 Reception: 100 W/R/		Wedding Coordinator (360) 254-5977

W=Wedding Ceremony   R=Reception   B=Banquet   S=Seminar   M=Meeting   P=Picnic

Please let these businesses know that you heard about them from the Bravo! Bridal Resource Guide.   **587**

ADDRESS	CAPACITY	GUEST ROOMS	CONTACT
Sheldon's Cafe at the Grant House 1101 Officers' Row Vancouver, WA 98661 *See page 191*	Indoor: Up to 115 (3 rooms) Outdoor: Up to 125 W/D/R/B/		Gary or Barbara Sheldon (360) 699-1213
Shilo Inn—Vancouver 401 E. 13th St. Vancouver, WA 98660	Up to 25 W/R/B/S/M/	120	Manager (360) 696-0411
Totem Pole Family Restaurant 7720 N.E. Hwy. 99 Vancouver, WA 98665	Up to 145 W/R/B/S/M/		Manager (360) 694-2541
Water Works Park on Reserve behind Clark College Vancouver, WA	No maximum Outdoor amphitheater W/R/P/		Facilities Coordinator (360) 696-8219
The Wedding Place 908 Esther St. Vancouver, WA 98660 *See page 325*	Indoor: Up to 50 W/R/B/S/M/		(360) 693-1798
Who-Song & Larry's 111 E. Columbia River Wy. Vancouver, WA 98661	Up to 70 W/R/B/S/M/		Manager (360) 695-1198

WASHOUGAL

ADDRESS	CAPACITY	GUEST ROOMS	CONTACT
Hathaway Park G St. & 24th Washougal, WA 98671	Outdoor (shelter): Up to 50 W/R/B/P/		Brenda Snell (360) 835-8501
Washougal Community Ctr. 1681 C St. Washougal, WA 98671	Indoor: Up to 108 Auditorium: 120 R/B/S/M/		City of Washougal (360) 835-8501

WOODLAND

ADDRESS	CAPACITY	GUEST ROOMS	CONTACT
Oak Tree Restaurant 1020 Atlantic Ave. Woodland, WA 98674	Up to 500 R/B/S/M/		Banquet Manager (360) 887-8661 Fax (360) 225-8454

W=Wedding Ceremony   R=Reception   B=Banquet   S=Seminar   M=Meeting   P=Picnic

TRADITION

In Medieval times,

as part of the bride's dowry,

a shoe was given to the groom,

who nailed it on the wall over

the wedding bed to symbolize

the transfer of authority of the

bride to her new husband.

ADDRESS	CAPACITY	GUEST ROOMS	CONTACT
Brooks Assembly of God P.O. Box 9099 9165 Portland Rd. N.E Brooks, OR 97305	Ceremony: Up to 425 W/R/		Wedding Coordinator (503) 393-2155 Fax (503) 393-0778
Calvary Baptist Church 1230 Liberty Rd. S.E. Salem, OR 97302	Up to 350 W/R/		Wedding Coordinator (503) 363-9246
Englewood United Methodist Church 1110 17th N.E. Salem, OR 97301	Up to 150 W/R/		Administrative Assistant (503) 364-4555
First United Methodist 600 State St. Salem, OR 97301	Ceremony: Up to 450 Reception: Up to 250 W/R/		Kay Kemper (503) 364-6709
Grace Baptist Church 4197 State St. Salem, OR 97301	Ceremony: Up to 450 Reception: Up to 150 Gymnasium: Up to 600 W/R/		Wedding Coordinator (503) 364-7764
North Salem Baptist Church 4290 Portland Rd. N.E. Salem, OR 97303	Up to 250 W/R/		Office (503) 399-0190 Fax (503) 588-3369
Lancaster Assembly of God 491 Lancaster Dr. NE Salem, OR 97301	Up to 300 W/		Wedding Coordinator (503) 363-3303 or (503) 393-5530
Micah Ballroom 680 State St. Salem, OR 97301	Sit-down: Up to 530 *Non-smoking *No alcohol R/B/P/M/S/W/		Todd Hedeen (503) 315-7990
Monmouth Christian Church 189 S. Monmouth Monmouth, OR 97361	Up to 250 W/R/		Church Office (503) 838-1145 Fax (503) 838-3453
Scottish Rite Masonic Center 4090 Commercial St. S.E. Salem, OR 97302	Sit-down: Up to 250 Reception: Up to 500 W/R/B/S/M/ *No alcohol		Building Manager (503) 363-9240 Fax (503) 363-2018
St. Joseph Catholic 721 Chemeketa Salem, OR 97301	Ceremony: Up to 600 W/		Wedding Coordinator (503) 581-1623
Woodland Chapel 582 High St. S.E. Salem, OR 97301 *See page 326*	Ceremony: Up to 125 W/R/M/		Office Administrator (503) 362-4139

W=Wedding Ceremony   R=Reception   B=Banquet   S=Seminar   M=Meeting   P=Picnic

Please let these businesses know that you heard about them from the Bravo! Bridal Resource Guide.

SALEM AREA
BANQUET SITE LISTINGS

ADDRESS	CAPACITY	GUEST ROOMS	CONTACT
DOWNTOWN SALEM			
Micah Ballroom 680 State St. Salem, OR 97301	Sit-down: Up to 530 *Non-smoking *No alcohol R/B/P/M/S/W/		Todd Hedeen (503) 315-7990
NORTHEAST SALEM			
Best Western Pacific Highway Inn 4646 Portland Rd. N.E. Salem, OR 97305	Two banquet rooms: Up to 65 M/S		Sales Office (503) 390-3200 Fax (503) 393-7989
O'Callahans Restaurant & Catering at the Quality Inn Hotel & Convention Center 3301 Market St. N.E. Salem, OR 97301 *See page 169*	Up to 450 W/R/B/S/M/P/	150	Sales & Catering (503) 370-7835 or (503) 370-7997
Canton Garden Restaurant 3225 Market St. N.E. Salem, OR 97301	Up to 120 R/B/S/M/		Mary or Simon (503) 588-1125
Elmer's Colonial Pancake House 3950 Market St. N.E. Salem, OR 97301-1940	Up to 25 B/S/M/		Owner (503) 363-3950 Fax (503) 362-2377
Henry Thiele's Prime Rib Riverside 103 Pine N.E. Salem, OR 97303	Stateroom: Up to 20 Reception: Up to 100 W/R/B/S/M/		Trudy Thiele/Owner (503) 399-7786
Heritage Tree Restaurant 574 Cottage N.E. Salem, OR 97301	Up to 90 W/R/B/S/M/		Owner (503) 399-7075
Izzy's Pizza Restaurant 2205 Lancaster Dr. N.E. Salem, OR 97305	Up to 35 R/B/S/M/		Manager (503) 399-0915
Oregon State Fair & Expo Center 2330 17th St. NE Salem, OR 97310	50 to 4,000+ W/R/B/S/M/P/		Events Manager (503) 378-3247 Fax: (503) 373-1788
Quality Inn Hotel & Convention Center 3301 Market St. N.E. Salem, OR 97301	Up to 450 W/R/B/S/M/	150	Catering (503) 370-7835 or (800) 248-6273
Reed Opera House 189 Liberty St. N.E. Salem, OR 97301	Up to 300 W/R/B/S/M/		Gloria Chambers (503) 391-4481

W=Wedding Ceremony   R=Reception   B=Banquet   S=Seminar   M=Meeting   P=Picnic

Please let these businesses know that you heard about them from the Bravo! Bridal Resource Guide.   **591**

SALEM AREA
BANQUET SITE LISTINGS

ADDRESS	CAPACITY	GUEST ROOMS	CONTACT
Salem Inn 1775 Freeway Ct. N.E. Salem, OR 97303 *See page 189*	Up to 50 R/M/S/	64	John and Dora Anderson (503) 588-0515 (888) 305-0515
Salem Senior Center 1055 Erixon St. N.E. Salem, OR 97303	Up to 300 W/R/S/M/		Center Secretary (503) 588-6303 Fax (503) 588-6377

NORTHWEST SALEM

ADDRESS	CAPACITY	GUEST ROOMS	CONTACT
Denny's 3155 Ryan Dr. S.E. Salem, OR 97301	60-75 B/S/M/		Management (503) 585-8424 Fax (503) 375-9618
Eola Inn 4250 Salem Hwy. Salem, OR 97304	50-150 R/B/S/M/		Owner (503) 378-7521
La Estrellita 1111 Edgewater St. N.W. Salem, OR 97304	Up to 80 R/B/S/M/		Manager (503) 362-0522
McGrath's Public Fish House 350 Chemeketa St. N.W. Salem, OR 97301	Up to 30 B/M/R/		Manager (503) 362-0736
Roth's Hospitality Meeting Center 1130 Wallace Rd. N.W. Salem, OR 97304	5 Banquet rooms: Up to 150 W/R/B/P/M/S/		Catering Dept. (503) 370-3790 Fax (503) 581-4762

SOUTH SALEM

ADDRESS	CAPACITY	GUEST ROOMS	CONTACT
Phoenix Inn—South Salem 4370 Commercial St. S. Salem, OR 97302	2 Banquet rooms Up to 50 D/R/B		Sales Dept. (503) 588-9220 Fax (503) 585-3616
Rudy's at Salem Golf Club 2025 Golf Course Rd. S. Salem, OR 97302	Sit-down: Up to 150 W/R/B/S/M/		Owner (503) 399-0449

SOUTHEAST SALEM

ADDRESS	CAPACITY	GUEST ROOMS	CONTACT
Alessandro's Plaza Restaurant 325 High St. S.E. Salem, OR 97301	Sit-down: Up to 300 R/B/S/M/		Chris (503) 370-9951
Big Horn Brewing Co. 515 12th St. S.E. Salem, OR 97302	Sit-down: Up to 40 Reception: Up to 75 R/B/		Wes Foulger (503) 363-1904 Fax (503) 375-9327
Black Angus 220 Commercial St. S.E. Salem, OR 97301	Up to 650 W/R/B/S/M/		Catering (503) 585-1101 Fax (503) 375-3988

W=Wedding Ceremony   R=Reception   B=Banquet   S=Seminar   M=Meeting   P=Picnic

SALEM AREA
BANQUET SITE LISTINGS

ADDRESS	CAPACITY	GUEST ROOMS	CONTACT
Chelsea's Restaurant 4053 Commercial St. S.E Salem, OR 97302	Up to 45 R/B/S/M/		Manager (503) 585-1175
Creekside Golf Club 6250 Clubhouse Dr. S.E. Salem, OR 97306	Up to 220 W/R/B/S/M/P/		Linda Little (503) 363-4653
Historic Deepwood Estate 1116 Mission St. S.E. Salem, OR 97302	Indoor: Up to 57 Outdoor: Up to 150 W/R/B/S/M/		Staff Director (503) 363-1825
Historic Elsinore Theatre 170 High St. S.E. Salem, OR 97301	Reception: Up to 200 R/B/W/S/M/		Jean Deems (503) 375-3574 Fax (503) 375-0284
Izzy's Pizza Restaurant 2990 Commercial St. S.E. Salem, OR 97302	Up to 50 R/B/		Manager (503) 581-9831 Fax (503) 316-3909
Mill Creek Inn— Best Western 3125 Ryan Dr. S.E. Salem, OR 97301	Up to 200 W/R/B/S/M/C/		Manager (503) 585-3332
Mission Mill Village 1313 Mill St. S.E. Salem, OR 97301	Ceremony: Up to 100 Reception: Up to 450 W/R/S/M/P/B/		Tracy Stroud (503) 585-7012
Rangler's Ranch House 3743 Commercial St. S.E. Salem, OR 97302	Up to 60 R/B/S/M/		Nancy Williams (503) 378-1738
Scottish Rite Masonic Center 4090 Commercial St. S.E. Salem, OR 97302	Sit-down: Up to 250 Reception: Up to 500 *No alcohol W/R/B/S/M/		Building Manager (503) 363-9240 Fax (503) 363-2018
Tropical Beach Cafe 2653 Commercial St. S.E. Salem, OR 97302	Up to 125 R/B/S/M/		Sam Koizumi (503) 362-1100
Willamette Valley Vineyards 8800 Enchanted Way S.E. Turner, OR 97392 *See page 207*	Indoor/Outdoor: Up to 600 W/R/B/S/M/P		Hospitality Coordinator (503) 588-9463 (800) 344-9463

DALLAS/RICKREALL

ADDRESS	CAPACITY	GUEST ROOMS	CONTACT
Eola Hills Wine Cellars 501 S. Pacific Hwy. 99W Rickreall, OR 97371 *See page 137*	Indoor: Up to 250 Outdoor: Up to 250+ P/R/B/S/M/		L.J. Gunderson (503) 623-2405
Polk County Fairgrounds 520 S. Pacific Hwy. W. Rickreall, OR 97371	Up to 1,000 W/R/B/S/M/P/ *Multiple bldgs. available		Manager (503) 623-3048 or (503) 745-7256

W=Wedding Ceremony   R=Reception   B=Banquet   S=Seminar   M=Meeting   P=Picnic

Please let these businesses know that you heard about them from the Bravo! Bridal Resource Guide.   **593**

SALEM AREA
BANQUET SITE LISTINGS

ADDRESS	CAPACITY	GUEST ROOMS	CONTACT
INDEPENDENCE			
Amador Alley 870 N. Main St. Independence, OR 97351	Up to 75 B/M/		Owner (503) 838-0170
Inn at Oak Knoll 6345 Salem-Dallas Hwy. Independence, OR 97351	Up to 93 R/B/M/		Jerry & Jan Alderson (503) 378-0102 Fax (503) 399-0348
KEIZER			
Collett's Restaurant & Bar 165 McNary Estate Dr., N. Keizer, OR 97303	Up to 200 W/R/B/S/M/		Banquet Coordinator (503) 393-4111
Izzy's Pizza Restaurant 3400 River Rd. Keizer, OR 97303	Up to 50 R/B/M/		Manager (503) 390-5002
Keizer Lions Auditorium 4100 Cherry Ave. N.E. Keizer, OR 97303	Up to 180 W/R/B/M/		Rental Committee Chairperson (503) 390-1172
MONMOUTH			
Gentle House 855 N. Monmouth Ave. Monmouth, OR 97361	Indoor: Up to 150 Outdoor: Up to 600 W/R/B/S/M/P/		Program Coordinator (503) 838-8673 Fax (503) 838-8289
SUBLIMITY			
Silver Falls Conference Center 20022 Silver Falls Hwy. S.E. Sublimity, OR 97385	Indoor: Up to 86 W/R/B/S/M/P/		Dayna Rich (503) 873-8875 Fax (503) 873-2937
Silver Falls Vineyards 4972 Cascade Hwy S.E. Sublimity, OR 97385 *See page 196*	Indoor/Outdoor: Up to 250 W/R/M/B/		Duane Defrees (503) 769-5056
WOODBURN			
Settlemier House 355 N. Settlemier Ave. Woodburn, OR 97071 *See page 190*	Indoor: Up to 85 Oudoor: 300+ W/R/B/M/		Sharon Walsh (503) 982-1897

W=Wedding Ceremony   R=Reception   B=Banquet   S=Seminar   M=Meeting   P=Picnic

SALEM AREA
PARK SITE LISTINGS

ADDRESS	CAPACITY	GUEST ROOMS	CONTACT
SALEM			
Bush Pasture Park **Rose Garden** 600 Mission St. S.E. Salem, OR 97301	Outdoor: Up to 100 *No tables or chairs W/P/R/		Bruce Bolton (503) 588-6261
Cascade Gateway Park 2100 Turner Rd. S.E. Salem, OR 97302	Covered: Up to 300 2 uncovered: Up to 150		Bruce Bolton (503) 588-6261
Minto Brown Island 2200 Minto Island Rd. (Off S. River Rd.) Salem, OR 97302	Outdoor (shelter): Up to 150 W/R/M/P/		Bruce Bolton (503) 588-6261
Spongs Landing **Marion County Parks** 2500 Niagra St., N. Salem, OR 97303	Up to 300 2 shelter areas W/R/P/M		Denise Clark (503) 588-5036 Fax (503) 588-7970
Willamette Mission **State Park** 10991 Wheatland Rd., N.E. Gervais, OR 97026	Up to 2,000 W/R/B/P/		(503) 393-1172 ext. 23 (800) 452-5687

W=Wedding Ceremony   R=Reception   B=Banquet   S=Seminar   M=Meeting   P=Picnic

Please let these businesses know that you heard about them from the Bravo! Bridal Resource Guide.   **595**

INDEX BY NAME & SUBJECT

P

Q

R

Y

Z